Governmentality Studies in Education

D1430329

CONTEXTS OF EDUCATION

Series Editors:

Michael A. Peters
University of Illinois at Urbana-Champaign, USA

Scope:

Contexts of Education is a new series of handbooks that embraces both a creative approach to educational issues focused on context and a new publishing credo.

All educational concepts and issues have a home and belong to a context. This is the starting premise for this new series. One of the big intellectual breakthroughs of post-war science and philosophy was to emphasise the theory-ladenness of observations and facts—facts and observations cannot be established independent of a theoretical context. In other words, facts and observations are radically context-dependent. We cannot just see what we like or choose to see. In the same way, scholars are argue that concepts and constructs also are relative to a context, whether this be a theory, schema, framework, perspective or network of beliefs. Background knowledge always intrudes; it is there, difficult to articulate, tacit and operates to shape and help form our perceptions. This is the central driving insight of a generation of thinkers from Ludwig Wittgenstein and Karl Popper to Thomas Kuhn and Jürgen Habermas. Increasingly, in social philosophy, hermeneutics, and literary criticism textualism has given way to contextualism, paving the way for the introduction of the notions of 'frameworks', 'paradigms' and 'networks'—concepts that emphasize a new ecology of thought.

This new series is predicated upon this insight and movement. It emphasises the importance of context in the establishment of educational facts and observations and the framing of educational hypotheses and theories. It also emphasises the relation between text and context, the discursive and the institution, the local and the global. Accordingly, it emphasizes the significance of contexts at all levels of inquiry: scientific contexts; theoretical contexts; political, social and economic contexts; local and global contexts; contexts for learning and teaching; and, cultural and interdisciplinary contexts.

Contexts of Education, as handbooks, are conceived as reference texts that also can serve as texts.

Governmentality Studies in Education

Michael A. Peters
University of Illinois at Urbana-Champaign, USA

A.C. Besley
University of Illinois at Urbana-Champaign, USA

Mark Olssen
University of Surrey, UK

Susane Maurer
Philipps-University of Marburg, Germany

Susanne Weber
University of Applied Sciences Fulda, Germany

SENSE PUBLISHERS
ROTTERDAM/BOSTON/TAIPEI

A C.I.P. record for this book is available from the Library of Congress.

ISBN: 978-90-8790-983-3 (paperback)
ISBN: 978-90-8790-984-0 (hardback)
ISBN: 978-90-8790-985-7 (e-book)

Published by: Sense Publishers,
P.O. Box 21858, 3001 AW
Rotterdam, The Netherlands
http://www.sensepublishers.com

Printed on acid-free paper

Cover: Fig. 11. Intérieur de l'Ecole d'enseignement mutuel, situeé rue du Port-Mahon, au moment de l'exercice d'écriture. Lithographie de Hippolite Lecomte, 1818. (Collections historiques de l'INRDP). Cf. p. 147 Eng. Edn.Picture in the French edition of Discipline and Punish omitted from Englishedition. Caption from French edition (Editions Gallimard, 1975); recovered from a website by Jeremy Crampton at http://monarch.gsu.edu/jcrampton/foucault/foucault_dp.html

CONTENTS

III. Foucault, Education and Governmentality: European Perspectives

ACKNOWLEDGEMENTS

This collection has taken much longer to assemble and edit than the editors first thought given the fact that we brokered the idea back in 2005 while attending a conference together in Germany. This was the first time that we entertained the idea of such a collection. The five of us thought that the attempt to bring together an omnibus collection on Foucault, governmentality and education, inviting contributors from around the world was a constructive enterprise and useful step in Foucault scholarship. Originally the collection focused on contributors from English-speaking countries, mainly US and UK, and Germany. The collection was extended when we decided to invite some of the foremost Foucault scholars to become involved and were delighted at the generous response from Colin Gordon, Jacques Donzelot, Thomas Lemke, Tom Osborne and others. The result is a larger and much more considered collection that has three sections: a general theoretical section comprised of scholars from France, Germany, UK, US, Finland, and China; a section that focuses on English-speaking, mainly Anglo-American contributors but also contributors from Australia, New Zealand and Canada; and a final section based on chapters written by contributors from Germany in the main, but also contributors from Belgium and Sweden. Colin Gordon kindly agreed to write the Foreword and Vivianna Pitton provided translations of the pieces by Gordon and Donzelot, although only one of her translations is included here. Tina Besley and Michael Peters would also like to thank Rodrigo Britez and Ergin Bulut, both PhD scholars at the University of Illinois, who did most of the formatting and some of the editing work of the collection as a whole. Jacques Donzelot's 'Michel Foucault's Understanding of Liberal Politics' ('Michel Foucault et l'intelligence du libéralisme') was first published in *Esprit* November, 2005 (trans. V. Pitton) and appears here with the permission of the autor and French Publisher. 'Neoliberal Governmentality: Foucault on the Birth of Biopolitics' by Michael A Peters first appeared in S. Weber & S. Maurer (eds.) *Gouvernementalität und Erziehungswissenschaft* (Governmentality and educational science), VS Verlag, Wiesbaden, Germany, pp.37-50.

COLIN GORDON

FOREWORD: PEDAGOGY, PSYCHAGOGY, DEMAGOGY

Cettui-ci apprend à parler, lors qu'il lui faut apprendre à se taire pour jamais.

On peut continuer à tout temps l'étude, non pas l'écolage: la sotte chose qu'un vieillard abécedaire!

This person is studying how to speak, when he should be learning to be silent for ever. One can always continue with study, but not school-work: how foolish for an old man to be learning his ABC!

Montaigne *Essays* 2:28: 'For everything there is a season.'

Tout le monde sait, et moi le premier, que nul n'a besoin de courage pour enseigner.

Everyone knows, and I know as well as anyone, that no one needs courage to teach.

Michel Foucault, Lecture given at Collège de France, 1st February 1984[1]

1.

None of Foucault's investigations has a central focus on the history, practice or politics of education. These themes, nevertheless, appear often in the course of some of the key developments in his work. And indeed it would be surprising if a career devoted to a Nietzschean history of thought never paid attention to the processes and mechanisms of the pedagogical communication and reproduction of knowledge.

The political events of May 1968 in Paris, which briefly shook the Gaullist state, were, in their immediate origins and in terms of their protagonists' immediate preoccupations, classroom revolts. Foucault embraced their cause to the extent of accepting, for a brief period, responsibility for organizing the philosophy department at the new experimental university of Vincennes, which was created as a direct response to the events. 1968 changed the political context of Foucault's work and writing, and gave a new inflexion to its style, its purposes and its themes.

No doubt Foucault was consciously writing the history of this present when he made the famous comments in *Discipline and Punish* on the mutual resemblance of the prison, the school, the factory and the convent. But just as his experience at Vincennes sharpened his sceptical opinion of socialist revolutionary politics, Foucault afterwards expressed some scepticism about the relative importance of educational institutions as loci of power in modern society: "One has to be really naïve to imagine that the effects of power linked to knowledge have their culmination in university hierarchies. Diffused, entrenched and dangerous, they operate in other places than in the person of the old *prof*".

Foucault's work has had a dynamic influence in several fields of study which were not directly his own. Educationists, in this sense not unlike geographers, have from an early date found there and adopted to their own concerns useful tools, concepts and styles of problematisation[2]; this volume demonstrates the range and continuing fruits of their work; but they can also find, dispersed across his output, a significant number of direct treatments of educational themes. As with the themes interesting to geographers, this available corpus has grown in recent years with the continuing publication of Foucault's shorter writings and lectures. As in the case with his work on governmentality, we can usefully consult, alongside these discussions, additional complementary sources including work by a certain number of Foucault's co-researchers which followed up on hints and suggestions in his work.A more extensive, accurate and coherent knowledge of Foucault's work may still offer us new ways of enhancing our capability to pose and explore new questions about our present and its history, in this domain as in others. In the hope of furthering this process, the following pages offer a quick, zigzag tour of some places where Foucault discusses education. There is a danger, as in all such exercises, of fabricating false coherences; genealogy teaches, among other things, the contingency and recency of our units of historical comparison, and we should be prepared to conclude from a survey of Foucault's observations on the subject that, just as there may be no simple formula to encapsulate Foucault's very distinctive capabilities as an educator[3], his analyses may assign no privileged or definitively identifiable place to the pedagogical in the problem-field of the technologies of individual formation and guidance.[4]

The title of this foreword proposes, for what it is worth, a triadic framework (inspired by the triadic domain-cluster of knowledge, ethics and government which Foucault several times uses in later texts and lectures when explaining the overall scope of his project) within which some of Foucault's observations on pedagogy and various sibling practices might be situated. Foucault uses the term 'psychagogy' in his 1982 lectures, defining it, specifically in contrast to pedagogy, as "the transmission of a truth whose function is not to endow an individual subject with aptitudes, but to modify that subject's mode of being". Foucault says here that pedagogy and psychagogy are often coupled practices in Hellenistic culture, but become decoupled in Christianity.[5] In the 1983 lectures Foucault speaks of "the problem of the government of the soul, of psychagogy. In order to conduct oneself and others, to conduct others well by conducting oneself well, what truths does one need? What practices and techniques are necessary? What knowledge, what exercises, etc.?"[6] 'Demagogy' is added here, on my own responsibility, as a third scoping term, understood in one of its less pejorative original usages, to mean discourse addressed to the people for its formation or edification: the care of the soul, or the conscience, of the citizen.[7] Foucault himself uses the term 'demagogy' in its pejorative sense, in one important discussion in his 1983 lectures, as the practice of 'false truth-telling' which is linked to the tendency of democracy – illustrated by the primal example of Athens – to put at risk the practice of (true) truth-telling on which its own survival depends: "true discourse, and the emergence of true discourse, is the very root of the process of governmentality. If democracy can be governed, it is because there is a true discourse'." (167)[8]

2.

In 1969 Foucault published an Introduction[9] to an edition of Arnauld and Lancelot's *Grammaire Générale et Raisonnée*. This essay forms a pendant to his preceding book, *The Order of Things*, in which a significant role was assigned to a companion treatise by the same two authors, the *Port-Royal Logic*. Foucault here links a mutation in the role attributed to grammar to a key component of sixteenth- and seventeenth-century educational reforms: the shift from the 'direct method' of teaching of Latin in Latin to the teaching of Latin and vernacular languages in the student's own vernacular. As a consequence, Foucault argues, the study of language is unburdened of a series of speculative preoccupations inherited from the Greek grammarians: the natural or artificial origins of words, the value of etymology, or the reality of universals, and finds itself instead with 'a previously unknown task: looking for the rationale of usages (*rechercher la raison des usages*)'. These remarks suggest a research question which would be worthy of attention, if it has not already been addressed: to what extent is the *episteme* of representation, a discursive regime analysed in *The Order of Things* as jointly governing a set of early-modern knowledges (general grammar, natural history and the theory of wealth), whose principles Foucault sees as being conceptually announced and summarised in the Port-Royal texts, a regime of knowledge and enquiry shaped by the agenda and requirements of a specific pedagogy?

3.

All cultural progress, by means of which the human being advances its education, has the goal of applying this acquired knowledge and skill for the world's use. But the most important object in the world to which it can apply them is the human being: because the human being is its own final end.

Kant, *Anthropology from a Pragmatic Point of View*, Preface

A book of daily exercise. Not of theory or the School.... The world being its own school, the purpose of anthropological reflection will be to situate man in this formative element... It teaches the human being to recognise in its own culture the school of the world. Here it can be said to have a kind of kinship with *Wilhelm Meister*, since it discovers, too, that the World is a School.

Foucault, Introduction to the *Anthropology [33/53f]*

The recent publication of Foucault's 1961 'complementary' doctoral dissertation, his preface to his translation of Kant's *Anthropology*, brings to light unnoticed lines of continuity and development running from the start to the end of Foucault's trajectory.[10]

In his last, newly published lecture series of 1984, Foucault locates the late 18th century as the point where a certain neoclassical notion of a 'philosophical life' reaches its end: philosophy becomes a university profession and the militant, missionary vocation of the Stoic or Cynic philosopher-hero, after a literary apotheosis in the personage of Goethe's *Faust*, migrates towards the political domain, to the figure of that different and new exemplary personage, the revolutionary. Foucault's 1961 commentary already locates, in the late Kantian text of 1798 (the final written form of a public lecture series delivered annually for 25 years) precisely such an end-point of a neo-Stoic conception of philosophy conceived as an art of dietetics or life-conduct, rather than as a theoretical or scientific doctrine (Kant explains his 'pragmatic' style of anthropological inquiry by comparing the unrealisable Cartesian ambition to explain the physical workings of human memory with the useful and practical study of the 'obstacles and stimulants' of memory which can lead to techniques for its cultivation and improvement.) Pragmatic anthropology is a user's guide to human capabilities. Foucault notes that Kant's letter 'On the power of the mind to master its morbid feelings by sheer resolution', setting out his 'Dietetic', or personal recipes of healthful daily living, overlaps in its core concerns, in time of its production, and in part of its content with the draft text of the *Anthropology*. [11] Likewise anticipating the terms of Foucault's later discussion of the care and 'usage' of the self and the aesthetics of existence are the terms in which he sets out the Kantian problematic of pragmatic anthropology. Kant had written in an earlier text that 'we investigate the human being here ... to know what it can make of itself and *how it can be used*'; by 1798 the question is no longer how the human being can be used but "what can be expected of it" and what the human being "can and should" make of itself. The connection between 'can' and 'should', Foucault writes, 'is ensured by the concrete movement of daily exercise: by *Spielen* [play]. This notion of *Spielen* is singularly important: man is nature's game, but he himself plays the game, and plays with it... So the game becomes a *"künstlicher Spiel"* [an artful/artificial play]'. [32f/52f]

Implicit in the 1961 commentary are many points of contact between the purposes of the *Anthropology*, focussed on the self-education of the human being as citizen of the world, and the theme of Enlightenment. Two famous Kantian questions come to prominence at different times in Foucault's thought: *'Was ist der Mensch?'* ('what is the human being?') and *'Was ist Aufklärung?'* ('what is Enlightenment?'). As far as I know, there is no published text where Foucault explicitly comments on the relation between these two questions; there is some work here for commentators. We can say that Kant himself connects the questions closely enough by defining Enlightenment as a key event in the history of humanity, the human being's exit from its state of self-imposed tutelage. In the commentary on Kant's essay *'Was ist Aufklärung?'* in the second lecture of his 1983 course, Foucault explicitly rejects the idea that the human being is considered by Kant to require some supplementary education or development in order to achieve enlightenment. Human beings continue to live in tutelage not because of our ignorance or immaturity, but because of our indolence and cowardice, and in particular our indolent tendency to entrust the guidance of our conduct to those who 'obligingly' offer us their services – a textbook author, a director of conscience or a medical advisor – not, Foucault adds, that such sources of advice or guidance are in themselves to be criticised as illegitimate: our fault is only to substitute these aids for the exercise of our own understanding, conscience and judgement. Foucault notes that Kant excludes the possible role as agents of Enlightenment of philosophers or public teachers who liberate mankind by educating it: such as process can end (Kant remarks in 1784) only in the subjection of the liberated to their liberators. On the other hand, Foucault draws attention, in his parallel discussion of a later text by Kant on the evidence for the prospects of human progress, to the decisive significance attributed by Kant in this respect to contemporary events – in particular, not to the event of the French Revolution, but to that of the popular and public responses of enthusiasm and sympathy to the news of that revolution.

Kant, it appears, did think that the capability for such disinterested sympathies and responses was something which could, and should, be taught. In his treatise on *Education* he states that youth should be encouraged to cheerfulness, even temper, dutifulness and 'in love towards others, as well as to feelings of cosmopolitanism. There exists something in our minds which causes us to take an interest in ourselves, in those with whom we have been brought up, and there should also be an interest in the progress of the world. Children should be made acquainted with this interest, so that it may give warmth to their hearts. They should learn to rejoice at the world's progress, although it may not be to their own advantage or to that of their country.'[12] Kant is opposed to the total state control of schools (and calls for a regime allowing for experimentation in schooling) because it is liable to impede this enlightening educational task: 'we are met by two difficulties—parents usually only care that their children *make their way* in the world, and Sovereigns look upon their subjects merely as *tools* for their own purposes. Parents care for the home, rulers for the state. Neither has as their aim, the universal good and the perfection to which man is destined, and for which he has also a natural disposition. But the basis of a scheme of education must be cosmopolitan.'

Foucault's early and late Kant discussions are linked by a sharp sensitivity to the network of new significations in Kant of notions of the *public* and the *popular*. Foucault cites an earlier passage in his *Logic* in which Kant characterises 'popularity' as a form of perfection in the presentation of knowledge, a balanced completeness which ensures its immediate and universal perspicuity and availability. In the Preface to the *Anthropology* where Kant alludes to the public or 'popular' status of his lectures, this notion is further linked to his conception of the pragmatic: 'An anthropology written from a pragmatic point of view that is systematically designed and yet popular (through reference to examples that can be found by every reader) yields an advantage for the reading public: the completeness of the headings under which this or that observed human quality of practical relevance can be subsumed offers readers many occasions and invitations to make each heading a theme of new observations, which can be placed in the appropriate section...'

Foucault adds that 'popular' has a further dimension here because it includes the idea of an exposition of 'popular knowledge', meaning that knowledge which humanity already collectively possesses, and that this aspect is developed in Kant's text through a relatively new relationship (distinct from that found in his major philosophical texts) to the vocabulary, with its distinctive semantic structures and expressive capabilities, of his own vernacular, national language – German. In this respect, and as a further stage in the disengagement of learned culture from Latinity which Foucault evokes in relation to the Port-Royal *Grammar*, pragmatic anthropology begins to function like a kind of ordinary-language philosophy.

4.

Foucault's most extended discussion of education is in the famous third section, 'Discipline', of *Discipline and Punish*. Most of the illustrative material is drawn from the two most influential French schooling manuals of the early modern period, De La Salle's *Conduite des Écoles chrétiennes* and the *Instruction méthodique pour l'école Paroissale*.[13] Foucault's purpose here is not so much to establish the distinctive features of these authors' pedagogical technique, as the methods shared with other institutions, and with those of one in particular. "Is it surprising that prisons resemble factories, schools, barracks, and hospitals, which themselves all resemble prisons?"

James Tully's remarkable chapter on Locke and the government of conduct, published after Foucault's death and dedicated to him, gives an account of Locke's programme for popular education which, within a Protestant theological and political context, and with particular emphasis on the link between popular education, enclosed institutions, compulsory labour and the policing of the poor, aptly identifies the same key elements of the disciplinary thematic analysed, from mainly French examples, in Foucault's survey.[14] Tully connects a mutation in pedagogical technique advocated in Locke's *Some thoughts concerning education* and *On the conduct of the understanding* to wider contemporary developments in disciplinary technique. The "assault on the Renaissance techniques of memorising rules, and its replacement with education as habit formation by repetition and drill, by 'exercises'", Tully writes, "is part of a much broader dispersion of techniques of discipline by drill throughout Europe from roughly the time of the revolutionary reform of training in the Dutch army in the 1590s." (p. 232)

The genealogy of the penal and the disciplinary perspectives is, however, only one of a set of linked approaches which Foucault brings to bear in his work of the 70s on the development of Western practices of individual formation and guidance. In the 1973-74 Lectures on *Psychiatric Power*[15], Foucault first discussed Bentham's *Panopticon* as a technical prototype, not of the modern prison, but of the 19th-century asylum. In the same lecture course, foreshadowing the governmentality lectures of 1978, he sketches an early modern problematic of individual 'government' which spans the same range of practical domains as *Discipline and Punish*, and which gives a prominent place to the developments in early modern schooling due, notably, to an ascetic and mystically inspired religious group founded in 14th-century northern Germany, the Brothers of the Common Life[16]. He links these developments to the historic process of the 'colonisation of youth' – the pacification, domiciling and segregation of the anarchic and itinerant mediaeval university student population. "We find the mould, the first model of the pedagogical colonisation of youth, in this practice of the individual's exercise on himself, this attempt to transform the individual, this search for a progressive development of the individual up to the point of salvation, in this ascetic work of the individual on himself for his own salvation. On the basis of this, and in the collective form of this asceticism in the Brothers of the Common Life, we see the great schemas of pedagogy taking shape, that is to say, the idea that one can learn things only by passing through a number of obligatory and necessary stages, that these stages follow each other in time, and that in this ordered movement through time, each stage represents a degree of progress. The twinning of time and progress is typical of ascetic practice, and it will be equally typical of pedagogical practice." (p. 67)

In *Discipline and Punish*, Foucault again cites the educational initiatives of this community, and their significance of their transposal of spiritual techniques to the educational domain for the modern history of discipline: "the theme of a perfection towards which the exemplary master guides the pupil became with them that of an authoritarian perfection of the pupils by the teacher; the increasingly rigorous exercises that the ascetic life proposed became tasks of increasing complexity that marked the gradual acquisition of knowledge and good behaviour; the striving of the whole community towards salvation became the collective, permanent competition of individuals being classified in relation to one another." (pp. 161–2).

Foucault's discussion in *Discipline and Punish* (1976) of the individualising technique of the examination can properly be understood, at least in part, a development and extension of a key theme in his earlier *Birth of the Clinic* (1963) which is made explicit in its subtitle, 'An archaelogy of the clinical gaze'. In his later work Foucault makes a key reference to Georges Canguilhem's book on the *Normal and the Pathological*, noting the extent to which normalizing and disciplinary practices can incorporate a quasi-clinical component – an individualising gaze which detects, measures and classifies the deviations of an individual, and of individual development, from a norm. In his earlier book, Foucault develops the idea that the organized space of the hospital where the clinical gaze holds sway, is not only a machine for cure and a machine for diagnosis and research, but a machine for teaching. "Clinical observation relies on the organization of two conjunct domains: the hospital domain and the pedagogical domain". The hospital works by arranging patients in series of similar cases so that the underlying common features of each pathology can be recognised. "The way that truth is made apparent through repetition also indicates the way that the same truth can be acquired. It offers itself to be learned by the same process that it offers itself to be cognized... the genesis of the manifestation of truth is also the genesis of the acquisition of truth. There is no difference in nature between the clinic as science and the clinic as pedagogy. In this way a group is formed, comprising the clinical teacher and his students, within which the act of recognition and the effort to learn are accomplished in a single process."[17] The clinic is a case, one among several which Foucault observes in his genealogies, of the hybridisation or symbiosis of pedagogy with other practices.

5.

The disciplinary history of the school is taken up in a study by three young French historians, Roger Chartier, Didier Julia and Marie-Madeleine Compère, in their book *L'éducation en France du XVIe au XVIIIe siècle*[18], published a year after Foucault's *Discipline and Punish*, and already citing it (the work is in turn cited in the editorial commentary by Michel Senellart on Foucault's 1978 lectures, *Security, Territory, Population*).[19] Roger Chartier, much of whose work has focussed on the material history of reading, writing, and printing, has been perhaps the most innovative mainstream French historian of the last 30 years to have acknowledged Foucault as a major influence. He was elected in 2007 by the Collège de France to a chair of Writing and Cultures in Modern Europe. Chapters in their 1976 volume by Chartier and Julia appear to both echo and anticipate strands of Foucault's research, notably the linked early-modern concerns with schooling, the Erasmian educational idea of Christian civility (the humanist *paideia* of conduct integrating piety and manners, public self-presentation and corporal decorum) and the education of princes and aristocrats. It is possible and perhaps probable that Foucault read this work at the time of its publication. Francois de la Noue formulated in late 16th-century France an influential plan for academies designed to provide the sons of the nobility with, in the words of Chartier and Julia, "an apprenticeship in the government of oneself and others." Not only do renaissance scholars (Erasmus and others) publish manuals for the education of the Christian Prince, but generations of the children of royal families are entrusted to high-profile educators who produce, for the occasion, dedicated treatises – in the case of Bishop Bossuet, appointed as 'director of political conscience' to the Grand Dauphin (heir apparent to Louis XIV), this included treatises on politics, grammar, history and logic (pp. 175–6). Education of the prince and advice to the prince are overlapping genres; a key component of royal advice (whose history, some of which Foucault was to explore in his later lectures, dates back to Plato) is the art of distinguishing true counsel from flattery; in his 1983 lectures, Foucault alludes to the mode of truth-telling required of the royal minister in the early modern monarchical state (8): reason of state (he may perhaps have been suggesting) might in this light be seen as one of the forms of early-modern political *parrhesia*. Good government, in turn, requires the virtue and education of the governed: citing Xenophon and Plato, Erasmus observes that "the chief hope of the state is founded in the proper training of its children" and "nothing is of greater importance for the prince than that he should have the best possible citizens."[20]

The education of the royal heir, whose set-piece experiences could include the direction of elaborate mock battles fought between sizeable armies of real combatants, could itself readily become an intellectual battlefield of dynastic and court policy. The prince, as Erasmus had explained, required a knowledge of his realm in order to be able to rule it; this could be acquired in part by geography lessons, in part by travelling. For the education of the Duc de Bourgogne, grandson and heir of Louis XIV, a grand survey of the state of France was commissioned, based on detailed reports commissioned from regional intendants. As Foucault records, the writer commissioned to summarise the reports, the duc de Boulainvilliers, interposed his own denunciation, on behalf of the dispossessed nobility, of the fraudulent historical and legal origins of the royal despotism, attacking in particular, the historical-administrative 'power-knowledge' wielded by the bureaucratic state through its monopolistic manipulation and exploitation of the public and legal archives.[21]

6.

Elsewhere in these remarkable 1976 lectures, the educational institution figures as a context for the changing politics of historical and other knowledges. (ibid 178-84) This is in the course of the first of two brief but striking 'digressions' in the 70s lectures – the second is in the 1978 lectures, *Security, Territory and Population* – where Foucault suggests a recontextualisation of the core themes of *The Order of Things* (and indeed also revisits, in an unusually direct way, part of the agenda of his 1970 inaugural lecture, *The Order of Discourse*). Foucault rapidly outlines here a view of how the changing regimes of knowledge of life, labour and language respectively entered into, and became stakes in historico-political debates and struggles over race, class and nation.

Foucault links these developments to the organization of the modern University (which he sets in France at the turn of the 18th and 19th centuries), setting the shifting politics of historiography against wider changes in the institutional regulation of knowledges and discourses – the shift from a system of norms governing the permitted *content* of statements (including religious censorship of science) to a system of academically administered norms governing the *form and conditions* of their enunciation – the regime shift, as he puts it, from an 'orthodoxy' to an 'orthology'.

7.

In the 1978 lectures on governmentality, Foucault again makes a point of linking his discussion back to the classical *episteme*, the early modern knowledges of grammar, natural history and wealth, and the transformations which mark its beginning and end. The 'man' of the human sciences, of philology, biology and political economy, is the knowable unit of population as an object of government. Just before this 'digression', Foucault makes a significant remark on the linkage between population, the public sphere and education:

> Taking the effects specific to population into consideration, making them pertinent if you like, is, I think, a very important phenomenon: the entry of a nature into the field of techniques of power, of a nature that is not something upon which, over which, or against which the sovereign must impose just laws. [...] We have a population whose nature is such that the sovereign must deploy considered procedures of government within this nature, with its help, and paying it due regard. In other words, with population we have something completely different from a collection of subjects of right differentiated by

their status, localization, goods, responsibilities, and offices: [we have] a set of elements that, on one side, are immersed within the general regime of living beings and that, on another side, offer a surface on which authoritarian, but considered and calculated transformative interventions can take hold. [...] With the emergence of mankind as a species, within a field of the definition of all living species, we can say that man appears in the first form of his integration within biology. From one direction, then, population is the human species, while from another it is what will be called the public. [...] The public, which is a crucial notion in the eighteenth century, is population seen under the aspect of its opinions, ways of doing things, forms of behaviour, customs, fears, prejudices, and requirements; it is what one can get a grip on through education and campaigns of proselytisation and persuasion. The population spans everything from the biological substrate, through species-life, to the graspable surface of the public. From the species to the public; we have here a whole field of new realities, realities in the sense that they are pertinent elements for mechanisms of power, the pertinent space within which and on which one must act. (p.75)

From the species to the public, or (we might also say) from population to the popular.

8.

Foucault's French editor adds a footnote reference here at the word 'public', to the celebrated early work by Jürgen Habermas on the *Public Sphere*, which in 1978 had just been translated in France. One may also think here of the well-known passage in the 1979 lectures where Foucault discusses Adam Ferguson's history of civil society as offering conceptual underpinnings for a liberal governmentality: the history of a human sociability whose nature includes the core characteristics of historical contingency, mutability and facticity, and characterises the new notion of civil society as a "transactional reality in the history of governmental technologies"; the location of "the mutual play of power relations and the things which continually eludeelude their grasp".[22] Three years earlier, Foucault had analysed Sieyès' *What is the Third Estate?*, and the bourgeois historiography of Thierry, as breaking with a polemical historico-political culture in which history is a weapon against the state for the righting of ancient wrongs, and becomes a conciliatory and triumphal narrative of the class which, out of its own resources and capabilities – "not only wealth, but administrative capacity, and also a morality, a certain way of living, a certain way of being, a will, an instinct for innovation" – becomes the architect of State and nation as historical incarnations of universality.[23] Common to Foucault's remarks on Ferguson and on Thierry is the perception of a new programmatic and pedagogical role assumed by liberal historical discourses, at once formulating and formative of a public space, and of the role of actors in that space.

In the 1978 lecture, after making his linkage back to *The Order of Things*, Foucault says in his concluding comments that the theme of man, and the human sciences that analyze man as living being, working individual, and speaking subject, should be understood on the basis of the emergence of population as the correlate of power and the object of knowledge. After all, 'man', as he is thought and defined by the so-called human sciences of the nineteenth century, and as he is reflected in nineteenth century humanism, is nothing other than a figure of population. (p. 79)

We are of course now familiar with bio-power (even if Foucault was by now apparently close to discarding this term) as the mode in which government deploys the knowledges of human and biological sciences to govern populations; but it is helpful to retain here Foucault's other remark that the dimension in which a population offers itself to governmental influence or intervention is the public sphere, and that the modes of that intervention include education. That might reasonably lead us to ask what can be said about the role of educational policy within governmentality in general, or within a specific form of governmentality: some suggested answers will be found in the contributions to this volume.

9.

Two years earlier, in the 1975 lectures, *Abnormal*[24], which centred on the genealogy of forensic psychiatry and criminology, Foucault refers (in his lecture on March 5th) to the wave of publications in later 18th-century France and Germany calling for the establishment of public, national or state-supervised systems of education (a notion about which Kant, as noted above, expressed significant reservations). Foucault was discussing here the changing governmental status and function of the early modern family (ideas afterwards developed in Jacques Donzelot's *The Policing of Families*) and the idea of an implicit compact between state and family over their respective roles in the formation of the young – a point of strong intersection between the history of governmentality and the history of sexuality.

The question of respective roles of parental nurture and schooling, this time as elements of investment in the formation of the non-genetically determined component of human capital, reappear in a contemporary setting the following year in Foucault's lectures on neoliberalism, where he draws attention to new analyses which highlight the level of investment in human capital as a determinant of the rate of economic growth in the postwar West, the developing world, and early modern Europe.[25]

10.

The present volume amply illustrates the ways in which Foucault's work, including the later work focussed on governmentality, offers hints, fragments and building blocks for a genealogy of pedagogical practice and knowledge. At the core of the enterprise as Foucault conducts it there is, of course, the linkage between investigation and problematisation. What is it that we wish to problematise when we study the genealogy of education?

There can be many answers, of course. One question which the preceding assemblage of scattered moments in Foucault's writings might help bring to mind, and which might merit further attention, is the role of education in modern societies as an axis linking the governability of societies to the formation of a public discursive space.

The 'public', Foucault tells us in 1978, is the surface via which the independent natural life of population offers itself to the educational interventions of government. The 'liberal' academic institution, formally independent of doctrinal censorship by church and state, is the place of production of normalising knowledges. The public thinker is, in some senses, by definition or by vocation, a public educator or moralist. Modern critique is, Foucault argues, originally and essentially critique and resistance of a way of being governed, and also, if not invariably, an argument for being governed otherwise, or less, or conceivably not at all. In his 1983 lecture, Foucault situates Kant's view of Enlightenment as a reconfiguration of the relation between the government of self and the government of others. But how to be governed is, as we have seen, the educational subject par excellence. Foucault's reflections on the status of the intellectual, which evolve into his investigations of truth-telling and the truth-teller, and are continuously linked to his Kantian thematic of Enlightenment as the problematisation of the present, are nor unrelated to this focal location of the public critical and intellectual function at the point of contact of the governmental and the educational. It is not accidental that Foucault chooses the trial of Socrates, and the tense, lateral and partly antinomic relations in ancient Greek culture between philosophical truth-telling and '*psychagogy*' on the one hand the political or pedagogical forms of *paideia* or 'conduction', on the other[26], as a main theme of his final lecture courses. It may not be over fanciful to read some of the critical responses to Foucault's work during his later and post-humous period of celebrity in the United States, by public thinkers and moralists such as Charles Taylor, Clifford Geertz, Richard Rorty, the heirs and survivors of the Frankfurt School and others, as reactions to a perceived subversion of, challenge to, or competing exercise of a function within modern societies of moral tutorship of the young which has been, from Goethe, Arnold, Thoreau and Ruskin through Tolstoy, Russell, Alain, Dewey, Gandhi and Wittgenstein to the recent present, a frequent, if not integral component of the life and preoccupations of the public intellectual.

In several of his lecture series, Foucault discusses Athenian, Shakespearean and classical French theatre as media for the exposition of 'public law', the narrative or doctrinal articulation of the foundations of sovereign authority. He criticises the Marxist analytical category of 'ideology' for its assumption that power is necessarily sustained by means of deceptions and mystifications. In his (as yet unpublished) 1980 lectures, he proposed that western societies are characterised by a recurring requirement, frequently varying in its concrete forms, to connect the governmental exercise of sovereignty with the public manifestation of truth: truth-telling (*parrhesia*) is one, but only one, of the possible modes of such manifestation of truth (*aleturgia*).There are clear hints from Foucault's last years that he wanted to go on to apply the analytical tools developed in his investigations of antiquity to the genealogy of early modern and contemporary politics. Some readers have felt irresistibly moved to sense a testamentary, valedictory pathos in Foucault's highly remarkable last lecture course. In fact, he began his opening lecture (delayed by illness) on February 1st 1984 by voicing an impatience to move on to a new phase of work, saying that his immediate intention was to conclude his five-year "Greco-Latin trip" and then to "return to a certain number of contemporary problems".[27] There are signs that one of the subjects of those planned investigations, which others might still want to carry forward, might have been the forms of manifestation and inculcation of public knowledge and public truth, administered, among others, by educational institutions and actors, which our societies require in order to function.

Foucault says that a defining character of *parrhesia* is that its performance entails risk and courage, because it consists of uttering a true discourse which is uncomfortable for its recipient – who may be a friend, patron, prince or the democratic majority of one's fellow-citizens.[28] Writing in praise of a journalist and friend, Jean Daniel, who he admired for these truth-telling qualities (this is one of the pieces where Foucault first discusses Kant's idea of Enlightenment as a critical semiology of the present moment), Foucault uses the phrase 'a morality of discomfort'.[29] The discourse of the flatterer or demagogue is the exact opposite – an opportunist discourse calculated to comfort and please the dominant audience of the moment. Public moral discourses addressed to the people ('demagogy' in the non-pejorative sense), and possibly particularly to the young, discourses designed to protect – perhaps with particular zeal during the period leading up to and following the end of the Cold War and the consequent depolarisation of an established global regime of moral orientation – against a range of dangerous intellectual, moral or political tendencies (cynical passivity and despair; sceptical relativism and nihilism; terrorist violence), may in some cases constitute a practice of *parrhesia*; they may also be versions of pastoral, missionary or militant discourse – Foucault provides partial genealogies of all three of these forms[30]; as such, they may in some cases be anti-parrhesiastic, and even (in the pejorative sense) demagogic discourses, if part of their function is to disqualify or silence other, less comfortable discourses or truths. Discourses of public edification, Foucault cautions (following Kant), may be prone to a self-corrupting flaw: pious, high-minded allegiance to the values of the Enlightenment can become 'the most touching of treasons'; the pedagogy of democratic virtue can in certain circumstances become (as Kant might have put it) the euthanasia of that democratic truth-telling which, Foucault tells us, is indispensable to a democratic governmentality. The art of telling a flatterer from a friend, a demagogue from a truth-teller, is as necessary in our time as in that of Plutarch or Erasmus.

NOTES

[1]   *Le Courage de la Vérité* (2009) ed. Frédéric Gros, Gallimard, Paris: p. 24.
[2]   This process began early on. Karen Jones and Kevin Williamson (1979) 'The Birth of the Schoolroom', *Ideology and Consciousness*, 6. This article appeared in the same issue as the first translation of a Foucault lecture on governmentality.

[3] See Thomas Osborne, 'Foucault as Educator', this book.

[4] Reading Foucault's most recently published and final lecture series of 1984, one finds more on this subject. Here, after distinguishing four general modes of 'veridiction' or true utterance, Foucault sees the mediaeval West as operating a new distribution in which the modalities of prophesy and parrhesia. Five volumes of the Collège de France lectures remain to be published in French, seven in English.

[5] In his as yet unpublished lecture course of 1980, *Le gouvernement des vivants*, Foucault situates this shift within the early development of Christianity, around the end 2nd century, between Clement and Tertullian. (Lecture of 13 February 1980).

[6] The German scholars Paul Rabbow (1914,1954) and Ilsetraut Hadot (1969) introduced this theme in modern scholarship under the terms 'Seelenleitung' and 'Seelenfuhrung'.

[7] Demogogy thus understood is the pedagogy and psychagogy of the citizen. C Gordon, 'The Soul of the Citizen: Max Weber and Michel Foucault on Rationality and Government', in S Whimster and S Lash eds., (1987) *Max Weber, Rationality and Modernity*, London: Allen & Unwin.

[8] I am grateful to Graham Burchell for reminding me of this remark, for other advice, and for discussion of these subjects over several decades.

[9] *Dits et écrits*, Gallimard, 1994, Vol 1 732-752 (a shorter version had appeared in 1967).

[10] *Kant*, Anthropologie du point de vue pragmatique, *tr. Michel Foucault; Foucault*, Introduction à l'Anthropologie, *edited by Daniel Defert, Francois Ewald and Frederic Gros, Paris, Vrin 2008.* Introduction to Kant's Anthropology, *ed. Roberto Nigro, tr. Roberto Nigro and Kate Briggs. Los Angeles, Semiotexte 2008. Kant, Anthropology from a Pragmatic Point of view, tr. and ed. Robert B Louden with an introduction by Manfred Kuehn, Cambridge UP, 2006.*

[11] Kant explicitly warns in the *Anthropology*, in the chapter on "Self-observation", against the dangers of the keeping of spiritual diaries. The "affected composition of an inner history of the *involuntary* course of one's thoughts and feelings" is "the most direct path to illuminism and even terrorism". He cites the case of the savant Albrecht von Haller, whose daily keeping of a spiritual diary induced a condition of acute mental anguish. "This eavesdropping on oneself is either a disease of the mind (melancholy), or leads to one and to the madhouse". (22)

[12] *Kant on Education* (Boston, 1900, tr Annette Churton) http://oll.libertyfund.org pp15ff (Foucault does not discuss this text.)

[13] The Port-Royal authors do not figure in this discussion.

[14] James Tully, (1993) *An approach to political philosophy: Locke in contexts*, CUP. Chapter 6, 'Governing conduct: Locke on the reform of thought and behaviour', pp. 179–241.

[15] Ed. Jacques Lagrange, tr. Graham Burchell, Palgrave Macmillan 2006.

[16] Erasmus was educated at one of the Brothers' schools.

[17] *The Birth of the Clinic*, (1973) tr. Alan Sheridan, Routledge, Chapter 7.

[18] Paris, 1976. See also Georges Vigarello's important study *Le corps redressé. Histoire d'un pouvoir pédagogique* (Paris, Delarge, 1978), a history of corporal pedagogies and orthopaedics, influenced by the agenda of *Discipline and Punish*.

[19] Ed. Michel Senellart, tr. Graham Burchell, Palgrave Macmillan, 2007.

[20] *Erasmus, (1997)* The Education of a Christian Prince, *Cambridge UP, tr. and ed. Lisa Jardine, p. 72. Jardine comments that the work "presents a manifesto for the crucial role of a 'philosopher' (or professional educator) in the administration of a properly run state" (xx). Erasmus makes clear that* parrhesia, *the fearless telling of truth to princely power, forms part of this educational package. The bound volume which Erasmus sent to Henry VIII containing his* Education *also included his translation of Plutarch's 'How to tell a flatterer from a friend', an essay discussed by Foucault in his lectures on* parrhesia *given in Paris and Berkeley in 1983.*

[21] Michel Foucault, (2003) *Society must be defended* tr. David Macey, Allen Lane: 127ff.

[22] Lecture of April 4th 1979.

[23] *Society must be defended*, ibid: 235 (translation amended).

[24] Ed. Valerio Marchetti and Antonella Salomoni, tr. Graham Burchell, Verso 2003.

[25] *The Birth of Biopolitics*, lecture of March 14th 1979.

[26] See, notably, the important discussion in *The Hermeneutics of the Subject* of Epicurus's critique of *paideia*. (238-244): the opinion of Montaigne cited in the epigraph above is in this tradition. (Foucault suggests that we re-read Montaigne "as an attempt to reconstitute an ethics and an aesthetics of the self".)Two of the Socratic dialogues which Foucault studies most attentively, *Alcibiades I* and *Laches*, are about young men or adolescents who have been badly educated. For the philosophical critics of, as Frederic Gros describes in his 'Course Context', quoting from Foucault's unpublished notes: 'one can only be led to oneself by unlearning what has been instilled by a misleading education… "Education is grounded on a basis of errors, deformations, bad habits and dependencies which are sedimented in us from the start of life."' (536)

[27] It would also be an excess of piety to assume that the purpose of that 'trip', and the vivid portrayals in the 1982-4 lectures of various versions of Greco-Roman philosophical life, is primarily to propose to modern readers a set of *exempla* for contemporary ethical practice. The arresting portrait of the Cynic philosopher, filtered through its revisionist rendering by the Stoic philosopher Epictetus, as a 'functionary of humanity', 'associated with the government of Zeus', might be taken to lend itself to critical and cautionary reflections as much as to the deduction of new moral agendas.

[28] The remark from the 1984 cited above as an epigraph implies a sharp partition between pedagogy and *parrhesia*, given that courage is declared unnecessary for the former and definitionally essential for the latter. The remark was no doubt intended to refer primarily to the conditions of western liberal democracies, not to all political and social circumstances. Foucault was at this time looking forward to paying a forthcoming visit, in the footsteps of other Western academics to the famous clandestine philosophy seminar in Prague. In the 1984 lectures he briefly discusses, praises and recommends *Plato and Europe*, the recently translated work by the founder of that seminar, Vaclav Havel's mentor, Jan Patocka. Although Foucault does not here discuss the fact that Patocka's recent death had followed a police interrogation relating to Patocka's signature of *Charter 77*, one may guess that his interest in Patocka and the reason for this reference is not exclusively in terms of Plato scholarship. It is hard to read these lectures without sensing a reference to Havel's (then unpublished) writings published shortly afterwards in the volume entitled *Living in Truth*. In his 1978 lectures, which included a citation from Andrei Sinyavski's *The Shade of Gogol*, Foucault expressed a marked scruple and reluctance to adopt the term 'dissident' as an analytic category, referring to its banalisation as an intellectual fashion ("After all, who doesn't have their theory of dissidence nowadays?" (201)) In 1977, Foucault had organized a public reception in Paris for exiled Soviet dissidents, at which Sinyavski was among the honoured guests.

[29] 'For an ethic of discomfort' (original title: 'Pour une morale de l'inconfort'), *Power*, pp. 443–448. In 1983, Foucault interviewed Edmond Maire, the leading figure in the non-communist left trade union federation CFDT, together with whom Foucault had publicly protested against the French socialist government's condoning of the declaration of martial law in Poland. In his questions, Foucault shows interest in both the pedagogical and the truth-telling roles played by Maire and the CFDT. ('La Pologne, et après?' *Dits et écrits*, IV: pp. 496–521.)

[30] In the lecture series of 1978, 1984 and 1976 respectively.

MICHAEL A. PETERS

INTRODUCTION

Governmentality, Education and the End of Neoliberalism?

THE BIRTH OF NEOLIBERALISM?

This collection of essays utilizes Foucault's notion of 'governmentality' to identify and analyze the main forms and characteristics of economic liberalism in its main geopolitical schools – Austrian, German, French and American – that have dominated the economic and policy landscapes of the post-war era, and also laid a template of sorts for the institutional world architecture called 'Bretton Woods' as the monetary system based on liberal conception of the 'open' market with its commitment to 'free' flows of capital and trade, the convertibility of currencies, and the formal apparatus of the International Monetary Fund (IMF) and World Bank (WB). After a general section comprising seven essays that together theorize Foucault's notion of governmentality in relation to liberalism and neoliberalism, this collection applies and develops Foucault's governmentality studies in relation to the field of education, providing both Anglo-American and European perspectives. Neoliberalism in the popular sense is a label for what is commonly understood as the doctrine of political and economic liberalism and set of policies originating in the 1970s that wielded together classical liberal political theory as exemplified by the Mont Pelerin Society after WWII and neoclassical economic theories that became identified with the so-called Chicago school under Milton Friedman in the 1960s.

It is not a unified and coherent doctrine and it has taken on different manifestations at different times and places sometimes with contradictory results. For an ultimately moral doctrine based on a classical account of political and economic freedom – a marriage of the 'free market' and the 'open society'– beginning Chile in 1973 where administrations and policy regimes based on the minimal state and open global market, paradoxically, were brutally established with force and coercion, against the rule of law and in a savagely anti-democratic way. This imposition became commonplace during the 1980s with 'structural adjustment' policies of the IMF and WB that 'forced' the transitional economies of Latin America and elsewhere to liberalize trade and monetary systems, to open up their economies and to privatize state assets and cut back state welfare.

For analytical purposes, we can postulate a rough chronology of neoliberalism:
– The development of the Austrian, Freiburg and Chicago schools in neoclassical economics as a continuance of classical liberalism in the first part of the twentieth century;
– The establishment of the Austrian school by Carl Menger with the publication of *Principles of Economics* (*Grundsätze der Volkswirtschaftslehre*) in 1871, his

'subjective theory of value' (theory of marginal utility) and the attack on historicism in the debate over epistemology (*Methodenstreit*) in economics that took place in the 1880s;
- Menger attracts Eugen von Böhm-Bawerk, Friedrich von Wieser and later Ludwig von Mises who extends marginal utility theory to money in *The Theory of Money and Credit* (1912) and recruits Friedrich von Hayek who develops Mises' business cycle theories and becomes Director of the newly formed Austrian Institute for Business Cycle Research in 1927;
- On the invitation from Lionel Robbins, Director of the London School of Economics, Hayek shifts to Britain, and in opposition to John Maynard Keynes develops his theory of spontaneous institutions, and engages in debates against socialist planning in the late 1930s;
- The founding of Freiburg School or the Ordoliberal School in the 1930s at the University of Freiburg in Germany by Walter Eucken, Franz Böhm and Hans Großmann-Doerth;
- The 'first globalization' of neoliberalism with the establishment of the Mount Pelerin Society in 1947 founded by Hayek who writes *The Road to Serfdom* as a tract against big government and totalitarianism;
- The establishment of the Chicago school in the with Frank Knight, Milton Friedman, George Stigler, Ronald Coarse, Gary Becker and others from the 1940s with an emphasis on the assumption of rationality in macroeconomics, monetarism, economics of education and human capital, the economics of information, innovation and political economy of property rights and contracts;
- The development of the 'Washington consensus' during the 1970s;
- The CIA sponsored coup against Salvador Allende in Chile and the subsequent imposition of neoliberal market reforms by General Pinochet from 1973-1990;
- The New Right ascendancy of the Thatcher-Reagan years during the 1980s and the 'export' of neoliberal ideology;
- The emergence of structural adjustment loans and institutionalization of neoliberalism through a series of world policy agencies such as IMF, WB, OECD (Organization for Economic Cooperation and Development) and WTO (World Trade Organization);
- The transition to 'knowledge economy' (OECD) and 'knowledge for development' (WB) in the 1990s and beyond;
- The collapse of neoliberal financial infrastructure and ethos, and the roll-back of neoliberal policies by Barack Obama's administration during the first term (2009-2013).

This is not the place to detail the growth of neoclassical economics in the Anglo-American and Continental traditions, but suffice it to say that standard economic history explains that the Austrian school emerged with Carl Menger in the late nineteenth century with its twin pillars of the subjective theory of value and the political defence of laissez-faire economic policy which became clearer in the hands of Friedrich Wieser, Eugene Böhm-Bawerk, and later, Ludwig von Mises and Friedrich von Hayek.[1] The neoliberalism of the Chicago school really emerged around George Stigler's leadership and Friedman's monetarism in the 1960s that was fiercely anti-Keynesian and against the concept of market failure. This school often referred to as the 'second' Chicago school included work on search theory (Stigler), human capital theory (Becker) and transaction cost analysis (Coarse) which then served as the basis for a series of innovations and new directions often characterized as the 'third' Chicago school including monetarism (Friedman), public choice theory (Buchanan), new classical macroeconomics (Lucas), new institutional economics (Coarse), new economic history (Fogel), new social economics (Becker), and Law-and economics (Posner).[2]

The Freiburg School or the Ordoliberal School was founded in the 1930s at the University of Freiburg in Germany by economist Walter Eucken and two jurists, Franz Böhm and Hans Großmann-Doerth. The founders of the school were united in their common concern for the question of the constitutional foundations of a free economy and society and were anti-naturalist in their conception of the market believing it was a legal-juridical construction.

FOUCAULT'S GOVERNMENTALITY

In his governmentality studies in the late 1970s Foucault held a course at the Collège de France on the major forms of neoliberalism, examining the three theoretical schools of German ordoliberalism, the Austrian school characterized by Hayek, and American neoliberalism in the form of the Chicago school (see Foucault, 2008). Among Foucault's great insights in his work on governmentality was the critical link he observed in liberalism between the governance of the self and government of the state – understood as the exercise of political sovereignty over a territory and its population.

Foucault's approach to governmentality including his analysis of German *ordoliberalism,* a source for the 'social market economy' and the EU's 'social model', begins with an analysis of the self-limitation of governmental reason which is takes to be synonymous with liberalism which he suggests should be understood very broadly as
- Acceptance of the principle that somewhere there must be a limitation of government and that this is not just an external right.
- Liberalism is also a practice: where exactly is the principle of the limitation of government to be found and how are the effects of this limitation to be calculated?
- In a narrower sense, liberalism is the solution that consists in the maximum limitation of the forms and domains of government action.
- Finally, liberalism is the organization of specific methods of transaction for defining the limitation of government practices:
  —constitution, parliament
  —opinion, the press
  —commissions, inquiries (Foucault, 2008, pp. 20–21)

Foucault's lectures on 'The Birth of Biopolitics' could easily have been called 'The Birth of Neoliberalism'. Liberalism Foucault suggests 'is a word that comes to use from Germany' (2008, p. 22) in the second half of the twentieth century. In later chapters he provides an understanding of German neoliberalism beginning with Ludwig Erhard in 1947 to examine contemporary German governmentality: economic freedom, the source of juridical legitimacy and political consensus. Foucault focuses on Erhard in retelling the story of German post-WWII reconstruction. After serving as economics minister for Barvaria (1945-46) Erhard becomes director both of the Advisory Committee for Money and Credit (1947–48) and the economic council for the joint Anglo-U.S. occupation (1948–49) where he is responsible for instituting currency reforms. As economics minister of the new Federal Republic of Germany under Chancellor Konrad Adenauer Erhard was responsible for policies of reconstruction successfully applying his social market system to problems of economic renewal.

What preserves liberalism in its new formation is the way in which neoliberalism picks up on the classical liberal political practice of introducing a self-limitation on governmental reason while departing from it in terms of a theory of pure competition and the question of how to model the global exercise of political power on the principles of a market economy. *Ordoliberalism* thus issues in a critique of the protectionist economy according to List, Bismarck's state socialism, the setting up of a planned economy during the First World War, Keynesian interventionism; and the economic policy of National Socialism.

The innovation of American neoliberalism for Foucault is the generalization of the model of *homo economicus* to all forms of behavior representing an extension of economic analysis to domains previously considered to be non-economic and the redefinition of *homo economicus* as entrepreneur of himself with an emphasis on acquired elements and the problem of the formation of human capital in education. Foucault goes on to discuss a resumption of the problem of social and economic innovation and the generalization of the 'enterprise' form in the social field.

Foucault (1991) uses the term 'governmentality' to mean *mentalities of rule* and, historically, to signal the emergence of a distinctive mentality of rule that he alleged became the basis for modern liberal politics. He begins to examine the problematic of government by analysing the *series*: security, population, government, maintaining that there is an explosion of interest on the 'art of government' in the sixteenth century which is motivated by diverse questions: the government of oneself (personal conduct); the government of souls (pastoral doctrine); the government of children (problematic of pedagogy) (Foucault, 1991). At the intersection of two competing tendencies – state centralisation and a logic of dispersion – Foucault says, the problematic of government can be located; a problematic which poses questions of the *how* of government and seeks "to articulate a kind of rationality which was intrinsic to the art of government without subordinating it to the problematic of the prince and of his relationship to the principality of which he is lord and master" (Foucault, 1991, p. 89). By the term 'governmentality' Foucault (1991, pp. 102–3) meant three things:

– The ensemble formed by the institutions, procedures, analyses, and reflections; the calculations and tactics that allow the exercise of this very specific, albeit complex, form of power, which has as its principal form of knowledge political economy and as its essential technical means apparatuses of security.

- The tendency which, over a long period and throughout the West, has steadily led toward the pre-eminence of this type of power that may be called government over all other forms (sovereignty, discipline, etc.) resulting, on the one hand, in the formation of a whole series of specific governmental apparatuses, and, on the other, in the development of a whole complex of *savoirs*.
- The process, or rather the result of the process, through which the state of justice of the Middle Ages, transformed into the administrative state during the fifteenth and sixteenth centuries, gradually became 'governmentalized.'

Liberal modes of governing, Foucault tells us, are distinguished in general by the ways in which they utilise the capacities of free acting subjects and, consequently, modes of government differ according to the value and definition accorded the concept of freedom. These different mentalities of rule, thus, turn on whether freedom is seen as a natural attribute as with the philosophers of the Scottish Enlightenment, a product of rational choice making, or, as with Hayek, a civilizational artefact theorised as both negative and anti-naturalist.

Hayek's conception of freedom, for instance, was one that characterized the market as neither natural nor artificial but rather the product of a spontaneous social order governed by rules selected in a process of cultural evolution. His conception of freedom and 'the constitution of liberty' has special application in the so-called 'knowledge economy' where, as Foucault also acknowledges, following a Kantian critique, the state is strictly limited in its power to know. Hayek argued that the price mechanism of the 'free' market conveys information about supply and demand that is dispersed among many consumers and producers and cannot be coordinated by any central planning mechanism. His early work emphasized that the key to economic growth is 'knowledge' and this insight provided him with the grounds for casting doubt on socialism and state planning, and for advocating that the market was the best way to organize modern society.

For neoliberals inspired by Hayek's insights the commitment to the free market involves two sets of claims: claims for the efficiency of the market as a superior allocative mechanism for the distribution of scarce public resources, and; claims for the market as a morally superior form of political economy. Neoliberalism as a political philosophy, it is often said, involves a return to a primitive form of individualism: an individualism which is 'competitive', 'possessive' and construed often in terms of the doctrine of 'consumer sovereignty'. It involves an emphasis on freedom over equality where freedom is construed in negative terms and individualistic terms. Negative freedom is freedom from state interference which implies an acceptance of inequalities generated by the market. Neoliberalism is both anti-state and anti-bureaucracy, and its attack on big government is made on the basis of both economic and ethical arguments (see Peters and Marshall, 1996). But this is to treat neoliberalism as a doctrine or ideology rather than a set of governmental practices.

CHARACTERISTICS OF NEOLIBERALISM

In *Poststructuralism, Marxism and Neoliberalism* (Peters, 2001), a book written for a U.S. audience and devoted to the proposition that poststructuralism is neither anti-Marxist nor anti-structuralist, I identified twelve features of neoliberalism from a viewpoint heavily influenced by Michel Foucault's (1979) notion of governmentality. Foucault uses the term 'governmentality' to mean the art of government and, historically, to signal the emergence of distinctive types of rule that became the basis for modern liberal politics. His starting point for the examination of the problematic of government is the series: security, population, government. He maintains that there is an explosion of interest on the 'art of government' in the sixteenth century which is motivated by diverse questions: the government of oneself (personal conduct); the government of souls (pastoral doctrine); and the government of children (problematic of pedagogy). Foucault says that the problematic of government can be located at the intersection of two competing tendencies: state centralisation and logic of dispersion. This is a problematic that poses questions of the how of government rather than its legitimation and seeks "to articulate a kind of rationality which was intrinsic to the art of government without subordinating it to the problematic of the prince and of his relationship to the principality of which he is lord and master" (Foucault, 1991, p, 89). It is only in the late sixteenth and early seventeenth centuries that the art of government crystallises for the first time around the notion of 'reason of state,' understood in a positive sense whereby the state is governed according to rational principles that are seen to be intrinsic to it. In charting this establishment of the art of government Foucault thus details the introduction of 'economy' into political practice (understood as 'the correct manner of managing goods and wealth within the family').

In line with this analysis, Foucault defines governmentality in terms of a specific form of government power based upon the 'science' of political economy, which over a long period, he maintains, has transformed the administrative state into one fully governmentalized, and led to the formation of both governmental apparatuses and knowledges (or *savoirs*). In elaborating these themes Foucault concentrates his analytical energies on understanding the pluralized forms of government, its complexity, and its techniques. Our modernity, he says, is characterized by the 'governmentalization' of the state. He is interested in the question of how power is exercised and, implicitly, he is providing a critique of the contemporary tendencies to overvalue the problem of the state and to reduce it to a unity or singularity based upon a certain functionality. This substantive feature – the rejection of state-centred analyses – has emerged from the governmentality literature as it has become a more explicit problematic. In outlining the main features of neoliberalism it is important to realise that there are affinities, continuities, and overlapping concepts as well as differences and theoretical innovations with classical liberalism.

I have previously focused on the 'new prudentialism' (O'Malley, 2002) in education based on the entrepreneurial self that 'responsibilizes' the self to make welfare choices based on an actuarial rationality (Peters, 2005). The promotion of the entrepreneurial self represents a shift away from a rights-based welfare model of the citizen to a consumer-oriented market individual (based on the rejuvenation of *homo economicus*) willing to calculate the risks and invest in herself at critical points in the life cycle. I have also analyzed Foucault's account of German *ordoliberalism,* a configuration based on the theoretical configuration of economics and law developed at the University of Freiberg by W. Eucken and F. Böhm that views the market contingently as developing historically within a judicial-legal framework. The economy is thus based on a concept of the Rule of Law, anchored in a notion of individual rights, property rights and contractual freedom that constitutes, in effect, an economic constitution. German neoliberal economists (Müller-Armack, Röpke, Rüstow) invented the term 'social market economy' which shared certain features with the Freiburg model of law and economics but also differed from it in terms of the 'ethics' of the market (as did Hayek in *The Constitution of Liberty*). This formulation of the "social market economy" proved significant not only in terms of the post-war reconstruction of the (West) German economy but through Erhard, as Minister and Chancellor, became important as the basis of the EEC's and, later, EU's 'social model'.

– Classical liberalism as a critique of State reason: A political doctrine concerning the self-limiting State; the limits of government are related to the limits of State reason, i.e., its power to know; a permanent critique of the activity of rule and government.

– Natural versus contrived forms of the market: Hayek's notion of natural laws based on spontaneously ordered institutions in the physical (crystals, galaxies) and social (morality, language, market) worlds has been replaced with an emphasis on the market as an artefact or culturally derived form and (growing out of the 'callaxy' approach) a constitutional perspective that focuses on the judicio-legal rules governing the framework within the game of enterprise is played (see Buchanan, 1991).

– The Politics-as-exchange innovation of Public Choice theory ('the marketisation of the State'): The extension of Hayek's spontaneous order conception (callactics) of the institution of the market beyond simple exchange to complex exchange and finally to all processes of voluntary agreement among persons (see Buchanan & Tullock, 1962).

– The relation between government and self-government: Liberalism as a doctrine which positively requires that individuals be free in order to govern; government as the community of free, autonomous, self-regulating individuals; 'responsibilisation' of individuals as moral agents; the neo-liberal revival of homo economicus, based on assumptions of individuality, rationality and self-interest, as an all-embracing redescription of the social as a form of the economic.

– A new relation between government and management: The rise of the new managerialism, 'New Public Management'; the shift from policy and administration to management; emulation of private sector management styles; the emphasis on 'freedom to manage' and the promotion of 'self-managing' (i.e., quasi-autonomous) individuals and entities.

– A 'degovernmentalisation' of the State (considered as a positive technique of government): Government 'through' and by the market, including promotion of consumer-driven forms of social provision (health, education, welfare), 'contracting out', and privatisation.

- The promotion of a new relationship between government and knowledge: 'Government at a distance' developed through relations of forms of expertise (expert systems) and politics; development of new forms of social accounting; an actuarial rationality; referendums and intensive opinion polling made possible through the new information and computing technologies; privatisation and individualisation of 'risk management'; development of new forms of prudentialism.
- An economic theory of democracy ('the marketisation of democracy'): an emerging structural parallel between economic and political systems – political parties have become entrepreneurs in a vote-seeking political marketplace; professional media consultants use policies to sell candidates as image products; voters have become passive individual consumers. In short, democracy has become commodified at the cost of the project of political liberalism and the state has become subordinated to the market.
- The replacement of 'community' for 'the social': The decentralisation, 'devolution' and delegation of power/authority/responsibility from the center to the region, the local institution, the 'community'; the emergence of the shadow state; the encouragement of the informal voluntary sector (and an autonomous civil society) as a source of welfare; 'social capital'.
- Cultural reconstruction as deliberate policy goal ('the marketisation of "the social"'): The development of an 'enterprise society'; privatisation of the public sector; the development of quasi-markets; marketisation of education and health; a curriculum of competition and enterprise
- Low ecological consciousness (Anthony Giddens): 'green capitalism'; 'green consumerism'; linear as opposed to ecological modernisation; 'no limits to growth'; market solutions to ecological problems
- Promotion of a neoliberal paradigm of globalisation: world economic integration based on 'free' trade; no capital controls; International Monetary Fund (IMF), World Bank (WB), World Trade organisation (WTO) as international policy brokers.

GOVERNMENTALITY STUDIES AND THE CHALLENGE OF GLOBALISATION

Foucault's concept of governmentality developed in the last years of his life has been developed by a range of thinkers including those who worked with him helping to prepare his famous lecture course, including Jacques Donzelot whose work features prominently in this collection both in a chapter and in interview with Colin Gordon, one of Foucault's English translators and the leading thinker of the Anglo-Foucauldian group that includes Graham Burcell, Peter Miller, Nikolas Rose, Barry Hindess and Mitchell Dean, among others. In Germany the work of Thomas Lemke has been essential reading and his work has been highly influential in governmentality debates around the world. We are fortunate to be able to include a chapter by Lemke. In the development and application of Focuault's work on governmentality we can discern a number of stages: its initial invention and development arising out of Foucault's late political and ethical thought in the late 1970s; the set of sustained reflections on the concept and its relations to biopolitics and neoliberalism in the course entitled 'The Birth of Biopolitics' delivered in 1978-79; the subsequent development of governmentality in a series of courses including *'Du gouvernment des vivants'* (1979-1980), *'Subjectivite et verite'* (1980-1981), *'Le gouvernment de soi et des autres'* (1982-1983), and *'Le gouvernment de soi et des autre: le courage de la verite'* (1983-1984) some of which have not yet been transcribed in French or translated into English. The book *The Foucault Effect: Studies in Governmentality* (1991) edited by Graham Burchell, Colin Gordon and Peter Miller combined three essays of Foucault's including the 1978 'Governmentality' with original an introduction by Colin Gordon and original essays by Pasquale Pasquino, Graham Burchell, Giovanna Procacci, Jacques Donzelot, Ian Hacking, François Ewald, Daniel Defert and Robert Castel. This was followed by Hunt and Wickham's *Foucault and Law* (1994), the collection by Andrew Barry, Thomas Osborne and Nikolas Rose (1996), *Foucault and Political Reason. Liberalism, neo-liberalism and rationalities of government*, and Mitchell Dean's (1999) *Governmentality: Power and rule in modern society.*

Since the end of the 1990s we have seen a flowering of governmentality studies with applications and development across the full range of the social science and humanities: in anthropology[3], politics (Lipschutz & Rowe, 2005); international studies (Larner & Walters, 2004; Sending & Neumann, 2006; Merlingen, 2006); rights and political freedom (Ciccarelli, 2008), cultural studies (Bratich et al, 2003), security (Leander & Rens, 2006) and 'terrorism' (Ventura et al, 2005; Tagma, 2006), development (Watts, 2003; Li, 2007), law (Pavlich & Wickham, 2001), geography (Crampton & Eldon, 2007), education[4] (Masschelein, 2007), everyday life (Nadesan, 2008), European governance (Walters & Haar, 2005) and environment (Death, 2006; Luke, n.d.). This is by no means a comprehensive list or summary.[5] The standard introductions to the concept of governmentality have been provided by Colin Gordon (1991; 2001; this volume), Nikolas Rose et al (2006) and most recently in a new collection by Ulrich Bröckling, Susanne Krasmann, Thomas Lemke (2009) entitled *Governmentality: Current Issues and Future Challenges* which explores the advantages and limitations of adopting Michel Foucault's concept of governmentality as an analytical framework. The workshop on which the book is based begins:

> The publication of *The Foucault Effect: Studies in Governmentality* in 1991 marked the beginning of a growing interest in the notion of governmentality in the social and political sciences. In the following years, 'governmentality' became a key term that inspired empirical analyses in different subject areas and academic disciplines. The so-called studies of governmentality offered quite a different perspective on state theory and political analysis: They went beyond traditional accounts structured by the opposition between state and civil society, public and private spheres, freedom and constraint by focusing on the interplay between processes of subjectivation and power mechanisms, political rationalities and governmental technologies. However, the concept

of governmentality also engendered serious criticism in recent years which may point to some limitations and shortcomings in this theoretical perspective. 16 years after the publication of *The Foucault Effect* the workshop shall provide the opportunity to discuss the theoretical and empirical achievements, future perspectives and persisting problems of an analytics of government. It takes up three major themes that encountered discussions and also critical attention in recent years (http://www. unikonstanz.de/ kulturtheorie/Workshop_TheStateofGovernmentality1.pdf).[6]

The brief for the workshop proceeds to highlight the three themes as: 1. Beyond the nation state: Sovereignty, bio-politics and trans-nationalisation; 2. Biological citizenship and the government of life; 3. The economy of government. One of the alleged limitations in Foucault's work, these authors argue, is the focus on the territoriality of the modern state, especially in an increasingly globalized world. Yet a number of authors have begun to apply the governmentality framework systematically beyond the territoriality of the modern state (Perry & Maurer, 2003; Larner & Walters, 2004; Walters & Haar, 2005).

Larner and Walters (2004) emphasized the way in which 'governmentality' has been used in two distinct ways in the literature: (1) "a form of power whose logic is not the defense of territory or the aggrandizement of the sovereign but the optimization of the health and welfare of the population" and (2) "an approach that explores how governing always involves particular representations, knowledges, and expertise regarding that which is to be governed" (p. 495). They develop the second sense of the notion as "the practice of government [which] involves the production of particular 'truths' about …. the constitution of our societies and ourselves" (ibid.). This 'governmentality' of the international allows Foucault's approach to be used and mapped onto current debates about gloablization where "the role of nonstate actors in shaping and carrying out global governance-functions is not an instance of transfer of power from the state to nonstate actors but rather an expression of a changing logic or rationality of government (defined as a type of power) by which civil society is redefined from a passive object of government to be acted upon into an entity that is both an object *and* a subject of government" (Sending & Neumann, 2006, p. 651). In a more porous and interconnected world governmentality can shed light on changing practices of political rule that define the identity and functioning of key actors in world politics. Such an understanding is crucial if we are to understand the new economization of the state which depends on networks and the complexity of network effects that challenge the space of pure economic rationality assumed by neoclassical economics and the ideal of rationally calculating economic man. Human capital theory based on this ideal then becomes the focus for an analysis of 'the entrepreneur of oneself' as a technology of indirect government control exercised *across* government policies that traverse national spaces, especially in the field of education and health where these indirect technologies are the substance of biopolitics.

Michael Merlingen (2006) provides a useful discussion of the attempt to extend governmentality beyond the state, reviewing three books: Larner and Walters

(2004) collection *Global Governmentality: Governing International Spaces;* Perry and Maurer (2003) collection *Globalization under Construction: Governmentality, Law, and Identity; and,* Walters and Haahr's (2005) *Governing Europe: Discourse, Governmentality and European Integration.* He identifies six strengths of "governmentality theory", which, as he argues "promise to provide some new interpretative purchase upon deterritorialised and de-stated politics" (p. 184). These he lists as: *Networked Governance* that enables governmentality theory with the aid of actor network theory (Latour, Callon) to study policy networks; a *Semiotics of Materiality* that enables "governmentality theory" to go beyond "discourse-centred poststructuralist and constructivist approaches in IR and EU studies" (p. 187); the *Denaturalisation of Governance* that helps "to strip political rule of its self-evident, normal or natural character" (p. 188); *Exploring the European/Global through Micropolitical Sites and Practices* "adds to the exploration of these microworlds is the excavation/mapping of all those little knowledges and humble and mundane technologies through which the European/global is articulated" (p. 189); *Resistance and the Fragility of Governance* "emphasises the likelihood of resistance and the reversibility of power relations" (p. 190). Perhaps most importantly, this feature in

> Its peculiar conceptualisation of the linkage between domination and people's capacity for self-control makes the theory well suited for bringing into focus the tensions and opposition between the government of others and self-government and for adding a new perspective on the diverse and often inconspicuous ways in which citizens resist being enrolled in governmental projects of order(liness) (p. 190).

Merlingen (2006) adds *Power and Domination* that understands strategic power as the "reciprocal attempt of people to shape each other's conduct and the correlated games of control and resistance", states of domination "which are asymmetric, institutionalised patterns of interaction, say, between the coloniser and the colonised, man and woman" (p. 190), and "technologies" as the third concept of power that together provides a toolbox for researchers.

Where researchers only a few years ago were attempting to demonstrate the policy convergence of neoliberalism, its 'export' and institutionalization, and its constitution of globalization (or at least one version), the wheel has turned again with the election of Barack Obama and his instant roll-back of many of Bush's policies, although not all neoliberal policies. Indeed, the crisis of Keynesianism and the welfare state has been followed by the crisis of neoliberalism and free market fundamentalism.

THE END OF NEOLIBERALISM?

George Soros, the Popperian financier, has warned that this is the age of 'the destruction of capital'. Already conservative estimates indicate that 50 trillion dollars have been wiped off the books worldwide (30 trillion in equity funds, 4 trillion in credit, 3 trillion in lost output, 3 trillion in the sub-prime housing market). The world economy still (at the time of writing in early April 2009) has not showed any consistent signs of improvement or growth. A groundswell of opinion from a variety of scholars point to 'the end of neoliberalism' and the beginning of a new age of state intervention, although there is fierce debate over the extent of further stimulus packages. The Nobel prize-winning economist Joseph Stiglitz (July 7, 2008)[7] in *Project Syndicate* begins his column with the assertion that the ideology of "market fundamentalism" has failed

> The world has not been kind to neo-liberalism, that grab-bag of ideas based on the fundamentalist notion that markets are self-correcting, allocate resources efficiently, and serve the public interest well. It was this market fundamentalism that underlay Thatcherism, Reaganomics, and the so-called "Washington Consensus" in favor of privatization, liberalization, and independent central banks focusing single-mindedly on inflation.

Writing before the collapse of Wall Street's investment banks—the bankruptcy of Lehmann Brothers, the sell off of Merryl Lynch, the Federal bridging loan of $85 billion to AIG, the 'stimulus package' and Obama's March 2009 budget requiring 3.6 trillion dollars—Stiglitz criticizes neoliberal policies and their costs to developing economies.[8] He faults the financial market allocation of resources to housing in the 1990s and the sub-prime crisis that has precipitated a global financial crisis and credit squeeze he thinks will be prolonged and widespread. He criticizes the selective use of free-market rhetoric used to support special interests and the way that Bush's policies have served the military-industrial complex. He concludes:

> Neo-liberal market fundamentalism was always a political doctrine serving certain interests. It was never supported by economic theory. Nor, it should now be clear, is it supported by historical experience. Learning this lesson may be the silver lining in the cloud now hanging over the global economy.

Others[9] such as John Quiggin (September 8, 2008)[10], the Australian social-democrat, have remarked:

> The fact that the credit crisis has reached this point marks the failure of the central claim of the neoliberal program, namely that private capital markets, free from intrusive government regulation, can enable individuals and households to handle the risks they face more flexibly and efficiently than a social-democratic welfare state.

In some sense the current series of crises that have rocked Wall Street to its foundations and threatened to destabilize the world financial system and its major banking and insurance institutions is just the latest round of failure for the global justice movement that has coordinated worldwide demonstrations against neoliberalism, 'the American imperialist project', the Iraq War, and strands referred to since the early 1980s as 'Monetarism,' 'Supply-Side Economics,' 'Reaganism/ Thatcherism.' Longtime critics of neoliberalism and its policies of privatization, state non-interference and deregulation summed up in the so-called 'Washington consensus'[11] such as the economists Stiglitz, and Robert Polin (2003), sociologist

Pierre Bourdieu (1998), geographer David Harvey (2005), philosopher/ linguist Noam Chomsky (1999), as well as the anti-globalization movement in general,[12] have consistently argued that neoliberalism is a class project that benefits the rich and leads to ever-increasing inequalities both within and between states.

A major overhaul of the financial system is almost certainly required and government regulation needs to be established, minimally, to ensure transparency and full disclosure, to spell out capital requirements and to avoid conflicts of interest. In 2009, Timothy Geithner as Obama's Treasury Secretary is currently implementing a plan to buy over $1 trillion in troubled assets and mortgages and the G20 under Gordon Brown is pushing for a new global framework for tighter regulation, spelling the end of global financial laissez-faire. The move to state-centric policies and to forms of regulation in the U.S. and elsewhere seems almost inevitable. Government intervention and (neo)Keynesianism is now suddenly back in fashion. The move to Federal regulation and a reform of the financial system seems to chime with the development of state capitalism elsewhere, especially in East Asia.[13]

As the centre of economic gravity shifts to East Asia it is not clear whether new Keynesianism will be embraced or whether in face of such intensive global competition and fierce economic nationalism whether Western economies can ever afford it. There is never the option of an innocent return historically and a return to the golden days of the welfare state in Scandinavia or New Zealand, or to the 'social model' in Europe, especially as new costly environmental and energy contingencies begins to bite. Some argue that what is required is a change of *ethos*—not 'confidence' and 'trust' of the market but rather the development of trust that comes with the radically decentred democratic collaboration that epitomizes distributed knowledge, political and energy systems. Yet all these explanations seem to be predicated upon understanding neoliberalism as a doctrine, ideology or set of policies and none have benefited from Foucault's notion of generality as a mentality of rule.

President Barack Obama has a strong vision for reclaiming the American dream and for a political and economic philosophy based on a combination of American pragmatism with a strong emphasis on 'what works' and an interventionist government-led emphasis on ethics and responsibility to change the culture of corruption in Washington. Obama's political philosophy is based on the notions of unity, community, equality and hope. He wants to transcend all divisions, to provide a new universalism of provision and encourage a greater inclusiveness that moves beyond the dualism and dichotomies that haunt the U.S. going back to the 1960s–white-black, male-female, Democrat-Republican—in order to assert the American moment and to provide global leadership.[14] Obama's administration is attempting to implement a progressivist egalitarian economic philosophy that is a managed form of capitalism oriented to crisis management in the short term with massive government assistance to banks, tax cuts to the middle class, and huge infrastructure investment aimed at economic recovery. In the longer term Obama is pursuing market-friendly innovation policies based on the reform of science and technology and structural reforms in green energy and universal health care.

The question is whether this really does mean the end of neoliberalism. Clearly, the IMF and WB are still pursuing their old structural adjustment policies especially in bankrupt states like the Ukraine and Latvia. Both internationally and within the U.S. the neoliberal mantra against big government has been given short shrift as governments world–wide has embarked on interventionist policies consisting in bail-outs, stimulus packages and in some cases wholesale nationalization of banking and insurance institutions or partnership with private interests. At the same time there is a clear set of policy intentions from Obama's administration to intervene directly in the economy by socializing and universalizing health as well as investing heavily in education, energy, science and technology. This means that the state under Obama has begun to move toward a model of greater collective responsibility reversing the earlier neoliberal strategy of making individuals responsible for social risks while at the same time resisting the move to Keynesian policies of full employment. The question is whether the concept of governmentality now provides the means to understand the constitution of new political forms and the reshaping of identities and subjectivities that follow from a community model.

Contemporary social theory, strongly influenced by Foucault focusing on identity studies seeks the constitution and manufacture of consciousness and subjectivity in more nuanced ways, emphasizing cultural processes of formation within larger shifts concerning globalization, the 'knowledge economy', and the mobility of peoples across national boundaries and frontiers. Economists have given greater attention to the world of social media and new technologies in relation to identity formation and the transformation of patterns of work and its definition in a post-industrial society. In economics there has developed an entire new field called 'behavioral economics' that repudiates aspects of neoclassical theory based on the simplifying assumptions of *Homo economicus*, importing and basing its insights on psychology.

At one time, at the very beginning of its disciplinary formation in the heyday of 'political economy', economics had a strong relationship to the other social sciences and, particularly, to questions of psychology. In *The Theory of Moral Sentiments* Adam Smith (1759) commented upon the psychological principles guiding human behavior providing the ethical and methodological principles for his later works. Broadly speaking, Smith followed his mentor, Francis Hutcheson, in dividing moral systems into two: nature (Propriety, Prudence, and Benevolence) and motive (Self- Love, Reason, and Sentiment). Smith, in contrast to Hutcheson, provides us with a psychological account of morality, beginning *Moral Sentiments* with the observation that however selfish a man may be supposed to be there are 'some principles in his nature, which interest him in the fortunes of others, and render their happiness necessary to him, though he derives nothing from it, except the pleasure of seeing it'. As the discipline developed, especially during the neoclassical phase, economists began to distance themselves from psychology as they sought to base their explanations on the hypothesis of rational agents, especially with the development of the concept of *Homo economicus* that appeared for the first time in the work of John Stuart Mill where the psychology of the postulated entity was defined as fundamentally rational. In 'On the Definition of Political Economy, and on the Method of Investigation Proper to It', Mill (1836) suggests that political economy is concerned with "...[Man] solely as a being who desires to possess wealth, and who is capable of judging the comparative efficacy of means for obtaining that end."

The essential aspect of *Homo economicus* is the 'rational' element in the sense that well-being is defined by the optimization of the utility function and is normally described in terms of three governing assumptions: individuality (all choices are made by individuals); rationality (these are conscious deliberative choices); and self-interest (they are made in the interest of the choicemaker). The rationality of Economic Man has been called into question by other disciplines that emphasize the cultural and gendered nature of rationality or point to the way in which economic agents act irrationally or in not rational optimal ways. The rejuvenation of Homo economicus as a basis for addressing public policy came during the decades of neoliberalism beginning under Thatcher and Reagan that so drastically restructured the public sector, reducing the number of public servants, commercializing and privatizing state enterprises, and selling off state assets. It also reshaped the global labor marketplace and restructured higher education in accord with its own globalization ideals. The building of 'enterprise culture' was as much a moral crusade to redefine the nature of society through a redefinition of work as were the first attempts to theorize the economic nature of humankind.

A new generation of social theorists and researchers now look for approaches that link discourse, power, psychology and the self with economics to explain the failings of assumptions of *Homo economicus*. Nowhere is this confluence of psychology and economics more important than the in newly emerging field of behavioral economics and finance. Robert J. Shiller, one of its ablest practitioners, writes, 'Behavioral economics incorporates insights from other social sciences, such as psychology and sociology, into economic models, and attempts to explain anomalies that defy standard economic analysis'. He treats behavioral economics alongside institutional economics as 'the study of the evolution of economic organizations, laws, contracts, and customs as part of a historical and continuing process of economic development' and notes that 'topics include economic fluctuations and speculation, herd behavior, attitudes towards risk, money illusion, involuntary unemployment, saving, investment, poverty, identity, religion, trust, risk management and social welfare institutions'.[15]

The fact is that the question of identity strongly influences economic thinking and behavior and people do not behave in the way that the strong rationality model of neoclassical economics has taught us to believe on the basis of *Homo economicus*. In this vein I am reminded of Foucault's (2008) lectures on the birth of neoliberalism and in particular lectures nine to twelve where he analyzes Amercian neoliberalism and the theory of human capital—the application of economics to the domain of social life (law and criminality) and the redefinition of *Homo economicus* as entrepreneur of himself, in effects, its generalization to every form of behavior. Foucault comments how *Homo economicus* emerged as the basic element of the new governmental reason in the eighteenth century as a correlate of the liberal art of government with its focus on civil society which he traces to Ferguson's (1787) *A History of Civil Society*.

When Obama (2009) asserts that ours is a market society in a strong sense he is also adverting to the deep institutionalization of *Homo economicus* in American society, the bi-partisan acceptance of human capital theory in economics and all spheres of life, especially in terms of a generalization of the form 'entrepreneur of himself' chiming with an embedded American ethos, even if under Obama this might come to mean a greater socialization of entrepreneurship and corresponding a greater personalization of services through social networks and social media.

THE ORGANIZATION OF THIS COLLECTION

Foucault (2008, p. 407) ends his lectures on the birth of biopower with the statement:

> You can see that in the modern world, in the world we have known since the nineteenth century, a series of governmental rationalities overlap, lean on each other, challenge each other, and struggle with each other: art of government according to truth, art of government according to the rationality of the sovereign state, and art of government according to the rationality of economic agents, and more generally, according to the rationality of the governed themselves. And it is all these different arts of government, all these different types of ways of calculating, rationalizing, and regulating the art of government which, overlapping each other, broadly speaking constitute the object of political debate from the nineteenth century. What is politics, in the end, if not both the interplay of these different arts of government with their different reference points and the debate to which these different arts of government give rise?

The essays of this collection focus on how neoliberal, third way and neo-conservative policies rely on a set of practices that might be termed 'government through the market' to produce 'responsiblized' citizens who harness their own entrepreneurial and self-governing capabilities. This collection while including general essays by some of the world's most renown Foucault scholars in the area of governmentality is primarily targeted at issues concerning the field of education and education policies. It is a landmark text in Foucault studies in education drawing on work currently being developed by scholars working in Germany, Belgium, Canada, Australia, China, Finland and New Zealand as well as the U.S. and United Kingdom. The collection fosters both internationalization and comparative policy analysis in education as well as general reflections on Foucault and the concept of governmentality. Many of the essays in this collection build upon previous research which has analyzed Foucault's approach to govern-mentality and 'the generalization of an "enterprise form" to all forms of conduct' (Burchell, 1996) and the way in which the promotion of enterprise culture has become a style of governance characteristic of both neoliberalism and Third Way politics.

The collection begins with a Foreword by Colin Gordon and a set of general chapters by Colin Gordon and Jacques Donzelot, Thomas Lemke, Risto Eräsaari, Mark Olssen, Michael A. Peters and Qizhi Yu. The next two sections comprise a set of chapters from Anglo-American perspectives and European perspectives. Anglo-American perspectives includes essays by Thomas Osborne, James D. Marshall, Robert Doherty, Tina (A.C.) Besley, Stephen J. Ball, Thomas S. Popkewitz, Jeff Stickney, David Lee Carlson, Adam Davidson-Harden, Lew Zipin and Marie Brennan, Bernadette Baker, Linda J. Graham, James Wong, and Majia Nadesan. The essays are comprehensive and wide-ranging examining 'Foucault as Educator' (Osborne), the shift from disciplinary to security society, social capital, the governmentality of youth, life-long leaning, university-school collaboration, the development of 'psychical science', brain-based-learning, possibilities of resistance for teachers, entrepreneurial subjects, neoliberalism and knowledge capitalism, secondary school strategy, special education and autism. European perspectives include a range of essays by Susanne Maria Weber, Susanne Maurer, Fabian Kessl, Daniel Wrana, Ute Karl, Thomas Höhne and Bruno Schreck, Andrea Liesner, Hermann J. Forneck, Andreas Fejes and Maarten Simons and Jan Masschelein. These essays, equally impressive in their range and depth, examine educational science in Germany, governmentality in social work, continuing education, older people and social work, modularised knowledge, governing the professor, adult education, organizational change, the fabrication of the European citizen, and self-study.

This collection on governmentality distinguishes between the different forms of neoliberalism in its historical and contemporary complexity in term of actual governmental practices. It also addresses forms of Third Way and neoconservative governmentality in the theoretical overview. The collection focuses on philosophical, historical and sociological understandings of 'governmentality' with an accent on *the entrepreneurial and enterprising self* and techniques of governing through the market. The theoretical overview will also trace the centrality of 'law and order', *ordnung*, and relation of the Rule of Law to economics, in liberal and neoliberal constitutions of 'freedom' and explore the field of constitutional economics, especially in relation to the funding, provision and regulation of public education.

Many of the essays in this collection are based on the theoretical promise of the problematic made explicit by the so-called Anglo-Foucauldians. I am referring mainly to the British and Australian neo-Foucauldians (including for example, Gordon, 1991; Burchell, 1993; Rose, 1993), as distinct from both the French and U.S. neo-Foucauldians, and as exemplified in an edited collection called *Foucault and Political Reason* (Barry et al., 1996). Besides the editors themselves, the collection edited by Barry, Osborne, and Rose (1996), includes the following contributors: Barry Hindess, Vikki Bell, Ian Hunter, Alan Hunt, Pat O'Malley, Mitchell Dean, and Barbara Cruikshank. (See also Dean, 1991, 1999; Hindess, 1996; Hunter, 1994; Hunt and Wickham, 1994; Rose, 1999, 2006). The Anglophone neo-Foucauldians might be distinguished from the French (e.g., Donzelot, 1979; Donzelot, 1991; Donzelot, this volume), and the U.S. neo-Foucauldians especially that based around the work of Paul Rabinow and Hubert Dreyfus (1983), and more recently the work on the anthropology of modernity by Paul Rabinow and his colleagues in the Anthropology department at the University of California, San Deigo.[16]

They may also be distinguished from various feminist appropriations of Foucault, which are both too diverse and complex for me to outline here. In terms of education the intention has been to include as many as possible of the Foucault theorists who have been writing in the field for some time and broadly to follow a neo-Foucauldian approach to the sociology of governance epitomized by *Foucault and Political Reason*. A neo-Foucauldian approach to the sociology of governance avoids interpreting liberalism as an ideology, political philosophy or an economic theory to reconfigure it as a form of governmentality with an emphasis on the question of *how* power is exercised. Such an approach makes central the notion of the self-limiting state, which in contrast to the administrative (or "police") state, brings together in a productive ways questions of ethics and technique, through the "responsibilization" of moral agents and the active reconstruction of the relation between government and self-government. It also proposes an investigation of neo-liberalism as an intensification of an economy of moral regulation first developed by liberals and not merely or primarily as a political reaction to "big government" or the so-called bureaucratic welfare state of the post-war Keynesian settlement. Indeed, as Andrew Barry et al (1996) point out, some who adopt this approach the era of post-war view welfarism as an aberrant episode that has little to do with liberalism *per se*. The approach enables an understanding of the distinctive features of neo-liberalism. It understands neo-liberalism in terms of its replacement of the natural and spontaneous order characteristic of Hayekian liberalism with "*artificially* arranged or contrived forms of the free, *entrepreneurial* and *competitive* conduct of economic-rational individuals" (Burchell, 1996: 23). And, further, it understands neo-liberalism through the development of "*a new relation between expertise and politics*" (ibid.), especially in the realm of welfare, where an actuarial rationality and new forms of prudentialism manifest and constitute themselves discursively in the language of "purchaser-provider", audit, performance, and "risk management".

Now the geopolitical world template has shifted in part as a consequence of neoliberal policies involving among other things the huge growth and collapse of finance capitalism, in the US and elsewhere in the West, there is a tendency towards community-building, providing jobs and a new focus on sustainability. It is too early to say whether this shift really signals the end of neoliberalism and the beginning of new forms of governmentality except to say there are clear signs that the emphasis of education to contribute to economic growth through research, innovation, and creativity is a development of historically deep-seated liberal notions about the expressive and creative self and the ways in which various freedoms to speak, teach and publish form a basis for governing liberal societies.

NOTES

[1] This description is drawn from 'Schools of [Economic] Thought' at http://cepa.newschool.edu/het/.

[2] See the Chicago Department of Economics website at, http://economics.uchicago.edu/index.shtml, where it makes the following description: 'Any definition of the "Chicago School" would have to find room for the following ideas (in chronological order from the 1940s to the present): the economic theory of socialism, general equilibrium models of foreign trade, simultaneous equation methods in econometrics, consumption as a function of permanent income, the economics of the household, the rationality of peasants in poor countries, the economics of education and other acquired skills (human capital), applied welfare economics, monetarism, sociological economics (entrepreneurship, racial discrimination, crime), the economics of invention and innovation, quantitative economic history, the economics of information, political economy (externalities, property rights, liability, contracts), the monetary approach to international finance, and rational expectations in macroeconomics.'

[3] See the work that originates with Paul Rabinow and others 'Critical Ethnographies of Globalization and Governmentality' http://ls.berkeley.edu/dept/anth/gandg.html.

[4] See also the website 'Contemporary Theory, Poststructuralism and Governmentality' at http://edtheory.ning.com/.

[5] For a more comprehensive summary see the journal *Foucault Studies* at http://rauli.cbs.dk/foucault_splash.html and the special issue on Neoliberal Governmentality (Issue No. 6, February, 2009) edited by Sverre Raffnsøe, Alan Rosenberg, Alain Beaulieu, Sam Binkley, Jens Erik Kristensen, Sven Opitz, Morris Rabinowitz, Ditte Vilstrup Holm.

[6] The workshop was held at the University of Leipzig, Dept. of Political Sciences, September 14-15, 2007.

[7] See Stiglitz's commentary at http://www.project-syndicate.org/commentary/stiglitz101.

[8] It seems almost inevitable that both Morgan Stanley and Goldman Sachs will also disappear. Morgan Stanley is in talks with the China Investment Corp. In the UK the Government rescued Northern Rock and Lloyds has bought out HBOS. Central banks around the world offered $180 billion to banks outside the US to weather the financial storm.

[9] See Lance Freeman's blog of March 2008 at http://www.planetizen.com/node/30187 and Robert Reich's Blog at http://robertreich.blogspot.com/. Both talk of the end of neoliberalism; see also Wallerstein's (2008) 'The Demise of Neoliberal Globalization' who argues the end of neoliberalism is a cyclical swing in the history of the capitalist world-economy, at http://www.monthlyreview.org/mrzine/wallerstein010208.html.

[10] See his blog at http://johnquiggin.com/index.php/archives/2008/09/08/the-end-of-neoliberalism/.

[11] The original consensus was based around the following tenants: 1. Fiscal discipline; 2. Reorientation of public expenditures; 3. Tax reform; 4. Financial liberalization; 5. Unified and competitive exchange rates; 6. Trade liberalization; 7. Openness to DFI; 8. Privatization; 9. Deregulation; 10.Secure Property Rights.

[12] I take Susan George's 'A Short History of Neoliberalism' as emblematic of this movement, see http://www.zmag.org/CrisesCurEvts/Globalism/george.htm.

[13] In this regard see, in particular, Parag Khana's (2008) *The Second World: Empires and Influence in the New Global Order*.

[14] Barack Obama, 'Renewing American Leadership' *Foreign Affairs*, July-August, 2007, at http://www.foreignaffairs.org/20070701faessay86401/barack-obama/renewing-american-leadership.html.

[15] See his course description of 'Behavioral and Institutional Economics' at http://www.econ.yale.edu/~shiller/course/527/ec52704.rl.htm.

[16] For the program and publications see the website at http://www.anthro.ucsd.edu/Divisions/modernity_anth.html.

REFERENCES

Baker, B. (2001). *In Perpetual Motion: Theories of Power, Educational History and the Child*, New York, Peter Lang.

Ball, S. (1994). *Education Reform: A Critical and Post-structural Approach*. Buckingham, Philadelphia: Open University Press.

Ball, S. (ed.) (1990). *Foucault and Education: Disciplines and Knowledge*. London: Routledge.

Barry, A., Osborne, T. & Rose, N. (eds.) (1996). *Foucault and Political Reason, Liberalism, Neo-liberalism and Rationalities of Government*. London: UCL Press.

Bourdieu, Pierre (1998). 'L'essence du néolibéralisme,' *Le Monde diplomatique* Mars 1998, http://www.monde-diplomatique.fr/1998/03/BOURDIEU/10167.

Bratich, J.Z., Jeremy Packer, Cameron McCarth (2003). *Foucault, Cultural Studies, and Governmentality*, New York, State University of New York Press.

Bröckling, U., Krasmann, S. & Lemke, T. (2009). *Governmentality: Current Issues and Future Challenges*, London, Routledge.

Burchell, D. (1997). "Liberalism" and Government: Political Philosophy and the Liberal Art of Rule. In C. O'Farrell (ed.), *Foucault, the Legacy*. Brisbane: Queensland University of Technology.

Burchell, G. (1993). Liberal Government and Techniques of the Self. *Economy and Society*, 22 (3), pp. 267-282. Also in: A. Barry, T. Osborne, N. Rose (eds.), *Foucault and Political Reason*, pp. 19-36. London, UCL Press.

Burchell, G., C. Gordon, & P. Miller (eds.) (1991). *The Foucault Effect: Studies in Governmentality*. Hemel Hempstead, England: Harverster Press.

Chomsky, N. (1999). *Profit over People – Neoliberalism and Global Order*. New York: Seven Stories Press.

Ciccarelli, R. (2008). Reframing Political Freedom: An Analysis of Governmentality, , *European Journal of Legal Studies*, 2008, 1, 3, Special conference issue.

Crampton, J.W. & Stuart Eldon (2007). *Space, Knowledge and Power: Foucault and Geography*, London, Ashgate.

Dean, M. (1991). *The Constitution of Poverty: Toward a Genealogy of Liberal Governance*. London: Routledge.

Dean, M. (1999). *Governmentality: Power and Rule in Modern Society*. London: Thousand Oaks.

Dean, M. and B. Hindess (eds.) (1998). *Governing Australia: Studies in Contemporary Rationalities of Government*. Cambridge: Cambridge University Press.

Dean, Mitchell (1999). *Governmentality: Power and Rule in Modern Society*. London: Sage.

Death, Carl (2006) .Resisting (nuclear) power? Environmental regulation and eco-governmentality in South Africa, *Review of African Political Economy*, 33 (109). pp. 407-424.

Defert, D. (1991). "Popular Life" and Insurance Technology. In G. Burchell, C. Gordon, P. Miller (eds.), *The Foucault Effect: Studies in Governmentality*, pp. 211-237. Hemel Hempstead, England: Harvester Wheatsheaf.

Deleuze, G. (1995). Postscript on Control Societies. *Negotiations 1972-1990*, trans. M. Joughin. New York: Columbia University Press.

Donzelot, J. (1979). *The Policing of Families*. Trans. R. Hurley, Foreword by G. Deleuze. New York: Pantheon Books.

Donzelot, J. (1991). The Mobilization of Society. In G. Burchell, C. Gordon, P. Miller (eds.), *The Foucault Effect: Studies in Governmentality*, pp. 169-180. Hemel Hempstead, England: Harvester Wheatsheaf.

Foucault, M. (1982). Space, Knowledge and Power: Interview. *Skyline*, March.

Foucault, M. (1991). Governmentality. In G. Burchell, C. Gordon, P. Miller (eds.), *The Foucault Effect: Studies in Governmentality*, pp. 87-104. Hemel Hempstead, England: Harvester Wheatsheaf.

Gordon, C. (1991). Governmental Rationality: An Introduction. In G. Burchell, C. Gordon, P. Miller (eds.), *The Foucault Effect: Studies in Governmentality*. Hemel Hempstead, England: Harvester Wheatsheaf.

Gordon, C. (1996). Foucault in Britain. In A. Barry, T. Osborne, N. Rose (eds.), *Foucault and Political Reason*, pp. 253-270. London: UCL Press.

Gordon, C. (2001). Introduction. *Michel Foucault: Power. The Essential Works*, Vol. 3, J. Faubion (ed.), pp. xi-xli. London: Allen Lane & The Penguin Press.

Harvey, D. (2005). *A Brief History of Neoliberalism.* New York: Oxford University Press.

Hindess, B. (1996). *Discourses of Power: From Hobbes to Foucault.* Oxford: Blackwell.

Hindess, B. (1997). Politics and Governmentality. *Economy and Society*, 26 (2).

Hunt, A. & Wickham, G. (1994). *Foucault and Law: Towards a Sociology of Law as Governance.* London, Pluto Press.

Hunter, I. (1994). *Rethinking the School: subjectivity, bureaucracy, criticism.* Sydney, Allen & Unwin.

Khana, P. (2008). *The Second World: Empires and Influence in the New Global Order.* New York: Random House.

Larner, W. & Walters, W. (2004). Globalization as governmentality, *Alternatives: Global, Local, Political*, vol 29, Special Issue - Governing Society Today, edited by Mitchell Dean and Paul Henman, pp. 495-514.

Larner,W. & William Walters (2004). *Global Governmentality*, London, Routledge.

Leander, Anna & van Munster, Rens (2006). 'Neo-Liberal Governmentality of Contemporary Security: Understanding private security contractors in Darfur and EU immigration control.' Paper presented at the annual meeting of the International Studies Association, Town & Country Resort and Convention Center, San Diego, California, USA, Mar 22, 2006 at http://www.allacademic.com/meta/p98828_index.html.

Li, Tania Murray (2007). *The Will to Improve: Governmentality, Development, and the Practice of Politics.* Duke University Press.

Lipschutz, R.D. & James K. Rowe (2005). *Globalization, Governmentality and Global politics: Regulation for the rest of us?* London, Routledge.

Luke, T.W. (n.d.). Generating Green Governmentality: A Cultural Critique of Environmental Studies as a Power/Knowledge Formation at http://www.cddc.vt.edu/tim/tims/Tim514a.PDF.

Marshall, J. (1996). *Michel Foucault: Personal Autonomy and Education.* Dorcrecht: Kluwer.

Masschelein, J. Simons, M., Brockling, U. & Pongratz, L. (2007). *The Learning Society from the Perspective of Governmentality, Educational Philosophy and Theory* Monograph series, Oxford, Blackwell.

Merlingen, Michael (2006). 'Foucault and World Politics: Promises and Challenges of Extending Governmentality Theory to the European and Beyond' *Millennium* 35 (1): 181-196.

Middleton, S. (1998). *Disciplining Sexuality: Foucault, Life Histories and Education.* New York & London: Teachers College Press.

Nadesan, M.H. (2008). *Governmentality, Biopower, and Everyday Life*, London, Routledge.

O'Malley, P. (1996). Risk and Responsibility. In Barry, A., Osborne, T. & Rose, N. (eds.), *Foucault and Political Reason: Liberalism, Neo-liberalism and Rationalities of Government*, pp. 189-208. London: UCL Press.

Peters, M.A. (2005). The New Prudentialism in Education: Actuarial rationality and the entrepreneurial self, *Educational Theory*, 55 (2): 123-137 (15).

Peters, M.A. & Marshall, J.D. (1996). *Individualism and Community: Education and Social Policy in the Postmodern Condition.* London, Falmer Press.

Olssen, M. (1999). *Michel Foucault: Materialism and Education.* Westport DT & London: Bergin & Garvey.

Pavlich, George and Gary Wickham (2001). (eds.) *Rethinking Law, Society and Governance: Foucault's Bequest*, Oxford, Hart.

Perry, R.W. & Maurer. B. (2003) (eds.), *Globalization under Construction: Governmentality, Law, and Identity*, Minneapolis, University of Minnesota Press.

Pollin, R. (2003). Contours of Descent: U.S. Economic Fractures and the Landscape of Global Austerity. *New York: Verso.*

Rabinow, P. & Dreyfus, H. (1983). *Michel Foucault: Beyond Structuralism and Hermeneutics.* Chicago, University of Chicago Press.

Rose, N. (1999). *Governing the soul: the shaping of the private self.* London, Free Associations Books, London.

Rose, Nikolas (2006). *Politics of life itself : biomedicine, power and subjectivity in the twenty-first century.* Princeton, Princeton University Press.

Rose, N., O'Malley, P. & Valverde, M. (2006). 'Governmentality,' *Annual Review of Law and Social Science*, December 2006, Vol. 2, Pages 83-104

Sending, Ole Jacob and Iver B. Neumann (2006). 'Governance to Governmentality: Analyzing States, NGOs, and Power', *International Studies Quarterly* 50 (3): 651-672.

Tagma, Halit Mustafa (2006). 'Sovereignty, Governmentality and the State of Exception: "Terrorism" and the Camp as the Constitutive Outside.' Paper presented at the annual meeting of the International Studies Association, Town & Country Resort and Convention Center, San Diego, California, USA, Mar 22, 2006 http://www.allacademic.com/meta/p100533_index.html.

Valverde, M. (1996). "Despotism" and ethical Legal Governance. *Economy and Society*, 25(3), pp. 357-372.

Ventura, H.E., Miller, J.M. & Mathieu Deflem, M. (2005). 'Governmentality and the War on Terror: FBI Project Carnivore and the Diffusion of Disciplinary Power,' *Critical Criminology* 13(1): 55-70.

Walters, W., & Haahr, J. H. (2006). *Governing Europe: Discourse, Governmentality and European Integration.* London, Routledge.

Watts, M. (2003). Development and Governmentality (p 6-34) *Singapore Journal of Tropical Geography*, Volume 24 Issue 1 , Pages 1 - 144

I. FOUCAULT ON GOVERNMENTALITY

JACQUES DONZELOT AND COLIN GORDON

1. GOVERNING LIBERAL SOCIETIES

The Foucault Effect in the English-Speaking World[1]

INTRODUCTION

On the occasion of the publication in France of Michel Foucault's 1978-9 lectures on the history governmentality, Jacques Donzelot invited Colin Gordon to discuss the extensive impact of these lectures in the English-speaking world, and the sources, scope and capabilities of the work which these lectures have inspired in the field of 'governmentality studies', particularly in relation to the contemporary impacts of liberalism and neoliberalism.

JACQUES DONZELOT In the two volumes of his lectures of 1978 and 1979, we see Michel Foucault making a major intellectual change of direction, moving away from an analysis of power as the formation and production of individuals towards an analysis of governmentality, a concept invented to denote the 'conduct of conducts' of men and women, working through their autonomy rather than through coercion even of a subtle kind. Out of this concept and the extended analysis of political economy which provides the material for its elaboration, Foucault never produced a published work. He broke off this series of investigations to occupy himself up to his death in 1984 with the writing of two books, which were evidently closer to his heart, of a history of the subject passing by way of the *Care of the self* and the *Use of Pleasure* (Foucault 1989a; 1989b). This however did not prevent this concept of governmentality from meeting with great success in the English-speaking world, in many ways stimulating there an intellectual dynamic more intense than in the case of his published works, which rapidly became classics and were treated as such and with the deference that status entailed, but not with the excitement which met the lectures on governmentality. In 1991 your volume *The Foucault Effect* (Burchell, Gordon, Miller, 1991) set off this dynamic by centring the 'effect' in question precisely on this notion of governmentality. But in France Foucault's lectures on the subject were not published until 2004 and without at first arousing great interest. So what accounts for this singular success of Foucault's reflection on governmentality in the Anglo-Saxon world?

COLIN GORDON We had a few advantages in Britain. In the first place, Foucault in his lifetime was more easygoing about foreign translations of his interviews and lectures than he was about their publication or reprinting in France. There may also have been more editorial latitude for juxtaposing this material with

M.A. Peters et al. (eds.), Govermentality Studies in Education, 3–15.

the work of people who were collaborating, virtually or actually, with Foucault. Some of Foucault's important later lectures and texts dealing with government were given in America and originally published there. In *The Foucault Effect* I was able to publish a summary, based on lecture notes and tapes, of his governmentality lectures: many people could certainly have done the same in France.

Secondly there is the difference in the national political conjuncture. In France after 1981 the dominant preoccupation remained socialism rather than liberalism, whereas Foucault had seen the importance of liberalism as a political issue and (I believe) conceived his 1979 lectures partly in response to the conjuncture of the Left's 1978 electoral defeat at the hands of Giscard d'Estaing. It is reasonable to suppose he would not have greatly lamented the defeat of a Left coalition in which the Communist Party played a major role. Here Foucault presents neoliberalism as a modern political rationality worthy of attention and a certain intellectual respect, while commenting that democratic socialism for its part has failed to engender a distinctive governmental rationality. This seemed a prescient and pertinent observation to some of us in Britain who were entering in 1979 on 18 years of Conservative government, whereas in 1981 France was to enter on twenty years of mainly socialist government, endowed with the legacy of the *'trente glorieuses'*, the three French post-war decades of notable socio-economic progress. Viewed from across the Channel, the French socialist governments seemed to be protecting, and indeed extending these enviable accomplishments, while a right-wing British government was busy dismantling the semi-corporatist post-war national system, and other English-speaking countries over the same period were getting a dose of the same medicine.[2]

JACQUES DONZELOT One can entirely accept this explanation of the success of governmentality studies in the Anglo-Saxon countries. There, neoliberalism triumphed and became an object of study whereas in France, given the relative dominance of the Socialist Party, we had to struggle for twenty years to produce a reflection on the social which uncoupled it from socialism and addressed it in terms of the governability of democracy. Showing that there existed an acceptable exit from socialism seemed to us more important than grasping the subtleties of liberalism as a political rationality. I have in mind a series of authors working to that agenda, including Robert Castel and myself, who were for a time close to Foucault, and others like Pierre Rosanvallon, who were not, who exemplify this national particularity of our relation to the question of government, in contrast to what you say about the destiny of that question in the English-speaking countries.

One can also wonder if the fact that Foucault's reflection was at odds with this French conjuncture might not have contributed to a certain hardening of his political stance in this terrain, a difficulty in positioning himself which led to abandoning this aspect of his reflection to concentrate on the care of the self? Because the context was a very delicate one : he had parted company with his 'revolutionary' links without lapsing into the kind of political philosophy which he hated, the question of regime, of the State, of all those official objects which he had been so well able to bypass. It was also the moment when the circle of friends around him in the 70s broke up and he contented himself with a few close supporters. In a way you invented a French Foucauldian school which never existed, or no longer exists in France, but, with this "Foucault effect" where you assembled texts from this loose group of friends in the 70s, weren't you fabricating an artefact which gave the illusion in Anglo-Saxon countries of a dynamic which no longer existed in France.... and thereby managed to produce one in those countries? Hence my second question – what was it that led to this interest in governmentality there?

COLIN GORDON It is quite true that in our volume we did not inform our readers about some political and personal disagreements between our authors, where we could not see that these were linked to a clear intellectual difference. My introduction to our book was (as I admitted) an attempt to construct a plane of consistence between the work of individuals who, in some cases, had never met, and in others were no longer collaborators or desiring to be perceived as such.[3] The fabrication of our artefact ended up taking some time, nearly a decade in all: Foucault's death in 1984 complicated and changed the terms of the project, which had been begun with his knowledge and approval, in various ways. Now that five volumes of Foucault's lectures from the 1970s have been published, however, one can more easily see how much of what became, for a time, a shared research programme was already well developed in his own work, in parts well before 1978.

As to Foucault's trajectory, I think it is with his 1976 lectures, at the latest, that he starts to distance himself from the militant ideal of the time. The discussion in those lectures of Sieyès and the Third Estate seems already to prefigure his later reflection on the formidable capabilities of liberalism as a political rationality. The intellectual path that led Foucault from the analysis of disciplines to that of governmentality is perfectly consistent, just as the theme of governmentality connects consistently in turn with his later themes of care of the self and truth-telling. Let's also remember that this 'late' or 'final' Foucault, who is supposed to have retreated into solitary study of the Church fathers and the history of the sacraments of penitence, was also the treasurer of the French branch of Solidarnosc, engaged in public discussion with the socialist trade union leader Edmond Maire, and in an institutional project with the law reformer and justice minister, Robert Badinter. It seems, as Michel Senellart rightly notes in his excellent editorial postscript to the 1978-79 lectures, that Foucault's interest in liberalism and neoliberalism is very much connected, around 1978, with his support for the East European dissidents. There is a marked anticommunist context in his lectures of 1978-9.

I have always been surprised that there was so little contemporary resonance at the time in France for Foucault's work on governmentality. In 1979 Foucault said that he would work in the following years' lectures on the genealogy of political parties – especially, I believe, that of the French Socialist party. I suspect that he was discouraged from pursuing this plan by the limited success of his dialogue with friends in, or close to, the Socialist Party. Perhaps his anticommunism still posed too many problems. But there was never any sign that he had repudiated this series of analyses. In the following years he encouraged and supported some young researchers he taught at Berkeley who did research into governmentality in America. At the time of his death, he had a book announced for publication with Editions du Seuil entitled *Le gouvernement de soi et des autres*.

I never thought that Foucault would have been in serious political disagreement with your work at around this time, or indeed that you would be likely to dissent from his views about security and autonomy in the Welfare State, as set out in his discussion with Robert Bono of the CFDT. Indeed I tried to show that Foucault's analyses of liberalism were consistent with the approach of your *L'invention du social* (Donzelot [1984] 1994), notably in the lecture he gave in 1979 on Fergusson's *History of Civil Society* where he sees emerging a notion of society as a « transactional reality », a mobile surface of engagement between the practices of government and the universe of the governed which constantly tends to escape their grasp. Whereas he had clear political differences with Deleuze – who was another philosophical genius, but no genius in politics. Nowadays, as you know, there as are many people in the world, academics in particular, who prefer a Deleuzian Foucault interpreted by Agamben or Negri, as there are people interested in governmentality studies. While the successive waves of posthumous publication and circulation of Foucault's work are reaching and inspiring new generations of readers, some of those who responded to his published work of the 70s and 80s may by now be looking elsewhere for stimulating novelty (unless, as is of course entirely feasible, Foucault's newly published work is reinterpreted and adapted to serve an agenda different from his own).

As for the results of English-speaking governmentality studies (not to speak of work in the rest of the world outside France), it is hard to give a short and summary answer. Nikolas Rose and Mitchell Dean published books which have been seen as aiming to systematise governmentality, to make it into a theoretical programme. But many people (and probably both of these authors) would deny that there is or was a 'governmentality school' in any clear-cut sense. Apart from the reference to a limited set of canonical texts by Foucault, there is typically a focus round the issue of liberalism and liberty, signalling the need to take liberalism seriously as an intellectual force which is also subject to historical transformation. Some original fields of research have been developed, such as the work of Peter Miller on the genealogy of management, and of Paul Rabinow and Nikolas Rose on bio-technologies; links have been made with other approaches, notably with Latour and actor network theory, in work on 'government at a distance'. James Tully, Duncan Ivison, Tom Osborne, Graham Burchell and I have been interested in the affinities between Foucault's works on governmentality and certain currents of English-language history of political thought, such as John Pocock's work on civic republicanism. Then there is work by people who were taught by Foucault at Berkeley, including interesting studies of modern governmentality by David Horn and Keith Gandal, and Jonathan Simon's important work on American penal justice.In recent years it is also becoming clearer that Foucault's legacy, and particularly his work on governmentality, has had major international impacts in the rapidly changing disciplines of geography[4] and anthropology and the new and important sector of postcolonial studies.

Does this work imply a distinctive political orientation? In broad terms we are a loose faction in the post-New Left diaspora which is still in search of its moral and ideological identity; more particularly, an episode in the experience of a Left coming to terms with a fresh advent and partial triumph of liberalism. There is not much evidence of a direct impact of this body of work on the political domain. I am not aware that Blair has read Foucault. Anthony Giddens, for a time the Blair-Clinton court philosopher, usually includes a caricature account of Foucault only as a marginal item in his doctrinal digests. But I think parts of the formulae of Clinton and Blair for a 'third way' may have effectively carried out a form of the operation which Foucault might have been taken as challenging the socialists to contemplate – the selective incorporation, in an updated and corrected social democracy, of certain elements of neoliberal analysis and strategy. In some ways it is the continuation of a trend initiated in the 70s by Schmidt in Germany, Giscard in France and Healey in Britain, and in her different way by Thatcher – the truth-telling role of government, in a world of global economic uncertainty and competition, as moral tutor of citizens in an ethic of enterprise and responsibility. The success of this formula in Britain seemed for a long time to be limited only by the irritability of citizens and the claims of the fourth estate, the media, to make and unmake governmental power (both of these reactions being severely aggravated, of course, by Blair's imprudent extension of his governmental agenda to embrace the neo-conservative enterprise of civilisation confrontation and global war on terror).

'Governmentality studies', where they are identifiable as such, have been an academic activity governed by prevailing institutional and discursive norms; Foucault's work, while inspiring to many, does not have the capacity to turn lead into gold. As part of this discursive order, there has been an ongoing discussion about which side such investigations are, or should be, on: that of a new rationalisation of government, or that of a critique of such rationality? No one has quite followed the trajectory of Francois Ewald, from a genealogy of social insurance to an ethical ontology of risk as the noble spirit of the enterprising class. All the same, the theme of governmentality has become involved in a debate where some are accused by others of seeking to legitimate, rather than to problematise, the idea of a 'risk society' considered as the ineluctable contemporary form of collective reality which all citizens and governmental techniques are necessarily obliged to confront.

The reception of Foucault's analysis of neoliberalism unfortunately often seems to be flattened into a set of polemical, ideological and globalising generalities, dispensing with the kind of descriptive investigation Foucault undertook in 1979 of the different avatars of neoliberalism with their national, historical and theoretical specificities. Indeed, neglect of post-war history seems to be a frequent feature of this polemical discourse: from a recent book on neoliberalism by David Harvey, a post-modern geographer who views Foucault's work as obsolete, one might think that neoliberalism had been an invention of the 1970s.

I hope the full publication of these lectures will revitalise this area of research. I think their publication will also show that this notion of governmentality can usefully be applied alongside Foucault's earlier and later ideas (power/knowledge, discipline, government of self, *parrhesia*). The theme of governmentality certainly needs to be seen in its continuity with the themes of the « late » or « final » Foucault (we are only talking here of an interval of five or six years): ethics, care of self, *parrhesia* or truth-telling, the conditions of existence of critical discourse. To understand these implications in full we will have to await the publication of the final lectures.

JACQUES DONZELOT After listening to this harangue, I plunged into the 'governmentality studies' for which you had pointed me to some of the key protagonists. And I emerged – at least for the moment – with mixed feelings of pleasure and unease.

The pleasure was especially in reading sections of the books co-edited and written by Nikolas Rose – *Foucault and Political Reason, The Powers of Freedom*, and the articles of Thomas Lemke. All of these show the pertinence of analysis in terms of governmentality in addressing neoliberalism. They all rely on the Foucauldian refutation of a fixed distinction between the domain of the State and the domain of civil society, between the domain of power and the domain of subjectivity. They use it to show that the 'retreat of the State' which is supposed to constitute neoliberalism in fact corresponds to an extension of government.

This extension is made possible by replacing the direct government of society by the State with a form of government at a distance. There is a destatification of government which goes in hand with the appearance of social technologies which delegate responsibility for individuals to other autonomous entities: enterprises, communities, professional organizations, individuals themselves. The use of contractual agreements, defined of objectives, measures of performance, combined with local autonomy, allows this shift of responsibility to governmental action at a distance. In this perspective,

> Individuals are to become 'experts of themselves', to adopt an educated and knowledgeable relation of self-care in respect of their bodies, their minds, their forms of conduct and that of the members of their own families. (Rose in *Foucault and Political Reason*, 1997, p. 59)

Individuals become 'entrepreneurs of themselves', and it is as such that they are bonded into society through the choices they make, the risks they take, and the responsibilities themselves and others which thereby arise and which they are required to assume. Citizenship is consequently no longer exercised in a relationship with the State or within a public space (such a space becoming indeed difficult to discern as such) so much as a varied range of private, corporate or quasi-public practices, ranging from work to consumption:

> the consumer citizen becomes an active agent in the regulation of professional expertise; the prudent citizen becomes an active agent of security, the citizen as employee becomes an active agent in the regeneration of industry. (ibid)

It is at this point, at this equation of the simultaneous growth of individual autonomy and responsibility – one believes oneself autonomous: what is worse, one is; but this autonomy is designed to make us into agents of the system – that my unease begins. Not because the analysis is false – I entirely endorse it as a necessary stage, as far as it does – but because it is presented as sufficient, whereas the underlying questions start just at the point where it stops, sure of itself and of its intellectual effect. The sophisticated social technologies of advanced neoliberal society, it tells us, contain an enlarged component of freedom along with an enlarged component of required responsibility in comparison with those of the Welfare State. Just as the latter marked an advance on old-style political economy, so political economy had represented a move beyond the model of reason of state. Each new model is evaluated only against the performance of its predecessor: they are always analysed at their 'technical' level, never in terms of a political criterion or in terms of value. This is the cost of the ability of governmentality studies to describe the materiality of social technologies while avoiding, for instance, the habitual denunciations of neoliberalism as an ideological rhetoric designed to mask a false economic theory and a practical anti-humanism, as Marxists and anti-globalisers like to put it. But doesn't the avoidance of that kind of simplification lead, in its turn, to a central ambivalence at the core of this kind of analysis? Isn't that what you yourself point out when you say that this kind of analysis can lead either to a critique of political rationality or to a rationalisation of this same set of policies?

In terms of political rationalities, in France we can all think of Francois Ewald's celebration of risk written from his current standpoint as a leading official of the national employers' organization. This is a classic case of counter-transference where the analyst falls blindly in love with his object, in this case the technology of insurance, and finds in it the key to all problems of social and political life.

But the other standpoint, the critique of political rationality, can be no less irritating when it is presented as a self-sufficient conclusion. I will give two examples which have struck me from my recent remedial reading course in governmentality studies.

The first is from Nikolas Rose's book *Powers of Freedom*. In a chapter called 'the community-civility game', he tries to establish a parallel between Bentham's famous Panopticon and the virtues claimed for it by Bentham in terms of preserving morality, stimulating industry and spreading education, and the qualities attributed to the notion of community promoted by authors like Etzioni, Putnam, Fukuyama and Belloch (already a somewhat hastily amalgamated group), or with that of the idea of associational networks considered as new diagrams of power, promoting 'moral' conducts in likewise subtly imperious ways. The 'we' of community is shown as exercising a technico-moral authority akin to that of the penitentiary Panopticon. At a stroke the Foucauldian analysis of governmentality as 'conduct of conducts', as action at a distance, loses its distinction from the disciplinary techniques of the 19th century. But more serious is the way this assimilation serves the cultivation of a posture of radical critique.

In Barbara Cruikshank's analysis of the function of the notion of empowerment in the USA, I found this same inclination to adopt a posture of radical critique at the cost of losing the subtle capabilities inherent in of this notion of the 'conduct of conducts'. When she denounces the invitation to self-empowerment, she is not so far from our own Jean Baudrillard and his celebration of the inertia of the silent majority as a form of resistance to the modern injunctions to participation and expression. One needs to be aware that she is analysing Californian 'Welfare to work' programmes which are more systems of forced labour under harsh conditions than steps to the empowerment of individuals over themselves or in their relation with others: whereas this theme of empowerment does also and above all have a dimension of acquisition of power over oneself thanks to the power which the collective one belongs to is able to produce. The collective in this case is not thought of as demanding a sacrifice from the individual, but rather as a necessary support for individual self-affirmation. But the choice as examples of these caricatured initiatives may also serve as indicating a wish to cultivate an exclusively critical posture.

One can also wonder if this ambivalence of these analyses in terms of governmentality may not lead them to incline towards one side or the other, the critical or the laudatory side, depending on the location where it is conducted. In Anglo-Saxon countries where neoliberalism was imposed from the start of the 80s, Foucault studies provide the means of a sophisticated critique, albeit one which is visibly lacking a capacity to propose alternatives. Does this political ambivalence in the notion of governmentality not condemn it to serving an ideological function, determined by political circumstance, whereas it aspires to be precisely the antidote of an ideological reading of forms of government?

COLIN GORDON One negative feature of the Foucauldian diaspora is that people can be seduced by the idea of revealing the truth of the present, but this is can be contaminated by a taste for hyperbolic discourses which exceed any critical purchase on the real. The leading example of this is no doubt the work Giorgio Agamben who detects in all government a virtual programme of extermination, and views the condition of the governed as universal reduction to the condition of *homo sacer*, and the like-minded commentators who in the UK see every Blairite innovation in the policing of families as a step on the road to serfdom.

As for the question behind your question, that is to say Foucault's critical standpoint vis-à-vis governmentality in terms of its potentiality for progressive technical invention, I suggest this brings us back to the distinctive quality of liberalism itself. Foucault says that the liberal art of government consists in the production and consumption of freedom, the creation and destruction of freedom. It is (as some say) the government of freedom and (as others remind us) the government of unfreedom[5] – or rather, the government of a freedom which is itself an unfreedom. Liberals (Keynes and Beveridge) were architects of the Welfare State : other liberals have been its critics and reformers. It is the paradox of liberalism in all its forms (neo, advanced, post...) that much action is necessary before one can *laisser faire* – action even to the extent of acting to bring into existence the reality (freedom, society) which it is desired to *laisser faire* – *'faire société'*, as indeed you have it in the title of your recent book. Hence one might partly counter some of your reproaches by saying that this kind of analysis brings out the ambiguity and ambivalence of liberal realities, in advance of any question of the practical consequences one chooses – or fails to choose – to infer from the analysis.

The detached, Weberian value-freedom of Foucault's description of the constitutive operations of liberalism as a governmentality may look to some like a disarming of the power of critique. You are asking whether and how, having unlearned the easy rhetoric of denunciation, one can then reintroduce a pertinent basis for critical evaluation.

In the first place, the very experience of a degree of discomfort at the paradoxes, antinomies and aporias of liberal liberty may help lead to healthy lucidity rather than moral incapacitation. Further, this element of detachment does not prevent, but even encourages the introduction of certain counter-analyses within the terms of the liberal paradigm: for instance, the theory of social capital invented by Robert Putnam (that is, of the resources which individuals draw from relational networks of solidarity and local and private forms of mutual support), or again, in relation to the Lockean theory of self-ownership as the necessary foundation of the liberal economy, the requirement that each person be endowed with the necessary resources to enable that self-ownership to be effective in practice (as Robert Castel argues in his recent book on *Social Insecurity*, in terms interestingly similar to those of Amartya Sen's work on 'capability rights').

Having said this, many who work in governmental studies do not feel called upon to take up the tasks you propose to them. In the book you quote, Nikolas Rose writes that in this type of work the aim is to destabilize and think beyond 'all those claims made by others to govern us in the name of our own well-being', and that studies of governmentality 'do not try to put themselves at the service of those who would govern better' [59-60]. This sounds like a form of knowledge which wants to serve only on the side of contestation. However, while recognising the critical contribution which his analyses have indeed made, others might wish at least to qualify those statements of position (which Nikolas himself firmly refuses to assert as group doctrines). Because it is hard to see why it should be a necessary axiom of the study of governmentality that all government (even one which claims to take account of the good of the governed) is an evil in itself, or that the wish to govern better should necessarily be something from which one ought ethically to disassociate oneself. Certainly, Foucault himself said that critique is not obliged to harness itself to the programming of a reform designed only to maintain an existing relation of forces, but he also said that in talking with a government one can be '*debout et en face*' – that is, engage in dialogue as an independent and equal interlocutor. In this view of things, critique, struggle, discussion and collective invention are compatible and complementary tasks. I suppose that it was not out of pure malice that Foucault suggested to the French Socialists in 1979 the project to invent a governmentality of their own; he indeed subsequently showed some evidence of willingness to assist with that task.

The seductive element in Foucault's rereading of liberalism was the thought that the art of better government was presented as the art of governing less, and that in this sense liberalism forms an autocritique of governmental reason: a governmentality which develops and corrects itself through its own critique. Alongside this there was his other seductive notion of critique (inspired by Kant's definition of Enlightenment as an emancipation from tutelage) as an indocility of the governed, a will not to be governed so much or in such a way. That is where the permanent task of critique would demand an inventive sequel: how to govern in order to be governed less, how to govern in order to be governed or to govern oneself in the way one wishes? Here we meet Foucault's refusal of the double blackmail, by the policy experts for whom a critique is invalidated if not accompanied by a prescription for reform, and by those who use the converse charge of recuperation, for whom every unprejudiced discussion of what is possible or desirable comes down to a capitulation of critique before the status quo.[6]

It is true that most of us have remained at a certain distance from the attempts, in the English speaking world as in France, to 'remoralise' politics through the injection of new or revived doctrines of civic and democratic virtue. Some thinkers, like William Connolly and James Tully, have made interesting attempts to incorporate values of difference and multiplicity in political ethics. My reading of your recent book *Faire société* suggests to me that you also subscribe to that general project.

Why have we kept our distance from these initiatives (apart from the consideration that today's civic pedagogues are sometimes too easily recognisable as recycled revolutionary ideologues)? For heuristic reasons Foucault drew a distinction between his field of research on governmental practices and the history of the political doctrine of sovereignty and its legitimate foundation, the history of citizens and their rights. This may have been initially necessary and effective as a means to establish and make visible a new object of study (except in respect of making that new object visible to historians of political thought), but I think it is time now for a more connected approach so that we can look, for instance, at what relation there might be between a certain notion of citizenship and a certain way of being governed[7]. This might help us to think more effectively about what we are becoming and what we wish or do not wish to become.

Another benefit of Foucault's initiative which has been noticed recently is that it anticipates the effects of globalisation in relativising the status of national state institutions. It surprised me that François Ewald and Blandine Kriegel said recently that Foucault was concerned with problems of his time and that now we have other concerns. Foucault's concerns in his later years seem to me to include notably neoliberalism, Islam, security, ethics, and the rights and global solidarity of the governed, all issues which I think we still recognise as pertinent today.

JACQUES DONZELOT I agree with this idea that the concept of governmentality has a prescient value in relation to globalisation, because it registers, in a sense in advance, the relativisation of States and nations, and I would also see in this advantage an enhanced possibility of linking the 'technical' analysis of governmentality with the 'moral' analysis of forms of citizenship corresponding to this new historical context.

The analysis of neoliberal governmentality shows a common orientation of developed countries striving to adapt to new realities. This orientation involves reducing the direct role of States in the economy and social relations, in favour of a new economy of social relations which emphasises autonomy and individual responsibility at all the local levels where autonomy and responsibility can be brought into interaction. In this sense, neoliberal governmentality is indeed a pure 'technical' product of critiques addressed to the Welfare State for the pasty forty years : left critics denouncing the creation in the name of progress of an order ever more disposed to control individuals, reducing their effective autonomy under the guise of an enhanced solicitude, and critics on the right who indicted the dismantling of the order necessary for progress through the deresponsibilising of individuals living under the increasing care of the State. The difficulty of sustaining an ever-rising burden of State revenues without affecting the global competitiveness of enterprises prompted governments to use and play off these two critiques against each other, to counter the growth of demands and recriminations addressed at the State.

The 'civic' question is so little foreign to this 'technical' solution that it arises out of the very fact of its application. For it is all very well to govern at a distance, relegating to the local level the play of encounters between the needs for autonomy and the demand for responsibility. That still requires that these 'localities', these diverse groupings, communities, enterprises, collectivities, form a society, and are not too disparate, too mutually estranged, too indifferent to anything outside of their own destiny, too incapable of a shared appreciation of what is right and just for all members of these constructed collectivities. Here there arises the question of consent to shared institutions, and therefore to the shared costs they impose. This consent is a form of civic engagement (*civisme*), its abstract incarnation, which we can counterpose to the direct mutual trust of people and citizens within the local frame of the specific community where they live.

Trust and consent are two relative values, the balance of whose roles can vary in the production of a civic society. They are in some sense the equivalents for citizenship of what autonomy and responsibility represent in the context of governmentality. They call for a similar concern for their mutual adjustment – what is the right relation of these two registers to permit the establishment of a civic society? And the intersection of these two registers, the 'technical' register of autonomisation and responsibility, and the 'civic' relation of consent and trust determines the way the concern for governmental effectiveness succeeds or fails to connect with the realisation of a civic society. Bringing together these two demands allows us to pose the question of how to make society exist in the context of neoliberalism. It seems to me that Europe is the place *par excellence* for the search for equilibrium between these two lines of transformation, the one which affects the governed and the one which affects the citizen.

COLIN GORDON Consent and trust and also, if possible, respect, are certainly things which every government today desires to produce and to enjoy – respect being incidentally the item which others most like to deny government, at least in Britain. The production of respect demands, in turn, persuasion and pedagogy. Persuasion for the social classes which are resistant to change because they feel insecure, and pedagogy for the minorities who may be inclined to disorder or revolt. On these subjects, alongside Foucault's accounts of the pastoral function of government it is worth reading Paul Veyne's essay on the irritability of the governed, 'When the individual is fundamentally affected by the power of the State' (*Economy and Society*, Vol. 34, No. 2, May 2005, translated by Graham Burchell). Veyne explains how Roman opinion was humiliated and violated by the spectacle of a ruler, the emperor Nero, who forced the ruled to serve as the audience of an aesthetic performance. In Britain we have had for a time a ruler who was the great tenor of what you in the 80s dubbed the coming 'civilisation of change': the man of truth as 'change-maker', telling the truth of global competition and the consequent obligation of all and each to be changed. But, just as Foucault taught us, it transpires that people can resist anything, even governmental *parrhesia*, even the pedagogy of reality and the ethic of change. The man of change and truth has not been assassinated, but he has been judged a corrupter and a liar. No governmentality will abolish resistance to government.

Could the currents of work and reflection we have been discussing contribute to the formation of a European political culture? 'It would be a good idea', as Gandhi said of Western civilisation. Foucault talked less about the common market than the social market (expect perhaps in that enigmatic question in one of his 1976 lectures: 'and what if Rome, once again, were to conquer revolution?'): is anyone writing the history of the linkage between those two themes?[8]

Foucault sketched the 20th-century international transfers (sometimes covert, often mediated by emigration and exile) of neoliberal techniques and formulae, much as he had outlined the international movement of ideas around 1900 on crime, security and social defence. It would be interesting today to continue this kind of analysis, tracing for instance the transfer between national and political camps of notions and techniques of social exclusion and inclusion.

Perhaps we need to enlarge our thinking even beyond the still growing European space. It is worth noting that the global (at least Anglophone) impact of the notion and theme of governmentality has coincided and in several cases interacted with the growth of the new discipline of postcolonial studies. The relation between proponents of postcolonial studies and Foucault's work have been, in a somewhat similar way to the situation in feminist studies, contested and often contestatory; sometimes one has the impression of a generation of fractious and needy orphans, afraid of their own freedom, who cannot forgive Foucault for failing to write their books as well as his, or for only having written the books he lived to write; nevertheless, the encounter has led to some promising beginnings of analyses of colonial and post- or neo-colonial styles of governmentality.[9] Perhaps we are also seeing the beginnings of a new analysis of the question which preoccupied Foucault, along with neoliberalism, in 1978-9, namely 'Islamic government', together with the now very current question of the possible civil and political modes of existence of Muslim citizens in societies with a liberal regime of government. If a European political culture was capable of accommodating and welcoming such reflections, it would be a step forward for Europe and the world.

Translated by Colin Gordon

NOTES

[1] Translated (with minor revisions to Colin Gordon's contribution) from *Esprit*, Novembre 2007, 82-95: 'Comment gouverner les sociétés libérales? L'effet Foucault dans le monde Anglo-Saxon'.

[2] Though Thatcher had fallen from power by the time The Foucault Effect was published; in the 80s the British Left's preferred intellectual guide for the understanding of Thatcherism was Gramsci, not Foucault.

[3] Sylvain Meyet (2006) points out, accurately, that no contributor to our volume except Foucault himself and the editors explicitly uses the term 'governmentality'.

[4] Legg (2006).

[5] Hindess (2001).

[6] To state what may be obvious: Foucault's insistence on recognising the critical and anti-essentialist components of liberalism and neoliberalism does not mean that these doctrines are therefore to be considered as the permanent homeland of critical thinking in general.

[7] As early as Histoire de la Folie, Foucault had identified the modern political problem of reconciling two incarnations of the citizen, the "man of law" and the "man of government".

[8] It is interesting that in his 1979 lectures on liberalism Foucault cites Kant's Perpetual Peace on the cosmopolitan right, prescribed by nature, of global free trade. "The guarantee of perpetual peace is, in effect, commercial globalisation (la planétarisation commerciale)" [2004, 60: my translation].

[9] For a useful survey see Legg (2006).

REFERENCES

Barry, A., Osborne, T., & Rose, N. (1996). *Foucault and political reason*. Routledge.

Burchell, G., Gordon, C., & Miller, P. (1991). *The foucault effect*. London: Harvester Wheatsheaf.

Cruikshank, B. (1999). *The will to empower: Democratic citizens and other subjects*. Cornell.

Dean, M. (1999). *Governmentality: Power and rule in modern society*. London: Sage.

Dean, M., & Hindess, B. (Eds.). (1998). *Governing Australia: Studies in contemporary rationalities of government*. Cambridge, UK: Cambridge University Press.

Foucault, M. (2004). *Naisssance de la biopolitique. Cours au Collège de France (1978–1979)* (Michel Senellart, Ed.). Paris: Gallimard/Le Seuil.

Hindess, B. (2001). The liberal government of unfreedom. *Alternatives: Social Transformation and Humane Governance, 26*, 93–111.

Ivison, D. (1997). *The self at liberty: Political argument and the arts of government*. Cornell.

Legg, S. (2006). Beyond the European province: Foucault and postcolonialism. In J. Crampton & S. Elden (Eds.), *Knowledge, and power: Foucault and geography*. Ashgate.

Rose, N. (1999). *Powers of freedom: Reframing political thought*. Cambridge.

Meyet, S., Naves, M-C., & Ribémont, T. (2005). *Travailler avec Foucault. Retours Sur Le Politique*. Paris: L'Harmattan.

Tully, J. (1993). *An approach to political philosophy: Locke in contexts*. Cambridge.

Jacques Donzelot
University of Paris X-Nanterre
France

Colin Gordon
Royal Brompton & Harefield NHS Trust
United Kingdom

JACQUES DONZELOT

2. MICHEL FOUCAULT'S UNDERSTANDING OF LIBERAL POLITICS

Last year, the 20th anniversary of Foucault's death was celebrated worldwide with large manifestations aiming to demonstrate the persistent currency of one of the greatest French intellectuals of the last century. However, they have missed, by only one year, the chance of coinciding with the issue that currently haunts us the most in France and that has pinnacled with the recent referendum on the subject of the European constitution, namely, the relationship between economic liberalism and politics. And, therefore, it is on this subject that his thinking could have appeared as the most current.

Michel Foucault has invented a unique method for reconsidering our ways of thinking about all of those objects supposedly universal such as madness, delinquency, sexuality and government. For him, it was not about showing their historical relativity, nor refusing their validity, as it is often argued, but rather, it was about claiming a priori their inexistence and unmaking all the certitudes of which they are object, such as their pure historicity. That has allowed him to wonder how what did not exist could take place, how a series of practices could been arranged to produce, in relation to each of those objects, a regime of truth, a fact of power and knowledge combined, which enabled to say, as long as the aforementioned regime of truth imposed its efficacy, what it was true or false in matters of madness, delinquency, sexuality and government. On each of these subjects, Michel Foucault produced canonic work…except for his work about government or his work taking into account his analysis of the relation between economic and political liberalism. Why this omission? Has his premature death prevented this analysis? It is difficult to say, because after having discussed this issue with unique passion, he suddenly abandoned it and devoted the rest of his life to the delight of a history of subjectivity whose interest, as considerable as it can be, nowadays one may think that it is not as important as the one he has abandoned along the way.[1]

In a certain way, posterity has censured his premature abandonment of the issue of the government of men in favor of the self-behavior. Everywhere the studies on governmentality constitute the most vivid part of his work[2]. This Foucauldian analysis of liberalism has been hardly taken into account in France[3]. We would like to remedy this by freely inspiring us from his analysis to comment on the current political conjunction, which is characterized in France both by the negative response to the referendum on the project of the European constitution that has revealed the extent to which liberalism is being rejected and by the Left's incapacity to adopt a position about globalization different of its withdrawal from it.

M.A. Peters et al. (eds.), Govermentality Studies in Education, 17–33.

In France, liberalism is viewed as a suspicious doctrine, tolerated by necessity, but strange to our thinking. One opposes it more than one thinks in function of it or starts from it. Compared to the brightest thinkers of the Republic, to many it looks like their opposite, the sign of their slackening, the mendacious promise of a harmony which would not be possible if it were not from the demanding imposition of the general interest by a State liberated from the influence of particular interests. Essentially, our political thinking is positioned at a calculated distance from this Anglo-Saxon doctrine: quite distant to succumb to its evil spells, but at the same time, not too far to sustain the principle of resistance to extremism which, otherwise, could repress the universal aspiration of our republican virtues in the narrowness of the national setting.

Because of our ideas against liberalism, without thinking about it, without taking into account the intelligence it contains, we go past the reasons that make its force and its unlimited expansion, and we adopt an increasingly fixed and sterile position in the future of the world. On the contrary, while in the Collège de France Foucault intended to recover the thread of liberalism as the thought of government and not as the opposite of the republican art of governing. This idea took up two years of his courses in the Collège de France, namely 1978 and 1979. The first one was entitled "Security, territory and population" and the second, "The birth of biopolitics". Seuil has edited both in 2004[4]. I have to say I started reading the transcription of my former professor's courses with the bizarre curiosity that one can experience about words that were once familiar and exciting before they became irritating and strange, and without having attended these two courses or any other afterwards and currently sustaining one of the most distant positions vis-à-vis the group of loyal followers who keep alive the cult of M. Foucault's memory. Very soon, though, the currency of his analysis on liberalism after 25 years of its formulation stunned me more than the past memories. This analysis shows wonderfully how the power of economics lies in an economy of power, as much during the emergence of liberalism at the end of the 18th century as when neoliberalism surfaced between the 30s and 50s. What aspects of Foucault's analysis are current and which ones are new? On the one hand, his analysis is current because of its remarks on the bifurcation of the French political thought vis-à-vis the Anglo-Saxon, its insistence about the law as the expression of a will, its view on the constitution as the result of the individuals' voluntary renunciation of their sovereignty, in sum, because of everything we have experienced about the referendum on Europe. On the other, what makes this analysis new is considering that neoliberalism calls for another kind of engagement with the idea of social justice, inherited through the 'welfare state' of the classical liberalism. Or rather, that this engagement calls for revision and adaptation in order to protect its resources and its efficacy and to avoid it is defended with tooth and nails. I would like to present first both moments of Michel Foucault's analysis on the birth of liberalism and its renewal in the half of the 20th century before drawing some remarks about our context, more than 25 years apart from his lectures.

THE INTELLIGENCE OF LIBERALISM ACCORDING TO MICHEL FOUCAULT

The beginning of the political economy constitutes the real object of the 1978 course, entitled "Security, territory, population". How are the title and the object related? They seem to be unrelated at first glance, which can be explained by the progressive detour of the course from an analysis of power towards an analysis of governmentality, a concept created in 1978 to account for the introduction of the political economy in the art of governing.

In the beginning of his course, Foucault intends to describe the passage, during the 18th century, from a power whose target is a territory to a power exercised over the population. The logic and the periodicity are similar to those used to deal with the history of punishment in *Discipline and Punish*—from *"l' éclat des supplices"* to *"la douceur des peines"*[5]—or in the conclusion of the first tome of the history of sexuality—"du droit de mort au pouvoir sur la vie"[6]—which announced a general reflexivity about bio-power of which this course must ensure its beginning. One is, thus, in known territory, ready to 'listen' to an author who masters his art and his object. However, he resolves to refuse the thesis of his main work, *Discipline and Punish*. For this occasion, he announces three subjects susceptible to support his argument in the case in point, that is, the displacement of the application of power over a territory to the population: the city, the famine and the illness.

Within the framework of a power aiming to secure a territory, each subject is discussed within a logic of demarcation, of separation, of fortification, as the territory is like a building that one must protect against internal and external threats. Cities must be fortified and protected from the outside in order to undertake commerce and craftsmanship. Also, they have to send their wealth to the capital, the place of the sovereign. The country too has to be controlled by the law of the landlord, of course, but also and above all, by the prohibitions of the sovereign in relation to anything related to the commerce of grain, whose costliness affects the inhabitants of the cities, thus, causing famines and arousing riots. Additionally, the sovereign outlaws the stock of grain by the peasants. In this way, the prix of grain can be increased and it can be sold to foreign countries. It is convenient that peasants make little profits so that the people of the cities can nourish themselves at the lowest price. Finally, vis-à-vis the epidemic illnesses such as smallpox, leprosy and cholera, it is better to proceed by separating and isolating the ills. In sum, the security of the sovereign's territory needs that he mainly resorts to separation and prohibition measures.

Foucault explains that the power mechanisms will change completely when the sovereign no longer worries about the security of the territory, but rather, about the security of the population. Regarding the cities, the problem would not longer consist in enclosing them with fortified borders, but in opening them to allow their growth and to avoid urban congestion. The concern shifts from caring about the limits imposed to caring about the facilitation of a good circulation of people, merchandise, and even the air. The same principle would prevail for avoiding famines: instead of limiting the commerce of grains to "iron collar" measures, it is better allowing the flux of merchandises and achieving the self-regulation of prices through the game of profits authorized in this way. As these profits would be invested in the new crops, the amount of grain for sale next year would increase, and concomitantly, its price would decrease. The possibility of importing, which had been agreed upon, would counteract better the attempts of stocking than its prohibition would. Certainly, this would not eliminate the revolts completely, but it would deprive them of its justification, as the sovereign would be acting conforming to "the nature of things" and not in terms of the prohibitions for whose inefficacy he could be accused. The nature of things can be found as well in the inoculation and vaccination, which consist in reducing illness by "authorizing" its entrance to the body. The body, thus, learns to protect itself, in the same way the authorized costliness of grain ends up leading to its decrease.

From needing his subjects' obedience to protect the security of his territory, the sovereign passes to a good use of freedom to secure the population. However, what supports the sovereign now? How does the notion of power applied to the population evoke the exercise of sovereignty? As Michel Foucault advances in his analysis, he feels uncomfortable mixing up the word sovereign with the word population: saying that the sovereign no longer reigns on his subjects but on a massive population makes these two terms clash. Also, he prefers using the term government in relation to the term population than to the word sovereign.

> As I talked about the population, there was a word which constantly returned—you may not say that I have done it deliberately, perhaps not entirely—. It is the word 'government'. The more I talked about the population, the more I avoided saying 'the sovereign'[7]

However, what are the implications of pairing up the words population and government? Essentially, it confirms that with the focus on the population not only the technologies of power changed, but also the model of government did. The government appeared as something different than a technology of power, at least as a frame for exercising it. Precisely, in the framework of sovereignty the model of reference for the exercise of power was the family, which raises this central question: How can the spirit of the head of the family be incorporated into the management of the state, that is, the economy, the wellbeing of all?

> The essential element in the prince's pedagogy is the government of the family, which one precisely calls economy...How can the economy be introduced, that is, how can one manage properly the individuals, goods and wealth, as one can do it in the family, as a good father of family who knows how to manage his wife, his children, his servants and to make prosper the family's fortune?[8]

This model of the family as a reference for the rule of the sovereign became questioned with the appearance of the population as the target of government. Being constructed as a governmental object, the population comprises several phenomena which surpass the familial model. How does a "good father of family" manage large epidemics? Especially, how can one integrate the spiral of work and the richness brought by the regulation of flows? Furthermore, how can one situate the old interdicts in a family logic? The family is no longer the model of approach of the population but a simple segment of it. For this reason, it becomes a means, a relay likely helping to control it (in the field of sexuality, demography, consumption...).

> At that moment, the family appears like an element inside the population and like a fundamental relay to control it... The family is no longer a model, but rather, it is a privileged segment because, when one wants to obtain something of the population in terms of sexual behavior, demography, or consumption, one needs to pass it through the family[9]

This analysis of the shift from the family as a model to a relay of the government is not new[10]. However, Michel Foucault extends it theoretically by creating and defining the concept of governmentality in opposition to the family model associated with sovereignty. For him, governmentality is "a complex form of power which has the population as its target, the political economic as its discipline and the security mechanisms as its techniques"[11]. From there, his course would take a completely different direction that the one he had announced. Instead of focusing, as envisaged, on the mutation of the techniques of power no longer targeting the territory but the population, the course was centered entirely on this new concept of governmentality and dedicated to show: 1) How the idea of government was born; 2) how this idea was introduced to the State under the cover of the model known as the *Raison d'Etat*, which appeared in the 16th century, and finally, 3) how this idea "conquered" the State thanks to the political economy in the 18th century, which constituted an accomplished form of "*governmentalization* of the State".

Where did the idea of government appear? It did not appear in Greece, where the king steered the city like a ship, but without being concerned about its inhabitants. Rather, it emerged among the Hebrews, who looked after their population, not their territory. They conceived their people as a herd in movement, on which the herdsman had to look over, taking care of each sheep.

> Who is the shepherd? Are those whose power burst in the eyes of men such as sovereigns, Gods, or Greek Gods who appear essentially for the gleam? Not at all. The shepherd "watches over". He watches over his herd intending to protect it from anything harmful, from anything bad. He is going to make sure that things turn out to be the best for each animal of the flock. The concern of the shepherd is directed towards the others, never towards himself[12].

The idea of government passes to the Christian culture and organizes its life in such a way that one can consider the religious wars as linked to this issue. It goes as well for the history of the Church, which can be interpreted as being organized entirely around the answers provided for counter-behaviors (or for resistances, if prefered) such as the asceticism, the communities, the mysticism, the return to the usury, the scatological belief...During this medieval period, the sovereign rules like a father leading his family, or like the superior of a convent leading his people towards the eternal happiness.

After the religion wars, the first discontinuity appeared with the idea of providing the sovereign with a supplement of power to command his subjects. This supplement would originate from the idea of the *Res publica* (public matters) understood as the stabilization of the State, and thus, the source of the model of the *Raison d'Etat*. With the *raison d'Etat*, the purpose of the government is no longer the heavenly happiness, but the State itself. But, what does then the word *d'Etat* mean? Sometimes it indicates a domain, sometimes a jurisdiction, sometimes a living condition (a statute), and sometimes the quality of a thing which...remains in the state, that is, immobile. Foucault argued that the sovereign Republic is nothing other than a territory, a group of rules, a group of individuals qualified by their statutes and living in the greatest stability.

> The sovereign is no longer defined in relation to the salvation of the herd and the final happiness of each sheep after its passage over this world. Rather, it is defined in relation to the State". "The purpose of the raison d'Etat is the State itself. If something like perfection, well-being or happiness truly exists, it will never be other than the State itself. There is not a final day... but only a united and final temporal organization[13].

Consequently, instead of following divine mandates, the sovereign rules with laws in order to preserve the State, to increase its force, its wealth, and hence, its population within its territory, which he defends vis-à-vis the other sovereigns.

It is against the model of the *Raison d'Etat* that liberalism will emphasize its superiority as a new governmental rationality. Foucault finds there the question of the population that had made his prior argument stumble and that he can integrate now with more confidence thanks to this detour via the history of the government. By considering this first form of governmentalization of the State, namely the raison d'Etat, it is possible to explain what changes in relation to the population from one regime of government to another. Within the framework of the *raison d'Etat*, what it counts is the quantity of the population. The population is an absolute commodity, a countable richness one should watch over because the wealth of the sovereign depends on its number, its work and its docility. Therefore, the goal of the security forces is taking care of the population by regulating its health, its production and its circulation. Mercantilism, the economic theory of the *Raison d'Etat*, requires that *"each country has the largest population possible, that its population is put to work entirely, and that wages are as low as possible, so that one can then sell abroad and ensure the import of gold"*[14]. On the contrary, within the framework of the political economy, the population is no longer a matter of numbers, but rather, it is a substance whose optimum number varies according to the evolution of wages, employment and prices. This substance cannot be regulated. However, it is controlled according to the extant resources, which depend on the development of trade between individuals as well as countries. It is more convenient to focus on the interactions between men than to command their actions, to lead their conduits, that is, to govern and not to regulate.

> For the economists, the number of the population is not a value in itself... One needs enough population to produce a lot. But one does not need too

much of it, so that the wages are not too low and people want to work and can support the prices with their consumption[15].

The "progress" governmentality made by passing from the raison d'Etat to liberalism consists on providing a reflection about the governmental practices. To govern is no longer to reign, to affirm a power, but to recognize that the truth is told elsewhere than in the center of the State, a truth—that of the market—which in any case invites to conceive action not in terms of the imposition of a will, but of the search for neither too much nor too little. The intelligence of liberalism as a form of government lies entirely on this pragmatism, on this search for what it is convenient to do (agenda) and what it is not (non agenda)[16]. The intervention of governmentality should be limited, but this limit would not be only one negative form.

In the field delimited by the concern of respecting natural processes, would appear a domain of lawful intervention...It would no longer be necessary to regulate, but to manage[17].

* *

For the political economy, the aim of the governmental reason is not the State anymore, or its wealth—like in the model of the *raison d'Etat*—but the society, its economic progress. Its role is no longer to restrain a liberty, expression of the fundamental bad nature of men, but to control it, and for this reason, to prohibit it, if necessary, through restrictions. It is a liberty which is produced and to be built. This construction takes place through interventions of the State, not by its pure and simple withdrawal. But how far can and should go this interventionism without risking becoming its opposite, a concealed or declared anti-liberalism? This question is the starting point of the neoliberal reflection, whose origin and reasoning Mr. Foucault analyzes and restores in the following course of 1979 entitled "The birth of bio-politics".

The increasing role of the State—frequent in all democracies though disparate in their demonstrations—causes the emergence of a neoliberal reflection which reached its pinnacle in the 20th century from the 30s to the 60s. The idea that this tendency needs to be contained, or even, reversed preoccupies liberal economists obsessively. Even if Keynes is, in his own way, a liberal, or at least, a thinker hostile to socialism, the fortune of his theories worries pure liberals, because they potentially position the State in the direction of the market instead of only producing it. This neoliberal fear, though, relies mostly on the abuses of democracy, and the emergence of Nazism and of Stalinism. What relationship does exist between a doctrine such as Keynesianism—which is overall liberal—and these monstrous figures of power? Only one but of importance: the increasing power of the state. According to the neoliberals, the fact that Nazism destroyed the internal State would prove only that it cannot face the demand of nationalization without falling apart... and that—contrarily to what one has believed—it does not constitute a rampart against the irrationalities associated with capitalism.

Neoliberals want to take up the challenge posited by what Max Weber named "the irrational rationality of capitalism". But, as Michel Foucault shows, they intend to do it in opposition to Marxists. During the 30s, Marxists in Germany gathered in the famous Frankfurt School led by Horkheimer and Adorno. They looked for a social rationality whose development would terminate with the economic irrationality of capitalism. At the same time, neoliberals gathered in another German city, Freiburg, and published in a journal entitled "Ordo". Among them, there were many economists who, for some, fueled the bearer reflection of the German Federal Republic after the war, and for others, they inspired the neoliberal school of Chicago organized around Milton Friedman. What they have in common is not proposing a corrective social rationality of capitalism's economic irrationality, but rather, they propose an economic rationality able to cancel its social irrationality.

> And history has caused, adds Michel Foucault, that in 1968 the last disciples of the Frankfort school collided against the police of a government inspired by the Freiburg School. Thus, they were distributed on both sides of the barricade, because such was the double, and at the same time, parallel, crossed and antagonist destiny of webberianism in Germany[18].

The "ordo-liberals" wondered about the weakness of the traditional liberal thought which forces the economy to undergo an increasing pressure for state inter-ventionism. They found this flaw in its "naïve" confidence in the virtues of the laissez-faire, that is, in the illusion of the market as a natural phenomenon which one should limit oneself to respect. This naturalist naivety makes the State intervene to deal with the problems and needs that the market cannot solve or satisfy. Treating the market as a natural entity turns it into the culprit of all that does not work and forces the "nature" of needs to play against the "nature" of the market. In short, it gradually disqualifies the latter in the name of the former. Because of the market, then, the State must intervene to compensate for the insufficiencies and to limit the excesses in the register of exchanges. But by so doing, the State is positioned against the market. Neoliberals argue this is a double mistake. In the market it is not important the principle of more or less satisfactory exchanges, but rather, the one of more or less effective competition. Exchange rejects equality

> in this sort of primitive and fictitious situation to which liberal economists of the 18th century committed... Essentially, the formula of the market lies elsewhere: It lies in competition. What counts, then, is not equality, but rather, it is inequality.[19]

Competition is not a natural phenomenon but a formal mechanism, a way of making play inequalities effectively and leaving none of them sure and in dominion of their position. Therefore, the role of the State is not to intervene because of the market, but for the market, so that it is always maintained and the principle of the equal inequality renders its effect[20]. Competition is not a fact of nature.

> It owes its effects to the essence it holds...Competition, is an eidos, a principle of formalization... It is to some extent a formal game between inequalities.[21]

What are the consequences of a theorization of competition in terms of governmental rationality? How does the role of the State change? In this framework, the
man of exchange, needs and consumption is replaced by the man of competition,
business and production. It implies, then, encouraging anything that shares the
spirit of the enterprise and relies on men as entrepreneurs of economic activities as
well as of themselves—salaried workers exploit their own human capital—, as
members of a collective regarded like an enterprise of co-owners taking care of
maintaining and increasing the value of their goods. What happens to the social—
this compensation of the economic—and the injustices generated by its irrationality? It is no longer intended as a remedy against the vices of competition and to
reduce inequalities. Rather, it serves only to maintain each individual within those
inequalities, so that individuals are retained in the register of the equal inequality
which allows competition. Thus, there is not exclusion a priori ... In short, social
policy is no longer a means for counteracting the economic, but one supporting the
logic of competition.

THE SOVEREIGNTY WAY AGAINST THE UTILITY WAY: THE EXAMPLE
OF THE REFERENDUM ON THE PROJECT OF THE EUROPEAN CONSTITUTION

In his analysis of the birth of liberalism and its revival in the mid 20th Century,
Foucault contributed to a better understanding of both by framing them within the
question of the art of government or "governmentality", Foucault's neologism
invented for the occasion. Created at the end of the 70s, this lecture is still
surprising because of its singularity linking methodically liberalism and politics
instead of distinguishing or opposing them as we use to do it in France. This is
precisely why in France we can comment on a recent topic marked foremost by a
confrontation between the supporters of politics, the role of the State, national
sovereignty, and of a European social model of which France would provide the
archetype, and the advocates of liberalism, the aforementioned national sovereignty
and the famous social model within the framework of globalization, at the time of a
project of European constitution which defied both with the pretext of their best
protection or/and the advancement of modernity. This does not imply, though, that
Michel Foucault's analysis had allowed deciding this debate in advance[22]. However,
it makes possible to clarify the assumptions of the forces involved.

What happens to public law when the political economy embraces an internal
principle of voluntary self-limitation? How can this self-limitation be established
legally? From this question, Foucault makes a distinction which allows understanding
a substantial difference in the attitudes about liberalism that, according to us, seems
to include those which had been unfolded during the recent referendum in France.
According to him, two systems of thought were forged to answer this question and
perpetuated until now with uneven luck[23].

The first system consists on renewing the foundations of law like in the *Raison
d'Etat*. Then, the law was used to contain the excesses of the *Raison d'Etat* by
relying *"on the natural or original rights inherent to any individual"* and to define,
thus, the absolute rights. From there, one could determine what depended on the

sovereignty's sphere, and hence, on the government's jurisdiction by the effect of a legitimate concession. Likewise, it was determined what did not appertain to it, which Foucault called the judicial-deductive way and assimilated to that of the French revolution and Rousseau.

> This approach departs from the individual, constructs the sovereign and finally defines governmentality. It is a way of setting, of entering the game by an ideal resumption of the social reality, the State, the sovereign, the government, the problem of legitimacy and the inalienability of rights.[24]

It is the way of sovereignty... but whereof insists on underlining, with a perceptible mischievousness, its retroactive nature—"reactionary", Foucault said—coming very close to insulting the fathers of the nation.

The second system does not focus on the right of the governed, but on the governmental practices and on the kinds of limits needed according to its objectives. It returns to a conception of the Law, not as the effect of the sovereign's will...or of the sovereign people's, but of a transaction between the legitimate sphere of the individuals' intervention and that of the public power. The Law is not the result of a cession or a division, but of a compromise, a common interest of both parts. Finally and foremost, it brings into play a conception of the individuals' freedom which is not as much juridical in essence as it takes into account the independence of the governed. *"The limit of government's competence will be defined by the boundaries of the governmental intervention's utility"*[25]. Of course, this is the way of the utility, the English utilitarianism and Bentham's, understood as the way of asking every time the following question to every government: what you do, is it useful? Within which limits? When does it become harmful? Evidently, it is not the revolutionary way, the way of sovereignty but that of utility.

Foucault asserts that between these two ways, the juridical-deductive of sovereignty and that of utility, there is heterogeneity and coexistence throughout history even if this coexistence sees the elements of the second taking it away:

> In the two systems, there is one which has been strong and other which, on the contrary, has regressed. The one which has been maintained, namely the "radical" English-like way, had tried to define the legal limitation of the public power in terms of governmental utility... Ultimately, utility will be the greatest criterion for creating the limits of the public power in an age where the utility problem increasingly covers all the traditional problems of the law.[26]

Now, putting aside Foucault's text, one may add that this progressive supremacy of the utility way over that of sovereignty throughout the 19th and the 20th century can be observed both in France and Great Britain. However, its dominance appears more clearly in France where it is confronted with a strong expression of the juridical-deductive way. It really only managed to establish itself as the way of sovereignty appears at an impasse. Its introduction—which cannot be done like the English utilitarianism for obvious reasons of national pride—then will justify resorting to a specific theorization. The impasse of the sovereignty way started in

France during the 1848 revolution when it was put face to face the partisans of a minimum State and those of a maximum State around the question of the right to work. And one sees well how, at the end of the 19th century, the solidarity doctrines inspired by Emile Durkheim constituted the French justification for the acceptance of the utility way because it subjects the State and its intervention to the question of its utility for society more than to its sovereign base. According to this doctrine, thus, the State must proceed to favor the solidarity of the society, but only that. It must know how to compensate for the shortcomings of the market in the protection of the population, but to restrain itself from going beyond the social and making the bed to the socialism understood like an alternative to the market. In France, the art of not too much, nor too little as a form of governmentality in the name of utility found a more methodical formulation than in the majority of other European countries—the United Kingdom included—since it mobilized a knowledge different to that of the political economy (i.e., sociology) and another terminology, that of solidarity[27].

The utility way carries this art everywhere in Europe, including in France, the land of the sovereignty way. Still, one should consider that the latter was never disavowed in its ideological preeminence. Not even has been socialism—at least democratic—, considered by many as the major form of sovereignty's achievement. The idea that a socialist governmentality is inconsistent and that it can lead only to an administrative government, updating, one may say, the *Raison d'Etat,* or shamefully endowing liberalism (Guy Mollet-like) takes only little consideration to this perenniality of the sovereignty way which remains minimally lived like the alternative against the "excesses" of liberalism. In his course, though, Michel Foucault insists greatly on the absence of a governmental rationality suitable for socialism.

Precisely, the sovereignty way seems to have been a useful recourse against the dangers of liberalism at the time of the last referendum. The powerful refusal of liberalism, in the French left at least, obviously testifies a resurgence of the sovereignty way. To provide a clear example of this, it is enough to recapture the three points around which the two ways can be distinguished and to apply them to the partisans of yes and no in the referendum. The utility way focuses on the governmental exercise, on the question of its desirable extent. It puts into action the mechanisms of compromise between what concerns the public and the individual's spheres. By freedom, it understands the effective independence of people. One finds these three characteristics in the arguments of the partisans of yes. The project of the constitution originates within the European government in response to the difficulties emerging from its scope, and thus, it argues about the utility of adopting a constitutional regulation which improves its governability. This is the first criterion, the starting point of the legislative concern. It originates in the interior of the governmentality, not from the sovereign will of the European citizens. Secondly, the project of constitution also returns to the utility way since it relies on an art of compromise. The term compromise is essential to the development of the project. It refers to the common rules and traditions of each country without forcing anyone beyond possible, for example, in terms of its social protection regime. And if in this respect there was a problem, it emerged more from fear of abusing the rule than from a problem of compromising like in the Polish mason affair. Finally, freedom is not as much juridical, a commodity which one yields or not, as a reality, the independence of people doing what they want according to their civil traditions, for example, regarding abortion.

As for the partisans of no, they methodically reproduced all the characteristics of the sovereignty way. For them, it was not about departing from the government and its problems but from people's constitutive rights. In their eyes, the first defect of this constitution was that it did not emanate from a Constituent Assembly, elected by the inhabitants of each country to decide the form of the collective sovereignty they would endow themselves with. For them, there was no way they would accept a law made from a compromise and not from the expression of their will. It should be collective and total or not to be at all. There was no chance they would yield their will unless the project was in agreement with their requirements. The discussion of each article of law and, a fortiori, of the former treaties they were asked to ratify reached passionate pinnacles as if it was about remaking the world and not about adapting to it as well as possible. As for the juridical conception of freedom, this discussion engaged with universal rights and duties incompatible with the maintenance of people's relative singularity in the domain of habits. In short, the partisans of no behaved as if the project of European constitution consisted in re-enacting the "social contract" against the *Raison d'Etat*.

FOR A LECTURE OF THE THIRD WAY

Liberalism goes hand in hand with progressive "techniques" in terms of governmentality in front of which the sovereignty way seems "retroactive" and the recourse to the State a manner of returning insidiously to the "*Raison d'Etat*". Does it mean that liberalism and, a fortiori, neoliberalism only raise reactive attitudes and gain partisans by making them lose the societies to which they belong? The question concerns particularly to neoliberalism and the role it plays in globalization. Does the political dilemma limit itself to choosing between adhesion to "ultra-liberalism"—the preferred name given by the *souverainists* and the extreme left to the neoliberal doctrines—or a reactionary attitude, antedated, incapable of offering an effective grasp on governmental practices? Between this retroactive way, precious to the traditional left, and that of neoliberalism, there is a middle way, precisely, the third way represented in its time by Bill Clinton and adapted to Europe by Tony Blair. But this famous third way is nothing more, as we have said often in France, that a copy hardly improved of neoliberalism, a recovery of the old liberal theories in their original hardness before the state had intervened to compensate for its misdeeds. It is on relation to this that the Foucauldian analysis can help the French political thinking to come off its impasse, because it demonstrates that neoliberalism is anything by the resumption of old liberal theories, as it shifts decisively the role of the state and of the exchange. This makes possible to tackle from a different perspective the question on the contents of the political option represented by the third way and to compare it advantageously with the solidarity philosophy of progress which serves as doctrine in the French left after more than a century.

Foucault's analysis of neoliberalism aims at countering the erroneous ideas about it and the relation between the economy and the social. For Foucault, among those erroneous assertions about neoliberalism, one would need to place first the ones for which neoliberalism represents a reactivation of old liberal theories in their original hardness. It is an important misinterpretation because the problem which neoliberals confront is no longer introducing a space free of regulation so that "laissez-faire" can take place, but creating the conditions of a competition without which the market is only a vain word. However, creating competition requires that the State not only allows laissez-faire practices, but also that it generates an adequate framework for them. To illustrate what neoliberals understand by the term "framework", he provides the example of the emergence of the common agrarian policy, which in 2005 does not lack flavor for us. In a 1952 text, Eucken, one of the most recognized neoliberals from the Freiburg school, explains all the reasons why German agriculture, as other European nations, has never integrated completely to a market economy: because of custom barriers and all kinds of protections rendered necessary due to their unequal degree of technical advance and also because of a manifest overpopulation. Thus, it is necessary to work on each one of those points, which implies intervening to facilitate migrations from the countryside towards the city, placing sophisticated equipment at people's disposal as well as the formation necessary for its use, transforming the juridical regime of exploitations and promoting their extent. In other words, the State must act on a level, not directly economic, but social in the broad sense of the term, to render competition possible. The fact that, afterwards, the common agricultural policy became more a system of subsidy to avoid competition than a means of social transformation to support it, however, does not remove the spirit of the initial approach. This implies that the government does not have to intervene as much on the effects of the market—through wellbeing policies—as on the society so that it can be controlled by the market.

Undoubtedly, it is possible to create a competitive capacity. But for how long? As the example of the common agricultural policy shows, there is no guaranteed duration for this capacity. It would be even assured to disappear in the long term according to Schumpeter, who with regret prophesied the advent of socialism as competition ineluctably causes monopolistic situations. Those situations justify the State's intervention as people's needs require to be satisfied by avoiding the hardness resulting from any situation in which the private supplier of the goods they need has absolute hegemony. According to Foucault, all the interest of the second time of the neoliberal reasoning is placed there. Neoliberals argue that if one wants to avoid the State's tendency to absorb the economic process, one needs to correct the initial error which provides its force. Which error? The one consisting in making prevail the man of exchange, the consumer, over the entrepreneur. The *homo economicus* of neoliberalism is an entrepreneur, even an entrepreneur of himself. Wages are generated by an entrepreneur whose capital is himself and who, then, has to maintain this human capital.

The *homo economicus* of traditional liberals was the man of exchange. He placed himself as a partner of another man during the exchange. On the contrary, given that the *homo economicus* of neoliberalism is an entrepreneur of himself, he has only competitors. Even consumption becomes an activity of enterprise according to which the consumer undertakes the production of his own satisfaction. Hence, the opposition between production and consumption, between the active character of the former and the passive, alienated, of the latter does not have sense. Denouncing the consumer society or the spectacle's society is to be mistaken about this epoch, to pretend that the man of neoliberalism is a man of exchange and consumption when he is first and foremost an entrepreneur. It is the problem of redistribution, of the incomes gap what creates men as consumers. On the contrary, the "politics of society" turns a man into an entrepreneur, somebody who is situated in a game and works to increase his success within a system in which inequalities are necessary and as much effective and stimulating as the large gaps are known.

However, neoliberals argue, there is a limit to the game of inequalities, namely, the limit of exclusion. One must do everything to prevent that some are not completely excluded from this game so it does not lose its sense and its credibility. Therefore, one needs to take care of those who are in the limits of this game so they can return to it. To maintain everyone in the game is increasing its dynamics and, thus, is a dimension of the politics of society. Much more than one charitable concern, the struggle against exclusion was initially, in the theoretical plan, an economic concern, impelled by the neoliberals[28]. Overall, though, it is important to stay in the game to remain a *homo economicus* according to neoliberals, that is, an entrepreneur, somebody eminently governable and different from its liberal predecessor, the man of exchange, who one had better let adjust himself "naturally". He is governable because he governs himself. He governs himself according to economic laws and one can take action on the environment in order to modify his conduits. With this purpose, one can establish "the conduct of conducts" because as entrepreneur of his life he is autonomous and, for this reason, one can make it responsible.

It was important restoring this analysis of neoliberalism to see that the third way is not completely what one has said, but a means of passing between the Caudine Forks of the old left and the new liberalism. One can appreciate its triple plan for the role of the State, the relation between the economic and the social, and finally, the form of government.

The question of the role of the State is a dimension which associates closely the third way to neoliberalism. For instance, it clearly rejects everything that the French left keeps maintaining like a domain of the state: nationalizations, public services set up as clergies of the State, etc. However, it does not mean that the third way wishes to reduce the State to a figurative role. It behaves as a declared advocate of "the politics of society" according to the neoliberal expression being used to name the interventionism intended to bring any social activity to the competition regime. In this, there is an acknowledged reason which is the negotiable benefit of this type of politics in a universe where globalization determines a nation's wealth and employment according to its competitiveness in any given sector. Laissez-faire and nationalizations are no longer deciding on this matter!

Neoliberalism only wants intervention at the service of competition. It neglects the social and condemns it even by accepting social policy only to fight against exclusion, under the condition, though, that it does not aim at reducing inequalities. Is not in the social field where one can blame the third way of a blind conformism? It seems obvious, for example, that the English government concentrates more its efforts against poverty than on the reduction of inequalities. Hardly installed, it has created a division for fighting against social exclusion and a relatively weak minimum wage, but it did nothing to directly increase workers' purchasing power or to protect legally their employment. It has not created many subsidized jobs, nor tried to boost the economy by consumption, that is, by increasing workers' purchasing power according to Keynesian recipes that have assured the support of the French left. Resigning to the canonical formulas of the social is not worth, though, abandoning the social. Rather, it implies a change in the nature of the relation between the economic and the social. Within the framework of the traditional Welfare state and, in agreement with the Keynesian theory, the relation between the economic and the social develops according to a spiraled scheme. The wealth development attained by the economic allows financing the social. In return, by increasing the income levels, the social allows maintaining or increasing the production as a consequence of the increase in the demand. This scheme has showed its limits on its two levels: the social deductions and the economic revival by the consumption. The first level can damage the capacity of investment if the dispensed benefits are massively deducted on behalf of the social. Sooner or later, this weakening of the investment capacity ends up affecting employment. In the framework of a global economy, the disadvantage of the second level can be the increasing consumption...of products coming from other countries. Does it imply then a cold disposal of the social? Rather, it implies the replacement of the Keynesian spiral model by a model of reciprocal but direct action between the economic and the social, not assembled by the virtuous dream of a progressive link between both: the philosophy of history has yielded the place to globalization much more uncertain of its effects in the period. In the spatial plan, strategy replaces dialectic. There will be winner and losers of whom one will take care later if the situation allows it. In fact, there is a first movement going from the social towards the economic and consisting in financing, on behalf of the social, the competitiveness of workers through education and training, as well as by launching the fight against unemployment. Also, there is a second movement going from the economic towards the social which ends up submitting the latter to a requirement of profitability of the investments carried out. This requirement is exemplified by the emphasis put particularly on prevention rather than on improving areas such as health, employment and retirement. This profitability minimally takes the form of the transparency requirement in the control and the outcomes of social policies, which the pure reasoning in terms of acquired rights renders difficult.

Regarding the third point, the one about governmentality, one sees easily which aspects of the neoliberal precepts irritate the traditional extreme left. Does not talking about autonomy and responsibility benefit individualism, that is, those individuals with better incomes and make the poor responsible for overcoming this condition? Undoubtedly, the advocates of the third way value autonomy and individual responsibility as eloquently as neoliberals. They see them as means to counteract the augment in services, which can increase absurdly if one remains in the current logic of automatic compensation for all the real problems we are brought to feel sorry. For them, though, they are only one means among many others. However, there is one mean which characterizes more directly this political current insofar as it constitutes as much an alternative to individualism as to the old left: it is the one which emphasizes the collective and political dimension of the prevention of damages. That is to say the one which stresses the notion of community action (in France one should state "collective" to avoid any misunderstandings of this expression, even if it is not an accurate translation). But as much as neoliberalism intends to lead "politics of society", the third way aims at rebuilding "a political society".

Translated by Vivianna Pitton

* *

NOTES

[1] Michel Foucault has discussed the issue of government for two years in his courses at the Collège de France in 1978 and 1979. Later, he has devoted himself to the history of subjectivity in the The Care of the Self and The Use of Pleasure which appeared in 1984, the year of his death.

[2] The mode of governmentality studies was first started in Great Britain and the U.S. by Colin Gordon, Graham Burchell and Peter Miller's book The Foucault Effect: Studies in Governmentality. Chicago: University Press (1991). It was retaken by Mitchell Dean in Governmentality: Power and Rule in Modern Society. London: Sage publications (1999) and it was followed in Germany due to Thomas Lemke's impulse in Neolibras Mus, Staat und Sellesttech… (2000).

[3] Two colloquia on the subject have been held in France during the 20th anniversary of Foucault's death: one at the MSH and the other at the IEP in Paris. The latter has been published: Meyet, S., Neves, M. C. & Ribemont, T. (2005). Trouvailles avec Foucault. L'Harmattan.

[4] Michel Foucault. Sécurité, Pouvoir, Population. Seuil 2004 and Naissance de La Bio-Politique. Seuil 2004.

[5] This can roughly be translated: "from the glare of tortures to the tenderness of sorrows."

[6] "[…] from the right to death to the control over life."

[7] M. Foucault. "Securite, Territoire, Population". Gallimard. Seuil 2004. P. 77-78.

[8] Idem, p. 98.

[9] Idem, p. 108.

[10] This idea is reflected in Jacques Donzelot's , La Police des Familles published a year later, in 1977. Chapter IV: "From a Government of Families to a Government by the Family".

[11] idem, p. 111.

[12] idem, p. 133.

[13] idem, p. 265.

[14] idem, p. 345.

[15] idem, p. 353.

[16] The expression on the agenda, so precious for politicians, appeared with the English utilitarianism, explains M. Foucault, when Bentham distinguished what needed to be done (from a liberal point of view), namely agenda, and what did not, that is, non agenda.

[17] idem, p. 360.

[18] In "The Birth of Biopolitics", p. 110.

[19] idem, p. 122.

[20] By using this strange formula of "equal inequality" Foucault refers to this neoliberal idea according to which we all need to endure situations of relative inequality and that this differential does not condemn the market, but makes it work...under the condition that anybody is persistently excluded of the game.

[21] idem, p. 124.

[22] The Foucauldian diaspora has right, left and extreme left-wing supporters. still, one needs to highlight that the most notorious among the latter, Antonio Negri, has requested to vote in favor of the European constitution project, because of hatred towards the national echelon, which hinders an awareness of the reality of "the empire", and to engage with the struggles on this supreme level. by so doing, then, he reinforced the beliefs of those supporting the sovereign nation and the French-like European social model...

[23] This analysis appears in the second volume of both courses, page 39 and the following ones.

[24] idem, p. 41.

[25] idem, p. 42.

[26] idem, p. 45.

[27] For this analysis, see J. Donzelot (1984) "The Invention of the Social. Essay on the Decline of Political Passions". Fayard: Seuil Point Essais. One notices, for example, that the issue of not too much, not too little in politics, recently promoted by Tony Blair and the Third Way between the old left and Thatcher's neoliberalism has been supported as well by a renowned sociologist: Anthony Giddens.

[28] It is sufficient to think about the precedence of Lionel Stoléru's book (Defeating Poverty in Rich Countries. Paris, 1974) adherent to the American neoliberal policy about the relative debates on exclusion emerging at the end of the 80s to agree upon this precedence.

THOMAS LEMKE

3. AN INDIGESTIBLE MEAL? FOUCAULT, GOVERNMENTALITY AND STATE THEORY

In his lectures of 1978 and 1979 at the Collège de France, Michel Foucault responded to some Marxist critics who had complained that the "genealogy of power" lacked an elaborated theory of the state.[1] Foucault remarked that he had refrained from pursuing a theory of the state "in the sense that one abstains from an indigestible meal" (2004b, p. 78).[2] However, a few sentences later Foucault states: "The problem of state formation is at the centre of the questions that I want to pose" (2004b, p. 79).

This article explores this apparent contradiction and investigates the contribution of an "analytics of government" to state theory. This approach takes up methodological and theoretical considerations that Foucault developed in his "history of 'governmentality'" (1991a, p. 102). It has three analytical dimensions. First, it presents a nominalist account that stresses the central importance of knowledge and political discourses in the constitution of the state. Secondly, an analytics of government uses a broad concept of technology that encompasses not only material but also symbolic devices, including political technologies as well as technologies of the self. Third, it conceives of the state as an instrument and effect of political strategies that define the external borders between the public and the private and the state and civil society, and also define the internal structure of political institutions and state apparatuses. After presenting the three analytical dimensions, the last part of the article will compare this theoretical perspective with the concept of governance and with critical accounts of neo-liberalism.

GOVERNMENTALITY AND TRANSFORMATIONS OF STATEHOOD

Foucault proposed the concept of governmentality for the first time in his lectures at the Collège de France in 1978 and 1979 (2004a; 2004b). The notion derives from the French word *gouvernemental*, meaning "concerning government" (see Senellart, 2004, p. 406). The word "governmentality" was known even before it figured as a central term in Foucault's work. Roland Barthes had already used the "barbarous but unavoidable neologism" (1989, p. 130) in the 1950s, to denote an ideological mechanism that presents the government as the origin of social relations. For Barthes, governmentality refers to "the Government presented by the national press as the Essence of efficacy" (1989, p. 130). Foucault takes up this "dirty word" (2004a, p. 119), but detaches it from the semiological context. Governmentality no longer refers to a mythological symbolic practice that

M.A. Peters et al. (eds.), Govermentality Studies in Education, 35–54.

depoliticizes social relations, but represents the "rationalisation of governmental practice in the exercise of political sovereignty" (2004b, p. 4).

Foucault deploys the concept of governmentality as a "guideline" for a "genealogy of the modern state" (2004a, p. 362) embracing a period from Ancient Greece up until contemporary forms of neo-liberalism. I wish to emphasize two points here, as they seem important for an adequate assessment of the innovative potential of an analytics of government. First of all, the concept of governmentality demonstrates Foucault's working hypothesis concerning the reciprocal constitution of power techniques and forms of knowledge and of regimes of representation and modes of intervention. Government defines a discursive field in which exercizing power is "rationalized." Ways in which this occurs include the delineation of concepts, the specification of objects and borders, and the provision of arguments and justifications. In this manner, government makes it possible to address a problem and offers certain strategies for managing or solving the problem.

Second: rather than presenting an analysis of the development and transformation of political-administrative structures, Foucault concentrates on the multiple and diverse relations between the institutionalization of a state apparatus and historical forms of subjectivation. He endeavors to show how the modern sovereign state and the modern autonomous individual co-determine each other's emergence. Like Norbert Elias (1976) he is interested in the long-term processes of co-evolution of modern statehood and modern subjectivity. But whereas Elias relies on a general theory of civilization presupposing a single historical logic of development ("the process"), Foucault analyzes heterogeneous and plural "arts of government" (2004b, p. 4). He refers to the older meaning of the term government (Sellin 1984; Senellart 1995). While the word has a purely political meaning today, Foucault is able to show that up until well into the 18th century the problem of government was placed in a more general context. Government was a term discussed not only in political tracts but also in philosophical, religious, medical and pedagogic texts. In addition to management by the state or administration, government also addressed problems of self-control, guidance for the family and for children, management of the household, directing the soul, and other questions. For this reason, Foucault defines government as conduct, or, more precisely, as "the conduct of conduct" and thus as a term which ranges from "governing the self" to "governing others" (Foucault, 2000a, pp. 340–342).

To mark the conceptual difference between this wider notion and the more recent concept of government, Foucault distinguishes between the "problematic of government in general" and "the political form of government" (1991a, p. 88).

To be sure, Foucault's "genealogy of governmentality" is more of a fragmentary sketch than an elaborated theory, and most of it is to be found in lectures that were never prepared for publication. Nevertheless, the concept of governmentaliy has inspired many studies in the social sciences and historical investigations. Especially in Great Britain, Australia, Canada and the US (Burchell, Gordon and Miller, 1991; Barry, Osborne and Rose, 1996; Dean and Hindess, 1998; Dean and Henman, 2004), but also in Germany and France (Bröckling, Krasmann and Lemke, 2000; Pieper, Gutiérrez Rodriguez, 2003; Meyet, Naves and Ribemont, 2005), scholars have sought to refine and extend Foucault's work as a tool for the critical analysis of political technologies and governmental rationalities in contemporary societies.[3]

A major focus of studies of governmentality has been the shift from the Keynesian welfare state toward so-called free market policies and the rise of neo-liberal political projects in Western democracies. An analytics of government helps to provide a dynamic analysis that does not limit itself to statements about the "retreat of the state" or the "domination of the market", but deciphers the apparent "end of politics" as a political program. As many scholars have noted, the critique of direct state interventions is a positive technique of government which entails a transfer of the operations of government to non-state actors. As a result, current political changes are understood not as a decline of state sovereignty but as a promotion of forms of government that foster and enforce individual responsibility, privatized risk-management, empowerment techniques, and the play of market forces and entrepreneurial models in a variety of social domains (Rose and Miller, 1992; O'Malley, 1996; Rose, 1996; Cruikshank, 1999; Henman, 2004).

While the concept of governmentality provides a very promising tool for the analysis of transformations in (contemporary) statehood, there are also some limitations and blind spots to be noted. To start with, it is mostly the territorially sovereign nation state that serves as the implicit or explicit frame of reference in the governmentality literature. This perspective is often informed by a Eurocentric approach excluding all forms of "fragmented" or "graduated sovereignty" (Ong, 2005) that characterize statehood in many parts of the world (Schlichte, 2005). Until more recently, studies of governmentality mostly neglected non-Western as well as non-liberal contexts (Sigley, 2006). Furthermore, there is rarely any consideration of how transformations of Keynesian forms of government on a national level are linked with international developments or of how the appearance of new actors on the global or European scale is paralleled by a displacement of the competences of the nation state.[4] Such an approach makes it impossible to investigate the new forms of government that are indicated by the increasing significance of international, supranational and transnational organizations like the UN, IMF and World Bank, and it does not account for the new role of transnational alliances of Nongovernmental Organizations. As James Ferguson and Akhil Gupta rightly stress, it is necessary to extend an analytics of government to include modes of government that are being set up on a transnational and global scale. They criticize the way in which "institutions of global governance such as the IMF and the WTO are commonly seen as being simply 'above' national states, much as states were discussed vis-à-vis the grassroots. Similarly, the 'global' is often spoken of as if it were simply a super-ordinate scale level that encompasses nation-states just as nation-states were conceptualized to encompass regions, towns, and villages" (2002, p. 990). As the recent discussions of "transnational" or "global governmentality" show, scholars are already rethinking and questioning spatial and scalar framings of sovereign states that are too often taken for granted in the literature on governmentality (Lippert, 1999; Ferguson and Gupta, 2002; Larner and Walters, 2004a; 2004b; 2004c; Perry and Maurer, 2004).

In the following, I will propose an analytics of government that takes up some of the insights of Foucault's work on governmentality while seeking to avoid the shortcomings in the conceptualization of contemporary statehood that I have mentioned. Three dimensions that will be briefly described in the remaining part of the article characterize this theoretical perspective.

THE HISTORICAL ONTOLOGY OF THE STATE

The point of departure of an analytics of government is "the 'governmentalization' of the state" (Foucault, 1991: 103). According to Foucault, government by state agencies must be conceived of as a contingent political process and a singular historical event in need of explanation rather than a given fact. A series of 'how' questions follow from this problematization. How does the state come to act, if at all, as a coherent political force? How is the imaginary unity of the state produced in practical terms? How does a plurality of institutions and processes become the state? How to account for the apparent autonomy of the state as a separate entity that somehow stands outside and above society?

To pursue these questions, Foucault proposes an analytical framework he sometimes calls "a political history of truth" or "historical nominalism" (e.g. 1991b, p. 86). This methodological-theoretical perspective informs not only his "genealogy of the modern state", as in the 1978-79 lectures at the Collège de France, but also his book on the *Birth of the Prison* and the first volume of the *History of sexuality* (Foucault, 1977; 1979).[5] Foucault's historical nominalism is a critical investigation consisting of a positive and a negative component. The latter is closely tied to subverting self-evidences and universal truth claims: "It means making visible a singularity at places where there is a temptation to invoke a historical constant, an immediate anthropological trait, or an obviousness which imposes itself uniformly on all. To show that things 'weren't as necessary as all that'." (1991b, p. 76) The second "theoretico-political function" of historical nominalism consists of

> rediscovering the connections, encounters, supports, blockages, plays of forces, strategies and so on which at a given moment establish what subsequently counts as being self-evident, universal and necessary (1991b, p. 76).[6]

This dual movement characterizes the specific profile of Foucault's nominalism. The objective of this approach is not to dispute that there is some "object" to which "state" refers; rather, the point called into question is whether this referent is identical to the "state" itself. In fact, the idea of a universal and neutral state can itself be comprehended as a specific "state effect." The concept of government is meant to historically situate statehood, to reflect on its conditions of existence and rules of transformation. An analytics of government studies the practical conditions under which forms of statehood emerge, stabilize and change – combining and connecting different and diverse "elements" in such a way that retrospectively an "object" appears that seemed to have existed prior to the historical and political process, presumably guiding and directing it. As Rose and Miller put it:

[T]he state can be seen as a specific way in which the problem of government is discursively codified, a way of dividing a 'political sphere', with its particular characteristics of rule, from other, 'non-political spheres' to which it must be related, and a way in which certain technologies of government are given a temporary institutional durability and brought into particular kinds of relations with one another. (Rose and Miller, 1992, pp. 176–177; Lascoumes, 2004)

According to Foucault, the state possesses the same epistemological status as politics and economy. These entities are "neither existing things nor illusions, errors or ideologies. They are something that did not exist and that is part of reality, [that is] the effect of a regime of truth that separates truth from falsity" (Foucault, 2004b, p. 22). The state is not an object that is always already there, nor can it be reduced to an illusionary or ideological effect of hegemonic practices. Rather, the state is conceptualized as a "transactional reality" [*réalité de transaction*] (Foucault, 2004b, p. 301), that is to say a dynamic ensemble of relations and syntheses that at the same time produces the institutional structure of the state and the knowledge of the state. An analytics of government investigates the "historical ontology" (Foucault, 1984, p. 45) of the state, searching for discontinuities and ruptures in the regimes of truth. The assumption that the state does not exist is followed by the question of how different elements and practices made it possible that something like *the* state possesses a historical reality and structural consistency over a longer period of time.[7]

It follows that an analytics of government takes seriously the historical and systematic importance of "political knowledge" (Foucault, 1997, p. 67) for state analysis. Historically, the emergence and stability of state agencies is intimately tied to the incessant generation, circulation, storage and repression of knowledge. The constitution of the modern state was closely connected with the rise of the human sciences and the production of knowledge about the population and individuals. It depended on information concerning the physical condition of the national territory, diplomatic and secret knowledge about the strengths and weaknesses of foreign states, and other forms of knowledge that made objects visible and rendered them into a calculable and programmable form. State actors and agencies used statistical accounts, medical expertise, scientific reports, architectural plans, bureaucratic rules and guidelines, surveys, graphs, and so on to represent events and entities as information and data for political action. These "inscription devices" (Latour, 1986) made it possible to define problems, specify areas of intervention, calculate resources, and determine political goals (Burke, 2000; Vismann, 2000; Desrosières, 2002; Collin and Horstmann, 2004).

In systematic terms, political knowledge plays a dual role in the constitution of the modern state. On the one hand, political rationalities provide cognitive and normative maps that open up spaces of government which are intrinsically linked to truth. State agencies produce and proliferate forms of knowledge that enable them to act upon the governed reality. On the other hand, the state is constituted by discourses, narratives, world-views and styles of thought that allow political actors to develop strategies and realize goals. What is more, these symbolic devices even define what it means to be an actor, who may qualify as a political actor and citizen (Nullmeier, 1993; Meyer, 1999; Steinmetz, 1999a; Müller, Raufer and Zifonun, 2002; Hajer and Wagenaar, 2003). Finally, it would be a misunderstanding to reduce political knowledge to scientific reasoning and rational argumentation since it is also embodied in routine action, cultural self-evidence and normative orientations. Thus the state is not only a material structure and a mode of thinking, but also a lived and embodied experience, a mode of existence (see Maihofer, 1995; Sauer, 2001, pp. 110–112).

This analytical perspective has two important theoretical merits. First, the commonplace contrast between state formation and policymaking loses credibility, since the former is not a single event but an enduring process in which the limits and contents of state action are permanently negotiated and redefined. It follows "that 'policies' that affect the very structure of the state are part of the ongoing process of state-formation" (Steinmetz, 1999b, p. 9; Gottweis, 2003). Second, this approach makes it possible to include the observer's position in the process of theory construction. Political and sociological knowledge, operating with dualisms like individual and state, knowledge and power, and so on, plays a constitutive role in the emergence and reproduction of concrete forms of statehood. It provides a symbolic infrastructure that maps possible sites of intervention, and it is also inside this cultural framework that subjects define and live their relation to the state (Demirovic, 1998, pp. 49–50; Mitchell, 1991, p. 94; Rose and Miller, 1992, p. 182).

TECHNOLOGIES OF GOVERNMENT: THE MATERIALITY OF THE STATE

As the focus on 'how' questions indicates, an analytics of government is particularly interested in examining governmental technologies as a way of accounting for state transformations and state policies. It proposes a concept of technology that seeks to grasp the materiality of technologies by circumventing two possible pitfalls that either reduce technologies to an expression of social relations or conceive of society as the result of technological determinations.[8] To counter expressivist and determinist accounts, an analytics of government extends the notion of technology in two ways.

First, an analytics of government examines how forms of subjectivity, gender regimes and life styles are produced in practical terms by distinguishing a plurality of governmental technologies. Foucault addressed four different forms of technology in his work. In *Discipline and Punish* (1977) and in *The History of Sexuality, vol. 1* (1979) he analyzed technologies seeking to discipline the individual body or to regulate population processes, and in his later work he was also sensitive to the workings of "technologies of the self" and "political technologies of individuals." While the former concentrate on processes of self-guidance and the ways in which subjects relate to themselves as ethical beings, the latter denote "the way by which [...] we have been led to recognize ourselves as a society, as a part of a social entity, as a part of a nation or a state" (Foucault, 2000b, p. 404).[9]

By focussing on diverse and distinct technologies, an analytics of government avoids the pre-analytical distinction between micro- and macro-level, individual and state. It conceives of both processes of individualization and practices of institutionalization as technologies of government. This approach makes it possible to ask questions about the relationships between different governmental technologies. For example, one can investigate how technologies of the self and political government are articulated with each other (see Foucault 1988; 1993, pp. 203–4). This line of inquiry also opens up empirical investigations of historical forms of articulation between physical being and moral-political existence: how and when do certain bodily experiences become a moral, political or legal problem? This is the theme of Foucault's last works on the History of Sexuality (1985; 1990). Finally, it is possible to investigate the "natural foundations" of national identities. For example, what relationship exists between biological characteristics and questions of citizenship? (see Rose and Novas, 2005.)

Second, an analytics of government operates with a concept of technology that includes not only material but also symbolic devices. It follows that discourses, narratives and regimes of representation are not reduced to pure semiotic propositions; instead, they are regarded as performative practices. Governmental technologies denote a complex of practical mechanisms, procedures, instruments, and calculations through which authorities seek to guide and shape the conduct and decisions of others in order to achieve specific objectives. These technologies include:

> methods of examination and evaluation; techniques of notation, numeration, and calculation; accounting procedures; routines for the timing and spacing of activities in specific locations; presentational forms such as tables and graphs; formulas for the organization of work; standardized tactics for the training and implantation of habits; pedagogic, therapeutic, and punitive techniques of reformulation and cure; architectural forms in which interventions take place (i.e. classrooms and prisons); and professional vocabularies (Inda, 2005, p. 9; Miller and Rose, 1990, p. 8; Rose and Miller, 1992, p. 183).

Let us once again note two theoretical implications of this perspective. On the one hand, the distinction between soft and hard, material and symbolic technologies, between political technologies and technologies of the self, becomes precarious. An analytics of government proposes an integral account that investigates the dynamic interplay of elements that are often systematically separated. On the other hand, this theoretical perspective questions the notion of a state apparatus confined to the structural and organizational characteristics of the state as an institutional ensemble. An analytics of government reverses this "institutionalocentric" (Foucault, 2004a, p. 120) account by conceiving of institutions as technologies. Instead of taking institutions as the point of departure, it focuses on technologies that are materialized and stabilized in institutional settings. Rather than attributing political transformations to the policies of an autonomous state, an analytics of government traces them in new technologies and forms of knowledge that provide the "very possibility of appearing to set apart from society the free-standing apparatus of a state" (Mitchell, 1991, p. 92).[10]

STRATEGIES AND STATE EFFECTS

The third feature of an analytics of government is that it conceives of the state as an effect and instrument of political strategies and social relations of power. The state is an *effect* of strategies since it cannot be reduced to a homogeneous, stable actor that exists prior to political action. Rather, *the* state is to be understood as an emergent and complex resultant of conflicting and contradictory governmental practices. Bob Jessop's idea of a plurality of state projects fruitfully illustrates this point. Jessop rightly reminds us that "whether, how and to what extent one can talk in definite terms about the state actually depends on the contingent and provisional outcome of struggles to realize more or less specific 'state projects'" (Jessop, 1990, p. 9; 1996). Like state projects, "arts of government" are not the objects of political theories or abstract ideologies, but an integral part of a regime of practices that specifies the objectives of governmental action and is regulated by continuous reflection (see Foucault 2004b, p. 4). But grounding the state in a network of governmental practices does not mean that the state is a secondary category that could be dispensed with. On the contrary, it occupies a strategic position:

> It is certain that, in contemporary societies, the state is not simply one of the forms of specific situations of the exercise of power – even if it is the most important – but that, in a certain way, all other forms of power relation must refer to it. But this is not because they are derived from it; rather, it is because power relations have become more and more under state control [...]. Using here the restricted meaning of the word 'government', one could say that power relations have been progressively governmentalized, that is to say, elaborated, rationalized, and centralized in the form of, or under the auspices of, state institutions (Foucault, 2000a, p. 345).

This strategic approach goes well beyond a juridical conception of the state. The state is neither the result of a social contract nor does it rely on the "active consent" of the governed, as Antonio Gramsci's concept of hegemony suggests; also, the state cannot be understood as a compromise between classes, gender or other group identities. "Compromise", "consent" or "contract" are the result rather than the origin of strategic articulation. These categories are in need of explanation rather than given facts (see Foucault, 2000a, pp. 340-348). Rather than understanding the state in juridical categories, we have to conceive of it within the logic of strategic relations that constitute a collective will that did not exist beforehand. While ideas of contract, compromise and consent are insufficient to understand the transformations and dynamics of state action, the concept of translation in actor-network theory might prove more helpful. In their critique of the Hobbesian model of the social contract and the concept of juridical sovereignty, Michel Callon and Bruno Latour propose "a sociology of translation." In their view the contract is merely a specific instance of the general phenomenon of translation. By translation they understand

all the negotiations, intrigues, calculations, acts of persuasion and violer
thanks to which an actor or force takes, or causes to be conferred on its
authority to speak or act on behalf of another actor or force (Callon a
Latour, 1981, p. 279).

From this perspective, translation does not mean the correct transmission of
already existing text or will into another, but something quite different: translat
produces this text or will by expressing in one's own language what others say a
want, why they act in the way they do (Callon, 1999, p. 81).

However, the state is not only an effect but also an instrument and a site
strategic action. It serves as an *instrument* of strategies insofar as it establishes
frontier regime that is defined by the distinction between inside and outside, state
and non-state. This borderline does not simply separate two external and independent
realms, but operates as an internal division providing resources of power. It
constitutes a differential frontier regime that establishes and reproduces structural
gaps between private and public, residents and foreigners, and so on (Mitchell,
1991, pp. 89–91; see Valverde, 1996, pp. 367–369). As a result, the fact that some
actors and processes are regarded as private may secure them a privileged role or,
alternatively, may deprive them of financial and organizational resources and legal
protection – a "bareness" that may in turn be exploited in economic or ideological
terms (see Agamben, 1998). Examples of this include the situation of illegal
immigrants in Western societies and male violence in the family. Concerning the
latter, feminist state theory has observed that modern statehood was marked by a
"dual face" (Sauer, 2004, p. 117): monopolization and centralization of the legitimate
means of violence in the hands of the state corresponded to the father's right to
employ physical violence in relations with other family members.

Furthermore, the state is also a *site* of strategic action. The inner structure of the
state is characterized by a materiality that Bob Jessop, drawing on Nicos
Poulantzas' account of the state as a social relation (1977) has defined as "strategic
selectivity." The term refers to the state's differential impact on the capacity of
different political forces to pursue their strategies and to realize their goals (Jessop,
1990, p. 9–10). It addresses the relational character of this selectivity and focuses
on the constraints imposed by existing institutional structures. As Jessop puts it:

Particular forms of state privilege some strategies over others, privilege the
access of some forces over others, some interests over others, some time
horizons over others, some coalitions possibilities over others. A given type of
state, a given state form, a given form of regime, will be more accessible to
some forces than others according to the strategies they adopt to gain state
power (Jessop, 1990, p. 10).

A certain type of state is more suited to the pursuit of some types of economic and
political strategies than others, because of the modes of intervention and resources
characterizing the structure of the state. However, this structure does not determine
the success or failure of political strategies. The differential impact is not inscribed
in the state apparatus as such, but is the result of the dynamic and mobile

structures and the strategies adopted by different forces
p. 260–262).[11]

ze two important consequences of such a "strategic logic"
4). First, if we take seriously the strategic dimension of
roblems and questions will be opened up for state theory that
garded as "private", reflecting a failure to recognize that the
s not signify a protected and separated space outside state
itself the object of the state's power of definition and regulation.
overnment asks what forms of identity are accepted, proliferated
y hindered or even suppressed by the state. What gender regime is
rete forms of statehood? What apparatus of sexuality, what forms
eproduction are promoted, marginalized or even repressed?
analytics of government goes well beyond the limits of both positivist
the state and theories that dispense with the category of the state
it proposes an approach to the state that does not take for granted the
ne originating subject that pre-exists and determines political processes
erred to as *the* state; nor does it simply denounce the statist account as an
or myth that doesn't correspond to the complexity of political and social
While it is necessary to refuse to take for granted the apparent autonomy of
te and the state-society distinction, an analytics of government goes one step
er. It not only criticizes "idealist" accounts of the state, but also seeks to
ain how the "myth" of an autonomous state is produced and reproduced in
ial relations at the same time as it remains an integral and organizing part of it.[12]

GOVERNMENTALITY, GOVERNANCE, AND CRITIQUE

An analytics of government enables us to overcome some theoretical blind spots of
the governance discourse that dominates contemporary accounts of state transformations and policies. The term "governance" was introduced into political science
and organizational theory as an academic term in the 1980s. Since then it has
enjoyed an impressive career, and is used today as a "catch-all term" (Smouts,
1998, p. 81) or a "buzzword" (Jessop, 1998, p. 29) to refer to any mode of co-
ordination of interdependent activities.[13] In a very general sense the word signifies
any strategy, process, procedure or program for controlling, regulating or managing
problems on a global, national, local or organizational level. The scientific
literature ranges from governance in public administration and public policy,
international relations and European goverance to corporate governance (Kooiman,
1993; Marks et al., 1996; Prakash/Hart, 1999; Willke, 2007). Governance involves
a shift in the analytical and theoretical focus from "institutions" to "processes" of
rule and announces the eclipse or erosion of state sovereignty. It accounts for the
growing interdependencies between political authorities and social and economic
actors capturing the policy networks and public-private partnerships that emerge
out of the interactions between a variety of bureaucracies, organizations and
associations. Governance encompasses on the one hand the displacement to
supranational levels of practices that were formerly defined in terms of the nation

state (e.g. the European Union or the United Nations); on the other hand, the governance literature stresses that there are important mechanisms of social regulation besides the state – such as the community, organizations and the market (Rose, 1999, pp. 15–17; Benz 2004).

There are several themes and topics the governance discourse shares with an analytics of government. First, a common feature of both approaches is an interest in 'how'-questions and a focus on governmental practices thereby taking a distance towards political studies that concentrate on attitudes, mentalities and opinions to understand politics. Second, governance and governmentality extend the scope of political analysis beyond the domain of the state and institutional politics. They are both investigating "political power beyond the state" (Rose/Miller, 1992) that is to say the forms of power that configure apparently non-political sites like the school, the prison or the family. Third, the two theoretical accounts are characterised by a relational understanding of power. Power is not conceived as a stable and fixed entity that could be "stored" at particular institutional sites but signifies the result of a mobile and flexible interactional and associational network (Walters, 2004, pp. 31–33).

Yet in spite of these similarities, there remain some important differences concerning the fundamental assumptions and the theoretical orientations between the governance discourse and an analytics of government. The first difference relates to the ontological status of the objects of governance. As Bob Jessop remarks, "much of the literature on governance assumes that the objects of governance pre-exist their coordination in and through specific governance mechanisms" (Jessop, 2003, p. 6). This realist approach to politics contrasts with the nominalism of an analytics of government. The latter does not start from the assumption that there is an external relationship between government and its objects; quite on the contrary, it recognises that government is also actively involved in constituting agents, identities and interests.

This brings us to a second difference that relates to the role of politics in governance literature. The governance discourse involves dialogue, participation, representation and the inclusion of "the governed". It seeks to give visibility to interests that are often ignored and extents the public sphere insofar as it promotes the consultation and implication of a whole range of societal and economic actors who are addressed as "partners" or "stakeholders". However, there are some serious shortcomings to be noted that limit the promise of an increasing democratisation. The governance literature assumes that political decisions are based on neutral facts or rational arguments, thereby ignoring the role of strategic options and political alternatives. As a consequence, it often marginalizes central conflicts between different social groups and classes or downplays contradictions between political interests and objectives – and is rightly criticized for "failing to take note of important aspects in the analysis of political processes that pertain to a sociology of domination" (Mayntz, 2004, p. 74; Smouts, 1998). For example, most of the literature on global governance takes it for granted that the political and social cleavages between those who profit from globalization and those who do not can be bridged by "modern" or "good" governance. In this view, poverty and wealth have nothing to do with each other, and economic growth, ecological considerations, political democracy, social solidarity, healthy living etc. appear to be equally achievable – without radically changing established political and social structures (Brunnengräber and Stock, 1999; Rucht, 2001; Brand, 2004). While an analytics of government endorses a strategic account stressing the constitutive role of political conflicts and confrontations, the governance discourse seeks to minimize "frictions" and is characterised by an "antipolitical politics" (Walters, 2004, pp. 33–7; Hirst, 2000; Mouffe, 2005).

It follows that the governance discourse promotes a technocratic model of steering and managing – this feature marks the third point where the governance discourse departs from an analytics of government. Most of the governance literature relies heavily on a certain kind of metanarrative. It claims to be a political response to the growing social complexity that calls for multilevel, networked, cooperative, heterarchic alternatives to hierarchic and state-centred forms of regulation (Jessop, 1998).[14] However, this account represents a rather distorted image of the past ignoring the multiple ways in which even the most interventionist welfare states governed by "indirect" mechanisms and forms of cooperation and implication:

> Governance theory works with a somewhat exaggerated conception of the power of the postwar welfare state. This has the effect, in turn, of over-emphasizing the novelty and significance of many of the phenomena of 'steering', 'regulation', and indirect control typically grouped under the rubric of 'new' governance (Walters, 2004, p. 38).

The caricature of a time when states were "whole" (and not yet "fragmented" and "decentred") serves as background for the claim of a decisive historical break: The diagnosis of a growing complexity of the social world – the globalisation of financial and other markets, the importance of informational and communicate technologies, the appearance of new forms of production etc. – is linked to an idea of the "end of politics", to a "post-ideological" world order that is no longer governed by fundamental conflicts and oppositions. In this view, governance is about steering and regulating a world without radical alternatives, it is animated by the search for "rational", "responsible" and "efficient" instruments of problem management. On this reading, strategic interests are reduced to technological concerns; politics just seems to follow the dictate of a structural logic of complexity. In contrast to this technocratic and managerialist approach, an analytics of government is more reflexive concerning the function of political knowledge and the intimate link between politics and technology. It does not take the "complexity" narrative at face value but investigates the role it plays in constituting and legitimising governance as a particular style of rule (Walters, 2004, pp. 40–41).

Seen from the perspective of an analytics of government, the governance discourse represents a particular "art of government" that is firmly rooted within a liberal concept of the state. It stresses political consensus, mutual accommodation and collective problem solving and searches for mechanisms that foster coordination, cooperation and harmonization. The governance discourse translates fundamental antagonisms and political oppositions into modes of articulation of different interests. It conceives of strategic confrontations as diverse "inputs" to reach a decision or to carry out a programme. In this conceptual frame, conflicts are not regarded as a threat to social order, but as a means of social progress:

> Governance [...] marks the space of a liberal game of assimilation. Where many political discourses seek to articulate a field of antagonistic forces as agents of political transformation, governance seeks to implicate them as 'partners' in a game of collective self-management and modulated social adjustment (Walters, 2004, p. 35).

Furthermore, a large part of the governance discourse seems still to accept the duality of state and society. Often governance is explicitly defined by a distance from the state, focussing on informal arrangements and decision-making processes below state institutions and beyond the competence of political authorities ("government"). Its proponents distinguish strictly between hierarchical interventions by the state and decentralized societal mechanisms exploring the interdependencies and networks between the two domains. By contrast, an analytics of government takes the state to be an integral part of governmental practices; it is an instrument and effect of these practices, not their foundation or counterpart. It follows that the opposition of state and civil society cannot be taken as a universal fact, but constitutes a contingent and internal element of governmental practices. On this reading, the government discourse illustrates what Foucault once described as an "overvaluing of the problem of the state" (1991a, p. 103) – the paradoxical result of reducing the state to an institutional ensemble and a hierarchical structure. As Wendy Larner and William Walters put it:

> [G]overnmentality can offer a particular kind of historical perspective that is often lacking in the global governance literature. This would involve seeing global governance as a particular technology of rule and placing it within the much longer trajectory of liberal political reason (2004b, pp. 16–17; see also Crowley, 2003).

But an analytics of government not only offers a critical account of the governance discourse, it also exposes some shortcomings of approaches that suffer from an inverse fixation. While the governance literature often caricatures the state as a hierarchical and bureaucratic apparatus, the anti-globalization literature and many critical accounts of neo-liberal modes of government tend to invoke a nostalgic image of the nation state as an actor defending public interests against powerful economic actors (see e.g. Bourdieu, 1998). The problem with this kind of analysis is that it also essentializes the state, being preoccupied with a territorial nation state that is supposedly being eroded by global economic regimes. The argument is that there is some "pure" or "anarchic" economy that should be "regulated" or "civilized" by a political reaction on the part of society. This critical account ironically shares the (neo-)liberal idea of a separation between politics and the economy. The concept of governmentality proves useful in correcting the diagnosis of neo-liberalism as an expansion of the economy into politics, since it helps us to go beyond a theoretical position that takes for granted the separation of state and market (see Lemke, 2002).

Taken together, the two opposing forms of analysis result in an interesting theoretical-political constellation. While some scholars demand a "reinvention of government" (Osborne and Gaebler, 1992) which includes a comprehensive deregulation and privatization of state functions and the downsizing of the political apparatus in the light of new global economic challenges, others call for the state to resist "the economic horror" (Forrester 1999) in order to protect citizens from the negative aspects of globalization. Neither of these approaches recognizes the necessity of a relational, technological and strategic approach that takes into account the fact that the state *and* the economy are themselves being reconfigured and reinvented in novel ways. Both consider the nation state as a prefabricated and stable form, failing to see that the relations between state and economy, global and local, as well as the categories themselves, require theoretical attention (Perry and Maurer, 2003).

CONCLUSION

This article started with Foucault's remark that he had refrained from pursuing a theory of the state "in the sense that one abstains from an indigestible meal." At the same time Foucault claims to provide nothing less than a "genealogy of the modern state." I have examined this apparent paradox in order to determine what an analytics of government might offer to state theory.

Foucault's analytics of government combines the "microphysics of power" (see Foucault, 1977), which remained centred on questions of discipline and normalization, with the macro-political question of the state (Lemke, 1997). This approach investigates how power relations have historically been concentrated in the form of the state without ever being reducible to it. Following this line of inquiry, Foucault sees the state as

> nothing more than the mobile effect of a regime of multiple governmentalities. [...] It is necessary to address from an exterior point of view the question of the state, it is necessary to analyse the problem of the state by referring to the practices of government (Foucault, 2004b, p. 79).

When Foucault focuses on the "governmentalization of the state" (1991a, p. 103), he does not assume that government is a technique that could be applied or used by state authorities or apparatuses; instead, he comprehends the state itself as a dynamic and contingent form of societal power relations. Thus, governmentality is

> at once internal and external to the state, since it is the tactics of government which make possible the continual definition and redefinition of what is within the competence of the state and what is not, the public versus the private, and so on; thus the state can only be understood in its survival and its limits on the basis of the general tactics of governmentality (1991a, p. 103).

In the light of this analytical framework, what we observe today is not a reduction of state sovereignty and planning capacities but a displacement from formal to informal techniques of government and the appearance of new actors on the scene of government. These processes indicate fundamental transformations in statehood and a new relation between state and civil society actors. In other words, the difference between state and society, politics and the economy does not function as a foundation or a borderline, but as an element and effect of specific governmental technologies (see Lemke, 2002).

As I have argued, an analytics of government is characterized by a triple movement of pluralization and decentralization that Foucault sums up as follows:

> Altogether, the perspective [...] consists in trying to expose the relations of power concerning the institution to analyse them in terms of technology; to expose them also concerning the function to reformulate them in a strategic analysis; and to free them from the privilege of the object to replace it by an interest of the constitution of fields, areas and objects of knowledge (2004a, p. 122).

Practices instead of object, strategies instead of function, and technologies instead of institution – this is certainly not a light snack, but it might be the recipe for a state theory that opens up new directions and research areas for political analysis and critique and provides a better understanding of current political and social transformations.

NOTES

[1] This paper has been accepted for publication in *Distinktion: Scandinavian Journal of Social Theory* and the final version of this paper will be published in No. 15, 2007.
I would like to thank William Walters for some valuable suggestions and comments as well as the journal's two reviewers whose remarks helped sharpen the argument. Research support for this paper was provided by a Heisenberg Grant from the German Science Foundation (DFG).

[2] Quotations from French and German have been translated by the author.

[3] For overviews of "studies of governmentality", see Dean, 1999; Lemke, 2000; Meyet, 2005.

[4] For a notable exception to this general tendency see Barry, 1993; 2001.

[5] Foucault's historical nominalism breaks with classical nominalism by taking up and radicalizing insights from French epistemology and the Marxist philosophy of Louis Althusser. On the difference between the two forms of nominalism see Phaller, 1997: 178–183. Ian Hacking proposes a similar distinction between "static" and "dynamic" nominalism (1986; 2004). See also Dean, 1998a.

[6] See Mitchell Dean's definition of an analytics of government: "An analytics is a type of study concerned with an analysis of the specific conditions under which particular entities emerge, exist and change. It is thus distinguished from most theoretical approaches in that it seeks to attend to, rather than efface, the singularity of ways of governing and conducting ourselves. Thus it does not treat particular practices of government as instances of ideal types and concepts. Neither does it regard them as effects of a law-like necessity or treat them as manifestations of a fundamental contradiction. An analytics of government examines the conditions under which regimes of practices come into being, are maintained and are transformed." (1999: 20–21; see also Gottweis, 2003).

[7] As Bob Jessop put it in a recent article: "In short, to study governmentality in its generic sense is to study the historical constitution of different state forms in and through changing practices of government without assuming that the state has a universal or general essence." (2007, p. 37)

LEMKE

[8] Andrew Barry (2001, p. 9) provides a very useful account of the relation between technology and politics: "To say that a technology can be political is not to denounce it, or to condemn it as a political instrument, or to say that its design reflects particular social or economic interests. Technology is not reducible to politics. Nor is to claim that technical devices and artefacts are 'social constructions' or are 'socially shaped': for the social is not something which exists independently from technology."

[9] See e.g. Barbara Cruikshank (1999) on "technologies of citizenship". Mitchell Dean has proposed a systematic account of different technologies of government (1998b, pp. 32–36).

[10] For a more detailed account, see Timothy Mitchell's critique of neoinstitutionalist concepts of the state (1991, pp. 91–94; also Foucault, 2004a, p. 123).

[11] See Jessop's comparison of Poulantzas' and Foucault's analysis of the state (2004).

[12] In a similar vein, Richard Warren Perry and Bill Maurer explain their approach to the analysis of globalization processes as follows: "To focus on the forms, as it were, of globalization, looking for the real behind the global hype or the global hope – misses the crucial question of why the global should assume such forms in the first place. We do not seek simply to demythologize Bourdieu's 'myth of globalization", or to "unmask" globalization, or to "de-dupe" those "blinded" by its wonders. We also seek to understand these wonders and their effects." (2003, p. xvii; Mitchell, 1991, pp. 89–91)

[13] Anne Mette Kjær (2004: 1–2) notes that between 1986 and 1998 "governance" appeared in 1,774 articles listed in the *Social Sciences Citation Index*. In the three years from 1999 to 2002, the Index had already registered 1,855 entries for the term.

[14] For a genealogy of "complexity" in European governance see Barry/Walters 2003.

REFERENCES

Althusser, L. (1994). *Sur la philosophie*. Paris: Éditions Gallimard.
Barry, A. (1993). The European community and European government: Harmonization, mobility and space. *Economy & Society, 22*(3), 314–326.
Barry, A. (2001). *Political machines*. London and New York: Athlone Press.
Barry, A., & Walters, W. (2003). From EURATOM to "Complex systems": Technology and European government. *Alternatives, 28*, 305–329.
Barry, A., Osborne, T., & Rose, N. (1996). *Foucault and political reason*. London: UCL Press.
Barthes, R. (1989). *Mythologies*. New York: The Noonday Press.
Benz, A. (2004). Einleitung: Governance – Modebegriff oder nützliches sozialwissenschaftliches konzept? In A. Benz (Ed.), *Governance - Regieren in komplexen Regelsystemen. Eine Einführung* (pp. 11–28). Wiesbaden: VS Verlag für Sozialwissenschaften.
Bourdieu, P. (1998). *Acts of resistance*. Cambridge, UK: Polity Press.
Brand, U. (2004). Governance. In U. Bröckling, S. Krasmann, & T. Lemke (Eds.), *Glossar der Gegenwart*. Frankfurt am Main: Suhrkamp.
Bröckling, U., Krasmann, S., & Lemke, T. (Eds.). (2000). *Gouvernementalität der Gegenwart*. Frankfurt am Main: Suhrkamp.
Brunnengräber, A., & Stock, C. (1999). Global governance: Ein neues Jahrhundertprojekt? *Prokla, 29*(3), 445–468.
Burchell, G., Gordon, C., & Miller, P. (1991). *The foucault effect*. Hemel Hempstead, Hertfordshire: Harvester Wheatsheaf.
Burke, P. (2000). *A social history of knowledge*. Cambridge, UK: Polity Press.
Callon, M. (1999). Some elements of a sociology of translation: Domestication of the scallops and the fishermen of St. Brieue Bay. In M. Biagioli (Ed.), *The science studies reader* (pp. 67–83). New York and London: Routledge.

Callon, M., & Latour, B. (1981). Unscrewing the big Leviathan: How actors macrostructure reality and how sociologists help them to do so. In K. Knorr-Cetina & A. V. Cicourel (Eds.), *Advances in social theory and methodology* (pp. 277–303). Boston: Routledge & Kegan Paul.

Collin, P., & Horstmann, T. (2004). *Das Wissen des Staates. Geschichte, Theorie und Praxis.* Baden-Baden: Nomos.

Crowley, J. (2003). Usages de la gouvernance et de la governementalité. *Critique Internationale, 21,* 52–61.

Cruikshank, B. (1999). *The will to empower.* Ithaca, NY: Cornell University Press.

Dean, M. (1998a). Questions of method. In I. Velody & R. Williams (Eds.), *The politics of constructionism* (pp. 182–199). London and Thousand Oaks, CA and New Delhi: Sage.

Dean, M. (1998b). Risk, calculable and incalculable. *Soziale Welt, 49,* 25–42.

Dean, M. (1999). *Governmentality.* London and Thousand Oaks, CA New Delhi: Sage.

Dean, M., & Henman, P. (2004). Governing society today: Editors' introduction. *Alternatives, 29,* 483–494.

Dean, M., & Hindess, B. (1998). *Governing Australia.* Cambridge, UK: Cambridge University Press.

Demirović, A. (1998). Staatlichkeit und Wissen. In C. Görg & R. Roth (Eds.), *Kein Staat zu machen. Zur Kritik der Sozialwissenschaften* (pp. 49–70). Münster: Verlag Westfälisches Dampfboot.

Desrosières, A. (2002). *The politics of large numbers.* Cambridge, MA and London: Harvard University Press.

Elias, N. (1976). *Über den Prozeß der Zivilisation. Soziogenetische und psychogenetische Untersuchungen* (Vols. 1–2). Frankfurt am Main: Suhrkamp.

Ferguson, J., & Gupta, A. (2002). Spatializing states: Toward an ethnography of neoliberal governmentality. *American Ethnologist, 29*(4), 981–1002.

Forrester, V. (1999). *The economic horror.* Cambridge, UK: Polity Press.

Foucault, M. (1977). *Discipline and punish.* London: Allen Lane.

Foucault, M. (1979). *The history of sexuality* (Vol. 1). London: Allen Lane.

Foucault, M. (1984). What is enlightenment? In P. Rabinow (Ed.), *The foucault reader* (pp. 32–50). New York: Pantheon.

Foucault, M. (1985). *The use of pleasure.* New York: Pantheon.

Foucault, M. (1988). Technologies of the self. In L. H. Martin, H. Gutman, & P. H. Hutton (Eds.), *Technologies of the self. A seminar with Michel Foucault.* Amherst, MA: University of Massachusetts Press.

Foucault, M. (1990). *The care of the self.* London: Penguin.

Foucault, M. (1991a). Governmentality. In G. Burchell, C. Gordon, & P. Miller (Eds.), *The foucault effect* (pp. 87–104). Hemel Hempstead, Hertfordshire: Harvester Wheatsheaf.

Foucault, M. (1991b). Questions of method. In G. Burchell, C. Gordon, & P. Miller (Eds.), *The foucault effect* (pp. 73–86). Hemel Hempstead, Hertfordshire: Harvester Wheatsheaf.

Foucault, M. (1993). About the beginning of the hermeneutics of the self: Two lectures at dartmouth (M. Blasius, Ed.). *Political Theory, 21*(2), 198–227.

Foucault, M. (1997). Security, territory, and population. In P. Rabinow (Ed.), *Ethics: Subjectivity and truth. Essential works of Michel Foucault, 1954–1984* (Vol. 1, pp. 67–71). New York: The New Press.

Foucault, M. (2000a). The subject and power. In P. Rabinow (Series Ed.), *Power. Essential works of Michel Foucault, 1954–1984* (Vol. 3, pp. 326–348). New York: The New Press.

Foucault, M. (2000b). The political technology of individuals. In P. Rabinow (Series Ed.), *Power. Essential works of Michel Foucault, 1954–1984* (Vol. 3, pp. 403–417). New York: The New Press.

Foucault, M. (2004a). *Sécurité, Territoire, Population: Cours au collège de France (1977–1978).* Paris: Éditions Gallimand et des Éditions du Seuill.

Foucault, M. (2004b). *Naissance de la biopolitique. Cours au Collège de France. 1978–1979.* Paris: Gallimard/Seuil.

Gottweis, H. (2003). Theoretical strategies of poststructuralist policy analysis: Towards an analytics of government. In M. Hajer & H. Wagenaar (Eds.), *Deliberative policy analysis. Understanding governance in the network society* (pp. 247–265). Cambridge, UK: Cambridge University Press.

Hacking, I. (1986). Making up people. In T. Heller, M. Sosna, & D. E. Wellberry (Eds.), *Reconstructing individualism. Autonomy, individuality, and the self in western thought* (pp. 222–236). Stanford, CA: Stanford University Press.

Hacking, I. (2004). *Historical ontology.* Cambridge, MA and London: Harvard University Press.

Hajer, M., & Wagenaar, H. (2003). Introduction. In M. Hajer & H. Wagenaar (Eds.), *Deliberative policy analysis. Understanding governance in the network society* (pp. 1–30). Cambridge, UK: Cambridge University Press.

Henman, P. (2004). Targeted! Population segmentation, electronic surveillance and governing the unemployed in Australia. *International Sociology, 19*(2), 173–191.

Hirst, P. (2000). Democracy and governance. In J. Pierre (Ed.), *Debating governance: Authority, steering, and democracy* (pp. 13–25). Oxford, UK: Oxford University Press.

Inda, J. X. (2005). *Anthropologies of modernity. Foucault, governmentality, and life politics.* Malden, MA: Blackwell.

Jessop, B. (1990). *State theory. Putting the capitalist state in its place.* Cambridge, UK: Polity Press.

Jessop, B. (1996). Veränderte Staatlichkeit. Veränderungen von Staatlichkeit und Staatsprojekten. In D. Grimm (Ed.), *Staatsaufgaben* (pp. 43–73). Frankfurt am Main: Suhrkamp.

Jessop, B. (1998). The rise of governance and the risks of failure: The case of economic development. *International Social Science Journal, 50*(155), 29–45.

Jessop, B. (2003). *The governance of complexity and the complexity of governance: Preliminary remarks on some problems and limits of economic guidance.* Retrieved June 4, 2007, from http://comp.lancs.ac.uk/sociology/soc024rj.html

Jessop, B. (2004). Pouvoir et stratégies chez Poulantzas et Foucault. *Actuel Marx, 36,* 89–107.

Jessop, B. (2007). From micro-powers to governmentality: Foucault's work on statehood, state formation, statecraft and state power. *Political Geography, 26,* 34–40.

Kjær, A. M. (2004). *Governance.* Cambridge, UK: Polity Press.

Kooiman, J. (Ed.). (2000). *Modern governance. New government - society interactions.* London and Thousand Oaks and New Delhi: Sage.

Larner, W., & Walters, W. (2004b). Introduction: Global governmentality: Governing international spaces. In W. Larner & W. Walters (Eds.), *Global governmentality* (pp. 1–20). London and New York: Routledge.

Larner, W., & Walters, W. (2004c). Globalization as governmentality. *Alternatives, 29,* 495–514.

Larner, W., & Walters, W. (Eds.). (2004a). *Global governmentality. Governing international spaces.* London and New York: Routledge.

Lascoumes, P. (2004). La Gouvernementalité: de la critique de l'État aux technologies du pouvoir. *Le Portique, 13/14,* 169–190.

Latour, B. (1986). The powers of association. In J. Law (Ed.), *Power, action and belief* (pp. 264–280). London and Boston: Routledge & Kegan Paul.

Lemke, T. (1997). *Eine Kritik der politischen Vernunft – Foucaults Analyse der modernen Gouvernementalität.* Hamburg and Berlin: Argument.

Lemke, T. (2000). Neoliberalismus, Staat und Selbsttechnologien. Ein kritischer Überblick über die governmentality studies. *Politische Vierteljahresschrift, 41*(1), 31–47.

Lemke, T. (2002). Foucault, governmentality, and critique. *Rethinking Marxism, 14*(3), 49–64.

Lippert, R. (1999). Governing refugees: The relevance of governmentality to understanding the international refugee regime. *Alternatives, 24,* 295–328.

Maihofer, A. (1995). *Geschlecht als Existenzweise.* Frankfurt am Main: Ulrike Helmer.

Marks, G., Scharpf, F. W., Schmitter, P., & Streeck, W. (1996). *Governance in the European union.* London and Thousand Oaks, CA and New Delhi: Sage.

Mayntz, R. (2004). Governance im modernen Staat. In A. Benz (Ed.), *Governance - Regieren in komplexen Regelsystemen* (pp. 65–76). Wiesbaden: VS Verlag für Sozialwissenschaften.

Meyer, J. W. (1999). The changing cultural content of the nation-state. In G. Steinmetz (Ed.), *State/culture: State formation after the cultural turn* (pp. 123–143). Ithaca, NY and London: Cornell University Press.

Meyet, S. (2005). Les trajectoires d'un texte: 'La gouvernementalité' de Michel Foucault. In S. Meyet, M.-C. Naves, & T. Ribemont (Eds.), *Travailler avec Foucault. Retours sur le politique* (pp. 13–36). Paris: L'Harmattan.

Meyet, S., Naves, M.-C., & Ribemont, T. (2005). *Travailler avec Foucault. Retours sur le politique.* Paris: L'Harmattan.

Miller, P., & Rose, N. (1990). Governing economic life. *Economy & Society, 19*(1), 1–31.

Mitchell, T. (1991). The limits of the state: Beyond statist approaches and their critics. *American Political Science Review, 85*(1), 77–96.

Mouffe, C. (2005). *On the political.* London and New York: Routledge.

Müller, M., Raufer, T., & Zifonun, D. (2002). Einleitung: Die Perspektive einer kulturwissenschaftlichen Politikanalyse. In R. Müller & D. Zifonun (Eds.), *Der Sinn der Politik. Kulturwissenschaftliche Politikanalysen* (pp. 7–14). Konstanz: UVK Verlag.

Nullmeier, F. (1993). Wissen und Policy-Forschung. Wissenspolitologie und rhetorisch-dialektisches Handlungsmodell. In A. Héritier (Ed.), *Policy-Analyse. Kritik und Neuorientierung* (pp. 175–196). Opladen: Westdeutscher Verlag.

Ong, A. (2005). Graduated sovereignty in South-East Asia. In J. X. Inda (Ed.), *Anthropologies of modernity. Foucault, governmentality, and life politics* (pp. 83–104). Oxford, UK: Blackwell.

Osborne, D., & Gaebler, T. (1992). *Reinventing government. How the entrepreneurial spirit is transforming the public sector.* Reading, MA: Addison-Wesley.

Perry, R. W., & Maurer, B. (2003). Globalization and governmentality: An introduction. In R. Perry & B. Maurer (Eds.), *Globalization under construction. Governmentality, law, and identity* (pp. ix–xxi). Minneapolis, MN and London: University of Minnesota Press.

Pfaller, R. (1997). *Althusser - Das Schweigen im Text. Epistemologie, Psychoanalyse und Nominalismus in Louis Althussers Theorie der Lektüre.* München: Fink.

Pieper, M., & Rodriguez, E. G. (2003). *Gouvernementalität. Ein sozialwissenschaftliches Konzept im Anschluss an Foucault.* Frankfurt am Main and New York: Campus.

Poulantzas, N. (1977). *L'État, le Pouvoir, le Socialisme.* Paris: PUF.

Prakash, A., & Hart, J. A. (Eds.). (1999). *Globalization and governance.* London: Routledge.

Rose, N. (1996). Governing "advanced" liberal democracies. In A. Barry, T. Osborne, & N. Rose (Eds.), *Foucault and political reason. Liberalism, neo-liberalism and rationalities of government* (pp. 37–64). London: UCL Press.

Rose, N. (1999). *Powers of freedom. Reframing political thought.* Cambridge, UK: Cambridge University Press.

Rose, N., & Novas, C. (2005). Biological citizenship. In A. Ong & S. J. Collier (Eds.), *Global assemblages. Technology, politics, and ethics as anthropological problems* (pp. 439–463). Oxford, UK: Blackwell.

Rose, N., & Miller, P. (1992). Political power beyond the state: Problematics of government. *British Journal of Sociology, 43*(2), 173–205.

Rucht, D. (2001). Global Governance – eine Antwort auf die Steuerungsprobleme internationalen Regierens? In J. Allmendinger (Ed.), *Gute Gesellschaft? Verhandlungen des 30. Kongresses der Deutschen Gesellschaft für Soziologie in Köln 2000, Band 2* (pp. 1010–1023). Opladen: Leske und Budrich.

Sauer, B. (2001). *Die Asche des Souveräns. Staat und Demokratie in der Geschlechterdebatte.* Frankfurt am Main and New York: Campus.

Sauer, B. (2004). Staat – Institutionen – Governance. In S. K. Rosenberger & B. Sauer (Eds.), *Politikwissenschaft und Geschlecht. Konzepte-Verknüfungen- Perspektiven* (pp. 107–1250). Wien: WUV.

Schlichte, K. (2005). *Der Staat in der Weltgesellschaft. Politische Herrschaft in Asien, Afrika und Lateinamerika.* Frankfurt am Main and New York: Campus.

Sellin, V. (1984). Regierung, Regime, Obrigkeit. In O. Brunner, W. Conze, & R. Koselleck (Eds.), *Geschichtliche Grundbegriffe. Historisches Lexikon zur politisch-sozialen Sprache in Deutschland* (pp. 361–421). Stuttgart: Klett-Cotta.

Senellart, M. (1995). *Les arts de gouverner. Du regimen médiéval aus concept de gouvernement.* Paris: Seuil.

Senellart, M. (2004). Situation du cours. In M. Foucault (Ed.), *Sécurité, territoire, population* (pp. 381–411). Paris: Gallimard and Seuil.

Sigley, G. (2007). Chinese governmentalities: Government, governance and the socialist market economy. *Economy & Society, 35*(4), 487–508.

Smouts, M.-C. (1998). The proper use of governance in international relations'. *International Social Science Journal, 50*(155), 81–89.

Steinmetz, G. (1999a). *State/culture: State-formation after the cultural turn.* Ithaca, NY and London: Cornell University Press.

Steinmetz, G. (1999b). Introduction: Culture and the state. In G. Steinmetz (Ed.), *State/culture. State-formation after the cultural turn* (pp. 1–49). Ithaca, NY and London: Cornell University Press.

Valverde, M. (1996). "Despotism" and ethical liberal governance. *Economy & Society, 25*(3), 357–372.

Vismann, C. (2000). *Akten. Medientechnik und Recht.* Frankfurt am Main: Fischer.

Walters, W. (2004). Some critical notes on "governance". *Studies in Political Economy, 73*, 27–46.

Willke, H. (2007). *Smart governance. Governing the global knowledge society.* Frankfurt am Main and New York: Campus.

Thomas Lemke
Social Sciences Department
Goethe-University
Frankfurt/Main
Germany

RISTO ERÄSAARI

4. OPEN-CONTEXT EXPERTISE

Und ist nicht alles, was wir wichtig nehmen, unser Verräter?
Es zeigt, wo unsere Gewichte liegen und wofür wir keineGewichte besitzen.
(Friedrich Nietzsche, *Die fröhliche Wissenschaft [The Gay Science]*)

INTRODUCTION

This chapter analyses what uncertainty and complexity has done to expertise. One effect is that a context with its horizon of experiences and expectations has been recognized as an important source for generation and validation of knowledge. While contributing to our uncertainty, helping to monitor that uncertainty and enabling us to live with uncertainty, expertise becomes tied to society in specific ways. This chapter will make this kind of conceptual space of expertise surveyable within three specific aspects, those of uncertainties, legitimation and context.

It is no longer clear why the expert's advice should be specially valued, and it cannot be constituted analytically through some pure influence of superior rationality and truth (Knorr Cetina, 2002, p. 12). Nobody can deny that expertise is closely related to experience, and that it was not turned into an actor and a noun until in an industrial society which put increasing emphasis on specialisation and qualification. Rather, we seem to be dealing with a case in which 'expertise' and 'experience' replace the old discourse on 'science' and 'truth'. How can we analyse modern expertise?[1] I will start from an insight provided by Wolf Lepenies:

The modern world was moulded primarily by four processes: secularisation, the rise of science and technology, industrialisation, and democratisation. These processes unfold at varying speeds and take locally specific forms; but they intertwine and influence each other worldwide. If we define modernity as the result of these processes, we can see that we are indeed at a turning point. When the increase in knowledge produced by science is no longer unquestioningly accepted as cultural enrichment but seen as a possible threat; when the core value of the labour-based society begins to weaken with the erosion of traditional patterns of work; when participation and involvement are no longer self-evident motives for action in the political sphere and participatory democracy is transformed into a democracy of absence; and finally, when fundamentalist creeds spread while established religions lose ground—then we are in a crisis of orientation that affects all the guiding principles of our economic and social activity (Lepenies,1998, pp. 17–18).

M.A. Peters et al. (eds.), Govermentality Studies in Education, 55–76.

If these processes are no longer unquestioningly accepted as enrichment but seen also as a threat, as a source of uncertainty as well as a source of alternative, then we must be prepared to recognise the effects of a lost coherence of the modern epoch and be able to create ways of talking and thinking about tracing this loss. It must have an effect on the conditions and performances of expert knowledge. For experts do not normally solve diagnostic questions and existential problems. Even if "creating new names and assessments and apparent truths is eventually enough to create new 'things'" (Nietzsche, 1974, Aphorism 58), the most crucial thing is not what we call such a condition—'crisis of orientation' (Lepenies), 'new obscurity' (Habermas), 'corrosion of character' (Sennett), 'discordant concordance' (Ricoeur)— but how we manage to identify a structuring and motivating idea that helps to make this condition intelligible in terms of the co-ordinates of uncertainty, achievement of definition, epistemic justification and contextual distribution. If semantics does not work, one has to invent new ideas or make space for thought experiments.

I imagine there must be at least a dozen different useful ways of classifying expertise, such as legitimacy, competence, interaction, contribution, context, authority, adherence, reliability, reasoning, distribution, mediation and extension. Every one of them can, moreover, be differentiated according to extension and intension, strength and style, thickness and thinness. Even if we decide to pick out a single dimension, let us say the last one, indicating a tendency to dissolve the boundary between experts and the public so that there are no longer any grounds for limiting the indefinite extension of technical decision-making rights, we cannot completely stick to this dimension and ignore the rest. While trying to solve the problem of extension we have to emphasise the role of expertise both as an analyst's category and as an actor's category (Collins & Evans, 2002), and in this the other dimensions, from legitimacy to mediation are certainly not irrelevant. Broader social and historical changes may prove necessary to explain legitimacy. Different contexts and environments may equally become necessary topics for explaining how expertise can or cannot be a powerful mediator. Thus expertise shows itself as a mechanism by which problems are framed, problems which incorporate not only scientific judgements or technical decisions but also more basic, deeper social and cultural predispositions and commitments.

In this article, I will suggest that a new constellation (configuration) of uncertainty is making its presence felt not only as different rational genres or types of uncertainty (risk, uncertainty, imprecision, ignorance, indeterminacy) but also as a kind of confusion in itself, as 'implicit orderliness' or as attempts to build commitment to anticipatory or precautionary regulation of uncertainty without reducing it to the category of risk; that is why I will, furthermore, make the suggestion that expertise has replaced facts and truths, or extended them into 'definitions' and definitory relationships. I am going to argue that as the truth regimes of 'post-normal' science have mutated, contemporary expertise has replaced the problem of legitimacy (credibility, confidence etc.) by the problems of extension (extended expertise; extended fact), communication and intertwined relationship between tacit and explicit knowledge and between the cultural models of actors and the operative models of analysts. Therefore I shall further argue that expert knowledge has become involved in social life and is appropriated within everyday life itself. Knowledge in other words is a real reflection of its social context but at the same time a way of tracing the apparent.

Finally in this article I attempt to broaden the contextual representation of expert knowledge, or at least provide a sketch in order to point out some fruitful new directions to go. To do so, an ethos or an invitation to establish a firm connection between the operational procedure and specific recommendations of advice, has to be expanded into a multi-contextual or a mediatory approach. Many writers (Knorr Cetina, 1999; Lash, 2002; Nowotny et al., 2002; Rip, 2002; Stichweh, 2000; Willke, 2002; Ziman, 2000) have spoken about a concept of knowledge that is multi-disciplinary, innovatory, sensitive towards social problems and generative and competent in the 'context of use' occupied by both producers and users.

This broadening of 'knowing how' and 'knowing what' is necessary because expert studies have tended to focus on institutionally defined scientific practitioners heavily dominated by science. Local, sticky and contextual elements of knowledge make it, however, possible to integrate experience and relevance in knowledge production (Willke, 2002). Multi-contextualism is also necessary because modern science is not monolithic but should be seen "as a patchwork of very different activities" (Rip, 1997, p. 617), for a particular time and place dependent on its particular historical and social circumstances. People's numerous descriptions of what they do is, moreover, multiplying unpredictability, which brings us to multi-complexity, challengeability and contestability (Strathern, 2000). As perhaps already visible here, this is a polemic article, and I will proceed in a direct manner. I will attempt to sketch a broad survey of ideas through making the conceptual space of expertise surveyable within three specific aspects—uncertainty, legitimation, context—of expertise.

EXPERTISE AS DEFINITION OF UNCERTAINTY

There is no general decline of cognitive authority (science, research, expertise, technology, knowledge creation and knowledge management). There is a new arrangement of it, or a new design of language. This has to do with converting knowledge through shared experiences, with crystallization of knowledge into concepts, diagrams and models so that it can be understood by others, with converting knowledge into more complex knowledge to enable communication, diffusion and systematisation and with embodying knowledge into practical skills by actualising concepts or encouraging thought experiments. The value of knowledge depends less on objective factors of meaning of knowledge than on how and for what the topical expert or the specialised citizen uses the knowledge (Willke, 2002). There is no foundation that gives decisive support for a vision of knowledge. In other words, it is not adequate to say that some basic conditions have taken away the underpinning necessary for the production of reliable knowledge, that unreliable knowledge is the result of some inherent incompleteness of science, or that some epistemological core crowded with many different norms and practices cannot be reduced to generic methodology or a privileged culture of scientific inquiry (Nowotny et al., 2002). Instead of linear knowledge development, gradual accumulation of knowledge or constant epistemological revolutions we have to look for spatial arrangements and transformations in the relationships between these arrangements. Hence questions like: What is closed? What is open? What is a threshold, a limit (cf. Brown, 2002)? Thus 'development' rather means that knowledge appears as a kind of crossroads or as points of interchange and that we do not learn to acquire wisdom from superior reason but through developing "a harmonious middle/milieu, a daughter of two banks, of scientific culture and of knowledge culled from the humanities, of expert erudition and of artistic narrative" (Michel Serres, quoted from Brown, 2002, p. 10).

Expertise consists of organising concepts that have to do with knowledge, belief, opinion, objectivity, detachment, argument, reason, rationality, evidence, even—as Hacking (2002a) points out—with facts and truths. All these suggest epistemological concepts that are not constants but have spatial, temporal and social dimensions with no clear boundaries. Organising concepts thus come into being through quite specific historical processes. Within the cognitive sphere we are always dealing with circles of epistemological problems: to specify what we know we need to specify how we know, and to specify how we know we need to specify what we know. We seem to depend more and more on nominal acts of naming, defining, creating, constructing. What things are called seems to have become more important or at least a more important source for innovation than what they are. Thus the interaction between 'practical knowledge' and 'explicit knowledge' is not confined to a single ontological depth but rather there are, for example, individual and institutional levels and their knowledge spirals. There are also forms of knowledge creation that become self-transcending processes. It is then far from clear how the new condition of uncertainty should be understood. Security, for example, is no stable or simple magnitude but a changeable social construction. If future expectations have become the important life horizon, security must also be seen in the same manner. Such 'expectation-securities' say very little about actual threats or confrontation with dangers, but in fact much about experiences or fictions of security (Bonss, Hohl & Jakob, 2001; Türcke, 2002). This kind of situative security does not correspond at all to our feelings about 'cumulative' or 'additive' security. We face the problem of "how can we communicate with the future about the dangers we have created?" and "what concepts can we form, and what symbols can we invent to convey a message to future generations?" (Beck, 2002, p. 40)

There are of course different kinds of uncertainties, but generally speaking uncertainty may refer to epistemological emptiness (heterogeneousity and distribution of the epistemological core), to ambivalence of or towards novelty, innovations, redundancy or requisite variety, to actual decline of cognitive authority due to development through which knowledge has been stripped of its metaphysical and culturally specific elements or, finally, to different images of knowledge motivated, for example, by a longing for secure knowledge, or by gaining a solid body of knowledge. We may also say that horizons of expectation will become visibly contingent (Strathern, 2000), that metaphysical explanations and practices of magic are re-experienced and that people more and more orientate themselves through contextual conceptions (Bonss, Hohl & Jacob, 2001). Such an epistemological predicament is of course not a new phenomenon, but part of the necessary and unavoidable epistemological reflection on boundaries and the scope of knowledge, even when dealing with the question of technical expertise. As a result of experienced generalised uncertainty there are, however, more creative as well as actively sceptic ways of confronting uncertainty, be it a question of cultural ambivalence (Dillon, 2001), analytic hierarchy (Collins & Evans, 2002) or a question of risk or precaution (Dean, 1998). Let me clarify each of these cases.

Uncertainty as cultural ambivalence: attempts to recognise and understand uncertainty become radical or at least loud with the extra excitement of confusion or ambivalence. This manifestation whispers in our ears that we should not expect any stable condition, expectation or orientation but something that is contingent or controversial and should for this reason be accepted as post-normal or beyond normality. Often this is followed by an invitation to see it as a construct or a mechanism that may make us learn order in new ways. This is clearly the case when Michael Dillon (2001) wants us to think that complexity should in fact be understood as 'implicit orderliness', in which order or certainty may be understood in nuanced and sensitive novel ways. Expertise is here 'realised' in the kinds of intellectual responsibilities it takes on: to attend to complexity as a condition of the way the world is, and thereby to hold up to society new frames of understanding and ways of living effectively with it. For example, do we give anteriority to radical relationality or do we think that the question is one of diversity and complexification of sense that escapes conventional measurement. If we prefer relativism to diversity, the whole world does not melt into air but there are taxonomies within which temporality or time is a parameter rather than an operator in itself. With taxonomies we gradually gain or enable others to make better informed judgements about whom to trust and whom not to trust, as I will show below when discussing analytic hierarchies of uncertainty. If we become interested in orderliness as diversity, we perhaps look for a diversity that has not, so far, been captured by definition or we are being curious about finding a way in which to discuss 'confused regularity'. In this case we are dealing with concepts or constructs that we use as regulatory ideas (in the Kantian way), in other words as operators of recognition and understanding. While thinking of uncertainty in this way, diversity not only differentiates elements but it also combines and recombines them in novel ways to produce new forms (Dillon, 2001).

Uncertainty as ambivalence is an epistemic state of not believing or knowing for certain. Just as information society is a more fitting epithet than knowledge society, it can be argued that 'uncertainty society' would be more accurate than 'risk society'. Science provides us with new knowledge and expertise is perhaps most often used to broaden, extend and reframe knowledge in the forms of technical know-how or other knowledge spirals. But this new knowledge generates further uncertainties (new unanswered questions, unintended side-effects), further complexity (a vast number of causal factors and potential mechanisms need to be taken into account when, for example, determining the effects of increased greenhouse effects in the atmosphere) and further unknown factors (we may have missed some process that should have been taken into account). When we turn to decision-making we have to take into account uncertainty of consequences, of reliance, of decision horizon and of values (Luhmann, 2000). Massive spread of information and the presence of uncertainties coexist: although old uncertainties are sometimes resolved, new uncertainties are being created at a much higher speed. Knowledge about uncertainty is a characteristic epistemic category of our age. Risk analyses, precautionary strategies, reversible decision options, involvement and intervention in the knowledge creation process, epistemic communities and the design of appropriate cognitive space are catchwords that give some indication of approaches that researchers and experts have developed. In the case of expertise as a particularly legitimate form of knowledge, the emphasis has moved onto 'contextualis-ation' (Nowotny et al., 2001; Giegel, 1993), 'extension' (Collins & Evans, 2002), 'broadening' (Rip, 1997), 'internalisation' (Nonaka, Konno & Toyama, 2001) or just implicit knowledge or counter-knowledge as the means for enhancing expectations for the relevance, validity and diagnostic strength of knowledge. One of the new slogans that has been applied to such an approach is 'robust knowledge' (Rip, 1997; Nowotny et al., 2002; McLennan, 2002).

Uncertainty as analytic hierarchy: the rational approach to uncertainty starts off with the idea of reducing systemic uncertainty or cognitive uncertainty through further research, alternative scenarios, professional consultancy etc. As these are potentially contestable, a more appropriate means lies in the conflation of the technical and political phases of the decision-making process. Even if a greater amount of research and technical expertise could ultimately reduce uncertainty, while drawing on a wide range of expertise could at least increase realism and abolish some threats and dangers, this would not resolve political problems in a realistic time-frame. Hence a separate process, based on different criteria, a kind of decisionistic scenario or simulation of phases, is needed to conduct the technical and political processes in parallel action. Expertise is brought in to replace facts or extended facts, of which Brian Wynne's (1996) work is an excellent example. His work is based on a distinction between different types of uncertainty: risk (where the odds are conceptualised), uncertainty (where parameters but not odds are known), ignorance (where not even parameters are known), and indeterminacy (where the way in which systems will be used by others cannot be guaranteed).

From this rationalistic perspective, scientific expertise appears as partial but can be helped by complementary expertise (local knowledge) to make better informed judgements about threats and doubts possible. In this way not only 'context', 'extension' and 'broadening' but also the criteria for inclusive expertise come to be based on social and cultural participation. The regulatory motivation is to attract attention to ignorance and indeterminacy, and to find ways of bringing these within the scope of precautionary or anticipatory schemes without reducing them to the category of risk. What in fact is thus created is a translation and the imposition of a model for which the public acceptance of experts or disagreement of critical views is irrelevant. The power that lies in the categorisation of uncertainty and knowledge is effective in structuring data, but there is no mechanism (algorithm) through which to turn these observations into an institutional response other than an *in casu* and local solution. It is possible to activate the focus groups to perform a peer review or an auditing, or provide a 'broader debate' about these issues. The extensional and contextual view seems, in technical terms, to go one step further and explicate or articulate some of the criteria.

Uncertainty as risk: knowledge about risk is a category characteristic of our age in a special way. The concept of risk has been invented to discover, conceptualise and organise threats and dangers or other uncertain expectations into manageable orientations. But that is only a half of the story. The risk-orientation is not always a problem of cognition, applicable methods and explicated meanings, but also a problem of recognition, namely an acknowledgement that within the observed phenomenon on the whole there exists an issue or a problem (Böschen, 2002). Niklas Luhmann (1992) has stressed that the intensity of 'ecological communication' is due to this sort of 'non-knowledge'. Thus risk-conception should not be seen primarily as some sort of a direct measure or indicator, as in quantitative risk analysis. What is significant about risk, as Mitchell Dean has pointed out, is that it is a way of ordering reality; "the significance of risk does not lie with risk itself but with what risk gets attached to." It is "a category of our understanding rather than intuition of sensibility" (Dean, 1998, p. 24). Contemporary risk analysis started by bundling the forensic and technical uses of risk out of sight, and in doing so this risk debate has uncovered many black boxes and paradoxes (Douglas, 1991). Risk became a key concept of modernity, a social construction in a world at risk, central to the constitution, ordering and intelligibility of the social itself.

Both individuals and whole societies may recognise themselves and define many of their problems in terms of technologies and semantics of risk. The language of danger and threat, sometimes even the whole landscape of uncertainty and a loss of orientation has been turned into the language of risk. Sometimes, as in the case of organisational knowledge management, this involves making spurious claims of being scientific and rational. In contemporary diagnostic sociology it has been acknowledged that our second modernity is a step beyond our conventional understanding and thus uncertain, but could be recognised and should be defined as risk society or even as world risk society (Beck, 2002). Thus our contemporary society is framed as a problem in which expertise may have a key role to play in problematising culture and information and constructing space for a pluralisation of experts and expert rationalities (Lash 2002). In this way the risk society also becomes a latent political society with a tendency towards oscillation between hysteria, indifference and reform (Nowotny et al., 2002). The mandate and the authority of experts are often vague depending on the applied logic of risk-sharing and the degree of actual threat. It is often difficult to explain—in other words 'contextualise', 'extend' and 'broaden'— the new concern with risk. Should it, for example, be conceived of as a public backlash against global corporations, as a generalised concern for fairness, a mode of constructing new institutional designs and cognitive spaces, or a way of inventing the calculations and probabilities necessary for taming chances?

EXPERTISE AS LEGITIMACY OF KNOWLEDGE

Experto credo—he who has experience knows all about it. Experience should then be included in the definition of expertise. It is an instance of truth, or rather an authentic kind of truth (Williams, 1988), that we may come across either as an experience (*Erfahrung*) that we get during the interchange of conversation, or as an experience (*Erlebnis*) due to language. "Experience-based expertise" (Collins & Evans 2002, pp. 251–252) originates, then, in some form of conventional wisdom where one's expertise has not been recognised by certificates. Thus experience may be a basis for implicit (tacit) knowledge or skills that cannot be reduced to analytic knowledge (guided by a scientific core), to critique (channelled by epochal trends) or to an overview (subsuming local trends and events). There is, however, no reason to turn experience into a sacred cow. Conditions of experience are, at the same time, the conditions of the objects of experience, i.e. experience and the constitution of its elements are subject to the selfsame reasons. Thus conditions of expertise are also the conditions of the objects of expertise. Illocutionary acts (mapping of context or order), prescriptions (imperative forces) and cognitions (judgements) are specific mechanisms through which reality becomes accessible. Here we come to see time as a parameter in itself, which was previously discussed in terms of uncertainty and intensification of temporality (Gumbrecht, 2002; Gumbrecht, 2001a). It provides us with—and perhaps makes us suffer from—the dynamic difference between 'past' and 'future'. This distinction is not without relevance when trying to specify the historical nature of skill and competence. On the one hand there is the competence or skill that belongs to 'past as a field of experience'. On the other hand there is the competence and skill that is linked to 'future as a horizon of chances'. The first aspect is about experiences as we have learned to understand them. The second aspect is about expectation, experiments and innovations on which we do not yet have any experiences.

Science, institutions and professions make up the traditional tripod of expertise. Science, because "experts represent dominant forms of knowing, and these dominating forms are scientific" (Schmidt, 1986, p. 30). Institutions, because "an expert is the representative of a trusted institution, and/or the bearer of trusted knowledge and competence" (Barnes, 1983, p. 234). Professions, because "the prototypical expert is the bureaucratic official, performing the specialized duties of his office" (Giddens, 1994, p. 83). This figuration shows convincingly that expertise represents forms of special competence, universal authority or cultural wisdom that can be called "contributory expertise" (Collins & Evans, 2002, p. 252). Perhaps we can list the following kinds of aspects as characteristic to it. First, this kind of expert knowledge becomes absorbed in and grows out of the ways in which scientifically qualified professionals try to promote institutional development in society. Second, it would in general be continuous with the core sciences, and it would be indebted to them both for its intrinsic possibilities and for its generous perspectives (Rose, 1994). Third, its energies and competence are distributed or applied according to the rules and norms of functionally differentiated society (Stichweh, 2000) which inevitably leads to decontextualisation and disembedding and thus to the topicality of expertise, trust and the professions.

This picture is not very far from the finalization thesis and its implementation towards scientification of all knowledge through the imposition of credentialism as well as monopolization of positions by scientifically trained experts (Rip, 2002; Redner, 2001). Striving for the professionalisation of non-scientific traditions has resulted in their transformation into scientific knowledge, but "the reason for this is not the superiority of science over other types of knowledge but the fact that in our society social opportunities are largely distributed according to certificates of knowledge" (Böhme, 1992, p. 61).

To pass through open doors of this type, it is necessary to respect the fact that they have solid frames, frames based on science, institutions and professions. Solid frames bring about credibility, cohesion and obligations. But their meaning and consequences have shifted over time (cf. Hacking, 2002a). Truth (science) is not just a restricted or confined entity or standard but something through which we constitute ourselves as objects of knowledge. Accordingly, power (profession) is not just a tool for control and surveillance but something through which we constitute ourselves as subjects acting on others, and ethics (institutions) is not only moral philosophy but something through which we constitute ourselves as moral agents.

Does the primacy of definition (or determination) put an end to the earlier primacy of finalization? The tripod produces the formal exclusivity of science and formal guidance or even rule by experts. Thus the structure of the tripod can also provide us with a structural explanation for the problem of legitimacy, but only formal ways of broadening its components, redefining its context(s), or replacing formal position-based credibility by extended credibility. In order to obtain an illustration of substantial changes within the constitution and functioning of expertise I need to take another approach. First I will take a look at these changes by considering illustrations offered by Collins and Evans (2002). Their recent article on the three waves of social studies of science in fact gives an excellent overview to new emphases in knowledge and being knowledgeable (Burke, 2000; cf. Audetat, 2001; Lenoir, 1999) and thus also into the legitimacy of expertise.

The first wave is described as "a golden age before the expertise problem raised its head." In the 1950s and 1960s the general aim was to explain science, not to question its basis. Sciences were thought of as esoteric as well as authoritative, and decision-making travelled only from the top down (Collins & Evan, 2002, p. 239). Under the second wave (from the early 1970s, continuing all the way to the present) it was necessary to draw on "extra-scientific factors to bring about the closure of scientific and technical debates." The attention was directed to the uses of scientific knowledge in social institutions. When expertise is discussed, the focus is often on the attribution of the label "expert" and on how expertise is made to travel between institutions (ibid., pp. 239–240). Wave three is concerned with finding "a special rationale for science and technology', namely that they are 'much more ordinary than we once thought" (ibid., p. 40; cf. Rip, 1997, p. 617). All in all, this story of the three waves can perhaps be read as the deconstruction or downfall of the previously mentioned tripod and its finality-oriented metanarrative. But it is mainly about the relationship between a scientific core and various expert positions. Maybe there is no change whatsoever in terms of the audience of expertise. Maybe in all cases, the cry begins when the expert is brought into the TV studio: 'Who does he think he is, why don't they call for an expert'! If someone certified as an expert or with the reputation of an expert is on the spot instead the cry will be raised 'what muscles does he have that he knows better than I do?'

The reconstructing of knowledge becomes necessary because the knowledge in the disciplines and discourses linked to expertise is no longer related to any pre-determined object-world, but instead constructs such worlds. Scientific practice based on such modifications of knowledge entails new problems, which often lead us to question conventional concepts. This eventually leads to new differentiation between basic science and application (Hörning, 2001): the introduction of new technologies no longer represents a mere application or use of a certain kind of knowledge, but instead continues and communicates the experimental phase in reality (Gibbons, 2000). That the expert is both an analyst and an actor under wave three seems to suggest that these circumstances turn out to be a melting pot: "The wider scientific community no longer plays any special part in the decision-making process," which means that it is seen as "indistinguishable from the citizenry in general" (Collins & Evans, 2002, p. 249). Whether we can trust these experts or whether they exert their influence in the same way as the institutions through which they are mediated, cannot be answered here while dealing with social relations between scientists and society.

Even if the problem of extension or broadening of relations between science and society is perhaps solved through inclusion in decision-making or in civil society, the question is still on 'insiders', on scientific practitioners and what they do, and even on scientific elites continuing their journey and making themselves reappear in new contexts. These immanent processes cannot be explained by network models. The extension of the expert process is not brought into the picture in terms of valid or adequately robust knowledge production or in terms of checking out who these insiders are, which operative models they stick to and what implicit sociology they find relevant. What perhaps is also necessary is to take configurations of local research and knowledge-producing and certifying fields as the units of analysis in the contextual picture (cf. Nowotny et al., 2001). These complementary elements reconfirm that expertise as an analyst's and as an actor's perspective consists of very different kinds of activities, and that knowledge is not produced through well-established channels but through different kinds of concrete applications and through communication. This will also lead us to a further observation: the extension and broadening of expertise cannot just be conceived as cognitive contextualisation, for it takes us to wonder about the place of people in our knowledge (Audetat, 2001), and to understand that it denotes context!

I will next speculate about the different directions I could go from here. One would be "the processing of meanings," but it would be very hard to obtain material about this in any other way than by attempting to reconstruct the rules that are being followed, i.e. the "unobservable internal decision rules, which vary from one agent to another" (Doran, 2001, p. 2), or from one context to another. Thus the extension or broadening of expert knowledge does not only happen in terms of social relations or in terms of knowledge production, but also in terms of how and with what kind of object communication occurs and what kind of internal decision rules—or rules of the game—are built into it. A second possibility would be to bring under discussion some of the meta-changes that may have actualised, such as 'transgressive competencies' (Nowotny), new forms of 'migratory' (Gibbons) or 'second' (Giddens) expertise, or the occurrence of some sort of 'displacement of expertise' (Eräsaari, 1998). Even if they might contribute to our understanding of what or who blurs the traditional frontiers between the grand categories of modern society such as the state, the market, the public and the private spheres, the arts and the sciences, they do not actually tell us what is happening to expertise either as analysis or as action. So, let me turn to specification of the relationship between expertise as analysis or cognition and expertise as action or culture.

The facts about the core competence of science should not be read as an indication of the impossibility of a round table for scientists and practitioners. The overwhelming hierarchies and complex disciplinary discourses seem to exclude lay practitioners from the science game. Even if the lay experts learned enough concepts and methods to play at the level of the scientific experts, they would no longer play on their home ground (van den Deale 2001) but run into difficulties in terms of communicating with the core context of science. But as has already been mentioned, modern science is no homogenous whole but a patchwork of different activities. Instead of saying that there is the duality of the core and the margin, the basic and the applied or the justification and the observation, we perhaps ought to say that there are several contexts and several interfaces. Perhaps there is no consensus among scientists and experts about the proper context, boundaries, gate-keepers and integrity of core activities such as discovery, justification, application, implication, competence and evidence (cf. Nowotny et al., 2001). Some contexts allow much historical variation and historical changes, robust criteria for assessment and comparison and critical discussion as reflexivity and pluralism, whereas within some other contexts processing and purification of arguments and counter-arguments is compulsory. There seems to be no space where the complex dynamics of scientific communication could be illustrated. Sometimes the norms or rules can be specified, but we do not know how they actually operate and what kind of effect they have on cultural codes. Even if the observable external rules and conduct can be clarified, the scientists and experts may obey unobservable internal patterns or make up their own rules which may also vary from one actor to another (Doran, 2001). Also from time to time these analysts or actors may spontaneously disappear from sites, some may be fixed and some travel between sites.

Individual beings have 'cultural' (cognitive) models for making sense of the world. Scientists, researchers and experts use 'operational' models to describe people and their activities in their natural environments with the help of assumptions and methods of the objective sciences. There may be particular cases where the cultural everyday meanings of lay actors (cf. Ricouer, 1991) and the operational models of science (cf. Redner, 2001; Eder, 1997) coincide. What people would do because of their practical knowledge and what they would have to do because of their images of social relations are then quite clearly overlapping. Most often, however, we expect them to contradict each other. In fact there is a need to have a third instance to make a reliable comparison or specification between these two constructs. Let me illustrate the case with perhaps the most central modern ritualistic discourse, the risk discourse. As we noticed in the previous chapter, risks (or precautionary principles) are conceptualisations of threats and dangers, they are constructs or calculations observed outside a natural order. A lay person cannot understand the meaning or the implications of risk within this context. His context of making sense of the world is based on the cultural model. So there should be some sort of exchange between these two contexts. Perhaps the same thing could be formulated as a need for space for situated knowledge, larger contexts for possessing knowledge, everyday life epistemology, and new divisions of knowledge (Burke, 2000).

Cultural models are very important for social order and integration because of their performative tasks. For the expert it is not only relevant to know what the practitioners or lay people think or expect, but also where they get tangled up in their own arguments and rhetoric. Risk and precaution do have an effect on ordinary life. They already increase the sheer quantity of cultural models—beliefs and ideas about nature, continuity, tolerance, security, existence, etc.—that are not concerned with scientific evidence or core science (Dean 1998; cf. Van Loon 2002). They guide, make or force us to become interested in something that is not just rules, conventions or norms and that perhaps is neither thick, solid nor durable in the manner of institutions or professions. In other words, they direct our observations and expectations to things that have in a way ceased to be constructs and things that have not turned into natural kinds of essences. There seem to be forms of knowledge that oddly fall between 'fact' and 'fiction'. The question is about the acquisition of non-propositional knowledge, skill or know-how (Kusch, 2001) that calls for a special epistemology. Sometimes this knowledge may fall either to fact or to fiction, or prove valid in one context but invalid in some other context, depending on the situation and the amount of attention it gets. Its vitality depends on its attractiveness in one or the other of its roles. This is a form of knowledge that aims at becoming a discussant or a mediator between two positions, or serves itself as a construction between 'science' and 'literature' (Lepenies, 1985).

Cultural models are neither burning down the tripod of science, professions and institutions nor rebuilding it. They come from and feel loyalty to a greater concern with implicit knowledge. This is concerned with social life, it can become appropriated within everyday life itself and it often has practical consequences even if it cannot be absorbed into a practical mechanism. But we cannot deny the fact that the 'results' of expertise not only produce decision-making over human heads but also may sometimes go directly into human heads, into their everyday consciousness (Noro, 2000). Clearly this is the case when experts explain—and simultaneously give orders linked to—the effects of BSE disease, new findings about cancer or alcohol, or a new interpretation of equality in social life. Even if we are the audience of expertise and expertise is discussion about us with us, I think we ought to observe certain important limits. Our ordinary consciousness cannot become thoroughly 'trans-scientificised' by operative models of objective science.

We live our everyday consciousness within narratives—in other words social constructions that make sense of the world—that may also be understood as morally binding.

EXPERTISE AS EXCHANGE OF CONTEXTS

Contextualisation does not stand for 'context' but is rather seen as an attempt to construct a mirror, an echo or a space that 'speaks back' or as an attempt to recognise a medium that has or even is the message. Through communication it is not only possible to give different kinds of meanings but also to deal with expectations in terms of doing things differently and finding oneself in new action horizons. The possibility of holding a justified belief and making observations and recognising alternatives is a specific way of making contextual or extended expertise intelligible. We do not need to lean on the cultural, mental, epistemic or virtual space, nor does its realisation lie in the materialisation of expert contributions. As constructive expertise the expert process itself carries this duality. It has an immanent space and it brings with itself its own agora. Thus there is no need to make the expert position into a top or a centre, or to furnish it with some generalist competence or other similar qualification. When the horizon of meanings actually widens and when reality can actually be communicated in different ways, we may speak about an indeterminate horizon of further possibilities. This is in fact a realistic mode of approaching society, commonality, things we do together, things we share, and a style of reasoning introducing new ways of finding out the truth and determine the conditions appropriate to the domains to which it applies. For these reasons I want to call it open-context expertise.

There is also another—in some sense a more dramatic—reason for speaking about open-context expertise. To illustrate this condition I will discuss the idea of common space or the *agora*. Nowotny, Scott and Gibbons (2001) present as one of their background motivations, the thesis that "the epistemological core is empty" by which they actually mean that "the epistemological core is crowded with many different norms and practices which cannot readily be reduced to generic methodologies or, more broadly, privileged cultures of scientific inquiry" (p. 199). Instead of saying that something is empty, or cognitively empty, they in fact seem to imply that the epistemological core is devoid of the capacity of giving epistemological or methodological orientation. But rather than saying, as they do, that science has to move into the agora, to the visible 'knowledge community', the open-context view would suggest moving calmly into open discussion on the issue of orientation, which in many ways comes very close to questions of uncertainty. This kind of discussion may reveal, for example, that the epistemological core is empty because its basic co-ordinates, such as the continuity of being, the reduction to unity and the essentially shared nature of the object-world (see Gauchet, 1997) have eroded and new or complementary co-ordinates have not been found for the core of the operational model.

The characterisation of the context is vitally important for the recognition and choice of repertoire of expertise. If its context is multiplied beyond recognition or fragmented (localised, globalised etc.), it can no longer be contained within the categories where the action to which expertise contributes—takes place. In such a case we can also speak about a displacement of expertise, which would put competence or a required contribution beyond the traditional tripod and its understanding of the capacity and the formulaic repertoire of expertise. What is needed is a new type of expertise, for example 'open expertise' (Giegel, 1993) or 'second expertise' (Giddens, 1995). This is exactly the situation that was discussed earlier. The cognitive or epistemological core is empty because the elements or the substance it contains are no more valid or solid. The foundation or the preconditions of expertise vacillate, or the idea of expertise is immediately substituted by a conceptual contrast to 'closed' and 'first' expertise. New vocabulary is, however, not very convincing. When speaking about 'open technology', 'second planning', 'wave three expertise', 'open professions' or 'fourth generation evaluation' we do not really know what is wrong with the previous version. But we cannot hope for any—at least quick—help from legislative or methodological assessment and comparison or from other ways of increased scientific justification.

The insidious erosion, the credibility crisis or the displacement of expertise does not perhaps happen because the experts have lost their competence or skill in the narrow or technical sense of the word. On the contrary, we have all the evidence to believe that they have gained more. It is the condition, the mode of preregulation, the mode of knowledge conversion or the mode of mediating expertise that has changed. Thus conceived, open-context expertise could well be seen as a constructive critique of the displacement of expertise (Eräsaari, 1998) or emptiness of the epistemological core. But how are we to specify this mode? I would put the focus on mediation and preregulation rather than, for example, mechanisms of conversion (transfer, dissemination, experimentation). The tradition (symbols of rules and rituals), the specific mechanisms (dynamics) or the routine (recurrent determination) of expertise are not irrelevant. And I wonder whether expertise is penetrated by a special kind of attitude or mentality, seriousness of knowledge creation, conversion and management, perhaps seriousness of knowledge crystallization and seriousness of confidence or trust through learning and experience.

Seriousness may in this context be understood as the embodiment of certain preconditions of communication, which prevails because of certain preregulated communicational (Baecker, 2000) and preregulatory metaphors, models and prototypes. Following this clue I will first discuss the way in which expertise is not only regulated through the ordinary rules and forms of governing. What I have especially in mind are the preregulations created to be obeyed by the tripod of science, professions and institutions. They obviously originate in disciplinary cultures, paradigms and discourses of science; they may also originate in certifications of competence and qualifications for different professions; and they could originate in mechanisms of governance that promote stability and consensus of social institutions. Even if these rules may heavily influence expert activities and may even become their internal rules of conduct, it is hardly possible to explain the displacement of closed-context expertise and thus the emergence of a crisis of credibility simply because of inadequate discipline, of transgressive demands for competence demands or of increase of instability in the institutional world. In fact, these trends have not been able to prevent us from having systematised and communicated, cognitively assimilable data around which professional experts and knowledge-producing occupations celebrate the emergence of an information society. It seems to me that communicative (or meta-communicative) preregulation is linked to the way expert knowledge and expert contribution is understood and specified and not just to the way they come into being or have been converted. Moreover, the role of these preregulations may previously have been latent but under the uncertainty condition it has remarkably strengthened.

Preregulation is both the condition that is taken seriously and also what creates seriousness. By this I am not referring to some sort of a new way of pre-understanding things and conditions, for example the more or less successful attack on the rational project of western culture or the attempts to understand the condition of postmodernity that seem to have led to increased confusion. Rather, I refer to different kinds of pre-commitments represented by norms, rules and discussion that grow out of a pre-organised binding of hands (Szompka, 1999). Pre-commitments make people purposefully change or have made the change the context of their own action, making it more rigid, demanding, and forfeiting than the conventional degree of social exchange. This may contain an inverse relationship between rules and trust (more dependence on rules, less trust, and vice versa), or rules and different tone, content, nuances and emphases on trust. It is both context-related and contains its own sequences. Thus there is, at least potentially, knowledge that is not only related to itself but actually constructs the corresponding object-worlds. Knowledge is to a great extent no longer related to pre-given object-worlds, but instead constructs such worlds. Within this kind of reality expertise has to be 'open' and it no longer represents the mere application or technical conversion of certain knowledge but will instead continue the experimental phase on its behalf in a reality created by uncertainty and by the necessity to construct continuity through expectations and open futures.

Discussion on the foundations and credibility of expertise may reflect the prominent position of seriousness in our European modernisation. Seriousness means 'being serious about truth' as Nietzsche (1974) wrote,

> ...it can happen that a man's emphatic seriousness shows how superficial and modest his spirit has been all along when playing with knowledge. – And does not everything that we take seriously betray us? It always shows what has weight for us and what does not. (Aphorism 88)

Seriousness is a kind of ghost of modernity. Serious matters become the experts' responsibility. Their essence may exist under very different kinds of social and cultural orders. A false, non-serious challenge turns into a silly joke, a betrayal or a political provocation. Its credibility and acceptability is carefully controlled and supervised. Any break or rupture in it is thought to bring security problems and destabilise trust and confidence. Seriousness is also surrounded by rationality campaigns, scientific evaluations and floods of information. Often the guardians of seriousness do not seem to be in any kind of agencies or offices. It is enough that you are under surveillance, but you do not know by whom or what. The atmosphere of seriousness makes us wonder whether we can ever reach this seriousness—the necessary condition of all communication, as Jürgen Habermas could have stated—and whether there is any other way assessing communication than the 'serious' one.

We seem to have no other choice than to go back to the professions and institutions that provide us with stable expectations and competence. They must prove sources of stable communication. There is no doubt about the fact that communication is conducted seriously in court, at the doctor's surgery, at a scientific conference, at a social worker's office, in a classroom and in a firm. As Dirk Baecker (2000) says, "in them they mean what they say and they say what they mean" (p. 390). If we, however, try to find out why this is the case, we will discover that the symmetry and coherence of saying and meaning is preregulated. Seriousness prevails because it is preregulated by pre-commitments. Within expertise it seems to be the case that preliminary knowledge and preliminary contracts have a decisive role in explaining why science (conceptions of truth), professions (criteria of competence) and institutions (stability and integration) on the one hand construct foundations for expertise and on the other hand also provide the reason for speaking about 'closed expertise' (Giegel, 1993).

Each of these components will through its choices—through its concepts, theories, models—construct the reality that it talks about. Hierarchies and discourses of science have an impact on communication, for example through the technical terminology that hides its power and necessarily excludes potential participants. Professions define and legitimate problem boundaries and chosen alternatives. Institutions act as intermediary mechanisms by creating frames for action and by bringing about integration. The expert is a true representative of the trusted tripod which processes 'closed' meanings that often carry a strict mentality and remain within their own context or in a world where objects and things are primary. It is at home in strongly preregulated and resurrective settings. There are very few ways in which everyday life and cultural models can be included in the procedure. In a way this is not only a tragedy of the closed-context mentality itself, but also of the society or the community, which has to rely on it. But it is exactly the breaking up or the gradual erosion of the preregulations based on seriousness that seems to provide an explanation for the corrosion of expertise.

We can make a distinction between first-order seriousness and second-order seriousness. This will help us in specifying the transformation from closed-context to open-context expertise. First order seriousness means the facticity of seriousness: it deals with the specification of conditions in terms of the actual matters and the object-world itself. First-order seriousness means the seriousness of the matter itself, tracing the conditions proscribing the intention of the matter in question, the seriousness of the world. It 'leaves open whether it means what it says, it only makes us understand that it says something and of course also means something', Baecker (2000) writes, "it invites to communication." First-order seriousness in other words "sees" the truth, but does not yet start to "speak" about it, (p. 393). According to Baecker (2000) second-order seriousness is always only the seriousness of the other, the other, who takes me seriously in relation to the situation, and who takes communication and relationships seriously. This seriousness is also seriousness of the conditions, but it is not seriousness of the world, but communication in the world and about the world. It is neither serious nor non-serious, neither ironic nor stupid; it is what it is. (p. 393)

Second order means consciousness, reflexivity, one's self-positioning in the environment, presenting oneself differently, even playing with reality. There is an element of pretension in it – that of assuming a distance or a role, or being oneself but also something else.

Seriousness is not a mental quality but the quality of communication. Thus we can say that communication itself takes care of its knowledge requirements. The idea that second-order seriousness is the seriousness of communication can be illustrated by a *Stammtisch* around which one can crack jokes. The vital point here is that jokes need not be taken seriously. However, one has to send a signal that one wants to be taken seriously, and one has to be ready to provide grounds or reasons that make this possible. One also has to send a signal that one recognises the fact that a decision about seriousness has to be taken up by others. This means that certain distances are being created in the act of signification. One has to communicate by all possible means, from gestures and facial expressions to irony or even stupefaction. It is not until these conditions are met that the other enters into communicative relations, i.e. is able to decide what the first means.

Seriousness becomes related to the quality of being convincing. Through communicative competence the expert can make a distinction between information and knowledge, or between denotative and performative statements. It is not so much a question of scientific quality, professional skill or institutional capability, as it is a question of competence to take part in communication, negotiation and deliberation. To say that science, professions and institutions are behind the credibility crisis of expertise is a triviality. It is a condition that has always existed. Expertise in this categorical sense is always a paradox (because lay people cannot have any effective means for checking its trustworthiness), a bottleneck (because technical speciality, terminology, hierarchies and discourses often go beyond lay understanding) and a rupture (because expertise always is without an adequate foundation and always suffers from disputed concepts).

CONCLUSION

It has been my argument here that the problem of legitimacy, credibility and the guiding capacity of expertise has been replaced by the problem of context, extension and the communicative broadening of expertise—that is, by a tendency to dissolve the boundaries between experts and the public so that there are no longer grounds for a strict instrumental rationality that resists the demonopolization of expertise, for the informalisation of access to discussions concerning social standards of relevance, for opening the structure of knowledge management, for the creation of publicity and community, for self-obligation and decision-making rights, all in all for open-context expertise.

In fact monopoly can be maintained only via abuse. Thus the problem is not in overcoming one type of wisdom by a superior form of (scientific) reason, but rather in learning to speak many languages and using many dialects, so that one may develop a tolerant ethics, a third instruction for preregulations, the possibility of a space that is not empty but a space for epistemological culture that makes our experience understandable.

Closed experience is a severe and unconditional strategy, ethos or mentality, which creates a strong link between core knowledge and specific advice or recommendations. Science is regarded as the custodian of rationality. This type of expertise is dominating, especially in contexts where technical authority or speciality and specific technologies are overwhelming (medicine, jurisprudence, engineering etc.). In this context there is little space for deliberation, interpretation, scepticism or hesitation. Solid proof and a set of preregulations valorise scientific objectivity as a prominent mechanism (Amann, 1993; Giegel, 1993). Within this context the lay person should follow the truths (science), competence (profession), and stability (institutions) provided by or reflected in expertise. The object as well as the ethos of expertise is constituted through truth, competence and stability. Within the study of closed expertise the knowledge operations are often formulated as products and results that speak the language of prescriptions and finalization that naturally define, justify and authorise themselves.

The closed context means, for example, an insensitivity or lack of basic tolerance towards phenomena and observations on which they have been based (Gauchet, 1997). This will then also have an influence on the ways in which uncertainty and indeterminacy are understood. Things and situations have got more complicated or arduous, but science itself is not innocent. The internal theory construction may also be in need of a renormalisation or restandardisation. But this is also done within the limits of core science, together with the effects to preregulation. This state of things and this order has also an effect on the formation of agendas within the public discussion as well as on controlling both the context of discovery and the operation through absorption of uncertainty and indecision. The adoption of absorption techniques (Luhmann, 2000) may always be legitimated through the stubborn need for rationality that is brought about by the pressure of contingency (Bogner & Menz, 2002). Despite the conditions of uncertainty, decisions have to be made constantly and quickly, and an expert system that is suitable for that purpose is therefore required. Sometimes the force of circumstances has to be obeyed. The analysis or interpretation of obscurity or anything that is difficult to understand needs to be left behind.

Within open expertise the context (the space for communication) is left open (to allow communication). This is not only a practical or pragmatic question but also a theoretical and an analytical one. Within this scheme there is often neither a chance nor a reason to get fixed into scientific preregulations or finalizations (Amann, 1993; Giegel, 1993). This is often the case in social sciences, anthropology and therapy, especially in the contexts and cases where obscurity and complexity become a challenge. In such a situation it is very difficult or problematical to adopt any fruitful distinction between internal and external absorption. To fall back on the scientific core would lead to elimination of the actual perspective (Giegel,1993). The approach has to be an epistemological one. Through use of cognitive and cultural processes the expert position is left open for the articulation, typifying and orientation of experiences to make them meaningful. Articulation increases meaningfulness: through performing for ourselves we increase our understanding, also collectively if it is shared with others (Demerath, 2002). Typification helps to make things appear more consistent and more distinctive. Orientation is the process of relating experiences to powerful meanings. We get more understanding if we understand our experience as contingent on other meanings. Open context practices do not appeal to preregulations. Instead they send a signal announcing that they are capable of shaping social conditions and living conditions by actively participating in expert communication without even excluding forms of counter-expertise or lay experiences.

Open expertise is in an exciting way contingent on context and action horizon. Through confronting things and situations it constitutes itself, creates its objects and gets its chances. Its way of anticipation cannot be based on objectification. It does not have (to have) a permanent basis, tradition or routine, or a scientific simulation. On the other hand it has to come out with symbolic forms of representation to prove adequately distinctive and meaningful as a testimony for the generative source of knowledge.

A FEW FINAL WORDS

The present age would hardly be possible without people's descriptions (Willke, 2002). People's descriptions of what they do multiply the unpredictability of outcomes. This will increase complexity without any genuine possibility to evade its implications. Supercomplexity (Strathern, 2000, p. 62; cf. Willke, 2002, p. 88; Urry, 2003) means "surfeit stacked and multiplied through a surfeit of frameworks for processing information." Systemic closures such as that generally offered by science in the form of expertise is no longer an option (Van Loon 2002), and 'Leave it to the experts' is no longer an acceptable slogan. Expertise contributes to uncertainty, helps to monitor and evaluate that uncertainty, and enables us to live with that uncertainty. The true context of robust knowledge? In a real world of uncertainties we could at least imagine the responsibility of experts to be attendant to supercomplexity as a condition of the way the world is, and thereby to hold up to society new frames of understanding and ways of living effectively in it (Barnett, 2000 cited in Strathern, 2000, p. 63). The experts' civic role or its reinvention in publicness is unique compared to views held by specific groups inside academia, enterprise and the government or by groups specialised in questions about the evolution of science and technology. The new interest in scientists' putative inclination to formulate promising research problems in terms of the 'novelties' that they may engender, the idea of socially robust knowledge is basically an effort to come out from the both fruitless and hopeless cycle of uncertainty—from more uncertainty to more knowledge, from more knowledge to increased complexity, from increased complexity to demands for abstraction, from demands for abstraction to increased uncertainty.

NOTES

[1] This article was initially prepared for the Helix 2000 Conference in Rio, and an earlier Finnish version was published in Ilkka Pirttilä and Susan Eriksson (Eds.), *Asiantuntijuuden areenat*, Jyväskylä: SoPhi 2002, pp. 21–38. Versions have been given at Copenhagen Business School, NAD-Seminar in Cothenburg, the University of Helsinki, the University of Graz, and at the research course on Evaluation Research on Public Policy Programmes, in Lammi. Thanks to participants for their comments and criticisms. Special thanks to Thomas Basboell for careful reading of the earlier draft and to Ilkka Pirttilä for comments on earlier versions of the paper.

REFERENCES

Amann, K. (1993). Wissensproduktion im sozialen Kontext. In W. Bonss & R. Hohfeld (Eds.), *Wissenschaft als Kontext—Kontexte der Wissenschaft*. Hamburg: Junius Verlag.

Audét, M. (2001). Re-thinking science, re-thinking society. *Social Studies of Science, 31*(6).

Baecker, D. (2000). Ernste kommunikation. In K.-H. Bohrer (Ed.), *Sprachen der Ironie—Sprachen des Ernstes*. Frankfurt a. M.: Suhrkamp.

Barnes, B. (1982). Science as expertise. In B. Barnes & D. Edge (Eds.), *Science in context. Readings in sociology of science*. Milton Keynes, Buckinghamshire: Open University Press.

Barnett, R. (2000). *Realizing the university in an age of supercomplexity*. Buckingham: The Society for Research into Higher Education and Open University Press.

Beck, U. (2002). The terrorist threat. World risk society revisited. *Theory, Culture & Society, 19*(4).

Beck, U., Bonss, W., & Lau, C. (2001). Theorie reflexiver Modernisierung—Fragestellungen, Hypothesen, Forschungsprogramme. In U. Beck & W. Bonss (Eds.), *Die Modernisierung der Moderne*. Frankfurt a. M.: Suhrkamp.

Bogner, A., & Menz, W. (2002). Wissenschaftliche Politikberatung? Der Dissens der Experten und die Autorität der Politik. *Leviathan, 30*(3).

Bonss, W., Hohl, J., & Jakob, A. (2001). Die Konstruktion von Sicherheit in der reflexiven Moderne. In U. Beck & W. Bonss (Eds.), *Die Modernisierung der Moderne*. Frankfurt a. M.: Suhrkamp.

Bradley, B. S., & Morss, J. R. (2002). Social construction in a world at risk. Towards a psychology of experience. *Theory & Psychology, 12*(2).

Böhme, G. (1992). *Coping with science*. Boulder, CO: Westview Press.

Böschen, S. (2002). Risikogenese. Metamorphosen von Wissen und Nicht-Wissen. *Soziale Welt, 53*(1).

Collins, H. M., & Evans, R. (2002). The third wave of science studies: Studies of expertise and experience. *Social Studies of Science, 32*, 2.

Dean, M. (1998). Risk, calculable and incalculable. *Soziale Welt, 49*(1).

Demerath, L. (2002). Epistemological culture theory: A micro theory of the origin and maintenance of culture. *Sociological Theory, 20*(2).

Dillon, M. (2002). Postmodernism, complexity and poetics. *Theory, Culture & Society, 17*(5).

Douglas, M. (1994). *Risk and blame. Essays in cultural theory*. London: Routledge.

Eder, K. (1997). Is there a reality out there? Realism versus constructivism in the social theory of nature. Manuscript.

Eräsaari, R. (1998). The displacement of expertise: The reflexions Elite meets with life politics. In S. Hänninen (Ed.), *Displacement of social policies*. Jyväskylä, FN: SoPhi.

Ewald, F. (1993). *Der Versorgestaat*. Frankfurt a. M.: Suhrkamp.

Gaucher, M. (1997). *The disenchantment of the world. A political history of religion*. Princeton, NJ: Princeton University Press.

Gibbons, M. (2000). Mode 2 society and the emergence of context-sensitive-science. *Science and Public Policy, 27*(3).

Giddens, A. (1994). Living in a post-traditional society. In U. Beck, A. Giddens, & S. Lash (Eds.), *Reflexive modernization.* Cambridge, UK: Polity Press.

Giegel, H.-J. (1993). Kontextneutralisierung und Kontextoffenheit als Strukturbedingungen der gesellschaftlichen Risikokommunikation. In W. Bonss, R. Hohfeld, & R. Kollek (Eds.), *Wissenschaft als context—Kontexte der Wissenschaft.* Hamburg: Junius Verlag.

Gumbrecht, H. U. (2001). How is our future contingent? Reading Luhmann against Luhmann. *Culture & Society, 18*(1).

Gumbrecht, H. U. (2001a). Die Gegenwart wird (immer) breiter. *Merkur, 55*(5/6), 629–630.

Hacking, I. (1999). *The social construction of what?* Cambridge, MA: Harvard University Press.

Hacking, I. (2002). Inaugural lecture: Chair of philosophy and history of scientific concepts at the Collège de France, 16 January 2001. *Economy & Society, 31*(1).

Hacking, I. (2002a). *Historical ontology.* Cambridge, MA: Harvard University Press.

Knorr Cetina, K. (2002). *Wissenskulturen. Ein Vergleich natutwissenschaftlicher Wissensformen.* Frankfurt a. M.: Suhrkamp.

Kusch, M. (2002). Testimony in communitarian epistemology. *Studies in History and Philosophy, 33A*(2).

Lash, S. (2002). *Critique of information.* London: Sage.

Lachenmann, G. (1994). Systeme des Nichtwissens. Alltagsverstand und Expertenbewusstsein im Kulturvergleich. In R. Hitzler (Ed.), *Expertenwissen. Die institutionalisierte Kompetenz zur Wirklichkeit.* Opladen: Westdeutscher Verlag.

Lepenies, W. (1985). *Die drei Kulturen. Soziologie zwischen Literatur und Wissenschaft.* München: Hanser.

Luhmann, N. (1992). *Soziologie des Risikos.* Berlin and New York: de Gruyter.

Luhmann, N. (2000). *Organisation und Entscheidung.* Opladen: Westdeutscher Verlag.

Lysaght, R. M., & Altschuld, J. W. (2000). Beyond initial certification: The assessment and maintenance of competency in professions. *Evaluation and Program Planning, 23*(2).

McLennan, G. (2002). Quandries in meta-theory: Against pluralism. *Economy & Society, 31*(3).

Nietzsche, F. (1974). *The gay science.* New York: Vintage Books.

Niinluoto, I. (2002). *Critical scientific realism.* Oxford, UK: Oxford University Press.

Nonaka, I., & Nishiguchi, T. (2001). Knowledge emergence. In I. Nonaka & T. Nishiguchi (Eds.), *Knowledge emergence. Social, technical, and evolutionary dimensions of knowledge creation.* Oxford, UK: Oxford University Press.

Nowotny, H., Scott, P., & Gibbons, M. (2001). *Re-thinking science, knowledge and public in an age of uncertainty.* Cambridge, UK: Polity Press.

Noro, A. (2000). Aikalaisanalyysi sosiologisen teorian kolmantena lajityyppinä [Zeitdiagnose as the Third Genre of Sociological Theory]. *Sosiologia, 37*(1).

Redner, H. (2001). Science and politics: A critique of scientistic conceptions of knowledge and society. *Social Science Information, 40*(4).

Ricoeur, P. (1991). Mimesis and representation. In M. J. Valdes (Ed.), *A Ricoeur reader: Reflections and imagination.* Toronto, ON: Harvester Wheatseaf.

Rip, A. (1997). A cognitive approach to relevance of science. *Social Science Information, 36*(4).

Rip, A. (2002). Reflections on the transformation of science. *Metascience, 11*(3).

Rose, N. (1994). Expertise and government of conduct. *Studies in Law, Politics and Society, 14*(3).

Schmidt, L.-H. (1986). *Vetandets politik. Experiment.* Stockholm: Symposium.

Schmidt, L. (2000). Varianten des Konstruktivismus in der Soziologie sozialer Probleme. *Soziale Welt, 51*(2).

Steiner, G. (2002). *Grammars of creation.* London: faber & faber.

Szompka, P. (1999). *Trust. A sociological theory.* Cambridge, UK: Cambridge University Press.

Stichweh, R. (2002). *Die Weltgesellschaft. Soziologische Analysen.* Frankfurt a. M.: Suhrkamp.

Strathern, M. (2000). Virtual society? Get real! *Cambridge Anthropology Journal, 22*(1).

Türcke, C. (2002). *Erregte Gesellschaft. Philosophie der Sensation.* München: Beck.

Urry, J. (2003). *Global complexity.* Cambridge, UK: Polity Press.

Van Loon, J. (2002). *Risk and technological culture. Towards a sociology of virulence.* London and New York: Routledge.

Williams, B. (1998). *Keywords. A vocabulary of culture and society.* Glasgow, Lanarkshire: Fontana Press.

Willke, H. (2002). *Dystopia. Studien zur Krisis des Wissens in der modernen Gesellschaft.* Frankfurt a. M.: Suhrkamp.

Wynne, B. (1996). Misunderstood misunderstandings: Social identities and public uptake of science. In A. Irwin & B. Wynne (Eds.), *Misunderstanding science? The public reconstruction of science and technology.* Cambridge, UK: Cambridge University Press.

Ziman, J. (2000). *Real science. What it is, and what it means.* Cambridge, UK: Cambridge University Press.

Risto Eräsaari
Department of Social Policy
Faculty of Social Sciences
University of Helsinki
Finland

MARK OLSSEN

5. GOVERNMENTALITY AND SUBJECTIVITY: PRACTICES OF SELF AS ARTS OF SELF-GOVERNMENT[1]

Although the self is constituted by practices, it is always possible to make something out of what it has been made into, once it learns how to pull the strings. This is the basis of ethical work. Ethical work, says Foucault, is the work one performs in the attempt to transform oneself into an ethical subject of one's own behaviour, the means by which we change ourselves in order to become ethical subjects. Such a history of ethics is a history of ascetics. In his interview 'On the Genealogy of Ethics' Foucault says that there is "another side to these moral prescriptions which most of the time is not isolated as such but is, I think, very important: the kind of relationship you ought to have with yourself, *rapport à soi*, which I call ethics, and which determines how the individual is supposed to constitute himself as a moral subject of his own actions" (1997a, p. 263). The question of how to conceptualise ethics and how to write its history lead Foucault to a study of ancient cultures in the tradition of historians of ancient thought such as Paul Veyne, Georges Dumézil, Pierre Hadot, and Jean-Pierre Vernant (Davidson, 1994, p. 64). His concern with ethics is the last two volumes of *The History of Sexuality*, constituted a reconceptualisation and reorientation of his original project on sex *in The History of Sexuality, Volume 1* (Davidson, 1994, p. 64). Now, sex would be conceptualised in relation to ethics, and ethics was to become, in his latter works, specifically the framework for interpreting Greek and Roman problematisations of sex. Ethics, as such, was a part of morality, but, rather than focus exclusively on codes of moral behaviour, it focussed on the self's relationship to the self, for the way we relate to ourselves contributes to the way that we construct ourselves and form our identities as well as the ways we lead our lives and govern our conduct.

Such a project, says Foucault (1997b) lies "at the intersection of two themes...a history of subjectivity and an analysis of forms of governmentality" (p. 88):

The history of subjectivity was begun by studying the social divisions brought about in the name of madness, illness and delinquency, along with their effects on the constitution of a rational and normal subject. It was begun by attempting to identify the modes of objectification of the subject in knowledge disciplines...such as those dealing with language, labor and life. As for the study of "governmentality," it answered a dual purpose: doing the necessary critique of common conceptions of "power"...; [and] analyse it rather as a domain of strategic relations focussing on the behaviour of the

M.A. Peters et al. (eds.), Govermentality Studies in Education, 77–93.

other or others, and employing various techniques according to the case, the institutional frameworks, social groups, and historical periods in which they develop (1997b, p. 88).

In this newfound concern with ethical action, there is on the surface a shift in relation to Foucault's interest away from knowledge as a coercive practice of subjection, to being a practice of the self-formation of the subject as an art of self-government. Hence, in his later works, Foucault applies the notion of govern-mentality as a set of strategic practices defining the relations of self to self, and of self to others. This links the "the question of politics and the question of ethics [to]…the analysis of governmentality – that is to say, of power as a set of reversible relationships – [which] must refer to an ethics of the subject defined by the relationship of self to self" (2005, p. 252). Yet this positing of a more active political, or "strategic" subject does not involve a radical break with his earlier work, nor is it inconsistent with it, says Foucault (1991a, p. 11; 1989b, p. 296). In *Madness and Civilization*, Foucault states that it was a matter of knowing how one "governed" "the mad" (1989b, p. 296); in his last two works, it is a matter of how one "governs" oneself. In addition, as he says:

> if now I am interested . . . in the way in which the subject constitutes himself in an active fashion, by the practices of the self, these practices are neverthe-less not something that the individual invents by himself. They are patterns that he finds in his culture and which are proposed, suggested and imposed on him by his culture, his society and his social group (1991a, p. 11).

My aim in this chapter is to demonstrate how the self utilises strategies of govern-mentality in relation both to self and others in order to demonstrate its agency in its effort to endeavour to effect change.

WHAT WE CAN LEARN FROM THE ANCIENT GREEKS

In both of the later volumes of *The History of Sexuality*, and in his writings on ethics in general, Foucault was inspired by the work of Pierre Hadot (1987, 1992, 1995, 1997). As Davidson puts it, "in order fully to understand Foucault's moti-vations and his object of study one must take into account the way in which Hadot's work on ancient spiritual exercises helped to form the entire project. . . . If, as is now widely recognised, the work of Georges Canguilhem is indispensable to understanding the early Foucault, the work of Pierre Hadot is crucial to understanding his last writings" (Davidson, 1997, p. 200, 201).

What Hadot did was to open up dimensions of ancient philosophy typically overlooked and forgotten. Foucault, being a keen reader of Hadot's work, sought to reinstate philosophy as "a mode of life, as an act of living, as a way of being" (Davidson, 1997, p. 195) by seeking to isolate philosophical and spiritual exercises that lead to the philosophical way of life. Hadot had argued that such exercises became eclipsed by the reduction of philosophy from a way of life to an abstract theoretical activity locked within a discipline. Similarly, Foucault argues, that "codes of behaviour became emphasised at the expense of forms of subjectivation"

(p. 201). In both *The Use of Pleasure* and *The Care of the Self*, Foucault borrows Hadot's notion of "spiritual exercises" directing his attention to the history of ethics as a history of *askēsis* or practices of self, focussing attention on classical Greece as well as Hellenistic and Roman philosophy as places where these elements of *askēsis* were most emphasised, strongest, and most dynamic (p. 201).

Hadot acknowledges in turn a debt to Pierre Courcelle's work on Hellenistic literature[2] which explored themes such as "self knowledge", historically following them "across the years . . . as they evolved in the western tradition" (Hadot, 1997, p. 206). An important concept was that of *philosophia* which as a form of life required spiritual exercises aimed at realising a transformation of one's vision of the world. Such exercises involved learning how to live the philosophical life (Hadot, 1997, p. 196). The lesson of ancient philosophy, Hadot says, consisted in "an invitation for a man to transform himself. Philosophy is conversion, trans-formation of the way of being and the way of living, the quest for wisdom" (Hadot, 1987, p. 227). Starting with Ancient Greece and traversing the Greco-Roman cultures, Hadot considers the philosophical orientations of the different schools – the Platonists, the Aristoteleans, the Epicureans, the Stoics, the Academicians – and notes how each school has its fundamental approach to life and regimen of exercises.

According to Arnold Davidson, "the idea of philosophy as a way of life . . . is one of the most forceful and provocative directions of Foucault's later thought" (1994, pp. 70–71). To emphasise philosophy as a "way of life" must be seen as distinct from everyday life, for, as Hadot has written with respect to the ancients, the idea of a way of life "implies a rupture with what the skeptics called *bios*, that is daily life" (cited in Davidson, 1994, p. 70). "It was this experience of philosophy as a way of life, and not simply as a theoretical doctrine, that brought Socrates into deadly conflict with the authorities" (p. 71). For Foucault, "philosophy was a spiritual exercise, an exercise of oneself in which one submitted to modifications and tests, underwent changes, in order to learn to think differently" (p. 71).

By ethics, Foucault refers not to morality in the narrow sense of the term, but rather *customs* and *practices* – what Kant meant by *Sitten* (Hacking, 1986, p. 239). Hence, ethics is not intended in the Kantian sense, as pertaining to something "utterly internal, the private duty of reason" (Hacking, 239) but more in the sense of Ancient Greece where ethics was concerned with the good life:

> The Greeks . . . considered this freedom as a problem and the freedom of the individual as an ethical problem. But ethical in the sense that Greeks could understand. *Ethos* was the deportment and the way to behave. It was the subject's mode of being and a certain manner of acting visible to others. One's *ethos* was seen by his dress, by his bearing, by his gait, by the poise with which he reacts to events, etc. For them that is the complete expression of liberty (Foucault, 1991a, p. 6).

In this regard, Hacking says that Foucault reverses Kant. Kant had held that we construct our ethical position by recourse to reason. As Hacking (1986, p. 239.) observes, "but the innovation is not reason but construction" (1986, p. 239). In other words, Kant taught us that we make the moral law, and that is what makes us moral. Foucault incorporates this constructionist dimension into his historicism, meaning that "morality leads away from the letter of the law of Kant, but curiously preserves Kant's spirit" (1986, p. 239). As Hacking concludes, "those who criticise Foucault for not giving us a place to stand might start their critique with Kant" (1986, p. 239).

Closely related to the Greek view of ethics, for Foucault, ethical action demands *stylization* which is an aesthetics of existence. In this sense, ethical self-creation of one's life as a work of art extends Nietzsche's conception that life has value as an aesthetic achievement and that one must give style to one's life by integrating the diffuse nature of oneself into a coherent whole. The question of style was crucial in ancient experience: there is the stylization of one's relationship to oneself, the style of conduct, and the stylization of one's relationship to others. In the Greco-Roman empire of the second and third centuries, style became thought of as a moral code (Foucault, 1989c, p. 319). According to Davidson this theme of aesthetics as involving a *style of existence* is another of Foucault's central ideas in his later writings[3]. (1994, pp. 70–71). Styles of existence refers to how one lives a life philosophically. The problem of ethics is in choosing a style of life. As Paul Veyne notes, "*style* does not mean distinction here; the word is to be taken in the sense of the Greeks, for whom artist was first of all an artisan and a work of art was first of all a work"(cited in Davidson, 1994, p. 67). One of Foucault's concerns was in the style of life of the homosexual community by which he sought to "advance . . . a homosexual askesis that would make us work on ourselves and invent, I do not say discover, a manner of being that is still improbable" (Foucault, 1989a, p. 206, cited in Davidson, 1994, p. 72). Hence, as Davidson points out, the homosexual style of life involves new forms of friendship and yields "a culture and an ethics aimed at the creation of a homo-sexual mode of life" (1994, p. 72).

THE HISTORY OF SEXUALITY VOLUMES 2 AND 3: EXPLAINING ETHICS

In *The Use of Pleasure* and *The Care of the Self* Foucault became concerned with the practices of the self that were very important in classical and late antiquity. These practices of the self were those practices "by which individuals were led to focus their attention on themselves, to decipher, recognise and acknowledge themselves as subjects of desire" (1985, p. 4). As such, it was part of his concern with the constitution of the subject: "the forms and modalities of the relation to self by which the individual constitutes and recognizes himself *qua* subject" (p. 6). Such a concern was an attempt to explain the historicity of ethical systems as the outcome of material forces across successive periods of history, focussing on Greek and Greco-Roman culture. *The Use of Pleasure* is concerned with the manner in which sexual activity was problematized by philosophers and doctors in classical Greek culture of the fourth century B.C. *The Care of the Self* deals with the same problematizations in the Greco-Roman cultures of the first two centuries of our era (the period known as the High Empire).

In *The Use of Pleasure* Foucault says, he is interested in "an analysis of the games of truth and error through which being is historically constituted as experience, that is, as something that can and must be thought" (1985, p. 6–7). Experience is defined as "the correlation between field of knowledge, types of normativity, and forms of subjectivity in a particular culture" (p. 4) Thus, Foucault asks "How and in what form was sexuality constituted as a moral domain?" (p. 10). His aim was "to define the conditions in which human beings "problematize" what they are, what they do, and the world in which they live" (p. 10). Not to study the codes, or ideologies, official interdictions, or successive conceptions of desire, "but rather to analyze the practices by which individuals were led to focus their attention of themselves, to decipher, recognize and acknowledge themselves as subjects of desire..." (p. 5). In this context, Foucault recognizes "*problematizations* through which being offers itself to be" (p. 11). Such problematizations were linked to a group of practices which were called "arts of existence" or "techniques of the self" which included "those intentional and voluntary actions by which men not only set themselves rules of conduct, but also seek to transform themselves, to change themselves into their singular being and to make their life into an *oeuvre*" (p. 10). It would be, says Foucault:

A history of the way in which individuals are urged to constitute themselves as subjects of moral conduct...concerned with the models proposed for setting up and developing relationships with the self, for self-reflection, self-knowledge, self-examination, for the decipherment of the self by oneself, for the transformations that one seeks to accomplish with oneself as an object. This...might be called a history of "ethics" and "ascetics", understood as a history of the forms of moral subjectivization and of the practices of self that are meant to ensure it (1985, p. 29).

Such an aesthetics of existence comprising various arts of life was developed in relation to dietetics, marriage, the management of the household, and erotics. It was around these and other practices that the Greeks "developed arts of living, of conducting themsleves, and of 'using pleasures' according to austere and demanding principles" (p. 249). This resulted in a series of flexible practices of self, aimed at self-mastery and self-regulation based on exercises whose purpose was to exact moderation in relation to diverse objects in diverse contexts. Such an account, says Foucault, would involve an "archaeology of problematizations" (p. 13), and a "genealogy of the desiring man" (p. 12).

The theoretical purpose was to both describe and account for these practices of self as regards to the use of pleasures. As Foucault explains:

[V]ery early in the moral thought of antiquity, a thematic complex – a "quadri-thematics" of sexual austerity – formed around and apropos of the life of the body, the institution of marriage, relations between men, and the existence of wisdom (p. 21).

This thematics maintained a constancy "crossing through institutions, sets of percepts, extremely diverse theoretical references, and in spite of many alterations"

(p. 21). Foucault dismisses what he believes to be a prevalent viewpoint with regard to the use of pleasures in Ancient societies. It is not true, he says (p. 14), that "Christianity strictly excluded such relationships, while Greece exalted them and Rome accepted them". As he puts it in the Conclusion to *The Use of Pleasure*:

> [T]he principle of a rigorous and diligently practised sexual moderation [can be found] ...as early as the fourth century [where] one finds very clearly formulated the idea that sexual activity is sufficiently hazradous and costly in itself, and sufficiently linked to the loss of vital substance, to require a meticulous economy that would discourage un-necessary indulgence. One also finds the model of a matrimonial relationship that would demand a similar abstention from all "extramarital" pleasure by either spouse. Further-more, one finds the theme of the man's renunciation of all physical relations with a boy (1985, pp. 249–250).

In *The Care of the Self* Foucault documents how the Socratic notion of "the care of the self" (*epimeleia heautou*) concerned with setting one's soul straight, as a preparation for political rule, in Plato's *Alcibiades*, became more widespread, encompassing all of life, in the imperial era. In was in these two centuries that austerity themes were strengthened pre-dating Christian societies. While there were many continuities with the Greeks of the fourth century B.C., Foucault makes the point that severe modifications were also perceptible, which "prevent one from considering the moral philosophy of Musonius or that of Plutarch simply as the accentuation of the lessons of Xenophon, Plato, Isocrates or Aristotle" (1986, p. 237). There was in short a growth of an art of existence increasingly emphasizing the fragility of the individual in the face of the dangers of sexual activity giving rise to new systems of knowledge and new dividing practices. In the Greco-Roman period, there arose a mistrust of pleasures, a more intense valoraization of marriage and martial roles, and a dissaffection with regard to the spiritual meanings imputed to the love of boys. There was "in a word...a more intense problematization of the *aphrodisia*" (p. 39) around a stricter observance of monogamous fidelity, a suspicion that sexual pleasure might be evil, a renewed ideal of chastity, and a general principle of moderation. In addition, there was a greater preoccupation with self – a growing inwardness – whereby life was not led to the same degree in public, accompanied by a more positive valuation of personal life and a greater intensific-ation of the values of private life. What essentially changed, says Foucault, was the arts pertaining to the "cultivation of the self", where relations to self were intensified and valorized, and the care of the self became a more general art of existence (*technē tou biou*) constituting a regular work of continuous preparation. Hence, this principle established its necessity in the Greco-Roman period very differently from the way that the principle functioned in Greek culture. The emphasis of the *Alcibiades* is replaced. Instead of being concerned with a function of perfecting oneself preparatory for one's political career, it became a life-long orientation, aimed at old age, involving the critical removal of habits. Instead of being based upon a pedagogical relationship between student and master, it became more curative, therapeutic and medical, and supported by a more varied set of social relations (educational organizations, private counsellors, family relations, relations of friendship). It referred to a whole mode of living. The final goal of the care of the self was a form of spiritual "conversion to self (for Epictetus, *epistrophē eis heautou*), involving a "return to the self", in an attempt to gain mastery of oneself. It was essentially this more general idea of the care of the self that came to characterize life in the Greco-Roman societies during the Golden Age of the Empire over the first two centuries. Such a conception is evident in all of the major writers of the period, including Seneca, Plutarch, Galen, Marcus Aurelius and Epictetus.

The concept "practices of the self" (*practiques de soi*) by which an individual constitutes him/herself as an ethical subject is central to all of Foucault's writings on ethics. By practices, Foucault refers to forms of action and behaviour that are socially and normatively governed, and which derive from the general rules and values in the culture. Practices of the self refers to "a set of practices by which one can acquire, assimilate, and transform truths into a permanent principle of action" (1997a, p. 239). When taken together they are essential to establishing an "aesthetics of existence". Such practices, as utilized by the Stoics, and other schools of Ancient philosophy, included a range of techniques and exercises, often carried out under a teacher, including a wide variety of actions such as studying, truth-relling (*parrhésia*) un-learning bad habits, adhering to principles, as well as activities such as listening, writing, self-reflection, memorising, as well as practical tests and activities such as abstinence, fasting, exercises of self-examination, keeping note-books (the *hupomnēmata*) confession, meditation and prayer. Rather than being seen in Weber's sense, as "abnegation", they constitute ascetical practices involving "the exercise of self on self by which one tries to work out, to transform oneself and to attain, a certain mode of being" (1991a, p. 2). Although, as practices of the self, they comprised techniques of self-formation, they are not represented individualistically as forms of subjective volition, but rather they aim to integrate and manage the relationship between the individual and the societal rules and practices of a period. As such, Foucault sees such a study as important to both the history of subjectivity as well as the study of governmentality, and its various forms and techniques. Such practices and techniques, he tells us, constitute an "art of self-government" (1997b, p. 88). It is a form of analysis where "power relations, governmentality, the government of the self and of others, and the relationship of the self to self constitute a chain" (2005, p. 252). The ability of individuals to learn the practices of the self which permit the navigation of the regulatory rules of a society reflects Foucault's view that "ethics can be a very strong structure of existence" holding a society together "without any relation with the juridical per se, [to]an authoritarian system, [to] a disciplinary structure" (1997a, p. 260).

THE CONFESSIONS OF THE FLESH

Such practices of self can be found in all cultures in different forms, says Foucault (1997a, p. 277). Although Foucault's intended fourth volume of *The History of Sexuality* (*Confession of the Flesh*) was never published, fragments of his thought and research presented in essays, seminar presentations and interviews indicate his general line of thought[4]. One important theme that Foucault emphasizes is the continuities between Greek, Greco-Roman and Christian ethics. In the conclusion of *The Use of Pleasure*, for instance, he seeks to link Greek and Christian ethics noting that the philosophical, moral, and medical thought that formed in the classical Greek and Greco-Roman eras "formulated some of the basic principles of later ethics – and particularly those found in Christian societies", and which the Christian societies "seem to have only had to revive" (1985, p. 250). Yet in that there were continuities around austerity and moderation, there were also differences. Just as Greco-Roman society differed from Athenian society in certain respects, so there were changes in the emergence of Christian experience. In Christian culture, strict obligations of truth, dogma and canon imposed a set of rules of behaviour for a certain transformation of the self. In that Christianity was an ethical system based more on a code, "subjectivation occurs in basically a quasi-juridical form, where the ethical subject refers his conduct to a law, or set of laws, to which he must submit at the risk of committing offenses that may make him liable to punishment" (1985, pp. 29–30).Christian experience implied an obligation to obey rules as the basis of ethical practice, embodied in such practices as the acknowledgement of faults, and the recognition of temptations. There was also an obligation to disclose the self as made obvious through the development of different forms of discovering and deciphering the truth about themselves. These included practices such as *exomologesis* which constituted an obligation of recognising oneself as a sinner and penitent through self-renunciation and expressing the truth about oneself (1997d, p. 244); *exagoreusis*, a form of permanent verbalization and confession involving "self-examination . . . reminiscent of the verbalizing exercises in relation to the teacher-master of the pagan philosophical schools" (245) and incorporating the Christian spiritual principles of obedience and spirituality; and practices that emerged later in the monastic communities such as the sacrament of penance and the confession of sins (243). Monastic life constituted a different technology of the self, based upon obedience and the contemplation of God, more concerned with "thought in itself" that is, with the "nature, quality and substance of his thoughts" (1997f, p. 218), related to "inner impurity" than with action, or self-mastery, or passions, or attitudes, and which represented a renunciation of self and a surrender of autonomy. The emergence of these technologies, says Foucault, was "the first time in history that thoughts are considered as possible objects for an analysis" (1997f, p. 220).

Foucault's 1980 course "On the Government of the Living" (Foucault, 1997e), as well as his 1981–82 lecture course (Foucault, 2005), also devoted attention to Christian practices of self, and witnessed a shift in ethics as a process of subjectivation, dictated by a subject's choice of existence, in classical or late Antiquity, to ethics as subjection to a higher power or truth, expressed in terms of a code, with Christianity. Foucault's interest in studying Christian techniques was related to his view that the modern hermeneutics of the self is rooted more in Christian techniques than Greek or Greco-Roman ones (1997f, p. 201; 2005, p. chps. 13–23).

FOUCAULT'S HISTORICAL MATERIALISM

For Foucault (1991b, p. 90), the idea of the art of government is also concerned with the issue of *security*, of stabilising the fragile link between ruler and ruled, of rendering it legitimate, "to identify dangers... to develop the art of manipulating relations of force that will allow the Prince to ensure the protection of his principality". The concept of *security* is, along with governmentality, a central concept for Foucault, and is concerned with the issue of how the state deals with unpredictable events, how it evaluates and calculates the costs and consequences, and how it manages populations within constraint, rather than through the imposition of rule. Indeed, "one need[s] to analyze the series: security, population, government" (1991b, p. 87) as part of a combined approach, he tells us. While sovereignty is concerned with the problem of rule through the imposition of law, security is concerned with the management of populations. The intersection of security and government occurs with the concern for the regulation of populations" and the search for "mechanisms capable of ensuring its regulation" (1997g, p. 67). While the issue of security is relevant in all periods of history, it became of increased concern in the 18th century, and affected the form and practice of government.

Just as security affects the governance of populations, so it relates to practices of the self, and influences the kinds of governance techniques the self employs. Foucault's treatment of ethics, like his analysis of modernity, constitutes an attempt to understand the importance of ethics as an autonomous domain of governance. In doing this, Foucault does not seek to relate such practices directly to modes of economic life, although he does recognize "the economic level below which a man might not hope to support a wife and family" (1986, p. 84) and other primary necessities of life as they influence the responses of individuals and communities to risks and dangers, well-being and survival. The emphasis on risks, dangers, survival and the self as material factors influencing the ethical and political structure of societies is a constant concern in these studies. The *aphrodisia* thus was in all times in these periods a potential source of disease and societal instability. Although in Greek times the sexual act had its normal and morbid forms, in Greco-Roman era, whilst still not an evil, it became "a permanent focus of possible ills" (p. 142); liable to "great excesses" (p. 142); requiring "extreme vigilance"; because more precariously lodged in a potentially unstable field of risks, dangers and disease. This provided a continuity in the discourses of austerity, but itself became overlaid with more subtle, yet distinct differences in form and practice, depending upon these specific factors as they developed under the Empire. While such differences gave rise to different practices of self, the common concern of themes such as "self-mastery", "self control" and on "self-regulation" was also apparent:

> The accent was placed on the relationship with the self that enabled a person to keep from being carried away by the appetites and pleasures, to maintain a mastery and superiority over them... (1985, p. 31)

The common concerns with austerity and regulation centred around *problematizations* around dietetics, health and disease, and a fear of sexual activity in relation to them. That this materialist tension constituted the central thesis of his later studies is supported by his comment in *Le Nouvel Observateur* (1st June 1984), as reported by Dosse (1997, p. 345) where he says that "[i]n *The Use of Pleasure* I tried to show that there was a growing tension between pleasure and health". Throughout these studies, Foucault utilises the concept of *problematization* to suggest an issue that was of concern or was seen to constitute a problem in the particular community studied. Thus, behaviour was problematized centering around "the way in which one managed one's existence" which "enabled a set of rules to be affixed to conduct" (1985, p. 101). In classical antiquity sexual activity and pleasure were problematized through practices of the self. In addition, he says, in the Greco-Roman era there was a "de-problematization" around the erotic and philosophical investments imputed to the love of boys conjointly with the instensification of investments around marriage, and a more intense problematization of the aphrodisia, its specific purposes, limits and functions[5].

Apart from the primary necessities of life in constituting a potential source of danger and instability, the core material factors were the body, the self, and the relationship to the collectivity in terms of its capacity to sustain the lives and existences of the citizenry, each in relation to the whole, and in relation to external and internal threats. The body affected ethics as a "health practice" (*hygieinē pragmateia*) "which constituted the permanent framework of everyday life" (1986, p. 101). There was in the Greco-Roman era a certain form of "pathologization" around sex that arose (p. 101). It was a fragile and precarious activity, of "unknown benificience", it was linked to an "open field of dangers and diseases", and could be "easily perturbed" (p. 101). Practices of the self are thus a response to material conditions and defined the context in terms of which practices of governmentality developed. What Foucault's materialism emphasizes, that earlier deterministic models had not, is the role of local and contingent factors, and the dynamic potentials of agency in interaction with the material.

Foucault also identifies changes in the structure of marital relations, and changes in the political game as two crucial material factors which accounted for changes in the practices of self in the Greco-Roman period. With relation to marital role there was a change in institutional role, a change in the organisation of the conjugal relationship and a change in value system. Foucault (1986, p. 73) describes a greater "publicizing" of marriage under the Hellenistic authorities in what constituted a growing interest in control as regards marriage by the authorities. There were a series of new legislative measures, of which the law *de adultoriis* was one manifestation. The consequence was that the wife's status gained compared with in the classical period in terms of juridical independence from her father, and in the strengthening of her economic role within marriage. Marriage became "more and more clearly a voluntary agreement entered into by the partners" (p. 75) This constituted a "significant evolution for Hellenistic Egypt" says Foucault (p. 76). Increasingly marriage looked to public authorities for its guarantees under the Empire. It became "more general as a practice, more public as an institution, more private as a mode of existence, a stronger force for binding conjugal partners and hence a more effective force for isolating the couple in a field of other social relations" (p. 77).

With regards to the political game there was a decline in city-states as autonomous entities; starting from the third century B. C., this decline corresponded to a growing valuation on private life. The new rules of the political game were ushered in because of the rise of a centralised imperialism under the Empire. One must approach the issue of explaining the changes that occurred, says Foucault (p. 82), in terms of the "organisation of a complex space": imperial society was "a space in which the centres of power were multiple". It was "much vaster", "more flexible", "more differentiated", "less rigidly hierarchized" and "much less closed" than was the case for small city-states, like Athens. As a consequence, Foucault suggests that the close community bonds of ancient Greece constituted one form of support for the differences:

> Broadly speaking, the ancient societies remained societies of promiscuity, where existence was led in public. They were also societies in which everyone was situated within strong systems of local relationships, family ties, economic dependencies, and relations of patronage and friendship (1986, p. 42).

As a consequence, changes in political and social life promoted a different model of the care of the self and a different model of governmentality. There is a more intense valuation of marriage and private life in Greco-Roman society which is in part an alternative to the civic activity and political responsibilities of Athenian society (p. 85). Marriage itself became characterised by greater equality and reciprocity between partners which undermined to a certain degree the traditional relation of male superiority (pp. 94–95). In addition, the importance of starting with the self as a basis for political rule was still emphasised, but in a different way. Hence, Foucault cites Plutarch who stresses that before they can be involved in public life it is necessary that the individual must "retreat within himself"; that before he can be involved in political rule he must "set his soul straight", and "properly establish his own *ēthos*" (pp. 91–92). Thus, in the Hellenistic period and during the Empire, the three types of authority – over self, household, and others – became modified, and a weaker public authority structure compared to Athens saw an individualistic withdrawal into "private life", and a greater emphasis on personal conduct and family relations (p. 96).

The exercise of power also changed in the Greco-Roman period. It was relativized in two ways, says Foucault (1986, p. 88). First, birth was less important as a denotation of status, and was not linked to status by right. Rather politics became a vocation of free and deliberate choice, based on judgement and reason. Secondly, power changed from being an *imperium* to a *procuratio* that is, from being a node, or centre, to being an intermediary, or delegated function. Power operated in the Empire as a "transition point" within a "field of complex relations" (p. 88). It was more defined as a "role", than as a "supreme authority". In Weber's sense, it was more "rational-legal" (p. 88). In short, the field of power relations had become more extensive and complex, resulting in a network of relations of greater equality and reciprocity.

SELF, OTHERS, ECONOMY AND POLITICS

In endeavoring to account for the use of pleasures and the ethical structures of different societies as embodied in practices of the self, Foucault makes it clear that practices of the self are linked to other institutions and groups: to marriage, the household, politics and to others. The very requirement for practices of the self requiring austerity, moderation and regulation or self-mastery reflect the vicissitudes of the self in relation to the tasks of survival, and the dangers facing particular societies at different periods. As Foucault explains:

> Self-mastery had an implied close connection between the superiority one exercised over oneself, the authority one exercised in the context of the household, and the power one exercised in the field of an agonistic society. It was the practice of superiority over oneself that guaranteed the moderate and reasonable use that one could and ought to make of the two other superiorities (1986, pp. 94–95).

Practices of the self also implied a particular ethical and political vision, for it is not possible to develop rules for living unless these make sense within a broader aesthetics of existence. To develop the ethical self as an aesthetics of existence is to develop "the purposeful art of freedom perceived as a power game" (1985, p. 253). It was problematized as centering on an axis of freedom, power and truth. In this sense, ethical practice was about the formation of character which was essential to freedom. A moral *askēsis* requiring moderation and self-mastery (*enkrateia*); a method or mode of subjection (*chrēsis*) involving the application of a *technē*, or *savoir-faire* relating to need, urgency, timeliness, and skills of comportment. Such ethical practices relating to sexuality bore a resemblence to a battle; the *aphrodisia* was made desirable and available in relation to an interplay of forces, whose potential was for revolt and excess in relation to the dangers in the field of social relations. Ethical relationships were in this sense agonistic, in that they involved struggle, suppression of appetites. The battle is between oneself and oneself, but only because the self always stood in a relation to others.

The relation of self to others is a constant theme in Greek and Greco-Roman societies manifesting itself in different ways in the different periods. "[I]t is not because it is care for others that it is ethical", says Foucault (1991a, p. 7). "Care for self is ethical in itself, but it implies complex relations with others, in the measure where this *ēthos* of freedom is also a way of caring for others." Thus, "the problem of relationships with others is present all along in this development of care for self" (p. 7). Moreover, the principle of the care for self came to operate as a general rule effecting how one conducted oneself, to an individual's rights, entitlements and duties, to the master of the household; to the ruler who looked after his subjects; as well as to a particular educational ideal, or "soul service" (1986, pp. 51–55). As he says: "educating oneself and caring for oneself are interconnected activities" (p. 55).

In one of his interviews (1989b, p. 296), Foucault states his central interest in *The Care of the Self* as being "how an experience is formed where the relationship to self and to others is linked". The care of the self, then, is always at the same time concerned with care for others. Ethical practice in this sense is communal, for "*ēthos* implies a relation with others to the extent that care for self renders one competent to occupy a place in the city, in the community . . . whether it be to exercise a magistracy or to have friendly relationships" (Foucault, 1991a, p. 7). Foucault notes how this indeed was the ethical imperative of Socrates. As he says, in Greek society, "one who cared for himself correctly found himself by that very fact, in a measure to behave correctly in relationship to others and for others. A city in which everyone would be correctly concerned for self would be a city that would be doing well, and it would find therein the ethical principle of its stability" (p. 7). There is a temporal and logical order, however: "one must not have the care for others precede the care for self. The care for the self takes moral precedence in the measure that the relationship to self takes ontological precedence" (p. 7).

Ethical action presupposes a certain political and social structure with respect to liberty. As Foucault puts it, "liberty is the ontological condition of ethics. But ethics is the deliberate form assumed by liberty" (1991a, p. 4). For liberty or civic freedom to exist there must be a certain level of liberation conceived as the absence of domination. In this, Foucault disputes the view "more or less derived from Hegel" in terms of which "the liberty of the individual would have no importance when faced with the noble totality of the city" (p. 5). The concern for liberty as expressed in ancient societies – in not being a slave for instance – was an absolutely fundamental theme, a basic and constant issue during eight centuries of ancient culture. Such ethical practices of self on self involve choices which are essentially moral choices, says Foucault (p. 5).

Just as ethical work presupposes liberty, it also is intrinsically political. As Foucault explains, "it is political in the measure that non-slavery with respect to others is a condition: a slave has no ethics. Liberty is itself political. And then it has a political model, in the measure where being free means not being a slave to one's self and to one's appetites, which supposes that one establishes over one's self a certain relation of domination, of mastery, which was called *arche*–power, authority" (1991a, p. 6).

Practices of the self are political also in that they constitute relations of power, they are ways of controlling and limiting, and imply different models of governance to sustain them. As such they raise the problem of the abuse of power, when one imposes on others "one's whims, one's appetites, one's desires":

> There we see the image of the tyrant or simply of the powerful and wealthy man who takes advantage of his power and his wealth to misuse others, to impose on them undue power. But one sees – at least that is what the Greek philosophers say – that this man is in reality a slave to his appetites. And the good ruler is precisely the one who exercises his power correctly, i.e., by exercising at the same time his power on himself. And it is the power over self which will regulate the power over others . . . if you care for yourself correctly, i.e., if you know ontologically what you are . . . then you cannot abuse your power over others. (Foucault, 1991a, p. 8)

The care of the self thus posits a politically active subject, involving practices of the self which include governance, with all of the associated problems of practical politics. These in turn involve managerial imperatives, at the level of the individual and of the state, including decision making, the interpretation and application of rules, gambits, risks, knowing when to act and when to hold back, or being able if necessary to attack or defend. These skills required *autarkeia* (self-sufficiency) which pertained in the ancient schools to a form of internal freedom "located in the faculty of judgement, not in some psychologically thick form of introspection" (Davidson, 1994, pp. 76–77).

Hence the care of the self does not just refer to attention to oneself in the narrow sense; nor is it concerned solely with the avoidance of mistakes and dangers; nor does it designate primarily an attitude toward one's self or a form of awareness of self. It constitutes both a principle and a constant practice: "We may say that in all of Ancient philosophy the care of the self was considered as both a duty and a technique, a basic obligation and a set of carefully worked-out procedures" (Foucault, 1997c, p. 95).In this sense it designates a "regulated occupation, a work with its methods and objectives" (p. 95). This work is by its very nature political, as it contains integral to it notions concerning the management of self and others. This is evident, says Foucault, in the meaning of the notion of *epimeleia* and its various uses. Xenophon employs the use of the concept to designate the work of a master of the household who supervises its farming, and it is an idea also used to pay ritual homage to the dead and to the gods. In addition, Dio of Prusa uses it to refer to the activity of the sovereign who looks after his people and leads the city-state (p. 95).

While I have on this basis of the reciprocal tie between self and other utlilized insights from Foucault to support my "thin communitarian" position (Olssen, 2002), one must be careful in attributing any conception of *community* to Foucault. The notion of *communio* suggests the establishment of a unity, and is premised in its traditional useage on the idea of a bounded and closed totality, which would be incompatible with Foucault's Nietzschean legacy. Having said this, the idea that people are socially constituted would seem to imply the ontological status of the social as constituted of particular institutional and political structures in terms of which both individual and group development takes place. Given this, how one is to conceptualise this space in which social beings are constituted raises an important question? My own concept of the 'thin community' was intended to capture this conception of an always open, unbounded social and institutional framework in which individuals develop and interact. It was, to use William Corlett's (1993) concept, a "community without unity"; or in Michael Oakshott's sense, it constituted a *societas* as opposed to a *universitas*[6]. For Oakeshott (1975, p. 203), whereas a *universitas* pertains to a tightly knit community with a common purpose, *societas* is marked by the fact that it does not presuppose a common or shared purpose. Rather than a common concern, what links them together is a "practice of civility", which Oakeshott calls *respublica*. It is a polity without a definite shape, or fixed borders, or a definite identity, but is in continuous re-enactment, and ultimately has possible links to a global polis.

Although the conception of a *societas* suggests a less Hegelian resonance than the traditional notion of community, I am not intending to suggest Foucault would accept that term. But that some such context must be presupposed would seem to be necessitated both (a) by the social character of selfhood, and (b) the institutional and political context necessary for the practices of the self to be enacted. What Foucault clearly conveys is that individuals create themselves in relation to social, political and regulatory structures of their environment, and the processes of this creation, although patterned and regular within limits, varies in different historical contexts.

Ethical action and agency are regarded as political, and as forms of power, which is itself represented as a force that circulates. In both his books and interviews Foucault presents a picture of individuals who are interconnected and interdependent with each other and to the structures of social and institutional control; where their ethical constitution is related to their participation in the world; where freedom, itself considered as political, is conceived of as self-mastery and control within a set of societal constraints. While patterns of withdrawal or commitment or involvement may vary between different societies, the ontolological status of the self in the world is not represented individualistically, as in Liberalism, seeing the self as a 'pre-social' subject, that invents itself from its own resources, but as a relation to an always open and ever changing complex social whole, itself structured by relations of power, and necessitating techniques of governance.

CONCLUSION

As with all his studies, Foucault's analysis in the latter volumes of *The History of Sexuality* reveals particular dimensions concerning his method. While self-constitution involves on the one hand particular techniques and practices of self, it is also evident that the process occurs in relation to particular social, institutional and political contexts. While such practices involve technologies of governance, governance refers to both "subjectivation" as well as to the social-institutional and political contexts (marriage, the household, the polis) in which subjectivation takes place. What is essential to see is that techniques of the self take place through strategies of governance just as the rule of populations takes place through strategies of governance. The relevance of governmentality attests to the ontological significance of power in history as defining the context in terms of which individuals and populations are shaped, and in terms of which human volition proceeds. It attests to the historicity of governance arrangements at any particular time.

In relation to both ethics and politics, Foucault uses the term *governmentality* to supplement pastoral power and biopower, in order to characterize this historicity. Governmentality has dual functions as *individualizing* and *totalizing*, in shaping both individuals and populations, in order to understand the strategic exercise of power as it is applied to situations. If 'bio-power' referred to disciplinary power introduced in the early modern period in order to rationalize the problems afflicting populations, governmentality pertains to the specificity of power relations with its concern to shape conduct as part of broader issue involving the *political* (i.e., volitional) exercise of power. It includes "techniques and procedures for directing human behaviour" (1997e, p. 81). It pertains, he says (1991b, pp. 87–88) to "a concern with the art of government...of how to be ruled, how strictly, by whom, to what end, by what methods, etc". In addition, the concept can be applied to the family, religion, the economy, as well as the state. In its most general sense it pertains to the "problematic of government in general" (p. 88) and articulates "a kind of rationality" (p. 89). In this sense, at it most simple level, governmentality expresses itself as an *art,* and also characterizes both practices of the self and forms of *state reason (raisson d'etat).*

NOTES

[1] This chapter draws significantly on Chapter 9 of my book *Michel Foucault: Materialism and Education,* Paradigm Publishers, Boulder, Colorado, 2006.

[2] *Les Lettres Creques en Occident de Macrobe a Cassiodore.*

[3] Foucault acknowledges a debt in his use of *style* to Peter Brown, *The Making of Late Antiquity* (Boston, Harvard University Press, 1978). See Foucault (1989s: 320).

[4] According to Davidson (1986: 230) Foucault originally announced that his *History of Sexuality* would be a six-volume study concentrating "on the eighteenth and nineteenth centuries and including volumes on children and perverts". Davidson (1994) further notes that five forthcoming volumes were listed on the back cover of The *History of Sexuality, Volume 1.* Foucault's interests changed after *Volume 1,* however, and he became interested more specifically in Ancient Greek, Greco-Roman and Christian ethics. Macey (1993: 446) notes that the intended fourth volume – *Confessions of the Flesh* – although started, will probably not ever be published.

[5] In an interview conducted in 1981 by André Berten in Belgium ("What Our Present Is"), Foucault simply defined this method as the "history of problems", or as "the genealogy of problems...why a problem, and why such a kind of problem, why a certain way of problematising appears at a given point of time" (see Foucault, 1997f: 165, 239).

[6] Oakeshott is using these terms which were used in the Middle Ages to describe two modes of human association.

REFERENCES

Corlett, W. (1993). *Community without unity: A politics of derridean extravagence.* Durhamm, NC: Duke University Press.

Davidson, A. (1994). Ethics as ascetics: Foucault, the history of ethics, and ancient thought. In J. Goldstein (Ed.), *Foucault and the writing of history* (pp. 63–80). Cambridge, MA.: Blackwell.

Davidson, A. (1997). *Foucault and his interlocutors.* Chicago and London: University of Chicago Press.

Dosse, F. (1997). *History of structuralism volume 2: The sign sets, 1967—present* (D. Glassman, Trans.). Minneapolis, MN and London: University of Minnesota Press.

Foucault, M. (1985). *The use of pleasure: History of sexuality* (Vol. 2, R. Hurley, Trans.). New York: Pantheon.

Foucault, M. (1986). *The care of the self: History of sexuality* (Vol. 3, R. Hurley, Trans.). New York: Pantheon.

Foucault, M. (1989a). Friendship as a way of life (J. Johnston, Trans.). In S. Lotringer (Ed.), *Foucault live.* New York: Semiotext(e).

Foucault, M. (1989b). The concern for truth. In S. Lotringer (Ed.), *Foucault live: Interviews, 1966–84* (pp. 293–308). New York: Semiotex(e).

Foucault, M. (1989c). The return to morality. In S. Lotringer (Ed.), *Foucault live: Interviews, 1966–84* (pp. 317–332). New York: Semiotex(e).

Foucault, M. (1991a). The ethic of care for the self as a practice of freedom: an interview (J. D. Gauthier, Trans.). In J. Bernauer & D. Rasmussen (Eds.), *The final foucault*. Cambridge, MA: MIT Press.

Foucault, M. (1991b). Governmentality. In G. Burchell, C. Gordon, & P. Miller (Eds.), *The foucault effect: Studies in governmentality* (pp. 87–104). Chicago: The University of Chicago Press.

Foucault, M. (1997a). On the genealogy of ethics: An overview of work in progress. In P. Rabinow (Ed.) & R. Hurley (Trans.), *M. Foucault, Ethics, subjectivity and truth: The essential works* (pp. 235–280). Allen Lane: The Penguin Press.

Foucault, M. (1997b). Subjectivity and truth. In P. Rabinow (Ed.) & R. Hurley (Trans.), *M. Foucault, Ethics, subjectivity and truth: The essential works* (pp. 87–94). Allen Lane: The Penguin Press.

Foucault, M. (1997c). The hermeneutic of the subject. In P. Rabinow (Ed.) & R. Hurley (Trans.), *M. Foucault, Ethics, subjectivity and truth: The essential works* (pp. 95–108). Allen Lane: The Penguin Press.

Foucault, M. (1997d). Technologies of the self. In P. Rabinow (Ed.) & R. Hurley (Trans.), *M. Foucault, Ethics, subjectivity and truth: The essential works* (pp. 223–251). Allen Lane: The Penguin Press.

Foucault, M. (1997e). On the government of the living. In P. Rabinow (Ed.) & R. Hurley (Trans.), *M. Foucault, Ethics, subjectivity and truth: The essential works* (pp. 81–86). Allen Lane: The Penguin Press.

Foucault, M. (1997f). *The politics of truth* (S. Lotringer & L. Hochroth, Eds.). New York: Semiotext(e).

Foucault, M. (1997g). Security, territory, population. In P. Rabinow (Ed.), *Michel Foucault: Ethics, subjectivity and truth* (pp. 67–71). London: Allen Lane and The Penguin Press.

Foucault, M. (2005). *The Hermeneutics of the Subject: Lectures at the Collège de France, 1981–1982* (F. Gros, Ed., G. Burchell, English series Ed., & A. Davidson, Trans.). New York: Picador.

Hacking, I. (1986). Self improvement. In D. Couzens Hoy (Ed.), *Foucault: A critical reader*. Oxford, UK: Blackwell.

Hadot, P. (1987). *Exercices spirituels et philosophie antique* (2nd ed.). Paris: Etudes Augustiniennes.

Hadot, P. (1992). Reflections on the notion of `the culturation of the self'. In T. Armstrong (Ed.), *Michel Foucault: Philosopher* (pp. 225–232). New York and London: Harvester and Wheatsheaf.

Hadot, P. (1995). *Philosophy as a way of life* (A. I. Davidson Ed. & M. Chase Trans.). Oxford, UK: Blackwell Publishers.

Hadot, P. (1997). Forms of life and forms of discourse in ancient philosophy (A. I. Davidson & P. Wissing, Trans.). In A. I. Davidson (Ed.), *Foucault and his interlocutors* (pp. 203–224). Chicago: University of Chicago Press.

Oakshott, M. (1975). *On human conduct*. Oxford, UK: Oxford University Press.

Olssen, M. (2002). Michel Foucault as thin communitarian: Difference, community, democracy. *Cultural Studies-Critical Methodologies, 2*(4), 483–513.

Olssen, M. (2006). *Michel Foucault: Materialism and education*. Boulder, CO: Paradigm Publishers.

Rabinow, P. (1997). Introduction: The history of systems of thought. In P. Rabinow (Ed.) & R. Hurley (Trans.), *M. Foucault, Ethics, subjectivity and truth: The essential works* (pp. XI–XLII). Allen Lane: The Penguin Press.

Rorty, R. (1991). *Objectivity, relativism, and truth*. Cambridge, UK: Cambridge University Press.

Taylor, C. (1989). *Sources of the self: The making of modern identity*. Cambridge, MA: Harvard University Press.

Veyne, P. (1997). The final foucault and his ethics. In A. Davidson (Ed.), *Foucault and his interlocutors* (pp. 225–223). Chicago: University of Chicago Press.

Mark Olssen
University of Surrey
United Kingdom

MICHAEL A. PETERS

6. NEOLIBERAL GOVERNMENTALITY: FOUCAULT ON THE BIRTH OF BIOPOLITICS

The political, ethical, social, philosophical problem of our days is not to liberate the individual from the State and its institutions, but to liberate ourselves from the State and the type of individualisation linked to it (Foucault, 1982, p. 216).

Power is exercised only over free subjects, and only insofar as they are free. (Foucault, 1982, p. 221).

INTRODUCTION

In his governmentality studies in the late 1970s Foucault held a course at the Collège de France the major forms of neoliberalism, examining the three theoretical schools of German ordoliberalism, the Austrian school characterised by Hayek, and American neoliberalism in the form of the Chicago school. Among Foucault's great insights in his work on governmentality was the critical link he observed in liberalism between the governance of the self and government of the state – understood as the exercise of political sovereignty over a territory and its population. He focuses on government as a set of practices legitimated by specific rationalities and saw that these three schools of contemporary economic liberalism focused on the question of too much government – a permanent critique of the state that Foucault considers as a set of techniques for governing the self through the market. Liberal modes of governing, Foucault tells us, are distinguished in general by the ways in which they utilise the capacities of free acting subjects and, consequently, modes of government differ according to the value and definition accorded the concept of freedom. These different mentalities of rule, thus, turn on whether freedom is seen as a natural attribute as with the philosophers of the Scottish Enlightenment, a product of rational choice making, or, as with Hayek, a civilizational artefact theorised as both negative and anti-naturalist. This paper first briefly discusses Foucault's approach to governmentality, before detailing and analysing Foucault's account of German ordoliberalism, a configuration based on the theoretical configuration of economics and law developed at the University of Freiberg by W. Eucken and F. Böhm that views the market contingently as developing historically within a judicial-legal framework. The economy is thus based on a concept of the Rule of Law, anchored in a notion of individual rights, property rights and contractual freedom that constitutes, in effect, an economic constitution. German neoliberal economists (Müller-Armack, Röpke, Rüstow) invented the term 'social market economy' which shared certain features with the Freiburg model of law and economics but also differed from it in terms of the

M.A. Peters et al. (eds.), Governmentality Studies in Education, 95–107.

'ethics' of the market (as did Hayek in *The Constitution of Liberty*). This formulation of the "social market economy" proved significant not only in terms of the post-war reconstruction of the (West) German economy but through Erhard, as Minister and Chancellor, became important as the basis of the EEC's and, later, EU's 'social model'.

Foucault's overriding interest was not in 'knowledge as ideology', as Marxists would have it, where bourgeois knowledge, say, modern liberal economics was seen as false knowledge or bad science. Nor was he interested in 'knowledge as theory' as classical liberalism has constructed disinterested knowledge, based on inherited distinctions from the Greeks, including Platonic epistemology and endorsed by the Kantian separation of schema/content that distinguishes the analytic enterprise. Rather Foucault examined practices of knowledge produced through the relations of power.[1] He examined how these practices, then, were used to augment and refine the efficacy and instrumentality of power in its exercise over both individuals and populations, and also in large measure helped to shape the consti-tution of subjectivity. Fundamental to his governmentality studies was the under-standing that Western society professed to be based on principles of liberty and the Rule of Law and said to derive the legitimation of the State from political philosophies that elucidated these very principles. Yet as a matter of historical fact, Western society employed technologies of power that operated on forms of disciplinary order or were based on biopolitical techniques that bypassed the law and its freedoms altogether. As Colin Gordon (2001, p. xxvi) puts it so starkly: Foucault embraced Nietzsche as the thinker "who transforms Western philosophy by rejecting its founding disjunction of power and knowledge as myth". By this he means that the rationalities of Western politics, from the time of the Greeks, had incorporated techniques of power specific to Western practices of government, first, in the expert knowledges of the Greek tyrant and, second, in the concept of pastoral power that characterized ecclesiastical government.

It is in this vein that Foucault examines government as a practice and problematic that first emerges in the sixteenth century and is characterized by the insertion of economy into political practice. Foucault (2001, p. 201) explores the problem of government as it "explodes in the sixteenth century" after the collapse of feudalism and the establishment of new territorial States. Government emerges at this time as a general problem dispersed across quite different questions: Foucault mentions specifically the Stoic revival that focussed on the government of oneself; the government of souls elaborated in Catholic and Protestant pastoral doctrine; the government of children and the problematic of pedagogy; and, last but not least, the government of the State by the prince. Through the reception of Machiavelli's *The Prince* in the sixteenth century and its rediscovery in the nineteenth century, there emerges a literature that sought to replace the power of the prince with the art of government understood in terms of the government of the family, based on the central concept of 'economy'. The introduction of economy into political practice is for Foucault the essential issue in the establishment of the art of government. As he points out, the problem is still posed for Rousseau, in the mid-18th century, in the same terms – the government of the State is modelled on the management by the head of the family over his family, household and its assets.[2]

It is in the late sixteenth century, then, that the art of government receives its first formulation as 'reason of state' that emphasizes a specific rationality intrinsic to the nature of the state, based on principles no longer philosophical and transcendent, or theological and divine, but rather centred on the problem of population. This became a science of government conceived of outside the juridical framework of sovereignty characteristic of the feudal territory and firmly focused on the problem of population based on the modern concept which enabled "the creation of new orders of knowledge, new objects of intervention, new forms of subjectivity and …. new state forms" (Curtis, 2002, p. 2). It is this political-statistical concept of population that provided the means by which the government of the state came to involve individualization and totalization, and, thus, married Christian pastoral care with sovereign political authority. The new rationality of 'reason of state' focussed on the couplet population-wealth as an object of rule, providing conditions for the emergence of political economy as a form of analysis. Foucault investigated the techniques of police science and a new bio-politics,

> Which tends to treat the 'population' as a mass of living and co-existing beings, which evidence biological traits and particular kinds of pathologies and which, in consequence, give rise to specific knowledges and techniques (Foucault 1989, p. 106, cited in Curtis, 2002).

As Foucault (2001) comments in "The Political Technology of Individuals", the "rise and development of our modern political rationality" as "reason of state", that is, as a specific rationality intrinsic to the state, is formulated through "a new relation between politics as a practice and as knowledge" (p. 407), involving specific political knowledge or "political arithmetic" (statistics); "new relationships between politics and history", such that political knowledge helped to strengthen the state and at the same time ushered in an era of politics based on "an irreducible multiplicity of states struggling and competing in a limited history" (p. 409); and, finally, a new relationship between the individual and the state, where "the individual becomes pertinent for the state insofar as he can do something for the strength of the state" (p. 409). In analysing the works of von Justi, Foucault infers that the true object of the police becomes, at the end of the eighteenth century, the population; or, in other words, the state has essentially to take care of men as a population. It wields its power over living beings, and its politics, therefore has to be a biopolitics (p. 416).

Foucault's lectures on governmentality were first delivered in a course he gave at the Collège de France, entitled 'Sécurité, Territoire, Population', during the 1977-78 academic year. While the essays "Governmentality" and "Questions of Method" were published in 1978 and 1980, respectively, and translated into English in the collection The Foucault Effect: Studies in Governmentality (Burchell et al, 1991), it is only in the last few months that the course itself has been transcribed from original tapes and published for the first time (Foucault, 2004a), along with the sequel Naissance de la biopolitique: Cours au Collège de France,

1978–1979 (Foucault, 2004b), although both books remain to be translated.[3] The governmentality literature in English, roughly speaking, dates from the 1991 collection and has now grown quite substantially (see, for example, Miller and Rose, 1990; Barry et al., 1996; Dean, 1999; Rose, 1999).[4] As a number of scholars have pointed out Foucault relied on a group of researchers to help him in his endeavours: François Ewald, Pasquale Pasquino, Daniel Defert, Giovanna Procacci, Jacques Donzelot, on governmentality; François Ewald, Catherine Mevel, Éliane Allo, Nathanie Coppinger and Pasquale Pasquino, François Delaporte and Anne-Marie Moulin, on the birth of biopolitics. These researchers working with Foucault in the late 1970s constitute the first generation of governmentality studies scholars and many have gone on to publish significant works too numerous to list here. In the field of education as yet not a great deal has focussed specifically on governmentality.[5]

Gordon (2001, p. xxiii) indicates three shifts that took place in Foucault's thinking: a shift from a focus on "specialized practices and knowledges of the individual person" "to the exercise of political sovereignty exercised by the state over an entire population"; the study of government as a practice informed and enabled by a specific rationality or succession of different rationalities; and, the understanding that liberalism, by contrast with socialism, possessed a distinctive concept and rationale for the activity of governing. Liberalism and neoliberalism, then, for Foucault represented distinctive innovations in the history of governmental rationality. In his governmentality studies Foucault focussed on the introduction of economy into the practice of politics and in a turn to the contemporary scene studied two examples: German liberalism during the period 1948-62, with an emphasis on the Ordoliberalism of the Freiburg School, and American neoliberalism of the Chicago School.

In this chapter I focus of Foucault's reading of German neoliberalism, the emergence of the 'social market' which has significance not only for understanding the historical development of an economic constitution and formulation of 'social policy' (and the role of education policy within it), but also the development of the European social model, more generally, and the continued relevance for Third Way politics of the 'social market economy.'

GERMAN NEOLIBERALISM AND THE BIRTH OF BIOPOLITICS

Naissance de la biopolitique (Foucault, 2004b) consists of thirteen lectures delivered by Foucault at the Collège de France (10 January-4th April, 1979). It is helpful to see this course in the series of thirteen courses he gave from 1970 to 1984. The first five courses reflected his early work on knowledge in the human sciences, concerning punishment, penal and psychiatric institutions: "*La Volonté de savoir*" (1970–71), "*Théories et Institutions pénales*" (1971–72), "*La Société punitive*" (1972–73), "*Le Pouvoir psychiatrique*" (1973–74), "*Les Anormaux*" (1974–75). The remaining eight courses focussed squarely on governmentality studies, with a clear emphasis also on the problematic (and hermeneutics) of the subject and the relation between subjectivity and truth: "*Il faut défendre la société*" (1975–76),

"Securité, Territoire, Population" (1977–78), *"Naissance de la biopolitique"* (1978–79), *"Du gouvernement des vivants"* (1979–80), *"Subjectivité et Vérité"* (1980–81), *"L'Herméneutique du subjet"* (1981–82), *"Le Gouvernement de soi et des autres"* (1982–83), *"Le Gouvernement de soi et des autres: le courage de la verite"* (1983–84). Even from this list of courses is become readily apparent that the question of government concerns Foucault for the last decade of his life and that for his governmentality studies, politics were inseparable in its modern forms both from biology – biopower and the government of the living – and truth and subjectivity. It is important to note that these same concerns in one form or another enter into Foucault's formulations in *Naissance de la biopolitique.*[6]

In the first lecture, having dealt with the question of method and reviewed the preceding year, Foucault signals his intention to pursue the question of how the introduction of political economy served as an internal (and defining) principle limiting the practice of liberal government. In the second lecture, he considers French radical jurisprudence and English utilitarianism as emerging solutions to the problem of the limitation of the exercise of public power. He begins to specify the novel features of the art of liberal government as consisting in three related aspects: the constitution of the market as a form of truth and not simply a domain of justice; the problem of the limitation of the exercise of public power; and the problem of equilibrium in the internal competition of European states. With Adam Smith and the Physiocrats he charts the birth of a new European model based on the principle of the 'freedom of the market' that surface with discussion of international trade, rights of the sea, and perpetual peace in the 18th century. I focus more heavily on lectures 4–8 in the course because they concern German neoliberalism and may be, therefore, more of interest to my German colleagues. They also contain the bulk of the references to Hayek. Lectures 9 and 10 focus of American neoliberalism, and lectures 11 and 12 investigate the model and history of *homo economicus* and the notion of civil society.[7]

Foucault begins the fourth lecture with a discussion of "fear of the State" or State phobia which had surfaced in the 1920s with the calculation debate of Mises and anti-Socialist sentiments of the Austrian School and which came to a head in Germany after the World War II with the experience of National Socialism, post-war reconstruction and the development of the Keynesian interventionist welfare state in Britain and Roosevelt's New Deal in the US. (Foucault also mentions the opposition between Keynes at Cambridge and Hayek at LSE. Hayek was recruited by the Director, Lionel Robbins in the early 1930s). In the context of post-war reconstruction Foucault details the Marshall Plan, adopted in 1948, and the Scientific Council set up in 1947 in Germany with the function, in the Anglo-American zone, of undertaking the reconstruction and administration of the economy. The Council comprised representatives of the Freiburg School (W. Eucken, F. Böhm, A. Müller-Armack, L. Miksch, A. Lampe, O. Veit and others) as well as members of the Christian Socialists. Much of his analysis of post-war Germany in these early years focuses on the role of Ludwig Erhard (1897–1977).

Erhard drafts the memorandum of war financing and debt consolidation and later as a member of the Bavarian Cabinet becomes Minister of Economics responsible for currency reform. As deputy of the Christian Democrats he is instrumental in introducing the politico-economic concept of the "social market economy" and becomes Minister of Economics in the first Adenauer government in 1949. He later becomes a council member of the Coal and Steel Community, Governor of the World Bank, appoints Müller-Armack as Secretary of State at the Economics Ministry in Bonn from 1958–63, plays a strong role in the EEC, and eventually is elected as the Federal Chancellor of the CDU in 1963 and remains so until 1967.[8] Foucault's emphasis is on the concept of the "social market economy" which Erhard established in 1948, fundamentally changing the West German economy, and with it the whole of post-war society. The social market economy was coined by the national economist Müller-Armack to define an economic system based on the free market principles, aimed at guaranteeing economic efficiency and social justice with a high degree of individual freedom. The crucial aspect for Foucault's governmentality studies is that the social market economy was devised as an economic system combining market freedom with social equilibrium, where the government played a strong regulatory role by creating a juridical-legal framework for market processes that both secured competition and ensured social equity.

In the fifth lecture Foucault begins to outline the German programme of neoliberalism by reference to the theoreticians, Eucken, Böhm, Müller-Armark and Hayek. Eucken was co-founder of the *ordoliberalen* Freiburg School with the jurists, Böhm and Hans Großmann-Doerth, who were united in their concern for constitutional foundations of a free economy and society, an approach that combined law and economics.[9] They were concerned to provide an institutional framework for the competitive order based on transparent rules for the efficient functioning of a private market economy embodied in the concept of "complete competition", which involved State monitoring of monopolies and anti-trust laws. Other aspects of the *ordoliberalen* framework included monetary stability, open markets, private property and ownership of the means of production, and freedom of contract between autonomous economic agents, including liability for one's commitments and actions.

The ordoliberal Freiburg School, as Vanberg (2004, p. 2) usefully notes, "while certainly part of the foundations on which the social market economy was created and generally subsumed under the rubric of German neoliberalism", also exhibited differences with neoliberal economists such as Müller-Armack, Röpke and Rüstow.

For the Freiburg School the market order, as a non-discriminating, privilige-free [sic] order of competition, is in and by itself an ethical order. As far as the need for "social insurance" is concerned, the Freiburg ordo-liberals recognized that the competitive market order can be, and should be, combined with a system of minimal income guarantees for those who are, temporarily or permanently, unable to earn a living by providing saleable services in the market. They insisted, though, that such social insurance provisions must be of a nondiscriminating, privilege-free nature, and must not be provided in ways – e.g., in the form of subsidies or other privileges granted to particular industries – that corrupt the fundamental ethical principle of the market order, namely its privilege-free nature. Müller-Armack, by contrast, regards the market order as an economically most efficient order, but not as one that has inherent ethical qualities. It is a "technical instrument" that can be used by society to produce wealth, but it does not make itself for a "good" society. It has to be made "ethical" by supplementary policies, in particular "social" policies. The important point is that in Müller-Armack's case, these supplementary "social provisions" that are supposed to make the market economy – beyond its economic efficiency – ethically appealing are not constrained, as they are in for the Freiburg ordoliberals, by the proviso that they must not be in conflict with the privilege-free nature of the rules of the game of the market.[10]

Foucault proceeds to discuss obstacles to political liberalism that had beset Germany since the 19th century, including economic protectionism, the socialism of the Birmarckian State, the role of WWI and economic reconstruction, a type of Keynesian rigidity, and the political economy of National Socialism. The neoliberal critique of National Socialism and State phobia is the starting point for an extension of this critique to both the New Deal in the US and Beveridge's Welfare State in the UK, that is, to the growth and development of the power of the State, and to standardization and massification as infringements of individual liberty defined through competition. Foucault claims that German neoliberalism enjoyed a novel relationship with classical liberalism through its constitutional theory of pure competition.

Lectures 4, 5 and 6 are devoted exclusively to "*le néolibéralisme allemande*" and Foucault in the last of these three lectures is concerned to discover what distinguishes neoliberalism from classical liberalism. He responds by arguing that the problem of neoliberalism is knowledge (savoir) of how to exercise global political power based on the principles of a market economy and he suggests that a major transformation occurred with the association between the principle of the market economy and the political principle of laissez-faire that presented itself through a theory of pure competition. Pure competition emerged as the formal structure of property that neoliberals saw as means for regulating the economy through the price mechanism.

He traces problems of government in this period in relation to monopolies and political society. He also examines the emergence in post-war Germany of what he calls "*politique de société*" or *Gesellschaftspolitik,* which I translate as "social policy", and the ordoliberal critique of the welfare state (*l'économie de bien-être*), where society is modelled on the enterprise society, and enterprise society and the good society come to be seen as one and the same.

The second aspect of social policy according to these German neoliberal thinkers is the problem of right in a society modelled on economic competition of the market which Foucault explores in lecture 8 by reference to a text by Louis Rougier and the idea of a legal-economic order, the question of legal intervention in the economy, and the development of the demand for a judiciary. The concept of order (*Ordnung*) is *the* central concept in the Freiburg school as it is at the basis of an understanding of *economic constitution*, or the *rules of the game*, upon which economies or economic systems are based. Eucken insisted that "all economic activity necessarily takes place within a historically evolved framework of rules and institutions" (Vanberg, 2004, p. 6) and that one improves the economy by improving the economic constitution or the institutional framework within which economic activity takes place. This was, in effect, the attempt to create conditions "under which the 'invisible hand' that Adam Smith had described can be expected to do its work" (Vanberg, 2004, p. 8). The major historical step for German neoliberals was the shift from feudalism to a civil law society where people enjoyed the same rights and status under the law and thus, had the *freedom to contract* with one another. This, in essence, represented their conception of free market economy, which was based on the natural order of free competition where all players met as equals and voluntary exchange and contract enabled coordination of economic activity.

GERMAN NEOLIBERALISM AND THE BIRTH OF THE EUROPEAN SOCIAL MODEL

Foucault's prescient analysis in 1979 of German neoliberalism focused on the Freiburg school of ordoliberalism as an innovation in the rationality of government by devising a conception of the market order based squarely on the Rule of Law. This conception, and its related versions in both German neoliberalism (after Müller-Armack and others) and Austrian economics going back to Mises and Hayek, was responsible for a form of constitutional economics that invented the 'social market economic' and shaped Gesellschaftspolitik or 'social policy', as an ethical exception to the rules of the market game. The challenge for scholars, especially in the German context or those with the language skills that permit them to analyse formations of German "social policy" is to provide the genealogical investigation of the change of values and shifting meanings underlying the development of educational policy as part of 'the social', and later its shift to being at the centre of economic policy, especially in the decade of 1980s and 1990s when Third Way and EU policies constitute education policy as an aspect of the 'knowledge economy'.

Foucault's analysis, formulated in the years 1978–79, and then developed in a series of subsequent themes as "the government of the living", "subjectivity and truth", and "the government of self and others", took up an account of the practices neoliberal governmentality as a set of novel practices introduced as a form of economic liberalism, that operated on the premise of a critique of "too much government", what Foucault describes as a permanent critique of State reason. Foucault would not have been unaware of the rise of a particular form of politics referred to as the New Right, which under both Thatcher and Reagan, combined elements of neoliberalism and neoconservativism in a contradictory formulation wielded together through 'great' statesmanship.

In this new neoliberal climate established at a popular level in an Anglo-American model that attained global ambitions under various guises through the old Bretton Woods institutions, the IMF and World Bank, and other formations like the "Washington consensus", the notion of the "social market economy", originally developed through German neoliberalism, offered some new hope as the basis of Third Way economic policies and, more generally, as the basis for the European social model (see, e.g., Joerges, Rödl, 2004).

In the United Kingdom, the Chancellor, Gordon Brown's foray into the discussion of the role and limits of the market in the context of globalisation has helped launch a new debate. In the new BBC4 series 'The Commanding Heights: The Battle for the World Economy' (2003) based on the book by Daniel Yergin and Joseph Stanislaw, Gordon Brown, who headed up the key policy-making IMF committee, told Yergin:

> The problem for the Left in the past was that they equated the public interest with public ownership and public regulation, and therefore they assumed that markets were not in the public interest ... [Markets] provide opportunities for prosperity, but equally they're not automatically equated with the public interest.

He went on to say:

> The idea that markets must work in the public interest, the idea that governments have a responsibility for the level of employment and prosperity in the economy, the idea that governments must intervene on occasions–these are increasingly the ideas of our time.

In an age of consumerism, a fundamental question is to what extent, if at all, the 'citizen-consumer' — a market-democracy hybrid of the subject – can shape privately funded public services in ways other than through their acts of consumption and whether acts of consumption can genuinely enhance the social dimensions of the market (see Peters, 2005c).

Foucault provides us with a means of analyzing the centrality of the rule of law to liberalism and the notion of individual property rights, the constitution of freedom in its different historical forms, and, crucially, the link between the government of the state and the government of the self that has become so important to understanding both neoliberalism and third way politics, especially insofar has it has institutionalised enterprise culture, the twin notions of performance and accountability, and the generalization of all forms of capitalization of the self, including most prominently the entrepreneurial self. In addition, in his most recently published lectures from the Collège de France Foucault provides us with a complex genealogy of the three main forms of contemporary economic liberalism in outline that confounds standard accounts of liberalism and neoliberalism.

NOTES

[1] In his Résumé du cours for 1979 (in Foucault, 2004b: 323) Foucault indicates that the method he will adopt is based on Paul Veyne's nominalist history and in this respect he writes:

Et reprenant un certain nombre de choix de méthode déjà faits, j'ai essayé d'analyser le libéralisme, non pas une théorie ni comme une idéologie, encore moins, bein entendu, comme une mannière pour la société de se\ représenter; mais comme une pratique, c'est-à-dire comme une manière de faire orientée vers objectifs et se régulant par une réflexion continue. Le libéralisme est à analyser alors comme principe et méthode de rationalisation de l'exercice de gouvernement–rationalisation qui obéit, et c'est là sa spécificité, à la règle interne de l'économie maximale.

Foucault (in 2001) explains in "Questions of method" his emphasis on practice with an accent on "eventalization" and "the problem of rationalities". He says, "Eventalizing singular ensembles of practices, so as to make them graspable as different regimes of 'jurisdiction' and 'verification'" (p. 230) and he ascribes the method to Veyne with the following remark "it's a matter of the effect on historical knowledge of a nominalist critique itself arrived at by way of historical analysis" (p. 238). The concept of practice here is crucial to understanding Foucault. Stern (2000: fn 33, p. 358) indicates in a footnote a reference to Dreyfus' course at the NEH Summer Institute on Practices on July 24 1997, under the title "Conclusion: How background practices and skills work to ground norms and intelligibility: the ethico-political implications" and summarises Dreyfus' account of five 'theories' (Wittgenstein and Bourdieu; Hegel and Merleau-Ponty; Heidegger; Derrida; and Foucault). He summarises Foucault's notion as follows: "Problematization. (Foucault) Practices develop in such a way that contradictory actions are felt to be appropriate. Attempts to fix these problems lead to further resistance. This leads to a hyperactive pessimism: showing the contingency of what appears to be necessary and engaging in resistance to established order." See also Schatzki et al (2001).

2 Rousseau's begin his famous 1755 text "Discourse on Political Economy" with the following remark: "The word Economy, or OEconomy, is derived from oikos, a house, and vomos, law, and meant originally only the wise and legitimate government of the house for the common good of the whole family. The meaning of the term was then extended to the government of that great family, the State." Rousseau, as you know, goes on to distinguish between the government of the family and the State, and to deny there is anything in common except the obligations that the head or sovereign owe to their subjects. They are, he argues, based on different rules and that "the first rule of public economy is that the administration of justice should be conformable to the laws" and to the general will. For the full text see: http://www.constitution.org/jjr/polecon.htm.

3 The Foucault archives have been recently relocated from the IMEC (Institut Mémoires de l'Édition Contemporaine) Paris address (9, rue Bleue, F-75009 Paris) to Abbaye d'Ardenne (14280 Saint Germaine la Blanche-Herbe), email: bibliotheque@imec-archives.com. Il faut défender la société, a course Foucault delivered in 1975–1976, was translated into by David Macey as Society Must Be Defended was published in 2003 by Penguin (Foucault, 2003). While courses for 1977–78, 1978–79, as previously mentioned, and 1981–82 (L'Herméneutique de sujet) have been recently published (in the Gallimand/Seuill series), courses for the years 1979–80, 1980–81, 1982–83, 1983–84 are still only available from the IMEC Foucault archive as recorded tapes.

4 The governmentality literature has grown up around the journal Economy and Society, and includes the work of Cruickshank, Hindess, Hunter, Larner, Minson, O'Malley, Owen, and others, as well as those referred to above, most of who have published in Economy and Society (for aims and scope, and table of contents, see http://www.tandf.co.uk/journals/titles/03085147.asp).

5 See my essay "Why Foucault?" (Peters, 2003c) where I discuss Foucault studies in the English-speaking world by reference to the work of Marshall, Olssen, Ball, Popkewitz & Brennan, Besley, Baker, Middleton and myself. My work on Foucault's governmentality dates from Peters (1994), with additional work in 1996 (with Marshall), Peters (1996), Peters (1997), and Peters (2001a, b, c). For additional work on Foucault see Peters (2003a & b), Peters (2005a & b). A special issue of Educational Philosophy and Theory will publish a special issue in 2006 entitled "The Learning Society and Governmentality" edited by Masschelein, Bröckling, Simons and Pongratz.

6 As he writes in his Résumé du cours (in Foucault, 2004b: 323):
Le thème retenu était doc la biopolitique: j'entendais par là la manière don't on a essayé, depuis le XVIII siècle, de rationaliser les problèmes posés à la pratique gouvenrement par les phénomènes propres à une ensemble de vivants constitutes en population: santé, hygiene, natalitié, longévité, races...

7 Foucault investigates the notion of civil society – a twin notion to homo economicus and indissociable elements of the technology of liberal government – by reference to Adam Ferguson (1996), a philosopher of the Scottish Enlightenment, whose An Essay on the History of Civil Society, first

published in 1767, as an inquiry into the "natural history of man", seeks to elucidate the general characteristics of human nature (including principles of self-preservation, union, war, etc.), provide a "history of rude nations", policy and arts, and comments on the advancement of civil and commercial arts, as well as "the decline of nations" and "corruption and political slavery".

[8] Foucault refers to the work of F. Bilger (1964) La Pensée économique libérale de l'Allemagne contemporaine. For a brief chronological biography of Erhard see http://www.dhm.de/lemo/html/biografien/ErhardLudwig/.

[9] Foucault (2004b) notes that Eucken knew and met with Husserl. Foucault refers to the phenomenological roots of German ordoliberalism.

[10] Vanberg (2004) argues that the constitutional approach of the ordoliberals distanced itself from laissez-faire economics and is closely modelled by James Buchanan's constitutional economics. Vanberg also notes differences that occurred in discussions at the Mont Pelerin Society between Eucken and Mises. While Eucken knew Hayek since the early 1920s, Vanberg argues that ordoliberalism was a German invention that was not influenced by Anglo-Saxon influences or the Austrian School. See also Broyer (1996) and Witt (2002). For the continued relevance of ordoliberalism and the social market model see Joerges, Rödl (2004).

REFERENCES

Barry, A., Osborne, T., & Rose, N. (Eds.). (1996). *Foucault and political reason: Liberalism, neoliberalism and rationalities of government.* London: UCL Press.

Becker, G. (1964). *Human capital: A theoretical and empirical analysis, with special reference to education.* New York: National Bureau of Economic Research; distributed by Columbia University Press.

Broyer, S. (1996). *The social market economy: Birth of an economic style.* Discussion paper FS I 96-318, Social Science Research Center, Berlin.

Buchanan, J. (1991). *Constitutional economics.* Oxford, UK: Blackwell.

Burchell, G., Gordon, C., & Miller, P. (Eds.). (1991). *The foucault effect: Studies in governmentality.* Chicago: University of Chicago Press and Harvester.

Curtis, B. (2002, Fall). Foucault on governmentality and population: The impossible discovery. *Canadian Journal of Sociology, 27*(4), 505–535.

Dean, M. (1999). *Governmentality: Power and rule in modern society.* London: Sage.

Ferguson, A. (1996). An essay on the history of civil society 1767 (D. Forbes, Ed.). Edinburgh, UK: Edinburgh University Press.

Foucault, M. (1977). *Discipline and punish: The birth of the prison* (A. Sheridan, Trans.). London: Penguin.

Foucault, M. (1977). *Language, counter-memory, practice: Selected essays and interviews* (D. Bouchard, Ed.). Oxford, UK: Blackwell.

Foucault, M. (1982). The subject and power. In H. L. Dreyfus & P. Rabinow (Eds.), *Michel Foucault: Beyond structuralism and hermeneutics* (pp. 208–226). Chicago: University of Chicago.

Foucault, M. (1984). What is enlightenment? In P. Rabinow (Ed.), *The Foucault reader* (pp. 32–50). New York: Pantheon.

Foucault, M. (1985). *The use of pleasure: The history of sexuality* (Vol. 2, R. Hurley, Trans.). New York: Pantheon.

Foucault, M. (1986). Kant on enlightenment and revolution. *Economy and Society, 15*(1), 88–96.

Foucault, M. (1989). *'Resume des cours 190–1982.* Paris: conferencs, essais et lecons du Collège de France', Paris, Julliard.

Foucault, M. (1997). The ethics of the concern for the self as a practice of freedom. In Rabinow (Ed.) & R. J. Hurley (Trans.), *Ethics: Subjectivity and truth. Essential works of Michel Foucault, 1954–1984* (Vol. 1, pp. 281–301). London: Penguin.

Foucault, M. (2001). *Power: Michel Foucault the essential works 1954–1984* (Vol. 3, J. D. Faubion Ed., R. Hurley & others Trans.). London: Allen Lane & The Penguin Press.

Foucault, M. (2003). *Society must be defended* (D. Macey, Trans.). New York: Picador.

Foucault, M. (2004a). Sécurité, Territoire, Population: Cours au collège de France (1977–1978), Édition établie sous la direction de Francois Ewald et Alessandro Fontana, par Michel Senellart, Paris, Éditions Gallimand et des Éditions du Seuill.

Foucault, M. (2004b). Naissance de la biopolitique: Cours au collège de France (1978–1979) [English Translation title]. Édition établie sous la direction de Francois Ewald et Alessandro Fontana, par Michel Senellart, Paris, Éditions Gallimand et des Éditions du Seuill.

Gordon, C. (2001). "Introduction" to Power. In J. D. Faubion (Ed.), R. Hurley & others (Trans.), *Michel Foucault the essential works 1954–1984* (Vol. 3, pp. xi–xli). London: Allen Lane & The Penguin Press.

Gray, J. N. (1982, Winter) F. A. Hayek and the rebirth of classical liberalism. *Literature of Liberty, 5*(4). Retrieved September 6, 2008, from http://www.econlib.org/library/Essays/LtrLbrty/gryHRC1. html

Hayek, F. A. (1960). *The constitution of liberty*. Chicago: University of Chicago Press.

Joerges, C., & Rödl, F. (2004). *'Social Market Economy' as Europe's Social Model?* European University Institute (Florence) Working paper LAW No. 2004/8 Retrieved September 6, 2008, from www.iut.it

Miller, P., & Rose, N. (1990). Governing economic life. *Economy and Society, 19*(1), 1–31.

Peters, M., & Marshall, J. (1996). *Individualism and community: Education and social policy in the postmodern condition*. London: FalmerPress.

Peters, M. (1994). Governmentalidade Neoliberal e Educacao [Neoliberal govermentality and education]. In T. Tadeu da Silva (Ed.), *O Sujeito Educacao, Estudos Foucaulianos*. Rio de Janeiro: Editora Vozes.

Peters, M. (1996). *Poststructuralism, politics and education*. London: Bergin and Garvey.

Peters, M. (1997). Neoliberalism, welfare dependency and the moral construction of poverty in New Zealand. *New Zealand Journal of Sociology, 12*(1), 1–34.

Peters, M. (2001a). *Foucault, neoliberalism and the governance of welfare, Chapter 4 of post-structuralism, marxism, and neoliberalism: between theory and politics*. Lanham, MD and Oxford, UK: Rowman and Littlefield.

Peters, M. A. (2001b). Education, enterprise culture and the entrepreneurial self: A foucauldian perspective. *Journal of Educational Enquiry, 2*(2). (Online-only journal).

Peters, M. A. (2001c). Foucault and governmentality: Understanding the neoliberal paradigm of education policy. *The School Field, 12*(5/6), 59–80.

Peters, M. A. (2003a). Truth-telling as an educational practice of the self: Foucault, Parrhesia and the ethics of subjectivity. *Oxford Review of Education, 29*(2), 207–223.

Peters, M. A. (2003b). *Educational Research, 'Games of Truth' and the Ethics of Subjectivity*. Ethical Educational Research: Practices Of The Self, Symposium: Michael A. Peters, Tina Besley, Clare Caddell, BERA. Unpublished.

Peters, M. A. (2003c). "Why Foucault? New Directions in Anglo-American Educational Research", Invited keynote at the conference "After Foucault: Perspectives of the Analysis of Discourse and Power in Education", 29–31 October, 2003, The University of Dortmund. In: Pongratz L. et al. (Eds.) (2004). *Nach Foucault. Diskurs- und machtanalytische Perspectiven der Pädagogik*. Wiesbaden: VS Verlag Für Sozialwissenschaften.

Peters, M. (2004). Citizen-consumers, social markets and the reform of public services. forthcoming in. *Policy Futures in Education, 2*(3 & 4), 621–632.

Peters, M. A. (2005a). Foucault, counselling and the aesthetics of existence. forthcoming *The British Journal of Counselling and Guidance*, special issue on Foucault and counselling, eds. Tina Besley and Richard Edwards, 33(3), 383–396.

Peters, M. A. (2005b). The new prudentialism in education: Actuarial rationality and the entrepreneurial self. 55(2), 123–137(15).

Pignatelli, F. (1993). Dangers, possibilities: Ethico-political choices. In *The work of Michel Foucault.* Retrieved September 6, 2008, from http://www.ed.uiuc.edu/EPS/PES-Yearbook/93_docs/ PIGNATEL. HTM

Rose, N. (1999). *Powers of liberty.* Cambridge, UK: Cambridge University Press.

Schatzki, T., Knorr, C. K., & Von Savigny, E. (Eds.). (2001). *The practice turn in contemporary theory.* London and New York: Routledge.

Vanberg, V. (2004). *The Freiburg school: Walter Eucken and ordoliberalism. Freiburg discussion papers on constitutional economics.* Retrieved September 6, 2008, from http://opus.zbw-kiel.de/ volltexte/2004/2324/pdf/04_11bw.pdf

Witt, U. (2002). Germany's 'Social market economy': Between social ethos and rent seeking. *The Independent Review, 4*(3), 365–375.

Michael A Peters
University of Illinois
Urbana Champaign
USA

QIZHI YU

7. REFLECTIONS ON GOVERNMENTALITY

The neologism 'governmentality' which means the new art of government based on the principle of *laisser faire* or neoliberalism, was created by Foucault[1] using the word 'government' and its relations, and was a main subject during Foucault's last years (1978-1984). It constituted the central concept of History of Systems of Thought in the series of eight courses, concerning society, security, territory, population[2], biopower, biopolitics, living, subjectivity, truth, subject, self, others, etc. (see Besley and Peters, 2007, p. 145 and p. 185, and Foucault, 2004, head page). This concept 'governmentality' is very important for enabling Foucault to reflect on the order of power and subjectivation, which is different from knowledge in the sciences of Man or *Order of Things*. It forms an important turning point or Foucauldian revolution: a project on the history of governmentality or a project on the history of systems of thought of 'governmentality'.

In the conferences from 21 to 25 May 1973, Foucault discussed the relation between government and rationality, in which we can see a possibility of combining these two terms:

I do not believe, however, that the procedure of investigation is simply the result of a kind of progress of rationality…The investigation in medieval Europe is especially a process of government, a technique of administration, a modality of management; in other words, the investigation is a given manner to exert the power (Foucault, 1994, p. 584).

Foucault establishes the intrinsic relationship between rationality (perhaps besides legitimacy) and government, and uses always the term "rationality of government" (governmental rationality or government rationality) almost inter-changeable with the term "governmentality" (art of government) (Gordon, 1991, p. 1–48, and Foucault, 1991, p. 89). The word 'governmentality' is made by the co-pattern of three parts 'govern'-'mental'-'ity' or that of two parts 'govern'-'mentality' or 'governmental'-'ity'. According to Hunt and Wickham, Foucault's idea is to include "reason of state, the problem of population, modern political economy, liberal securitization, and the emergence of the human sciences" (http://en.wikipedia.org/wiki/Governmentality).

What does this word 'govern' mean? It means that "one governs things" (*on gouverne des choses*). Foucault quotes Guillaume de La Perrière's statement: "government is the right disposition of things, arranged so as to lead to a convenient end" (cited in Foucault, 1991, p. 93).

I would like to pose a question: what exactly does one govern? For Machiavelli, one doesn't govern 'things' (*choses),* but governs the territory (above all) and its inhabitants (consequently), in other words, "prince's relation with what he owns, with the territory has inherited or acquired, and with his subjects", "the territory

M.A. Peters et al. (eds.), Govermentality Studies in Education, 109–122.

is the fundamental element", and is "the very foundation of principality and sovereignty" (Foucault, 1991, p. 93 and p. 90). However, for La Perrière, one doesn't govern "territory", but "things". Foucault has further seen and thought that what government has to do with "a sort of complex composed of men and things" (Foucault, 1991, p. 93). This is a smart convergence of subject and his object, not a divergence of subject and object. I don't think this is a disappearance of their differences, but their "eternal repetition of differences" (used by Gilles Deleuze), which shows a kind of organic pleat "men-things", or "subject-object", or again "governor-governed". He has written:

> The things with which in this sense government is to be concerned are in fact men, but men in their relations, their links, their imbrication with those other things which are wealth, resources, means of subsistence, territory with its specific qualities, climate, irrigation, fertility, etc.; men in their relation to that other kind of things, customs, habits, ways of acting and thinking, etc.; lastly, men in their relation to that other kind of things, accidents and misfortunes such as famine, epidemics, death, etc. (Foucault, 1991, p. 93).

Foucault introduces 'men' clearly into the structure of government with 'things', and renovates Machiavelli's and La Perrière's definitions of government. "What counts essentially is this complex of men and things; property and territory are merely one of its variables" (Foucault, 1991, p. 94). According to this point, I would like to give a new Foucauldian definition of government: to govern means to govern the complex of men and things, not only to govern things, in other words, government is the right disposition of the complex of men and things, arranged so as to lead to a convenient end. This is an important turning point of the definition of government here. For Foucault, government has a complicated and dual finality of its own. We can see that government becomes men-things government because they coexist and have a sort of co-pattern and co-destiny, and it becomes anthropo-government because for Foucault the things concerning government are really men (body/human body, population/human beings, life, etc., which compose the ensemble of bios in their relations with other things).

"One governs things" is a relational proposition or statement. It establishes the governmental relations which converge three series of imbrications of concrete elements of men-things: a) wealth, resources, means of subsistence, territory... b) customs, habits, ways of acting and thinking...c) famine, epidemics, death...We will see that the government is always open for these three series and disposes them in the different fields, for example, a ship, a household, a country, etc. These series interweave each other and become a governmental labyrinth of men-things containing everything. I would like to think we can see a space where men and things coexist, namely men-thingstopia. One governs everything, and government is everywhere.

Men and things imbricate and inevitably invoke the metaphor of ship. "The fact that government concerns things understood in this way, this imbrication of men and things, is I believe readily confirmed by the metaphor which is inevitably invoked in these treatises on government, namely that of the ship" (Foucault, 1991,

p. 93). I think there is not only a metaphor but also an analogy among a ship, a household, a country, etc., although this metaphor is superior to the analogy. Governing a ship resembles governing a household, governing a country, which all resemble governing a ship. The ship can become a model of the other things. As he writes: "Is it surprising that prisons resemble factories, school, barracks, hospitals, which all resemble prisons?" (Foucault, 1979, p. 228) The metaphor and analogy of the ship let us find resemblances or identities among all the different fields (ships, households, factories, school, clinic, barracks, hospitals, prisons, countries, etc.) of government of the complex of men and things, so as to reach the finality.

According to La Perrière's definition and Foucault's concept "complex of men and things", my definition of government is that "government is the right disposition of the complex of men and things, arranged so as to lead to a convenient end". "Right disposition" means that we must apply a good manner, "complex of men and things" means that men and things are indivisible, "convenient end" means that government is for each element of the complex of men and things who/what are governed. These words have to do with a new art of government which is different from the traditional art of that. Foucault has found a neologism 'governmentality' based on principle of *laisser faire* or neoliberalism.

Foucault saw that the form of 'reason of state' (*Raison d'État, ratio status*) was a kind of obstacle to the development of the art of government until the early eighteenth century. There are many reasons: strictly historical reasons (Thirty Years War, peasant and urban rebellions, financial crisis), "mental and institutional structures of sovereignty" (Foucault, 1991, p. 97). "Contract theory enables the founding contract, the mutual pledge of ruler and subjects, to function as a sort of theoretical matrix for deriving the general principles of an art of government. But...it (contract theory) remained at the stage of the formulation of general principles of public law" (Foucault, 1991, p. 98). Foucault poses a question: "How then was the art of government able to outflank these obstacles?", and he says: "The art of government found fresh outlets through the emergence of the problem of population; or let us say rather that there occurred a subtle process, which we must seek to reconstruct in its particulars, through which the science of government, the recentring of the theme of economy on a different plane from that of the family, and the problem of population are all interconnected" (Foucault, 1991, p. 98). We see that the imbrication of population and economy is formed in the development of the science of government; conversely, the science of the government is possible in this imbrication. There is a solid triangle, population-economy-government.

Foucault poses further another question: "In what way did the problem of population make possible the derestriction of the art of government?" (Foucault, 1991, p. 99). He gives us the following answers: a) "What makes it possible for the theme of population to unblock the field of the art of government is this elimination of the family as model" (Foucault, 1991, p. 100); b) "Interest at the level of the consciousness of each individual who goes to make up the population, and interest considered as the interest of the population regardless of what the particular interests and aspirations may be of the individuals who compose it, this is the new target and the fundamental instrument of the government of population: the birth of a new art, or at any rate of a range of absolutely new tactics and techniques" (Foucault, 1991, p. 100); c) "The transition which takes place in the eighteenth century from an art of government to a political science, from a regime dominated by structures of sovereignty to one ruled by techniques of government, turns on the theme of population and hence also on the birth of political economy" (Foucault, 1991, p. 101). For Foucault, this doesn't signify that sovereignty and discipline have passed, on the contrary, sovereignty and discipline are more important than ever.

"The notion of a government of population renders all the more acute the problem of the foundation of sovereignty (consider Rousseau) and all the more acute equally the necessity for the development of discipline" (Foucault, 1991, p. 102). Foucault says: "In reality one has a triangle, sovereignty-discipline-government" (Foucault, 1991, p. 102). The population is the ultimate end of government and primary target of this triangle, the apparatuses of security is the essential mechanism of this triangle. Evidently, one has also a triangle of society, society of sovereignty-society of discipline-society of government, which are coexistent, and the population becomes the centre of this triangle. So the population and society are pluralistic. In this sense, we can say that government is the right disposition of population as a complex of men and things, arranged so as to lead to a convenient end of population itself, or to govern is to govern population which has to do with things (welfare of the population, improvement of its condition, increase of its wealth, longevity, health, etc.), the most important one of things is economy, just as Quesnay's graceful expression "good government as economic government" (Foucault, 1991, p. 92).

From a genetic point of view we can consider the notion of 'discipline' as a prehistoric notion of governmentality or as a sort of 'pregovernmentality.' We can also think that the word 'governmentality' is a generalized result of the word 'discipline'; for an origin of the word 'governmentality' we can return to *Surveiller et Punir* (*Discipline and Punish*), in which Foucault analyzed all the history of the discipline, and *Histoire de la Sexualité* (*The History of Sexuality, V.1*). Thus, the concepts 'government' and 'art of government' or 'governmentality' posed by Foucault are simply further developments of 'discipline' or 'art of discipline'. If the concept 'discipline' in *Surveiller et Punir* was mainly a concept of partiality, topicality, particularity and materiality, and prepared the scientific conditions of totalization, integration, generalization and abstraction of this concept, in *Security, Territory, Population*, Foucault has completed its totalization, integration, generalization and abstraction. It signifies that the special discipline has been elevated to the general discipline, in other words, discipline in a narrow sense expanded into a wide sense, namely government. The disciplinary society is precisely integrated into the society of government (see Yu, 2007, p. 23). For governmentality, territory is one variable of the complex of men and things or population and economy, body of the individuals is integrated into the population (the human beings), an anatomo-politics of individualized body into a biopolitics of generalized population.

The sovereignty is exerted within the limits of a territory, the discipline is exerted on the body of the individuals, and finally the security is exerted on the whole of a population... The scholastic discipline, the military discipline, the penal discipline also, the discipline in the workshops, the worker discipline, all that, it is a certain manner of managing the multiplicity, of organizing it, of fixing its points of establishment, coordinations, side or horizontal trajectories, vertical and pyramidal trajectories, hierarchy, etc. (Foucault, 2004, p. 13–14).

Foucault defines the governmentality as "singular generality" (généralité singulière, see Senellart, 2004, p. 407–408). Thus governmentality is in fact a general art of right disposition/government (e.g., discipline) of men and things. Senellart quotes Foucault's manuscript on governmentality: "A singular generality: it has only evential reality and its intelligibility can only implement a strategic logic" (see Senellart, 2004, p. 408). Senellart says:

It remains to wonder which bond links, in Foucault's thought, these types of eventiality: that which falls under a particular historical process, specific to the Western society, and that which finds its theoretical anchorage in a general definition of power in term of 'government' (Senellart, 2004, p. 408).

Governmentality is the liberal rationality inherent with the micropower and anatomo-politics, and it has not eliminated the discipline. "Nevertheless, discipline was never more important or more valorized than at the moment when it became important to manage a population" (Foucault, 1991, p. 102). Before Foucault created the concept governmentality and drafted "a project on the history of systems of thought of governmentality", namely discussed the "mechanism of security" or "apparatuses of security" in the course on 25 January 1978, he had attempted to explain how the problem of specific population was born. If we want to explain effectively the specific problems of population, we need to systematically analyze the problem of government or that of the following series: security-population-government (Foucault, 2004, p. 91). Henceforth, government and governmentality become the essential concepts of the project on the "history of systems of thought" in the lectures given by Foucault at the Collège de France.

Further, I would like to say that "one governs things" means "one governs population", population and things which are identical to men and things, are inseparable and become the complex composed of men and things of government. "The population is the subject of needs, of aspiration, but it is also the object in the hand of government" (Foucault, 1991, p. 100). This signifies that government becomes self-government, and art of government is that of governing the self, governmentality is egogovernmentality or self-governmentality, governmental culture is culture of self, governmental care is care of self, governmental technology is technology of self...

According to governmentality, government is government of population, which has to do with things, especially their most important element 'economy'. So we can say that government constitutes the imbrication of population and economy (or men and things), but does not cause their opposition. Clearly, population becomes economic population (economic men or homo œconomicus). The term 'economy', namely 'government of the family', has the central position in the art of government of continuity: an upwards continuity (governing himself- his goods- his patrimony-the state) and a downwards continuity (the state- his patrimony- his goods - governing himself). Foucault believes that the essential issue in the establishment of the art of government is to introduce economy into political practice. "And if this is the case in sixteenth century, it remains so in the eighteenth" (Foucault, 1991, p. 92). I would like to say that it is equally so in our century, or in the era of a globalization of economy, because the development of economy with the problem of territory is a central variable of concerning directly the condition of population or livelihood of people and that of alleviating the poverty.

What is governmentality? We can follow Clare O'Farrell's simple definition and that provided by Wikipedia:

> Foucault originally used the term "governmentality" to describe a particular way of administering populations in modern European history within the context of the rise of the idea of the State. He later expanded his definition to encompass the techniques and procedures which are designed to govern the conduct of both individuals and populations at every level not just the administrative or political level
>
> (http://www.foucault.qut.edu.au/concepts/index.html).
>
> In his lectures at the Collège de France, Foucault often defines governmentality as the 'art of government' in a wide sense, i.e., with an idea of 'government' that is not limited to state politics alone, that includes a wide range of control techniques, and that applies to a wide variety of objects, from one's control of the self to the 'biopolitical' control of populations. In the work of Foucault, this notion is indeed linked to other concepts such as biopolitics and power-knowledge
>
> (http://en.wikipedia.org/wiki/Governmentality)

Further, Foucault gives us a definition of governmentality (we see here the place of birth of this beautiful term after using the term 'art of government' from the beginning to here in the lecture on 1 February 1978) which means three following things:
- The ensemble formed by the institutions, procedures, analyses and reflections, the calculations and tactics that allow the exercise of this very specific albeit complex form of power, which has as its target population, as its principal form of knowledge political economy, and as its essential technical means apparatuses of security.
- The tendency which, over a long period and throughout the West, has steadily led towards the pre-eminence over all other forms (sovereignty, discipline, etc.) of this type of power which may be termed government, resulting, on the one hand, in formation of a whole series of specific governmental apparatuses, and, on the other, in the development of a whole complex of *savoirs*.
- The process, or rather the result of the process, through which the state of justice of the Middle Ages, transformed into the administrative state during the fifteenth and sixteenth centuries, gradually becomes "governmentalized" (Foucault, 1991, p. 102–103, and Foucault, 2004, p. 111–112).

For Foucault the governmentality, which means the new art of government or liberal art of government, is based on the government concerning for the domains of application the function of states and a politico-military technology and a police. From the eighteenth century to our present, government, population and political economy compose a solid triangle, and Foucault tries to find the inherent relationship among movement of government, movement of population and movement of political economy in this triangle. In the process of three movements, it is the governmentality which has established their relations.

> Maybe, after all, the state is no more than a composite reality and a mythicized abstraction, whose importance is a lot more limited than many of us think. Maybe what is really important for our modernity — that is, for our present — is not so much the *étatisation* of society, as the "governmentalization" of the state (Foucault, 1991, p. 103).

Foucault thinks that the governmentalization is more important than the *étatisation* in our present time. This is an inevitable contemporary tendency, but in China there is an imbrication of *étatisation* and governmentalization, or a link between quasi-*étatisation* and quasi-governmentalization which coexist. According to Foucault, "We live in the era of 'governmentality' first discovered in the eighteenth century" (Foucault, 1991, p. 103). The pastoral and the new diplomatic-military techniques where the governmentality was born out of, and the police which was contemporaneous with the art of government, make the Western state governmentalized. But I would like to believe that the governmentality, namely new technology of power based on liberalism, integrates the art of government. It's the governmentality which reduces the function of the state, which makes the state of justice and state of administration become the state of government, which makes the society of laws and society of regulation and discipline become the society of population. Thus the population becomes a central object of government.

Until now, we have almost understood Foucault's notions of government and governmentality. Foucault has answered this essential question: "How to govern?" ("*Comment gouverner?*") This is a philosophical question what Foucault was interested in. As Gordon says:

> Foucault …was interested in government as an activity or practice, and in arts of government as ways of knowing what that activity consisted in, and how it might be carried on. A rationality of government will thus mean a way or system of thinking about the nature of the practice of government (who can govern; what governing is; what or who is governed); capable of making some form of that activity thinkable and practicable both to its practitioners and to those upon whom it was practised. Here, as elsewhere in his work, Foucault was interested in the philosophical questions posed by the historical, contingent and humanly invented existence of varied and multiple forms of such a rationality (Gordon, 1991, p. 3).

According to the idea of new art of government or governmentality as rationality of government or governmental rationality, we see obviously there is a problem of just measure of government. That is a just measure, which means governmental rationality, between the governor and the governed. The governor refers to who can govern or governs the governed and the governed means what or who can be or is governed. The governor governs the governed (men or things). According to La Perrière, "governor can signify monarch, emperor, king, prince, lord, magistrate, prelate, judge and the like" (see Foucault, 1991, p. 90). According to the other writers, the governed can signify household, souls, children, province, convent, religious order, and family (see Foucault, 1991, p. 90). The question of the art of government is in fact that of 'how to govern', that is the following question: 'how does the governor govern the governed?' At the beginning of the lecture concerning 'governmentality' on 1 February 1978, Foucault posed a series of questions about the art of government: "How to govern oneself, how to be governed, how to govern others, by whom the people will accept being governed, how to become the best possible governor" (Foucault, 1991, p. 87). After his lecture, Foucault gave another lecture "What is Critique?" (I think this essay merits special discussion, as did Butler, see Butler, 2002) at the *Société Française de Philosophie* on 27 May 1978 At the beginning, he posed again another series of questions interlinked with the above-mentioned series of questions:

How to govern the children, how to govern the poor and the beggars, how to govern a family, a household, how to govern the armies, how govern the various groups, the cities and states, how to govern his proper body, how to govern his souls (Foucault, 1990, p. 37).

It's wonderful that Foucault, in view of the question "how to govern?" poses a new question which was not posed in the lecture on 'governmentality' on 1 February 1978: "how not to be governed?" (Foucault, 1990, p. 37). In connection with 'government', he finds a competition point: not to be governed or not to be governed like that and at this price, that is antigovernment or degovernment, correspondingly, in connection with 'governmentality', he advances "the art of not being governed or again art of not being governed like that and at this price", namely 'antigovernmentality' or 'degovernmentality'. In fact this is a game between the governor and the governed, who are partner and adversary. Face to face with "governing so much" of the governor, the governed dares to use own reason or understanding to say "yes" at the same time said "no". "Yes" here means "obey the government", "no", "not to obey the government like that". This is without doubt a kind of noble critical attitude as virtue in general, also is a kind of valuable Enlightenment mentality. The governed shouts again the motto of Enlightenment: "*Sapere Aude*![dare to know] Have courage to use your own understanding!" (*Was ist Aufklärung?*, Kant, 1784) The critique is "the art of not being governed like that", isn't "the art of not being governed at all", it's a result of the bidirectional movement of the struggle and compromise between the governor and the governed, namely their interactive result. In this sense, there are limits of the right to govern the governed, this means that the rights of the governed or rights of man are possible: the governed can say to his governor: "I don't want to be governed by you so much."

Therefore, the governor and the governed have reached a balance point, which is precisely the competition point. The appropriate government or rational government will be really possible. This is a convenient end that the governmentality will lead us achieve. It is this critical attitude which the governor and the governed imbricate each other, but do not separate each other. "The governor governs the governed", what does it mean? It means the mutual pledge, game and imbrication. We see here a kind of new complex of subject and object (the governor and the governed), who are in their relation to the critique/criticalattitude and the Enlightenment/Enlightenment mentality.

Foucault defines the critique by *"l'art de n'être pas tellement gouverné"*: the critique is the art of not being governed so much (Foucault, 1990, p. 38). This is a new definition and new proposition of critique. "How not to be governed so much", means "how not to be governed like that, by that, in the name of these principles, for such objectives and by the means of such procedures, not like that, not for that, not by them (*comment ne pas être gouverné comme cela, par cela, au nom de ces principes-ci, en vue de tels objectifs et par le moyen de tels procédés, pas comme ça, pas pour ça, pas par eux* (Foucault, 1990, p. 38))". As Foucault says: "Things must be disposed" (Foucault, 1991, p. 95), things must be criticized, that is to disbelieve, to challenge, to limit, to transform, etc. all the pedagogical, political and economical arts of governing so much. This is a "critical attitude" called by Foucault.

He fixes three following senses, namely precise and historical points of anchorage (*points d'ancrage précis et historiques*), of the critical attitude (Foucault, 1990, p. 38–39):
– The first point of anchorage: in a era when the government of men was essentially a spiritual art, or essentially a religious practice in relation with the authority of the Church and that of the Bible, to not want to be governed like that, this was essentially to seek from the Bible another relation which linked up with God's function of the dogma.
– To not want to be governed, this is here the second point of anchorage, to not want to be governed like that, this is not any longer to want to accept these laws.
– Finally, "to not want to be governed", this is certainly not to accept as truth, where I am going to pass very quickly, what an authority tell you be true, or at least this is not to accept it because an authority tell you what it is true.

These three points proposed by Foucault tell very clearly us that the critique is respectively biblical, juridical and anti-authoritative. We can say that the critique is the art of refusing, challenging and limiting the Bible, the writing, and the authority of the Church; the right, the nature, and the law; the science, the relation with oneself, and the authority of dogmatism. For Foucault, the focal point of critique is in essence the relationship net composed of power, truth and subject. The governor, such as monarch, emperor, king, prince, lord, magistrate, prelate, judge, educator, *pater familias* and the like, has the aid of the mechanisms of power that adhere to a truth for subjugating the individuals as subject or governed. The critique is to say "no" in face of governor and his authority, and takes a kind of general responsibility. Therefore the critique is a virtue in general. To say "to not want to be governed like that" is to express and practise this *critical virtue*. By the critical virtue, "the subject gives himself the right to question truth on its effects of power and question power on its discourses of truth" (Foucault, 1990, p. 39, and see Butler, 2002). Just as Butler writes:

> To be governed is not only to have a form imposed upon one's existence, but to be given the terms within which existence will and will not be possible. A subject will emerge in relation to an established order of truth, but it can also take a point of view on that established order that retrospectively suspends its own ontological ground (Butler, 2002).

Governmentality studies, created and developed roughly by Foucault and continued and deepened by the other thinkers, for example, 'neo-Foucauldians' Gordon, Burchell, Rose, Miller, Dean, Barry and al. (see Besley and Peters, 2007, p. 132 and p. 183, and Senellart, 2004, p. 409–410), belong to a high Kantian enterprise or critique, and is one of some possible roads (Foucault, 1990, p. 36–37). In his essay "What is Critique?" Foucault developed further his notion of governmentality (new art of government) and idea of relation between critique and Enlightenment which prepared his very important course, "What is Enlightenment?" (the first course in 1983, which became his more well-known text as his badge (*blazon*) or amulet (*fétiche*), published in Rabinow, P. (ed), *The Foucault Reader*, 1984) at the Collège de France. "What is Critique?" and "What is Enlightenment?" are two equally important and essential questions, and they are internally relational.

The importance of the lecture "What is Critique?" is to explain the profound relation between critique and Enlightenment. Foucault thinks that this definition of critique, "the critique is the art of not being governed so much", is not very different from that of the Enlightenment given by Kant:

> Enlightenment is man's emergence from his self-imposed immaturity. Immaturity is the inability to use one's understanding without guidance from another. This immaturity is self-imposed when its cause lies not in lack of understanding, but in lack of resolve and courage to use it without guidance from another. *Sapere Aude!* [dare to know] "Have courage to use your own understanding!"—that is the motto of Enlightenment[3], *Beantwortung der Frage: Was ist Aufklärung? Berlinische Monatsschrift,* Kant, 1784, 2, S. 481–494).

By this definition of Enlightenment, Foucault discovers the coherence between definition of critique and that of Enlightenment. Maybe, we think that Foucault has defined the critique based on Kant's definition of Enlightenment (*Aufklärung*). Foucault indicates that Kant has founded the connection between Enlightenment and immaturity — "Immaturity is the inability to use one's understanding without guidance from another" — here the word "guidance (guide)" (*Leitung/ leiten, conduite/conduire*) has a religious sense. It is very characteristic that Kant has defined the *Unvermögen* (inability incapacity) by way of a relation between exercised authority and authority in the self-imposed immaturity of man, and a relation between excess authority and lack of decision and courage. It is very characteristic that Kant points out the examples of man's immaturity: religion, right, and knowledge, which correspond to the precise and historical points of anchorage (*points d'ancrage précis et historiques*) of the critical attitude: the Bible, the writing, and the authority of the Church; the right, the nature, and the law; the science, the relation with self, and the authority of dogmatism.

Evidently, the Enlightenment and critique have the co-points of anchorage and are consistent. Just here, the Enlightenment makes immature man as the guided become the adult or Man, and the critique makes man as the governed have a good command of the art of not being governed so much or say "not to want to be governed like that". Foucault further says:

> Having to do with the Enlightenment, the critique will be for Kant what he is going to say to the knowledge: do you know well until where you can know? Reason as much as what you want, but do you know well until where you can reason without danger? (Foucault, 1990, p. 41)

We see that, when Foucault spoke of the obstacle to the development of the art of government, he wrote:

> It is the population itself on which government will act either directly through large-scale campaigns, or indirectly through techniques that will make possible, without the full awareness of the people…the population the subject of needs, of aspirations, but it is also the object in the hands of the government, aware, *vis-à-vis* the government, of what it wants, but ignorant of what is being done to it (Foucault, 1991, p. 100).

Kant restates "*Sapere aude* [*wage es verständig zu sein*/dare to know]!", but another contrary voice which comes of Frédéric II is similarly important: "Argue as much as you want and about what you want, but obey!" (http://www.english. upenn.edu/~mgamer/Etexts/kant.html, and see Foucault, 1990, p. 40).

Foucault skilfully connects critique, Enlightenment and government. Foucault's definition of critique — "the critique is the art of not being governed so much" — is original, distinctive and creative because he has not simply repeated Kant's definition of critique. Either we may say that, he further confirmed and advanced Kant's philosophical enterprise of critique through the Kantian Enlightenment, and through giving a negative dimension of government — not to be governed like that (so much) — he has further made a connection between the critique and the Enlightenment, or he has relieved the distance and opposition between them, thus caused them to establish the relation: the critique and the Enlightenment not only are the matches, but also are the partners. We felt that, the relations between them are quite complex, surpass our imagination.

'Critique', 'Enlightenment' and 'government', like 'security', 'territory', 'population', form a new trinity/triangle. We see here man must persist in the principle of autonomy, and the principle of autonomy belongs to the critique and the Enlightenment. Foucault writes:

> Lorsqu'on se sera fait de sa propre connaissance une idée juste, que l'on pourra découvrir le principe de l'autonomie et que l'on n'aura plus à entendre le *obéissez*; ou plutôt que le *obéissez* sera fondé sur l'autonomie elle-même. /When one forms for his own knowledge a right idea, that one will be able to discover the principle of autonomy and that one will not have to hear any

more the *obey*; or rather than the *obey* will be founded on autonomy itself (Foucault, 1990, p. 41).

"The *obey*" takes autonomy itself as its foundation. Only if the governed persists in the principle of autonomy, he can say "not to be governed like that" to his governor and doesn't accept the government like that; only if he persists in the critical attitude and the Enlightenment mentality, he can avoid into the governor's slave without the autonomy; the desubjugation (*désassujetissement*) is possible, Foucault says: "critique essentially insure the desubjugation of the subject...in a word, the politics of truth" (quoted by Butler, 2002).

Further, the trinity "critique-Enlightenment-government", as an idea, has specifically manifested the governmentality effect. The governmentality is the art of governing everything, including idea, notion, theory, knowledge, etc. Thus we can get a notion of "governmentality of the idea". As if we can understand the "government of the state" and the "governmentalization of the state", we can understand the government of the "idea" and governmentalization of the "idea".

Obviously, on the one hand, the "idea" becomes the object of the government or that of the governmentalization, and the question is posed here: how to govern the "idea" (notion, theory, knowledge, etc.)? The question of government of the "idea" should be integrated into the field of the "governmentality" in general and that of the "governmentalization" in general. "Government of the state" and "government of the idea" are inseparable. On the other hand, the state itself and its security, its territory, its population and so on are integrated into our discussion, they become the idea, the concept, the word, the thought, the theory, the knowledge, and they all are subject to the government, similarly, we must consider "critique", "Enlighten-ment" and "government itself" as the objects of the government and those of the governmentalization. Government itself has also its problem of government, since all of the things — in which government is an important element — wait for the government. The things must be disposed or governed. The problem of government as the object of government is: "How to govern our idea?" Government must become its object; this is a sort of reflexivity. This is in fact a problem of meta-government, i.e., that of government of governments. Maybe, the critique ought to help us resolve this problem.

Foucault unfolds a negative dimension of the government through the definition of critique: 'Not to be governed', namely 'to degovern like that' or 'degovernment'. The word 'degovernment' is a partner and a match for 'government'. The 'govern-ment', 'not to be governed like that', must be artistic; at the same time, as the 'government', the 'degovernment' ('not to be governed like that') also has its history, namely the history of degovernment, relates and synchronizes with the history of government; similarly, 'the art of not being governed like that', namely the art of degovernment, as the governmentality, also has its history, namely a history of critique, which relates and synchronizes with the history of govern-mentality. This degovernmentality, wholly as the governmentality, must be bring into our reflections and concerns the governed. Maybe, we live in the era of a complex composed of governmentality and degovernmentality which always interact.

With degovernmentality, governmentality is very important because "the state can only be understood in its survival and its limits on the basis of the general tactics of governmentality" (Foucault, 1991, p. 103), thus the notion (or perhaps theory) of governmentality created and researched by Foucault is equally important for our postmodernity, and "has given rise to a vast field of research, since ten years, in the Anglo-Saxon countries, and more recently in Germany, the '*governmentality studies*'" (Foucault, 2004, p. 409). Governmentality studies and their generalization and application by neo-Foucauldians, are on the rise, including a few neo-Foucauldian concepts, for example, biogovernmentality, ecogovernmentalty, etc. The term "biogovernmentality" is used by João Biehl, who writes:

> After briefly historicizing the development of this novel form of bio-governmentality, I will examine concrete situations in which the AIDS policy is involved and the ways in which it affects local trajectories of the epidemic both institutionally and in lived experience, particularly in urban poor contexts where AIDS is spreading most rapidly (Biehl, 2005, p. 249–250).

'Ecogovernmentality' means environmentality: art of environmental protection.

> Ecogovernmentality (also spelled Eco-governmentality) is a term used to denote the application of Foucault's concepts of biopower and governmentality to the analysis of the regulation of social interactions with the natural world. Begun in the mid 1990s by a small body of theorists (Luke, Darier, and Rutherford) the literature on ecogovernmentality grew as a response to the perceived lack of Foucauldian analysis of environmentalism and environmental studies. Ecogovernmentality focuses on how government agencies, in combination with producers of expert knowledge, construct 'The Environment'. This construction is viewed both in terms of the creation of an object of knowledge and a sphere within which certain types of intervention and management are created and deployed to further the government's larger aim of managing the lives of its constituents. This governmental management is dependent on the dissemination and internalization of knowledge/power among individual actors. This creates a decentered network of self-regulating elements whose interests become integrated with those of the State (http://en.wikipedia.org/wiki/Governmentality#Ecogovernmentality).

Evidently, 'biogovernmentality' is the integration of life in governmentality, and 'ecogovernmentality' is the integration of environment in governmentality. Governmentality proves to be a very fruitful concept – one that we will continue studying and applying extensively in diverse fields – a very open concept.

NOTES

¹ An Italian version of this lecture, given at the Collège de France on 1 February 1978, is published in *Aut-Aut* 167-8, September-December 1978, p. 12–29; the English version by Rosi Braidotti is published in *Ideology and Consciousness*, № 6 (Autumn 1979), then revised by C. Gordon, in Graham Burchell, Colin Gordon and Peter Miller (Eds). 1991, p. 87–104; the first French version is edited in *Actes*, № spec. 54: *Foucault hors les Murs*, été 1986, p. 6–15, and reincluded in *Dits et*

Ecrits, 1954–1988, III, № 239, p. 635–657, and the new and complete French edition in *Sécurité, Territoire, Population* (2004) is totally revised according to the record and manuscript; the Chinese version translated from the English version, is published in Min'an Wang, Yongguo Chen and Yunpeng Zhang (Eds), *Modernity: The Reader II*, Henan University Press, 2005, p. 383–398.

² The word 'population' means "a global mass (a large number of people, a mass of living and co-existing beings, l'homme vivant, l'homme être vivant, l'homme-espèce versus l'homme-corps — my notation), affected of processes of ensemble which are specific to the life, and which are processes like the birth, the death, the production, the disease, etc." (Foucault, *'Il faut défendre la société'*, Paris: Seuil/Gallimard, p. 216). Foucault tries to integrate the human body of individualization into the human beings of totalization, an anatomo-politics of human body into a biopolitics of human beings.

³ This English traduction from http://www.english.upenn.edu/~mgamer/Etexts/kant.html.

REFERENCES

Besley, A. C., & Peters, M. A. (2007). *Subjectivity & truth: Foucault, education and the culture of self.* New York: Peter Lang.

Biehl, J. (2005). Technologies of invisibility: Politics of life and social inequality. In J. X. Inda (Eds.), *Anthropologies of modernity: Foucault, governmentality, and life politics.* Malden, MA: Blackwell Publishing Ltd.

Butler, J. (2002). What is critique? An essay on foucault's virtue. In D. Ingram (Ed.), *The political: Readings in continental philosophy.* London: Basil Blackwell.

Foucault, M. (1979). *Discipline and punish.* New York: Vintage Books Edition.

Foucault, M. (1990). Qu'est-ce que la Critique?, a lecture given at the Société Française de Philosophie on 27 May 1978, published. In *Bulletin de la Société Française de Philosophie*, 80ᵉ Année, № 2 (pp. 35–63). Paris: Armand Colin.

Foucault, M. (1991). Governmentality (R. Braidotti Trans. & C. Gordon Rev.). In G. Burchell, C. Gordon, & P. Miller (Eds.), *The Foucault effect: Studies in governmentality* (pp. 87–104). Chicago: University of Chicago Press.

Foucault, M. (1994). La Vérité et les Formes Juriques. In D. Defert & F. Ewald (Ed.), *Dits et Ecrits. 1954–1988 II (1970–1975).* Paris: Editions Gallimard.

Foucault, M. (2004). *Sécurité, Territoire, Population. Cours au College de France. 1977–1978.* Paris: Seuil/Gallimard.

Gordon, C. (1991). Governmental rationality: An introduction. In G. Burchell, C. Gordon, & P. Miller (Eds.), *The Foucault effect: Studies in governmentality* (pp. 87–104). Chicago: University of Chicago Press.

Senellart, M. (2004). Situation des Cours, in Foucault, M. (2004). *Sécurité, Territoire, Population. Cours au College de France. 1977–1978.* Paris: Seuil and Gallimard.

Yu, Q. (2007). How does Foucault treat Marx? *Modern Philosophy* (China), *93*(6), 19–27.

Qizhi Yu
Institute of Philosophy
South China Normal University
People's Republic Of China

**II. FOUCAULT, EDUCATION AND GOVERNMENTALITY:
ANGLO-AMERICAN PERSPECTIVES**

THOMAS OSBORNE

8. FOUCAULT AS EDUCATOR

Of all the offence Schopenhauer has given to numerous scholars, nothing has offended them more than the unfortunate fact that he does not resemble them (Nietzsche, 1874).

The argument of this paper is simple and probably obvious. It can be briefly and bluntly stated. It is that Michel Foucault was not only and straightforwardly a thinker and a researcher, but was also – and fundamentally – an educator.

STYLE

Our most basic source of evidence for this is Foucault's own obviously educational work; his teaching, his lectures (see Foucault 2003; 2004; 2006 and 2007). Some distinctive aspects of these shall be our main focus in what follows (cf. Osborne, 2008; chapter 3).

In discussing Foucault's lectures I want to invoke the notion of *style*. The lectures raise the question of educational style most obviously because here we have – as it were, directly – the author's personal voice. This is to invoke the notion of style in what Ian Hacking would call a personalising rather than a generalizing sense (Hacking, 1992); it is style as the personal signature of the teacher. Perhaps this distinction is, as Hacking himself suggests, a rather crude approach to the topic. And certainly style in this context cannot *just* be a matter of personal voice. It is not just that the lecturer is present in person and that it is indeed *his* voice we can hear – although this can hardly be irrelevant to an author's style. The sense of a live performance is certainly integral to the lecture as an event, yet this is a precarious relation – as Erving Goffman showed. For if a lecture were simply and only a performance, simply a question of the speaker's own personal style, then nothing – or at least nothing serious – would get conveyed. What counts is a certain combination of content and form. As Goffman wrote:

> [L]ectures must not be presented as if engrossment were the controlling intent. Indeed, lectures draw on a precarious ideal: certainly the listeners are to be carried away so that time slips by, but because of the speaker's subject matter, not his antics; the subject matter is meant to have its own enduring claims upon the listeners apart from the felicities or infelicities of the presentation (Goffman, 1981, p. 166).

So the style of a lecture has to do with more than just the surface effects of speech itself. Style relates also to subject-matter, to content, to the concepts and ideas which give that subject-matter its shape and which are inseparable from it. Style inheres in the movement of the concepts and ideas that are presented, their velocity, their directionality, their rhythm, their juxtaposition.

M.A. Peters et al. (eds.), Govermentality Studies in Education, 125–136.
© *2009 Sense Publishers. All rights reserved.*

What is specific to Foucault's lectures in terms of their style? Of course this question cannot be separated from that of Foucault's style as a whole; in his books and interviews as well as his lectures. It was Gilles Deleuze who alluded most probingly to this question. Foucault, observed Deleuze, was a great stylist. Deleuze noted the manner in which Foucault's style as a whole evolved from the "shimmerings and scintillations of the visible" in his early work to his last books, where "the style tends towards a kind of calm, seeking an ever more austere, an ever purer line..." (Deleuze, 1995, p. 101). For Deleuze, style itself is linked not least to a certain capacity for variation in relation to linguistic norms. In this sense, style is not a property of individuals but is the expression of a sort of language within a language, "the procedure of a continuous variation" (Deleuze and Guattari, 1987, p. 97). Style, in this sense, always relates to something outside of itself. "Style is a set of variations in language, a modulation, and a straining of one's whole language toward something outside it" (Deleuze, 1995, p. 140).

Adapting Deleuze's formulations to our own uses, let us say that the particularity of style here entails something outside language in two senses; *demonstration* and *variation*. Together these make up much of the force of what Foucault is up to in his lectures, and elsewhere.

DEMONSTRATION

This is the sense of something 'outside' language in that – referring to an opposition favoured by Deleuze – it refers to the realm of the visible rather than simply the articulable. This sense of style is not just linguistic but is, as Deleuze puts it, 'audiovisual', involving particular forms of content (visibility) as well as expression (sayability). Much of the force of Foucault's lectures and books, thinks Deleuze, rests upon this sense of visuality. It is not just that Foucault is adept at descriptive tableaux, although this is certainly true; it is, rather, a feature of Foucault's particular *style*, especially with regard to what he calls Foucault's 'description-scenes', those of the chain gang, the asylum, the prison van, the Panopticon – "as though these were scenes and Foucault were a painter" (Deleuze, 1988, p. 80). But there is more to the emphasis on visuality than this. The Wittgensteinian distinction between showing and saying comes to mind in this connection. For Foucault's work – and this, we might note, is especially so of the lectures – seems to function, as it were, by acts of demonstration; by showing rather than saying. This is why there is a paucity of methodological reflection in Foucault's work. And when there is methodological reflection, it is usually – precisely – *reflection*, after the fact; as in *The Archaeology of Knowledge* (Foucault, 1971). Generally-speaking, Foucault preferred to show – especially in his lectures – how he practiced his work, not to set it out formally and methodologically in advance. Style should be *opposed* to methodology in this sense. We could even say that those with methodologies rarely have style.

The lectures are particularly exemplary of this principle of demonstration as opposed to explanation. The result is something like a picture or a map of affiliations and contestations within particular discursive formations. Foucault's aim is to exhibit this map for us, to show it to us – to show us that there *is* a map of this or that sort. Thus for instance in the 1976 *Society Must Be Defended* series – which shall be the main focus in our remarks here – we are presented with a sort of historical morphology of historicism, a map of historicism. The research question is simple (and not strictly-speaking genealogical). "Who, basically, had the idea of inverting Clausewitz's principle ... that what is going on beneath and in power relations is war?" (Foucault, 2002, p. 47).

Foucault discovers the formative principles of historicism emerging after the religious wars of the Sixteenth Century; in Britain this occurs above all in the petty-bourgeois context of the radicals of the English Revolution, whereas in France the discourse is one of aristocratic reaction against the monarch. The first truly historicist discourse emerges where truth itself is conceivable as a historical phenomenon; "a discourse that develops completely within the historical dimension" (ibid, p. 55). This is a discourse of "pure time"; "deployed within a history that has no boundaries, no end and no limits" (ibid, p. 55). Above all, it is a historicism of war between races. The function of the lectures is to trace the history of this historicism of race war; "during the French Revolution and especially in the early nineteenth century with Augustine and Amédée Thierry and to show how it underwent two transcriptions": a biological transcription, and a transcription into the idea of a social war. Finally, the aim is to trace the emergence of a biologico-social racism, one which will ultimately – for instance, in the phenomenon of Nazism – re-centre the discourse of power, inverting it so to speak, such that this discourse of race struggle will become the discourse of power itself (ibid, p. 61). Throughout this demonstration we are *shown* – rather, one might say, than *told* – the extent to which historical discourse is not a neutral affair, describing the world in propositional terms, but is rather a matter of engagement with the positions of others, weapons in struggle. Discourse itself is always directed, aimed, targeted at some or other alternative form of discourse. Discourse is itself a matter of strategy and struggle.

One is reminded in this context of Foucault's comments on the English analytical school of language and his affinities with it; the analysis, as he puts it, of "discourse as strategy, somewhat in the manner of the Anglo-Saxons, in particular Wittgenstein, Austin, Strawson, Searle" (Foucault, 1984, vol. II). But whereas, as Foucault comments, these analyses are rather limited by their parochial Oxbridge concerns, Foucault's own task is to expose the strategic element of discourse within the real dimension of history. As he put it later in a piece a few years subsequent to the *Society Must Be Defended* lectures, the task is to produce a kind of analytical philosophy of politics.

Anglo-Saxon philosophy tries to say that language never either deceives or reveals. Language, it is played. The importance, therefore, of the notion of game... Relations of power are also played; it is these games of power that one must study in terms of tactics and strategy, in terms of order and of chance, in terms of stakes and objectives. (Foucault, 1984, vol. III: 541–2; also Davidson, 1997: 4–5, where this passage is quoted at greater length).

Foucault's work both shows and exemplifies this strategic notion of discourse without either exactly theorising it or constituting it methodologically in advance. It is rather a question of an immanent description, a portrait of kinds of discourse in their functioning, co-existence and struggle.

VARIATION

So much for the first sense of style. But a second element of this sense also reaches 'beyond language' in that it sets some or other dominant discourse into a state of variation with itself; not, then, so much beyond language as such, but in a relation of variation to some or other dominant language. This is *variation*.

In terms of Foucault's books, the principle of genealogy itself performs this function. Take, briefly, the example of *Discipline and Punish*; not to put forward a new conception of punishment but to use a certain kind of historical nominalism to question the self-evident status of the prison (Foucault, 1979). The genealogy of the modern punitive system does not use the teleologies of history to explain the present, but is a history of the present; one that uses history against itself, one that pitches the dominant forms of historicism against itself; that puts the dominant meliorist histories of penality into a sort of negative variation. In the lectures – and let us continue here with the example of the *Society Must Be Defended* series – we can see that this principle of variation corresponds less to a determinate methodology than to a certain kind of performance; a waging of war on certain other conceptions of the relations between power and knowledge, as well as to other conceptions of history. As regards power, we can see that the whole demonstration in *Society Must Be Defended* is also a question of a variation on the dominant, sovereign, discourse of power; as well as a genealogy of historicism, *and* a kind of archaeology on Foucault's part; an archaeology of Foucault's own prejudice against sovereign conceptions of power. As regards knowledge, Foucault provides in the 1976 lectures some striking reflections on the image of knowledge in the Enlightenment and the extent to which genealogy entails 'outwitting' this image. Instead of taking at face value the Enlightenment view that knowledge was a question of illuminating darkness with light, we need, he argued, to think of knowledges in terms of multiplicity. The Enlightenment invented the image of Science and, of course, the disciplines. Genealogy functions as a kind of corrective to these images of knowledge, just as it functions as a corrective to other forms of sovereign conceptions of power.

But Foucault is also, so to speak, using the example of political historicism in these lectures to wage war on dominant conceptions of history. Take Foucault's two examples of dialectics, on the one hand, and of the modern discipline of history on the other.

One of the functions of Foucault's genealogy of historicism in *Society Must Be Defended* is to indicate the distance that separates political historicism from misapplied assumptions of kinship; for instance, those of Hobbes, Machiavelli or the dialectic. Taking the example of Hegelianism and Marxism, far from being an instance of the discourse of political historicism, the dialectic, Foucault says, had the effect of taking it over and displacing it into the old form of philosophico-juridical discourse. Basically, the dialectic codifies struggle, war, and confrontations into a logic, or so-called logic, of contradiction; it turns them into the twofold process of the "totalization and revelation of a rationality that is at once final but also basic, and in any case irreversible" (Foucault, 2002, p. 58). Only a genealogical analysis of the discourse of political historicism could indicate the distance that separates them from the superficially apposite conceptual kin of the dialectic, or the work of Machiavelli or Hobbes. But this is not really a question of theorizing such distance, but of *showing* it, just as one shows distances on a map; indicating that these phenomena which seem so proximate in some terms, for instance in the discourse of the history of ideas, in fact inhabit different terrains altogether. Or rather, these dubious conceptual kin in fact serve opposite interests more often than not, so far as Foucault is concerned. Hobbes's work, for instance, is represented as an attempt to avert grounding all social relations in war but to re-activate the old juridical principles of sovereignty precisely against the proponents of the race war since the Conquest. The dialectic, meanwhile, is represented by Foucault as being "philosophy and right's authoritarian colonization of a historico-political discourse that was both a statement of fact, a proclamation, and a practice of social warfare" (ibid, p. 58). So much for dialectics, and – one supposes – Marxism.

The relations between political historicism and the discipline of history itself are more complicated. Here, it is most certainly a question of variation rather than outright opposition, for the relations between history as a discipline and political historicism, it seems, have been integrally ambivalent. This whole theme should really be the focus of a separate study in its own right, one that would focus on the value of the *Society Must Be Defended* series for an analysis of the emergence of orthodox 'liberal' historiography. The modern discourse of history, Foucault observes at one point, sits somewhere at the confluence of the discourse on race war and the idea of sovereignty; that is, it oscillates between political historicism and something like State history (ibid). This means that modern history as a discipline remained both disciplinarised and tied, for instance, to questions of administrative knowledge, but also, as Foucault puts it, potentially combative, especially with its concerns for the question of society and the phenomenon of revolution; for close to the idea of history is the notion of the ubiquity of war (ibid). The practice of history it seems is a double-edged enterprise.

Would that be so of Foucault's own attitude to historical work? Some critics are purported to have found a sense of performative contradiction in Foucault's attitude to history. Foucault undermines all truths, yet claims himself to be telling some sort of truth. This, it seems, is the predicament of the genealogist.

For some, it is an intrinsically unfortunate predicament. For instance, Alasdair MacIntyre in *Three Rival Versions of Moral Inquiry* argues that the genealogist – and Foucault himself is his exemplar here – is in an anomalous teaching position in the University. Either genealogists have to remain outside the university as something akin to nomadic thinkers, or they accept absorption into the university "but saying and being heard to say only what the standard formats of the current academic mode permitted" (MacIntyre, 1990, p. 220). MacIntyre envisages a genealogical lecture as follows:

> From a genealogical standpoint what is needed is some way of enabling the members of an audience to regard themselves from an ironic distance and, in so separating themselves from themselves, to open up the possibility of an awareness of those fissures within the self about which and to which genealogical discourse is addressed. But in achieving this the genealogist cannot avoid opening up the question for his or her audience of what mask or masks the lecturer is, has been, and will be wearing. So the lecture will perhaps be transformed into, perhaps abandoned in exchange for, a theatre of the intelligence, a theatre in turn requiring critical commentary from both its adherents and opponents. And among the purposes to be served by both theatre and genealogical commentary will be the undermining of all traditional forms of authority, including the authority of the lecturer (ibid, pp. 232–3).

On the evidence of Foucault's own lectures, it is certainly a misconception to think of these as presenting some sort of ironic mask. The lectures certainly present something recognisable as research and, if not certainly in an 'authoritarian' manner then perhaps in a processual one. The lectures certainly aim at truth, albeit a truth that would be of a different sort to some of our more settled, established truths. At the beginning of the 1976 lectures, Foucault invokes a sense of futility in relation to his work. Of interest here is the sense of research as a question only of a "useless erudition"; of "fragments of research, none of which was completed, and none of which was followed through; bits and pieces of research... always falling into the same rut, the same themes, the same concepts" (Foucault, 2002, p. 3). Clearly what was at stake here, then, was not research of an orthodox, positive or 'scientific' sort.

KNOWLEDGES

So what was it? Foucault pointed to two themes in particular that had concerned him in his work; the recovery of buried knowledges on the one hand, and of subjugated knowledges on the other. In each case, what was involved was the exposure of the lines of battle and force that traversed the production of forms of knowledge. In short, it was a question not of posing in a mask of irony but of producing genealogical knowledges. And if for Foucault such genealogical knowledges were specifically to be countered to the image of Science – conceiving of them, in fact, as anti-sciences (ibid.) – then they were not to be counter-veridical as such; ironic, indifferent to the truth. Rather, genealogies pertain to their own norms of truth. In the 1976 *Society Must Be Defended* lectures Foucault's alternative ethic of knowledge, his methodology of thought, is of course integrally connected to the discourse of war. These lectures should be read, in this case, not just as an excavation of themes of war in the history of philosophy and other forms of thought but as problematisations of Foucault's own practice as a particular kind of philosopher, historian and intellectual. In this sense, the 1976 lectures effect a kind of reflexive work or work upon the self on Foucault's part; a form of work that in its own way could be said even to prefigure the theme of practices of self in his later writings. This is a question of Foucault's thought, as it were, folding back upon itself to become a reflection on his own practice. This, not least, is the role of Foucault as educator; a figure devoted not simply to the discovery of positive truths – to 'research' – but who exemplified a certain attitude to knowledge in his own practice. This practice – as instanced so wonderfully in his lectures – never took a final form, but always presented itself as an exercise, an on-going apprenticeship, a search; a kind of ethics of truth in fact (see Osborne, 1998).

So if there is some truth in MacIntyre's idea that the lectures are about gaining a sense of distance from the usual idea of authoritative teaching, then rather than this relating to the idea of some sort of mask of ironism we should regard it as an ethics of truth; a process of reflexive work – an integrally educational enterprise, not just in the sense of education others but in the sense of an education of the self. That is not least of the effects that the lectures achieve. And the difference between the lectures and the books on this score may simply be that in the lectures one can see the process as it unfolds. The machinery of thought is laid bare in a way that is not the case with the books. What appears in the lectures is not so much thought itself as the work of thought; a work that is really something like an ethical work, even an ordeal of knowledge – in the sense sometimes invoked by Max Weber.

SPIRITUALITY

One can even argue that Foucault himself invokes – demonstrates – something of this sense of an on-going ethical, educational work in the distinction between philosophical forms of knowledge and spirituality that he invokes so memorably in *L'Hermeneutique du Sujet* (Foucault, 2001). In a sense, the concept of spirituality is – once more – a means of invoking the outside as variation on more orthodox forms of knowledge.

> Let us call philosophy the form of thought which reflects upon that which permits the subject to have access to truth, the form of thought which tries to determine the condition and the limits that are entailed for the subject to have access to truth. And if one can call this philosophy, then I believe we can call spirituality the research, the practice, the experience through which the subject imposes on himself the necessary transformations to gain access to the truth. (Foucault, 2001, p. 16).

Of course this is a practice that is internal to philosophy not exterior to it. This is not a question of being against philosophy, of resisting it with an ironic mask – as in the terms of MacIntyre. It is rather a question of invoking a sort of outside to philosophy, but one that is – to sound like Deleuze – folded into it internally in so far as the opposition between philosophy and spirituality becomes a sort of running issue throughout *L'Hermeneutique du Sujet*, with various aspects of the philo-sophical tradition – Spinoza, Hegel, for example – invoked as attempts to reconcile the two or at least engage the one with the other.

Moreover, it would be foolish completely to assimilate Foucault's own conception of his work to this idea of spirituality; not least because in the *'Courage de Vérité'* series Foucault distinguishes between the kinds of spiritual self-transformation connected on the one hand to stoicism and on the other to the Cynics; the one a slow, laborious transformation the other more akin to a rupture, a burst of laughter, the incursion of a sense of the scandalous. Spirituality, in other words, is not a uniform phenomenon any more than is philosophy. One could argue that there are elements of Foucault's style in both these themes of transformation, but the main issue is simply the invocation, the disclosure, the *showing* of this principle of self-transformation itself.

Variation, style – these do not just relate to language, to discourse, to power, to knowledge, but to our very sense of selfhood. There is no theory of the self in Foucault's work, but there are various exercises of the self – the lectures themselves are examples of this. They are educational exercises in self-transformation; but, so to speak, a collective self-transformation, one involving an audience that participates in the performance by being present at it. This sense of self-transformation is integral to Foucault's sense of his work as being a series of variations, in this sense upon the self itself. Which is why Deleuze is right, at least in Foucault's context, to connect the notion of intellectual style with that of the style of life. "But if there's a whole ethics in this, there's an aesthetics too. Style, in a great writer, is always a style of life too, not anything at all personal, but inventing a possibility of life a way of existing" (Deleuze, 1995, p. 100). Deleuze also invokes the 'searing phraseology' of *The Use of Pleasure*:

> After all, what would be the value of the passion for knowledge, if it resulted only in a certain amount of knowledgeableness and not, in one way or another and to the extent possible, in the knower's straying afield of himself? (Foucault, 1998, p. 8).

The books, one might say, are the products of this principle; the lectures are its demonstration as process, even performance.

GOVERNMENT

Ultimately, too, the lectures relate to matters of government. Certainly, the theme of education, as invoked here, may seem a long way from the famous concept of governmentality that so marked the later years of Foucault's research and which has been so influential in the Anglo-Saxon world, but in fact education is, so to speak, quite fully a governmental matter so long as we take government in its broadest sense as the shaping of conduct including conduct that is nominally 'free'.

Now, education is not least a matter of critique. If we think of Foucault's work as being related not just to the production of positive forms of knowledge but as being educational work – exercises in thought, exercises in gaining a distance in thought – then that work obviously has a relation to the activity of critique. This is critique not in the negative, denunciatory sense but critique as work that one does upon the limits of one's thought, critique as resistance to received forms of government. As such critique is itself, in a way, a form of government (see Foucault, 1990). Foucault conceived of intellectual work as being closely integrated with the exercise of freedom; it can be, amongst other things, a means of freeing oneself from given norms and rationalities of government. In this sense, Foucault was quite traditional in his concerns; holding, in almost Kantian vein, that critical autonomy was a fundamental value, albeit one that could not be taken for granted in any dogmatic way but which, rather, had to be the object of cultivation, of work, of exercise. Genealogical work is critical in precisely this ethical kind of sense. Instead of being a denunciatory form of critique it is a form of distancing, of self-distancing, a corrective to received forms of understanding, to supposed constants that we might otherwise take for granted and leave unexamined. I think that Foucault probably felt that the exercise of thought in this sense was fundamental to the very idea of critical ethics in a free society.

GENEALOGY

Having invoked the idea of genealogy as a form of educational critique, I want to say a little more, in closing, at this point concerning the specificity of Foucault's lectures. For actually it seems that the lectures are not the same sort of genealogies, it seems, as are the books. This is difficult to specify beyond saying that Foucault's lectures handle time in a particular way. It would be a little misleading to make out that, in contrast to the lectures, the books all handle time in some uniform Nietzschean manner. Foucault's *originality* in relation to Nietzsche seems to me if anything to have been under-rated on this score. Yet broadly speaking it is true that the books, at least until the last books on Antiquity, employ methodologies that can be related to Nietzschean genealogy. *Discipline and Punish* most conspicuously. Putting it very schematically, we can say that this is so in at least two ways. First, in that what is described takes the form not of something elevated and transhistorical, but something lowly, worldly and tied to the exigencies of power. The prison, for example, emerges not as a result of the enlightened reasonings of philosophers, but as a result of very particular circumstances to do with transformations in the prevailing technologies of power. Second, in that the mode of description is not linked to some kind of 'origin' but to a series of emergences that do not necessarily have any ultimate continuity. Thus there is no 'essence' to the prison that can be found in its 'origin', even if the antimonies of prison discourse can be traced back to the circumstances of the emergence of the prison. All this means, in effect, that there is a sense in which time in Foucault's books is Nietzschean conceptual time. It is time that runs – however it is presented – methodologically-speaking backwards. One begins with a tension in the present and one works back along its fault-lines. Even the earlier 'archaeological' work can be understoodin this sense of a backwards-moving time; to the extent, for instance, that this work was indebted to Georges Canguilhem's idea of 'recurrent history', tracing concepts back along their lines of development rather than chronologically in terms of their 'maturation'. *The Birth of the Clinic* can be conceived more or less as recurrent history in this sense.

PROBLEMATOLOGY

But Foucault's lectures for the most part do not seem to operate quite in this way. One might say, generalizing far too much of course, that whereas the books are predominantly archaeological or genealogical, the lectures are problematological (see Osborne, 2003). Foucault takes problems and then analyses them, typically in chronological rather than genealogical time, in terms of their transformations, bifurcations and variations.

In *Society Must Be Defended* the discourse of historicism, for example, is not really subjected to the rigours of a genealogy. Note that the initial question: 'who first thought of reversing Clausewitz's dictum?' is not really a genealogical one. On the contrary; it seems to be conspicuously a question to do with origins. Foucault maps out an evolving and repeatedly bifurcating problem space in order to illustrate the developmental morphology, so to speak, of the discourse of historicism. Even the lectures on political reason work in something of a similar manner. For instance, with the problem of neo-liberalism, especially American neo-liberalism: this is something far closer to the history of ideas than to genealogy. Note that the last two books on Antiquity are also, in effect, like problematologies. The last books become more like the lectures.

Now, perhaps we should refrain from making too much of this distinction between genealogy and problematology. It is certainly not absolute. And no doubt the books are problematological too in their own way. Perhaps it is no more than a difference of emphasis, a reflection only of the obviously different contexts of production that are entailed with regard to books, on the one hand, and to lectures on the other. But certainly this difference of emphasis allows Foucault to do something in the lectures which he did not tend to do in his books; and that is, so to speak, to step out of both chronological and genealogical time and to introduce something of the order of a notion of the invariant. The lectures seem to be full of excursuses, invoking from initially limited materials quite general phenomena. These are of two main sorts; let us call them, the lateral and the projective forms of the excursus. The lateral ones are those such as the reflections on Shakespeare, Racine and public right in the *Society Must Be Defended* lectures; or the reflections on the Gothic novel there and in the *Abnormal* series. These examples serve to show that problems are not confined by genre or discipline but operate laterally, across forms of genre. Perhaps the best example is what Foucault says of the Gothic novel in the 1976 lectures. The Gothic novel does not really belong to literature, or not only to literature. Rather, these are 'political' novels. "They are always about the abuse of power and exations; they are fables about unjust sovereigns, pitiless and bloodthirsty seigneurs, arrogant priests, and so on" (ibid, 212).

The projective excursuses are perhaps more interesting. These serve to isolate something like invariant forms that cross passages of time. One thinks of the invocation of Hitler in *Society Must be Defended*; and also again in *Abnormal*. In the latter text we have, for instance, the invocation of the principle of the 'infamy of sovereignty'. Ubuesque or ridiculous power is understood here not as limiting the idea of sovereignty but of showing its necessity; "a way of giving striking form of expression to the unavoidability, the inevitability of power, which can function in its full rigour... even in the hands of someone who is effectively discredited" (Abnormal, 13). But this is a form of power that crosses historical periods; from Nero to "the little man with trembling hands crowned with forty million deaths who, from deep in his bunker, asks only for two things, that everything else above him be destroyed and that he be given chocolate cakes until he bursts..." (13)

But what is intriguing is the way in which Foucault is able to use these excursuses to develop new concepts and angles on his material. Perhaps the very best example of this is, again, this theme of the weakness of power and "despicable sovereignty" in the opening lectures of *Abnormal*. The freedom of the lectures seems to give Foucault the scope to develop an entire – and quite general – picture of power here; one which would stress not, as it were, the 'powerfulness' of power, but the functionality of its weakness. Hence the transition in the argument from Clastres's analysis of kingship and authority in certain forms of tribal society with the functioning of psychiatry, as essentially a weak science; or the unforgettable account of grotesque sovereignty; that power can be laughable. Of course these are not reflections of any theory of power in Foucault's thinking; rather they illustrate the extent to which thinking through the question of power was not least a question of a patient, on-going documenting of its varied forms; a form of documentation that was not simply the pious un-masking of the critic but, ultimately, the humorous satire of the genealogist, the one who divides up discourses – as Foucault does at the beginning of *Abnormal* – into "discourses of truth and discourses that make one laugh."

REFERENCES

Davidson, A. (Ed.). (1987). *Foucault and his interlocutors*. London: Routledge.

Deleuze, G. (1988). *Foucault*. Minnesota: University of Minnesota Press.

Deleuze, G. (1995). *Negotiations*. New York: Columbia University Press.

Deleuze, G., & Guattari, F. (1987). *A thousand plateaus: Capitalism and schizophrenia*. London: Athlone Press.

Foucault, M. (1971). *The archaeology of knowledge* (A. Sheridan-Smith, Trans.). London: Tavistock.

Foucault, M. (1979). *Discipline and punish: The birth of the prison* (A. Sheridan-Smith, Trans.). Harmondsworth: Peregrine.

Foucault, M. (1984). *Dits et Ecrits* (Vol. 4). Paris: Gallimard.

Foucault, M. (1990). What is critique? Tr. K.P. Geiman. In J. Schmidt (Ed.), *What is enlightenment? Eighteenth-century questions and twentieth-century answers*. Berkeley, CA: University of California Press.

Foucault, M. (2003). *Abnormal* (G. Burchell, Trans.). London: Verso.

Foucault, M. (2004). *Naissance de la Bio-politique*. Paris: Gallimard & Seuil.

Foucault, M. (2006). *The Hermeneutics of the subject* (G. Burchell, Trans.). London: Palgrave Macmillan.

Foucault, M. (2007). *Security, territory, population* (G. Burchell, Trans.). London: Palgrave Macmillan.

Goffman, E. (1981). *Forms of talk*. Oxford, UK: Blackwell.

Hacking, I. (1992). 'Style' for historians and philosophers. *Studies in History and Philosophy of Science, 23*(1), 1–20.

MacIntyre, A. (1990). *Three rival versions of moral inquiry*. London: Duckworth.
Osborne, T. (1998). *Aspects of enlightenment*. London: UCL Press.
Osborne, T. (2003). What is a problem? *History of the Human Sciences, 16*(4), 1–17.
Osborne, T. (2008). *The structure of modern cultural theory*. Manchester: Manchester University Press.

Thomas Osborne
Department of Sociology
University of Bristol
United Kingdom

JAMES D. MARSHALL

9. MICHEL FOUCAULT ON POWER: FROM THE DISCIPLINARY SOCIETY TO SECURITY

INTRODUCTION

Discipline and Punish was published in France in1975. Foucault said that this represented five years work on the analysis of power. Almost immediately after publication, in his opening lectures in January 1976 at Le Collége de France, he begins to reconsider the 'How' of power and to pursue and develop a military model of war and struggle, which differs from the account of power in *Dicipline and Punish* (Foucault, 2003, chapter 2). In an unpublished lecture in 1967[1] – *Structuralisme et analyse littéraire* – Foucault invokes J. L. Austin (amongst other British philosophers) and accepts that the analysis of a statement was not complete when the linguistic structure had been given. (He was also aware of American John Searle's work). Discourse extended beyond that and must take account of the *effects* of statements. Whilst he identifies some effects of language in *Discipline and Punish* he does not really offer an account of *how* this happens, of *how* the effects *emerge*. In 1976 he begins to talk of answering this by recourse to a military model where discourse functions as a weapon, involving war and struggle.

Foucault was then well aware of J. L. Austin's approach to performative utterances. He was also aware of the work of American John Searle. Searle's *Speech Acts* published in 1969 was developed from his D.Phil submitted at Oxford in 1959.[2] Thus it is not surprising that Austin's *How to Do Things with Words* (1962) is often referred to by Searle in this 1969 source (though he disagrees with Austin on a number of issues[3]).

Furthermore, in a lecture in Japan in 1978,[4] and considering ordinary language British philosophy explicitly,[5] Foucault suggested that philosophy might cease asking whether power was good or evil and instead pose questions as to *how* relations of power were constituted. Arnold Davidson says, in relation to this lecture, that for Foucault the Anglo-American ordinary language model of philosophy provided,

> A basis of analogy for two of Foucault's central claims: first, we should not assume that relations of power have only one function; we should describe power, in all of its diversity and specificity, as it actually works; second, we should take seriously the notion of games, employing the ideas of tactics, strategies, stakes, and so on as tools for the analysis of power relations. Thus, Foucault calls for a descriptive analytic of our *jeux de pouvoir* rather than a global theory, a fixed picture, of how power must work (Davidson, 1997, p. 4).

M.A. Peters et al. (eds.), Govermentality Studies in Education, 137–152.

Davidson continues as follows:

> I do not know how the Japanese audience reacted to his no doubt unanticipated analogy, but I suspect that both American and French audiences will be unprepared to find Foucault supporting his task 'quite modest, quite empirical, quite limited," with the model of analytic philosophy of language, more specifically with the analysis of our everyday language games (Davidson, 1997, p. 4).

I will pursue these changes in his analysis of power from *Discipline and Punish*, to governmentality and into his account of security. Finally I will look briefly at Agamben and how security might degenerate into terrorism.

THE DISCIPLINARY SOCIETY

In discussing the unpublished lecture given in Tunisia in 1967, Davidson also refers to a 1967 letter from Foucault to Daniel Defert in which, referring to "les analystes anglais" he said: "They allow me indeed to see how one can do nonlinguistic analyses of statements. Treat statements in their functioning." (Davidson, 2003, p. xx).

Foucault referred to these effects as occurring at a level of strategic intelligibility, i.e, known or logically possible of being known, and used this to formulate his strategic and 'militaristic' model of power (Davidson, 2003, p. xviii). But essentially this comes after the publication of *Discipline and Punish*.

Foucault said that this book represented five years work on the analysis of power (2003, p. 23). But almost immediately, in the 1977 lectures, he begins to reconsider the 'How' of power and to develop a military model of power relations based upon war and struggle in *Society Must be Defended* (Foucault, 2003, chapter 2). Foucault says that he has been

> Trying to look at since 1970–1971...the "how" of power...trying to understand its mechanisms" which set the limits of "the rules of right that formally delineate power"...and..."the truth effects which in their turn, reproduce that power. So we have the triangle: power, right, truth (Foucault, 2003, p. 24).

Discipline and Punish had provided a new and an important analysis of power, in opposition to what Foucault called the 'classic juridical theory of power'. (He is later to say that elements of that approach remained in and after that book – see below.) This term captures the juridical conception and the liberal notion of power to be found in the 18th century and in Marxism. These he says have much in common – what he calls 'economism.' Power is a *right* which, like a commodity, can be possessed or exchanged, i.e., which can be transferred (or alienated), or a right founded, through a juridical act. Running through the versions of juridical power and of liberal power, there is a common analogy between power and commodities, between power and wealth, and between power and 'sovereignty' (be it a King or a parliament) (Foucault, 1976, p. 13). In Marxism we find what he calls the 'economic functionality' of power. The role of power is to perpetuate the relations of production and to perpetuate class domination through the relations of production. But clearly both positions have economic bases.

So to summarise this conception of power: power is imposed upon another by someone who *owns* it as a commodity – akin to economic ownership (e.g., a sovereign or a school principal); it is top down from a macro level; power is seen as repressive (or at best in liberal education as a necessary evil [Peters, 1966]); repressive power acts upon beliefs often with bodies as conduits (the army); and finally power is 'exercised' in disciplinary blocks. This top down ownership turns 'enquiry' outwards away from particular instances of power relations towards wider theories of legitimacy, perhaps to a version of contract theory and, thereby, away from the politics of everyday life. This in turn affects discussion of power relations because it then occurs at an abstract and philosophical level.

In contrast Foucault wishes to look at the extremities of the exercise of power and power/knowledge where the effects of power relation become more explicit from empirical or historical instances and from the resurrection of subjugated knowledges. By taking this turn to the micro level Foucault can study the actual *effects* of power/knowledge. Thus the classical analyses of power, concerned with the contractual and legal limits of power, ask archaic and wrong types of questions. But the state, immersed in those questions, can only operate 'on the basis of other, already existing power networks that invest the body, sexuality, the family, kinship, knowledge, technology and so forth (Foucault, 1980, p. 122). Foucault does not see power relations as always repressive; if that were the case then the state would hardly be able to operate. They may be oppressive but they can also be *productive,* as exemplified in *Discipline and Punish,* in the production of learned young people, such as teachers and soldiers. True they are *normalized,* but this is not to predict, or determine what they will do, but to say they have qualified to be a teacher or a soldier and will function as expected of a teacher, soldier etc.

In *Discipline and Punish* the prison has more than one place of birth. As Macey puts it (using Bentham's panopticon at the end of the quote):

> A whole range of institutions and discourses contribute to the emergence of a pervasive notion of discipline...the soldier becomes a manufactured object whose every movement, real and potential, can be measured and recorded ...(and the)... slightest movements can be observed and corrected....From this multiplicity of discourses, practices and institutions there emerges a disciplinary power...it functions like machinery. Discipline itself is neither an institution nor an apparatus; it is a type of power "a 'physics' or an 'anatomy' of power, a technology... The ultimate expression of the disciplinary society is of course Jeremy Bentham's 'panopticon.' (Macey, 1993, p. 332–3).

Panopticism was not based on negative functions but became *the* discipline-mechanism. It was a functional mechanism that was to improve the exercise of power by making it lighter, more rapid, more effective, a design of subtle coercion for a society to come (Foucault, 1979, p. 209). "It was a way of defining power relations in terms of the everyday life of men" (Foucault, 1979, p. 205). Furthermore, the movement towards a generalized surveillance, rested upon an historical transformation which involved,

> the gradual extensions of the mechanisms of discipline throughout the seventeenth and eighteenth centuries, their spread throughout the whole social body, and) the formation of what might be called the disciplinary society (Foucault, 1979a, p. 209).

But what has happened to Foucault's projected analysis of discourse and its effects? Of course the discourses of disciplinary blocks had effects in *Discipline and Punish,* but those effects are the production of qualified or normalized subjects, as efficiently as possible and with efficiency in power relations – for example the panopticon required only one guard in the central pillar to place a number of inmates under surveillance. The effect of normalizing people is to make them malleable and to lead useful, docile and productive lives. Foucault has not really tackled the 'how' of power/truth in *Discipline and Punish.* There is no analysis of statements like that of performative utterances in Austin (1962). Thus we are left in *Discipline and Punish* with panopticism and its effects.

Indeed, Foucault says on 7 January 1976: "everything I have said to you in previous years is inscribed within the struggle-repression schema…or contract – repression schema… which is, if you like, the juridical schema" (Foucault, 2003, p. 17). This seems to be almost and admission that, on his own criteria he didn't get it 'right.'

GOVERNMENTALITY

The Military Model of Power Relations

As we saw above, Foucault begins in 1976 to talk of answering the "how" of power by recourse to a military model where discourse functions as a weapon, involving metaphors of *forces,* of wars and of struggles, through the establishment of discourses of truth, which did not exclude rhetoric and polemics (Foucault, 2003, chapter 2). "It was a type of power which presupposed a closely meshed grid of material coercions" (Foucault, 2003, p. 36). This is clearly not what he calls an answer to his typical juridical and philosophical question, "How does the discourse of truth establish the limits of power's right?" In this section I will pursue the answers he gives to his questions of power relations into the account of governmentality and, briefly, into security.

Foucault distinguishes a philosophical approach to this question, as stated above, from a more factual question, "a question from below" He formulates two versions of his question, as follows: "What are the rules of right that power implements to produce discourses of truth?" Or in an *alternative* formulation: "What type of power is it that is capable of producing discourses of truth that have, in a society like ours, such powerful effects?" (Foucualt, 2003, p. 24). His answer depends upon how society is organized.

In a society such as ours – or in any society come to that – multiple relations of power traverse, characterize and constitute the social body; they are indissociable from a discourse on truth, and they can neither be established nor function unless a true discourse is produced, accumulated, put into circulation, and set to work. Power cannot be exercised unless a certain economy of discourses of truth functions in, on the basis of, and thanks to, that power (Foucault, 2003, p. 24).

Thus his overall domain of enquiry covers, "rules of right, mechanisms of power, truth effects. Or rules of power and the power of true discourses" (Foucault, 2003, p. 25).

In his earlier writings he talks of power existing only when we might say it is being exercised. His analysis begins at the micro level in disciplinary blocks such as the prison, the army and the school, and not from the macro level. Yet in talking of the organization of society it might be thought that he is considering power not only at the micro level but also at the macro level – the organization of society – which grounds discourses of truth and provides disciplinary institutions that establish rules of right (that in turn produce discourses of truth). Foucault does not waver in his beliefs and discussions of power that it exists initially at the micro level (Foucault, 2003, p. 30), though he begins to incorporate discussions of macro power, which lead eventually, via *The History of Sexuality,* Vol. 1, and the turn to population, to *governmentality* (Foucault, 1979b).

The military model of power relations is an alternative conceptualization of power relationships, seeking to discover a basis for the intelligibility of politics (and reason of state) in terms of a general form of war. Carl von Clausewitz had given several formulations of a relationship between war and politics in *On War* (1982). Some of these formulations are:
– War is merely or is nothing more than, the continuation of policy by other means;
– War is simply a continuation of political intercourse with other means;
– War is part of policy;
– War can never be separated from political relations.

If it is not clear who first reversed the place of the key terms – 'war' and 'policy'/ or politics – in formulations such as (1) and (2). Nevertheless, by 1976 Foucault, as a first step, gives this reading of Clausewitz's proposition, as being; "Power is war, the continuation of war by other means." But Foucault immediately inverts his reading of Clausewitz's proposition to say: 'Politics is the continuation of war by other means" (Foucault, 2003, p. 15), He is not interested in who initially inverted Clausewitz's principle. Rather it is the inverted principle itself.

At the end of 1976 Foucault had further amended his earlier position on the military model (Davidson, 2003, p. xviii).

Should one then turn around the formula and say politics is war pursued by other means? Perhaps if one wishes always to maintain a difference between war and politics, one should suggest rather that this multiplicity of force-relations can be coded – in part and never totally – either in the form of 'war' or in the form of 'politics'; there would be here two different strategies (but ready to tip over into one another) for integrating these unbalanced, heterogeneous, unstable, tense force relations (Foucault, 1979b, p. 93).

It should be noted that Foucault differs from Clausewitz's (3) and (4).over the relation between war and politics as Foucault wishes to distinguish between war and politics. There is no necessary logical relationship between the two, but they are always 'found' together as either power elicits truth, or truth elicits power.

Thus discourse of truth functions as a weapon, involving forces of war and struggle, Power relations establish discourses of 'truth,' through forces that resemble war, and as discourses, did not exclude rhetoric and polemics (Foucault, 2003, chapter 2. Finally, "It was a type of power which presupposed a closely meshed grid of material coercions" (Foucault (2003, p. 36).

Governmentality

Foucault extends his use of the military model as he begins to talk in the late 1970s of governmentality, government rationality and the art of government. According to Gordon (1991, p. 2) by 'government' Foucault meant something like 'the conduct of conduct' or 'a form of activity aiming to shape, guide or effect the conduct of some person or persons. In one sense the effects are *subjects*. But the process is different from, e.g., *Discipline and Punish* because within governmentality there is a pastoral element which guides thinking (on such matters as welfare, education and happiness) and thereby shapes individuals because of the discourses of truth which suggest paths for individuals as to how to attain health, education and happiness. But it also individualizes and produces identifiable individuals as subjects. Yet if it was to *individualize* and to *normalize,* through discourses of truth and the underlying grid of coercions it produced subjects who would lead useful docile and productive lives. Governmentality is concerned also with ensuring the right distributions of 'things' so as lead to, or provide, an end convenient or suitable for each of the things that are to be governed. In this pastoral role, in 'predicting' prosperity and happiness governmentality suggests to subjects, if not coerces them, about how to attain these 'goods' in various ways – e.g., computers are almost becoming compulsory in schools and in obtaining qualifications, and the professionalism of sport, with its increasing media hype brings enjoyment if not pleasure to increasing numbers. Thus rationality of government acquires a way or system of thinking about government not only in its practices but also making it practicable to its functionaries or officials and for those upon whom it was practised. Later governmentality is to become part of the 'science' of economic management theory.

Foucault (1979b) discussed three models of governmentality. First, for Machiavelli's Prince the things which are to be governed are first and foremost territory and, secondly, the inhabitants of the Prince's territory. Foucault rejects Machiavelli and turns to discuss, second, the account of the family as offering a model of good governance. But this was inappropriate for the governing of the complex 'modern' state and the 'modern' economic theories that were emerging in the late 18th and early 19th centuries. A new form of rationality of state was needed.

In his third example of the rationality of state Foucault does not draw upon territory or upon the family as model. Instead it is the inhabitants through the families, their complex relations and their links with property and culture in the widest senses. The links included misfortunes and disasters, accidents, famines, and war (Foucault, 1979 b, p. 11). Governmentality clearly required more than the implementation of power and knowledge entangled in Sovereignty, and its juridical type theories of power relations.

But the move from *Discipline and Punish* to *The History of Sexuality,* Vol. 1, also involves a shift from analyses of techniques of domination towards analyses of techniques of the self, i.e., how we come to aid and abet our becoming *subjects.* This shift is caught by his distinction between *technologies of domination and technologies of the self* (Foucault, 1988).

Thus Foucault (1979 b) advances a notion of governmentality which abandons political theories about the state, its legitimation (juridical power and liberalism) and its implementation of general principles of justice, wisdom and prudence. The new knowledge which was required needed to be concrete, precise and specific.

As states from the early 17th century entered into competition, strengths and weaknesses of both the state and of individuals, became important historically as states faced an indefinite future through struggle and competition with other states. Thus political knowledge and, if individuals were to be utilized, knowledge of capacities, abilities and propensities became very important. Not only were human beings now considered as a species but, thereby, by attention to the phenomena of population, individuals became an important aspect or means, towards the ends of the state.

Of course power relations and some form of domination would be necessary. But this was new for the analysis here of power as the continuation of war by others means becomes apposite. War itself undergoes a marked and visible change. War, instead of being controlled and conducted from the centre of a territory is dispersed to the boundaries of the territory in order to control better incursions, attempted wars and wars. But at the boundaries territories we find the disaffected, those who have not been coerced, and subjugated knowledges. We would also find inhabitants who wee more closely affiliated with those on the other side of the boundary, as a result of previous seizures, boundary changes, and confrontations. Thus war becomes aligned with the disaffected, the 'delinquents', and through the resurrection of subjugated knowledges, individualization, attention to population and the protection of society, relations of power and discourses of truth come to require notions of struggle and war.

Governmentality to Security

At the Collége de France in 1978 Foucault began to change course again in his lectures. He studied the emergence of the early modern state though he would have seemed to have covered aspects of this topic – reason of state – in earlier works such as *Discipline and Punish* and *Madness and Civilization.* But what has changed is his standpoint again, on power relations.

Discipline and Punish was groundbreaking in that it proposed a new account of power, but after its publication Foucault began to shift ground gently. Indeed his new views in the late 1970s "placed Foucault in opposition to his own positions of ten years earlier" (Paras, 2006, p. 88). After the events of 1968 Marxism ceased to be a major intellectual force in France, though Sartre clung doggedly to it. Yet there remained a group of non repentant but rudderless group of leftists. Foucault may be said to have been a member of that group especially if we consider his actions at Vincennes and at Le Collége de France. (These philosophical acts are well documented by Didier Eribon [1991, Chapters 17–20] and David Macey [1993, chapters 9, 12, 13 & 15]).

But there was also a different view of philosophy, arising from the leftist remnants of 1968. This group was known as the *nouveaux philosophes* and André Glucksman and Bernard-Henri Levy were well known members of this leftist group (Levy named it, and Glucksman denied he was ever a member). Glucksman had been an ultra-Maoist but he had abandoned Maoism by 1974. From then on "he systematically denounced gulags, forms of totalitarianism and the philosophies tending in this direction" (Eribon, 1991, p. 262). In 1972/3 Foucault, who had flirted "since May '68 with the most savage kinds of political violence...like Glucksman pulled back and quietly began to rethink his position" (Miller, 1993, p. 233) In what was his most significant gesture of support Foucault, in 1977, was to review favourably Glucksman's *The Master Thinkers,* the argument of which was that 19th, century German philosophers, including Marx And Nietzsche, were the 'mentors' of the 20th century tyrants – Hitler and Stalin. But whereas Deleuze's anger with Glucksman's book was philosophical, Foucault's position was more political. Their different attitudes towards *The Master Thinkers* led Foucault and Deleuze to hold radically different and opposed positions on political questions, and to destroy their friendship.[6] The point here is that by 1977 at the least Foucault had abandoned violence.

By1976 Foucault was advocating an analysis of power relations in terms of a military model. This was a new response to juridicio power and sovereignty, so as "to release or emancipate this analysis of power from three assumptions – of subject, unity, and law – and to bring out...what I would call relations or operators of domination" (Foucault, 2003, p. 45). To a certain extent this turn to the military model has at last paid attention explicitly to the positions and comments by Anglo-American ordinary language But this analysis was concerned with the conditions which permitted things to be said and the effects of discourse were not to be given a causal analysis.

The starting point (for this critique) is Clausewitz's assertion on war and politics, discussed above. But the second notion to be considered is that of police. According to Gordon (1991, p. 10) Foucault suggests that what permitted *raison d'état* in Continental Europe to rise above earlier forms of governmentality and "become a knowledge of the state's strength," was the corpus of theory, pedagogy and codification of what could be called *Polizeiwissenscaft, or* 'science of police.' The modern notion of policing is included but the science of police covered much more than that. Perhaps, Gordon says, one could say that

> Reason of state's problem of calculating detailed actions appropriate to an infinity of unforeseeable and contingent circumstances is met by the creation of an exhaustively detailed knowledge of the governed reality of the state itself, extending (at least in aspiration) to touch the existences of its individuals...The idea of prosperity or happiness is the principle which identifies the state with its subjects...it emphasizes that the real basis of the state's wealth and power lies in its population (Gordon, 1999, p. 100).

But this is paradoxical because on the one hand an aim of government is to develop the aspects of individual lives which strengthen the state and on the other is the notion of pastoral care brought forward from the pastoral model of the good family. Thus the provision of welfare and education are not merely humane responses to certain rights. Therefore, according to Gordon, we must see police as striving towards the prudential by cultivating the pastoral. Foucault however sees Police Science as aspiring to a knowledge of inexhaustibility detailed and continuous control. Foucault (borrowing from Mitterrand) described government further, in the Police State, as a 'permanent coup d'état.' A defining characteristic of the Police State was, for Foucault, 'the marginalization of the distinction between government by law and government by decree' (Gordon, 1991, pp. 10–11).

LIBERALISM

The 'How' questions, discussed above are important, first, because they shift the terrain of problematising away from more traditional political and philosophical concerns. According to Foucault,

> The elaboration of juridical thought has essentially centered around royal power ever since the middle ages. The juridical edifices of our societies was elaborated at the demand of royal power, as well as for its benefit, in order to serve as its instrument or its justification. In the West right is the right of royal command. (Foucault, 2003, p. 25)

The second major and later outcome was his critique of neoliberalism. Foucault had noted that the left had had no answer to the march of neoliberalism and a planned book with Pierre Bourdieu did not eventuate. Nevertheless there is a critique of neoliberalism in his later work.

Sir Isaiah Berlin held a pluralist position towards liberalism and liberal values. In one of his many discussions of liberalism Berlin gave this list of liberal values; "liberty, equality, property, knowledge, security, practical wisdom, purity of character, sincerity, kindness, rational self-love."[7] However, Berlin did not believe in either Enlightenment views that harmony between competing liberal values could be attained or that human perfectibility was possible in practice. Berlin raised these issues in "Herder and the Enlightenment":

What is the best life for men? And, more particularly, what is the most perfect society? There is, after all, no dearth of solutions. Every age has provided its own formulae...in sacred books or in revelation or in the words of inspired prophets or the tradition of organized priesthoods; others found it in the rational insight of the skilled metaphysician, or in the combination of scientific experiment and observation... in the 'natural' good sense of men not 'scribbled over' by philosophers or theologians, or perverted by 'interested error'...(or that)...only trained experts could discover great and saving truths...But one assumption was common to all these views: that it was, at any rate common in principle, possible to draw some outline of the perfect society or the perfect man (sic), if only to define how far a given society or a given individual fell short of the ideal. (Berlin 2000a, p. 232)

Because of this and his belief that experience over several centuries had shown that there were irresolvable conflicts between human ideals and values, resulting in competing and often violent practices, pluralism were the only possible political outcome. Thus for Berlin we must learn how to live with pluralistic and potentially competing values, because there were no agreed upon criteria for ranking or prioritizing these values. Therefore as the pursuit of one value, freedom from say, may conflict with justice, constraints may need to be placed upon the former. No one value, including negative freedom which he defended so strongly (Gray, 2006) could be of ultimate value.

Obviously this poses problems for neo-liberalism with its fundamental emphasis on freedom *from,* the free market and the notion of individual choice.

NEOLIBERALISM

Foucault's early behaviour and his *The Order of Things* (Foucault, 1973) had convinced some friends, colleagues and commentators that he was right wing, but he was essentially always a man of the left, who believed that liberalism provided a sufficiently fertile problematic for a sustained critique of neoliberalism. Although a fierce individualist he was not a minimalist individualist like Robert Nozick, but believed that liberalism's strength historically was its critique of the extension of unwarranted power by the state. In his 1978 lectures at Le Collège de France he begun to address criticisms of his earlier work on power/knowledge (e.g., Foucault, 1979 b; 1980), by an abrupt shift to the new topic of *Governmentality.* One major outcome of this new material was the important article, 'Governmentality' (Foucault, 1979 b), in which he poses a series of interrelated questions about *how* we govern – ourselves and others – and *how* we come to be governed and accept being governed. The second major and later outcome was his critique of neoliberalism. Foucault had noted that the left had had no answer to the march of neoliberalism in Europe and a planned book with Pierre Bourdieu did not eventuate. Nevertheless there is a critique of neoliberalism in his later work.

Neoliberalism differs markedly from liberalism. The early versions of neoliberalism which emerged in the 18th century, and Marxist theory, share, according to Foucault, 'economism' in the analysis of power (Foucault, 2003, p. 13). They share this feature because classical juridical power conceptualised power as a right "which can be possessed...as a commodity, and which can therefore be transferred or exchanged" (ibid.), in a similar manner as an exchange of contracts. "There is therefore an obvious analogy, and it runs through all these, between power and commodities, between power and wealth" (Foucault, 2003, p. 13). In Marxism there is what he calls the 'economic functionality' of power, the role of which is to perpetuate the relations of production and to reproduce a class domination that is made possible by the relations of production. Thus political power "finds its raison d'être in the economy."

> Broadly speaking, we have...in one case a political power which finds its formal model in the process of exchange, in the economy of the circulation of goods; and in the other case, political power finds its historical raison d'être, the principle of its concrete form and of its actual workings in the economy. (Foucault, 2003, p. 14)

Foucault's immediate question was, "What tools are currently available for a non-economic analysis of power?" To which his own answer was "I think that we can say that we really do not have a lot" (Foucault, 2003, p. 15).

Foucault provides a genealogical argument to show that neo-liberal economic theory, is not the inevitable outcome of earlier economic theory suggested by the Scottish 'philosopher historians', and especially as propounded by Adam Smith. Even if Smith was the leader on many matters, his contemporaries – Adam Ferguson, James Steuert and David Hume in particular – held ideas which were different from his. Foucault saw liberalism as a collection of concepts and theories which were not always compatible (cf. Berlin) and, thereby, provided a fertile critique for neo-liberalism, but his critique did not start from philosophical analyses of key concepts where differences could be established – e.g., the concepts of freedom, equality and community. Any such argument would always be inconclusive because establishing that liberals and neoliberals held different concepts of e.g., 'freedom' and 'equality', does not tell us which version of a concept to hold. Furthermore, if such concepts are contested then it is always open to the neoliberals to propose new theoretical concepts. Indeed Hayek proposed this in general terms and with the concepts of 'catallaxy' and 'demarchy' in particular (Hayek, 1967).

Instead, beginning in 1979, Foucault proposes a genealogical argument against Smith's version of neoliberalism. But this argument is not compelling, and needs to be extended in at least two general directions to account for why the 'truths' of such neoliberal theories are accepted. Denis Meuret (1988) suggests why Smith's account was acceptable in the 18th century but that too needs to be supplemented by arguments from performative accounts of language (Austin, 1962).

FOUCAULT'S GENEALOGICAL ARGUMENT AGAINST NEOLIBERALISM

Foucault's genealogical argument is designed to show that there is not a steady line of descent from the times of Adam Smith to Hayek and the neoliberals. There are two strands to this argument. First, there are substantive differences between Smith's position and modern neoliberalism which cannot just be described as a 'progression'. Second, there was no reason why Adam Smith's position should have won the day over, e.g., his contemporary Adam Ferguson.

In similar fashion to the events of Damiens' execution in 1757 and the treatment of young offenders in Faucher's reformatory some eighty years later, Foucault argues in *Discipline and Punish* that there is not a continuous and progressive line of descent from the economic theories of Adam Smith to the present economic and economically based management theories, e.g., Hayek. It would be mistaken to see this line of 'descent' as a progression. We can see this by considering some reasonably clear differences – there are of course others. First, Smith's individual of *The Wealth of Nations* (1969) is not the manipulable man of modern economic theory. Second, the hidden hand of the 18th century philosophers is not the catallaxy of Hayek (see below). Finally, there has been the extension of what was an economic theory to cover all spheres of non-random human activity (for a fuller discussion see Gordon, 1991).

Smith's individual was driven by self interest but he was also conceived as autonomous, choosing in the market 'rationally' in accordance with self interest. Smith's position on the individual was then reductionist to this metaphysical core of self interest, which was conceived as inviolable and not to be open to, or coerced by, the activities of governments. But there has been an invasion of the central metaphysical core by the positing of a faculty of *choice* (Gordon, 1991: 43: Marshall, 1996) and the political invasion of the autonomy and self interests of such individuals by governments. Along with the positing of a faculty of choice, which is not merely that of personal autonomy – being able to decide for oneself – has come the notion that we can and must make *continuous* choices, that the modern life of the individual is an enterprise constituted by continuous choices. This is far from the *homo economicus* of Smith.

The hidden hand argument was advanced before Smith's version appeared. Adam Ferguson also held to a version of it, arguing that the progress of society is a spontaneous process, not the result of any single plan or human scheme, but a product of a number of diverse purposes and plans which emerge from the fundamental *differences* between human beings. Progress did not depend therefore upon merely economic concerns and economic competition in a free market. It is precisely because men scheme and plan – they "are sufficiently disposed to occupy themselves in forming projects and schemes" – that "man will find an opponent in every person who is disposed to scheme himself" (Ferguson, 1966, p. 122), and that progress is the outcome of this *diversity*. He continues that men "seldom are turned from their way, to follow the plan of any single projector". Thus "nations stumble upon establishments, which are indeed the result of human action, but not the execution of any human design" (ibid.). Smith's version of the human hand however depended upon the economic interests of individuals who were self interested as part of their very nature'

Hayek developed the notion of catallaxy. It differs from the hidden hand in that whereas the hidden hand was used to describe and explain the hidden effects of market exchanges, catallaxy is a technical concept used to describe "the spontaneous ordering forces of the market". It is not something then which can be ordered and controlled so as develop and control the efficiency of the market (Hayek, 1967, p. 91). "The ordered structure which the market produces is, however, not an organisation but a spontaneous order or cosmos..." (loc.cit). A cosmos has no purpose, and no regulating system outside of itself and is thus self organising or self regulating. Hayek believed that such a concept was necessary for the open society into which we were evolving. In that case Smith's *The Wealth of Nations,* with all its suggestions for economic order is otiose. Furthermore neoliberalism has been concerned to extend these economic theories beyond their original 'home' to all forms of non-random action, especially to management.

Thus there are fundamentally different ontological and metaphysical assumptions between Smith and Hayek. But should modern views of neoliberalism just be seen as a linear development of those earlier ideas? Foucault's answer would be 'no' because, in the interlude from Smith to Hayek, we can see the emergence and the exercise of *bio-power,* that form of power which operates on both individuals and populations. "The disciplines of the body and the regulations of the population constituted the two poles around which the organization of power over life was deployed" (Foucault, 1980).

SECURITY

Foucault later sees notions of *raison d'état* differently, seeing liberalism as being understood and utilised as a critique of the state. It challenged the existing forms and exercises of state sovereignty but, as Foucault notes, if it set limits to state governmentality and state activity it did not succeed in, or even attempt to formulate a positive liberal art of *government.* The concern of jurists was "less with the development of an autonomous art of government than with finding ways of codifying government within the conceptual and institutional structures of sovereignty" (Burchell, 1991, p. 125).

According to Foucault it is the idea of the phenomena of population as being possible of consideration as a political problem that renewed development of governmental thought, or *raison d'état,* which became both possible and actualised. This arises in a shift in the conceptualisation of power from the power of death of the sovereign, to the notion of *power over life,* which evolved in two basic forms, or two poles of development, in the 18th century, and which were indispensable for the development of capitalism (Foucault, 1980, pp. 140–1).

> The first to be formed ... centred on the body as a machine; its disciplining, the optimization of its capabilities, the extortion of its forces, the parallel increase of its usefulness, ... *an anatomo-politics of the human body.* The second, formed somewhat later, focussed on the *species* body, the body imbued with the mechanics of life and serving as the basis of the biological processes; propagation, births and mortality, the level of health, life expectancy and longevity...Their supervision was effected through an entire series of inter-ventions and *regulatory controls; a bio-politics of the population* (Foucault, 1980, p. 139; my emphasis).

What governmentality has to ensure in the modern self regulating state is the individual. But this modern individual has a myriad of interests and desires, as reflected by, e.g., differing life styles, tourist destinations, sports, and the myriad offerings in music, literature, films and TV channels. As Burchell says:

> Liberty is thus a *technical* requirement of governing the natural processes of social life and, particularly, those of self-interested exchanges. The security of laws and individual liberty thus presuppose each other. The government of interests must of necessity be government of a 'system of natural liberty…it finds the principle for limiting and rationalising the exercise of political power in the operations of the freedom and rationality of those who are to be governed … The liberal principle of security-liberty might be described as one which provides a formula for a mutual adjustment of the antimonic principles of law and order. (Burchell, 1991, p. 139).

Security must be considered *alongside,* in relation to, liberty. How can we understand this coupling? If we take a simple law about not stealing there is a corresponding punishment for those found guilty of the crime. This involves a binary division and relationship, between the crime and the punishment. This binary is an outcome of the legal-juridico approach to power and sovereignty; "The legal system is the archaic form of the penal order, the system we are familiar with from the Middle Ages until the seventeenth and eighteenth century" (Foucault, 2007, p. 6) However, apart from binary type questions about the relationships between the severity of the crime and the severity of the punishment, Foucault says that these further questions can, at least, be asked: (1) "What is the cost of repressing these thefts?"; (2) Is it "more worthwhile to tolerate a bit more theft or to tolerate a bit more repression?"; and (3) what is a socially and economically acceptable limit for a punishment in relation to a crime? Thus

> [t]he general question basically will be how to keep a type of criminality, theft for instance, within socially and economically acceptable limits and around an average that will be considered as optimal for a given social functioning. (Foucault, 2007. p. 5)

If these three questions are pursued (and there are others) there is no longer just a binary relationship between crime and punishment because,

> A third personage, the culprit, appears within the binary system of the code, and at the same time outside the code, and outside the legislative act that establishes the law… a series of adjacent, detective, medical, and psychological techniques appear which fall within the domain of surveillance, diagnosis…" (Foucault, 2007, p. 5)

Thus Foucault distinguishes between the penal, the disciplinary or modern, and the contemporary. This third form is what Foucault calls security. It inserts the example of theft into a probable set of events – other thefts; it is costed, and; compared to an average considered as optimal and a bandwidth of the acceptable punishments which must not be exceeded. "In this way a completely different distribution of things and mechanisms takes place" (Foucault, 2007, p. 6). However these forms are not to be strictly and temporally ordered, for there are vestiges of the other two forms to be found in any one form. Thus the penal, in the execution of the regicide Damiens in *Discipline and Punish,* for example, carries elements of discipline (behave yourselves) and a costing of the worth of his public execution (for example, will it provoke riots by the populace?) (Foucault, 2007, p. 7).

It is these elements of 'costing' which underlie or initiates the wider problem of security. This problem involves a couple – liberty and security. Costing is not just dependent upon an actual crime but involves analysis of known crimes and possibilities, and predictions of possibilities. In a liberal society, or at least one in which freedom *from* is seen as very important (Berlin, 1969), then in the name of *security* freedom *from* may be violated. At present terrorism presents serious problems to citizens, who may find their particular and general liberties curtailed, if not violated. This has already happened through legal channels in many Western States. However a more general problem, for those that believe strongly in freedom *from,* is that such intrusions upon the freedom of citizens may, itself, be construed as terrorism. But that important and complex issue must be pursued elsewhere.

NOTES

[1] Available on tape at Centre Michel Foucault. I am grateful for this reference to Arnold Davidson.
[2] He had published some of this material in the 1960s – e.g., in Mind and The Philosophical Review.
[3] Austin and Peter Strawson (later knighted) were his supervisors for the D.Phil
[4] Published 1978 as 'La Philosophie analytique and politique' *Dits et Ecrits,* 1954–1988, ed. Deniel Defert and Francois Ewald, Vol. 3: 541–542.
[5] In this 1978 paper he exhibits knowledge of Wittgenstein, without due credit, and how British ordinary philosophy differs from, e.g., Humbolt and Bergson. See Davidson, 1997, 2–5.
[6] They scarcely spoke again. But after Foucault's death Deleuze wrote his magnificent book on Foucault. Replying to a question "Why this book?" Deleuze replied that it was "out of my own necessity. Out of admiration for him, out of emotion over his death, over this interrupted work" (Eribon, 1991, p. 262).
[7] Sir Isaiah Berlin, Political Ideas in the Romantic Age, quoted in Gray, 2006, 20.

REFERENCES

Austin, J. L. (1961). *How to do things with words.* Oxford, UK: Oxford University Press.
Berlin, I. (1969). Two concepts of freedom. In I. Berlin (Ed.), *Four essays on liberty.* Oxford, UK: Oxford University Press.
Berlin, S. I. (2000). Herder and the enlightenment. In H. Hardy (Ed.), *Three critics of the enlightenment.* London: Pimlico.
Burchell, G. (1991). Peculiar interests: Civil society and governing. In G. Burchell, C. Gordon, & P. Miller (Eds.), *The system of natural liberty* (pp. 119–150).
Clausewitz, C. von. (1832). *On War.*
Davidson, A. I. (1997). Introduction. In A. Davidson (Ed.), *Foucault and his interlocuters.* Chicago and London: The University of Chicago Press.
Davidson, A. I. (2003). Introduction. In M. Bertaini, A. Fontana, (Eds.), & D. Macey (Trans.), *Michel Foucault, Society must be defended.* New York: Picador.
Eribon, D. (1991). *Michel Foucault* (B. Wing, Trans.). Cambridge, MA: Harvard University Press.

Ferguson. (1966). *An essay on the history of civil society*. Edinburgh, UK: Edinburgh University Press, with an Introduction and Edited by Duncan Forbes. Originally published 1767.

Foucault, M. (1978). La Philosophie analytique and politique. In D. Defert & F. Ewald (Eds.), *Dits et Ecrits, 1954–1988* (Vol. 3).

Foucault, M. (1979a). *Discipline and punish: The birth of the prison* (A. Sheridan, Trans.). New York: Vintage. Originally published in France by Editions Gallimard, 1975.

Foucault, M. (1979b). Governmentality. *Ideology and Consciousness, 6*, 5–21.

Foucault, M. (1980). *The history of sexuality* (Vol. I). Vintage: New York. Originally published in France by Editions Gallimard, 1976.

Foucault, M. (1988). *Technologies of the self* (L. H. Martin, H. Gutman, & P. H. Hutton, Eds.). Amherst, MA: The Univesity of Massachusetts Press.

Foucault, M. (2003). *Society must be defended* (M. Bertaini, A. Fontana, Eds., & D. Macey Trans.). New York: Picador.

Foucault, M. (2007). *Security, territory, population: Lectures at the college de France, 1977–78* (G. Burchell, Trans. & M. Senellart, Ed.). New York: Palgrave MacMillan.

Gray, J. (2006, July 13). The case for decency. *New York Review of Books*, 20–22.

Glucksman, A. (1980). *The master thinkers; The Manifesto of 'New Philosophy' from France* (B. Pearce, Trans.). New York: Harper and Row. Originally published in France by Editions Grasset et Fasquelle, 1977.

Gordon, C. (1991). Government rationality: An introduction. In G. Burchell, C. Gordon, & P. Miller (Eds.), *The Foucault effect: Studies in governmentality*. Chicago: The University of Chicago Press.

Hayek, F. A. (1947). *Collective economic planning: Critical studies on the possibility of socialism*. London: Routledge.

Hoy, D. C. (1986). *Foucault: A critical reader*. Oxford, UK: Blackwell.

Macey, D. (1993). *The passions of Michel Foucault*. London: Hutchinson.

Marshall, J. D. (1996). *Michel Foucault, personal autonomy and education*. Dordrecht, The Netherlands: Kluwer.

Meuret, D. (1988). A political genealogy of political economy. In M. Gane & T. Johnson (Eds.) (1993), *Foucault's new domains*. London and New York: Routledge.

Miller, J. (1993). *The passion of Michel Foucault*. New York: Simon and Schuster.

Paras, E. (2006). *Foucault 2.0: Beyond power and knowledge*. New York: Other Press.

Peters, R.S. *The ethics of education*. London: George, Allan and Unwin.

Smith, A. (1969). *The wealth of nations, Books I–III*. Harmondsworth: Penguin.

Walzer, M. (1983). The politics of Michel Foucault. *Dissent, 30*, 481–490. Reprinted in Hoy (1986), pp. 51–68.

James D. Marshall
The University of Auckland
The University of North Carolina at Chapel Hill

ROBERT DOHERTY[1]

10. SOCIAL CAPITAL: GOVERNING THE SOCIAL NEXUS

INTRODUCTION

This chapter sets out to offer some reflections on the translation of social capital theory into policy innovation within the project of New Labour drawing on the critical resources provided through an analytics of Governmentality (Rose, 1999, Foucault, 2007). It proceeds upon the idea that forms of 'state reason' incubate a view of the secure, ordered and prosperous State. Such an intellectual architecture in turn establishes an idealised outline that creates and sustains a disposition to recognise and categorise certain activities, behaviours, outcomes or social positions as constituting what is to be viewed as a problem, a threat, or as being desirable and often essential.

GOVERNMENTALITY

Studies that are approached from a horizon of governmentality have a deliberate focus on the rationalities and intellectual resources that constitute governmental reason together with all forms of knowledge co-opted towards the task of governing. Ultimately such forms of reason must be rendered practical, must be materialised in practices, arrangements, spaces and designs. It is unsurprising that Foucault (Burchell, Gordon et al., 1991) is drawn to the task of giving an account of the systems of ideas that constitute 'government reason,' its historical periodization, its evolving nature, its changes and discontinuities. Each new schema, having achieved influence, provides for a novel or elaborated formulation of a practical art of governing. Such a history of government reason maps onto an account of the changing pattern and form of the State's intervention into the lives of its citizens. For Foucault, the State in modernity is characterised by an increasing 'governmentalization' of the social order as the State intervenes on behalf of what it perceives as its own interest, essentially mindful of the need to maximise its resources (crucially what becomes visible by the emergence of population as the object of government).

Arising out of the breakdown of the restrictions of the feudal order and the emergence of capitalism, Foucault presents the establishment of liberalism as the instigator of a unique and distinctly modern form of government. Central to liberal rule is the 'freedom' of the citizen as they internalise norms and directions for the regulation of their own behaviour. Liberty, therefore, becomes a resource for government; liberal governmentality is as much about what subjects do to themselves as what is done to them. As Peters (2001) puts it, '. . . government in

M.A. Peters et al. (eds.), Govermentality Studies in Education, 153–163.

this sense only becomes possible at the point at which policing and administration stops; at the point where government and self-government coincide and coalesce'. This is a novel understanding of the operation of freedom in the theorisation of how the State can be governed. Liberal governmentality evolves in reaction to a realisation of the limits and incongruity of a 'police state' that seeks to know, to see, to govern through an all-pervading inspection, modulation and instruction in every detail of life. The liberal state is made workable by a certain formulation of the citizen, a responsiblized, socialised citizen whose conduct within the imagined spaces of freedom will act to serve the well-being of the State.

Rose (1996; 1999) writing from a governmentality perspective takes up the liberal problematic of government, the dilemma over how to govern when there are clearly demarcated sectors across the borders of which government must not extend. The rights of the citizen, the productive equilibrium of the space of economic activity and the space of civil society, fundamental to liberalism's internal logic, are imperilled by the ingress of the State. The innovative liberal solution, that so engaged Foucault, was to govern by and through freedom. Central to this rationality is the necessity to regulate and shape the free individual; altering the ways in which the subject comes to understand it-self as a self, and is fashioned to take an active role in governing their own conduct. Rose (1996) highlights liberal rule as a form that operates through a particular relation to forms of knowledge, in particular all manner of knowledge of human conduct that became increasingly available to the State form a burgeoning human sciences. The commandeering of forms of knowledge may be a constant feature of the exercise of sovereignty throughout the history of rule and government, nevertheless the modern is made possible and characterised by its insatiable appropriation of expanding fields of knowledge into schemes of government. While simultaneously placing it-self at arms length from the spaces of economic and civil activity, delegation to 'expert' authorities is a second feature of the liberal ethos of government. Institutionalised, professionalized authority is licensed to intervene, to ameliorate, to reform and to engage with problem spaces and detrimental conducts. Independent authorities are set at large to actively instigate a mesh of programmes, strategies, regimes and arrangements to maintain the well-being of society, regulating and governing free citizens. This strategy of governing at a distance, at a safe interval from the 'political,' serves to shield the liberal settlement from hazarding its legitimacy.

Our modern or late modern age unfolds under an ethos of government whose architecture remains unmistakably liberal in its form. Historically it is possible to trace a liberal passage that moves forward from a proto-liberal political rationality into full classical liberalism; giving way in the late 19[th]century to a reconfiguration into a 'new or 'social' liberalism and further compromising after 1945 into an 'embedded' form of liberalism (Harvey, 2005). Rose (1996; Dean, 1999) has characterised the most recent alterations to the structural design of liberal government in terms of an 'advanced liberalism.' What identifies advanced forms of liberal government is a new matrix of arrangements, forms of intervention and strategies of governing. This new phase is represented most clearly by the rediscovery of the market as a mechanism for control and efficiency and its insertion into spaces of activity within a blurring public private domain. Quasi forms of the market are accompanied by the application of new forms of accountability and the precise statement of what is to be understood as 'quality' or as the desired output, together with systems of legitimating metrics. Forms of advanced liberal government have seen the elevation of management theories and techniques to become the *zeitgeist* of the public sector, the marker of the modern, and the driver of projects of 'modernisation' together with the extensive introduction and novel extension of older technologies of accountancy and audit.

Peters (2002) in examining neoliberal governmentality identifies among its essential characteristics such elements as: retaining the liberal commitment to a perpetual critique of the state; the movement from naturalism toward an understanding of the market as an artefact shaped by cultural evolution and a focusing on the legal, regulatory framework of the economic sphere; the extension of economic rationality as a basis for the political; a revival of the rational, self-interested, utility-maximising subject of classical economics; the unleashing of the techniques and rationality of business, the commercial, the private, into the public services and operations of the State. Rose's analysis of advanced liberalism encapsulates both the neoliberal strain of governmentality, through which it emerged, together with the subsequent project of government put into motion in a form recognisable in the UK context as *Third Way governmentality*. The triumph of the market and the domination of neoliberalism have conspired to evaporate faith in socialism, putting classical forms of social democracy to rout in the process. The 'rediscovery of the market,' as part of what Sassoon (1996) has characterized as neo-revisionism, has centred on a profound shift by the left away from a political economy of common ownership and state provision to one that positively embraced and celebrated the market, a 'modernised social democracy.'

Blair's (1998) modernised social democracy claims continuity with the values of the progressive centre left (previously expressed in forms of embedded liberalism), while recognising that the means to achieve them must radically alter in the faced of a new, sociologically distinct, historical condition. New Labour has come to stand for the importance of economic success in the context of market capitalism, 'seeking prosperity for all.' In turn, the welfare arrangements of the Third Way state have been restructured around a new ethic of individual rights and responsibilities. Key to understanding the project of New Labour is its disengagement with the economic sphere, opting for a role as regulator, guarantor of fiscal stability and the conditions in which business can operate successfully. Conversely, Third Way proclaims a belief in the State as an agent of progress and mechanism for ensuring social cohesion and social justice defined in terms of opportunity for all. The move towards the 'social investment state' (Giddens, 1998) signals a revision of government itself, its purpose and means of effect. Under a politics of Third Way the locations where the citizen, the consumer, encounters the State becomes a key terrain of intervention; consequently, the health facility, the welfare service, the educational institution become fundamental locations for 'modernisation', the insertion of new practices and regimes of government. Third Way governmentality can be viewed as a form of advanced liberalism distinguished by a refocusing on the imperative of the economic space and its successful operation in a climate of global competition. In particular the governing of the social space, the disposition of civil society, now operates in relation to the fixed datum of success in the economic sphere. To such an end, a form of state reason, under an idealised Third Way schematic, comes to be formulated into a project of government in which the freedom of the citizen must be shaped and nurtured in such a way as to mobilise the populations' resources of human capital, health and culture. Government of the national community must ensure security and prosperity through supporting and sustaining the social base of economic activity and therein 'release the full potential of the information economy.'

In attempting to sketch a Third Way governmentality, or the reason of state inherent within a modernised social democracy a trajectory emerges that, under an analytics of governmentality, offers an explanation as to why certain forms of knowledge or products of social science, become visible and are appropriated; while other innovations remain obfuscated, or are seen as unproductive. The direction of a Third Way project of governance carries its own instinctive orientation to formulate, to know (*savoir*), what is to be seen as troubling in the social domain and an openness to technologies and forms of knowledge that can in turn be mobilised in response to the need to govern, to bring order, to ensure containment, or to make certain security and productivity.

THIRD WAY AND SOCIAL CAPITAL

A concern with knowledge and intellectual resources draws our attention to the individuals and assemblages that innovate and act as conduits for new and elaborated forms of reason, those who produce, interpret and speculate in the marketplace of ideas. The development of a liberal 'modern' art of government deliberately involved practices and arrangements that sustain and reap knowledge innovations as part of the machinery of government. The process of 'governmentalization of the state' advanced upon the appropriation and application of forms of knowledge and expertise to the tasks, problems and fields of government variously conceived. An analytics of governmentality is instantly drawn to elucidate the contingent and opportunistic convergence of the climate of ideas and the evolving practice of government. This line of inquiry draws attention to the role of the individual, the intellectual, the academic, the think tank or the epistemic community in the promotion or transfer of forms of knowledge and other epistemological resources into the mechanisms and practices of government. This process of adoption is well illustrated by the recent appropriation of forms of *social capital theory* within state reason, together with subsequent emergent attempts to govern the locations, activities, and dispositions made visible by such forms of knowledge.

Governmentality studies has a historical orientation, alert for and sensitive to the evolving and changing ways in which the 'art of government' is understood, reinvented and rendered practicable. At the core of the Third Way project articulated by Giddens and Blair is the reform, or 'modernisation,' of the State and 'government'. It is in the light of a particular sociological interpretation of economic and social change, which makes truth claims based on having decoded the nature of this new set of conditions, that the need for a shift in the 'rationality of government' is premised.

> Government needs to build a 'knowledge base' that will release the full potential of the information economy. Old-style social democracy concentrated on industrial policy and Keynesian demand measures, while the neoliberals focused on deregulation and market liberalization. Third Way economic policy needs to concern it-self with different priorities – with education, incentives, entrepreneurial culture, flexibility, devolution and the cultivation of social capital (Giddens, 2000:73).

Giddens can be acknowledged as making the central architectural contribution to the intellectual foundations that supported the weight of the Third Way project of Blair's New Labour. Social capital holds a double attraction for Third Way. For Giddens, in the first instance, social capital recommends itself in arguing a strategy for the 'new economics' that forms the central plank of Third Way. Szreter (2001) advocates social capital as essential to the political project of New Labour providing, 'critical assistance to the Third Way by providing it with its own distinctive political economy.' In the context of knowledge capitalism, social capital illuminates the operation and sensitivity needed towards networks, flows of information, forms of organisation, and low transaction costs, all essential for success. Moreover, the applicability of social capital goes beyond the economic to provide Third Way with a means of linking up policy across 'individual and State, society and economy' (Finlayson, 2003).

Located in the Cabinet Office of the Blair government, the Performance and Innovation Unit (PIU) serves to illustrate the ongoing engagement of Third Way with social capital. A 'strategic thinker's seminar' in March 2002 organised by the PIU reviewed trends in social capital together with examining 'the potential import-ance of social capital for a range of economic and social outcomes' (Cabinet Office, 2002). The seminar presentations listed the potential benefits of social capital as including: growth in GDP; labour market efficiency; higher educational attainment; reductions in crime; improvements in health; and institutional performance. David Halpern (2005, an academic seconded to the PIU) and in particular Geoff Mulgan, the director of the PIU and a key New Labour advisor, standout as academic entrepreneurs who have made use of social capital theory in framing policy innovation and schemes of government. However, it is a particular reading of social capital that has been established and put to work within sectors of a schema of Third Way governmentality.

SOCIAL CAPITAL

In approaching the primary literature on social capital there emerges what perhaps could be characterised as a clear fault line. This fissure can be thought of as demarcating two broad discourses of social capital reflecting the differing contexts and theoretical milieu from which forms of social capital theory have emerged and developed. On one side, around a reproductive conflict orientation, there is a vertical orientation to social capital theory, associated with the innovation of Bourdieu (1986). This vertical orientation can be contrasted with a horizontal more functionalist orientation associated with Coleman (1988) and taken up by Putnam (2000) who, in turn, has become synonymous with the notion of social capital circulating in the policy climate.

Bourdieu developed his formulation of social capital within the thrust of an intellectual project that sought, operating within a broadly Marxist framework, to recognize the dynamics of a hierarchically structured social order, its operation and in particular, its mechanisms of reproduction. For Bourdieu the existence, stability and recreation of social inequality was decisively unmasked when examined through the operation of capital, primarily the possession of economic capital. However, economic capital was only part of a much more ambitious endeavour to articulate the nature of a new totalising account of an economy of forms of capital. Using this original multi-capital scheme, including ideas of, economic, cultural, symbolic and social capital developed to differing degrees of theoretical precision, Bourdieu set out to explain the operation of the different forms of exchanges that reproduced the social order. Bourdieu's is a vertical formulation of social capital in that it captures differences in power, status and resources, drawing attention not only to the accessible resources available through social bonds but to the fundamentally different 'aggregate of the actual or potential resources.' For Bourdieu, the value or worth, or the power of such diverse resources accessible within social networks corresponded to, and was mediated by, class position in the social structure:

> The volume of the social capital possessed by a given agent thus depends on the size of the network of connections he can effectively mobilise and on the volume of capital (economic, cultural or symbolic) possessed in his own right by each of those to whom he is connected (Bourdieu, 1986, p. 248).

James Coleman stands as a key figure in the launch of a horizontally orientated social capital theory in the English speaking world, notably through a paper entitled *social capital in the creation of human capital* (Coleman, 1988) and a book, *foundations of social theory* (Coleman, 1990). It is hard not to believe that, along with the lucid articulation of its meaning, Coleman's established eminence as a sociologist played an important part in drawing attention to this idea (Field, 2003). Again, Coleman's intellectual biography is essential to understanding his formulation and use of social capital. A distinct feature of Coleman's social theory is his commitment to methodological individualism, in seeking to explain the social Coleman remained steadfast in a commitment to rational choice theory. Notable in Coleman's work predating his venture into social capital is his involvement with social exchange theory (Fine, 2001) and his collaboration with Gary Becker (1964) at the University of Chicago.

Coleman's formulation of social capital must be understood as part of a more general attempt to integrate economics and sociology underpinned by rational choice. Fine (2001) draws attention to Coleman's contribution to social exchange theory and the lack of consideration given to its significance and continuity with his development of social capital. At its heart social exchange theory, operating on the basis of methodological individualism, sought to explain the social in terms of the cumulative behaviours of individuals. This project drew on a theorisation of exchange and on behavioural psychology. In moving on to social capital Coleman engages in a new partnership with economics in the enterprise of explaining the relation of the individual to the macro. While finding the use of aggregation within economics to be inadequate, Coleman also admires this solution as being constructive, but strives to go further in explaining the social structures that frame individual rational actions. Social capital therefore operates for Coleman as a form of public good, a resource, arising as a by-product of the actions and relations of free self interested individuals who create obligations, reciprocity, trust and norms providing benefits that can have a wider impact and sanctions and reinforcements that can prevent free riding. For Coleman, social capital could explain aspects of the development of human capital, and can exist in different forms and importantly in differing quantities. Coleman's definition of social capital points toward the dimensions of the relational and the efficacious:

> A particular kind of resource available to an actor comprising a variety of entities which contained two elements: they consist of some aspect of social structures and they facilitate certain actions of actors – whether persons or corporate actors within the structure (Coleman, 1990, p. 98).

Robert Putnam, a political scientist by discipline, has been elevated from the shadows of academia to the status of public intellectual on the basis of his articulation of social capital theory. His first modest venture into the explanatory property of social capital, *Making Democracy Work* (Putnam, Leonardi et al., 1993), a study of regional government in Italy, only gained semi-canonical status in retrospect when he turned his attention to the civic climate of the US using a social capital framework. It was a paper (Putnam, 1995) and a subsequent book; both provocatively titled *Bowling Alone* (2000) that propelled social capital into the mainstream of political and educated popular thought. Putnam's message was that contemporary America was experiencing an ongoing decline in its social capital, exemplified in the demise of associational life; a view supported by a plethora of indices of falling membership, lack of trust, encapsulated in the change from organised bowling leagues to the motif of the individual bowler.

Putman's approach to social capital is informed by Coleman, acknowledging the influence of Coleman's study (1988) of its relation to educational outcomes. Putnam defined social capital in terms of the establishment of networks, norms and trust and shares a broadly public goods conception with Coleman:

> Firstly social capital allows citizens to resolve collective problems more easily. ...These and other coordination challenges go by various names-collective action problems, the prisoner's dilemma, the free-rider problem...

> Second, social capital greases the wheels that allow communities to advance smoothly....everyday business and transactions are less costly.

> A third way in which social capital improves our lot is by widening our awareness of many ways in which our fates are linked. People who have

active and trusting connections to others...develop or maintain character traits that are good for the rest of society. (Putnam, 2000, p. 288)

In Putnam's application of social capital there is an up-scaling of the level of analysis. In the Italian study Putnam focuses on the operation of regions in the North and South, and in turning his attention to the US he makes use of the state level as a subunit of the national. The existence and vitality of networks, norms and trust are presented by Putnam as key dimensions of the strength of society and its ability to generate wealth, health and provide contentment. Putnam (2000) made use of a 'social capital index' including components measuring participation, volunteerism, sociability and trust, to produce a gradated map of social capital across America's states. This array of social capital scores was then correlated by Putnam with a range of other indices (including education, crime, prosperity and democracy) to conclude that there is a positive relation between high levels of social capital and other desirable outcomes. Putnam gives an unequivocally affirmative answer to his question; 'does social capital have salutary effects on individuals, communities, or even entire nations?'

Contemporary research in the social sciences has seen an explosion of social capital literature, to the extent that social capital now operates as a form of meta-concept across disciplines in much the same way as the idea of globalisation. The conceptual assemblage of social capital has been forcefully attacked on such grounds as its lack of definition, confusion between what it is and its effects, its reliance on inference and resistance to measurement, it's eschewal of history, its neofunctionalism, romanticism and its blindness to questions of power, politics, culture and the role of the State. The relentless inflation of social capital within and across different theoretical enterprises has so far seemed immune to accounts of its inadequacies, dangers and biting critical appraisals (Arneil, 2006; in particular see Fine, 2001). The critical purchase of Bourdieu's vertical social capital has been extinguished and submerged by a remarkably flexible neo-functionalist, rational choice species. By far the dominant (perhaps only) social capital discourse in play within the policy climate is horizontal in orientation.

THIRD WAY AND THE ATTRACTION OF SOCIAL CAPITAL

Social capital is a theoretical set of ideas about the properties and resources that adhere within social bonds. There is little by way of firm or established evidence that social capital can be fabricated or synthesised, and in particular there is caution even among its adherents, or the classical liberal assumption of perverse outcomes, over the capacity of the State to intervene in pursuit of desirable social capital (Gamarnikow, 1999a). From an empirical perspective the measurement of social capital is deeply problematic, moreover there is a recognition of the dark side to social capital as found in parochialism, cartels and organised crime. Significantly such inconvenient features have not deterred governments and theorist of left and right from designing new schemes and visualizing potential spaces in which to apply political power towards ends made thinkable by the concept of social capital.

Horizontal social capital harmonises powerfully with the essential assemblage of other knowledges, economic, political, social and ethical, that make Third Way government thinkable. In attempting to explain something of the attractiveness of social capital to Third Way, and particular its architects at differing levels of invention, two broad virtues emerge as notable. The sociological nature of Third Way's claims to truth and the social theory relation of social capital provide a neat articulation. Classical social democracy relied on a strong moral foundation to its claims to power and programme for change. Third Way asserts it-self on the grounds of having precisely diagnosed new times, characterised by individualism, postfordism, knowledge capitalism and the consumer citizen, and in turn, being capable of governing and positioning the State to succeed in this new condition. Secondly, Third Way claims continuity with classical social democracy in its most un-neoliberal of convictions towards the pursuit of inclusiveness, equality and the protection of the vulnerable. Importantly this social agenda requires that 'the intervention of government is necessary to pursue these objectives' (Giddens, 2001). Horizontal social capital theory holds out the possibility of providing Third Way with a means of acting on concerns of security linked to economic success together with devising responses to social disintegration and the loss of societal cohesion.

GOVERNING THE SOCIAL NEXUS

The course to a secure and prosperous State, through the appropriation of social capital, gives a new imperative to the need to govern the social nexus. Notably, this sector of bio-politics looks to the structure and action of relational bonds that exists between the elements of population as a resource and site of intervention. This can be understood as a reflection of advanced liberal government's redefinition of the ethic of citizenship. Advanced liberalism (Dean, 1999) is marked out by its remoralisation of the relation between citizen and society. The hapless citizen of welfare rights is eligible for a helping hand from the State in the face of hardships inflicted by uncontainable structural forces. The citizen in conditions of advanced liberalism is reconceived as, assumed to be, an active agent primarily responsible for making a success of their own life, the self actualising citizen of choices, opportunities and self-fulfilment.

Changing the conception and ethical design of the citizen is clearly not a new innovation. However, advanced liberalism is concerned with a particular energetic citizen who becomes the end of an active strategy of intervention and formation by government. Noteworthy is the rearrangement of the technologies of formation available to government towards the establishment of this new active subject citizen. Attention, through horizontal social capital, to the social bonds and relational networks of the citizen, assumed or implored to be active agents in the space of the economic or the civil, opens up to advanced liberal governments of both left and right an irresistible surface of intervention. It is conceivably a natural expansion of government under advanced liberalism to extend its array of schemes, devices and technologies used to shape conduct towards the maximisation of those policy goods made tantalisingly visible through knowledge of social capital.

In discussing the nature of an analytics of governmentality Rose (1999) posits its interest in, 'lines of thought, of will, of intervention, of programmes and failures, of acts and counter acts.' The existence of failure and counter acts in rational attempts to govern conduct is not perhaps surprising. In relation to attempts to govern the relational bonds of particular targeted groups under the inspiration of a horizontal social capital the experience of Third Way seems to be closer to failure or at least a grappling with the elusiveness of the social capital prize. This is clearly illustrated by attempts to reduce social exclusion (another load bearing component of Third Way political reason) through an education policy innovation informed by horizontal social capital. Education Action Zones (EAZ) sought to reduce educational underachievement by funding a range of innovative and flexible bottom up strategies to 'raise standards' in schools that operated in 'challenging circumstances.' To be designated as socially excluded in an EAZ carried clear assumptions of low or deficient resources of social capital. However, building or altering social capital within the EAZs has not turnout to be an uncomplicated or uncontested activity (Gamarnikow, 1999b). Gewirtz (2005) and her colleagues, in an evaluative study, found that if…'social inclusion is to become a reality, then policy and practice needs not only to be responsive to the material constrains faced by those defined as socially excluded but also must be based on, and informed by, respect for the values and choices of these people.' Notwithstanding the complications that are emerging from attempts to devise practices and technologies that operate on social capital, horizontal social capital continues to function as an active component of political reason altering the policy climate in which projects and interventions are being devised. A governmentality perspective draws attention to Third Way's actions and incursions aimed at maximising the virtuous resources thought to be accessible through the modulation of relational bonds.

NOTES

[1] The author would like to acknowledge the opportunity to engage with the social capital literature provided through a research fellowship within the Applied Educational Research Scheme.

REFERENCES

Arneil, B. (2006). *Diverse communities: The problem with social capital.* Cambridge, NY: Cambridge University Press.

Becker, G. S. (1964). *Human capital. A theoretical and empirical analysis, with special reference to education* (pp. xvi, 187). New York: National Bureau of Economic Research.

Blair, T. (1998). *The third way: New politics for the new century.* London: Fabian Society.

Bourdieu, P. (1986). The forms of capital. In J. E. Richardson (Ed.), *Handbook of research for the sociology of education.* New York: Greenwood Press.

Burchell, G., Gordon, C. et al. (1991). *The Foucault effect: Studies in governmentality: With two lectures by and an interview with Michel Foucault.* Chicago: University of Chicago Press.

Cabinet Office. (2002). *Social capital a discussion paper.* London: Performance and Innovation Unit.

Coleman, J. S. (1988). Social capital in the creation of human capital. *American Journal of Sociology, 94,* 95–120.

Coleman, J. S. (1990). *Foundations of social theory*. Cambridge, MA and London: Belknap Press of Harvard University Press.

Dean, M. (1999). *Governmentality: Power and rule in modern society*. London: SAGE.

Field, J. (2003). *Social capital*. London: Routledge.

Fine, B. (2001). *Social capital versus social theory: Political economy and social science at the turn of the millennium*. London and New York: Routledge.

Finlayson, A. (2003). *Making sense of new labour*. London: Lawrence & Wishart.

Foucault, M. (2007). *Security, territory, population*. Basingstoke, Hampshire: Palgrave Macmillan.

Gamarnikow, E., & Green, A. (1999a). Developing social capital: Dilemmas, possibilities and limitations in education. In A. Hayton (Ed.), *Tackling disaffection and social exclusion: Education perspectives and policies* (pp. viii, 226). London: Kogan.

Gamarnikow, E., & Green, A. (1999b). The third way and social capital: Education action zones and a new Agenda for education, parents and community? *International Studies in Sociology of Education, 9*(1), 3–22.

Gewirtz, S., Dickson, M. et al. (2005). The deployment of social capital theory in education policy and provision: the case of education action zones in England. *British Educational Research Journal, 31*(6), 651–673.

Giddens, A. (1998). *The third way: The renewal of social democracy*. Malden, MA and Cambridge, UK: Polity Press.

Giddens, A. (2000). *The third way and its critics*. Malden, MA: Polity Press.

Giddens, A. (2001). *The global third way debate*. Cambridge, UK: Polity Press.

Halpern, D. (2005). *Social capital*. Oxford, UK: Polity.

Harvey, D. (2005). *A brief history of neoliberalism*. Oxford, UK and New York: Oxford University Press.

Peters, M. (2001). Foucault and governmentality: Understanding the neoliberal paradigm of education policy. *The School Field, XII*(5/6), 61–72.

Peters, M. (2002). *Poststructuralism, marxism and neoliberalism*. Lanham, MD: Rowman & Littlefield.

Putnam, R. (1995). Bowling alone: America's declining social capital. *Journal of Democracy, 6*, 65–78.

Putnam, R. D. (2000). *Bowling alone: The collapse and revival of American community*. New York and London: Simon & Schuster.

Putnam, R. D., Leonardi, R. et al. (1993). *Making democracy work: Civic traditions in modern Italy*. Princeton, NJ: Princeton University Press.

Rose, N. (1996). Governing "advanced" liberal democracies. In A. Barry, T. Osborne, & N. S. Rose (Eds.), *Foucault and political reason: Liberalism, neo-liberalism, and rationalities of government* (pp. x, 278). Chicago: University of Chicago Press.

Rose, N. (1999). *Powers of freedom: Reframing political thought*. Cambridge, UK: Cambridge University Press.

Sassoon, D. (1996). *One hundred years of socialism: The West European left in the twentieth century*. London: Fontana.

Szreter, S. (2001). A new political economy: The importance of social capital. In A. Giddens (Ed.), *The global third way debate* (pp. xiv, 431). Cambridge, UK: Polity Press.

Robert Doherty
University of Glasgow
UK

TINA (A. C.) BESLEY

11. GOVERNMENTALITY OF YOUTH: BEYOND
CULTURAL STUDIES

I don't feel that it is necessary to know exactly what I am. The main interest
in life and work is to become someone else that you were not in the beginning.
If you knew when you began a book what you would say at the end, do you
think that you would have the courage to write it? What is true for writing
and for a love relationship is true also for life. The game is worthwhile
insofar as we don't know what will be the end. My field is the history of
thought. Man is a thinking being.

Michel Foucault (1982) *Truth, Power, Self: An Interview with Michel Foucault*
http://en.wikiquote.org/wiki/Michel_Foucault

INTRODUCTION

When I talk with students, teachers, counselors about young people, most people
seem to have something to say and I hear multiple descriptions, clichés, truisms
and so forth. So I begin by pondering how discourses position youth in the 21st
century. A genealogy of discourses of youth reveals shifts over time in how they
are viewed and positioned. In writing this chapter, I pose the question: How do
understandings of governmentality play out in discourses of youth?

The first section of the chapter briefly discusses the emergence of Foucault's
notion of governmentality which links two sets of ideas: government and self-
government; and neoliberalism and the entrepreneurial self. Governmentality acts
as a bridge between Foucault's early work on the self and disciplinary societies and
his later work on economic liberalism. As a naturalised Kantian, Foucault wants to
understand the self as a cultural and historical construction created or fabricated, in
part, through the disciplines that take as central the freedom of the subject and his
or her autonomy. Autonomy in this context, as Foucault reminds us, is a byword
for self-regulation (where auto = self, nomos = law). The notion of self-regulation
and autonomy can be explored in a collective sense and I use the term as a means
of exploring the genealogy of discourses of adolescence/youth. This fulfils Foucault's
double–sensed notion of a 'discipline', the first based in sociologically oriented
criteria for the development of a discipline, usually known as some variation of
'youth studies' and the second in terms of notions of subjectivity of the self that
encourages and is itself predicated upon the subject's freedom.

The second section examines the formation of discourses on youth and their
discursive processes in two dominant paradigms. It begins with a subsection on

M.A. Peters et al. (eds.), Govermentality Studies in Education, 165–199.

what I call 'psychologizing adolesence' at the start of the 20th century, moving to another subsection, 'sociologizing youth'– a set of contemporary discourses that initially developed around the concept of 'sub-culture' established by Dick Hebdidge and others in the 1970s and which I explore in more detail in my book, *Counseling Youth: Foucault, Power and the Ethics of Subjectivity* (Besley, 2002). The chapter also makes some brief observations on the disciplinary formation of 'youth studies' (see Besley, 2002).

In the third section, Managing 'Risky' Youth Subjects I examine one of the dominant discourses of youth, that of youth 'at risk'. I start with definitions of this, a range of socio-psy programs and interventions which are voluntary and community based.. One aspect of governmentality concerns social security, risk assessment, risk management and insurance, thus involving the not only economic aspects but also therapeutic discourses of ways of managing risk, of using technologies of the self that include interventions of the psy sciences, to promote or enhance personal health and well-being and self-realization (O'Malley, 1996). Such a view will encompass understanding of the lifestyle choices as self-regulation and agency that young people make as they fashion their ever-changing identities, as they develop their sense of self amid conflicting and opposing societal forces that tend to emphasize notions of youth at risk rather than more positive, hopeful discourses that affect the majority of youth. This forms the first part of my argument that I argue that in the 21st century neoliberal context of consumer capitalist societies, discourses of youth need now to move beyond the valuable earlier understandings based on psychological and cultural/subcultural studies to harness Foucault's notion of governmentality. In terms of governmentality, if youth cannot or will not control their conduct, they cease to be 'docile bodies' and 'useful' to the state (see Foucault, 1976). If their behavior becomes unacceptable and criminal, the state will step in and attempt to control their conduct (at least for a while), administering its biopower in the form of the youth justice system – governmentality in action which is probably the biggest risk of all for youth, especially in the disciplinary, punitive way it is formulated in much of the USA, where it totally ignores the theoretical findings of youth development that have been established in psychological discourses.

Beyond cultural studies – the fourth section – brings the two earlier sections of the chapter together by analyzing the importance of changing economic conceptions of the self which demand something more than perspectives garnered solely from cultural studies alone. In particular I will argue that cultural studies needs a Foucauldian history of *homo economicus* that Foucault gives in the last four lectures of *The Birth of Bio-politics* (2008) and a critical engagement with the economics of the self where the dominance of pure rationality models have given way to a consideration of a range of psychological attributes that influence our economic decision-making.

I address the contemporary significance of governmentality under neoliberalism, which currently operates in most advanced capitalist nations, providing the context within which youth now exist in the 21st century. This condition is markedly different from the welfare state and has seen the expansion of deregulated markets, vastly increased consumer cultures at the same time as the influence of state has changed, in some aspects decreasing, but in others extending its gaze, surveillance, power and control. Quite how things will proceed following the global financial crisis of 2008–09, which has seen governments finally acknowledging the folly of financial deregulation which is hurting most capitalist economies in the world, is yet to be played out. Most governments are now acting pragmatically, reluctantly ditching some of their neoliberal ideologies and acting in direct contrast by using bail-out taxpayer funds to shore up banks, car companies (GM & Chrysler in USA), enormous transnational insurance companies like AIG and financial institutions and in the process often buying a stake in these institutions. Plans to regulate are to follow, so maybe the 21st century will become 'post-neoliberal.'

THE EMERGENCE OF GOVERNMENTALITY: LINKING GOVERNMENT AND SELF-GOVERNMENT; NEOLIBERALISM AND THE ENTREPRENEURIAL SELF

Foucault examines government as both a practice and a problematic that first emerges in the 16th century, as a general problem dispersed across quite different areas of life, coining the term 'governmentality' as a neologism for government rationality, one that links both 'govern' and 'mentality'. rationality, one that links both 'govern' and 'mentality'. Mitchell Dean discusses these divisions of 'govern' and 'mentality', or mentalities of governing – mentality being a mental disposition or outlook, a view taken by Jaques Donzelot and Colin Gordon (this book). The French word *mentalitie* has a similar meaning in English referring to one's mental attitude, mindset, outlook, beliefs, rationality, way of thinking, one's interiority which sets out how individuals interpret and respond to situations. One's mentality may be unwittingly constructed and/or intentionally created.

Today the term 'government' holds primarily a political meaning, but Foucault showed that up until later in the 18th century it had much wider connotations being discussed 'not only in political tracts, but also in philosophical, religious, medical and pedagogic texts.'

Jacques Donzelot (2009, this book) states that governmentality is:

a concept invented to denote the 'conduct of conducts' of men and women, working through their autonomy rather than through coercion even of a subtle kind. Out of this concept and the extended analysis of political economy which provides the material for its elaboration, Foucault never produced a published work.

Colin Gordon (2009, this book) adds:

The intellectual path that led Foucault from the analysis of disciplines to that of governmentality is perfectly consistent, just as the theme of governmentality connects consistently in turn with his later themes of care of the self and truth-telling.

In Foucault's view, governmentality means the complex of calculations, programmes, policies, strategies, reflections, and tactics that shape the conduct of individuals, 'the conduct of conduct' for acting upon the actions of others in order to achieve certain ends (Foucault, 1991). Governmentality is not simply about control in its negative sense (such as controlling, subduing, disciplining, normalizing, or reforming people) but also in its positive, constitutive sense, in its contribution to the security, health, wealth, and well-being of society (Foucault, 1979; 1991). Governmentality involves "'governing the self' and "governing others'" (Lemke, 2002, p. 49).

Rather than the old style binary oppositions, governmentality replaces the 'or' with 'and' creating twin or linked notions such as autonomy and responsibility, trust and consent and respect (see Donzelot and Gordon, this book). It involves the 'how' of governing the state, **and** how an individual governs their own mentality or interiority in this process – linking technologies of power or domination with technologies of the self (Foucault, 1988). The state governs its subjects and in turn produces or constructs the citizens it requires or desires through a wide range of political technologies and government supported practices and institutions (e.g. laws, policies, interventions, initiatives, statistics and techniques) – that is its 'biopower' and 'biopolitics'[12] and associated discourses (Foucault, 1981). The individual governs him or herself by their subjectivity and mentality.

From Dean, we can understand that governmentality is not just a tool for thinking about government and governing but also incorporates how and what people who are governed think about the way they are governed. Such thinking holds a collective component, that is, the sum of the knowledge, beliefs and opinions held by those who are governed, but this mentality is not usually "examined by those who inhabit it" (p. 16). This raises the interesting point that those who are governed may not understand the unnaturalness of both the way they live and the fact that they take this way of life for granted – that the same activity in which they engage in "can be regarded as a different form of practice depending on the mentalities that invest it" (Dean, 1999, p. 17). He explains:

On the one hand, we govern others and ourselves according to what we take to be true about who we are, what aspects of our existence should be worked upon, how, with what means, and to what ends. On the other hand, the ways in which we govern and conduct ourselves give rise to different ways of producing truth (Dean, 1999, p. 18).

According to Dean any definition of governmentality should incorporate all of Foucault's intended ideas – not only government in terms of the state, but government in terms of any "conduct of conduct" (Dean, 1999: 10). It must incorporate the idea of mentalities and the associations that go with that concept: that it is an attitude towards something, and that it is not usually understood "from within its own perspective" and that these mentalities are collective and part of a society's culture. It must also include an understanding of the ways in which conduct is governed, not just by governments, but also by ourselves and others (Dean, 1999, p. 16). The semantic linking of governing and mentalities in governmentality indicates that it is not possible to study technologies of power without an analysis of the mentality of rule underpinning them.

Foucault considered that an explosion of interest in the 'art of government' in the 16th century was motivated by four diverse questions: the government of oneself or one's personal conduct; the government of souls and lives or pastoral conduct; the government of children, which subsequently involved pedagogy and their education; and the government of the state by its prince or ruler (Foucault, 1991). Self-government is connected with morality; governing the family is related to economy and ruling the state to politics. Foucault discusses the Stoic revival focusing on the government of oneself; the government of souls elaborated in Catholic and Protestant pastoral doctrine; the government of children and the problematic of pedagogy; and, last but not least, the government of the State by the prince. Foucault believed that in the mid-18th century the family became 'the privileged instrument for the government of the population and not the chimerical model of good government' (Foucault, 1991, p. 100) thus enabling population to become the ultimate end of government. This put government in a position to concentrate on the welfare of its population, to embark on large-scale campaigns such as vaccinations, marriage, employment, improving its health, wealth, mortality. In turn this made it possible for technologies of the self such as the psy sciences and counseling to emerge. It also enabled the study of youth to emerge, arguably beginning with G. Stanley Hall's classic work, *Adolescence: its relations to physiology, anthropology, sociology, sex, crime, religion and education* in 1905, foregrounding the emergence of the discipline of youth studies.

Foucault (1982) commented on the 'disciplining' of European society since the 18th century by playing on the double meaning of 'discipline'. He referred to "blocks" of "disciplines" in which "the adjustment of abilities, the resources of communication, and power relations constitute regulated and concerted systems," citing the example of an educational institution (Foucault, 1982, p. 218). Foucault argued that it was not that society had become increasingly obedient, nor that society had set up disciplinary institutions such as barracks, schools or prisons, but rather that an increasingly invigilated process of adjustment had been developed: "More and more, rational and economic relations have been set up between productive activities, resources of communication, and the play of power relations" (Foucault, 1982, p. 219). Foucault (1977) suggested that the operation of institutions such as prisons, factories, and schools can be understood in terms of techniques of power that are a form of 'power/knowledge' that observes, monitors, shapes, and controls the behavior of people within these institutions.

Disciplinary mechanisms, such as "hierarchical observation, normalizing judgement and the examination," develop within disciplinary institutions and enable disciplinary power to be achieved by both training and coercing individual and collective bodies (Smart, 1985, p. 85). The examination observed individuals and, in turn, produced a compilation of written reports, files, and registers that enabled populations to be documented, described, analysed and classified. Through it, each individual and ordinary people became a "case", a change from "regimes of sovereign power in which only the celebrated and noble were 'individualized' in chronicles and fable ... a lowering of the threshold of description and the construction of a new modality of power" (Smart, 1985, p. 87). Foucault's notion of governmentality, its link with the sociohistorical context and with one instrument of the disciplinary technology of power – the 'examination' – enabled the 'psy' sciences (e.g. psychiatry, psychology, psychotherapy, counselling etc.) to emerge in the late 19th and subsequently to expand in the 20th century (Foucault, 1979, 1989c; Rose, 1989, 1998). On top of his earlier formulation, Foucault's later analysis of power as a form of ethical self-constitution and governmentality allows us to understand youth in the 21st century in ways that differ from earlier theorizing, in particular the forms of sub-cultural analyses that emerged from the 1960s onwards. The notion of governmentality serves to analyse and understand how discourses of youth involve a form of disciplinary power with its own form of power/knowledge.

Foucault's notion of governmentality concentrates on understanding the pluralised forms of government, its complexity, and its techniques in the question of how power is exercised whereby the rationality of government involves both permitting and requiring the freedom of its subjects. "I believe that the concept of governmentality makes it possible to bring out the freedom of the subject and its relationship with others which constitutes the very stuff [*matière*] of ethics" (Foucault, 1991, p. 102). Foucault analyzes ethics in terms of the free relationship to the self [*rapport à soi*], emphasizing the historical and conceptual relations between truth, freedom, and subjectivity. Yet, in terms of freedom, the political philosophy of neoliberalism involves a competitive, possessive form of individualism that is often construed in terms of 'consumer sovereignty' and emphasizes freedom over equality and individual freedoms over community freedoms (Peters & Marshall, 1996). The notion of freedom is often individualistic, with negative implications in terms of 'freedom from' rather than 'freedom to'—especially freedom from state interference (Besley, 2002). The power relations between government and self-government, public and private domains coincide and coalesce at the point where 'policing' and 'administration' stops and where the freedom of the subject becomes a resource for, rather than a hindrance to, government. In liberal democracies, governing others has always been linked to subjects who are constituted as being 'free' to simultaneously practice liberty and take responsibility for governing the self (Rose, 1998).

Foucault's governmentality goes beyond fixed distinctions of the state and civil society, of power and subjectivity (Dean, 1996; Rose, 1996; Gordon, 1996). Gordon (this book) points out that 'trust and consent ... are in some sense the equivalents for citizenship of what autonomy and responsibility represent in the context of governmentality.' With the addition of respect, trust and consent are what

> ...every government today desires to produce and to enjoy – respect being incidentally the item which others most like to deny government, at least in Britain. The production of respect demands, in turn, persuasion and pedagogy. Persuasion for the social classes which are resistant to change because they feel insecure, and pedagogy for the minorities who may be inclined to disorder or revolt. (Gordon, this book).

Analyses in terms of governmentality then involve problematisation, critique, and contestability about these practices of governance of the self and of others. The

Foucauldian notion of power, as formulated in his later work, is not a simply repressive one, as power is usually conceptualised in traditional liberal sociology and Marxist political thought. While the 'juridico-discursive' conception of power is repressive, for Foucault power is not only repressive or negative, but also 'positive', not in the sense of being good or benign or something to aspire to, but in the sense of being constitutive in the shaping of peoples' lives and ideas (Foucault, 1980). Foucault is less concerned with a theory of power than with "an 'analytics' of power: that is, toward a definition of the specific domain formed by relations of power, and toward a determination of the instruments that will make possible this analysis" (Foucault, 1980, p. 82). Foucault is primarily interested in how power is exercised, in "actions upon actions" which constitute power relations (Foucault, 1982, p. 220) and how it involves creative aspects in relationships, discourses and consciousness. Foucault's later analysis of power shifted to understanding power as a form of ethical self-constitution and governmentality which sheds some light on understanding the shift in discourses of youth. Governmentality both individualizes and also later totalizes people. For example students are individualized when they expose their personal experiences in classroom exercises or therapeutic situations and later, if this work is part of psychological intervention or for grading purposes, they are totalized when their experiences are compared to others, with norms.

Foucault's work on governmentality in *The Birth of Bio-Politics- Lectures at the Collège de France 1978–79* addresses neoliberal governmentality in the very early days of its emergence, before it was adopted by so many advanced capitalist societies following from Thatcher and Reagan in the 1980s (Foucault, 2008; Lemke, 2001, 2002). Under neoliberalism which has the avowed aim of 'rolling back the state' especially the public sector (Kelsey, 1993), creating the minimal state or instituting small government, the state has in fact extended its role. Instead of governing directly, neoliberal states now govern at a distance through forms of indirect government through 'an agenda that is characterized by competition, privatization, and the reform of public institutions using managerialist ideologies that emphasize the four "D's—decentralization, devolution, deregulation, and delegation—and codifying policy and accountability which enable government at a distance under the guise of local autonomy" (Besley, 2002, p. 177). Moreover, the population is subject to indirect government through multiple private, corporate or quasi-public practices, through "social technologies which delegate responsibility for individuals to other autonomous entities: enterprises, communities, professional organizations, individuals themselves." (Gordon, this book). In neoliberal regimes individuals become "experts of themselves", adopting "an educated and knowledge-able relation of self-care in respect of their bodies, their minds, their forms of conduct and that of the members of their own families" (Rose, 1996, p. 59). Chapter 8 of our book *Subjectivity and Truth: Foucault, education and the culture of self*, focuses upon a 'new prudentialism', 'on an entrepreneurial self that 'responsibilizes' the self to make welfare choices based on an actuarial rationality (Besley & Peters, 2007). It is a form that seeks to 'insure' the individual against risk, since in this instance the State has transferred this risk to the individual. Such moves constitute new types of subjectivity – nothing less than what/how we become as human beings' (Besley & Peters, 2007, p. 155–6). Such new entrepreneurial self became vitally important once the state's self-limited role decreased its power to mediate in the market to achieve the traditional welfare goal of full employment or of equality of opportunity in education. At the same time that neoliberals were attempting conceptually to remoralize the link between welfare and employment and to 'responsibilize' individuals for investing in their own education, neoliberal governments began to dismantle arrangements for state arbitration in the labor market, substituting individualized employment contracts, and exposing workers to the vagaries of the market – i.e. to more risk.

There has been a proliferation of risk management strategies and education especially regarding security at all levels—national, personal and institutional – since 9/11. The notion of the 'risk society' first described by Ulrich Beck (1992) focused on environmental, health and personal risk and was extended to include security by Anthony Giddens (1990, 1991). Yet notions of 'at risk youth' and 'nation at risk' predate Beck's and Giddens' uses of the term. The USA *Nation at Risk: Imperative for Educational Reform* Report, 1981 posed concerns about the place of education in maintaining America's pre-eminence as a world leader both economically and technologically (see: http://www.ed.gov/pubs/NatAtRisk/risk. html). Fifteen years later in 1998 the same rhetoric was revived in *A Nation Still at Risk: An Education Manifesto* (http://edreform.com/pubs/manifest.htm). The risks posed to 'tomorrow's well-being' by 'educational mediocrity' is now defined as 'economic decline' and 'technological inferiority'. The Report reads: 'Large numbers of students remain at risk. Intellectually and morally, America's educational system is failing too many people'. The main renewal strategies mentioned are: '*standards, assessments and accountability*' on the one hand, and '*pluralism, competition and choice*', on the other (italics in original).

> Neoliberalism, considered as a risk management regime, involves the distrust of expert knowledges, especially those traditionally involved with the welfare state such as social workers and teachers. Under neoliberalism there is a shift to the creation of a uniform structure of expert knowledges based on the calculating science of actuarialism and accountancy ('the audit society'). 'The social' is promoted as that which is capable of being governed— traditionally, the regulation of 'the poor' and 'pauperisation'. 'Work' and 'unemployment' have become fundamental modern categories of social regulation (Besley & Peters, 2007: 159).

> The regulation of risk takes place through insurance and the responsibilization of the individual consumer who increasingly is forced to become responsible for his/her own safety, health, employment and education. We might called this a prudentialization of social regulation – we are made to be prudent (as part of a wider moral discourse) and risk management of the social hazards facing us in modernity is based on the self-constituting prudential citizen under economic and contractual conditions (Besley & Peters, 2007, p. 160).

A genealogy of the entrepreneurial self reveals that it is the relationship, promoted by neoliberalism, that one establishes to oneself through forms of personal invest-ment (for example, user charges, student loans) and insurance that becomes the central ethical component of a new individualized and privatized consumer welfare economy. In this novel form of governance, responsibilized individuals are called upon to apply certain management, economic, and actuarial techniques to themselves as subjects of a newly privatized welfare regime. At one and the same time enterprise culture provides the means for analysis and the prescription for change: education and training are key sectors in promoting national economic competitive advantage and future national prosperity. They are seen increasingly as the passport for welfare recipients to make the transition from dependent, passive welfare consumer to an entrepreneurial self. In the past, so the neoliberal argument goes, too much emphasis has been placed on social and cultural objectives and insufficient emphasis has been placed on economic goals in education systems. Henceforth, the prescription is for greater investment in education and training as a basis for future economic growth. Such investment in human skills is underwritten by theories of human capital development and human resources management. The major difference from previous welfare state regimes is that education, increasingly at all levels but more so at the level of tertiary education, is no longer driven by public investment but, rather, by private investment decisions. The uptake of education and training grants by able-bodied welfare recipients, especially women who are single parents, now becomes mandatory after a given period within countries where neoliberal policies have been adopted, in what some see as a shift from a welfare state to a Schumpetarian workfare state (Besley & Peters, 2007: 164).

Above all, the theme of 'responsibilizing the self,' a process at once economic and moral, is concomitant with a new tendency to 'invest' in the self at crucial points in the life cycle and symbolizes the shift in the regime and governance of education and welfare under neoliberalism. Risk and responsibility have been thematized in new ways. There has been a shift from a disciplinary technology of power, first, to welfarism – to programs of social security as governmentalized risk management and to new forms of actuarial or insurance-based rationalities – and, second, to new forms of prudentialism (a privatized actuarialism) where risk management is forced back onto individuals and satisfied through the market. O'Malley comments 'Within such prudential strategies, then calculative self-interest is articulated with actuarialism to generate risk management as an everyday practice of the self' (O'Malley, 1996, p. 200). The duty to the self – its simultaneous responsibilization as a moral agent and its construction as a calculative rational choice actor - becomes the basis for a series of investment decisions concerning one's health, education, security, employability, and retirement. The responsibiliz-ation of the self and its associated new prudential strategies go hand in hand with two related developments: a substitution of 'community' for 'society' and the invention of new strategies for government through information (Besley & Peters, 2007: 165–6).

DISCOURSES OF YOUTH: 'PSYCHOLOGIZING ADOLESENCE'
AND 'SOCIOLOGIZING YOUTH'

Psychologizing Adolescence

Western societies historically have used adult values and understandings of the world, rather than any code formulated by youth themselves to construct meanings of 'adolescence' or 'youth'. Young people have been defined against traditional humanist philosophical notions of the 'normal' adult self which views the subject or agent as a stable, fixed, rational, autonomous being who is independent, fully transparent to itself and responsible for his/her actions and exercising conscious 'choices'. This Enlightenment view derives from Cartesian-Kantian philosophy is a highly value-laden, and thus contestable view of what adults, are or should be and what adolescents or youth should become. Contrary to popular belief, this view is not a universal 'truth', but an ideal that originated in Classical Greek society with the institutionalization of philosophy. More recently different versions—the Kantian ethical subject and *homo economicus* of liberal political economy—have been re-emphasized by Western capitalist democracies. These views of the adult citizen, a product of a particular culture, have become the standard against which serve as ideals for maturing young people in politics and education.

Strong criticisms of the Enlightenment self have been mounted against its individualism, the mind/body dualism which privileges the mind or intellect, especially in education; and the rationality and autonomy that is particularly challenged by various forms of social theory including critical theory, poststructuralism and feminism (see, for example, Foucault, 1980, 1985; Meyers, 2000). In contrast to the Enlightenment self, twentieth century philosophy and social theory, especially since WW II, has provided an understanding of the self more in terms of its temporality and finitude; its corporeality (embodiedness); its spatial and cultural location (situatedness); its intersubjectivity, otherness or relatedness; its gendered subjectivity and sexuality; its libidinal forces and emotionality; new forms of cultural and ethical self-constitution; emerging patterns of global production and consumption; and the constitution and positioning of identity in discourse.

Chronological definitions of youth are commonplace as are biological ones but both are limiting since the former tends to reflect status and arbitrary bureaucratic conventions while biological ones generally equate the start of adolescence with attaining sexual maturity. In order to understand the construction of discourses of adolescence and youth in the early twenty-first century in Western and industrialized societies, I argue it is necessary to understand the specific historic-cultural conditions of consumer-oriented societies where the combinations of markets and new information and communications technologies strongly shape the identities of youth people.

Both the psychological and sociological paradigms continue in uneasy tandem with psychological discourses tending to use the term 'adolescence' while sociological discourses differentiate themselves by tending to use the term 'youth'. The critique of accepted 'truths' of these dominant discourses and the taken-for-granted assumptions about the categories of 'adolescence' and 'youth' begins by considering how such categories are constructed and how young people are generally positioned in social science discourses. This approach, then, opens up new ways of rethinking the constitution of youth with some theorists arguing that in the postmodern world 'hybridised' youth–combining elements of local culture and globalized consumer world culture centered around the concept of 'style'– are emerging (Giroux, 1996; Best & Kellner, 1998; Besley, 2003).

The rapid industrialization and urbanization of the USA and the developed world beginning in the late 19th century heralded the emergence of 'adolescence' as an object of 'scientific' study alongside the establishment of psychological discourses. In studying and observing young people, the discursive construction of an age-related group tended to focus on the abnormal, the deviant, the clinical and the pathological. It was a problem saturated approach with 'juvenile delinquency' specified as a distinctively modern problem. G. Stanley Hall's (1905) classic work entitled simply *Adolescence* carried the subtitle 'Its relations to physiology, anthropology, sociology, sex, crime, religion and education', clearly demonstrating how in discourse categories are formulated and devised that are often based on values and norms which have the power to specify, position and define people in various ways. These 'new' definitions became the basis for policies and laws that regulate and control the behavior of young people.

The challenge to official and accepted discourses about the nature of adolescence and youth often entail assumptions that tend to naturalize these categories as 'given' and unalterable. For instance, Lesko (1996) talks of 'denaturalizing adolescence' as a process of exposing the politics of contemporary representations of adolescence around three dominant forms: 'coming of age', being 'hormonally driven', and peer orientation. Lesko deconstructs the predominant recurring notion of adolescence as a 'natural', universal and ahistorical stage with immutable characteristics, arguing that the prevailing discourse ignores the social processes and constructs that created the notion of adolescence and which can and do change over time.

The categories 'adolescence' and 'youth' have been constructed from a combination of different theoretical discourses – philosophical, psychological, biological, sociological, anthropological, and criminological. Theories of adolescence, for instance, can be considered as the discursive effects of certain sets of social practices, of power/knowledge that occur across numerous contemporary social domains – the family, school, law, medicine. These categories also are open to change and redefinition as, for example, the World Health Organization reflecting the prolongation of adolescent dependency in the developed world has extended 'youth' to include young adults up to 24 years.

Traditional approaches to understanding adolescence have been based on both developmental and humanist-existentialist psychological discourses. Schools have readily adopted these definitions even although they have serious limitations. Universalizing stage theories of child and adolescent development, such as those of Jean Piaget, have been probably the most influential in how the adolescent was theorized in individual, positivist, naturalist and functionalist terms. Developmental psychology has established taken-for-granted truths about how I conceptualize youth and in turn, education. The adolescent was seen as an individual trying on personae to find an identity or true self that becomes established for life. However, the effect has been to label, diagnose, categorize, calculate, normalize, judge, totals and even pathologise young people as, for example, attention deficit disordered, maladjusted, dyslexic, conduct disordered, oppositional-defiant, emotionally handicapped, severely emotionally disturbed, learning disabled etc. Yet linear sets of stages of development towards becoming a fully autonomous, independent individual do not fit women's experiences of growing up, and do not deal with ethnicity nor power relations. Since the late 1970s a contextualized approach based on the work of Jerome Bruner, Lev Vygotsky and Urie Bronfenbrenner has been favored in developmental discourse. The social emphasis has major implications for how adolescents are understood as social beings that operate both individually and in groups, interdependent with others and how education has a place to play in their development. But the social context is still seen as adaptive and so still appeals either implicitly or explicitly to functionalist biology.

Despite a considerable body of critique, developmental notions re-surfaced in the 1990s, providing the concepts, institutions and practices (e.g., standardized testing and targeting regimes) that are designed to provide resources and programs for selected youth. Yet these inadvertently marginalize some young people through such current labels as 'mainstream', 'gifted and talented' and 'at risk' youth. These deny the effects of power relations in terms of ethnicity, class or gender on the outcomes of schooling – outcomes that are not simply dependent on various individual capacities such as intelligence, ability, appearance, attitude, motivation, self-esteem and so on. Schools as sites where young people not so much mature but where they negotiate class, gender, ethnicity and other relationships, need to become aware the practices they adopt that are derived from the hidden unquestioned assumptions of development theories.

One frequently hears of medico-psychological diagnoses and labels in schools where students are also commonly described by their academic performance, their socio-economic background, classroom dynamics, and sub-cultural or peer groupings. It has been only recently, especially through the work of Michel Foucault and other poststructuralist theorists writing on feminism, social constructionist psychology and narrative therapy that these 'truths' have been strongly contested. Nikolas Rose's work on the genealogy of the 'psy' sciences (e.g., psychology, psycho-analysis, clinical psychology, social work, psychotherapy, counseling) has revealed the problematic nature of much of this discourse and its labeling of young people. Yet many people involved in the psy sciences still consider adolescence to be a stage when cognitive and emotional development takes place amid emotional storm and stress. As a result the focus continues to be on an individual adolescent's problems and on those who do not reach expected norms, leading to the dominance of remedial/adjustment ways for dealing with adolescents in psychological practice and in schools. But these inadvertently blame the victim instead of suggesting how society should adjust to better accommodate the adolescent. Rose's arguments show how psychological discourses not only became key ways of understanding the self, childhood and adolescence, but also how, in the process, the soul (subject/self) of the young citizen has become the *object* of government – the government of the self and the government of the state (Rose 1989; 1998).

Sociologizing Youth

Sociological notions of youth differ from most psychological approaches that, except for recent social, discursive and constructionist psychological approaches, mostly focus on the individual. In sociological and postmodern literature youth is conceptualized as *relational*, as 'social processes whereby age is socially constructed, institutionalized and controlled in historically and culturally specific ways.' (Wyn & White, 1997: 11). However, youth is still often idealized and institutionalized as a deficit state of 'becoming' that exists and has meaning in relation to the adult it will 'arrive' to be. Structures play a role in the governance of society in general and in particular for youth, but the impact of agency, the capacity for acting intentionally in our modern world need to be acknowledged so the politico-socio-economic contexts in which youth exist need to be understood. While the physical and psychological changes that occur in youth are important, the way these are constructed by society and in turn negotiated by individuals is equally important.

In the 1950s, 1960s and 1970s 'youth', motivated by an ethic of rebellion ('cool') against the uniformity of adult society, by protest against the Vietnam war, and by the development of youth markets for music, clothing and youth style, experimented with new values and 'life-styles' (e.g., the commune, hippies, 'free love' in multiple and same-sex relationships), turning to forms of behavior often misunderstood by adults and the authorities. Such developments were described in terms such as the 'generation gap' and theorised as 'moral panics' based on perceptions of an increase in juvenile delinquency and moral decline. Youth were often described as 'alienated', 'non-committed', 'undisciplined', 'pleasure-seeking' and unwilling to engage in the work ethic characteristic of white Anglo-American Protestantism.

Stanley Cohen's (1980) work uncovered the role of the media in formulating both 'moral panics' and 'folk devils' in confronting societal fears of the threat of the Other and pointing out how tabloid sensationalism can demonize youth. The way the news pays attention to negative behavior, violence and deviance of youth in sensational terms of strange happenings, bizarre behavior, scandals and exceptional crimes reinforces existing perceptions and prejudices and a resultant adult public outcry often ensues as youth become positioned as 'at risk' or as problems. The media is not neutral, nor innocent. It provides information, and possibly vicarious pleasure, but also displays society's moral expectations of right and wrong and the bounds of acceptability, in turn defining and shaping society and social problems. Often moral crusaders use the media to get their concerns and messages across and to gain public support. Whilst the media may well express moral indignation and outrage it is not above exaggerating sensational events in order to increase its ratings. Consequently, youth culture is to a large extent, morally constituted by the media.

Until the emergence of postmodern theorists in the late 1980s and 1990s, from the 1970s, youth studies had been dominated by the paradigm established by cultural/subcultural studies of youth from the Birmingham Centre for Contemporary Cultural Studies (CCCS). The CCCS studies utilized ethnographic methods and Marxist analysis to describe and analyze the contours of youth culture and subcultures in the post-war period – a time when youth came to be seen as a social problem that reflected considerable social change in lifestyle and values. Stuart Hall and Tony Jefferson (1976), Paul Willis (1981) and Dick Hebdige (1979) used Gramsci's concept of hegemony to interpret a series cultural styles of youth in post World War II Britain as spectacular symbols of resistance that were symptomatic of widespread but largely submerged dissent.

Subcultural studies focused on the interplay of ideology, socio-economic status adult middle-class culture through style as discourse. They examined how adolescents develop meaningful identity through developing their own subcultures in response to marginalization, incompleteness, race, class and meaninglessness in the roles that adult society grants them. The more that mainstream adult culture ignores youth subcultures, the more these will use symbols such as language, clothing, music, jewelry, and behavior to reject and negate conventional adulthood. The problem is that the more involved with and the more radical the subculture, the less able is the adolescent to enter mainstream society and consequently social dislocation becomes entrenched.

To be sure, some youth subcultures may be devoted to and shaped by protest/resistance, but to see youth only in this way is no longer appropriate as our world changes and notions of a mainstream culture are replaced by notions of a plurality of cultures. Therefore youth would not be resisting any single dominant class, political system, or adult culture. Despite highlighting the problems of adolescent marginalization and adjustment, the CCCS subcultural viewpoint has been criticized for: romanticizing youth while ignoring 'ordinary kids' who are too drab or passive to warrant investigation; focusing on class and age while neglecting other variables such as gender and ethnicity; universalizing from studies that focused only on a minority of youth – working-class males – unconsciously reflecting the researcher's class background. Subcultural analysis tends to essentialize the cultural formation of youth, ignoring the experience of females while over-emphasizing the differences and dichotomies of domination/subordination, expression/repression or regulation and normal/delinquent in the focus on styles (McRobbie, 1991). Furthermore, they ignore commonalities, continuities and the active choices that young people make, despite personal agency being circumscribed by the diversity of structures, institutions, values, family and peers that one interacts with.

Dick Hebdige (1979) criticized the over-emphasis on the intergenerational opposition between young and old instead focusing on style and life-style in the construction of youth subcultural identity. The names of some youth subcultures – teddy boys, bodgies, widgies, mods, rockers, punks, skinheads, rastafarians, hipsters, beatniks, hippies, hip hoppers, rappers, surfies, homies, metallers – are notable for the way they focus on the style of dress, mannerisms and the type of music that provide some of the cohesiveness for the group and invoke images of particular types of behavior, which is usually perceived by adults as rebellious, negative and even violent.

Hebdiges's work, by focusing on style and lifestyle seems to maintain its relevance far more today when understanding youth than many of the other CCCS works, now that times have moved on under neoliberal environments with accompanying changes in work, cultures and society in the late 20th and early 21st century. It still resonates now that the old forms factory work have largely disappeared especially in UK and USA youth are forging their identities in a globalized consumerist world. The old understandings of working class no longer hold in the 21st century now that many youth are involved in higher education until their early 20s. Others of course are employed in low paying 'McJobs' in the service industry. The CCCS class analysis fails to acknowledge or even consider distinctions, contradictions, multiplicities and complex variations within the category 'working class' – not even considering ethnic, sexuality and gender differences nor spatiality and the effects of private and public spaces. It ignored the impact of migration on the working class especially of people of colour from former British colonies such as West Indies, Pakistan, India and Africa who in many cases gained work in factories and became part of the industrial working class. Instead of assessing the impact of globalization, what it maintained was "an ethnic and nationalist myopia planted firmly in the soil of an agrarian England transcoded onto the urban setting" (McCarthy & Logue, 2009, p. 151).

Postmodern approaches tend to emphasize the dual cultural processes of constructing youth identity, through the market as an aspect of the culture of advanced consumerism and through the agency of youth themselves. The categorization of youth, in relation to the market – be it the young cosmetics and beauty market, the youth fashion market, or the latest music fad – is highlighted as a socio-cultural construction based on the concept of style, and life style, an emphasis on what Foucault called the 'aesthetics of existence'. Foucault, influenced by both Nietzsche and Heidegger (who are often considered forefathers of postmodernism) talked of making one's life a work of art. Here is the basis for a new sociology of youth beginning from Nietzschean premises that emphasizes an 'aesthetics of self' and questions of self-stylization.

MANAGING 'RISKY' YOUTH SUBJECTS

There seems to be a continuing theme in discourses of youth that positions them as either 'bad' or 'good' with few positioned in any middle ground between these binary extremes. Moreover, contemporary discourses are dominated by negative views that position youth as either victims or perpetrators, as being 'at risk', alien, or dangerous, as drug using, gang- oriented, over-sexed, as dominated by consumer and popular culture (the MTV generation). Adult observers seem to not notice that youth behave in largely the same manner as adults, but seem more than content to blame youth for bad behavior ignoring that many adults behave in the same manner and in fact 'framing' youth in order to control them (see Males, 2002). Social analysis that tend to view youth as victims sees them, according to Mike Males, a 'scapegoat' generation in USA, or as Henry Giroux argues, a 'fugitive culture' that has had its innocence stolen by corporate culture and been 'abandoned' in a post

9/11 world. Ronald Strickland's edited collection argues that neoliberalism makes war on the young (Males, 1996; Giroux, 1996, 2000, 2004; Strickland, 2002).

There has been considerable effort and debate by social theorists in describing and naming successive generations of youth. Those born since the Post World War II baby boom (i.e., after 1964) are variously described as Generation X, followed by then Gen-Y (born 1977–1995), and finally Millennials (1982–2001) (Howe & Strauss, 1992, 2000; Strauss & Howe, 2006). Jean Twenge (2006) combines GenX and GenY calling them 'Generation Me' and accuses those born after 1970 of being more narcissistic,believing they can be anything they want to be, are more open sexually, disrespectful of authority, but more stressed and depressed than earlier generations because they have been brought up with too much emphasis on self-esteem and too little reality.

There are some, but far fewer positive discourses about youth. Favorable views about youth seem to appear less frequently, not surprisingly because the media tends to overwhelmingly present the views of many adults who see youth as, strange, alien, exotic, savage, even feral as Stanley Cohen pointed out several decades ago when he talked about moral panics and folk devils (Cohen, 1981). In effect the media primarily portrays youth as the 'Other' which is unable to control or govern themselves. What is at play is a variation on notions of the evil or the innocent child that emanate from deep-seated dualities and fears that adults have about young people and their behavior and which result in all manner of attempts to control or govern youth behaviors. Such a negative depiction of youth is frightening, so by gathering knowledge about youth various interventions and techniques can be devised and applied in order to monitor, analyze, contain, correct and if necessary, confine or incarcerate youth as seems appropriate. Information and knowledge about youth is collected from a myriad of sources and from professionals in all fields e.g., psy sciences, medical, legal, economics, socio-logists, geographers, demographers, marketing and advertising etc. Could it be that in academia and associated publishing, as in other areas of the media, positive stories don't 'sell' or launch careers as well as those about 'bad' things and excess? (a topic for future research maybe?) On the positive discourse side, some youth are described as responsible, rational and even politicized (especially during the 2008 US elections) although being politicized is by no means simply seen as positive.

The notion of 'risk' as applied to youth has two main interpretations. One involves 'being risky' or undertaking behavior perceived as risky. It holds a psychological dimension and is often held as a defining feature of youth, willingness to take risks rather than simply ill-considered. A second interpretation involves multiple dis-courses of youth 'at risk' and consequent sets of interventions that institutions put in place to deal with youth so labeled. The first interpretation is an important aspect of political agency and therefore of political (community) service is compromised by the second. Government discourses about educational risk have played out recently in policy such as No Child Left Behind. In the current neoliberal environ-ment, to avoid and mange educational risk, a prudential rationality has evolved whereby youth are now expected to invest in their own education, taking out student loans and selecting educational courses at the best colleges – a self-investment that is forced upon them and aided by guidance counselors and others. To understand this new form of risk, we need to go beyond cultural studies to the changing economics of the self, to governmentality. This will be examined in a later sub-section, following this brief examination of discourses of 'at-risk' youth.

Considerable attention has been paid to the notion of 'at-risk' youth in recent years, with the emphasis being on problems such as youth crime, violence, gangs, drug and alcohol abuse, academic performance, dropping out and teen pregnancy etc, in effect continuing the discourse of youth a problem begun by G. Stanley Hall in 1905. What defines 'at risk' youth? The media and many social critics strongly promote a view that youth face more serious and critical risks than previous generations, focusing on the problems listed above. Parents, teachers and many psychologists and social theorists understandably worry that exposure to gangs, bullying and violence in schools; poverty; poor schools; changing and deteriorating family structures; substance abuse; violent and sexualized media images are likely to put youth at risk. Moreover, youth who have a higher level stresses in life are more likely to be less resilient than their peers and to cope by abusing substances; becoming sexual active; engaging in gangs and/or crime; self-harming and attempting suicide. At-risk youth who run away from home and live on the streets are subject to and engage in dangerous activities just to survive and may eventually find themselves subject to youth justice system and incarcerated. Being labeled 'at risk' tends to reinforce youth as dangerous, to themselves and both to and from others; as relatively powerless yet with power, albeit in its negative form as resistance, rebellious, anti-social even criminal and marginalized.

A brief review of 'at risk' youth websites is informative. The US site, http://www.at-risk.org/ is "a resource for parents and the general public in search of information about at-risk youth. This site will present you with information and articles about helping at-risk youth." The site's pages include: "resources" with links to related sites; "who is at risk?"; "development of juvenile justice"; "who is to blame?" It then lists at-risk youth articles respectively: "Oppositional-Defiant Disorder; Peer Pressure; Options for troubled teens; Teen Depression; Teen Suicide; Teen Violence; Teens & Alcohol; Teens that Runaway; Teen Drug Abuse; ADD; ADHD; Anorexia; Bulimia." The site's home page asks:

Whats [sic] Being Done?

Over the past decade, more and more attention has been given to the issues associated with "at-risk youth" including youth crime, violence, sex, substance abuse, poor academic performance, etc. Research shows that at-risk youth struggle with complex issues and scenarios that are brought on by peers, mentors, family members, and difficult social environments. The increased complexity of today's at-risk youth has forced parents and federal agencies to work together to find solutions. There has been growing interest in community-based efforts that help to educate and direct at-risk youth and families to a variety of helpful services. This is evident by the recent support of at-risk youth programs or initiatives by federal agencies such as the OJJDP (Office of Juvenile Justice and Delinquency Prevention). The OJJDP has recently joined with other federal agencies to help bring about the SafeFutures initiative and the Children at Risk initiative. (http://www.at-risk.org/)

A link is provided for parents to access Help for Troubled teens at http://www. helpfortroubledteens.net/, which has blogs, phone numbers and links for "suggestions for families; How Badly is your Teen Struggling? Common Teen Drugs; Boarding Schools for Trouble Teens; Teenage Abortion." This site links with psychological diagnoses as per the DSM and social analysis and comment and suggested interventions.

The American Bar Association (ABA), Commission on Youth at Risk at http://www.abanet.org/youthatrisk/, with the slogan "America's youth are our most important asset", provides links to "ABA policies concerning youth; ABA activities that support youth; partnership with Girl Scouts; National Roundtable series; Programs across the nation; what lawyers can do." The ABA makes clear links for youth at risk in terms of education and law, for example:

ABA Criminal Justice Section's Juvenile Justice Committee recently sponsored "From Truancy to Zero Tolerance: The Changing Border of Education and Juvenile Justice." The program, held on Aug. 23 in Washington, D.C., featured ABA President Karen J. Mathis as moderator.

Expert panelists presented information on a truancy intervention program, and addressed zero tolerance, special education and disability rights vis-à-vis delinquency, and alternative remedies to court referrals. http://www. abavideonews.org/ABA372/podcasts.php

The Introduction to Morley & Rossmans' report (2006) states that assessing that youth at risk and their families have multiple needs, has meant that many collaborative, community-based interventions have developed, now that use "case management, parental involvement, using volunteers for tutoring and mentoring, integrating services and comprehensive rather than narrow services." Furthermore:

Support for such initiatives by federal agencies and foundations underscores the interest in exploring these approaches and in communicating lessons learned to assist similar efforts. For example, the U. S. Department of Justice's (DOJ) Office of Juvenile Justice and Delinquency Prevention (OJJDP) provides support for the SafeFutures initiative. A federal interagency partnership, including the U.S. Departments of Commerce and Health and Human Services and OJJDP, supported Communities in Schools (CIS). The Annie E. Casey Foundation funded the New Futures initiative in five cities. OJJDP and two other DOJ agencies, the Bureau of Justice Assistance and the National Institute of Justice, joined a consortium of foundations, trusts, and other organizations to support the Children at Risk (CAR) initiative. Another community-based collaboration supported by the Bureau of Justice Assistance is the Comprehensive Communities Program, which addresses overall community crime prevention and includes a youth crime prevention component (see http://www.urban.org/publications/307399.html).

Another example of a US program which has a 30 year history of dealing with at risk youth is the Crossroads Programs, begun in 1978, which "has worked to build better futures for disadvantaged children and their families. Our mission is to empower youth who are homeless, abandoned, abused, or at-risk to lead healthy, productive lives." (http://www.crossroadsprograms.org/). Their programs, which are listed on the website as: "Capable Adolescent Mothers; Cinnaminson House [homeless youth, 16– 21]; Community Care for Kids [Specialized foster homes for emotionally disturbed children who are at risk of placement in a residential treatment facility]; Flexible Solutions [temporary placement foster care during an emergency or for a respite period]; Just for You Learning Lab; Preteen Promise; Project DISCOVERY [homes for LGBTQ (lesbian, gay, bisexual, transgender and/or questioning) youth]; Rites of Passage Transitional Housing Program [intensive life skills training, job coaching and placement, case management, and transitional housing]; Second Chance Homes [transitional housing program for homeless teen mothers and their children] ; Transitional Living Program; Trinity Place Host Homes [for runaway and homeless youth while family reunification is negotiated and/or other needed services are put in place.]" have a distinct Rogerian emphasis:

> Our programs are designed to encourage the personal development of children and youth while working to strengthen and support healthy relationships among family members. We believe that all youth deserve a chance to discover and put to use their inherent strengths and talents in order to become successful, contributing adults. Our approach is to promote positive, healthy child and adolescent development by fostering responsibility, resiliency, and respect for self and others. Safe housing, counseling, and appropriate referral and follow-up services are delivered in an atmosphere of positive regard and care. (http://www.crossroadsprograms.org/)

There are many other initiatives, sources of information and programs aimed at assisting youth at risk and examples on the Internet e.g., Teen Help Us – http://www.teenhelp.us/; The Bureau for at risk youth – http://www.sunburst-media.com/hminfo.aspx?M=s&index=131&selection=20: Hot Topic: At-Risk Youth – http://www.servicelearning.org/instant_info/hot_topics/at-risk/index.php; a wilderness camp in Selkirk Mountain Range, Idaho – http://www.ascent4teens.com/; selected bibliography, Mentoring Youth at Risk, at http://www.west.net/~jazz/mentor/biblio.html. Such programs have laudable aims and varying degrees of effectiveness, but when all else fails, unfortunately the next stop for at risk youth tends to be the youth justice system and the possibility of incarceration, especially for males and non-white youth. The USA criminal justice system exerts a heavy disciplinary power, currently incarcerating more youth than any other country in the world. These youth are largely male with minorities disproportionally represented. As Wikipedia notes:

> On any given day more than 126,000 youth are serving time in jails and prisons based on rates from the year 2007 (http://gatheringforjustice.ning.com/). Approximately 500,000—half a million—youth are brought to detention centers in a given year (Homan, & Ziedenburg, 2006, p. 3) Minority youth

are disproportionately represented in incarcerated populations relative to their representation in the general population. A recent report from the National Council on Crime and delinquency found that minority youth are treated more severely than white youth at every point of contact with the system— from arrest, to detention, to adjudication, to incarceration—even when charged with the same crime (Poe-Yamagata, & Jones, 2000). In 1995 , African American youths made up 12% of the population, but were arrested at rates double those for Caucasian youths (The Trauma Foundation, 2004). The trend towards adult adjudication has had implications for the racial make-up of the juvenile prison population as well. Minority youth tried in adult courts are much more likely to be sentenced to serve prison time than white youth offenders arrested for similar crimes (Males& MacAllair,2000).

(http://en.wikipedia.org/wiki/Prisons_in_the_United_States#Incarceration_rate)

US youth justice is generally a state mandated affair. A study comparing Texas and California youth incarceration policies from 1995–2006 reveals very different policies but little difference in reducing crime; Texas has increased imprisonment for younger offenders for less serious crimes while California has diverted and used non-custodial sentences for many youth, while placing older youth committing more serious crime in correctional facilities (Males, Stahlkopf, & Macallair, 2007).

This result suggests that juvenile crime control policies that emphasize incarceration and similar punitive measures need to be reconsidered, and that Texas's current youth incarceration policy is unjustified and unnecessary. Given the recent human rights abuses occurring in Texas and California youth correctional facilities, crime control policies that emphasize non-incarcerative options should be given greater priority. The savings achieved by reduced incarceration could be reinvested in a range of community-based interventions. (Males, Stahlkopf, & Macallair, 2007 – http://www.jdaihelpdesk. org/Docs/Documents/Crime%20Rates%20and%20Youth%20Incarceration% 20in%20Texas%20and%20California%20Compared.pdf).

Many states have increased the numbers of laws so they now try youth as adults. There has been a particularly punitive approach rolls back of the very notion of youth justice which separates youth under age 18 from adults in the justice system and is intended to rehabilitate as well as punish, instead putting thousands of young people at risk of harmful consequences that are often permanent because it limits their education, future employment prospects and disenfranchises them – often for minor and non-violent offences. The US national statistics are alarming (see Appendix) and the situation is being challenged by various campaigns within the US and beyond (e.g., Campaign for Youth Justice, http://www.Campaign4 youthjustice.org/; Youth Justice in Action, http://www.youthjusticeinaction.org/; Building Blocks for Youth, http://www.soros.org/initiatives/usprograms/focus/ justice/articles_publications/publications/public_opinion_youth_20011001).

In contrast to the way youth justice operates in USA, the New Zealand Youth Justice system, for a much smaller country of course, still maintains a very separate system for youth and one which emphasizes rehabilitation and restorative justice practices [3] (see http://www.justice.govt.nz/youth-justice/system.html; also, Morris &Maxwell, 1998; http://www.cyf.govt.nz/youthjustice.htm). Just as New Zeal and aims to reduce provide alternatives to incarceration for youth so they do not start their adult lives with criminal records, the move to allow for youth development and community treatment is favored by The Juvenile Detention Alternatives Initiative (JDAI) (see: http://www.aecf.org/MajorInitiatives/JuvenileDetention AlternativesInitiative.aspx):

A private-public partnership being implemented nationwide, with pilot programs in California, Oregan, New Mexico and Illinois. Their goal is to make sure that locked detention is used only when absolutely necessary.

Their approach is multi-faceted, including multiple emphases on: Intergovernmental collaboration; reliance on data; creation and implementation of objective admissions screening for detention facilities; expedited case processing to reduce pretrial detention; improved handling of "special cases"; express strategies to reduce racial disparities; improving the conditions of confinement; and researching, testing, and endorsing alternatives to confinement.

Alternatives to confinement are sensitive to family and culture, and treatment is often built around the strengths of the youth and their families. Alternative treatment methods might include any combination of the following, as well as other approaches: diversion, mentorship, Aggression Replacement Training, Functional Family Therapy, and multi-systemic therapy.

The JDAI has produced some promising results from their programs. Detention center populations fell by between 14% and 88% in JDAI counties over the course of 7 years 1996–2003). These same counties saw declines in juvenile arrests (an indicator of overall juvenile crime rates) during the same time period ranging from 37–54% (Holman and Zeidenberg, 2006, p. 14–15). They are succeeding in reducing youth incarceration and youth crime. (http://en.wikipedia.org/wiki/Prisons_in_the_United_States).

In effect, if youth cannot or will not control their conduct with or without the assistance of others, the state will control it for them. If youth do not use their agency, autonomy and self-regulate to become docile bodies and subjects that are useful for the state, then the state will administer its disciplinary biopower in the form of the youth justice system – governmentality in action.

BEYOND CULTURAL STUDIES: THE CHANGING ECONOMICS OF SELF

Just as adults have problems, youth clearly they do too, but the at risk youth discourse tends ignore that problems are not limited to youth and tends to produce totalizing descriptions of youth, which completely ignores the fact that in USA and UK the vast majority of youth are involved in education. They are in effect responsible, 'docile' young people, mostly following expected and even prescribed paths of youth development, e.g., in the USA, "About three-quarters of the freshman class graduated from high school on time with a regular diploma in 2004–05" (http://nces.ed.gov/pubs2008/2008032.pdf). While closer to 100% may be the goal, and the statistics indicate different completion rates between states in effect highlighting problem areas which happen to be mostly in the south where there are large African-American populations and in agriculturally oriented states. "Status dropout rates for Whites, Blacks, and Hispanics ages 16–24 have each generally declined between 1972 and 2006. Rates for Whites remained lower than rates for Hispanics and Blacks" (http://nces.ed.gov/pubs2008/2008032.pdf). Some young people who do not complete "on time" or drop out will do so later at adult high schools and others will be employed. Furthermore participation in higher education is higher than ever in the western world (see USA indicators[4]).

> The rate at which high school completers ages 16–24 enrolled in college in the fall immediately after high school was approximately 50 percent in most years between 1972 and 1980. By 1997, this rate had increased to 67 percent and has fluctuated between 62 and 69 percent since then. Although immediate college enrollment rates increased overall between 1972 and 2006 for both Whites and Blacks, there has been no overall change in the White-Black gap. For Hispanics, the rate has fluctuated over time but increased overall between 1972 and 2006. Nonetheless, the gap between Hispanics and Whites has widened over this period. In 2006, the immediate college enrollment rate was 58 percent for Hispanics, compared with 69 percent for Whites. (http://nces. ed.gov/pubs2008/2008032.pdf)

These young people are following expected paths of development in mostly finishing High school – the expected standard in USA. Subsequently over half enter university and most enter adult life as responsible citizens, getting jobs, setting up homes, families and so on – chasing the American Dream. They appear to have exercised agency and have made rational decisions (maybe with help from parents, teachers, guidance counselors) in their own self-interest as to what course in education suits them the most and will fulfil their potential and dreams of happiness the 'good life'. They invest in themselves by taking student loans to obtain a university education, opting for courses that will hopefully and eventually maximize their earning potential. They are in effect becoming entrepreneurs of the self.

Traditional conceptions of rationality that govern agental models of the self emphasize not only simplifying assumptions of individuality, rationality and self-interest, but also risk-averse activity or at least a calculation of risk as part of a rationality assumption. Indeed it is the case that the risk taking agent is the paradigm of the model of the entrepreneur beginning with Callon and Schumpeter and the entrepreneurial self. In other words the management of risk is an integral part of rationality and decision-making designed to enhance self-interest in the neo-classical model. In this section, I use the discourse of 'risk' as the background against which to bring into alignment Foucault's notion of governmentality and his emphasis on the government of self with two aspects of risk discourse – 'being risky' or 'at risk' as already discussed in the previous section, and calculating and managing risk, i.e., the entrepreneurial self.

There are serious grounds now for doubting the theoretical centrality of *homo economicus* and its extension into the social realm through the concept of the entrepreneurial self. Not only is this figure of rationality open to question on the basis of advances in behavioral economics and finance (see especially the work of Shiller, 2000), but also the overturning of principles of neoliberalism by the Obama administration now leads to speculation about a new socialized or community self where risk is once again socialized although differently from the Keynesian welfare state. This explains for instance new Obama policy programs to extend and socialize health insurance, to introduce community service for young people, and to emphasize the values of equality, community and unity that transcend the old 1960s dualisms between black/white; males/females; and North/South. In these latest policy constructions, the driving logic of identity formation is much more anchored in the concepts of belonging, participation, and collaboration which are all relational characteristics that de-emphasize processes of individualism and individualization. These principles and this new collective logic of identity gels well with the new reality of networks and the application of social media and social networking to a whole host of problems in education, democracy promotion, community building and politics.

This new socialized self is different from any unvarnished socialist or Keynesian welfare state notions of self. It is also different from nationalist notions of self by virtue of the logic of networks and by the new ethic of participation and collaboration that are sparked by the web as platform. Perhaps a better term for this social fabrication of the self is 'neo-social' self or 'participatory' self.

Contemporary identity studies now view the constitution and manufacture of consciousness and subjectivity in the light of current cultural processes of formation including globalization, the 'knowledge economy', and transnational migrations of not just companies and finance but of people. Accordingly, new social media and new technologies also play a part in identity formation and new patterns of work in post-industrial societies and new discourses are emerging:

> ...concerning questions of power and identity, especially in relation to rising unemployment, to social media, to globalization, and to new forms of work. A new generation of social theorists and researchers look for approaches that link discourse, power, psychology and the self (Peters, 2009, p. 131).

One of these new discourses is 'behavioral economics' which has evolved using insights from psychological discourse – cognitive and emotional behavior in relation to rationality and decision-making, self-interest and public choice – while, rejecting some aspects of neoclassical theory based on the homo economicus (see http://en.wikipedia.org/wiki/Behavioral_finance). Peters states that :

> ... the question of identity strongly influences economic thinking and behavior and people do not behave in the way that the strong rationality model of neoclassical economics has taught us to believe on the basis of *Homo economicus* (Peters, 2009, p. 131).

What behavioral economics does is introduce the emotions to traditional concepts of rationality, something that feminist theorist such as Diana Meyers (2000) had already established in philosophical understandings of the self in her work, 'Feminist perspectives on the self,' (see: http://plato.stanford.edu/entries/feminism-self/). The emotional context has been expanded somewhat with the former Federal Reserve Board Chairman, Alan Greenspan unintentionally contributing a key notion, "irrational exuberance" to behavioral economics in a speech given in 1996 during a stock market boom. The phrase, describing "a heightened state of speculative fervor", become popularized as a result of the stock markets in Tokyo, Hong Kong, Frankfurt, London and New York slumping immediately after his speech; Robert Shiller's 2000 book, *Irrational Exuberance*, and now with the 2008-09 financial crisis, it signifies the excesses of a past era (Shiller, http://www.irrationalexuberance.com/definition.htm).

In Chapter 8, 'Enterprise Culture and the Entrepreneurial Self', of our book, *Subjectivity and Truth, Foucault, Education and the Culture of Self* (Besley & Peters, 2007), these ideas are discussed in some detail and I only briefly point to some of these here. In the 1980s 'enterprise culture' which emerged in the UK under Margaret Thatcher – a profound shift away from the Keynesian welfare state to a neoliberal model of the entrepreneurial self, based on the rejuvenation of *homo economicus*.

A genealogy of the entrepreneurial self reveals that it is the relationship, promoted by neoliberalism, that one establishes to oneself through forms of personal investment (for example, user charges, student loans) and insurance that becomes the central ethical component of a new individualized and privatized consumer welfare economy. In this novel form of governance, responsibilized individuals are called upon to apply certain management, economic, and actuarial techniques to themselves as subjects of a newly privatized welfare regime. In this context Burchell's remark made in the context of a Foucauldian analysis of neoliberalism that an 'enterprise form' is generalized to all forms of conduct and constitutes the distinguishing mark of the style of government, could not be more apt (Burchell, 1996, p. 275). At one and the same time enterprise culture provides the means for analysis and the prescription for change: education and training are key sectors in promoting national economic competitive advantage and future national prosperity (Besley & Peters, 2007, p. 164).

Neoliberalism promoted a deliberate policy shift from a 'culture of dependency' to one of 'self-reliance' and 'responsibilization'. In effect what has emerged is a

'New prudentialism' in education that focuses on an entrepreneurial self that 'responsibilizes' the self to make welfare choices based on an actuarial rationality. It is a form that seeks to 'insure' the individual against risk, since in this instance; the State has transferred this risk to the individual. Such moves constitute new types of subjectivity – nothing less than what/how we become as human beings (Besley & Peters, 2007, p. 155–156).

Neoliberalism can be seen as an intensification of moral regulation based on the radical withdrawal from government and responsibilization of individuals through economics and it emerges as an actuarial form of governance that promotes an actuarial rationality through the encouragement of a political regime of ethical self-constitution as consumer-citizens (Besley & Peters, 2007, p. 159).

In this form of government, the citizen-consumer, became 'responsible' for making 'choices' about their "lifestyles, their bodies, their education and health", calculating the risks and investing in themselves "at critical points in the life-cycle—birth, 'starting school,' 'going to university,' 'first job', marriage, retirement," – i.e., paying for higher education and taking out student loans if necessary (p. 160). We point out that under neoliberalism,

'Choice' is not simply 'consumer sovereignty' but rather a moralisation and responsibilization—a regulated choice-making transfer responsibility from State to the individual in the social market. Its specific forms have entailed a tearing up of labour law under the welfare state and an emphasis upon more privatised forms of welfare often involving tougher accountability mechanisms and security/video surveillance. The 'risk society' is put in place through actuarial mechanisms and there is an emphasis on all forms of insurance as a means of reducing risk to the individual (in areas of employment, education, accident, security, retirement). In one sense, this is the primary link between government and the government of the self, which is promoted in its relation to choice making through cybernetic and information systems. Neoliberalism has a suspicion of autonomous form of self-regulation. Actuarialism is a mobilisation of one predominant structure of expert knowledge and an interrogation of the autonomy, which accompanies other expert knowledges of teachers, social workers (traditional forms under the welfare state). Prudentialism refers to the new form of insurance against risk, which is 'forced' onto individual as consumers in the social market. The mode of 'forced choice' which encourages a 'responsibilization' Peters calls 'actuarial rationality' as in making consumer choices concerning education as a service individual consumers in effect become actuaries calculating the risks of their own self-investments (Besley & Peters, 2007, p. 160).

In recent years the UK in a move to create enterprise culture which has more recently been formulated as a move towards a 'knowledge economy'. It has been embarking on a move from only the elite and middle class being able to afford to attend university, to mass higher education and has also instituted enterprise education in school curricula. The UK aims to catch up with the USA in terms of numbers attending higher education and has instituted mechanisms for them to pay for this to invest in themselves, as has been required for years of American young people who wished to attend college:

About one third of young people go on to higher education at age 18 (with almost 50% of students in Scotland), and an increasing number of "mature" students are studying either full-time or part-time for university degrees. Higher education is a current policy priority for the government, with a target set to attract 50% of 18- to 30-year-olds to higher education by 2010. (http://www.britishcouncil.org/usa-education-uk-system-k-12-education.htm)

In this manner young people and sometimes their families are holding the risk that this will pay off. Ulrich Beck defined risk defined "as a systematic way of dealing with hazards and insecurities induced and introduced by modernization itself" (Beck, 1992, p. 21). Further, he coins "the risk society", which "is characterized essentially by a lack: the impossibility of an external attribution of hazards. In other words, risks depend on decisions, they are industrially produced and in this sense politically reflexive" (Beck, 1992, p. 183).

Such 'risk' is not limited to individuals, but can also play out nationally. Fore example, the 1981 report *Nation at Risk* considered that the USA's pre-eminence as a world leader both economically and technologically was at risk and worried that:

> The educational foundations of our society are presently being eroded by a rising tide of mediocrity that threatens our very future as a Nation and a people. What was unimaginable a generation ago has begun to occur – others are matching and surpassing our educational attainments. (http://www.ed. gov/pubs/NatAtRisk/risk.html).

In 1998 the same rhetoric was revived in *A Nation Still at Risk: An Education Manifesto* (http://edreform.com/pubs/manifest.htm). This document outlines the risk management regime for US education systems in terms of 'ten break-through changes for the 21st century' including the now familiar, 'national academic standards', 'standards-based assessment' and 'tough accountability systems,' alongside 'school choice', charter schools, deregulated teacher force, differential teacher pay systems, and 'essential academic skills.' The rhetoric and the national risk management strategy is very similar to the UK's approach to education policy (Besley & Peters, 2007). In the process of becoming governable, both 'youth' and 'risk' become categories problematizing young people such that new forms of knowledge are created and interventions devised and applied.

NEW SOCIAL MEDIA AND POLITICIZED YOUTH IN 21ST CENTURY

In earlier work (Besley 2006; Besley & Peters, 2007) I discussed the way youth in UK used new media in 2003 to mount protests against the start of the Iraq war, in particular the 'Hands Up for Peace' campaign initiated by London schoolgirls Neela Dolezalova and Rowenna Davis (http://www.sustnable.org.uk/newact7.htm; http://www.bbc.co.uk/videonation/articles/u/uk_handsupforpeace2.shtml). Prior to this adults seem to have despaired that youth were disengaged politically, but the Iraq war and US presidential election have dispelled this notion.

A further example of politicization of youth and the use of new media technologies has occurred in 2008 USA Presidential elections and has begun to change perceptions about youth. The campaign of Barack Obama in both the

Primaries and the Presidential election has involved the engagement of youth (under 30s) of all ethnicities on a scale unprecedented since the 1960s. The youth cultures of the Internet generation, Generation Y, or Millennials, has been harnessed via new social media such as YouTube, Facebook, MySpace, Twitter and blogs. For example:

Before the rally [at George Mason University more than a week before announcing his Presidential campaign], Obama's campaign already knew they had a massive presence on Facebook. Students for Barack Obama (SFBO) had around 60,000 members, and even more astonishingly, a 26-year-old named Farouk Olu Aregbe had assembled more than 200,000 in his Facebook group "Barack Obama (One Million Strong for Barack)" in little more than two weeks (the group now has more than 272,000 members) (http://www.thenation.com/doc/20070305/graham-felsen).

Obama's slogans 'Change we can believe in', "Yes We Can" and "We're the Ones We've Been Waiting for", resonate with youth who see positive comparisons to John F. Kennedy's slogan, "the torch is being passed" in what seems to hark back to the revolutionary ideals and changes of the 1960s. It may however be to a certain extent, a romanticising of the past, seeking a return to a golden age, much simpler and more certain. Nevertheless the spirit of change of the 1960s in terms of civil rights, women's rights and a belief in peace and working together is attractive to many young people. Michael Delli Carpini, (Dean, Annenberg School for Communication, University of Pennsylvania), sees that "on campuses across America, the Boomer legacy of social development is coming to fruition," (Lubrano, 2008). As some students say:

"Older people see color as an issue," said Melissa Smyth, 18, a Rowan University freshman from Dennisville, Cape May County. "With my generation, electing a black president would be a positive. It says to black people there are no differences." Agreeing completely, Talia Sykes, 25, a Rowan graduate student from Mount Laurel, said: "My generation is all about change and diversity. I go to a diverse college, a diverse workplace. My partying is diverse. We're a generation that holds hands and sits with each other, and you don't have to look like me."

On campuses across America, the Boomer legacy of social development is coming to fruition, said "One of the biggest differences of this generation is its incredible open-mindedness to diversity," he said. (Lubrano, 2008)

Obama's appeal to a wide cross-section of America's youth is based on many things: his personal charisma and youth (he is 46); being bi-racial (Kenyan and white) and his emphasis on diversity with an appeal to a broad section of people; his intelligence and inspiring words (educated at both Colombia and Harvard and the first African American to lead the Harvard Law Review); an aversion to the way dynasties seem to be occurring in presidential politics; opposing the Iraq war and his message of change and hope for both domestic and foreign policies. As a warning note, Mark Bauerlein, sees an appeal to the vanities of youth or'the youth temptation' in the suggestion that

> They are special, the smartest generation yet, occupying not only a unique point in time, and that they can fix what their predecessors were unable to do. 'When Obama talks about change, adults hear policy adjustments on Iraq, taxes, health care, etc. When 18-29-year-olds hear "change," it means erasure of the old, the irrelevance of the past.' (http://chronicle.com/review/brainstorm/bauerlein/the-obama-appeal).

Nevertheless, it was with the support of the youth vote as well as others that saw the historical election of Barack Hussein Obama as the 44th president of the USA. No wonder youth feel special and engaged with democracy at long last. They are democratized, politicized and responsible citizens. They are not only governed but are engaged in the selection process of who shall govern them and under which conditions.

CONCLUSION

Under late capitalism, in the postmodern era, where the culture of consumption has taken over from the culture of production, youth can be better understood in terms of them consuming their identities in the global marketplace where style and identity become inextricably mixed. From the early 1980s we have seen multinational corporations targeting niche markets of specific age or interest groups (e.g., pre-teens, tweenies, kidults, generation X, rappers, hip hoppers, homies, surfer) and focusing on their multiple identities, differences, desires and buying-power. The central idea here is the way the market infiltrates the social fabric, probing into sensitive zones, from preschool to youth, from the barely linguistic in order to 'train' young market populations in the habits and disciplines of consumerism. Now, more than ever, kids find their identities and values in the marketplace, rather than in traditional sources such as the family, church, school that comprise a locality, and moreover, that marketplace is an increasingly globalized one. Style is clearly influenced by fashion, the cult of celebrity – including celebrities, TV or movie stars, royalty or sports stars – advertising, music, video games and the plethora of multi-media and social networking sites. A characteristic of style is the use of bricolage, assembly, pastiche, blending or hybridization where although a particular stylistic theme may be adopted, there is often some element of difference devised by youth in an attempt to assert their individuality (and maybe even an element of control) within the choices that are available and the statements about themselves and identity that they are making.

New tools are needed to explain and understand youth in our current and future world that is globalized, multi-lingual and multi-cultural, where humanist theories of the self and much of both psychologized and sociologized paradigms have become obsolete and therefore stand in need of refinement. If we follow postmodern theorists we move away from universalizing notions about youth towards acknowledging plurality and difference (age, gender, sexuality, ethnicity, religion etc.). It is also necessary to acknowledge contradictory tendencies: while Western youth seem to be gaining more personal autonomy within familial and educational structures that is partly a result of new forms of income, they are not necessarily gaining increased freedom as centralized forms of control based on the surveillance state and the dominance of the global multi-national market become ever more sophisticated in manipulated their needs. There is also move in the new discourses about youth to move away from an emphasis on temporality as development to acknowledging concerns of spatiality and cultural situatedness. Youth discourses also tend to emphasize becoming rather than being, identity rather than self and focus on cultural formations of subjectivity. Foucault's notion of power/knowledge leads us to understand better the inseparability of discourses, institutions and cultural practices, and to seek a more holistic understanding of youth in terms of subjugated knowledges. In examining youth today we need to not only to actually speak with them to gain their perspectives, but also to listen for the little narratives, still largely unwritten, which should not be forced into a consensual metanarrative. Rather than seeing youth as resisting through rituals, and styles, might the use of Foucault's work on power relations, power-knowledge and governmentality now be more fruitful lines of analysis of youth.

NOTES

[1]   These terms are explored more fully in Chapters 3 and 4 in my earlier book, *Counseling Youth: Foucault, Power and the ethics of subjectivity* (Sense Publishers, 2002).

[2]   Foucault's term 'biopower' refers to 'an explosion of numerous and diverse techniques for achieving the subjugations of bodies and the control of populations' (Foucault, 1980: 140). Biopower is a technology of power involving the way the state regulates the population through practices that relate to human life - practices concerning customs, health, sexuality, reproduction, genetics, family, well-being and risk regulation etc. 'Biopolitics' is the style of government that regulates populations through biopower and in his work, *The Birth of Biopolitics (Michel Foucault: Lectures at the College De France)* Foucault addressed neoliberalism (Foucault, 2008).

[3]   The Youth Justice System (http://www.justice.govt.nz/youth-justice/system.html) New Zealand's youth justice system is governed by the *Children, Young Persons and Their Families Act 1989* (the Act). The Act sets out two principles relating to child and young offenders: they are held accountable, and encouraged to accept responsibility, for their behaviour: and they are dealt with in a way that acknowledges their needs and that will give them the opportunity to develop in responsible, beneficial, and socially acceptable ways.

   The youth justice system takes a diversionary approach and aims to keep young people out of the formal justice system (courts), unless the public interest requires otherwise. The system aims to resolve offending and hold a young offender to account without them receiving a criminal conviction, as they would under the criminal justice system. Experience shows that, once a young person has a criminal record, they tend to carry on breaking the law and their offences may get more serious. The aim is to avoid that.

   When a child or young person is apprehended the Police have a range of responses available to them. Children under 10 years of age cannot be prosecuted (taken to criminal court) for any criminal offence, but the Police can respond to the offending through warnings and alternative action. Serious offending by this group will normally be dealt with as a care and protection matter through Child, Youth and Family.

   An apprehended child aged 10 to 13 can only be prosecuted for murder or manslaughter. Other offending by children may be dealt with by police through a warning or diversionary action. More

serious offending can result in a Family Group Conference (FGC) and may be referred to the Family Court, where a wide range of orders is available to the Court to address the child's offending.
An apprehended young person (someone aged 14 to 16 years old) can be:
warned by frontline Police;
referred to the Youth Aid division of Police for alternative action (diversion);
referred for a youth justice FGC to decide whether a charge should be laid; or
arrested and charged in the Youth Court.
For very serious offences, the Youth Court may transfer the young person to the adult court system. Where a young person is charged with murder or manslaughter they are automatically dealt with in the High Court. Alleged offenders aged 17 years and over are dealt with in the adult court system.

[4]   Total undergraduate enrollment in degree-granting postsecondary institutions has generally increased since 1970 and is projected to reach 15.6 million students in 2008 and 17.0 million in 2017. This increase has been accompanied by changes in the proportion of students who are female. From 1970 to 2006, women's undergraduate enrollment increased over three times as fast as men's, surpassing men's enrollment in 1978. During this period, women's enrollment rose from 3.2 to 8.7 million (an increase of 178 percent), while men's enrollment rose from 4.3 to 6.5 million (an increase of 53 percent). From 2007 to 2017, both men's and women's undergraduate enrollments are projected to increase, with women maintaining 57 percent of total enrollment. (http://nces.ed.gov/pubs2008/2008032.pdf)

REFERENCES

Adam, B., Beck, U., & Loon, J. V. (2000). *The risk society and beyond: Critical issues for social theory.* London: Sage.
Ascent for troubled teens. Retrieved from http://www.ascent4teens.com/
At Risk Youth. Retrieved from http://www.at-risk.org/
Bauerlein, M. (2008). The Obama appeal. *The Chronicle of Higher Education.* Retrieved from http://chronicle.com/review/brainstorm/bauerlein/the-obama-appeal
Beck, U. (1992). *Risk society: Towards a new modernity.* London: Sage.
Besley, T. (2002). *Counseling youth: Foucault, power and the ethics of subjectivity* (2nd ed.). Rotterdam, The Netherlands: Sense Publishers. (pbk ed.).
Besley, T. (2003). Hybridized and globalized: Youth cultures in the postmodern era. *The Review of Education/Pedagogy/Cultural Studies, 25*(2), 75–99.
Besley, A. C. (Tina). (2006). Technologies of the self and parrhesia: Education, globalization and the politicization of youth in response to the Iraq War 2003. In M. A. Peters (Ed.), *Education, globalisation and citizenship in an age of terrorism* (pp. 111–144). Boulder, CO: Paradigm Publishers.
Besley, A. C., & Peters, M. A. (2007). *Subjectivity and truth: Foucault, education and the culture of self.* New York: Peter Lang.
Best, S., & Kellner, D. (1998). Beavis and Butt-Head: No future for postmodern youth. In J. Epstein (Ed.), *Youth culture: Identity in a postmodern world* (pp. 74–99). Oxford, UK: Blackwell.
Campaign For Youth Justice. Retrieved April 2009, from http://www.campaign4youthjustice.org/.
Cieslik, M., & Pollock, G. (Eds.). (2002). *Young people in risk society: The restructuring of youth identities and transitions in late modernity.* Aldershot, Hampshire: Ashgate.
Cohen, R. (2008, January, 28). Obama's youth-driven movement. *International Herald Tribune,* Retrieved from http://www.iht.com/articles/2008/01/27/opinion/edcohen.php
Cohen, S. (1980). *Folk devils and moral panics: The creation of the mods and rockers* (2nd ed.). New York: St. Martin's Press.
Crossroads Programs. http://www.crossroadsprograms.org/
Dean, M. (1996). Foucault, government and the enfolding of authority. In A. Barry, T. Osborne, & N. Rose (Eds.), *Foucault and political reason: Liberalism, neo-liberalism and rationalities of government* (pp. 209–229). London: UCL Press.

Dean, M. (1999). *Governmentality: Power and rule in modern society.* London: Sage.

Foucault, M. (1977). *Discipline and punish: The birth of the prison.* London: Penguin.

Foucault, M. (1980). *The history of sexuality: The will to knowledge* (Vol. I). New York: Vintage Books.

Foucault, M. (1985). *The history of sexuality: The use of pleasure* (Vol. II). New York: Vintage Books.

Foucault, M. (1988). Technologies of the self. In L. H. Martin, H. Gutman, & P. H. Hutton (Eds.), *Technologies of the self: A seminar with Michel Foucault* (pp. 16–49). Amherst, MA: The University of Massachusetts Press.

Foucault, M. (1988). *The history of sexuality, Vol. 3: The care of the self* (R. Hurley, Trans.). New York: Vintage Books.

Foucault, M. (1991). Governmentality. In G. Burchell, C. Gordon, & P. Miller (Eds.), *The Foucault effect: Studies in fovernmentality* (pp. 87–104). Chicago: The University of Chicago Press.

Foucault, M. (1997). *Ethics: Subjectivity and truth* (P. Rabinow, Ed.). New York: New Press.

Foucault, M. (2008). *The Birth of Biopolitics—Lectures at the College de France, 1978–1979* (M. Senellart, Ed., & G. Burchell, Trans.). London: Palgrave Macmillan.

Giroux, H. A. (1996). *Fugitive cultures: Race, violence and youth.* New York: Routledge.

Giroux, H. A. (2000). *Stealing innocence: Corporate culture's War on children.* New York: Palgrave.

Giroux, H. A. (2004). *The abandoned generation: Democracy beyond the culture of fear.* London: Palgrave Macmillan.

Gordon, C. (1996). Foucault in Britain. In A. Barry, T. Osborne, & N. Rose (Eds.), *Foucault and political reason: Liberalism, neo-liberalism and rationalities of government* (pp. 253–270). London: UCL Press.

Graham-Felsen, S. (2007, February 15). *Obama's impressive youthroots.* The Nation. Retrieved from http://www.thenation.com/doc/20070305/graham-felsen

Hall, S. G. (1905). *Adolescence: Its psychology and its relations to physiology, anthropology, sociology, sex, crime, religion, and education.* New York: Appleton.

Hall, S., & Jefferson, T. (Eds.). (1976). *Resistance through rituals: Youth subcultures in post-war Britain.* London: Hutchinson.

Hebdige, D. (1979). *Subculture: The meaning of style.* London: Methuen.

Hicks, R., & Hicks, K. (1999). *Boomers, X-ers, and other strangers: Understanding/generational differences/divide us.* Alexandria, VA: Focus.

Homan, B., & Ziedenburg, J. (2006). *The dangers of detention: The impact of incarcerating youth in detention and other secure facilities.* Washington, DC: Justice Policy Institute. Retrieved April 2009, from http://en.wikipedia.org/wiki/Prisons_in_the_United_States#Incarceration_rate

Howe, N., & Strauss, W. (1992). *Generations: The history of America's future, 1584 to 2069.* New York: Harper Perennial.

Howe, N., & Strauss, W. (2000). *Millennials rising: The next great generation.* New York: Vintage.

Kelsey, J. (1993). *Rolling back the state: The privatisation of power in Aotearoa/ New Zealand.* Wellington, NZ: Bridget Williams Books.

Lemke, T. (2001). "The Birth of Bio-Politics" – Michel Foucault's Lecture at the Collège de France on Neo-Liberal Governmentality. *Economy and Society, 30*(2), 190–207. Retrieved from http://www.thomaslemkeweb.de/engl.%20texte/The%20Birth%20of%20Biopolitics%203.pdf

Lemke, T. (2002). Foucault, governmentality, and critique. *Rethinking Marxism, 14*(3), 49–64.

Lesko, N. (1996). Denaturalizing adolescence: The politics of contemporary representations. *Youth and Society, 28*(2), 139–161.

Lesko, N. (2001). *Act your age: A cultural construction of adolescence.* New York: RoutledgeFalmer.

Lubrano, A. (2008, February 2). An appeal to youth: Obama's message of change makes politics "relevant again" for young voters. *Philadelphia Inquirer - Philly.com.* Retrieved May 2008, from http://www.philly.com/philly/news/homepage/15131916.html

Males, M. A. (1996). *The scapegoat generation: America's war on adolescents.* Monroe, ME: Common Courage Press.

Males, M. A. (2002). *Framing youth: 10 myths about the next generation*. Monroe, ME: Common Courage Press.

Males, M., & MacAllair, D. (2000). *The color of justice*. Washington, DC: Building Blocks for Youth.

Males, M. A., Stahlkopf, C., & Macallair, D. (2007, June). *Crime rates and youth incarceration in texas and California compared: Public safety or public waste?* Center on Juvenile and Criminal Justice. Retrieved March 2009, from www.cjc.org.http://www. jdaihelpdesk.org/Docs/Documents/Crime% 20Rates%20and%20Youth%20Incarceration%20in%20Texas%20and%20California%20Compared. pdf

McCarthy, C., & Logue, J. (2009). Reading against the grain: Examining the status of the categories of class and tradition in the scholarship of British cultural studies in light of contemporary popular culture and literature. *Policy Futures in Education, 7*(2), 145–160. Retrieved from http://dx.doi.org/ 10.2304/pfie.2009.7.2.145

McRobbie, A. (1991). *Feminism and youth culture: From 'Jackie' to 'Just Seventeen'*. London: Macmillan.

Meyers, D. (2000). Feminist perspectives on the self. In *Stanford encyclopedia of philosophy*. Retrieved March 2002, from http://plato.stanford.edu/entries/feminism-self/

Morley, E., & Rossman, S. B. (1998). Helping At-risk youth: Lessons from community-based initiatives. *Urban institute*. Retrieved March 2009, from http://www.urban.org/publications/ 307399.html

Morris, A., & Maxwell, G. (1998). Restorative justice in New Zealand: Family group conferences as a case study. *Western Criminology Review, 1*(1). [Online]. Retrieved from http://wcr.sonoma.edu/ v1n1/morris.html

O'Malley, P. (1996). Risk and responsibility. In A. Barry, T. Osborne, & N. Rose (Eds.), *Foucault and political reason: Liberalism, neo-liberalism and rationalities of government* (pp. 189–207). London: UCL Press.

Peters, M. A. (2005). The new prudentialism in education: Actuarial rationality and the entrepreneurial self. *Educational Theory, 55*(2), 123–137. Retrieved from http://dx.doi.org/10.1111/j.0013-2004.2005.00002.x

Peters, M. A. (2009). Global recession, unemployment and the changing economics of the self. *Policy Futures in Education, 7*(1), 129–133. Retrieved from http://dx.doi.org/10.2304/pfie.2009.7.1.129

Peters, M. A., & Marshall, J. D. (1996). *Individualism and community: Education and social policy in the postmodern condition*. London: FalmerPress.

Poe-Yamagata, E., & Jones, M. (2000). *And justice for some: Differential treatment of minority youth in the justice system*. Washington, DC: Building Blocks for Youth. Retrieved April 2009, from http://en.wikipedia.org/wiki/Prisons_in_the_United_States#Incarceration_rate

Rogoff, B. (2003). *The cultural nature of development*. Oxford, UK: Oxford University Press.

Rose, N. (1989). *Governing the soul: The shaping of the private self*. London: Routledge.

Rose, N. (1998). *Inventing our selves: Psychology, power, and personhood*. Cambridge, UK: Cambridge University Press.

Rose, N. (1996). Governing 'advanced' liberal democracies. In A. Barry, T. Osborne, & N. Rose (Eds.), *Foucault and political reason: Liberalism, neo-liberalism and rationalities of government* (pp. 37–64). London: UCL Press.

Rose, N. (1999). *Powers of freedom: Reframing political thought*. Cambridge, UK: Cambridge University Press.

Shiller, R. J. (2000). *Irrational exuberance*. New Haven, CT: Princeton University Press.

Shiller, R. J. (2005). *Definition of irrational exuberance*. Retrieved from http://www.irrationalexuberance. com/definition.htm

Strickland, R. (Ed.). (2002). *Growing up postmodern: Neoliberalism and the war on the young*. Lanham, MD: Rowman & Littlefield.

Strauss, W., & Howe, N. (2006). *Millennials and the pop culture*. LifeCourse Associates.

Teen Help Us: Retrieved from http://www.teenhelp.us/

The Trauma Foundation. (2004). Young people—incarceration and death at home in the U.S. Retrieved from http://www.traumaf.org/featured/5-21-04youthincarceration.html

Twenge, J. M. (2007). *Generation me: Why today's young Americans are more confident, assertive, entitled--and more miserable than ever before*. New York: Free Press.

US Dept of Education. (2008). The condition of education 2008- in brief. National Center for Education Statistics (NCES). Retrieved August 2008, from http://nces.ed.gov/pubs2008/2008032.pdf

Vogel, J. (2007). *The Obama movement: Why Barack Obama Speaks to America's youth*. Lincoln, NE: iUniverse.

Willis, P. (1981). *Learning to labor*. New York: Columbia University Press.

Wyn, J., & White, R. (1997). *Rethinking youth*. London: Sage Publications.

Youth Indicators. (2005). *Trends in the well-being of American youth*. Retrieved August 2008, from http://nces.ed.gov/PUBSEARCH/pubsinfo.asp?pubid=2005050

Youth Justice, Ministry of Justice, NZ. Retrieved April 2009, from http://www.justice.govt.nz/youth-justice/system.html

Youth Justice, Ministry of Child Youth & Family, NZ. Retrieved April 2009, from http://www.cyf.govt.nz/youthjustice.htm

Youth Justice in Action. Retrieved April 2009, from, http://www.youthjusticeinaction.org/

APPENDIX

Campaign for Youth Justice, USA

http://www.campaign4youthjustice.org/nationalstats.html (accessed April 2009)

National Statistics

These national statistics reflect the reality of trying, sentencing and incarcerating children in the adult criminal justice system.

Youth Crime

Youth commit only a small portion of the nation's crime. For example, in 2006, 12.6 percent of violent crime clearances and 19.1 percent of the property crime clearances nationwide involved only youth. According to the FBI, youth under age 18 accounted for only 15.4% of all arrests.

Youth crime has also been going down for many years. The number of adults arrested in 2006 and in 1997 was virtually the same, whereas the number of juveniles arrested dropped a staggering 24% during that same time frame.

Juvenile Justice System

Every year, juvenile courts in the U.S. handle an estimated 1.6 million cases in which the youth was charged with a delinquency offense.

After arrest, many youth are detained in a detention or residential facility to await a hearing in juvenile or adult court, depending on how they are charged. While in out-of-home placement, youth are separated from their community and their normal day-to-day life (school, jobs, family, etc.).

1 out of every 5 youth who are brought before the court with a delinquency case is placed in a juvenile detention facility.

Detention facilities are meant to temporarily house youth who are likely to commit another crime before their trial or who are likely to skip their court date. Unfortunately, many of the youth held in the 591 detention centers across the country do not meet these criteria and should not be there.

Seventy percent of youth in detention are held for nonviolent charges. More than two-thirds are charged with property offenses, public order offenses, technical probation violations, or status offenses (crimes that wouldn't be crimes if they were adults, like running away or breaking curfew).

The overuse of detention is particularly harsh on youth of color. In 2003, African-American youth were detained at a rate 4.5 times higher than whites. Latino youth were detained at twice the rate of whites.

Nearly 70% of children in public detention centers are in overcrowded facilities holding more youth than they were designed for.

A one-day snapshot of juvenile offenders in detention found that roughly 5% were status offenders.

After adjudication, many youth are sentenced to juvenile correctional facilities or state training schools. On any given day, over 90,000 youth are incarcerated in juvenile correctional facilities.

Adjudicated youth sent to residential placements such as juvenile correctional facilities increased by 44% from 1985 to 2002.

There are less severe alternatives to incarcerating youth, and they work. Community-based programs, including diversion programs, drug treatment, evening reporting centers, treatment clinics and family programs, have been shown to be less costly than detention or incarceration and to help youth stay out of trouble and to not re-offend.

Youth in the Adult Criminal Justice System

An estimated 200,000 youth are tried, sentenced, or incarcerated as adults every year across the United States.

Most of the youth prosecuted in adult court are charged with non-violent offenses.

Research shows that young people who are kept in the juvenile justice system are less likely to re-offend than young people who are transferred into the adult system. According to the Centers for Disease Control and Prevention, youth who are transferred from the juvenile court system to the adult criminal system are approximately 34% more likely than youth retained in the juvenile court system to be re-arrested for violent or other crime.

Currently, 40 states permit or require that youth charged as adults be held before they are tried in an adult jail. In some states, if they are convicted, they may be required to serve their entire sentence in an adult jail.

On any given day, nearly 7,500 young people are locked up in adult jails.

A significant portion of youth detained in adult jails before their trial are not convicted as adults. As many as one-half of these youth will be sent back to the juvenile justice system or not be convicted. Yet, most of these youth will have spent at least one month in an adult jail and one in five of these youth will have spent over six months in an adult jail.

On any given day, more than 2,000 young people are locked up in adult prisons.

Tina (A. C.) Besley
University of Illinois at Urbana Champaign
USA

STEPHEN J. BALL

12. LIFELONG LEARNING, SUBJECTIVITY AND THE TOTALLY PEDAGOGISED SOCIETY

The lifelong learner is a much over-burdened and over-determined social subject within current education policy and within some current versions of social theory. Lifelong learning indeed is subject to a constant stream of 'over blown policy statements' (Edwards & Nicoll, 2001, p. 104) and lifelong learning texts are saturated with policy fictions[1]. These statements and texts sketch the outlines and some dimensions of what may be a new social totality, of which lifelong education is a significant component. This chapter explores some of the major elements of this new social totality and is organised around a trajectory of lifelong learning and focuses in particular on three 'moments' or scenarios of learning and subjectivity; the pre-school learner and 'total mothering'; the post-compulsory learner and workfare society; and the adult learner and 'self help'. Across these moments four inter-weaving discursive themes are identified; enterprise, responsibility, trainability and commodity.

Introduction: The Rhetorics and Discourses of Lifelong Learning (LLL)

The LLL policy industry is framed and driven at a variety of levels and from a diversity of sites by a remarkably stable and incessantly repetitive rhetoric. An English example to begin (DFEE, 1998) from a document called *The Learning Age*

> Learning is the key to prosperity ... investment in human capital will be the foundation of success in the knowledge-based global economy of the twenty-first century' (p. 7). 'To continue to compete, we must equip ourselves to cope with the enormous economic and social change we face, to make sense of the rapid transformation of the world, and to encourage imagination and innovation (p. 10).

In another example, the Swedish Ministry of Education intend that adult education should:

> ... provide opportunities for continuing education and personal development, both in the role as a citizen and in the role as a worker. It should consist of knowledge and creativity, and aptitude to learn new things and handle change. (Ministry of Education, 1998, p. 8)

And of course the EU:

> The lifelong learning approach is an essential policy Strategy for the development of citizenship, social cohesion, employment and for individual

M.A. Peters et al. (eds.), Govermentality Studies in Education, 201–216.

fulfilment (*European report on quality indicators of lifelong learning*, European Commission, 2002).

UNESCO declaim in even more forthright and imperative terms:

> The sheer pace of technological change has convinced business communities and nations alike of the need for flexibility in the quality of the labour force. Education systems can therefore no longer be expected to train a labour force for stable industrial jobs; they must instead train individuals to be innovative, capable of evolving, adapting to a rapidly changing world and assimilating change (UNESCO 1996 p. 71 *Open and Distance Learning: Prospects and Policy Considerations*, Paris).

Within these dextrous texts LLL is constituted in relation to the fuzzy fictions of 'the knowledge economy' within which a new kind of worker, who is innovative, creative and enterprising, is hailed. As always real economies are "far more complex and messy" (Edwards & Nicoll, 2001, p. 111) and uneven than these texts project and we need to regard all of these pronouncements as partial fictions rather than simple truths, although they are not outside of the true but the 'real' economies of real nations and the realities of work for most, bear only a passing resemblance to what is described here (see Keep, 1997). At the core of all this seething of discourse around the lifelong learner is the enterprising individual.

> An enterprising individual has a positive, flexible, adaptable disposition towards change, seeing it as normal, and as an opportunity rather than a problem. To see change in this way, an enterprising individual has a security borne of self-confidence … etc. (OECD report *Enterprising Culture: A Challenge for Education and Training*).

These texts also outline a 'policy machinery' of mechanisms, procedures and tactics that is assembled and deployed within programmes of LLL. The "work of politics or government is partly done in the materiality of [such] texts" (Furlough, 2000, p. 158) and becomes part of their texture. Urgency, inevitability and radical change are part of this texture. Any lack of clarity and coherence in these statements, and how the elements are joined-up, is unimportant and is overcome by reiteration within and between discursive sites. These texts work, "[b]y furnishing a novel language and set of techniques for thinking about the objects, targets, mechanisms and limits of government" (du Gay, 2004, p. 40).

What is produced in these documents and what is the subject of the policies which stem from them is nothing less than a new kind of person and a new "ethic of personhood"; for within lifelong learning "an entire self must be completely made over as an enterprising individual" (McWilliam, 2002, p. 292). What these texts articulate is the production of a new kind of worker, citizen, learner with new dispositions and qualities, what Kuhn and Sultana (2006) call the European Learning Citizen. In effect what is being constructed is a new ontology of learning and of policy and a very elaborate 'technology of the self' through which we shape our bodies and subjectivities to the needs of learning, "developing not only a 'sense' of how to be, but also 'sensibility': requisite feelings and morals…" (Colley, James et al., 2003, p. 471). The lifelong learner exists within a new moral environment (Haydon, 2004) inside of which values, social relations and self-worth are tightly tied to the imperatives of an enterprising life and "enterprise is positioned as a principle of the 'good life'" (Edwards, 2002, p. 357). Indeed, "the 'economic politics' of Enterprise appears to know no boundaries either in terms of where it might be applied" (du Gay, 2004, p. 40) or to whom. Inside these policies we are as Falk (1999) puts it: 'Sentencing Learners to Life'. That is, we are moving inexorably towards 'the learning society', a society in which "every adult possess[s] a personal learning plan, written down and monitored with a chosen mentor; every organization seek[s] to become a learning organisation" (Keep, 1997, p. 457); what Tuschling and Engemann (2006) call the "regime of learning" with its concomitant "regime of documentation of oneself." Through data bases, portfolios, self-evaluations and learning reviews and audits lifelong learners are "subjects which have to be seen" (Foucault, 1979, p. 187).

In Bernstein's terms (2001) these are the outlines of a "totally pedagogised society" and the "pedagogisation of life" in which learning is an activity that is conducted endlessly, "in which the State is moving to ensure that there's no space or time which is not pedagogised" (Bernstein, 2001, p. 377). A social system within which individuals make themselves available for re-education and re-trainability – "the ability to profit from continuous pedagogic reformations" (Bernstein, 2001, p. 365), which rest in turn on the forgetting of prior habits, and a commitment to "de-learning" (Bauman, 2004, p. 22) for the duration of life. LLL "is largely a project of economic, social and epistemological recuperation dedicated to delimiting rather than expanding the subjectivities of learners" (Falk, 1999, p. 7). What is required here is a personal depthlessness, an unaccumulated self, which can shuffle off the burdens of experience, for indeed experience is an obstacle to change. Rather, flexibility, innovation, creativity, evolution and adaptability within the 'unfixed maze' (Bauman 2004) of learning are all mobilised through the policy tropes of LLL and are becoming the new technologies for managing whole populations in economic and social conditions of instability and uncertainty (Bernstein 2001) and thus "the ordering of human multiplicities" (Foucault, 1979, p. 218). This is a kind of economic Darwinism (Edwards & Nicoll, 2001); adapt, evolve or become irrelevant.

Within all this as many commentators have pointed out the acquisition, development and "up-dating" of skills and competences become the personal responsibility of the individual worker based upon "a virtuous, disciplined and responsible autonomy" (Dean, 1999, p. 155). Concomitantly institutions and governments are increasingly less responsible for their workers and citizens in these and other respects.

Starting in the late 1970s, the nation's leaders sought to break a corrosive cycle of rising inflation and stagnating output by remaking the U.S. economy in the image of its frontier predecessor – deregulating industries, shrinking social programs and promoting a free-market ideal in which everyone must forge his or her own path, free to rise or fall on merit or luck. On the whole, their effort to transform the economy has succeeded.

But the economy's makeover has come at a large and largely unnoticed price: a measurable increase in the risks that Americans must bear as they provide for their families, pay for their houses, save for their retirements and grab for the good life.

A broad array of protections that families once depended on to shield them from economic turmoil – stable jobs, widely available health coverage, guaranteed pensions, short unemployment spells, long-lasting unemployment benefits and well-funded job training programs – have been scaled back or have vanished altogether. (Los Angeles Times)

In other words, "The educable subject today is created in relation to a new rationality of governing where it is constructed through its own choices and actions" (Fejes, 2006, p. 676). This subject "is to interpret its reality and destiny as a matter of individual responsibility, it is to find meaning in existence by shaping its life through acts of choice" (Rose, 1998, p. 151); "responsibilised individuals are called upon to apply certain management, economic, and actuarial techniques to themselves as subjects of a newly privatised welfare regime" (Peters, 2001, p. 60). LLL is a micro-technology of power which works to this end, mobilising subjects in ways that promote self-reliance and enterprise, enabling them to develop capacities and constantly re-making themselves, a form of continuous "optimisation" (Dean, 1999, p. 20), which works on, through and with them as active subjects; and within which "The enterprising self will make an enterprise of its life" (Rose, 1998, p. 154). As a category of person and as an ethical personality, du Gay argues the entrepreneur now *"must be seen as assuming an ontological priority"* (du Gay, 1996, p. 181). Enterprise as it is diffused through the social fabric becomes "the generalised principle" (Gordon, 1991, p. 42) of the functioning of governmentality. And the enterprise narrative insinuates itself every where and into the heart of learning and childhood:

To foster the entrepreneurs of tomorrow, by 2006 every school in the country will offer enterprise education, and every college and university should be twinned with a business champion (2005 Labour Party Election Manifesto, p. 23).

As (McWilliam f/c) points out all of this has two underpinnings. First, that "the market is the best way to achieve effective organisational arrangements" it has "paradigmatic status" (du Gay, 1991, p. 45). Second, that "the ethics of wealth creation" is a final measure of success and worth (the new heroes of economics and education policy are "business champions", self-made entrepreneurs). This is, a "highly individualist form of capitalism" (Heelas & Morris, 1992, p. 3) based on a "headlong pursuit of relevance as defined by the Market" (Falk, 1999, p. 1).

Let me briefly now put this new enterprising, lifelong learner into a general economic and social context or at least within the discursive contexts of the economic and the social which policy texts and some social theory conjure up.

THE ECONOMIC

The necessity and inevitability of LLL is driven discursively by the repetitious deployment of the urgent demands of globalisation. As Tony Blair asserted in an interview with Newsweek: "Complaining about globalization is as pointless as trying to turn back the tide. Asian competition can't be shut out; it can only be beaten. And now, by every relative measure of a modern economy, Europe is lagging". This is, the 'necessarian logic of New Labour's political economy' (Watson & Hay 2003) and that of the EU and OECD and UNESCO, articulated through the sorts of "persuasive texts" (Edwards & Nicoll, 2001, p. 111) quoted previously. That is the subordination of "social policy to the demands of labour market flexibility and/or employability and the perceived imperatives of structural or systemic competitiveness" (Jessop, 2001, p. 298) through which and in the name of which "the individual and 'its' society become ever more interwoven" (Tuschling & Engemann, 2006, p. 452).

And of course as 'educators' we are ourselves imbricated in and 'hailed' by these texts. The learner and the organisations of learning (like universities) must be re-made to respond to the exigence (Edwards & Nicoll 2001), that is to globalisation, and to play their part in the economics of competition. All individual and institutional actors and their dispositions and responses are tied within these texts to the fate of the nation within the global economy. These are the limits to our sense of and imagination about learning within the contemporary "'general politics' of truth" (Foucault, 1980, p. 131). We must give up on the past, and give ourselves up to be re-formed, to be re-made as subjects of globalisation and global subjects, moving in and across a 'borderless Higher Education' (http://www. unesco.org/iiep/virtualuniversity/files/chap3.pdf).

There is an easily graspable narrative in the other texts I have quoted, an "insistent singularity" (du Gay, 2000, p. 78) which links the everyday intimacies of educational practices ever more closely to the global economy. There is a dialogue that places the 'old' public sector in contrast to a 'modern' public sector and the 'new' economy and as a threat to competitiveness, it is cast as an anachronism, an irrelevance.

> Do we take modest though important steps of improvement? Or do we make the great push forward for transformation? Let me spell it out. In education…we open up the system to new and different ways of education … There's nothing wrong with the old principles but if the old ways worked, they'd have worked by now (Tony Blair, Labour Party Conference, Autumn 2002).

THE SOCIAL

The lifelong learner also makes perfect sense when the new learning, adapting, flexible self is relocated in the post-traditional social world, torn asunder from the constraints of class and community, to become a project of its own realisation. And there is much that is attractive in this. The new learning/enterprising self is a set of unrealised possibilities and opportunities, for in place of tradition, there is merit.

Success and failure is a matter of being enterprising or not, having talent or not and no longer a matter of who you are but what you might become.

> Enterprise and fairness thence sit 'naturally' together Enterprise and fairness. That is our goal. ("Knowledge 2000" – Conference on the Knowledge Driven Economy. Tony Blair. (http://mbbnet.umn.edu/doric/economy.html)

Giddens refers to the policies of a "learning society" as about the "redistribution of possibilities" rather than of resources, but he also acknowledges that: "In such a social order, the privileged are bound to be able to confer advantages on their children – thus destroying meritocracy" (Giddens, 1998, p. 102). Post-welfare policies are no longer concerned with the redistribution of wealth, but rather with its creation.

All of this is, of course, more than simply a phenomenon of LLL and is represented and refracted, and in Giddens' case, as a 'policy intellectual' enacted, as part of the metaphysics of what Beck calls the 'second modernity' or 'reflexive modernization' with its 'disembedding mechanisms' (Giddens, 1991). These dissolve traditional parameters and social and political institutions and 'protective frame-works' and generates a 'social surge of individualism' with the effect that "people have been removed from class commitments and have to refer to themselves in planning their individual labour market biographies" (Beck, 1992, p. 87). Social certitudes are subject to interrogation. There is a concomitant loss of social ties and increasing sense of social isolation. As Bauman puts it human identity is being transformed from a 'given' to a 'task'. The individual is made responsible for performing that task and dealing with its side effects, as we search through "a portfolio of identities" within an "ambivalent social structure" and confront rampant uncertainties and with incomplete knowledge; "The standard biography becomes a chosen biography, a do-it-yourself-biography" (Beck, 1994, p. 15). This then both enhances the desire for "a life of one's own" and an "experimental life" and "biographic solutions" but leaves the individual feeling "bereft and alone in a world lacking psychological supports" (Giddens, 1991, p. 3).

However, there are two important caveats to Beck's and Giddens' analyses which are often left aside. First, the 'bewildering imperative of self-determination' produces its own particular inequalities. Uncertainty is experienced differently from different social positions and different social groups have different sorts of access to the resources, skills and capitals that are needed to cope effectively with ambivalence, futurity and responsibility. Those outside of choice and/or lacking in the key competencies of choice are 'socially excluded'. Second, the "runaway world" is one of very peculiar freedoms within which individuals are "condemned to activity" (Beck, 1992, p. 162) and the necessity to choose, and must live up to the guidelines for living a "responsible life" (p. 135). They are "compelled" (p. 88) to make themselves the centre of their own planning. We are "obliged to be free" (Rimke, 2000, p. 73)[2]. There are conditions of freedom and of individualism within which the "responsible life" is tightly specified if not necessarily "obvious" and within which "we will never know enough and never develop all the necessary capacities and competences" (Bernstein, cited in Bonal, 2003)[3]. The capacity to change "becomes nowadays the index of fitness" (Bauman, 2000, p. 19). Individuals are required "to make something of their lives and use their ability and potential to the full" (Tony Blair, 2002) – where "something" and "ability" and "potential" are already narrowly circumscribed; "… no one can 'opt out' of the transformations brought about by modernity" (Giddens, 1991, p. 22). Those deemed unfit within these conditions of freedom are subject to interventions of remediation, and enforced 'activation' within workfare social policies which are aimed at cultivating appropriate personal attributes – like self-esteem, self-confidence, self-motivation, ambition and efficacy. For the social excluded, without 'protective structures' this can easily become "an individualism of dispossession, an inexorable form of destitution and loneliness" (Santos, 1995). You get blamed for your failure to inhabit the new persona successfully. Those who fail, are seen as having 'diminished selves' (Ecclestone, 2007), as vulnerable, 'at risk', 'fragile', they are both pathologised and stigmatised. Falk argues that LLL now acts to make education more intrusive and more damning of those who choose not to engage in it (Falk, 1999). It is at this point that the state acts – when there is a failure of responsibility "a process at once economic and moral" (Peters, 2001, p. 61) – the state intervenes, as an authoritarian moral agent.

I want now to try to make all of this more practical and develop and ground the lifelong learner within a trajectory of scenarios – from the cradle to the grave; although these scenarios are differently classed.

TOTAL MOTHERING

Lifelong learning is starting increasingly earlier. For more and more families parenting is focused on making a project of their children and the mother becomes the 'planning office' for the production of a particular kind of educational subject, especially in the middle classes and especially at a time of generalised subjective insecurity and fear of falling (Ehrenreich, 1989). Within such families the work of the inculcation of cultural capital and self-formation is hectic, even frantic, and deliberate, in contrast to Bourdieu's portrayal set at an earlier point in time by (Bourdieu, 2004). It is a product of 'intensive mothering' or 'total mothering' – the heavy investment of the mother's time, energy, money and emotional commitment into enhancing the child's intellectual, physical, social and emotional development; "the maximum free time being harnessed to maximise cultural capital" (Bourdieu, 2004, p. 19). It is primarily mothers who take on the responsibility for researching, arranging and monitoring the care and education of the children (see Vincent & Ball, 2006). "It is women's role to convert economic capital into symbolic capital through the display of tastes" (Skeggs, 2004, p. 142).

The "making up" of the child in terms of particular "talents" or "abilities" is then "the product of an investment of time and cultural capital" (Bourdieu, 2004, p. 17) and also money. And increasingly this 'making up' – the ways in which we conceptualise and realise who we are and what we may be (Hacking, 1986) – involves drawing upon a whole range of commercial activities and entertainments and is certainly not entirely dependent "on the cultural capital embodied in the whole family" (Bourdieu, 2004, p. 19). The buying-in of learning or developmental experiences and advice and support (like activities or entertainments, or tutoring or parenting classes) are made possible by economic capital which is converted into cultural capital.

The activities available to children are many and varied but focus in particular on the aesthetic – music, drama, art and dance. The role of the aesthetic in this is as a vehicle of accumulation of culture for exchange – "making culture into a property of the middle class itself" (Skeggs, 2004, p. 135) although at the same time there is enjoyment and fulfilment to be had for the children. The two things are not mutually exclusive. Indeed aestheticization involves "a particular relation to culture as a resource, which is used to generate the self" (p. 137) – a form of extension – and accumulation of value to the self. The two aspects may indeed be inseparable, as part of what is being acquired is the ability to enjoy; to know what is good and what is good for you; an investment of oneself in activities of legitimate taste and oneself as investment.

For some parents the activities provided for their children is part of a process of experimentation of making and finding the child, ensuring that talents and abilities are located and made the most of. The parents work within a logic which draws on the idea of "the pursuit of self-making" (Jordan, Redley et al., 1994, pp. 5–6) which lies at the heart of liberal individualism - the idea, as (Bauman, 1993, p. 4) puts it, of individuals with "identities not-yet-given" which in their construction over time involve the making of choices. This is a particular kind of individualism, and a particular kind of freedom, embedded in the specialness and particularity of the young child and the idea that the young child should be able to realise their inherent capabilities or potential and become a self-developing subject, a person of categoric value. Opportunities are provided, choices made, a style and orientation of action towards the social world is initiated. Responsibilities to the self are being worked at and established.

As noted already, part of the work of transmission and inculcation takes place outside the family, through the use of commercial, specialist services. These include private tuition, as well as enrichment activities (e.g., StageCoach[4], Tumbletots and Cresendo). Expertise is bought-in alongside the selling of educational products and services directly to parents and learners; learning materials (books and software) and educational toys and materials or what (Kenway & Bullen, 2001) call "edutainment" – "fun with a purpose" which encourage parents to "seek consumerist solutions to parenting problems" (p. 85). Intuitive parenting is no longer good enough. Indeed, parenting itself is increasingly politicised and commercialised. Middle class parents must live up to the models that they are held up to be to others. (For example, parenting courses are not only for those deemed by the state to be deficit in parenting skills, in the UK companies such as The Parent Company offer evening seminars for £45 per person on topics such as 'Raising Boys' and 'Raising Girls'. They also offer parenting classes over the telephone. The Parenting Practice, offer 'Skills for Transforming Family Life' – "Would you like to be a more effective, calmer parent with happier, more cooperative children?" Upcoming Workshops (all £38 per person, £60 per couple) include 'Reducing Sibling

Squabbles' and 'Improving Adult-Child Relationships'). Bernstein sees this as another 'pedagogic translation' part of the T.P.S in which' family units' become parenting skills' (Bernstein 2001 p. 365). For those parents deemed by the state to be 'failing parents' various remedial and disciplinary interventions are possible including compulsory attendance at parenting classes (see Home Office, 2003. *Respect and Responsibility – Taking a stand against Anti-social Behaviour.* London, Stationery Office).

POST-COMPULSORY LEARNER – THE TRAINABLE/FLEXIBLE/DEVELOPMENTAL YOUNG PERSON

In this stage of LLL "At the centre of attention is no longer the curriculum that learners have to master but their abilities to organize themselves and to perceive and use their circumstances as learning opportunities" (Tuschling & Engemann, 2006, p. 458). Opportunities which are intended to produce a "highly flexible worker who possesses requisite skills in management, information handling, communication, problem-solving and decision-making" (Peters, 2001, p. 66). "The global economy has made largely extinct the notion of a 'job for life'. The imperative now is employability for life" (DfES, 2003) and its concomitant "trainability": that is, "the ability to be taught ... the ability to respond effectively to concurrent, subsequent and intermittent pedagogics" (Bernstein, 1996, p. 73) – a "totally pedagogised person."

This is a person who has the appropriate 'social competencies', or 'key qualifications' or 'basic self-organizational dispositions' (see Tuschling and Engemann, 2006). In this way of thinking about the subject Gordon (1991, p. 43) argues "economic government joins hands with behaviourism" and works to "replace inner commitments and dedications by short-term instrumentalities" (p. 76)[5].

In order to influence the trend in youth and long-term unemployment the Member states will intensify their efforts to develop preventive and employability-oriented strategies, building on the early identification of individual needs (Council of the European Union, 2000, p. 3).

Within this social world of learning everything is possible but nothing is stable. There are no certitudes or complacencies upon which we may rest and draw, we must become developmental rather than 'situated subjects' capable of a different realisation of self in different and changing contexts, a giving up of modernist essentialisms. Increasingly, learning is less about SOMETHING than **being something**. It is about 'learning to be employable' (Garsten & Jacobsson, 2003) and becoming trainable, and acquiring attributes and dispositions towards this end. For 'skills' and knowledge are now 'perishable goods' (Garsten & Jacobsson, 2003) unless they are generic and 'transferable'. The social and collective commitments of a situated identity are now redundant and obstructive. Young workers must constantly work on themselves to make themselves employable in their struggle to avoid 'the zone of precarity' (Dorre, 2006)[6]. They must internalise and take responsibility for the needs of the state and personal histories and social conditions of learning are typically eradicated in all this. The future is dissolved into uncertainty and precarity, and 'limitless postponements' (Deleuze, 1990), we are left only with short-termism and a readiness to be different, to change, we are 'de-centred'.

Indeed some Back to Work courses 'teach' the maintenance of a neutral persona and self-presentation as skills necessary to obtain certain sorts of work. Bernstein (2001) contrasts this 'ability' to be taught, and reformation in response to contingencies with the capacity of the actor "to project himself/herself meaningfully rather than relevantly or instrumentally into" the future (p. 366) and goes on to argue that: "The concept of trainability, the key to lifelong learning and lifelong learning itself, the mode of socialisation into the Total Pedagogised Society, erodes commitment, dedications, and coherent time, and is therefore socially empty" (p. 366). Change itself becomes desocialised and depoliticised, it just happens, it is globalisation, it is technological change, it is inevitable, irresistible and necessary. As a result experiences are abstracted "from the power relations of their lived conditions and negate the possibilities of understanding and criticism" (Gordon, 1991, p. 73). Problems of employment become problems of employability – what Coffield (2006, p. 6) calls "an empty, unsatisfying concept ... a readiness to be trained and re-trained for whatever types of employment are available, which leaves learners searching for individual solutions to systemic problems ... In the language of C. Wright Mills, employability turns the public issue of the dearth of good jobs into the private trouble of constant retraining." This is what Bourdieu calls "flexploitation", that is a mode of domination of a new kind, based on "the creation of a generalized and permanent state of insecurity aimed at forcing workers into submission, into the acceptance of exploitation" (Bourdieu, 1998, p. 85). This is increasingly achieved through the new and more intimate pedagogies of advice, mentoring, personalised learning and bespoke vocational programmes, which enable and required learners to think about themselves in new ways. While much of this is in particular focused upon the post-compulsory learner within the fluidities of further and vocational education, but there is an increasing convergence between further and higher education, especially within policy texts.

THE EDUCABLE AND SELF-HELPING ADULT LEARNER

You are constructed as learning all the time, during leisure time, at work and in education. Such a way of reasoning about learning seems to indicate a new way of reasoning about how to govern and what to govern (Fejes, 2006, p. 698)

As the final 'moment' within lifelong learning I want to consider the phenomenon of self help. As Rimke (2000) argues, self-help literature may be viewed as a strategy "for enlisting subjects in the pursuit of self-improvement and autonomy" (p. 61) and one which is done best "by evading or denying social relations" (p. 61), we must rely on ourselves and not others, we are responsible to no one but "our self" and which is based on the postulate "that people can exercise control and mastery of themselves and their lives" (p. 62). It "negates the inherent sociality of being" (p. 62). What Rimke calls "hyper-individuality" (p. 67) or Bernstein (1996) calls a "therapeutic identity" that is "an internally self-regulated construction ... a truly symbolic construction ... an open narrative which constructs internal linearity" (p. 77).

At the same time, as with parenting "Self help projects also require external forms of textual authority and expert knowledge" (Rimke, 2000, p. 62). Self-help is thoroughly commodified, in the form of self-help books and software and through the work of life-coaches, counsellors and therapists or advisers and mentors of various kinds. We can self-help to the limits of our competence and then 'buy-in' expertise or support in order to know how to work on ourselves better. That is the productive application of the skills of our own subjectification, through the liberties of self-determination. This assumes a further form of flexibility, or re-making, as we chose who we want to be and become who we want to be in a never-ending project of self-reflection and self actualisation. Life is made meaningful and of value "to the extent that it can be rationalized as the outcome of choices made or to be made" (Rose, 1996, p. 57). Again the power relations which shape personhood are erased. Through the calculative techniques of the self- help manual we turn 'the gaze' upon ourselves to see if we 'add-up', we audit ourselves. We learn about ourselves, and self-confess through hybridised, psychologically-based knowledges. Without that self-knowledge we are always in danger of repeating our mistakes. Such knowledge is the priority as we strive to live up to 'perfection codes' of mind and body.

Thus, self-help takes place at one of the many "interconnections between multiple domains of government and self formation" (Rimke, 2000, p. 71) constituting new forms of bio-power for managing populations, for achieving docility and productivity as governments continually "extend their capacities to produce healthy, productive and flexible populations" (Edwards, Nicoll & Tait, 1999, p. 625).

DISCUSSION

From this dystopian account of the world of lifelong learning I want to draw four specific points of conclusion and offer one speculative generalisation.

1. This world of lifelong learning is populated by learners who are alone and lonely. It is a world devoid of community and commitment within which, increasingly, social relations are valued solely for their extrinsic worth. A move to what Wittel (2001) calls 'network sociality' which is 'informational' rather than narrational, and primarily based on the exchange of data. Furthermore, there is an individuation of educational institutions as they compete with one another to recruit and perform, **and** of the educational workplace – with more and more short term projects, freelancers, consultants, agency-workers, fixed term contracts, skill-mixes – these new kinds of workers are 'with' and 'for' the organisation, rather than 'in' it as Wittel (p. 65) puts it. Social ties within educational work become ephemeral, disposable, serial, fleeting – we live as Bauman terms it in "the age of contingency" (Bauman, 1996). Within the liquid modern social world the work of keeping social relations "eminently dismantleable" (Bauman, 2004, p. 22) is as

important as their assembly. This further contributes to the dissolution of moral obligations. This is pointed up in the increasing perception of social relationships as social capital, a form of investment in social relations for individuals and for the state. This is a form of the displacement of use values (a qualitative relation) into exchange values (a quantitative relation) – a ratio of exchange between commodities – so much social capital gets you so much output in terms of levels of employment, or reductions in crime. Here social relations themselves are a commodity – something to be 'invested in', that produces 'returns'. They have to be 'done' because they are not **there**, not natural, they do not have their **own** materiality, their own history, they do not have a narrative, they do not have a basis in mutual experience or common history. Rather, they are continually and deliberately produced and reproduced and 'consumed'. They are what Knorr-Cetina (2000) calls 'post-social relations'. We no longer simply *have* social relationships, we *do* them, and such relationships have to be *managed*.

Increasingly social relations can be managed at a distance. There are ever more new ways of being lonely in the e-world of distance learning. Social relations are 'de-localised', based on communication technologies rather than face-to-face encounters what Lury (1997) calls ' a prosthetic culture' of social engagement. We can be anyone and anything on the internet and need look no-one straight in the eye. "We can no longer speak of the social without speaking of the technological" (Castells, 2001, in McWilliam, 2005, p. 2). We become emotionally attached to and learn from distant "others" media "role models" who serve as "regular and dependable companions" (Thompson, 1995, p. 220).

2. All of this can lead to a "diminished moral responsibility" (Mason, 2001, p. 47) as we fashion ourselves within a consciously contrived style of conduct and let go of out-moded authenticities and become ever more responsive to market signals. We are left to struggle with the antagonism of functionality and morality (Wittel, 2001)[7]. In Bauman's (1991, p. 197) terms, there is "the privatisation of ambivalence" which, "casts on individual shoulders calls for a bone structure few individuals can boast." Sennett (1998) describes this as a 'corrosion of trust' and loyalty and mutual commitment. We are responsible to and for no-one but ourselves and focused on our goals. We are made into liquid social subjects with the necessarily flexible morals and loyalties; "the public sphere and the public responsibility to which citizenship refers. The inter-identified subjectivities to which citizenship has obligations and on which it depends, are negated by a life of self-help" (Rimke, 2000, p. 73).

> 3. It is not that 'initiative', 'enterprise', 'responsibility' or 'activity' are not worthwhile human capacities … Rather, it is that within the frame of entrepreneurial selfhood … [they] are narrowly imagined in relation to the performance of exchange relations in the extended order of capitalist markets (Kelly, 2006, p. 29).

The assertion of exchange relations is a recurrent facet of this account. Falk argues that lifelong learning is now working as vehicle for selling commodities and as a profitable commodity in itself (McWilliam, 2002) – a privatisation of learning, in a variety of senses. In relation to this students of all sorts from nursery to higher education have been explicitly constituted as 'customers', a development that further reinforces the idea that their learning experience itself is a commodity that (hopefully) can be exchanged at some point of entry into the labour market (Willmott 1995). This is the transformation of social relations into a thing. As part of seeking after new 'markets' and the re-orientation to the customer, new forms of 'delivery' and consumption of education are being created which can result in learning becoming increasingly fragmented. The curriculum is reorganised as a sequence of knowledge gobbets (Bytesize as it is on the BBC revision website) which can be transferred as 'credits' and combined in novel ways with no guarantee of internal coherence – they are made 'readable' in the jargon of the Bologna Declaration – a 'cut and paste HE curriculum' as David Robertson (2000) calls it, fluid and non-linear. Nonetheless, Robertson is optimistic about the effects of this in terms of 'organizational flexibility and professional academic cross-fertilization' (Robertson, 2000). More pessimistically it may be that pedagogic relationships and values are marginalised. Lyotard in *The Post Modern Condition,* his 1984 review of higher education, refers to this as 'exteriorisation' and is summed up in his terms as a shift from the questions 'it is true' and 'it is just' to 'is it useful, saleable, efficient' (Lyotard 1984). Knowledge is no longer legitimated through "grand narratives of speculation and emancipation" (p. 38) but, rather, in the pragmatics of "optimization" – the creation of skills or of profit rather than ideals or what Lyotard also calls the "merchantalization of knowledge."

4. As indicated at various points in the text, the sensibilities and motivations which are coming to inform LLL are subtly and not so subtly 'classed'. The discourses of LLL celebrate and reward the classed mobile liberal subject, very much a middle- class subject with disposable resources social, cultural, emotional and financial and particular 'style of life' and repertoire of commitments. The inability to deal with the uncertainties and instabilities involved is likely to elicit remedial interventions. They thus re-affirm old inequalities and divisions and produce new ones.

AN EPISTEMIC SHIFT

Finally if we put all of this together, Perhaps then what we are witnessing is a profound Epistemic shift from a modernist to postmodernist education paradigm – leaving behind the 'authentic' modernist/welfare learner to create a depthless, flexible, lonely, responsive and responsible learner (collectively represented as human capital), devoid of 'sociality', the ultimate commodification of the social. The logic of all of this is the end of "the age of education" (Tuschling & Engemann, 2006, p. 465). In these terms as Gordon (1991) suggests rational thought and action "entailing strategic choices between alternative paths, means and promises' are reimagined in the manner of economics, as part of the 'territory of economic theory" (p. 43). This is what Kelly (2006, p. 23) calls the "dangerous conceit" of neoliberalism, subject to which "the framework of relations between individuals and governments is currently undergoing a profound transition" (Tuschling & Engemann, 2006, p. 451).

This is a profound change in the underlying set of rules governing the production of discourses, the conditions of knowledge, in a single period – a cultural totality or multi-dimensional regularity if you like; social structures and social relations that take shape as the flesh and bones of the new dominant discourse – a general transformation in the nature of social relations – based on the removal of many of the key boundaries which have underpinned modernist thought and a concomitant collapse of moral spheres and a total subordination of moral obligations to economic ones (Walzer, 1984). A dislocation within which a new kind of citizen is produced in relation to new forms of government and governance – and a concomitant loss of 'citizenship capacity'(Crouch, 2003). More specifically, new kinds of relations to and within education and learning are being enacted – 'there is a crisis, and what is at stake is the very concept of education itself' (Bernstein, 1996).

This is not just a process of reform, it is a process of social transformation. Without some recognition of this and attention within public debate to the insidious work that is being done, in these respects, by the T.P.S. – we may find ourselves living and working in a world made up entirely of contingencies, within which the possibilities of authenticity and meaning in teaching, learning and research are gradually but inexorably erased.

NOTES

[1] 'Factual and fictional stories share many of the same kind of textual devices for constructing credible descriptions, building plausible or unusual event sequences, attending to causes and consequences, agency and claim, character and circumstance' Edwards, D. (1997). Discourse and Cognition. London, Sage.

[2] Triantafillou, P. and M. Risjerg Nielsen (2001). "Policing empowerment: the making of capable subjects." History of the Human Sciences(14): 2. argue 'that the more effective empowerment is – the more the subject participates in taking charge of herself to promote the well-being of herself and her family – the more profoundly she is enmeshed in relations of power'.

[3] Stagecoach Theatre Arts founded in 1988 now operates from 355 UK schools and in 2001 was floated on AIM (the Alterative Investment Market).

[4] And Richard Sennett has shown how the principle of "no long term ... corrodes trust, loyalty and mutual commitment" (1998:24).

[5] Precarity is more and more becoming a living situation that is not only characterized by material deficits, insecurity, adverse working conditions and lack of recognition, but above all by dwindling possibilities for people to make long-term plans (see 'the zone of precarity'. (Klaus Dörre november 2006 http://www.goethe.de/ges/soz/dos/arb/pre/en1870532.htm).

[6] Although Giddens might see these conditions as the bases for 'active trust'.

REFERENCES

Bauman, Z. (1993). *Postmodern ethics*. Oxford, UK: Blackwell.
Bauman, Z. (1996). Morality in the age of contingency. In P. Heelas, S. Lash, & P. Morris (Eds.), *Detraditionalization: Critical reflections on authority and identity*. Oxford, UK: Basil Blackwell.
Bauman, Z. (2000). *Liquid modernity*. Cambridge, UK: Polity Press.

Bauman, Z. (2004). Liquid sociality. In N. Gane (Ed.), *The future of social theory*. London: Continuum.

Beck, U. (1992). *Risk society: Towards a new modernity*. Newbury Park, CA: Sage.

Beck, U. (1994). *The reinvention of politics: Towards a theory of reflexive modernization*. Cambridge, UK: Polity Press.

Bernstein, B. (1996). *Pedagogy symbolic control and identity*. London: Taylor and Francis.

Bernstein, B. (2001). From pedagogies to knowledges. In A. Morais, I. Neves, B. Davies, & H. Daniels (Eds.), *Towards a sociology of pedagogy*. New York: Peter Lang.

Bernstein, B. (2001). Video conference with Basil Bernstein. In A. Morais, I. Neves, B. Davies, & H. Daniels (Eds.), *Towards a sociology of pedagogy*. New York: Peter Lang.

Bourdieu, P. (1998). *Acts of resistance: Against the tyranny of the market*. New York: The New Press.

Bourdieu, P. (2004). Forms of capital. *The RoutledgeFalmer reader in the sociology of education*. S. J. Ball. London: RoutledgeFalmer.

Colley, H., James, D. et al. (2003). Learning as becoming in vocational education and training: Class gender and the role of vocational habitus. *Journal of Vocational Education and Training, 55*(4), 471–496.

Crouch, C. (2003). *Commercialisation or citizenship*. London: Fabian Society.

DfES. (2003). *The future of higher education: White paper*. DfES: DfES.

Dorre, K. (2006). *The zone of precarity*. Retrieved February 23, 2007, from http://www.goethe.de/ges/soz/dos/arb/pre/en1870532.htm

du Gay, P. (1996). *Consumption and identity at work*. London: Sage.

du Gay, P. (2004). Against 'Enterprise' (but not against 'enterprise', for that would make no sense). *Organization, 11*(1), 37–57.

Ecclestone, K. (2007). Resisting images of the 'diminished self': The implications of emotional well-being and emotional engagement in education policy. *Journal of Education Policy, 22*(4), 455–470.

Edwards, D. (1997). *Discourse and cognition*. London: Sage.

Edwards, R. (2002). Mobilizing lifelong learning: Governmentality in educational practices. *Journal of Education Policy, 17*(3), 353–365.

Edwards, R., & Nicoll, K. (2001). Researching the rhetoric of lifelong learning. *Journal of Education Policy, 16*(2), 103–112.

Ehrenreich, B. (1989). *Fear of failing: The inner life of the middle class*. New York: Pantheon.

Fejes, A. (2006). The planetspeak discourse of lifelong learning in Sweden: What is an educable adult. *Journal of Education Policy, 21*(6), 676–716.

Foucault, M. (1979). *Discipline and punish*. Harmondsworth: Peregrine.

Garsten, C., & Jacobsson, K. (2003). Learning to be employable: An introduction. In C. Garsten & K. Jacobsson (Eds.), *Learning to be employable: New agendas on work, responsibility and learning in a globalizing world*. London: Palgrave Macmillan.

Giddens, A. (1991). *Modernity and self-identity*. Cambridge, UK: Polity.

Gordon, C. (1991). Governmental rationality: An introduction. In G. Burchell, C. Gordon, & P. Miller (Eds.), *The Foucault effect: Studies in governmentality*. Brighton, Brighton and Hove: Harvester and Wheatsheaf.

Hacking, I. (1986). Making up people. In T. Heller, M. Sosna, & D. Wellbery (Eds.), *Autonomy, individuality and the self in western thought*. Stanford, CA: Stanford University Press.

Haydon, G. (2004). Values education: Sustaining the ethical environment. *Journal of Moral Education, 33*(2), 116–129.

Heelas, P., & Morris, P. (Eds.). (1992). *The values of the enterprise culture: The moral debate*. London: Routledge.

Jessop, B. (2001). What follows Fordism? On the periodization of capitalism and ites regulation. In R. Albritton, M. Itoh, R. Westra, & A. Zuege (Eds.), *Phases of capitalist development: Booms, crises and globalisations*. Basingstoke, Hampshire: Palgrave.

Jordan, B., Redley, M. et al. (1994). *Putting the family first: Identities, decisions and citizenship*. London: UCL Press.

Keep, E. (1997). 'There's no such thing as society...': Some problems with an inividual approach to creating a Learning society. *Journal of Education Policy, 12*(6), 457–471.

Kelly, P. (2006). The entrepreneurial self and 'Youth-at-risk': Exploring the horizons of identity in the 21st century. *Journal of Youth Studies, 9*(1), 17–32.

Kenway, J., & Bullen, E. (2001). *Consuming children: Education-entertainment-advertising.* Buckingham: Open University Press.

Knorr-Cetina, K. (2000). Postsocial theory. In G. Ritzer & B. Smart (Eds.), *Handbook of social theory.* London: Sage.

Kuhn, M., & Sultana, R. (Eds.). (2006). *Homo Sapiens Europaecus: Creating the European learning citizen.* New York: Peter Lang.

Lury, C. (1997). *Prosthetic culture.* London: Routledge.

Lyotard, J.-F. (1984). *The postmodern condition: A report on knowledge.* Manchester, Lancashire: Manchester University Press.

Mason, M. (2001). The ethics of integrity: Education values beyond postmodern ethics. *Philosophy of Education, 35*(1), 47–69.

McWilliam, E. (2005). Unlearning pedagogy. *Journal of Learning Design, 1*(1), 1–11.

McWilliam, E. (2002). Against professional development. *Journal of Educational Philosophy and Theory, 34*(3), 289–300

Peters, M. (2001). Education, enterprise culture and the entrepreneurial self: A foucualdian perspective. *Journal of Educational Enquiry, 2*(2), 58–71.

Rimke, H. M. (2000). Governing citizens through self-help literature. *Cultural Studies, 14*(1), 61–78.

Robertson, D. (2000). Students as consumers: The individualization of competitive advantage. In P. Scott (Ed.), *Higher Education Reformed.* London: FalmerPress.

Rose, N. (1996). Governing advanced liberal democracies. In A. Barry, T. Osborne, & N. Rose (Ed.), *Foucault and political reason: Liberalism, neo-liberalism and rationalities of government.* London: UCL Press.

Rose, N. (1998). *Inventing ourselves.* Cambridge, UK: Polity Press.

Sennett, R. (1998). *The corrosion of character: The personal consequences of work in the new capitalism.* New York: W.W. Norton.

Skeggs, B. (2004). *Class, self, culture.* London: Routledge.

Thompson, J. B. (1995). *The media and modernity. A social theory of the media.* Cambridge, UK: Polity Press.

Triantafillou, P., & Risjberg Nielsen, M. (2001). Policing empowerment: The making of capable subjects. *History of the Human Sciences, 14*(2), 63–86.

Tuschling, A., & Engemann, C. (2006). From education to lifelong learning: The emerging regime of learning in the European Union. *Educational Philosophy and Theory, 38*(4), 451–469.

Vincent, C., & Ball, S. J. (2006). *Childcare, choice and class practices: Middle-class parents and their children.* London: Routledge.

Walzer, M. (1984). *Spheres of Justice: A defence of pluralism and equality.* Oxford, UK: Martin Robertson.

Watson, M., & Hay, C. (2003). The discourse of globalisation and the logic of no alternative: Rendering the contingent necessary in the political economy of New Labour. *Policy and Politics, 31*(3), 289–305.

Willmott, H. (1995). Managing the academics: Commodification and control in the development of university education in the UK. *Human Relations, 48*(9), 993–1027.

Wittel, A. (2001). Towards a network sociality. *Theory, Culture and Society, 18*(6), 51–76.

Stephen J. Ball
Institute of Education
University of London

THOMAS S. POPKEWITZ

13. WHY THE DESIRE FOR UNIVERSITY-SCHOOL COLLABORATION AND THE PROMISE OF PEDAGOGICAL CONTENT KNOWLEDGE MAY NOT MATTER AS MUCH AS WE THINK[1]

ABSTRACT

Teacher education and school reforms leave unexamined the politics of the system of reason that orders and divides. The political is embodied in the partitioning of sensibilities, shaping and fashioning what is known, to be done, and hope for as the possibilities of schooling and professional education. That politics, however, is not only about what 'we' should be, but also about processes of casting out and excluding what does not 'fit' into the normalized spaces. The discussion first examines two problematics about contemporary research to consider the principles generated in research about what can be known, what must be done, what may be hoped. The subsequent analysis is of standards curriculum reforms and equity research in school-university partnerships as embodying a system of reason with double inscriptions of inclusion and exclusion: inscriptions of cultural theses about the hoped for child and the simultaneous enunciation of fears about the dangers and dangerous populations that threaten the future. The final two sections focus on the thesis about schooling serving 'all children' as processes of abjection. The 'all' is the thesis of the child as the unfinished, cosmopolitan 'lifelong learner' that at the same time embodies and requires its other, abjected child who is signified as 'he child left behind' who is recognized for inclusion but placed outside in unlivable spaces. The study considers the limits of 'the reason' of contemporary reforms as instantiation of governing principles rather assumptions of inclusion and democratization.

INTRODUCTION

The National Commission on Teaching (1996, 2003) captures much of the hope of contemporary reforms. The hope of reform is clearly in the title *No dream denied: A pledge to America's children* (2003). The dream is for an inclusive schooling that eliminates academic "gaps across racial, ethnic, and economic groups" (p. 43; also see American Council on Education, 2003). The dream's fulfillments are reforms that produce "clear and consistent visions of teaching and learning", the integration between university instruction and clinical practices, and performance standards to guarantee adequate professional and subject matter knowledge. Professional education entails commitments to analytical and reflective skills.

M.A. Peters et al. (eds.), Governmentality Studies in Education, 217–234.

Further and an important element of such reforms is increased sensitivity to cultural diversity in the political and ethical obligations of professional education.

The 'dream' of inclusive schooling, however, embodies not only the expression of social and moral commitments in teacher education. It is assembled by particular principles generated to order, differentiate and divide the objects of reform as knowable components of reality. The partitioning of sensibilities is the political, shaping and fashioning what is known, to be done, and hope for as the possibilities of schooling and professional education. That politics, however, is not only about what 'we' should be, but also processes of casting out and excluding what does not 'fit' into the normalized spaces (Popkewitz, 2008). The latter, I will argue, simultaneously enunciation of fears of the dangers and dangerous populations that threaten the envisioned future.

I begin the discussion with the principles that order two problematics about contemporary research. My use of problematic is to consider the principles generated in research about what can be known, what must be done, what may be hoped. I first direct attention to the *equity problematic* as an exemplar for consider overlapping principles about research in contemporary reform. I then explore the problematic about systems of reason that enable a consideration of the rules and standards that research on *equity problematic* as it relates to school and professional reforms. The subsequent analysis standards curriculum reforms and equity research in school-university partnerships as embodying a system of reason with double inscriptions of inclusion and exclusion: inscriptions of cultural theses about the hoped for child and the simultaneous enunciation of fears about the dangers and dangerous populations that threaten the future. The hope and fears, I argued, embodied its other through processes of abjection that cast out and radical differentiate and divide to produce inclusions/exclusions.[2] The final two sections focus on the thesis about schooling serving 'all children' as processes of abjection. The 'all' is the thesis of the child as the unfinished, cosmopolitan 'lifelong learner' that at the same time embodies and requires its other, abjected child who is signified as 'the child left behind.' The latter child is recognized for inclusion but placed outside in unlivable spaces.

The analysis of the double gestures of inclusion/exclusion draws on Foucault's (1991) of governmentality. The study considers the limits of 'the reason' of contemporary reforms as instantiation of governing principles rather assumptions of inclusion and democratization (also see, Popkewitz, 1991, 2008). The commitments of this research to engage in study that seeks possibilities other than those already in the present. To borrow from Foucault, research is the

> ...matter of shaking this false self-evidence, of demonstrating its precariousness, of making visible not its arbitrariness, but its complex interconnection with a multiplicity of historical processes, many of them of recent data (Foucault, 1991, p. 75).

TWO PROBLEMATICS IN THE STUDY OF SCHOOLING AND PROFESSIONALIZATION: EQUITY AND REASON OF REASON

Two different problematics to reform and research in schooling and professional education are discussed. One is 'the equity problematic.' As part of a European Union research project on educational governance and social exclusion in nine countries, we did an extensive review of Anglo-American educational research to examine the principles that order research problems and methods about inclusion and equity (Popkewitz & Lindblad, 2000). This is followed by a discussion of the problematic of 'reason' to direct attention to what is assumed as necessary, natural or neutral in the subjects of reform about inclusion and equity.

The Equity Problematic

Schematically, the equity problematic entails research directed to change the conditions of school to produce a more equitable society.[3] Research is to identify the necessary knowledge for understanding the factors that increase or hinder representation and access social groups handicapped in existing school programs. The assumption of research is that once the factors and mechanism of inequity are made apparent, more efficient policies and programs are possible to bring forth progress. The assumptions of the Equity Problematic circulate in policy and research through four overlapping principles.

First is *the politics of representation*. Research identifies those groups that are excluded through low academic scores, academic graduate rates, or participation in areas given high priority, such as mathematics and sciences. Research functions to understand the practices that produce and/or redress that exclusion. Statistical reporting in cross-national reports of education, for example, compare different characteristics of populations to school performance indicators; comparing ethnic, racial groups and gender populations to norms about school attendance, achievement levels, and graduation rates, among others. Qualitative research provides narratives of the interactions, communications and cultures of classrooms to understand how bias is mobilized to prevent social inclusion.

Gender and social mobility studies exemplify this focus on representation. Early gender research on teaching mathematics, for example, identified differences between girls and boys participation in advanced classes. The statistical information about enrolments was complemented by ethnographic studies of classrooms to understand the processes by which differentiation are produced. The findings were used to create school policies, program development and professional training to increase girls' participation. A different example relates to social mobility. Swedish research on the comprehensive school reforms and American War on Poverty in the late 1960s and early 1970s sought to identify economic and social groups' participation in schools and to increase graduation rates and attendance in college. The school district's decentralization in the New York City to create community schools, the U.S. Teacher Corps program to provide teachers for schools in areas of poverty, and research on the teaching of reading were to increase participation, efficacy among the poor, and school success. Much contemporary research on neoliberalism follows this pattern of examining how policies of marketization disadvantages marginalized groups in society.

Second, change is finding the right mixture of policies to produce an inclusionary institution and thus eliminate (at least theoretically) exclusion and inequities. Standards and performance based curriculum reforms and research, for example, are to provide for an inclusionary schooling in which "all children to learn". The research strategies are to identify who is "falling behind", and then create programs to remediate and rescue the child left behind. From one ideological position, research that calls for "the gold standard" of randomized experiments to identify "evidence based" reforms about what works operates on the assumption of finding the mixtures that eliminates exclusions. Research is to identify the right set of procedures that will close the achievement gap between the advantaged and disadvantaged students. Design Research, a seemingly different ideological and methodological approach than "the gold standard", maintains the purpose of research finding the right mixture of practices through a constant process of monitoring of classrooms so as to achieve "desired results" (see discussion in Popkewitz, 2008, chapters 7–9).

The third principle is that knowledge serves human purposes and intention. The idea is that knowledge is 'useful' through efficient planning that brings into alignment school practices with system goals. The gold standards and design research are possible and plausible as points of debate as they exist within a grid of practices that assumes a consensus, stability and harmony about the goals to which action is directed.

The notion that research has practical implications crosses ideological positions. The principles are found in research about seeking more effective classroom instruction and it research that is to contribute to a more democratic society and emancipatory classroom. The policy maker, researcher, and teacher, for example, look to research (and the researcher) as providing knowledge that is in service of 'desired' social purposes of schools. The teacher asks "What does this research tell us for improving classroom teaching?" The university researcher is heard to say "How can this research be made relevant to what teachers do in the classroom?" The political activist implores that research serves as an agent of change and social reconstruction.

The different expressions have the unspoken principle that knowledge is the servant of people to effect agency and social progress. The notion of use is captured in the phrase "Knowledge is power!" coupled with the more general belief the language, ideas, discourse are epiphenomena to material life.

Fourth, inclusion and exclusion are *separate categories in planning*. The increase in one decreases the other with the potential to provide for the unity of the whole. The game is sum-zero; inclusion is to eliminate exclusion. The distinction between inclusion and exclusion is embodied in the common reform phrase that 'all children learn.' The unspoken assumption is that proper planning will erase all distinctions and differences. The erasure of difference is signified in reforms about school partnerships between schools and universities in which a more culturally sensitive curriculum and teacher will increase children's achievement and produce a more inclusive society.

Fourth and finally is the premise that reform and research is to change society by changing people (Popkewitz, 2006). School voucher programs are envisioned by conservatives as enabling children of the poor to emulate the wealthy and provide for the cosmopolitan unity where there is no difference. Critical pedagogies draw on the Great Depression's pedagogical reformer George Counts (1932/1980) who wrote "Dare the school build a new social order?" to argue for new social visions that counteract capitalism.Current references to Counts argue about the need to remake society with the emancipatory visions of cosmopolitanism. Paulo Freire's "pedagogy of the oppressed" is transferred from the Brazil Catholic liberation theology for rural setting into American urban schools as a bottom up strategy for a cosmopolitan world bound to social justice and equality.

My outlining the principles of the equity problematic is to diagnosis the limitations of its practices through examining its rules and standards of reason as they circulate in the governing of school and professional reforms and research. While the equity problematic is important in its focus on excluded populations, it is not sufficient and, ironically, may miss the very principles that order school change and the problem of social exclusion. The knowledge about including the child "left behind" and university and school collaboration are not 'merely' instruments to achieve desired goals. To recognize those for inclusion does not exorcize exclusion.

The Problematic of "Reason"

How we think and order the things of the world and our self as not merely something of logic or ideas that describe events or people. Foucault argued that it is possible to think about reason as an inscription device in which different cultural practices come together to govern, shape, and fashion the conduct of conduct. The reason of reform, then, is an effect of power through the principles generated about reflection and action.

The structuring principles of 'reason' in schooling can be initially considered with the notion of adolescence. Adolescence emerges as a significant category of planning in the early 20th century through the child study of G. Stanley Hall. That category fabricated a particular human kind that the school was to administer.[4] The word fabrication directs attention to three qualities or nuances of "reason" itself. One, adolescence is a fiction. Adolescence is a fiction created to think about things in the world that require our attention. G. Stanley Hall (1924) used the notion of adolescence to respond to the changing characteristics of the children coming to mass schooling. Dramatic changes in the school child were seen as urban populations associated with European immigrants and African Americans from the south entered northeastern U.S. classrooms at the turn of the 20th century. Adolescence was a way to think about the modes of living of the child whose qualities of development and growth were thought of as most significant in the governing of the adult.

A second quality of fabrication is as manufacturing or making. The notion of adolescence was not merely a fiction. It responded to things of the world and also entered into everyday practices as principles of child development and growth. Books, theories, programs and assessments for teachers and parents were produced to ensure adolescents' psychological health and cognitive development and to treat the problems that arose from deviations. And children began to think of themselves through the distinctions and categories of 'adolescence.' Today what parent does not look at her child's actions or teacher assessments of classroom learning through lens of adolescent development and growth?

Third, Hall's writing historically enunciated particular solutions and plans for action in social, cultural and educational arenas that go beyond its particular approach. Adolescence is a cultural thesis about how one should live. That thesis is produced through assembly and overlapping of different historical trajectories. Hall's child study carried cultural theses about agency and reason that mutated from Northern European Enlightenment into an evolutionary story of an American Exceptionalism, the later as the telling of the nation as an epic of a unique human experiment in the development of the highest ideals of cosmopolitan values. The new discipline of psychology in which Hall wrote was a response to and part of these political efforts concerned with the morality of society and 'the civilizing mission' of the school. Child study was part of American Protestant progressive reformist projects concerned with altering the perceived moral disorder of the city and its immigrant populations.

The educational reforms enunciated through notions of adolescence were to remake "'the soul' of the child, a phrase that Hall as well as Dewey used in their educational projects.[5] Pedagogical practices embodied the hope of the future citizen **and** worries and anxieties about the child, family life, juvenile delinquency, sexual habits, and other morally threatening behaviors. These worries, anxieties and fears were inscribed in Hall's studies as racialized and gendered distinctions about the threats of the uncivilized urban populations who did not fit in the space of the American Exceptionalism, its "American race" and its citizens as "the Chosen People" – women not in the home, immigrants from non-Protestant countries, Irish Catholic immigrants, African-American, and Chinese American.

The 'civilizing mission' embodied hopes and fears that excluded in the desire to include. Hall's child study and the notion of adolescence addressed the city reforms of the turn at the 20th century. American Progressive reforms were to reassert Christian ethics into public life perceived as undermined through the emergence of organized capitalism laid bare with muckraking literature. Science was central. As the natural sciences provided mastery of the physical world, the social sciences would provide master in changing society through changing people. Psychology was part of this broader reformist project (Popkewitz, 2005, 2008).[6]

Today the hopes and fears refer to a different civilizing mission of the school that today speaks about the citizen of the nation in a global world (Popkewitz, 2000). Let me provide an initial illustration before proceeding further. The professional reform report *What Matters Most. Teaching for America's Future*

(*National Commission on Teaching & America's future,* 1996) is to change the conditions of teacher education that is also about changing teachers.

> We must reclaim the soul of America. And to do so, we need an education system that helps people forge shared values, to understand and respect other perspectives, to learn and work at high levels of competence, to take risks and persevere against the odds, to work comfortably with people from diverse backgrounds, and *to continue to learn throughout life* (p. 12, my italics).

The reorganizing teacher preparation brings to bear collective cultural thesis about collective belonging that expresses both hope and fears in its rhetoric of 'reclaiming the soul of America.' The rhetorical 'reclaiming the *soul*' of the nation is not about the past. It is a cultural thesis about modes of living, ordered through conduct that forges values, respects others, takes risks, works with diverse people, and an individuality that continues to learn throughout life. The cultural thesis about the hope of society in the making of the child differentiates and distinguishes the universal child who takes risks and respects others from 'others' that I explore below.

The fabrications of the adolescence in child study and today's 'soul' of the nation are not natural categories for curriculum planning and professional education but are historically inscribed cultural theses about modes of living that include and exclude.The following pursues the argument about inclusion and exclusion, first, in the U.S. curriculum standards reform about an equitable education for *all* children. Second I examine pedagogical discourses about the lifelong learner and the child left behind as two distinct cultural theses about who the child is and should be. I use these examples to consider the double practices of exclusion and inclusion that circulate and are elided in discussions of school – university – community collaboration and curriculum standards reforms.

THE STANDARDS OF CURRICLUM AND MAKING AN EQUITABLE SOCIETY THROUGH FABRICATING THE STANDARD CHILD

Curriculum standards are central to issues of quality and equity in U.S. contemporary school and professional reforms. Standards outcome criteria establish what children should know, for example, about music composition, basic arithmetic computation or geometry, and the historical understanding of the nation's development. Standards are also fundamental in teacher education reforms. The University of Wisconsin-Madison's teacher education programs, for example, list performance outcomes mandated by Wisconsin's state educational authority.[7] The standards are seen as improving the quality of teaching and to ensure that students from diverse backgrounds are treated equally.

The advocates and critics of standards maintain the principles about exclusion and inclusion discussion earlier in the equity problematic. The assumptions are related to the politics of representation and the sum-zero game in which inclusion and exclusion are treated as analytically distinct categories – practices to reduce exclusion create greater inclusion. Further, it is assumed that the right mixtures of reforms will change the conditions of society by changing people. The hope of those advocating standards is to ensure *all* children receive an equal education (Ravich, 1995). Critiques of the standards reform movement are framed generally with the hope that schooling will increase participation and success (and thus decrease exclusion) of children of the poor, racial minorities, and certain ethnic groups (Boaler, 2000). Curriculum standards are faulted as they are seen as carriers of cultural bias or structural forces that marginalize economical and social groups.

The issue at hand in these reforms is not the question of standards, but what is taken as standards in school reforms. The standards that are significant are not necessarily in what is given as performance outcomes of schooling. Standards are historically related to the condition of governing who people are and should be that were part of the forming of the modern state.[8] Before the 18th century, it was difficult to govern a state because of variable measurements. Each local area had its own units of measurement *(a hand, a foot, a cartload, a basketful, a handful, a within earshot)* that resisted any central administration. People without patronyms could not be tracked. In what might seem ironic, the modern notions of the Republic, and the freedom and liberty of the modern citizen were dependent on the creation of standards. Standardizing to measure and compare people was to enable the European sovereign to provide consistent receipts into the treasury. Prior to the French Revolutions, The Encyclopedists saw the inconsistency among measurements, institutions, inheritance laws, taxation, and market regulations as the greatest obstacle to making the French a single people with equal rights (Scott, 1998, p. 32). Standardization of the metric system was not only to bring administrative centralization and commercial reform. It was to promote cultural progress and democratic change by treating all citizens equally. The uniform measures were to transform the people of the nation into citizens of the nation in the belief that "the uniformity of customs, viewpoints, and principles of action will, inevitably, lead to a greater community of habits and predispositions" (citing the historian Ken Adler in Scott, 1998, p. 32).

Ignored in the debates about standards are the comparative systems of recognition and difference that frame the hopes of reform. The founders of the American and French Republics acknowledged that the practices of liberty and freedom required educational system that produced the dispositions that made possible the citizen's participation upon which the new regime depended. The freedom of the citizen was not something innate to the person. It had to be produced. The standards of curriculum embody cultural theses about different modes of living that differentiate children that require exploration. Educational standards are part of the process of governing through making the citizen.

STANDARDS, RECOGNITION AND PROCESSES OF ABJECTION: THE UNFINISHED COSMOPOLITAN AND THE CHILD LEFT BEHIND

At this point, I want to consider the particular cultural theses in current reforms through the notions of the lifelong learning and 'no child left behind.' Standards reforms embody a continuum of values in which there are cultural theses about who the child is and should be. These values can be made visible initially through the question: If there is a child left behind to be included with *all* children, what are distinctions and categories to differentiate the hope of the *all children* from its *Other*? To answer this question of division and exclusion in the practices of inclusion, I draw on analyses of reform in the European Union and U.S. (Popkewitz, & Lindblad, 2004; Popkewitz, 1998; also, Simon & Masschelein, 2006). At one end of the continuum is the child who stands as the universal *all*. That child thinks, speaks, feels and acts as *the unfinished cosmopolitan,* a lifelong learner who responds actively to the global changes occurring, engages in the social construction and reconstruction of Learning Society and as a global citizen. That is the hope inscribed in pedagogy as the cosmopolitan is a continual image and narrative in modern republics and schooling.[9] The fear of pedagogy is the child recognized and differentiated from the lifelong learner. That child who is *left behind,* not fitting into the space occupied with the "all children." The two cultural theses are folded into the other as each requires its Other.

THE CULTURAL THESIS OF THE LIFELONG LEARNER: THE UNFINISHED COSMOPOLITAN

Who is this unfinished cosmopolitan who acts as the lifelong learner in 'The Information Society'and 'The Learning Society'?

The lifelong learner is a discourse about the individual is continually pursues knowledge and innovation in a never ending chase for the future. Choice becomes a goal of life and problem solving and working collaboratively in communities as the avenues for continual seeking personal fulfillment.Pedagogy narratives about problem solving and community link *all* individuals to social or economic progress and the revitalization of democracy. Stories of the problem solving child, for example, are about a mode of life faced with constant changes in society. The child acts autonomously (seemingly) and responsibly (hopefully) in continuous decision making. The child inhabits the Learning Society with "a cosmopolitan identity which shows tolerance of race and gender differences, genuine curiosity toward and willingness to learn from other cultures, and responsibility toward excluded groups within and beyond one's society" (Hargreaves, 2003, p. xix).

The seduction of this mode of living is its political register about "voice" and empowerment by working continuously on self improvement and self-actualization.[10] The subjectivity of the lifelong learner is spoken of as an entrepreneurial individual. It would be mistaken, however, to think of this register as an economic reduction of humanity. The classroom community becomes a 'participation structure' concerned with creating fluid identities associated with lifelong learning.

The notion of the lifelong learner is related to mutations of the Enlightenment's cosmopolitan in ascribing a life organized through reason and rationality in the pursuit of individual empowerment and a universal progress. In the present, that cosmopolitanism has particular sets of principles and connections that I think of as an unfinished cosmopolitan (Popkewitz, 2008). That cosmopolitanism is one that entails the continual capacity to innovate and cope with change in the never ending processes of making choices and problem solving.

The narratives of the unfinished cosmopolitan connect the scope and aspirations of public powers with the personal and subjective capacities of individuals. Earlier 20th century classrooms were places of socialization where the child internalized pre-established collective and universal norms of identity; today they are a redesigned space of living. The location of responsibility is no longer traversed through the range of social practices directed toward a single public sphere– the social. Responsibility is located today in communities, diverse, autonomous and plural communities perpetually constituted through one's own practice in communities of learning.

Whatever the merits of problem solving and community, they are not merely descriptive of some natural reasoning of the child that the research merely recoups. The words are assembled in a system of reason to relate individuality to collective belonging. The mathematics education standards literature, for example, places problem solving and communities of learners in a particular cultural thesis about living in a 'ubiquitous' uncertain future for which learning mathematics prepares the child. In a statement resonating across American school reforms, the National Council of Teachers of Mathematics (2000) model for curriculum standards argues that the student needs to be prepared for the future where change is "a ubiquitous feature of contemporary life, so learning with understanding is essential to enable students to use what they learn to solve the new kinds of problems they will inevitably face in the future" (pp. 20–21).

The child who acts to plan for the ubiquitous future is a particular mode of living. The project of life is to design one's biography as a continuous movement from one social sphere to another, as if life were a planning workshop that had a value in and of itself. Action is a continual flow of problem solving to design not only what will be done but also the future of what that person will be. Agency is directed to problem solving that chases desire in the infinite choices of pursuit of continuous innovation.

The empowerment of freedom is talked about as if there are no enclosures. Yet freedom of choice expresses a fatalism of the processes of globalization. The unfinished cosmopolitanism is the inevitable march of globalism that teachers respond to in curriculum changes. Teachers, school administrators and government officials in a European Union study expressed that fatalism (Lindblad & Popkewitz, 2004). The new child was one who makes choices to be happier and successful in a globalization that had not author or need to explain. The ubiquitous future of globalism makes it not possible for the individual, to quote a French high school textbook, "to escape the flux of change" (Soysal, Bertiloot, & Mannitz, 2005, pp. 24–25). Globalism was naturalized to intern and enclose the spaces of the participation.

THE FEAR OF THE FUTURE IN THE PRESENT: THE CHILD LEFT BEHIND
AND THE URBAN CHILD

If the unfinished cosmopolitan is the hope of the future, another type of hope exists in school reforms. It is the hope of an inclusive society through reforms that eliminate marginalization and failure of *particular populations* of children. That hope of an inclusive society is captured in the phrase 'no child left behind' that recognizes particular groups of children in need of rescue. This section will focus on the system of recognition to include groups as simultaneously a system that inscribes difference. The recognition and difference places the child in a double space that is both inside and outside of norms that embody what is constituted as civility. This civility, however, is not some formal notion of ethics or morality. Rather it is generated in relation to the distinctions associated with what the child left behind is **not** – the unfinished cosmopolitanism of the lifelong learner.

To consider the complex and comparative qualities assembled in the phrase 'the child left behind' entails turning to constant reiteration of reforms to treat *all* children equal in their opportunities and conditions of learning. The reiteration of 'all' signals rhetorically the commitment to an equal and inclusiveness of society. The Principles and Standards for School Mathematics, for example, states that "*All* students, regardless of their personal characteristics, background, or physical challenges, must have opportunities to study—and support to learn—mathematics" (National Council for Teachers of Mathematics, 2000, p. 12, *italics added*). The American Council on Education (1999) teacher education reform report re-asserts this hope in its appeal for an education "available to *all* students, not just the affluent and the lucky . . ." (p. 5, *italics added*)

The inscription of the phrase "all children" is not only an ethical commitment. It gives expression to an assembly of distinctions that classify who the child left behind is *not*. The *all* unites all parts of the social whole into a particular sameness from which individual children are classified and measured. That qualities of the unity is expressed as the lifelong learner that function as the 'civilized' individuality – the child who has esteem, self-responsibility in making choices, problem solves and continually innovating as a mode of living. The sameness is inscribed in the psychological theories and categories of pedagogy that calculate and order teaching and learning.

A digest of personal facts fashions territories of membership and nonmembers in the *all* children. The child left behind bears the same sets of distinctions and classifications of the lifelong learner but in spaces outside of its normalcy as what psychologically is lacking. These principles of difference and division overlap with those given to the 'the urban child' In American education. If I use an ethnographic study of an alternative teacher education program for urban and rural schools (Popkewitz, 1998), the urban child is a determinate category of a human kind and a cultural thesis of difference. Urban is not a geographical place but a cultural space and thesis about who does not 'fit' those of the unfinished cosmopolitan child. In other nations, that child might be called disadvantaged, at-risk, or the 'needy' child. This cultural thesis of difference in the U.S. is to understand by comparing its cities as spaces with great wealth and a cosmopolitan urbaneness that coexist with the spaces of poverty and racial segregation. Children who live in the high rise apartments and brownstones of American cities appear as 'urbane' and cosmopolitan (and not 'urban'). Children living in suburbs, rural areas as well as the inner city are 'seen' and talked about with the distinctions of difference: having 'low expectations', low self-esteem, family dysfunctions, and poverty. The significance of 'urban', then, is in its cultural thesis about the child rather than as a geographical distinction.

The comparative distinctions that differentiate the unity of 'all children' from the *urban, child left behind* has multiple and paradoxical functions. It sanctifies political and cultural values about inclusion and respect for the Other through erasing and re-inscribing difference. If I return to the lifelong learner and The Learning Society, there seems as if there are no differences as all children will problem solve and work collaboratively in a continual process of choice and innovation. Yet standing with the 'all' children are distinctions and differentiations that name the qualities and characteristics of those who do not qualify as among the *all* children.

What is the cultural thesis about the mode of life in the children recognized for inclusion but constituted as different from *all children*?

The dangers and dangerous populations overlap social, cultural and psychological distinctions. There are overlapping categories and distinctions, for example, in federal websites on 'what works' that is to identify reforms consistent with the goals of the No Child Left Behind legislation, and research about equity in teaching the 'urban' child.[11] The dangerous child has psychologically low self-esteem and poor self-concepts. The psychological qualities are assembled with social/moral categories to express central cultural fears such as, for example, dysfunctional families, single parent households, poverty, and juvenile delinquency. The urban child left behind is recognized as living

> In poverty, students who are not native speakers of English, students with disabilities, females, and many nonwhite students [who] have traditionally been far more likely than their counterparts in other demographic groups to be victims of low expectations" (National Council of Teachers of Mathematics, 2000, p. 13).

The problem of the failing child is reduced to a psychological commonplace – low expectations.

The hope of rescue is also the fear of moral disorganization related to reach into one of the most sacred spaces of modern life, the family. The child left behind is not only about the child who does not succeed in schools. It is also the family left behind and which is recognized in need of special help and different. Research on the family and childrens' school failure, for example, focus on the families of children who fail in school as the "fragile family", and the "vulnerable families" (Hildago, Siu, Bright, Swap & Epstein, 1995; p. 500). The parents are differentiated and normalized as having a lower level of education and socioeconomic status, are immigrants (the length of time living in country), live in poor areas of residence, and are ethnically defined (living or not living in ethnic enclaves), among others (Hildago, Siu, Bright, Swap & Epstein, 1995). The social and economic classifications of the child and family are linked to structural relations within the gender relations and communications patterns that relate to gender, such as whether the mother is a single or teen parent (Hildago, Siu, Bright, Swap, & Epstein, 1995, p. 501, David and Lucille Packard Foundation, 2002).

The various categories of the child and family are a determinate classification of deviance that has succinct chronological, cultural, physiological and psychological characteristics. The aggregate of the 'fragile' and 'vulnerable' family acquires the abstraction of the sciences or impersonal management to reason about the group and personal capabilities and capacities of people.

MAKING EXCLUSION IN THE MAKING OF REFORMS TO INCLUDE

The title of this chapter, 'Why The Desire for University-School Collaboration And The Promise of Pedagogical Content Knowledge May Not Matter As Much As We Think' directs attention to the limitations of the equity problematic. The promise of collaboration and participation in the reforms seem as the living out of democratic commitments. They are to bring together major stake holders in making decisions that are important to their lives.

While the overt purposes of the narratives of reform are to include the excluded child, the system of reason in the reforms generate principles about who the child is, should be, and who is not that child. The seductiveness of the sacred words of education in mobilizing people should not be confused with the necessary historical and analytic work to consider the assemblies and connections that govern what is constituted as our very humanness through pedagogical projects. The very questions of differentiations and divisions require, to borrow from Algerian Frantz Fanon that "people must give up their too-simple conception of their overlords" in the constructions of given identities (cited in Gilroy, 2006, p. 57).

Participation and empowerment, to use two of the sacred words of contemporary reforms, are not merely instrumental practices of negotiations, dialogue and representation of diverse groups. Participation entails the circulation of prior principles in giving intelligibility to reflection and action. Judith Butler (1991), the feminist philosopher spoke about this as the double quality of the pronoun 'I.' There is the autobiographical 'I' as the actor who make decisions. That 'I' is also historical. There are grids of ideas and institutional patterns through that the practices of learning, pedagogy and professional actions are made plausible.

Let me pursue this historical specificity further. While it is fashionable to talk about neoliberalism, markets, and privatization in policy studies as an explanation and causal fact of reforms, its notions of participation and collaboration entail a particular assembly, connections, and disconnections related to particular governing practices that has little to do with markets per se. The end of *laissez faire* and market economy in the middle of the 19th century America produced a state in care of the self that are maintained and which mutate in today's reforms.Governing expressed relationship with civil society and the state designed to circumvent the predominant systems of local government, party control, and court systems in place since the 18th century. Mutations of these administrative patterns of governing that relate state and civil institutions are evident in the production of national curriculum standards. The standards are written in an overlapping of professional teacher organizations with foundations like the Carnegie and federal and state agencies.

The much heralded democratization and equalization in professional reforms of collaboration and participation cannot be adequately considered outside of the administrative pattern of governing. The speaking of 'closer ties between clinical practices and schools', and the call 'for clear and consistent visions and performance standards' in teaching are strategies that function to provide stability and consensus that leaves unscrutinized the re-structuring qualities of the "reason" of schooling and its principles of inclusion and exclusion.[12] The call for teacher subject matter knowledge and pedagogical knowledge, another focus in professional reforms, assume that the problem of schooling is the need for greater competence in the 'what' and 'how' of teaching. Again, the conclusion reaches into an almost undeniable but potentially controversial 'truth.'[13] Elsewhere I argue that the reforms on teacher subject matter knowledge and pedagogical content knowledge stabilize the knowledge of science or mathematics through its psychological principles (Popkewitz, 2004a). Without considering the rules and standards through which participation and reflection are shaped and fashioned,[14] the solutions embodied in reforms are, at best, about organization and institutional activities that leave unquestioned the comparative system of reason in which the child recognition and differentiated.[15]

Finally, there is a need to rethink the orthodoxy of research as an expertise in designing people. The designing of people underlies phrases such as 'what works,' 'empirically based knowledge,' and the certainty that science can produce models of 'replication' in school life. Science as useful for directing change, is valorized in the distinction of theory/practice that collaboration in teacher education is to overcome.

This view of scientific knowledge as social administration has not always been there. It emerges in the late 19th century reforms concerned with the moral disorder of the city. The expertise of the human sciences was to change the social conditions that produced strategies to change people (Popkewitz, 2006). Beside the empirical 'fact' that such planning and ideas of replications have never worked,[16] the changing of people vacates the moral and political implications of planning people. It disenables the very notion of democracy sought in efforts of collaboration and participation. While planning is necessary to modern notions of liberty and democracy, the expertise of science that speaks of its authority in governing as empowerment and freedom is paradoxical. Despite the good and even sometimes radical intentions of curriculum reforms to empower others, the empowerment of pedagogy is an effect of power (see, e.g., Cruikshank, 1999). Any attempt to promote subjectivity through governing thought cannot overlook the subject who is to be reformed and how that subject is constituted in the school curriculum. .

The focus on systems of reason is to address the politics of schooling and the work of the intellectual (Popkewitz, 1997). Rose (1999) argues, for example, against the prevailing view of expertise by suggesting that inquiry is "to disturb that which forms the very groundwork of our present, to make the given once more strange and to cause us to wonder how it came to appear so natural" (p. 58; also see). To borrow from Foucault (1989):

The work of an intellectual is not to mold the political will of others; it is, through the analysis that he does in his own field, to re-examine evidence and assumptions, to shake up habitual ways of working and thinking, to dissipate conventional familiarities, to re-evaluate rules and institutions and starting from this re-problematization (where he occupies his specific profession as an intellectual) to participate in the formation of a political will (where he has his role as a citizen to play) (pp. 305–306).

If we take Foucault's work that embodies his notion of governmentality, it can be considered as a practice of resistance. This notion of resistance is different from that of the equity problematic. That latter is concerned with struggling against those not represented in public life and denied access and opportunities. This politics of schooling is important but not sufficient. It does not recognize that resistance is also in denaturalizing the habitual ways of organizing life, making fragile what has seemed unquestionable and evitable. Resistance in this latter sense is through contesting what are taken as natural and thus opening up possibilities other than those that already exists.

NOTES

[1] I would like to acknowledge the comments on earlier drafts from Marianne Bloch, Carl Grant, Amy Sloan, Ruth Gustafson, Jamie Kowalczyk. I have limited references central to the thesis and to places where I have discussed more fully the specific textual and empirical analyses so as not to overwhelming the text. Proceeding this way is to merge the French tradition of limiting references to what is only essential and the American tradition of citing each element in the argument. I am not sure what is correct or whether how I have proceeded helps. I hope so.

[2] This term emerged in work that I did with Jamie Kowalcyck (see, e.g., Kowalczyk & Popkewitz, 2005) and related to Kristeva (1982; also see Butler, 1993) . Our use is to explore systems of reason. Other uses or related concerns, see Shimakawa (2002) study of Americanness and the Asian body as "abjection" and Shapiro's (1999) concern with the doubles of inside and outsides as fluidities and contingencies in which individual and collective subjects are constituted.

[3] An extensive citation list of the following is found in Popkewitz & Lindblad (2000) and provide here the analytical distinctions that order the problematic, with specific references when appropriate .

[4] The notion of human kinds is borrowed from Hacking (1986).

[5] I do not mean to suggest that the particular applications of theories of the child and teaching are the same in the iconic figures of American education. It is to suggest that there is a family of resemblance, to borrow from Wittgenstein, that can be discerned historically. The resemblances and their principles of governing are discussed in a book that I am writing, *The Reason of Cosmopolitanism Reason: School Reforms, Science and Making Society through Making the Child*

[6] The euphemisms of research do not talk directly of changing people, but rather of the attitudes and dispositions of a teacher who respects diversity, or can live in a world continually changing, or who engages in problem-solving. But to have these qualities is to link the planning strategies of the classroom to planning who the child is and should be.

[7] The Elementary Certification Program Standards to meet the State's certification requirements are below. They are general enough to allow seemingly different practices, respond to the commitment to diversity and community, yet are the assembled and connected to particular discourses of psychology and curriculum that produce cultural theses that links the teacher to narratives of

planning who the child is and should be, some of which I discuss in the following section. The nine of the fifteen standards are:

STANDARD 1: INCORPORATES UNDERSTANDING OF HUMAN LEARNING AND DEVELOPMENT

STANDARD 2: UNDERSTANDS SOCIAL CONTEXT OF SCHOOLING

STANDARD 3: DEMONSTRATES SOPHISTICATED CURRICULAR KNOWLEDGE

STANDARD 4: DEMONSTRATES PEDAGOGICAL KNOWLEDGE IN SPECIFIC DOMAINS

STANDARD 5: EXPLAINS AND JUSTIFIES EDUCATIONAL CHOICES

STANDARD 6: CONNECTS SCHOOL AND COMMUNITY

STANDARD 12: ACCOMMODATES FOR ALL STUDENTS

STANDARD 13: IS A REFLECTIVE PRACTITIONER

STANDARD 14: RELATES WELL WITH STUDENTS, FAMILIES, AND COMMUNITIES

[8] My use of governing borrows from Foucault's (1979) notion of *governmentality*.

[9] I argue this in a current book that I am writing, as well as in Popkewitz, 2004.

[10] The word "empowerment" is another *topoi* of contemporary reforms in multiple social arenas, crossing ideological positions in policy analyses and research (see, e.g. Hargreaves, 1993). My use of this and other such terms is to interrogate their deployments in professional practices rather than to argue normatively for or against.

[11] The following discussion is drawn from (Popkewitz, 1998).

[12] I discuss the notion of systems and its structural notions of change in Popkewitz, 1984. In this article, the study of reason can also be considered as embodying notions of structure and system related to the earlier discussion of fabrication and which is different from the theoretical position of, for example, "realist" philosophy.

[13] I say controversial to bring forth the discussions of Rancière (1987/1991) who argues models of schooling are bases on notions of "replication" that work against the libratory qualities of education.

[14] This distinction is one of political philosophy and discussed in relation to school reforms in Popkewitz (1978).

[15] While psychology as a technology of instruction may be necessary, other models of thinking about school subjects are possible from, for example, technology and science studies. The latter provide models of thinking about production of knowledge in disciplinary fields as cultural practice that regulate how judgments are made, conclusions drawn, rectification proposed, and the fields of existence made manageable and predictable (see, e.g., Knorr Cetina, 1999; Latour, 1999; Nasar, 1998).

[16] Without being exhaustive in the list of historical examples, one can take early 20th century urban planning that leaches into the present, progressive reforms from Thorndike to Dewey, and the 1960s War of Poverty as suggesting empirically some hesitation with this notion of expertise. But to use "the gold standard," the complexities of medical drug testing and its unanticipated effects suggests that the certainty of engineering the future needs to be cautiously approached (This is discussed in Popkewitz, 2004b; Popkewitz, 2006).

REFERENCES

American Council on Education. (1999). *To touch the future: Transforming the way teachers are taught: An action agenda for college and university presidents.* Washington, DC: American Council on Education.

Boaler, J. (Ed.). (2000). *Multiple perspectives on mathematics teaching and learning.* Westport, CT: Ablex Publishing.

Butler, J. (1991). Contingent foundations: Feminism and the question of "Postmodernism." In J. Butler & J. Scott (Eds.), *Feminists theorize the political* (pp. 3–21). New York: Routlege.

Cruikshank, B. (1999). *The will to empower: Democratic citizens and other subjects.* Ithaca, NY: Cornell University Press.

David and Lucille Packard Foundation. (2002). Welfare reforms and children. *The Future of Children, 12*(1).

Foucault, M. (1989). Foucault live: Interviews, 1966–84. In S. Lovtringer (Ed.). New York: Semiotext(s).

Foucault, M. (1991). Governmentality. In G. Burchell, C. Gordon, & P. Miller (Eds.), *The Foucault effect: Studies in governmentality* (pp. 87–104). Chicago: University of Chicago Press.

Hall, G. S. (1924). *Adolescence: Its psychology and its relation to physiology, anthropology, sociology, sex, crime, religion, and education* (Vol. 1). New York: Appleton and Co.

Hargreaves, A. (2003). *Teaching in the knowledge society: Education in the age of insecurity.* Maindenhead, England: Open University Press.

Hidalgo, N., Siu, S., Bright, J., Swap, S., & Epstein, J. (1995). Research on families, schools, and communities: A Multicultural perspective. In J. Banks (Ed.), *Handbook of research on multicultural education* (pp. 498–524). New York: Macmillan.

Gilroy, P. (2006). *After empire: Melancholia or convivial culture.* New York: Routledge.

Lindblad, S., & Popkewitz, T. (2004). Educational restructuring: (Re)thinking the problematic of reform. In S. Lindblad & T. Popkewitz (Eds.), *Controversies in educational restructuring: International perspectives on contexts, consequences, and implications* (pp. vii–xxxi). Greenwich, CT: Information Age Publishing.

National Commission on Teaching and America's Future. (1996). *What matters most. Teaching for America's future.* Washington, DC: Author.

National Commission on Teaching and America's Future. (2003). *No dream denied: A pledge to America's children.* Washington, DC: Author.

National Council of Teachers of Mathematics. (2000). *Principles and standards for school mathematics.* Reston, VA: Author.

Popkewitz, T. (1997). A changing terrain of knowledge and power: A social epistemology of educational research. *The Educational Researcher, 26/9,* 5–17.

Popkewitz, T. (2008). *Cosmopolitanism and the age of school reform: Science, education, and making society by making the child.* New York: Routledge.

Popkewitz, T. (2006). The idea of science as planning was not planned: A historical note about American pedagogical sciences as planning society and individuality. In R. Hofstetter & B. Schneuwly (Eds.), *Education nouvelle—Sciences de l'Education. The New Education and Educational sciences. Fin du 19ᵉ –milieu 20ᵉ siécle* (pp. 143–169). Bern: Peter Lang.

Popkewitz, T. (Ed.). (2005). *Inventing the modern self and John Dewey: Modernities and the traveling of pragmatism in education.* New York: PalgraveMacmillan.

Popkewitz, T. (2004). The reason of reason: Cosmopolitanism and the governing of schooling. In B. Baker & K. Heyning (Eds.), *Dangerous coagulations: The uses of Foucault in the study of education* (pp. 189–224). New York: Peter Lang.

Popkewitz, T. (2000). Reform as the social administration of the child: Globalization of knowledge and power. In N. Burbules & C. A. Torres (Eds.), *Globalization and education: Critical perspectives* (pp. 157–186). New York: Routledge.

Popkewitz, T. (1998). *Struggling for the soul: The politics of education and the construction of the teacher.* New York: Teachers College Press.

Popkewitz, T. (1991). *A political sociology of educational reform: Power/Knowledge in teaching, teacher education, and research.* New York: Teachers College Press.

Popkewitz, T., & Lindblad, S. (2000). Educational governance and social inclusion and exclusion: Some conceptual difficulties and problematics in policy and research. *Discourse, 21*(1), 5–54.

Rancière, J. (1987/1991). *The ignorant schoolmaster. Five lessons in intellectual emancipation* (K. Ross, trans. and with an introduction). Stanford, CA: Stanford University Press.

Ravitch, D. (1995). *National standards in American education: A citizen's guide.* Washington, DC: Brookings Institution.

Rose, N. (1999). *Powers of freedom: Reframing political thought*. Cambridge, MA: Cambridge University Press.

Scott, J. (1998). *Seeing like a state: How certain schemes to improve the human condition have failed*. New Haven, CT: Yale University.

Simons, M., & Masschelein, J. (2006). *The governmentalization of learning and the assemblage of a learning apparatus*. Paper presented as Foucault and adult education/adult learning, Linköping University, 8th to 10th February.

Soysal, Y., Bertiloot, T., & Mannitz, S. (2005). Projections of identity in French and German history and civics textbooks. In H. Schissler & Y. N. Soyal (Eds.), *The nation, Europe, and the world: Textbooks and curricula in transition* (pp. 13–34). New York: Berghahn Books.

Thomas S. Popkewitz
The University of Wisconsin-Madison
USA

JEFFREY STICKNEY

14. CASTING TEACHERS INTO EDUCATION REFORMS AND REGIMES OF INSPECTION

Resistance to Normalization through Self-Governance

INTRODUCTION

The topics of teacher supervision and professional development offer fertile ground for Foucaultian consideration of the ethics and politics of education reforms (see Larsen, 2005). Instead of surveying this literature or adding to it with another example, I set out various related, philosophical questions bequeathed to us by Foucault. From a Foucaultian position, I want to ask, what are teacher-subjects' relations to truth, power and their 'own' professional selves within curriculum reforms, as school districts administer and police these initiatives through regimes of training and inspection? The chapter shows that governmentality within education systems, a rather elusive phenomenon ("the conduct of conduct"), opens to consideration, in its multiplicity, by looking at teachers' comportment to various pedagogic games of truth – an opening of the professional's world that is especially poignant while undergoing the invasive measures of supervision.

Governmentality, as a locus of freedom and control, is manifest in what conceivable and practical stances teachers can take up, in terms of revealing to inspectors the truth about or concealing their relations to veridical discourses and sanctioned practices within education reforms.[1] As a practicing teacher, I am concerned with teachers' compliance and resistance to normalization within games of accounting and causality (e.g., 'effective schools' and character education rhetoric), but also with professional obligations in terms of telling the truth about oneself, either to one's self or to others who may also govern one's conduct. Without imposing the language of 'authentic' or 'inauthentic' modes of being, we may nevertheless see in the intersection of techniques of domination and techniques of self-formation an awakening of the critical subject: first, by problematizing his subjection to mis-education, or to normalization through top-down forms of professional development and inspection; and, second, by his own subjectification through various arts of resistance and self-stylization (Foucault, 1990, pp. 4–8).[2]

As an academic, I am stung by Foucault's reminder that philosophical activity, and the essay in particular as "a modifying test of oneself in the game of truth" instead of merely a "simplifying appropriation of others," must direct thought not "to legitimating what one already knows," but "to undertaking to know how and to what extent it would be possible to think differently" (Foucault, 1990, pp. 8–9).[3] Investigating the intersection of current education reforms with regimes of teacher development and inspection, in writing this paper I follow Foucault's advice to

M.A. Peters et al. (eds.), Govermentality Studies in Education, 235–256.

work at "the limits of ourselves" – a philosophical ethos demanding "work carried out by ourselves on ourselves as free beings" (Foucault, 1994a, p. 316). The discipline (*askesis*) involved in writing requires that I not only legitimate my immanent criticism of education systems through Foucaultian dress, but that I turn that very philosophy on myself in order to fashion my own thought.

The broader project, beyond the limits of this paper, is to survey actual education reform landscapes – a genealogy of current pedagogic discourse and technique that "opens up a realm of historical inquiry," even "putting it to the test of contemporary reality" in order to create spaces of professional freedom within education systems (Foucault, 1994, p. 319).[4] Evaluative practices in education set up rules that act as 'limit-conditions', elucidating the complex sets of relations gathered into Foucault's concept of governmentality (Tully, 1999). Like Foucault's "privileged example" of sexuality, pedagogic limits (e.g., marking off 'sound' from 'unsound' forms of teaching) offer "a refracting surface" on which to show the general problem of the relations between subjectivity and truth (Foucault, 2006, p. 2; see Stickney, 2005). Using the refectory lens of teacher development and inspection, I will briefly untangle these links between governmentality, subjectific-ation and truth, showing how they tie up with Foucault's concepts of problematiz-ation, power relations, eventualization, educational blocks, pastoral supervision, and the role of the specific intellectual or truth-sayer.

CARE OF THE SELF AS PEDAGOGICAL

Instead of stretching Foucault's discussion to make applications to education, we find that throughout the 1982 lectures, pedagogy in relation to governmentality is a central theme. He also kept dossiers for these lectures in which he reflected on the topics of pedagogy and *paideia*.[5] The dossier on "Government of self and others" contains a passage that parallels a theme running through his exploration of the *Alcibiades*: the need for a master to bring out, not a "lost origin" but a "distinct nature" in the course of overcoming the negative effects of mis-education (Foucault, 2006, pp. 45–6; cf. nt.10).

> Education is imposed against a background of errors, distortions, bad habits and dependencies which have been reified since the start of life. So that is not even a matter of returning to a state of youth or infancy where there would still have been the human being; but rather of referring to a "nature" …which has never had the opportunity to emerge in a life immediately seized by a defective system of education and belief. The objective of the practice of the self is to free the self, by making it coincide with a nature which has never had the opportunity to manifest itself in it. (Foucault, in Gros, 2006, p. 536)

Foucault shows "care of the self" (*epimeleia heauton,* or *cura sui*) to be deeply rooted beneath what we have come to understand from Socrates and Plato as the Greek *telos*: the Delphic oracles' admonition to "know thyself" (*gnōthi seauton*) in order to gain access to the truth (Foucault, 2001, p. 107; Besley, 2007). In "The Subject and Power," this broad historical survey of Western philosophy forms the backdrop for discussion of the subject's agency within modern pedagogical institutions, and for clarification of what "care of the self" means if the self is constituted largely by discourses and non-discursive practices. From this ancient lineage emerges my central question: How do teachers care for and to a limited extent govern themselves, in terms of their own professional development and innovation of practice, 'being truthful' to themselves and others as they are ushered through transformative practices and discourses by school administrators, department heads and education consultants? The terminology lingering around 'authenticity' here is philosophically loaded. Many of Foucault's readers would answer, reasonably: "What self?" Or, doesn't Foucault mean "to become what one is *not*?"

> From philosophy comes the displacement and transformation of the limits of thought, the modification of received values and all the work done to think otherwise, to do something else, to become other than what one is. (Foucault, 1996b, p. 307)

Moving away from phenomenology, Foucault explicitly rejected Sartrean "authenticity" in favour of the more Nietzschean themes of the history of truth and self-stylization (Foucault, 1994b, p. 262). Foucault approached these Nietzschean, genealogical topics and their potential for leading subjects out of normalization through self-problematization by moving through Heidegger's analysis of the subject's (*Dasein's*) everyday, in-authentic "tranquilization" in discourses and "entrapment" in the "public they-self" (on Heidegger, see Foucault, 1996, pp. 470–1; Olssen, 2006, p. 4; Heidegger, 1996, pp. 35–8, 136, 255; Stickney, 2008a).

Alternately, one might ask: Which Foucault? 'Governmentality' emerges in "The Subject and Power" as a way of addressing, in part, criticism that his middle works emphasize hegemonic power to the exclusion of autarchy (Foucault, 2006). To what extent do epistemic structures define possibilities within disciplines, and do power/knowledge complexes normalize subjects within pernicious regimes of truth?Some readers see in *Discipline and Punish* rather hapless selves, constituted by what Charles Taylor called "monolithic discourses" and invasive disciplinary practices (Taylor, 1986). Attention to Foucault's later writings redirect focus on 'arts' or 'technologies of the self' in which subjects have some agency in their own process of subjectification and self-creation. Instead of adopting a picture of the 'divided Foucault,' or a 'turning point' in his philosophy, he constructs a plausible explanation. Although we might question an author's re-description of his work, a unified position emerges in the 1980s that gives us a better starting point for problematizing the subject's relations to truth and power, located specifically within educational settings (Foucault, 1994c, pp. 214–5; 1994d, p. 459; Gros, 2006, p. 525).[6]

Throughout Foucault's work, he recalls, the goal was not to analyze the phenomenon of power, per se. The "objective, instead, has been to create a history of the different modes by which, in our culture, human beings are made subjects" (Foucault, 1994e, p. 326, cf.p. 327; see 1994f, p. 201; 1994g, p. 452; Gros, 2006, p. 512). This includes the delineation of various dividing practices we carry out, as in normatively sorting the 'sane' from the 'insane', or for my purposes, the 'sound' from the 'unsound' pedagogies and teachers during education reforms and classroom inspections (Stickney, 2007). Foucault clarifies the links as follows, explaining that in spite of the emptiness of such phrases as "getting back to oneself, "freeing the self," "being oneself" or "being authentic" there is no other "first or final point of resistance to political power than in the relationship one has to oneself" (Foucault, 2006, pp. 251–2).

> In other words, what I mean to say is this: if we take the question of power, of political power, situating it in the more general question of govern-mentality understood as a strategic field of power relations in the broadest and not merely political sense of the term, if we understand by governmentality a strategic field of power relations in their mobility, transformability, and reversibility, then I do not think that reflection on this notion of governmentality can avoid passing through, theoretically and practically, the element of a subject defined by the relationship of self to self. Although the theory of political power as an institution usually refers to a juridical conception of the subject of right, it seems to me that the analysis of governmentality – that is to say, of power as a set of reversible relationships – must refer to an ethics of the subject defined by the relationship of the self to self. (Foucault, 2006, p. 252)

Foucault reaffirms this unifying re-description in several 1980s radio interviews (Foucault, 1996, pp. 409, 448, 450–5). Instead of the neo-Kantian, liberal-Enlightenment focus on the universal rights of the 'autonomous,' rational individual, Foucault follows Nietzsche's history of truth to its consummation in the subject's arts of self-creation within various, historically localized games of truth and power relations of governance (Olssen, 2006). It is not just a matter of whether the subject has certain rights or not, as in a matter of law or the study of political institutions (the legal subject), but whether a ground for possibilities exists at certain junctures, and whether actors themselves can see opportunities for "freedom within the rules" (Foucault, 1994h, p. 300; see Tully, 2002).

Considering how designations and dividing practices arise – hence an "historical ontology of the present" – Foucault shows how the search for an authentic, core identity, too, is a historically emergent game or charade (Foucault, 1994i, p. 389, cf. pp. 380, 386–7). He speaks in deference to the notion of people "uncovering their identity" as this game closes the realm of possibilities – the range of possible selves – through a medieval picture of essentialism (e.g., baring 'the soul'; Foucault, 1994j, p. 166). It is hard to avoid these considerations and the authenticity rhetoric surrounding them, however, when inspectors asks teachers to self-evaluate their performance along predetermined criteria, assess and demonstrate their degree of implementation of various reforms (e.g., 'authentic learning and assessment') or compliance with local initiatives and policies, and then set them 'at ease' by assuring teachers that what inspectors really want to see in the classroom visit is their 'actual' teaching style.[7] In Foucault's historical demonstrations of normalization through discourses and disciplinary practices, and in his genealogical presentation of liberty as an invention of the ruling classes instead of something essentially in man's nature (Foucault, 1994i, p. 371), he presents subjects as always being subject to various forms of domination (discursive and non-discursive), and having practices of self-control (*enkratia*) or capacities for freedom on the other. For Foucault, the central 'agonism' between "power relationships" on the one side, and "the recalcitrance of the will" or "the intransigence of freedom" on the other, is "a mutual incitement" or "permanent provocation" from which the subject cannot escape (Foucault, 1994e, p. 342).[8]

A similar tension occurs in teaching when alternating between different kinds of pedagogical relationships: when the classroom teacher or consultant breaks from authoritatively conveying knowledge to the group, not to tutor individuals in those same general truths but to offer guidance (truth about the self) to a chosen student or teacher initiate (Foucault, 2001, pp. 113–4). The latter practices are chronicled by Foucault as Greek forms of 'confession' (self-diagnosis) and 'salvation' (self-testing or being true to oneself), essential to the training of the truth-sayer (*parrhesiastes*) who would later occupy a critical role in public life. Instead of focusing on Western philosophy's obsession with correct reasoning and the truth of statements, an analytic approach to truth, he turns attention to the critical tradition in which truth is an activity in which people train and engage: "the importance for the individual and society of telling the truth, of knowing the truth, of having people who tell the truth, as well as knowing how to recognize them" (Foucault, 2001, p. 170). Foucault asks:

> Who is able to tell the truth? What are the moral, ethical, and spiritual conditions which entitle someone to present himself as, and to be considered as, a truth-teller? ...Should truth-telling be brought into coincidence with the exercise of power, or should these activities be completely independent and kept separate? (Foucault, 2001, p. 169)

Re-conception of power as productive in Foucault's later work allows for a revaluation of education as, potentially, a creative place for truth and self-formation. Advocating a 'polymorphic connection' between people and culture in which subjects are not submitted to information as much as they are exposed to it – where 'the right to knowledge' is not restricted to certain stages in life or certain categories of individuals but is rather a right 'exercised continuously in multiple forms' – Foucault remarks:

> One of the principle functions of teaching was that the formation of the individual be accompanied by the determination of his place in society. Today we ought to conceive it in such a way that it would permit the individual to modify himself according to his own will, which is possible only on the condition that teaching be a "permanently open" possibility. (Foucault, 1996b, p. 306)

Without falling into the traps of authenticity discourse and identity politics, Foucault elicits and qualifies the crucial links connecting the political and ethical aspects of subjectification and truth-telling. Foucault explains: "the kind of analysis I have been trying to advance for some time you can see that power relations, governmentality, the government of the self and others, and the relationship of the self to self constitute a chain" (Foucault, 2006, p. 252). For my topic, this chain includes teacher normalization by means of professional development and inspection: discourses and apparatuses that school systems bring to bear on teachers in pursuing administrative visions of 'performance excellence', system and school 'plans for continuous improvement' and practices intended to enhance 'student success.' When one wants to alter an education system, either as a top-down reformer within a Ministry or School Board, or through immanent critique and 'agonistics of reform' from the bottom up, one has to find something on which one can set to work. Those seeking effectiveness and accountability, as well as those seeking greater professional autonomy have the difficult task of concep-tualizing the overlapping sets of relations – the micro circuitry – that make up a governance structure within something as localized and yet complex as a school system. This micro-political realm is not, necessarily, less complex than the macro, even though the magnitude and stakes may differ (Rose, 1999).

Where do we begin to unravel the whole ensemble of reformatory and disciplinary practices intended to both ensure learning and shape behaviour? Foucault offers a vantage point on this complexity in showing three types of overlapping relationships, joined into various 'blocks': power relations, relationships of communication, and objective capacities. Education serves as an example of the general concept of a capacity-communication-power *nexus*, but exemplifying more particularly 'blocks':

> In which the adjustment of abilities, the resources of communication, and power relations constitutes regulated and concerted systems. Take, for instance, an educational institution: the disposal of its space, the meticulous regulations that govern its internal life, the different activities that are organized there, the diverse persons who live there or meet one another, each with his own function, his well-defined character – all these things constitute a block of capacity-communication-power. Activity to ensure learning and the acquisition of aptitudes or types of behavior works via a whole ensemble of regulated communications (lessons, questions and answers, orders, exhortations, coded signs of obedience, differential marks of the "value" of each person and of the levels of knowledge) and by means of a whole series of power processes (enclosure, surveillance, reward and punishment, the pyramidal hierarchy). (Foucault, 1994e, pp. 338–9; cf. 1994k)

Five points are then considered in the analysis of power relations, to which the reader may draw familiar examples from educational settings:
- systems of differentiation
- types of objectives pursued by those who act upon others
- instrumental modes
- forms of institutionalization
- degrees of rationalization (Foucault, 1994e, p. 344).

Within pedagogical institutions, these domains of control and communication have increasingly come under state purview and thus become "governmentalized" – that is to say, elaborated, rationalized, and centralized in the form of, or under the auspices of, state institutions" (Foucault, 1994e, p. 345; re: 'govermentalization', 1994f, p. 221).

Preceding the description of educational blocks, Foucault emphasizes the plethora of possible combinations: relationships between communication-capacity-power are "neither uniform or constant"; "rather, there are diverse forms, diverse places, diverse circumstances or occasions in which these interrelationships establish themselves" (Foucault, 1994e, pp. 338–9). Although education systems attempt to decant regularities across their jurisdictions, among the many schools and districts it is exceedingly hard to get people to act in concert. Despite the intended rationalization and limitation of options within tightly 'welded', "authoritarian high-modernist" reforms of the educational 'block' (the *omnes et singulatim* or "for one and for each"), within educational reform movements we find, in fact, diverse mutations and localized adaptations within schools and school systems (Scott, 1998; Foucault, 1994l). Instead of picturing this ensemble as a tightly organized block – an interlocking piece of machinery or a disciplinary matrix that stamps out clearly delineated types of persons – we might better imagine the constitution of subjects occurring within an archipelago of diverse modes of implementation and improvisatory response (Stickney, 2005).

The chain also includes teachers' resistance to normalization through relations they carry out with themselves and others. Freedoms can be discovered or negotiated within a seemingly monolithic block, because of its complexity and 'strange multiplicities' (Tully, 1995) – the dispersal of limits that comes with diverse personnel and institutions within an overall education system (at either the local or the provincial level; Foucault, 1994l). In the final section, I apply this chain to the analysis of educational concatenations: overlapping curriculum reforms and regimes of inspection in which school systems cast their teachers, developing a Foucaultian perspective on freedom as 'reversibility' within the teacher subjects' ethical and political relations to power and truth.

QUESTIONS OF TRUTH, CONTINGENCY AND RELATIVISM

A related set of questions come into play when the inspection event is turned outward, shifting perspective from teacher performance onto the mandated curriculum reforms they are supposed to implement. Are some education reforms, indeed, better than others are, or are they all arbitrary 'games of truth'? Does truth telling in the form of contestation presuppose that some people are better able to render a faithful account of events, and does this recognition make 'truth' something outside the game, on which some agents gain better purchase than do others? The subject's comportment to truth, as a central aspect of governmentality, connects with the question of teacher agency within the rules or mandates of an education system. Questions of historical contingency, constructivism and relativism, related to those around authenticity and degrees of agency within matrices of power/knowledge, come together as interrelated aspects of the same inquiry.

In posing these kinds of questions, attention settles on how veridical discourses and dividing practices actually play out and establish boundary conditions in relation to educators – ostensibly governing and normalizing those cast into various pedagogic reforms by what *holds* or *counts* as true-or-false (see Stickney, 2008b). Instead of verification, we get an 'historical survey of the present', or ethical and political inquiry of subjectification within various pedagogic games of truth and their power relations. Foucaultian epistemology does not answer whether a rule is necessarily or even sufficiently right, but asks after 'veridiction' or truth telling: "The way in which the individual establishes his relation to the rule and recognizes himself as obligated to put it into practice" (Foucault, cited by Rabinow, 1994, p. xxxiii; re: 'veridiction', Foucault, 1996c, p. 413).

During Foucault's 'middle period' we find him addressing the question of truth in relation to his concept of *power/knowledge*, by which he did not mean to reduce the one to the other but to show how truth (in terms of the *true-and-false*) is produced within certain power relations. Relational terms point us toward a two-way stance with regard to knowledge: ones in which the subject may actively partake in its production or in its inscription upon him or her self.In this way, we see both the social construction of knowledge(s) and the subjectivization of persons who freely enter into these domains or discourses, or have them imposed upon them. Foucault refers to these productive processes of power as 'regimes' and a general 'politics of truth':

> That is, the types of discourse which it accepts and makes function as true; the mechanism and instances which enable one to distinguish true and false statements, the means by which each is sanctioned; the techniques and procedures accorded value in the acquisition of truth; the status of those who are charged with saying what counts as true. (Foucault, 1994m, p. 131; cf. p. 133)

Locating the subject within regimes of truth and the power relations that sustain them is an apt description for pedagogic knowledge and its dissemination in school systems. From this earlier perspective we can imagine the teacher's relations to the purveyor's of pedagogic wisdom, whether guests speakers at colloquia or curriculum consultants who convey the initiatives and sanctioned practices gleaned from educational texts and superintendents of education. It is harder to see within these top-down regimes of truth teachers' subtler work on their own, professional selves.

Later, in the introduction to *The Use of Pleasure,* Foucault refers to "the games of truth and error through which being is historically constituted as experience; that is, as something that can and must be thought. What are the games of truth by which man proposes to think his own nature...?" (Foucault, 1990, pp. 6–7). He explores four components of this problematic: ethical substance, the aspect of the self one alters; ethical work, the means by which one transforms oneself; *telos,* the aim of the ethical subject given its circumstances; and, mode of subjectification or self-stylization and form-giving – "The way in which the individual establishes his relation to the rule and recognizes himself as obligated to put it into practice" (Foucault, 1990, pp. 26–8; see Rabinow, 1994, p. xxxiii). Although governance entails all four, it is this last component that I am primarily concerned with in addressing teacher comportment to mandates handed down during education reforms: how administrators expect the professional to conduct him or her self in relation to these rules and to willingly participate in transformative practices and or adopt new discourses in order to comply. How might these rules and modes of "professional development" conflict with the professional's own ethical work and aims, given his or her trajectory (*telos*) of self-transformation?In "The Subject and Power," Foucault offers three modes of 'subjectivization': another way of approaching the teacher's relation to official pedagogic knowledge and sanctioned practices, power relations within school systems and teachers' own self-transformative agendas.

- modes of inquiry that try to give themselves the status of sciences, e.g., the objectivizing of the speaking or productive subject:
- the objectivizing of the subject in "dividing practices", where the subject is either divided in himself or divided from others; and,
- the way a human being turns him or herself into a subject (Foucault, 1994e, pp. 326–7).

These appear as an organizing principle in his later work, used as themes for the three-volume collection of Foucault's *Essential Works* (Foucault, 1990, p.4; 1994b, p. 262–3). They comprise what Foucault calls in "What is Enlightenment?" the three axes of a "critical ontology of ourselves": "How are we constituted as subjects of our own knowledge? How are we constituted as subjects who exercise or submit to power relations? How are we constituted as moral subjects of our own actions?" (Foucault, 1994a, p. 318; cf. 1990, p. 4).

Social discourse and practices do not constitute the subject wholly nor does the subject simply create itself in utopian fashion, *ex nihilo* (see Hekman, p. 145). As Foucault uses the term, 'power relations' only occur where there is the two-way possibility of freedoms or mobility, not where rule is absolute under a form of despotism or subjugation (Foucault, 1994h, p. 291). His concern is with cases where freedoms are possible even though "power is always present," as in 'reversible relations' between people of different ages. Such conditions of reversibility are inherent in teaching students but also in the process of initiating teachers into pedagogic reforms and their particular games of truth. The process is corrupt if it infantilises the student or teacher initiate, but the presence of power relations itself is not corrupting or evil. As with amorous relations, where power may also reverse, he adds:

And let us take, as another example, something that has often been rightly criticized – the pedagogical institution. I see nothing wrong in the practice of a person who, knowing more than others in a specific game of truth, tells others what to do, teaches them, and transmits knowledge and techniques to them. The problem in such practices where power – which is not itself a bad thing – must inevitably come into play is knowing how to avoid the kind of domination effects where a kid is subjected to the arbitrary and the unnecessary authority of a teacher, or a student put under the thumb of a professor who abuses his authority. I believe that this problem must be framed in terms of rules of law, rational techniques of government and *ethos*, practices of the self and of freedom. (Foucault, 1994h, p. 298)

Substituting 'teacher' for 'kid', we can imagine Foucault not condemning (outright) professional development that prescribes 'best practices' for others to follow, but rather the use of arbitrary and unnecessary authority in the process – something one finds all too often within infantalizing forms of teacher development and inspection.[9]

Foucault also explained that the "practices through which the subject constitutes itself in an active fashion" are "not invented" by the subject; rather, "They are models that he finds in his culture and are proposed, suggested, imposed upon him by his culture, his society, his social group" (Foucault, 1994h, p. 291). Teachers engage in such practices, conducting work on themselves, when they network on shared courses of study, join book clubs, learn new software, take workshops, attend seminars and or upgrade their qualifications at universities and institutes, etcetera. Under conditions of neoliberalism, however, we are wary that in these practices of the self, too, subjects might be duped into aligning their skills with the needs of the organization in order to minimize personal and institutional risk (Peters and Marshall, 1996).

Lastly, Foucault's references to the 'production of truth' or 'games of truth' were not intended to suggest, either, that there is no such thing as truth, that truth is not serious (just a trivial game) or that there is no such thing as external reality. The "political production of truth" does not reduce truth to power: "...I am absolutely not saying that games of truth are just concealed power relations – that would be a horrible exaggeration" (Foucault, 1994h, p. 296). Connecting the capacity to formulate truths with power does not mean "that what the person says is not true, which is what most people believe. When you tell people that there may be a relationship between truth and power, they say: 'So it isn't truth after all!'"(Foucault, 1994h, p. 298).The sense in which truth is produced in 'games' has more to do with openness to play or modification over time, as some games "are permitted to the exclusion of all others. In a given game of truth, it is always possible to discover something different and to more or less modify this or that rule, and sometimes even the entire game of truth" (Foucault, 1994h, p. 297).

In addressing the problematic of how the 'mad' subject is constituted and ethically transforms it self, Foucault made a crucial, deflationary remark on the matter of social construction. Showing "how truth games are set up and how they are connected with power relations" and institutions "in no way impugns the scientific validity or the therapeutic effectiveness of psychiatry: it does not endorse psychiatry, but neither does it invalidate it" (Foucault, 1994h, p. 292). The discussion continues, revolving around the subject, who – based on playing out these games and following their rules and principles – can arrive at results that are "considered valid or invalid, winning or losing." To say "considered true" raises the penultimate question with which Western culture has a preoccupation – whether 'holding as true' satisfies the "obligation to truth," as Foucault refers to it (Foucault, 1994h, p. 295). To the question "So is truth not a construction," he answers:

That depends. There are games of truth in which truth is a construction and others in which it is not. ...On the basis of what can be said, for example, about this transformation of games of truth, some people conclude that I have said that nothing exists.... (Foucault, 1994h, pp. 296–7)

Foucault is showing here how the care of the self is connected with the concern with truth, and how certain consequences may result from playing various games of truth. Here the genealogist can point to "other reasonable options, by teaching people what they don't know about their own situation, their working conditions, and their exploitation" (Foucault, 1994h, pp. 295–6). In saying this, he makes a connection between truth and power relations without negating 'truth' or adopting relativism and anti-realism.

A second theme, then, related to the formation and governance of subjects, is Foucault's defence against accusations of naïve or self-refuting forms of relativism. In "The Subject and Power," the Collège de France lectures gathered in *The Hermeneutics of the Subject* (1981–02) and in the Berkeley lectures compiled in *Fearless Speech* (1983) – together with the radio interview "The Concern for Self as a Practice of Freedom" (1984) – Foucault repeatedly dissociates himself from an excessively constructivist reading of his work (Foucault, 1994e, p. 330; see Faubion, 1994, pp. xiii, xxxii, xxxvii; Gordon, 1994, p. xvii). Intent not to appear either a determinist or relativist, in these later writings methods of self-transformation meld with both governmentality and the subject's relation to truth.

Foucault's discussion of educational blocks set out in the previous section – "the deployment of technical capacities, the game of communication, and the relation-ship of power" – also addresses this second guiding question. Unlike his earlier work, "Truth and Power" (1976), in "The Subject and Power" he now refers to "objective capacities" within institutions, raising the question of whether truth has any basis outside the games played at various periods of history. He clarifies that by "objective capacities" he means aptitudes – abilities inherent in the body or relayed by external instruments – using the example of students within educational settings.[10] Educational jargon that levels all learners and teachers or that extends 'success' and 'mastery' beyond ranges of normal usage can be appraised, from this perspective, as ignoring (becoming tranquil to) the specificities of individual students and teachers. Taking these topics up as they fold into one another, we see how governance within education reforms (various games of truth) helps us to understand the subject's agency or capacity within such "blocks", avoiding problems of subjugation, over-determinism and relativism.

Ian Hacking crosses this quagmire by engaging the later philosophies of Wittgenstein and Foucault in "a critical ontology of ourselves" (Foucault, 1994a, p. 316; Hacking, 2002, p. 25). Adopting Hacking's approach to historical ontology, we may question the extent to which teacher development and appraisal processes (their prescriptions and evaluation criteria) constitute or make up the teachers ostensibly reformed and judged. Instead of seeing our labels for either student aptitudes ('gifted' or 'learning disabled') or teacher suitability ('exemplary' or 'unsatisfactory') as being 'natural kinds' cleaved by nature or merely social constructions, we can follow Hacking in attending to the interface between what he calls "dynamic realism and historical nominalism" (Hacking, 2002, pp. 26, 48). Our dividing practices in education reforms, such as the delineation of sound versus unsound pedagogies, may be based on both the 'robustness of fit' with external reality and the political production of truth and power relations that sustain the true-and-false (Hacking, 1999). Many of the claims made on behalf of the reformers amount to political rhetoric, like socialist realism, achievable only in the self-congratulatory, *paper theatre* of the reform. Others I am not in a position to challenge or falsify, such as the cognitive and neuro-scientific basis of such discourses as 'brain compatible learning,' but can nevertheless ask how this discourse leads us to constitute teenagers differently and to arrive at different sets of normative practices or possibilities within our schools (Wong, 2009 – this volume).

Applied to teacher agency within education reforms, administrators see resistance to 'innovative practice' as 'retrenchment in outdated paradigms' – a form of parochialism to be overcome by regimes of professional development and inspection (Stickney, 2006). The teacher who contends with new pedagogic methods and designations may, indeed, be held within the grip of folk pedagogies that are no more, perhaps less, valid than those officially proposed.Remaining "true" to one's established "best practices" may be regressive: the result of blind habit, or herd mentality, instead of foresight (Dewey, 1944, pp. 102–03, 107, 145, 340–1). The point here is that Foucaultian genealogy of subjugated, disqualified and popular knowledges – those found struggling with erudite, sanctioned or globalizing forms of knowledge, does not seek to disprove – in positivistic or scientistic fashion – the latter, nor, as he puts it, "vindicate a lyrical right to ignorance and non-knowledge" (Foucault, 1980a, pp. 83–84). Instead of the rightness of forms of knowledge, his problem is rather "what rules of right are implemented by the relations of power in the production of discourses of truth?" (Foucault, 1908a, p. 93). The purpose in doing a critical history of the present is not to offer up better or more genuine solutions than those mandated; that would be playing the same game of the modernist reformers who govern education systems.It is, rather, as Foucault remarks, to "grasp the points where change is possible and desirable, and to determine the precise form this change should take" (Foucault, 1994a, p. 316).

The same tension between the given and the constructed is found in *problematizations*. A "problematization," Foucault writes, "does not mean the representation of a pre-existent object nor the creation through discourse of an object that did not exist. It is the ensemble of discursive and non-discursive practices that make something enter into the play of the true and false and constitute it as an object of thought (whether in the forms of moral reflection, scientific knowledge, political analysis, etc.)" (Foucault, 1994n, p. 670, cited by Rabinow and Rose, 2003, p. xviii). By a "problematization" of truth he meant "how and why certain things (behaviour, phenomena, processes) became a *problem*" (Foucault, 2001, 170). As examples, he notes how at given historical moments certain behaviours become characterized as 'mad' or 'criminal', whereas at others they are neglected. He then refutes the accusation that this historical ontology results in a form of "historical idealism":

For when I say that I am studying the 'problematization' of madness, crime, or sexuality, it is not a way of denying the reality of such phenomena. On the contrary, I have tried to show that it was precisely some real existent in the world which was the target of social regulation at a given moment. The question I raise is this one: How and why were very different things in the world gathered together, characterized, analyzed, and treated as, for example, 'mental illness'? ...And even if I won't say that what is characterized as 'schizophrenia' corresponds to something real in the world, this has nothing to do with idealism. For I think there is a relation between a thing which is problematized and the process of problematization. The problematization is an 'answer' to a concrete situation which is real. (Foucault, 2001, pp. 171–72)

They are creations, "but a creation in the sense that, given a certain situation, you cannot infer that this kind of problematization will follow. Given a certain problematization, you can only understand why this kind of answer appears to reply to some concrete and specific aspect of the world. There is a relation of thought and reality in the process of problematization" (Foucault, 2001, pp. 172–3).

The term 'politics of truth', then, is open to misinterpretation, as it may conjure up images of either truth by referenda, consensual agreement or plebiscite. In this section, I have tried to show that we must read the political aspect in terms of what Foucault says about games of truth, power relations and governance. He elaborates on these connections using the concept of *eventualization*, to which I next turn our attention.

To put the matter clearly: my problem is to see how men govern (themselves and others) by the production of truth (I repeat once again that by production of truth I mean not the production of true utterances but the establishment of domains in which the practice of true and false can be made at once ordered and pertinent.

Eventualizing singular ensembles of practices, so as to make them graspable as different regimes of 'jurisdiction' and 'verification': that, to put it in exceedingly barbarous terms, is what I would like to do. ...I would like, in short, to resituate the production of true and false at the heart of historical analysis and political critique. (Foucault, 2003, p. 252)

EVENTUALIZATION

The depictions Foucault gives us through genealogy show what numerous and perhaps inconsistent archives reveal as various possibilities for thought and action at a certain time, or what problems could then be articulated and what 'positivities' given to discourses on insanity and incarceration (Foucault, 2003, p. 248). By comparison, a survey of curriculum reforms and regimes of professional development and inspection would also open our gaze unto what educators currently deem possible to think or do, not in order to say that they are 'not true' after all, but to show the limits cast through the political production of truth (see Tyack and Cuban, 1995). The purpose of Foucault's historical vignettes, as with an assay of contemporary education initiatives in a locale, is to capture the dispersal of possibilities – what he calls 'eventualization':

> It means making visible a *singularity* at places where there is a temptation to invoke a historical constant, an immediate anthropological trait, or an obviousness that imposes itself uniformly on all. To show that things "weren't all as necessary as that"; it wasn't a matter of course that mad people came to be regarded as mentally ill; it wasn't self-evident that the only thing to be done with a criminal was to lock him up…. (Foucault, 2003, p. 249)

Foucault describes the "breach of self evidence" as the first theoretico-political function of 'eventualization'; the second "means the rediscovering of connections, encounters, supports, blockages, plays of force, strategies, and so on, that at a given moment establish what subsequently counts as being self-evident, universal, and necessary. In this sense one is indeed effecting a sort of multiplication or pluralization of causes" (Foucault, 2003, p. 249). What this 'causal multiplication' means is analyzing the multiple processes that constitute an event, such as finding the relation between the penal institution and penalization as a practice, to the "formation of closed pedagogical spaces functioning through rewards, punishments, and so on" (Foucault, 2003, p. 249). *Eventualization* results in a "polymorphism" of elements, relations and domains of reference. Moving away from historical explanations that search for simplicity and singular causes, he sees a need to 'traverse the sphere' of what is given as 'objectivities' and to sort the "tangle" of a 'plethora of intelligibilities' instead of universal necessities (Foucault, 2003, juxtaposing p. 258 with p. 250).

Importantly in terms of subject agency, Foucault shows the surroundings of singular events as a multiplicity of causes or alternate possibilities: for instance, in connecting the pedagogical practices of a culture to those of its judicial, penal and medical institutions, making what seemed explicable now multidimensional or (metaphorically) a "polyhedron of intelligibility." For instance, Foucault draws the connection between the justice system and practices of incarceration with pedagogical institutions and practices of discipline in schools (Foucault, 1994o, pp. 56–57, 72, 75–6, 78–80, 83–4). As in hospitals and prisons, in schools we take control of the temporal element in student's lives, resulting in a sequestering of the subject into a highly controlled environment. Within such institutions, there is a kind of 'epistemological power' in which knowledge is extracted from the subjugated individuals operating there. Administrators study the subject's own micro-adaptations to controls in order to either better conduct work (an economy of labour) or make adaptations to institutional life itself. Those running the institution turn around the 'successful' subjects' coping behaviour as a form of second order knowledge: extracting, re-transcribing and accumulating new knowledge for controlling others. It is precisely this kind of feedback loop one finds operating within the interview and inspection processes used to hold teachers accountable, in which they are to reveal (self-identify) both their coping strategies and degrees of fit with sanctioned education reforms.

In like fashion, we can look back over the last twenty years of education reform and critique the global changes occurring with the spread of the accountability movement. Michael Power points out that although accountability and account giving are ordinary enough – part of normal experience and practice – there has been an "audit explosion" in the United Kingdom and abroad during the 1980s and 1990s (Rose, 1999, pp. 153–5).The transference of accounting practices to all sectors of our lives transforms our administrative practices into costly "rituals of verification" and our citizens into an increasingly distrustful *Audit Society* (Power, 1997, pp. 1–3). We incur a hefty social cost, Power argues, when we move from positions of trust (e.g., acting in good conscience) to the proliferation of formal auditing practices. Performances of teachers or university academics become measurable, auditable outputs, as elements that have worth in relation to the audit process itself. In other words, the auditing practice transforms the original purpose of the performative activity or technique audited. "The power of auditing is therefore to construct concepts of performance in its own image" (Power, 1997, p. 119; see also pp. 120–21).

A picture of 'accountability' holds us captive – calling for genealogical investigation of its foundations as a game of truth (paraphrasing Wittgenstein, 1968, §115). Describing how school systems try to make educators more accountable and measurable through reforms, or deliver quality assurance to education consumers, several authors refer to the emergence of technocratic rationalities: what Michael Peters calls "actuarial reasoning" and the "new prudentialism" (Peters, 2005). Educators and academic educationists must exercise forms of self-discipline (*askesis*) to over-come its enthralling hold; in order to see other pictures as possibilities – those offered up through historical example or through comparison with alternative images (Owen, 2003). Instead of debunking myths through ideology critique, the Foucaultian question is rather: To what extent can school systems actually govern and enforce the mandated practices and knowledge they promote in education reforms, and what "spaces of possibility" do they open or close to educators? These questions are ethical, political and epistemological, in that they ask after the freedoms we come to have or lose, in relation to what we now hold or count *as* true-or-false.

PASTORAL SUPERVISION, DISSIMULATION AND CONTESTATION

On the surface, teacher inspection offers contemporary examples of what Foucault described as panopticism and pastoral supervision (Hunter, 1993). Good accounts have been given of panoptic approaches to teacher evaluation, such as the '360 degree program' of 'multiple-data feedback' used in Taiwan and elsewhere (Blaidon, 2006; Ball, 1990). More importantly, combined techniques of pastoral supervision and panoptic control of subjects within educational institutions help us frame the interrelated topics of the subject's relation to truth, power and freedom.

Foucault described "pastoral power" as a legacy of the Church – the shepherd and the flock relationship – that has now spread and multiplied outside ecclesiastical institutions. It operates insidiously at the level of both supervision and conscience (the epitome of which is the confessional): "...this form of power cannot be exercised without knowing the inside of people's minds, without exploring their souls, without making them reveal their innermost secrets. It implies a knowledge of the conscience and an ability to direct it" (Foucault, 1994e, p. 333). Vestiges of pastoral power play out in various practices in education: for instance, through journaling practices in courses where students reveal their "inner" thoughts to teachers or professors – after carefully constructing them, of course, to fit anticipated expectations from the examiner (e.g., presenting facades to gain favourable recognition; see Gore, 1993, pp. 150–51). Pastoral supervision is also manifest in regimes of teacher inspection: "supervision for growth" or "annual growth" plans in which teachers confess their weaknesses to administrators and then establish benchmarks for their own professional development. On the surface, both practices – which encourage reflective practice – can be self-empowering and transformative, or self-indicting and servile (surrendering to expectations).

Another way of looking at it, however, is that the subjects under purview are merely acting out 'public transcripts' (Scott, 1990). The public scripts may be in sharp contrast to the hidden transcripts they freely perform in their classrooms or staff rooms; like slaves genuflecting to their masters, they are prudently enacting these public transcripts (feigning respect) out of reasonable fear of reprisal by some hegemonic class or authority figures.Schools are excellent hiding places. Power relations and techniques of pastoral supervision do not obviate the exercise of considerable freedom and frequent reversals of power within pedagogic institutions; cameras don't panoptically reach into the classroom itself and dissimulation is relatively easy in brief inspections, usually a one-off observation and pre and post interview. A formal inspection once every three to five years, as in Ontario's *Teacher Performance Appraisal* system, does not subjugate or outright constitute the teacher-self within the three axes: pedagogic knowledge, power relations, and technologies of the self. Within this game of truth – its discourses and non-discursive apparatuses – there are myriad possibilities, polyhedrons of intelligibility or alternate, criss-crossing paths. In other words, the educational block is also an opening for teacher agency in negotiating or creating possible freedoms instead of accepting what is presented as 'necessities', 'uniformities' and 'inevitabilities': the meeting place of diffuse alternatives Foucault referred to as "Eventualizing singular ensembles of practices" (Foucault, 2003, p. 252).

Under conditions of reversibility within regimes of teacher inspection, the teacher may not only dissimulate compliance with mandated reforms and sanctioned pedagogic techniques, but also find ways of openly contesting these politically produced 'truths.' Educators may exercise degrees of agency in playing the role of what Foucault calls the "specific intellectual."The specific intellectual is, first, in a position to offer immanent critique of a field or institution within which she works. Foucault explained that his own work on psychiatry, for instance, stemmed from his interest and familiarity with the field. That is what gave it its political meaning and practical impact – not an aseptic quality. He was "aware of the combats, the lines of force, tensions and points of collision which existed there"; consequently, "...The problem and the stake there was the possibility of a discourse which would be both true and strategically effective, the possibility of a historical truth which could have a political effect" (Foucault, 1980b, p. 64). The suggestion here is that the local actor may gain critical purchase on predominant regimes of truth, not only showing weaknesses in what are commonly held to be vouchsafed truths but helping to transform social games of truth through truth-saying (*parrhesia*).

In this kind of battle for or around truth, Foucault means not "the ensemble of truths to be discovered and accepted" but, rather, "the ensemble of rules according to which the true and false are separated and specific effects of power attached to the true" (Foucault, 1994m, pp. 131–2). The latter qualifications are all-important, as he is not just conducting ideology critique in order to root out "false consciousness," but rather to show "the status of truth and the economic and political role it plays" (Foucault, 1994m, p. 132; re: Gramsci, see Olssen, 2006, pp. 95–118). The presumption of "correct consciousness" is not there: rather than declare a universal truth, he is in a position to call into question how subjects normally stand in relation to accepted truths.

> The work of an intellectual is not to form the political will of others; it is, through the analyses he does in his own domains, to bring assumptions and things taken for granted again into question, to shake habits, ways of acting and thinking, to dispel the familiarity of the accepted, to take the measure of rules and institutions and, starting from that re-problematization (where he plays his specific role as intellectual) to take part in the formulation of a political will (where he has his role as citizen). (Foucault, 1996d, pp. 462–3)

Subjects to the political production and inscription of the true-and-false within power relations can enter into contestation. A 'specific intellectual' may bring immanent critique to bear on regimes of truth, offering revelations as to how seemingly certain, necessary or universal discourses and practices could be seen as otherwise: as uncertain, local and arbitrary. In these later writings, however, Foucault is linking discipline (*askesis*), in which the subject has an obligation to speak the truth about himself, to speaking truths to those in power. There is a connection which develops relatively late in the history of the West, he argues, between the subject's obligation to tell the truth about himself and his relation to the truth in general, in which it is instrumental for the subject to confess truthfully in order to make himself a worthy subject of true discourses (Foucault, 2006, pp. 364–65).

CONCLUSION: CASTING TEACHERS WITHIN REFORMS

In keeping with my opening theme, each teacher in a particular school district takes a stance in relation to what are presented as self evident pedagogic truths, governing him or her self in relation to this 'knowledge' and its power base. The machinery of the local education system – the block of communication-capacity-power – aligns in such a way that it makes it prudent for teachers and administrators to comply, even if disingenuously, with these various initiatives and to signal allegiance (become less conspicuously deviant) by adopting or prominently displaying their slogans.

School and board plans, like the Ministry of Education's package of reforms and teacher inspection policies, form a matrix of interlocking initiatives. As I indicated earlier, the modernist machinery of reform does not always align as intended, but forms instead an archipelago of locally diverse, improvisatory (site-based) responses to mandated reforms. What our school does is somewhat different from another, and how I interpret the plan for my department or my department members adopt from me varies significantly. In other words, there are ranges of freedom in our relations to these many overlapping initiatives and their sets of rules. I want to *problematize* the effect of educators being *multiply cast* in these fragmentary discourses and initiatives, often in ways that may interfere or discord with their prior membership or *thrownness* in larger language-communities and societal *games of truth* (see Heidegger, 1996, I.V-VI). Being governed within an education system is to be thrust or compelled into several, overlapping sets of specific discursivities (technical languages), disciplinary practices, apparatuses and institutions that constitute, in part, various kinds of professional selves. The multiple castings of the reforms do not constitute the professional self, outright; rather, discourses of education reform and apparatuses of professional development and inspection tend to fragment teacher selves into a polyhedron of possibilities, opening spaces of possibility depending upon the specific individual's public and private responses to these veridical discourses and their games of truth (Rose, 1998).

With this picture of education reform, its concatenation of interlocking components fused into a block or matrix, I have tried to show generally how governance links up with questions of subject formation and the subject's relations to truth and power.I am seeking to articulate how, in James Tully's formulation, "subjects raise a problem about a rule of the practice in the languages of communication and legitimation or challenge a relation of governance on the ground, enter into the available procedures of negotiation, deliberation, problem solving, and reform with the aim of modifying practice" (Tully, 2002, p. 540). The purpose of doing a historical ontology of present teacher selves is not just to describe the pervasive limit-conditions that normalize contemporary teachers through professional development and inspection; rather, as a specific intellectual, it is to contest actively those boundaries by entering into the negotiation of freedoms within actual governance systems, problematizing games of truth within specific blocks of education.

When school districts multiply cast teachers within top-down, overlapping initiatives, teachers not only inscribe upon themselves these politically driven sets of discursive formations and non-discursive practices; subjects of reforms also judge the reasonableness of the reforms. Educators react to these as sensible or senseless in relation to their societal games of truth, giving them a critical basis for truth-telling and action. The locus of freedom and truth in a change initiative is relational in that new rules, entities or words stand as adequate, or fall, in accordance with the political production of truth.Foucault helps us to think about the political process of opening our rules and practices to revision by assaying the rough ground of possibilities within veridical discourses – various games of truth orchestrated in education reforms. Critically speaking, I want to rethink education systems as sites or 'blocks' of contingent improvisation (see Hunter, 1994): realms of governance and the political production of truth within which educators can potentially inaugurate freedoms (Zerilli, 1995), without imagining these 'spaces' in our rules as something created entirely anew.

NOTES

[1] The term 'veridical discourses' is credited to Georges Canguilhem, and deployed by Quentin Skinner and James Tully (Rose, 1999, pp. 29–30).

[2] See Gros (2006, p. 526 & 548, nt.30) on this intersection: "In the first, unpublished version of the 1981 lecture, Foucault defined 'governmentality' as precisely the 'surface of contact on which the way of conducting individuals and the way they conduct themselves are intertwined'."

[3] See Davidson (2006, p. xxviii).

[4] The larger project continues from my dissertation (Stickney, 2005).

[5] Foucault kept dossiers on these and other thematic studies (government of self and others, "age, pedagogy, medicine," etc.), which he was only able to gloss over in his summary of the course. See Gros (2006, p. 516).

[6] Foucault (1994d) masks himself, for instance, under the pseudonym Maurice Florence.

[7] These anecdotes are based on my own experiences of undergoing teacher supervision.

[8] In Heideggerian terms, our normal, daily existence is one of being inauthentic, or falling prey to the tranquilizing language of the public they-self. Authenticity is not escape but momentary awareness of this permanent, 'factical' condition of our being-here (Heidegger, 1996, pp. 35–8, 167, 255, 320).

[9] For example, I was once given a sticker of a pony for successfully completing a pencil and paper bar graph showing my grade distribution, something I can do on the computer with a keystroke. I continue to fight for the adult right to go out to lunch, at restaurants instead of having "laid-on lunches," during professional Development days in my district.

[10] Foucault uses the terms 'objective finality' and 'objective capacity' in this segment of the essay (1994e, p. 339). See Wong (2007).

REFERENCES

Besley, T. (2007). Foucault, truth telling and technologies of the self in schools. In M. A. Peters & T. Besley (Eds.), *Why Foucault? New directions for educational research* (pp. 55–70). New York: Peter Lang.

Baildon, M. (2006). *Troubling data: A Foucaldian perspective of 'a multiple data source approach' to professional learning and evaluation.* Paper presented at the American Educational Research Association Annual Conference, San Francisco.

Ball, S. J. (Ed.). (1990). *Foucault and education.* London: Routledge and Kegan Paul.

Davidson, A. (2006). Introduction. In F. Gros (Ed.) & G. Burchell (Trans.), *The hermeneutics of the subject.* New York: Picador.

Dewey, J. (1944). *Democracy and education.* New York: The Free Press.

Faubion, J. (1994). Introduction. In J. Faubion (Ed.), *Essential works* (Vol. 2). New York: The New Press.

Foucault, M. (1980a). Two lectures. In C. Gordon (Ed.), *Power/knowledge.* New York: Pantheon.

Foucault, M. (1980b). Questions on geography. In C. Gordon (Ed.), *Power/Knowledge.* New York: Pantheon.

Foucault, M. (1990). *The uses of pleasure. History of sexuality* (Vol. 2, Robert Hurley Trans.). New York: Random House.

Foucault, M. (1994a). What is enlightenment? In P. Rabinow (Ed.), *Essential works* (Vol. 1). New York: The New Press.

Foucault, M. (1994b). On the genealogy of ethics. In P. Rabinow (Ed.), *Essential works* (Vol. 1). New York: The New Press.

Foucault, M. (1994c). What is an author. In J. Faubion (Ed.), *Essential works* (Vol. 2). New York: The New Press.

Foucault, M. (1994d). Foucault. In J. Faubion (Ed.), *Essential works* (Vol. 2). New York: The New Press.

Foucault, M. (1994e). The subject and power. In J. Faubion (Ed.), *Essential works* (Vol. 3). New York: The New Press.

Foucault, M. (1994f). Govermentality. In J. Faubion (Ed.), *Essential works* (Vol. 3). New York: The New Press.

Foucault, M. (1994g). Structuralism and post-structuralism. In J. Faubion (Ed.), *Essential works* (Vol. 2). New York: The New Press.

Foucault, M. (1994h). The ethics of the concern for self as a practice of freedom. In P. Rabinow (Ed.), *Essential works* (Vol. 1). New York: The New Press.

Foucault, M. (1994i). Nietzsche, genealogy, history. In J. Faubion (Ed.), *Essential works* (Vol. 2). New York: The New Press.

Foucault, M. (1994j). Sex, power, and the politics of identity. In P. Rabinow (Ed.), *Essential works* (Vol. 1). New York: The New Press.

Foucault, M. (1994k). Subjectivity and truth. In P. Rabinow (Ed.), *Essential works* (Vol. 1). New York: The New Press.

Foucault, M. (1994l). *'Omnes et singulatim'*: Toward a critique of political reason. In J. Faubion (Ed.), *Essential Works* (Vol. 3). New York: The New Press.

Foucault, M. (1994m). Truth and power. In J. Faubion (Ed.), *Essential works* (Vol. 3). New York: The New Press.

Foucault, M. (1994n). *Dits et e'crits* (Vol. 4). Paris: Gallimard.

Foucault, M. (1994o). Truth and juridical forms. In J. Faubion (Ed.), *Essential works* (Vol. 3). New York: The New Press.

Foucault, M. (1996a). The return of morality. In S. Lotringer (Ed.), L. Hochroth, & J. Johnston (Trans.), *Foucault Live. Collected interviews, 1961–1984*. New York: Semiotext(e).

Foucault, M. (1996b). The masked philosopher. In S. Lotringer (Ed.), L. Hochroth, & J. Johnston (Trans.), *Foucault Live. Collected interviews, 1961–1984*. New York: Semiotext(e).

Foucault, M. (1996c). What our present is. In S. Lotringer (Ed.), L. Hochroth, & J. Johnston (Trans.), *Foucault Live. Collected Interviews, 1961–1984*. New York: Semiotext(e).

Foucault, M. (1996d). The concern for truth. In S. Lotringer (Ed.), L. Hochroth, & J. Johnston (Trans.), *Foucault Live. Collected Interviews, 1961–1984*. New York: Semiotext(e).

Foucault, M. (2001). *Fearless speech* (J. Pearson Ed.). Los Angeles: Semiotext(e).

Foucault, M. (2003). The question of method. In P. Rabinow & N. Rose (Eds.), *The essential writings*. New York and London: The New Press.

Foucault, M. (2006). *The hermeneutics of the subject* (F. Gros, Ed. & G. Burchell, Trans.). New York: Picador.

Gordon, C. (1994). Introduction. In J. Faubion (Ed.), *Essential works* (Vol. 3). New York: The New Press.

Gore, J. (1993). *The struggles for pedagogies: Critical and feminist siscourse as regimes of truth*. New York and London: Routledge.

Gros, F. (2006). Course context. In F. Gros (Ed.) & G. Burchell (Trans.), *The hermeneutics of the subject*. New York: Picador.

Hacking, I. (1999). *Social construction of what?* Cambridge, MA and London: Harvard University Press.

Hacking, I. (2002). *Historical ontology*. Cambridge, MA: Harvard University Press.

Hekman, S. J. (1999). *The future of difference: Truth and method in Feminist theory*. Cambridge, UK: Polity Press.

Heidegger, M. (1996). *Being and time* (J. Stambaugh, Trans.). Albany, NY: State University of New York Press.

Hunter, I. (1993). The pastoral bureaucracy: Towards a less principled understanding of state schooling. In D. Tyler & D. Meredith (Eds.), *Child and citizen: Genealogies of schooling and subjectivity*. Brisbane: Institute for Cultural Policy Studies, Griffith University.

Hunter, I. (1994). *Rethinking the school. Subjectivity, bureaucracy, criticism*. Sydney and St. Leonards, Australia: Allen and Unwin.

Larsen, M. A. (2005). A critical analysis of teacher evaluation policy trends. *Australian Journal of Education, 49*(3), 292–305.

Olssen, M. (2006). *Michel Foucault: Materialism and education* (Updated ed.). Boulder, CO: Paradigm.

Owen, D. (2003). Genealogy as perspicuous representation. In C. Heyes (Ed.), *The grammar of politics. Wittgenstein and political philosophy*. Ithica and London: Cornell University Press.

Peters, M. A. (2005). The new prudentialism in education: Actuarial rationality and the entrepreneurial self. *Educational Theory, 55*(2), 124–137.

Peters, M. A., & J. D. Marshall (1996). *Individualism and community: Education and social policy in the postmodern condition*. London and Washington: Falmer.

Power, M. (1997). *The audit society. Rituals of verification*. Oxford, UK: Oxford University Press.

Rabinow, P. (1994). Introduction. In P. Rabinow (Ed.), *Essential works* (Vol. 1). New York: The New Press.

Rabinow, P., & Rose, N. (Eds.). (2003). Introduction. In *The essential Foucault*. New York and London: The New Press.

Rose, N. (1998). *Inventing ourselves. Psychology, power, and personhood*. Cambridge, UK: Cambridge University Press.

Rose, N. (1999). *Powers of freedom. Reframing political thought*. Cambridge, UK: Cambridge University Press.

Scott, J. C. (1990). *Domination and the arts of resistance: Hidden transcripts*. New Haven, CT: Yale University Press.

Scott, J. C. (1998). *Seeing like a state: How certain schemes to improve the human condition have failed*. New Haven, CT: Yale University Press.

Stickney, J. (2005). *Judging teachers: A philosophical investigation of Teacher Performance Appraisal*. Dissertation: University of Toronto.

Stickney, J. (2006). Deconstructing discourses on 'New *Paradigms* of teaching': A foucaultian and Wittgensteinian perspective. *Educational Philosophy and Theory, 38*(3), 327–372.

Stickney, J. (2007). *Crazy and fuzzy things in the name of teaching*. Paper presented at University of Toronto, *Agency After Foucault* conference (April). (Forthcoming publication.)

Stickney, J. (2008a). *The paradox of freedom through learning behind truth-telling and self-stylization*. Unpublished paper submitted to the Philosophy of Education Society.

Stickney, J. (2008b). Wittgenstein's 'relativity': Training in language-games and agreement in forms of life. *Educational Philosophy and Theory, 40*(5).

Taylor, C. (1986). Foucault on freedom and truth. In D. C. Hoy (Ed.), *Foucault: A critical reader* (pp. 69–102). Oxford, UK: Basil-Blackwell.

Tully, J. (1995). *Strange multiplicity. Constitutionalism in an age of diversity*. Cambridge, UK: Cambridge University Press.

Tully, J. (1999). To think and act differently. Foucault's four reciprocal objections to Habermas's theory. In S. Ashendon & D. Owen (Eds.), *Foucault contra Habermas: Continuing the Critical Dialogue*. London: Sage.

Stickney, J. (2002, August). Political philosophy as a critical activity. *Political Theory, 30*(4), 533–555.

Tyack, D., & Cuban, L. (1995). *Tinkering toward Utopia. A century of public school reform*. Cambridge, MA and London: Harvard University Press.

Wittgenstein, L. (1968). *Philosophical investigations* (3d ed., G.E.M. Anscombe, Trans.). Oxford, UK: Basil Blackwell.

Wong, J. (2007). Paradox of capacity and power: Critical ontology and the developmental model of childhood. In M. A. Peters & T. Besley (Eds.), *Why Foucault? New directions for educational research* (pp. 71–90). New York: Peter Lang.

Wong, J. (2009). Growing dendrites: Brain-based learning, governmentality and ways of being a person. In this text, M. A. Peters (Ed.).

Zerilli, L. M. G. (2005). *Feminism and the Abyss of freedom*. Chicago and London: University of Chicago Press.

Jeffrey Stickney
Ontario Institute for Studies in Education
University of Toronto
Canada

DAVID LEE CARLSON

15. PRODUCING ENTREPRENEURIAL SUBJECTS: NEOLIBERAL RATIONALITIES AND PORTFOLIO ASSESSMENT

INTRODUCTION

My aim in this chapter is to shed some light on the subtle forms of rationalities of rule in a large-scale portfolio assessment system in the United States. After years of public debate, corporate-sponsored community forums on education, and the state supreme court declaring the public schools unconstitutional, the state of Kentucky institutionalized portfolio assessment throughout K-12 education as a form of high-stakes, large-scale testing in 1989. Doing so challenged school reform movements throughout the United States; deviating from the standard multiple-choice test commonly used to evaluate vast numbers of students to the more laborious, time-consuming, paper-heavy portfolio represented a significant shift in what constitutes a "student," how that student demonstrates what s/he knows, and how students are governed. What's most unique about the school reform that took place is that it selected portfolio assessment as a testing instrument to demonstrate the state's obligation to provide a fair and equitable public school system.

The portfolio represented a historical rupture, leaping onto the educational arena with humanistic intensions to liberate students from the limitations of the multiple-choice test and the one-time, timed essay examination, and provide a new grid of intelligibility from which to demarcate the lines of the sayable and knowable. Using a Foucauldian lens of governmentality, this chapter completes an analytic of government, one that examines the rationalities of rule, or the multiple and intersecting ways to institutionalize assessment practices in this context, and examines the heterogeneous components that permitted the portfolio as a viable assessment practice in a large-scale accountability system. The chapter looks as the portfolio as an analytic of power and, thus, at its effects on governing populations within the state, specifically with regards to prudentialism, risk, and social security and insurance. It assumes that the implementation of the portfolio is a strategic move and emerged to meet an "urgent need" to produce a certain neoliberalsubject that is supposed to practice their freedoms in specific ways.

Portfolio assessment operates as a technology of government, as a form of governmentality, laced with specific rationalities of rule, as the "conduct of conduct" (Foucault in Dreyfus & Rabinow, 1983, pp. 220–221); one that individualizes and totalizes subjects. It posits that assessment practices are not simply pedagogical instruments used to diagnose or reveal a student's writing abilities, for example, but are also political technologies implemented to produce subjects. This notion

M.A. Peters et al. (eds.), Govermentality Studies in Education, 257–269.

challenges the view that school reform occurs in the halls of the state-legislature or the federal branches of government, but appears in the everyday practices of schooling. Even though portfolio assessment is a relatively recent form of evaluating students, the very fact that it was selected among other forms of assessment at this time reflects the intricate relationship between prevailing political ideology of the late1980s and the rationalities of rule in schools. Furthermore, the school reform in Kentucky was a complete redesign of the educational system in the state; however, this chapter focuses on the elements that relate to teaching and learning in class-rooms, specifically pieces that effect the production of the twelfth-grade writing portfolio, which functions as a gate-keeper for secondary students. It is in these places that we see how power functions in the capillary, where government governs at a distance, at the everyday spaces that effect individual and wholesale bodies materially. Thus, while it may appear that the portfolio provides students with a greater opportunity to express themselves freely, or to compose essay on topics that are personally relevant, or "authentic," the effects of portfolio assessment may elide any humanistic intensions, or the rhetoric of care and aid, we may have for using them in schools.

GOVERNMENTALITY

Foucault argues that a shift occurs in between the sixteenth and eighteenth centuries in the relationship between the role of the state and its obligations to the citizenry. Due to the various failures of sovereign power (Foucault, 1975 (DP and Governmentality essay), population explosion, and the rise of a mercantile class, sovereign power, represented by the monarch, could no longer secure the territory and could no longer know who or what it was governing. As Foucault suggests, it was actually due to a failure of the sovereign to perform its most basic and sacred duties that led to the dawning of new manner of governing. Even though an "avalanche of numbers" (Hacking in Burchell et al., 1991) emerged as a way to know the life styles of both individuals and populations at this time, an anxiety about the welfare, aspirations and health of individuals within the populations still occurred. The various strategies and techniques used to "govern at a distance" the "conduct of conduct" of individuals and populations along with the caution to not "govern too much" is what Foucault calls governmentality (Foucault in Burchell et al., 1991). Embedded within the various assemblages of techniques are 'rationalities of rule' or ways of thinking or rationalizing how and why governing is occurring this or that way. In many ways, to speak about schooling in almost any way without making reference to governing becomes a bit of a challenge; and becomes even more so when we include the 'life' of both populations of students and the individual student. Describing or articulating the various ways that students are encouraged to behave, think and feel without utilizing words about populations becomes very difficult. Thus, even though portfolio assessment is an important tool to evaluate a student's abilities, it represents a grid of intelligibility for how students should govern themselves and practice their freedom. More specifically, portfolio assessment in Kentucky induces students to perform their freedoms as neoliberal subjects.

The development of neoliberal governments, specifically in the United States, Great Britain, and China represented a shift in the role that the state plays in relations to individual subjects, in the prominence it is willing to play to secure the welfare of its citizens, and its ability to influence individual freedom (Harvey, 2005). Perhaps the ideology was most clearly articulated by Margaret Thatcher's claim that "...there is no such thing as society", only individuals and families. While her main point she asserts in a later statement was to dispel people of the myth that the role of government is to help individuals when they have a problem, or when they are "casting their problems on society" (Dean, 1999, p. 151), her summation of the government's role typifies the neoliberal turn in the 1980s. While there are and have been various forms of liberalism, they all agree that government should appear less in the lives of individuals, and should encourage individual perseverance rather than state welfare.

A major development or offshoot of liberal rationalities of rule is the development, through various research techniques and strategies, of experts who were able to create 'complex devices of rule' that shaped the individual in a social form. They were able to assume the role of governing institutions that sought to shape individual behaviors through environment and market forces. This does not mean that the ordoliberal dream of state manipulation became realized through these various experts, where the tentacles of central state extended themselves throughout the populous. Instead, what happened was a refiguring of the role of the state. Experts began to answer the problem of how to govern without governing too much, and individuals in the state began to be governed "through society" and through a "social norm," where their experiences were constituted in a "social form" (Rose in Barry et al., 1996, p. 40). They were also able, through parceling out aberrant behavior, to determine abnormalities and propose solutions to those abnormalities. In short, experts begin to develop what Foucault calls, regimes of truth about whole populations and codify and disseminate information about normal experiences. They serve as the governing agents in the society, supplying governing institutions with valuable information about individual cases and whole populations, each of which can now be governed "at arm's length" (Rose in Barry et al. 1996, p. 40). Educationalists are one iteration of these experts, and the portfolio becomes a assessment instrument to govern at a distance, through social norms, and to sift-out deviant thoughts and behaviors.

The desire for stability and security, also known as social security, social insurance, and economic security, drive both the rationality and technologies (self and domination) of governance (Burchell et al., 1991; Dean, 1999). The human sciences, specifically psychology and education, support this dynamic in that they provide knowledge that directs the subjectivities of the individual and provide information about the population that the government sets out to govern (Cruikshank in Barry et al., 1996). On this note, then, Castell (1997) argues that due to the emergence of risk as a social phenomenon, the subject disappears and an assemblage of factors that calculates both individual and collective levels of risk. The portfolio, while employing the rhetoric of individualizing instruction, allowing students to write about their personal experiences, to show what they know, eventually becomes totalized according to levels of potential risk. Students who compose novice or apprentice portfolio exhibit an inability to present themselves in such a normalize, rubricized manner that they deemed at risk of living independently and being owners of themselves. They lack, in short, the ability to be entrepreneurial subjects, ones that can manage themselves to be low-risk to themselves, others, and the state. Risk is determined based on their (student) ability to dependent upon state agencies, or ones that could potentially be a threat to the stability of the state.

RISK AND INSURANCE

Due to its emphasis on the limited role of government in the lives of individual people, and on its assertion that laws structure the relationships between people in society, neoliberal rationality of rule coincides with concerns for risk, the need for insurance to secure the state. Risk is a fairly recent phenomenon. Beck (1992) argues that social class and inequalities of wealth are no longer the most important features to understand society; instead our relationships to various environmental and health risks determine how we act. Giddens (1991) links risk to issues of security, positing that while risk provides individuals with more freedoms, it has become embedded within social institutions. Hence, no longer does the state provide the necessary welfare to support individuals through such social programs as public education, housing development, and Medicare/Medicaid; instead, privatization and deregulation make the individual responsible for his/her level of risk and how to manage that risk. Perhaps the most telling example in the United States is the high number (embarrassingly) of people without health insurance. Finally, Castel (1991) posits that risk emerges in response to the limits of diagnostic methods to avert deemed 'dangerous' individuals from carrying out harmful acts. The paradox of dangerousness, Castel claims, is that a diagnosis of a 'dangerous' individual is that it is a prediction of future events based on present symptoms; dangerousness assumes a probability that an individual will commit a certain harmful act in the future. While difficult to implement such assumptions on a large population, risk and insurance technology spreads the potential effects of unforeseen events to the individuals associated within a certain factored group. Risk and insurance imply one another, meaning that how risk is created and calculated impacts the amount and type of insurance one receives. Insurance thus is a "calculus of possibilities" (Ewald in Burchell et al, 1991, p. 200), or the "art of combinations" (p. 197) that estimates the probability that certain events will occur with a certain population. Individuals become categorized among various types of risk and at different levels. Insurance, thus functions only when calculations of risk can determine the chances that specific groups will experience a certain event; hence, individuals receive insurance based on their individual risk in comparison to the other members of his/her determined group. The level of risk dictates the amount and type of insurance. Due to the emergence of risk technology that the subject disappears and is replaced by a collection or assemblages of factors, placing individuals within certain specific risk/insurance groups (Castel, 1991).

NEW PRUDENTIALISM

With its emphasis on deregulation and individual freedom and independence from state agencies, neoliberal rationalities of rule encourage a new prudentialism (O'Malley, 1996; Dean, 1999; Rose, 1999; Harvey, 2005). Prudentialism means that individuals and communities assume their own risk (physical and mental health; educational performance etc.). Rather than intervening and regulating health and population welfare, the role of the state is to provide knowledge and skills to help individuals make rational and responsible decisions as they continually manage their own risk by recognizing the "irrationalities of irresponsibility" (O'Malley in Barry et al., 1996, p. 201). Leaving the individual to manage his/her own risk and to encourage communities to devise local solutions to local problems engenders an entrepreneurial spirit within the individual and throughout the community. Thus, the 'prudent subject' will accumulate the necessary resources and find relevant information to minimize and manage his/her personal risks (Rose, 1999; Peters, 2005). In advanced liberal societies such as the United States, the responsibilization of risk management has created a greater passivity and less risk-taking on the part of those unable to provide insurance for themselves. As Rose (1999) points out, this new prudentialism generates a greater division between those wealthy enough and able enough to take care of oneself and those who cannot. Each individual is forced to assume one's own risk, and thus be responsible for insuring oneself against future or potential harm. It is this dynamic, this relationship between responsibility, risk, and personal insurance, that one's abilities to problem-solve, make appropriate choices, and to be "independent" vital to surviving in an advanced liberal society. Schools, as we see in Kentucky play an important function in ensuring that students are able to have these capabilities when they graduate. The portfolio, it appears, serves as the best instrument to know if they are able to. The next section of this chapter demonstrates this point in more detail.

EMERGING FORCES

Portfolio assessment emerges from a milieu of risk and uncertainty. *A Nation at Risk* (Bell, 1983) report indicates a link between education and the security and order of a country. The report claims that while secondary schools and colleges have had significant achievements historically, they are at this time being "eroded" by a "rising tide of mediocrity," and as a result the United States is losing its competitive edge in the world. Similar sentiments were expressed in Kentucky at this time. In fact, a failure of government as sovereign power allowed neoliberal rationalities and techniques to disseminate throughout the state.

Molly A. Hunter (1999) reports that in addition to parents, local politicians and educational experts, the business community began to take an interest in public schooling in Kentucky. Predictions of an undereducated workforce and poor public school system prevented 90% of companies interested in relocating to the state from doing so. Many companies saw a 'black cloud of doom' of high school graduates. So much so, that such companies as Ashland Oil and UPS contributed significant amounts of money to local citizen groups to explore ways to reform Kentucky's educational system. In addition, the Fifth Congressional District reported in 1985 that its district was the "nation's worst" (Hunter, 1999, p. 3) which sparked business leaders who had grown up in this area to study the causes. The Mountain Association for Community Economic Development (MACED) learned that this particular region (Fifth Congressional District) had the "highest dropout rate" (Hunter, 1999, p. 4) and students only succeeded if they left the area. MACED recommended the founding of the "Forward in the Fifth," a "private nonprofit Local Education Fund and member of the national Public Education Network" (Hunter, 1999, p. 4).

This particular group established affiliates chapters in each school district in the local area. Its mission was to "raise educational levels in the region; encourage life-long learning by providing opportunities for parents, educators and community members; and to foster partnerships between communities and schools" (see http:/www.fif.org/about_us.htm). This particular citizens group "trains" parents to support their children. Reliance on the state switches to reliance on specific experts to "advise on how communities and citizens might be governed in terms of their values, and how their values shape the ways they govern themselves" (Rose, 1999, p. 189). Thus, technologies of community (Dean, 1999), organized to govern themselves, through various expert practices teach parents how to use computers, deal with "defiant" children, and how to serve as a "teacher" for their child. In addition to providing "Parent Teacher Conference Workshops" and "Active Parenting Classes," they also offer "Cooperative Parenting" classes to "enable families to shield their children from conflicts as parents go through divorce. It offers tools to manage anger, negotiate agreements and illustrates ways parents can remain child-focused" (see http:/www.fif.org/about_us.htm). These techniques of community where the experts get dispersed to help govern a community, demonstrates how the subject's conduct of conduct is governed at a distance. A dispersion of governing strategies and instruments occurs throughout the state and through media outlets.

The mainstream media also took an interest in public education. The Lexington *Herald-Leader* exposed the "nepotism and tax-fraud" in "local tax assessment practices" (Hunter, 1999, p. 4). In addition, the media allowed the Prichard Committee to investigate the state of education in Kentucky. This committee would later file an *amicus* brief in the *Rose. V. Council* Supreme Court case. On November 15, 1984, the Prichard Committee held statewide forums on the education, broadcasted on the Kentucky Educational Television (Hunter, 1999, p. 4). Ashland Oil provided the capital for advertisement and media announcements for the forums, in which 20,000 people participated. After the forums, people began to mobilize around the issue of public education, and the Prichard Committee hired Roberts & Kay, a consulting firm to run regional "Citizen Action Workshops" (Hunter, 1999, p. 4) and help people to begin to run their own grass-roots organization. As a result of these forums, the Prichard Committee published *The Path to a Larger Life:*

Creating Kentucky's Educational Future (1990) and began a large "public awareness campaign" (Hunter, 1999: 5) to motivate citizens to reform public education in Kentucky. They also generated an entire advertisement campaign to support their educational efforts. Here again, we see the technologies of community, where on the advertisements we see "How you can help..." a population at risk. These advertisements disseminate expert information on teaching and learning to the corporate body. For example, the advertisement entitled: "Feedback helps our brains grow and develop" the advertisement reads, "Feedback is especially important when learning new things. Students need to know if they are on the right track or if they have given an appropriate answer. Bad habits can develop if students don't receive feedback in a timely manner." The advertisement goes on to tell its audience to give "specific" feedback and "Instead of saying, 'Good Job,' say something specific like, 'Your work shows that you understand the steps for adding fractions.'" (see Partnership for Kentucky School online).

This brief and incomplete history provides with an overview of the neoliberal strategies at play in Kentucky at the time of their educational reform. What is important is that Kentucky's urgent need was due to a failure of government, and as a result, their employed other governing strategies to ensure the security of the state, its economic future, and the well-being of its population. Secondary school graduates played an important role in the calculations of well-being, and the public school system had a profound responsibility to guard the community against future risks, specifically risk of dependence upon state welfare institutions. Doing so meant an instrument that could give each teacher 'x-ray' vision (Sunstein, 200b) into each student's "unique as a thumbprint" (Rief et al., 2000, p. 63). Thus, shifting the spaces of students and teachers proved to be important components of the reform movement in Kentucky. Making the student the owner, or sovereign of his/her work, and making the teacher the coach, or pastoral guide, represents a strategic way to produce neoliberal subjects who are independent, entrepreneurial subjects equipped to take care of themselves, and by doing so, allows the state to function. The school provides social insurance against the future risk of dependence on state institutions.

A key piece to the reform movement in Kentucky was the writing portfolio. Although Kentucky was not the first state to implement a statewide accountability system with portfolios, it has been the only one within the United States to keep it. Despite serious questions regarding both validity and reliability of portfolios, Kentucky continues to use portfolios to assess their students and their schools. Furthermore, even though the state has change the required years for completing the portfolio (initially, students submitted portfolios at the end grades 4, 8, and 11, which was later changed to grade 12), the format and the desired result have remained consistent. The portfolio was just a piece to a larger accountability system throughout the state. Combined cognitive (portfolio scores) and non-cognitive (retention rates, attendance) scores affected the rewards or sanctions a school would receive. In addition, students include six pieces in their final portfolios, of which two must come from another class besides Language Arts (Kentucky Department of Education, 1997). They must write a Letter to the Reviewer, one personal expressive writing (memoir, personal essay), one imaginative writing (short story, poem), and three additional pieces (defend a position, solve a problem) (Kentucky Department of Education, 1997). While there are many elements to the system that one could investigate, for the purposes of this chapter, I would like to limit my comments to the portfolio, mainly to highlight the mentalities of rule embedded within it to challenge or subvert commonly held views about its emancipatory effects on students in schools. The portfolio, it will be argued, represents an instrument to neoliberal rationality of rule designed to measure levels of for risk and social security based on the principles of entrepreneurship and responsibility.

KENTUCKY WRITING PORTFOLIOS

The writing portfolios were part of the KIRIS (Kentucky Instructional Results Information System), which is under the sphere of assessment of KERA. Originally, under KERA, the writing portfolios were completed and scored after the 4th, 8th, and 11th grades. However, the writing portfolios switched to the 12th grade after the first accountability cycle in 1993. For the majority of the time, writing portfolios have been assessed during the 12th grade, and the format of the portfolio has not changed since its inception. The portfolio, it appears, monitors not just student work, but "local curriculum and instruction" and illustrates the "strong connection to student's classroom experiences and the strong involvement of teachers" (KIRIS, Chapter 12). The portfolio was designed to expand student writing from the "traditional" forms of writing, such as "reports, essays, research papers," to "personal experience writing; imaginative writing; reflective writing; and, trans-active writing for real-world purposes and audiences" (KIRIS, Chapter 12). Instead of being a one-time writing task, the portfolio is a collection of student's work over time. Students have the opportunity to re-write their papers before they put them in the scored portfolio, thus it is seen as their best work. In addition, portfolios were assessed "holistically", where each criteria (purpose/ audience awareness; idea development, organization, correctness etc.) is weighed equally, and students are given a score of novice, apprentice, proficient, and distinguished. Students must score proficient to graduate.

Teachers play an important role in helping students develop their writing abilities and compose their portfolios. The space of the teacher shifts in the neoliberal classroom. As the pseudo-sovereign in the classroom, the traditional role as the authority wielding power over the students takes a dramatic turn in the classrooms in Kentucky. Instead of being responsible for the students' work, writing pedagogy, and content curricula, the primary role of the teacher is to help students become the "owners" of their work, or to be "independent thinkers and writers" (KDE, 2003). Any direct intervention in the student's work diminishes the student's ability to own his/her own work. Teachers act more as mentors or coaches or colleagues rather than as authorities. They govern at a distance, letting the students to be the sole arbiters of their work. They must provide students with ample opportunities to write, with the requisite skills to engage with different audiences, teaching both informal and formal writing, and with direct feedback on student work. In addition, students select the final pieces that go into the final portfolio. This *laissaiz-faire* approach to teacher produces a greater view of a student's ability to problem-solve, placing them in their natural, authentic environment, which allows the teachers with a valid view of their abilities to practice their freedoms in very specific ways. Students practice entrepreneurship, generating their own topics, shaping and molding their work as they see fit. They are encouraged to take risks, to explore what they know and decide how to present their work. The teacher acts as a coach, while the student represents their level of 'ownership' and 'independence' in their portfolio. What's at stake is not simply 'good' writing, but managing subjectivities, organizing experiences, problem-solving independently, and reinventing oneself. Writing becomes merely a means to demonstrate one's ability to be a proper neoliberal subject. To explain these ideas more clearly, this paper discusses the novice and proficient writers in greater detail.

THE NOVICE AND PROFICIENT WRITERS

To unpack the rationalities of rule in the Kentucky portfolio, this section examines the scoring criteria of the novice and the proficient portfolios. Keeping in mind that the teacher plays a minimal role in preparing students to write their portfolio pieces, and that students must maintain complete ownership of their work, we begin to see how the portfolio became an important tool to prepare students to be independent subjects in a neoliberal state. Student portfolio reveal their abilities to problem-solve, to think logically, to organize their thoughts and their experiences, to relate to an audience, and to reinvent themselves. Each of the criteria can be interpreted with the neoliberal rationalities in mind. The novice and apprentice writers display a high level of risk, and thus must remain in high school until they are able to be otherwise, while the proficient and distinguished writers display low levels of risk, and are thus permitted to graduate.

A novice portfolio represents the individual who is incapable of exhibiting characteristics of the entrepreneurial subject, capable of making independent decisions, problem-solving, and relating to a variety of audiences. The pieces are brief, limited in scope, poorly organized, with few details, and fails to consider audience in the writing, using the inappropriate voice for a genre. From a neoliberal perspective, the novice student fails to demonstrate the necessarily qualities to take care of her/himself. The student did not harness the necessary resources to learn how to compose pieces for the portfolio, and is unable to organize her subjective and personal experiences into a cohesive, organized manner, indicating the student's inability to be rational. In addition, because the student is unable to compose a variety of pieces for different audiences, the student's lacks the ability to reinvent her/himself. Re-inventing oneself is important in a neoliberal state because without the safety-net of state welfare institutions, and the instability of markets, the individual may be forced to interact with different types of people in order to survive. If the student is unable to think clearly, problem-solve, collect necessary resources, organize thoughts, reinvent oneself, they become a high risk. The novice student has a higher probability, based on their entire portfolio, to be dependent upon the state, is not able to take responsibility for his/her own risk, and is a risk to him/herself to others. The portfolio provides social insurance against individuals who are unable to take care of themselves in the neoliberal state.

The proficient writer, on the other hand, represents the minimal level of competency that students must exhibit in order to graduate from high school. Students who compose a proficient portfolio demonstrate the ability to produce authentic writing, or writing for the real-world or for a real purpose, communicate effectively with an audience, recognizing the needs of the audience, are able to follow the format of a variety of genres, use a variety of voices, demonstrate critical thinking by providing in depth use of details in their work, are able to put subjective experiences in a logical, rational, organized fashion, they are able to make sense of subjective experiences and ideas, and are use appropriate language and follow rules. They demonstrate the minimal competence and skills needed to function in a neoliberal state.

What becomes evident after closer examination of these criteria is that what gets assessed and evaluated in the Kentucky portfolio is not simply the student's ability to compose various forms of writing. In fact, it appears that the writing is merely a reflection of a student's ability to perform itself as a neoliberal subject; one that must be prepared and fashioned to live as an independent subject. Novice writers represent the most at-risk subjects, ones who are unable to manage their experiences, ones who cannot present their ideas effectively, ones who cannot problem-solve and can't organize their thoughts and put them in a logical sequence. If allowed to leave public schools, they would demand the hand of a dwindling state. The proficient student manages themselves quite well and is able to exist independently and manages his/her subjectivities 'proficiently.' They are not at risk, but the school has ensured that they will not be so in the future.

PORTFOLIOS, RISK AND NEW PRUDENTIALISM

What we witness with the emergence of the portfolio as a form of assessment and in particular as a main element in a large-scale accountability system is the implementation, the enmeshing of neoliberal mentalities of rule in educational practices. In addition, the purpose of the portfolio is not make sure that students accumulate a certain body of knowledge or practice certain fundamental skills, but to demonstrate that they can be independent constructors of their own experiences and assume responsibility for their own decisions and choices. The teacher moves to the margins of the classroom, functioning as unobtrusive guides, as invisible facilitators, as people who arrange spaces for equal opportunity for students to express themselves. They abide by strict rules of conduct, leaving the student alone to be the sole decision-maker in the composition of the portfolio.

As a form of accountability, producing independent subjects capable of making appropriate decisions about one's care represents "enterprise education" (Peters, 2005, p. 135). The portfolio, laced with its neoliberal rationalities of rule. Inducing students to use personal experiences and desires to reflect their decision-making, problem-solving capabilities, allowing teachers, parents, and administrators x-ray vision into each student (Sunstein, 2002b). What makes the portfolio a form of entrepreneurial education is that is encourages the students to make an "investment in the self" (Peters, 2005, p. 134), ones that demonstrates how one can engage in "personal transformation" (p. 134). In addition, the portfolio allows administrators to calculate risk by grouping students based on their collective characteristics of how effectively they can take care of themselves. What is being measured in the writing portfolio is not just a student's writing abilities, but also their abilities to be independent owners of their work, and thus, entrepreneurs of oneself. Welfare institutions such as public education prepare students to be self-reliant and not dependent upon governmental agencies. By granting students the liberties to compose themselves, by forcing students to write a variety of writing assignments, and by collating their work into a rational rubric, the portfolio in Kentucky represent a new prudentialism; one where individuals and communities assume their own risk, become responsible for insuring against harmful dangers, preparing students to make appropriate decisions so that they may practice freedom to monitor their own well being. Finally, while the portfolio may serve as empirical evidence of how well a student can write, it also reflects the dominant rationalities of rule of the current moment; one that may force freedoms and produce confinement.

REFERENCES

Amodeo, J. (1998). Rising to the challenge of high-stakes assessment. In G. O. Martin-Kniep (Ed.), *Why am I doing this?: Purposeful teaching through portfolio assessment* (pp. 121–133). Portsmouth, NH: Heinemann.

Bell, T. H. (1983). *A nation at risk: The imperative for reform.* Washington, DC: Department of Education.

Barry, A., Osborne, T., & Rose, N. (Eds.). (1996). *Foucault and political reason: Liberalism, neo-liberalism and rationalities of government.* Chicago: University of Chicago Press.

Bell, V. (1996). The promise of liberalism and the performance of freedom. In A. Barry, T. Osborne, & N. Rose (Eds.), *Foucault and political reason: Liberalism, neo liberalism and rationalities of government* (pp. 81–97). Chicago: The University of Chicago Press.

Berthoff, A. E., Murray, D., Gere, A. R., & Kirby, D. (1984). Facets: The most important development in the last five years for high school teachers of composition. *The English Journal, 73*(5), 20–23.

Black, L. et al. (Eds.). (1995). *New directions in portfolio assessment: Reflective practice, critical theory, and large-scale scoring.* Portsmouth, NH: Heinemann Publishers.

Burchell, G., Gordon, C., & Miller, P. (Eds.). (1991). *The Foucault effect: Studies in governmentality.* Chicago: University of Chicago Press.

Burchell, G. (1996). Liberal government and techniques of the self. In A. Barry, T. Osborne, & N. Rose (Eds.), *Foucault and political reason: Liberalism, neo liberalism and rationalities of government* (pp. 19–36). Chicago: University of Chicago Press.

Callahan, S. (1996). *Using portfolios for accountability: The ethic of care collides with the need for judgment.* Paper presented at the Annual Meeting of the Conference on College Composition and Communication (Milwaukee).

Callahan, S. (1997). Kentucky's state-mandated writing portfolios and teacher accountability. In K. B. Yancey & I. Weiser (Eds.), *Situating portfolios: Four perspectives* (pp. 57–71). Logan, Utah: Utah State University Press.

Castel, R. (1991). From dangerousness to risk. In G. Burchell, C. Gordon, & P. Miller (Eds.), *The Foucault effect: Studies in governmentality with two lectures by and an interview with Michel Foucault* (pp. 281–298). Chicago: University of Chicago Press.

Cole, D. J., Ryan, C. W., & Kick, F. (1995). *Portfolios across the curriculum and beyond.* Thousand Oaks, CA: Corwin Press, Inc.

Cruikshank, B. (1996). Revolutions within: Self-government and self-esteem. In A. Barry, T. Osborne, & N. Rose (Eds.), *Foucault and political reason: Liberalism, neoliberalism and rationalities of government* (pp. 231–251). Chicago: University of Chicago Press.

Dean, M. (1999). *Governmentality: Power and rule in modern society.* London: SAGE Publications.

Donzelot, J. (1977). *The policing of families.* Baltimore and London: Johns Hopkins University Press.

Dreyfus, H. L., & Rabinow, P. (1983). *Michel Foucault: Beyond structuralism and hermeneutics* (2nd ed.). Chicago: The University of Chicago Press.

Elbow, P., & Belanoff, P. (1997). Reflections on an explosion: Portfolios in the 90's and Beyond. In K. Yancey & I. Weiser (Eds.), *Situating portfolios: Four perspectives* (pp. 21–34). Logan: Utah State University Press.

Ewald, F. (1991). Insurance and risk. In G. Burchell, C. Gordon, & P. Miller (Eds.), *The Foucault effect: Studies in governmentality with two lectures by and an interview with Michel Foucault* (pp. 197–210). Chicago: The University of Chicago Press.

Foucault, M. (1983). Afterword: The subject and power. In H. L. Dreyfus & P. Rabinow (Eds.), *Michel Foucault: Beyond structuralism and hermeneutics* (2nd ed., pp. 208–226). Chicago: The University of Chicago Press.

Foucault, M. (1991). Governmentality. In G. Burchell, C. Gordon, & P. Miller (Eds.), *The Foucault effect: Studies in governmentality with two lectures by and an interview with Michel Foucault* (pp. 87–104). Chicago: University of Chicago Press.

Foucault, M. (2003). "Omnes et Singulatim": Toward a critique of political reason. In P. Rabinow & N. Rose (Eds.), *The essential foucault: Selections from the essential works of foucault 1954–1984* (pp. 180–201). New York & London: The New Press.

Fu, D. (2000). The connected "I": Portfolios and cultural values. In B. S. Sunstein & J. H. Lovell (Eds.), *The portfolio standard: How students can show us what they know and are able to do* (pp. 105–115). Portsmouth, NH: Heinemann.

Gordon, C. (1991). Governmental rationality: An Introduction. In G. Burchell, C. Gordon, & P. Miller (Eds.), *The Foucault effect: Studies in governmentality with two lectures by and an interview with Michel Foucault* (pp. 1–51). Chicago: University of Chicago Press.

Graves, D. (2000). Forward. In B. S. Sunstein & J. H. Lovell (Eds.), *The portfolio standard: How students can show us what they know and are able to do.* Portsmouth, NH: Heinemann.

Hacking, I. (1990). *The taming of chance.* Cambridge, UK: Cambridge University Press.

Hunter, M. A. (1999). All eyes forward: Public engagement and educational reform in Kentucky. *Journal of Law & Education, 28*(4), 485–516.

Hayek, F. A. (1944). *The road to serfdom.* London: Routledge & Kegan Paul.

Kentucky Education Reform Act Resources. (1989). *Rose versus council for better education.* Retrieved from http://www.schoolfunding.info/states/ky/ROSEvCBE.PDF

Kentucky Department of Education. (1990a). *Kentucky instructional results information system (KIRIS).* Retrieved from www.education.ky.gov

Kentucky Department of Education. (1990b). *Transformations: Kentucky's curriculum framework.* Retrieved from www.education.ky.gov

Kentucky Department of Education. (1997). *Sharpening your child's writing skills: A guidebook for Kentucky's parents.* Retrieved from www.education.ky.gov

Kentucky Department of Education. (1998). *Saving time with writing portfolios: An idea book for administrators and classroom teachers.* Retrieved from www.education.ky.gov

Kentucky Department of Education. (2003). *Kentucky writing: Helping students develop as proficient writings—writing development teacher's handbook.* Retrieved from www.education.ky.gov

Mahoney, J. (2002). *Power and portfolios: Best practices for high school classrooms*. Portsmouth, NH: Heinemann.

Martin-Kniep, G. O. (1998). *Why am I doing this?: Purposeful teaching through portfolio assessment*. Portsmouth, NH: Heinemann.

O'Malley, P. (1996). Risk and responsibility. In A. Barry, T. Osborne, & N. Rose (Eds.), *Foucault and political reason: Liberalism, neo-liberalism and rationalities of government* (pp. 189–207). Chicago: University of Chicago Press.

Partnership for Kentucky School Reform. (1998). *Basic skills for kentucky jobs*. Retrieved from www.pfks.org

Peters, M. A. (2005). The new prudentialism in education: Actuarial rationality and the entrepreneurial self. *Educational Theory, 55*(2), 123–137.

Rief, L., Finnegan, M., & Gannett, C. (2000). Who's the teacher? In B. S. Sunstein & J. H. Lovell (Eds.), *The portfolio standard: How students can show us what they know and are able to do* (pp. 62–76). Portsmouth, NH: Heinemann.

Rose, N. (1989). *Governing the soul: The shaping of the private self* (2nd ed.). London & New York: Free Association Books.

Rose, N. (1996). Governing "Advanced" liberal democracies. In A. Barry, T. Osborne, & N. Rose (Eds.), *Foucault and political reason: Liberalism, neo-liberalism and rationalities of government* (pp. 37–64). Chicago: University of Chicago Press.

Rose, N. (1999). *Powers of freedom: Reframing political thought*. Cambridge, UK: Cambridge University Press.

Sunstein, B. S., & Lovell, J. H. (Eds.). (2000a). *The portfolio standard: How students can show us what they know and are able to do*. Portsmouth, NH: Heinemann.

Sunstein, B. S. (2000b). Be reflective, be reflexive, and beware: Innocent forgery for inauthentic assessment. In B. S. Sunstein & J. H. Lovell (Eds.), *The portfolio standard: How students can show us what they know and are able to do* (pp. 3–14). Portsmouth, NH: Heinemann.

Terwilliger, J. S. (1997). *Portfolios and classroom assessment: Some claims and questions*. Paper presented at American Educational Researchers Association Conference.

Tierney, R. J., Carter, M. A., & Desai, L. E. (Eds.). (1991). *Portfolio assessment in the reading writing classroom*. Norwood, MA: Christopher-Gordon Publishers.

Wiggins, G. (1992). Creating tests worth taking. *Educational Leadership, 49*(8), 26–33.

Yancey, K. B., & Huot, B. (1998). Construction, deconstruction, and (over) determination: A foucaultial analysis of grades. In F. Zak & C. C. Weaver (Eds.), *The theory and practices of grading writing: Problems and possibilities* (pp. 39–51). Albany, NY: State University of New York Press.

David Lee Carlson
Arizona State University
USA

ADAM DAVIDSON-HARDEN

16. NEOLIBERALISM, KNOWLEDGE CAPITALISM AND THE STEERED UNIVERSITY: THE ROLE OF OECD AND CANADIAN FEDERAL GOVERNMENT DISCOURSE

It is fitting that the terms 'knowledge economy' and 'knowledge worker' were likely first coined by the business management thinker Peter Drucker (1969; 1998). Drucker attempted to prophesy the future of capitalism for the good of its protagonists – corporations – in order to help them anticipate the demands of a changing economy and adapt to be profitable. Given the fact that epistemology has puzzled philosophers for millennia, we can be confident that the use of the term 'knowledge' in capitalist discourse has been limited in its scope and depth, that is, confined to understanding knowledge as an input and a good which enhances pro-fitability. It is not the purpose of this chapter to examine competing epistemologies in order to compare them with the discourse of the knowledge economy as it relates to education. Rather, I seek to unpack the thematic and conceptual thrusts behind the knowledge economy discourse as it is found in both national (principally Canadian) and international policy levels (using the OECD as a case example) in order to interrogate their use in shaping education, and particularly public universities in Canada. To aid this unpacking, I will employ an eclectic mix of Marx-inspired political economy and critical theory (Morrow, 2006; Schugurensky, 2006; 1999), Foucault-inspired neoliberal governmentality (Peters, 2001a; 2001b), as well as critical pedagogy perspectives to interrogate the knowledge economy in the context of neoliberalism. This particular work, in addition to its theoretical emphasis, is also founded upon tenets of critical discourse analysis (Fairclough, 1995) since it is (in the case of the government of Canada and the OECD) discourse, in the form of texts and policy recommendations, that I am interrogating in particular, in order to elicit the particular flavour of neoliberalism in its knowledge economy phase.

I will argue here that talk of the knowledge economy represents, at its root, merely an extension or transformation of neoliberal capitalist discourse which works to deepen a perception of education seen through the lens of 'instrumental rationality', following the insights of critical theory (Marcuse, 1968), and also to cultivate the behaviour of faculty and the policies of universities to conform with market models, needs and demands, a trend I interpret using the idea of neoliberal 'governmental rationality' (or 'neoliberal governmentality'), building on Foucault's work (1983; 1991). As such, I locate it as an extension of neoliberal social and economic policy discourse, still the hegemonic policy discourse of our times. With its programmatic focus on shaping state-funded education to suit the needs of capitalism and particularly scientific and technological innovation with commercial

M.A. Peters et al. (eds.), Governmentality Studies in Education, 271–302.

and market applications, the knowledge economy represents a new wineskin for an older ideology of tying national competiveness and prosperity to specialized industries that are held up as keys to prosperity. When it comes to universities, the idea of governmentality helps us to explore how 'we' as faculty and teachers, as well as administrators in public education settings, 'fit' into the vision of the knowledge economy or knowledge capitalism, which, building on a critical theory perspective, conceives education as an instrumental good toward the principal and paramount end of accumulating capital for national competitiveness in a global economy. Within a framework of political economy, Schugurensky's conception of 'heteronomy' (1999; 2006) as a constraining envelope of increasing demands from the market and government on universities is useful to understanding the larger picture of decline in state funding over time during the growing ascendancy of neoliberal policy. The chapter will proceed by first laying out a synthesized theoretical foundation for analysis rooted in neoliberalism and mentioned above, followed by an exploration of the use of the knowledge economy discourse in the hands of key international organizations as well as the Canadian government and other a few other Canadian stakeholder organizations, including the Canadian Federation of Humanities and Social Sciences. Having accomplished this, I will end with a brief discussion of implications for public universities, as well as faculty and administrators.

UNDERSTANDING NEOLIBERALISM

Since neoliberalism plays such a strong role in my analysis, it is necessary to start with this much-used concept in order to lay a proper foundation for an appreciation of how the knowledge economy is situated as an extension of neoliberal discourse for education. Indeed, the term is, one might say, too often used without a necessary mapping or genealogy of its roots and significance. The specific term neoliberalism has been in use for at least a half-century (Friedrich, 1955), as prominent European economists began to articulate their own particular version of a policy founded in the tenets of economic liberalism, yet suggestive of new trends in thought (Peters, 2001b). This latter body of thought of course stretches back to founding thinkers of the 18th century such as Adam Smith, whose theories foreshadowed the massive industrial development in the 19th century which was to propel capitalism far beyond the domestic economy that Smith, for one, idealized. Similarly, economic liberalism has been historically associated with conceptions of liberalized trade or free trade, also a common term in the 19th century. The idea that capital and investment ought to be free from as much intervention and regulation as possible, stands as a kernel conception behind economic liberalism. However, as alluded to above, within a thinker like Smith's paradigm there were articulated necessary constraints on capital; in his case an idea of free markets was decidedly restricted to the national economy where investors were expected to re-invest in the productive capacity of a particular nation-state (McMurtry, 1999, pp. 42–44). As capitalism exploded beyond national barriers to become truly global, economic liberalism as key *modus operandi* for nation-states transformed until eventually it little resembled the ideal which a founding thinker like Adam Smith envisioned in his *Wealth of Nations*.

Marx-inspired critiques of capitalism and its development identified these expansive interests and tendencies of capital to grow beyond borders, constantly opening up new frontiers and markets, ever-expanding into more diverse areas of the natural world and human life (Marx & Engels, in McLellan, 1977, p. 224)[1]. Hayek (1944) can certainly be characterized as one of the 'founding' thinkers of the new adaptation of economic liberalism, an adaptation that emphasized less state intervention toward the welfare model which Keynes advocated, and a concomitant encouragement of free markets (Peters, 2001b). Complementing this trend in thinking was the crucial acknowledgement by thinkers such as Hayek that markets need critical intervention from the state in terms of the rule of law, regulatory institutions, and subsidies of various sorts to facilitate and promote trade. Arguably, the paradigmatic idea behind neoliberalism stems from a core conception that markets are somehow inherently superior at ordering an economy, and that states ought not to intervene in economies by attempting to play the role of 'guarantor of welfare' in capitalist societies, as per a Keynesian approach.

A later generation of economists would pick up on these ideas, such as Friedman of the Chicago School (1963), Tullock and Buchanan (1962) (public choice theory), and Becker (1964) (human capital theory). These economic theoretical frameworks increasingly pictured individuals in a free market society principally as consumers, and extolled markets and an economistic way of analysing society while criticizing governments in terms of participation (or intervening) in aspects of the economy. The emergence of these types of ideas foreshadowed their coming rise to hegemony, which was in turn facilitated by concrete historical factors.

Appreciating this context, and following the work of scholars such as George (1999) and Harvey (2005), Teeple (2000) and others, neoliberalism can be characterized as an umbrella term for an economic policy trend which has emphasized shifting roles for public and private sectors in a context of attacks on the welfare state since the early 1970s. Taking cues from Teeple's understanding of neoliberalism, the conception represents a policy shift accompanying the decline of the long economic postwar boom after World War II in North America. Teeple (2000) suggests a view of the welfare state as a tenuous entity in a capitalist system. In particular, he suggests that in the context of economically booming post-WWII capitalist economy, the social achievement of the welfare state represents not a stage in inevitable historical progress but rather a particular phase in which wealthier capitalist societies could accommodate increased state intervention for greater common well-being. This mode of intervention is based on a Keynesian economic and social policy paradigm legitimating the goal of full employment through state deficit financing of social programs of various sorts, comprising what Marshall termed the new form of 'social citizenship' (Marshall, 1950). This period has been referred to as one of 'tripartisan' compromise, between government, labour, and business (Teeple, 2000, p. 38). This achievement is transient, however, as it has rested upon the profitability of the capitalist system. This transience has shown itself more and more in recent years, having been kicked off as the postwar economic boom began to recede in the early 1970s. With the decline of other sources for expansion and accumulation, the interests of capital have increasingly turned their eyes onto the public institutions of the welfare state, in the interests of privatization and marketization (i.e., in the neoliberal interest). As this attention has shifted, an increasing tension has developed which pits a conception of public services such as health and education as social rights or entitlements for citizens against one which sees these things as commodities to be purchased by consumers, in the same way as any other item available in the 'free market'. As the language or discourse of market relations and commodities has further enveloped more areas of society and education in particular, this tension has grown. In a sense, this type of scenario reflects the imperialistic and colonizing forces of imperial nation-states from the 15th century onward, as indigenous peoples, land and resources were appropriated and exploited in the interest of hegemonic colonial and imperial powers. In the contemporary context, formerly untapped areas of economic growth (and plunder) are subsumed by this logic under a growing sphere of market relations which shifts attention away from the Keynesian welfare state conception of social citizenship and social rights and toward markets as the principal form of social co-ordination. The growth of the 'market society' – an idea put forward by Polanyi (1944) – has encompassed over time the increasing absorption of more social activities and institutions into the domain and purview of capital accumulation. Teeple (2000) characterizes these types of shifts as the decline of social reform under neoliberalism, arguing that the tenuously won achievements of welfare state social citizenship have experienced retrenchments under the new policy hegemony.

Neoliberalism (agreeing with Pannu, 1996), is best understood as the dominant (or hegemonic) economic ideology and policy agenda of our times. As a general observation, a good analogy or comparator for neoliberalism can be found in Marx's ideas. If Marxism is best understood as a philosophy, economics and politics for unfettering the worker, then neoliberalism is a philosophy, economics and politics for unfettering the market, or the economy, from any perceptible constraints imposed by governments. Indeed, as mentioned earlier, neoliberalism seeks to transform the capacity of the state to intervene away from facilitating welfare toward primarily facilitating markets, although in a capitalist society, as a thinker such as Teeple argues (2000), these two tendencies can be seen as in a state of perpetual tension. The discourse of economistic freedom that neoliberalism represents agitates for social change toward increased reliance on, and use of, market forms in social policy and public governance. Marx's ideas, in contrast, can be argued to represent a discourse that agitates for social change in a contrary direction, toward expansion of social rights through measures such as public control over an economy, the redistribution of wealth, and the ensuring of universal access to critical social services. Applied to education, one discourse fights for the supremacy of a conception of education as commodity while the other fights for the supremacy of a conception of education as a social right. Underlying this conflict in conceptions, further, are disparate conceptualizations of freedom: as touched upon below, an economistic perspective of freedom frames the individual and society as factors in a vast economic calculus of self-maximization and profit. In contrast, freedom as conceptualized under the banner of increased social rights celebrates, rather than vilifies collective projects to ensure achievement and expansion of these things as necessities for a measure of 'freedom'[2]. 'Freedom' is an important term in the vocabulary of neoliberalism ('free trade', 'free market', economic 'freedom'), as it is claimed that toward economic growth, markets and trade must be made 'free' in order for countries to achieve maximum output, measured in GDP/GNP (Gross Domestic Product/Gross National Product). Political programs of privatization and deregulation are encouraged and imposed under neoliberal policy regimes toward the ultimate (professed) purpose of 'letting the market alone', an idea summed up in the classical economic notion of *laissez-faire* capitalism. Another contemporary term used to represent neoliberal economic ideology is 'trade liberalization' or just simply 'liberalization'. These terms again hit upon 'freedom' as a discursive catch-word within neoliberal discourse. The conception of freedom underlying this type of discourse is of course exclusively economistic: individuals, framed by orthodox economics through the lens of *homo economicus,* are conceptualized primarily as rationally self-interested calculators of material advantage, while the idea of freedom is centred on the ability not only of the individual but of business entities to freely choose how they may conduct their self-maximizing affairs as 'free' as possible from state intervention. Operationalizing the belief that any government involvement in the market leads to inefficiency and mismanagement in economic terms, neoliberal policies seek to both decrease government intervention in the market as well as to change governments' mode of involvement to encourage marketization.

Behind the scenes of today's neoliberal ascendance is a history of economic ideas in flux, as alluded to above. Peters (2001c) suggests that the move from Keynesianism to "neoliberal monetarism" in economic policy during the 60s and 70s represented a paradigm shift in economics and society (p. 4). Whereas Keynesian economics endorsed state investment in the economy as a way to encourage development, monetarism restricts state intervention in the economy to control of interest rates and inflation. George traces this history by highlighting the fact that during the ascendance of Keynesian thinking about the economy, neoliberal thinkers were among the ostracized group:

In 1945 or 1950, if you had seriously proposed any of the ideas and policies in today's standard neoliberal toolkit, you would have been laughed off the stage or sent off to the insane asylum. At least in the Western countries, at that time, everyone was a Keynesian, a social democrat or a social-Christian democrat or some shade of Marxist. The idea that the market should be allowed to make major social and political decisions; the idea that the State should voluntarily reduce its role in the economy, or that corporations should be given total freedom, that trade unions should be curbed and citizens given much less rather than more social protection–such ideas were utterly foreign to the spirit of the time. Even if someone actually agreed with these ideas, he or she would have hesitated to take such a position in public and would have had a hard time finding an audience. (George 1999, p. 1).

In additional feature of neoliberalism is a myopic concern with economic growth, expressed in measures such as GDP/GNP, which together are taken as the primary measure of nations' success according to neoliberal prescriptions. As a measure of total economic activity with no further specification, however, these measures can be said to measure little with respect to the well being of people and environments. In a report on trade and poverty released around the time of the recent People's Summit coinciding with the meeting around the (now defunct) Free Trade of the Americas (FTAA) in Québec city in 2001, the Canadian Centre for International Co-operation (CCIC) typified the shortcomings of economic growth measures in this way, relating a disturbing case study:

> ...there is the problem that even if an economy grows–something that you can measure by looking at its gross domestic product (GDP)–that doesn't mean that poor people within it are better off. GDP doesn't account for distribution of wealth within an economy. GDP can grow if an economy sells arms or requires the clean up of a major environmental disaster. GDP will also grow if a few companies generate high profits, but these factors don't mean that the economy's poor people are benefiting. Angola is a perfect example of this dichotomy. Thanks to oil and diamonds, Angola's economy has grown significantly in 2000. Yet a third of Angolan children still die before their fifth birthday; the UN's Human Development Index rates the country 160th of a possible 174, and UNICEF considers it "the worst place in the world to be a child". Angola's GDP is growing even as most of its people derive no benefit from oil or diamonds. Indeed, it is growing even as many people are further impoverished... (CCIC, 2001, p. 6).

Toward the penultimate goal of economic growth, neoliberal policy calls for the implementation of liberalization measures through privatization and deregulation as means to achieve the goal of a lessened role for the state in regulation of market activities. DeMartino outlines how through the concept of "government failure" advocates of neoliberalism call for a decreased role of the state in providing services, where market forces or the private sector could do the same, for profit (1999, p. 73). Citing government inefficiency, waste and bureaucracy, neoliberal advocates call for the abolition of what they call 'natural monopolies'. This term is meant to refer to public services set up by governments to meet various citizen needs, from transportation, to health care, to education. Requiring large investments and extensive government co-ordination, public services are perceived as "anti-competitive" in a capitalist environment (George, 1999, p. 4). However, when as in Britain, newly privatized and formerly public services raise rates for services dramatically (as in the case of telecommunications in that country), imposing monopoly rates on the public – something we have seen recently in North America with the privatized electricity scheme of California – conditions for private investors' increased profits are increased, but the accessibility of a service is concomitantly scaled back. In this way a market good (profit) can prevail over a public good (universally accessible services) under neoliberalism.

As a policy discourse which is emblematic of these types of shifts, and taking into account the context offered above, this research seeks to define neoliberalism – for the purposes of this analysis – as comprised of various constituent trends which characterize it as a policy trend. Thus, within this context, 'marketization' is a broad term which been used commonly to denote the expansion and import of market forms and mechanisms onto different social spheres, in this case education, resulting in the adoption of competition measures, incentives, and 'choice' as key components of governance. 'Commodification', representing the move to transform formerly non-traded or commercial entities and services into 'buyable' and profit-oriented schemes, is obviously related to marketization. 'Deregulation' in this sense also refers to the removal of barriers in the form of public regulation and control of services with a concomitant shift toward increased private sector roles, or privatization. Finally, a continuum of 'centralization' and 'decentralization' refers to the respective concentration of governance in education at certain governmental levels or, correspondingly, a shift away (or devolution) from central authorities to more local levels in matters of policy and practice. In addition to these understandings of constituent trends or discourses within neoliberalism as a general policy discourse, I also add my own interpretation to the term. I suggest that neoliberalism represents – as alluded to above – a colonizing and imperialistic force as a discourse and set of policy trends.

As the constituent trends within neoliberalism work to reframe aspects of social life – including public institutions and services – in the image of the market, these trends seek to 'translate' aspects of the social into marketable commodities and processes open to forms of competition and choice. I characterize this type of process as 'colonizing' in the sense of the dynamic of one set of 'languages' or policy discourses, that of the market, acting to redefine aspects of the social according to the mode of the market. That is to say, neoliberal policy discourses, with their focus on commodification, privatization and markets as a preferred mode of conducting social policy and arranging modes of governance, can be seen to have colonized the domain of social policy discourses, gaining hegemony in terms of prevailing policy regimes across many contexts, both in richer and poorer states. In turn, the use of the term 'imperial' connotes these discourses' current supremacy as a prevailing mode of policymaking and restructuring processes. In addition, a connotation of neoliberalism as imperialistic also infers motivation and intent; with neoliberalism we are not simply referring to vague policy processes but active policy campaigns and restructuring initiatives with real actors and real motivations driving them. This type of perspective acknowledges that there are actors within society who stand to benefit from the increased shift to market forms under globally hegemonic neoliberal policy regimes, accomplished through the erosion of social rights and programs as funded publicly in a welfare state context. In addition, the terms 'colonizing' and 'imperial' also serve to denote my open characterization of neoliberalism as a policy trend which represents entrenched powers and interests in advanced capitalist societies. I understand the ever-increasing imperial and colonizing force of marketizing further social and public spheres toward profit-making and commerce as a central feature of neoliberalism as a policy discourse.

NEOLIBERAL GOVERNMENTALITY AND POLITICAL ECONOMY, FOUCAULT AND MARX, AND TOWARD A MATERIAL-DISCURSIVE DIALECTIC

Foucault's ideas about governmentality, and neoliberal governmentality specifically, form an important extension of his work into the realm of the state and how power is exercised through a 'governing at a distance' in contemporary societies (Bratich et al., 2003). I will first explore Foucault in particular before explaining how I blend an approach of governmentality with a political economy perspective building on Marx's thought. These frameworks help to situate the current analysis further by honing in on a specific use of neoliberalism as it applies to educational work in universities under the discourse of the knowledge economy.

Tracing the evolution of state power from Christianity-based medieval societies ('pastoral power') through to emergent critiques of 'state reason' in the Renaissance and through to Enlightenment liberalism, Foucault poses that contemporary states govern through a special sort of rationality which, while keeping subjects/citizens at a 'distance' through conferral/concession of personal liberty, sought concomitantly to 'responsibilize' individuals and encourage 'self-regulation' (Gordon, 1991; Foucault, 1991). In this sense control is not so much realized through the relation of a sovereign ruler to his/her subjects or through government as an institution to a citizenry, but rather governmentality as a rationality and technique of control is employed as a tool whereby individuals are implicated in societal webs of control and co-ordination through their own liberty and self-regulation.

Further, continuing this theme of his later work, Foucault posited that neoliberal theorists of the German and U.S. (Chicago) economic schools sought to introduce the idea of economy as a prime organizer and conceptual anchor for understanding individuals in society. Coupled with this increasing incorporation of economics as a mode of governmentality, the new neoliberal governmentality sought to introduce economics as *the* preferred mode of societal organization over and above any other in contemporary governance. Neoliberalism's economic models of choice, competition and the 'rational actor' of *homo economicus* reinforced the conception of individuals as primarily economic subjects (Lemke, 2001).

Educational theorists and researchers such as Peters (2001a; 1996; with Marshall & Fitzsimmons, 2000) have explored how in particular, a Foucauldian type of neoliberal governmentality can be seen to operate in the educational domain, as forces of commodification, privatization and marketization (congruent with this paper's conception of neoliberalism) have colonized social spheres of all kinds with logics of competition, self-management and an entrepreneurial ethos. A table is reproduced in Appendix 1 showing Peters' interpretation of the application of the idea of neoliberal governmentality, with specific attention to education. This table compiles a view of various mechanisms of neoliberalism from this Foucauldian perspective, moving from the idea of liberalism as a critique of state reason toward the application of market modes and imperatives as organizing modalities of the state itself under neoliberalism. Such a frame offers a deliberately and fruitfully complex means of approaching problems of education restructuring and neoliberalism in education policy discourses. Through its emphasis on how such discourses seek to govern at a variety of levels through the construction of individuals and groups through specified economistic discourses, such a model of analysis supplements the two first frames, which in turn focus more on how education governance in the broader sense may be restructured along neoliberal lines. The notion of neoliberal governmentality, then, provides a distinctly useful frame in its attention to how restructuring accomplishes changes in governance through the re-figuring of individuals as subjects of this change.

Varieties of Marx-inspired and Foucault-inspired theory and research have often been interpreted as too disparate to reconcile, although thinkers in fields such as cultural studies have attempted to bridge the divide; some examples of this type of endeavour will be discussed below. In this spirit, it is argued here that both Foucault's understanding of discourse as well as his explorations of governmental rationality or governmentality – and specifically neoliberal governmentality – provides a potential nexus with Marx-inspired lines of thinking wherein a fruitful link can be made toward exploring neoliberalism's effects upon education through restructuring processes. It will be argued here that both realms of theorizing and modes of analysis together provide for a powerful and integrative perspective on contemporary education policy shifts and changes.

It has often been noted, of course (including by himself), that Foucault's novel and influential theorizing – to a significant extent – emerged through a dialogue and struggle with many of Marx's ideas and foundational theories of capital and its role in the growth of western industrial societies. In the following oft-cited remark of Foucault's, he affirms his own critical interactions with Marx's framework as a core critic of economy and society:

> I often quote concepts, texts and phrases from Marx, but without feeling obliged to add the authenticating label of a footnote with a laudatory phrase to accompany the quotation. As long as one does that, one is regarded as someone who knows and reveres Marx, and will be suitably honoured in the so-called Marxist journals. But I quote Marx without saying so, without quotation marks, and because people are incapable of recognising Marx's texts I am thought to be someone who doesn't quote Marx. When a physicist writes a work of physics, does he feel it necessary to quote Newton and Einstein? (Foucault 1980, p. 52).

Nevertheless, Foucault emphasized an irreverent (in a positive, critical sense) approach to any foundational theory of system of ideas and always attempted to appraise and re-appraise thinkers by placing them in a critical historical and social context, tracing the genealogies of ideas and practices in a complex and detailed mode of analysis. Foucault's conception of discourse as power/knowledge represents this aim of fleshing out, rather than over-generalizing, modes of power and control in society. His idea of a 'principle of discontinuity', the idea that forms of power/knowledge in discourses can be both an "instrument of domination" and a "point of resistance", represents a significant attempt to describe relations of power as diffuse and heterogeneous in contemporary society (Foucault, 1983; in Ball, 1990, p. 2). Through his book-length explorations, he analyzed various social institutions and practices through these new lenses of thought, which have subsequently reverberated throughout the social sciences as a new critical tool in exploring modes of control and discipline in society.

Neoliberal governmentality importantly emphasizes the role of various discursive strategies – or "tactics", in Foucault's terms (Foucault, 1991, p. 95) – which form the instruments whereby individuals' social practices are regulated and shaped by neoliberal discourses and ideas. Lemke's recounting of Foucault's analysis of the German and U.S. neoliberal schools through this frame emphasizes this type of perspective:

> Foucault suggests that the key element in the Chicago School's approach is their consistent expansion of the economic form to apply to the social sphere, thus eliding any difference between the economy and the social. In the process, they transpose economic analytical schemata and criteria for economic decision making onto spheres which are not, or certainly not exclusively, economic areas, or indeed stand out for differing from any economic rationality. Whereas the *Ordo*-liberals in West Germany pursued the idea of governing society in the name of the economy, the U.S. neo-liberals attempt to re-define the social sphere as a form of the economic domain. The model of rational-economic action serves as a principle for justifying and limiting governmental action, in which context government itself becomes a sort of enterprise whose task it is to universalize competition and invent market-shaped systems of action for individuals, groups and institutions (Lemke, 2001, p. 197).

Seen in this way, neoliberal governmentality intersects well with an analytical mode of appreciating how various discursive (legal, policy document, etc.) instruments – and the individual agents that mediate them – are implicated in education restructuring processes that reflect neoliberal elements. It is also in this nexus of neoliberal governmentality that I propose a linkage between Foucault's complex and novel views and one of the core themes of Marx's view of political economy within a capitalist society. Marx's views of the expansionist tendencies of capitalism and the 'commodity form', touched upon in Chapter 1, are evident in this passage from the *Communist Manifesto:*

> The need of a constantly expanding market for its products chases the bourgeoisie over the whole surface of the globe. It must nestle everywhere, settle everywhere, establish connections everywhere. The bourgeoisie has through its exploitation of the world market given a cosmopolitan character to production and consumption in every country. To the great chagrin of reactionists, it has drawn from under the feet of industry the national ground on which it stood. All old-established national industries have been destroyed or are daily being destroyed. They are dislodged by new industries, whose introduction becomes a life and death question for all civilized nations, by industries that no longer work up indigenous raw material, but raw material drawn from the remotest zones; industries whose products are consumed, not only at home, but in every quarter of the globe. In place of the old wants, satisfied by the productions of the country, we find new wants, requiring for their satisfaction the products of distant lands and climes. In place of the old

local and national seclusion and self-sufficiency, we have intercourse in every direction, universal interdependence of nations. (Marx & Engels, in McLellan, 1977, p. 224).

Of course, particularly when viewed in broad relief, Marx's ideas or Marxism taken in any sense is not an unproblematic frame. I choose, for instance, to remain 'agnostic' on questions of 'historical necessity' in the progress of society in Marx's formulation. I also avoid the notion of 'false consciousness' as I wouldn't be prepared to claim what might be 'true'. The Marxist idea of the declining rate of profit in capitalism, though not necessarily appreciable as a 'lawlike' formulation, still has insight in appreciating reasons and dynamics of the neoliberal push or 'profit myopic' motive. This said, I still argue passionately for the legitimacy and insight of modes of analysis derived from Marx's critique of capitalism and accept the central lines of this critique of capitalist economies and societies as based on exploitation both of people and planet.

Alongside the neo-Marxist frames for analysis offered, I argue that neoliberal governmentality perspectives can be balanced with the more structural or material emphasis of Marx-inspired theoretical frameworks. On the one hand, governmentality leads one to consider how discourses operate to subjectify individuals into modes of self-governance according to neoliberal principles and conceptions of individuality, in a marketized, commodified context. On the other, neo-Marxist views lead one to consider the role of entrepreneurial and corporate/actors within political settings, acknowledging the fundamental goal of neoliberalism in transforming areas of the public sphere into commodified and privatized 'markets', as well as the actors who drive this agenda of accumulation. Connecting with the conception of neoliberalism offered above, both modes of analysis connect to the notion of the imperialistic and colonial aspects of neoliberalism offered above, as individuals and arrangements for public governance are both shifted toward discourses and modes of the market.

With respect to Foucault, where many writers view his thought as antithetical to frames of Marxist analysis, I instead view it as a significant extension and innovation of the Marxist notion of the class struggle, ideology and power relations. However, having argued that Foucault's notion of power/knowledge in discourses and his principle of discontinuity – coupled with his conception of neoliberal governmentality – are both useful as parts of a complementary analytical method for the purposes of this thesis, it is necessary to specify which parts of Foucault's conceptions I feel are not useful toward conceptualizing this framework. For while I have emphasized through this section a balancing perspective of the macro and micro processes of neoliberalism, I feel a simplistic reading of Foucault reduces the social dangerously and unnecessarily to the discursive. This reading is in accord with Smith's view of some of the vagaries of postmodern/post-structuralist thought (1999), as well as Fairclough's statement of reservation within his framework of critical discourse analysis (CDA):

> In tying ideology to social relations of power, I am alluding to asymmetrical relations of power, to domination. Foucault's work in particular has popularized a different understanding of power as a ubiquitous property of the technologies

which structure modern institutions, not possessed by or attached to any particular social class, stratum or group (Foucault, 1979). My concern is that this sense of power has displaced the former, more traditional one, and more importantly has helped divert attention from the analysis of power asymmetries and relations of domination. An important objective for critical analysis is the elision of power/domination in theory and analysis. (1995, p. 17).

A total 'relativizing' notion of power goes beyond Foucault's point about discourse as a form of power/knowledge, to claim an (early) Nietzschean reading of truth, which admits of a form of nihilism and incommensurability of views. Rather than take this radical step as a reading of Foucault, I choose to appropriate his characterization of discourse as embodying forms of power/knowledge as a useful way of characterizing neoliberalism's manifestation in texts and social practices as a socially-mediated construction of subjectivity. As the economic subject (Du Gay, 1997, 2000) is consistently named and formed in social settings, concomitant forms of subjectivity and individualistic/economically rational views of human nature are reified and enacted socially. These processes, facilitated by an atmosphere of hegemonic neoliberalism, are related to neoliberalism's facilitation of the same asymmetries of power relations that Fairclough mentions. For the purposes of this work, I propose an understanding of these relations with explicit reference to a Marx-inspired framework and critique of capitalism.

In this way, though recognizing how power/knowledge is named intersubjectively and socially in different ways at local levels, I recognize that these local manifestations are tied to a larger story and process of facilitating asymmetrical relations of ruling with capitalism. In this sense I employ Foucault's principle of discontinuity in understanding how locally and textually-mediated social encounters vary, but also move beyond it toward an understanding of neoliberalism as a marketizing macro-theme, directed toward facilitating the reproduction of asymmetrical social relations (macro-structures).

An example of an educational scholar who might disagree with this type of analytical synthesis might be Thomas Popkewitz. The blending of Marx-inspired frames of analysis into a theoretical approach for present purposes would likely fit into a scheme of theorizing and research which Popkewitz (1999) would characterize as "critical modernism" (p. 3), for him a pejorative label. His criticism has its roots in a conviction that Foucault's social thought represents an 'inversion' of Marx's – inasmuch as Marx posited the 'productive characteristics' of labour and Foucault, the 'productive characteristics' of discourse through forms of power/knowledge (Ball, 1990; Foucault, 1983, 1984). The discussion above emphasizing compatibility of these frameworks touches upon the criticism Popkewitz raises in this case. Instead of reading Foucault the way he does, as a negation or inversion of Marx, again I read Foucault as a significant extension and as a point of intersect with Marx's thought. The combination of a discursive perspective without the necessary transcendence of the usefulness of Marx-inspired critiques of capitalism with their materialistic basis, this balance, is what I term a 'material-discursive dialectic'.

UNIVERSITIES UNDER NEOLIBERAL DISCOURSE AND POLICY: THE RISE OF THE KNOWLEDGE ECONOMY

The demands of the knowledge economy, it would seem, fall significantly on the shoulders of universities. In a book with the telling title *Creating Knowledge, Strengthening Nations*, the editors in their introduction observe the following:

> The university is being repositioned in terms of its relationship to the state and industry because it is now viewed as a key player in a global economic system where new knowledge and highly skilled human resources are perceived as the fuel of economic development (Jones et al, 2005, p. 7).

Being accountable to the requirement to act as the "fuel of economic development" has meant universities adopting what is perceived as an inevitable shift to closer links to the market, and accountability to the needs of the knowledge economy both in the nominal terms of churning out skilled labour, as well as contributing to capital accumulation through technology transfer and the marketing of potentially profitable technologies and other forms of intellectual property.

There is a large body of literature that critically analyzes the impact of neoliberalism on the function and behaviour of universities as institutions, and individual faculty and administrators as individuals in advanced capitalist countries (Lynch, 2006; Levidow, 2005; Canaan & Shumar, 2008; Olssen & Peters, 2005; Giroux, 2007; Hayes & Wynward, 2002; Taylor et al, 1997; Sit, 2008). Literature looking at U.S., Canadian, and international contexts has looked at the expansion of 'enterprise culture' and the increasing market/business-oriented behaviours of universities and faculty, as well as the commodification of knowledge in the work of universities (Lewis, 2008; Slaughter & Leslie, 1997; Slaughter et al, 2004; Peters, 2001a; Smyth, 1999; Newson, 1998; Fisher & Atkinson-Grosjean, 2002; Torres & Schugurensky, 2002, Porter & Vidovich, 2000; Ibarra-Colado, 2007). Such trends are also referred to as 'corporatization' of education (Turk, 2000) or as the trend to 'managerialism' (Currie & Newson, 2000; Peters et al, 2000) in their effective attempt to incorporate neoliberal ideologies into education restructuring. These types of trends have seen increasing pressure from university administration and governments for institutions and faculty to behave along 'entrepreneurial' lines, emphasizing increased 'partnering' with the corporate private sector and reliance on private funding, with concomitant implications for privately-funded (and owned) research and intellectual property, particularly in disciplines and program areas that are 'close to market' in the knowledge economy, such as biotechnology, pharmaceuticals, computers, and other applied sciences (Etzkowitz & Leydesdorff, 1997; Bocking, 2006; Fisher & Atikinson-Grosjean, 2002; Gould, 2003; Lynskey, 2005; Vallas & Kleinman, 2007; Healy, 2008). Another branch of literature sees the trend to increasing commercialization of research and the pushing of universities 'to market' as a betrayal of core values of discovery-based research and traditional liberal education (e.g., Axelrod, 2002).

The impetus for restructuring has an economic base: the same atmosphere of significant federal funding cuts to the provinces (through the move to the Canada Health and Social Transfer in 1995[3]) which served as a precipitating factor for some of the trends mentioned above has also affected university finances in more broad strokes. For instance, universities and colleges across Canada have increasingly shifted the onus for operating finances onto students through increased tuition with average debt load increasing by more than 100% over the ten-year period starting in 1990 (Statistics Canada, 2003; Doherty-Delorme and Shaker, 2000). These types of shifts both in education and other social sectors have been described by proponents of restructuring at the global level as moves to demand-side financing, where the individual – framed as the consumer of goods or commodities in this context – is looked to as the financer of social services through increased user fees of various kinds (Patrinos & Ariasingam, 1997). In developing countries, demand-side financing initiatives and mechanisms have been touted by researchers within organizations such as the World Bank for their supposed effect of increasing equity in education systems. This type of logic has been challenged seriously on several fronts, including that of postsecondary education with respect to tuition and private universities (Schugurensky, 2000), where critics argue that underfunding and social polarization result from increased privatization and more demand-side financing in education systems.

A global backdrop to these movements and debates in educational restructuring policies and initiatives can be found in the move toward the formalized commodification of education through global, supranational processes. These debates are partly focused around international trade agreements such as the General Agreement on Trade in Services (GATS) of the World Trade Organization (WTO)[4], as well as complementary regional trade agreements which are currently seeking to legally enshrine rules governing trade in educational services, with higher education as a particular focus for action due to its perceived profitability relative to other educational levels (Grieshaber-Otto & Sanger, 2002; Sauvé, 2002; Robertson, Bonal, & Dale, 2002). As these agreements seek a binding global framework for encouraging the growth of private opportunities for providing education services, shifts in policy aimed at incorporating universities into the knowledge economy through various means and settings form the local foreground to this global backdrop in international trends affecting postsecondary education.

The rise of the discourse of the knowledge economy, with its emphasis on building national systems of innovation through improved research capacity and university-private sector partnerships particularly in academic disciplines that are close to the market, has been an effective tool in various governments' policy chests for working to reshape universities, academic work, and the culture of public universities. Since at the present time I am involved in an ethnographic study looking at active and retired faculty and administrators' perceptions of changes in their own work and institutions from 1980 to recent times, I await an interesting experience-derived portrait of what exactly some changes have been at three particular institutions under the rise of this discourse. Further, it is not my ambition – as stated at the outset – to embark on a deconstruction and genealogy of this term and its cognate conceptions ('information economy'/society, 'knowledge society'). There are others who have done good work in this regard, and I would recommend specifically Peters and Besley (2006) for a wonderful history of the concept and a careful placement of its role in neoliberal discourse. For the moment, however, it is useful to consider a more specific setting for the use of the term as emblematic of its common usage and meaning, and for this I go to outspoken institutions that have been protagonists pushing for neoliberal policy – in this case the OECD and World Bank. Again, in the following discussion of these organization's knowledge economy platforms I draw on the work of Peters and Besley (2006) who, among others, have done great work unpacking their particular use of the discourse. A few comments regarding the shape of the discursive terrain are warranted, however, pertaining to its use as a lever for public policymaking.

GLOBAL 'KNOWLEDGE ECONOMY' DISCOURSE, AND CANADIAN NEOLIBERAL GOVERNMENTALITY

The central proclamation accompanying knowledge economy discourse concerns the growing pre-eminence of knowledge over capital as a factor in capital accumulation. On the surface, this point is not a novel one: some kind of knowledge (if we accept the distinction of this term as "true', justified belief' as opposed to information or data) has always been implicit in any form of capital accumulation and the labour that supports it. This constitutes an interesting point of divergence for some knowledge economy enthusiasts who zealously gush over the new 'weightless economy'[5], where knowledge has somehow become disarticulated from labour[6]. In a critical paper that dissects some of the ambiguities and discourse surrounding talk of knowledge economies, Smith comments pointedly that the term is "At the outset, it must be said that there is no coherent definition, let alone theoretical concept, of this term: it is at best a widely-used metaphor, rather than a clear concept" and "rhetorically, rather than analytically useful" (2002, p. 5–7). Most commonly, intangible assets such as the internet, ICTs, patents, copyrights and all sorts of intellectual property, databases and media libraries, as well asbiotechnology are pointed to as constituting key parts of the knowledge economy. Labour, of course, as a form of capital, is implicit in all of these things, however this is where the rhetorical or metaphorical value of the term 'knowledge economy' comes to the fore. Its principal value seems to be employed as a discursive tool for steering policy change, when it is wielded to recommend as much as to describe changes in capitalist economies. Thus the dot-com boom of the 1990s saw an effervescence of the discourse, only to have it brought back down to earth, but not abandoned. Consonant with talk of a post-industrial economy and society, talk of the knowledge economy sought to both to describe and prescribe changes that accompany the flight of manufacturing interests predominantly to periphery countries, where surplus value from exploitation of labour could be most efficiently maximized (leading to the rise of China and India as global industrial centers), while centre corporations reaped increasing profits from consumer society's continued addiction to overconsumption and waste.

With respect to intellectual property and particularly biotechnology, writers such as Shiva (2001; 1997) have effectively laid bare the exploitive and imperialistic designs of corporations on parts of the natural commons – whether seeds, life forms or curatives – that have formed an integral part of the life of indigenous peoples and communities for millennia. The knowledge economy cannot, in fact, be uncoupled from the capitalist economy itself; thus my preference for viewing it as an extension or transformation of capitalist discourse.

The OECD waded forcefully into this discourse with its report *the Knowledge-Based Economy* (1996). The overarching definition of a 'knowledge-based economy' or 'knowledge economy' offered in this work is impossibly vacuous: "economies which are directly based on the production, distribution and use of knowledge and information" (OECD, 1996, p. 7). The lack of an intelligible definition (Smith, 2002), however, has not prevented the OECD's policy recommendations on the subject from carrying force. The OECD has recently published a two volume analysis of 'tertiary education for the knowledge society'. Under a heading of 'main challenges for tertiary education', and a sub-heading of 'steering tertiary education', the authors list several salient points to consider[7]:

> Articulating clearly the nation's expectations of the tertiary education system Aligning priorities of individual institutions with the nation's economic and social goals Creating coherent systems of tertiary education Finding the proper balance between governmental steering and institutional autonomy Developing institutional governance arrangements to respond to external expectations (OECD, 2008, p. 16).

These five points are paired with a subsequent table that details key 'policy directions', which includes another five points under the suggestive label 'steering tertiary education: setting the right course':

> Develop a coherent strategic vision for tertiary education Establish sound instruments for steering tertiary educationEnsure the coherence of the tertiary education system with extensive diversification

> Build system linkages Strengthen the ability of institutions to align with the national tertiary education strategy

> Build consensus over tertiary education policy (OECD, 2008. p. 17).

Finally, the following excerpt from the report captures well the sense of urgency attached to the 'tertiary education sector' for contributing to the health of the economy as a whole:

> A country's ability to generate and exploit knowledge is an increasingly crucial factor determining its economic development. While natural resources and cheaper labour used to form the basis of comparative advantages, innovations and the use of knowledge are becoming more important. Economic growth is increasingly based on knowledge accumulation. Knowledge-based intangibles such as training, research and development, or marketing account for about one-third of the investment of firms. Economies of scope, "derived from the ability to design and offer different products and services with the same technology" (Salmi, 2000), are an increasingly important driving force

for expansion. This is particularly true in the case of high-technology industries such as electronics, where economies of scope outweigh the importance of economies of scale (Salmi, 2000). Increasingly knowledge-based economies and the need to improve a country's international competitiveness put tertiary education systems under increasing pressure to contribute to economic growth (OECD, 2008, p. 53).[8]

The 'knowledge accumulation' described in a system of 'knowledge capitalism' that is vital to the wider success of the capitalist economy is a factor that is taken as a basis for the type of advocacy that the OECD puts forward in this case, concerning appropriate 'steering' of tertiary education to suit 'national social and economic objectives'. While the 'social' in that phrase is seen to play a part in the enumerating of demands for how tertiary education must make a contribution, economic objectives seem to occupy a discursive position of pre-eminence, given the central tenets of the knowledge economy and the profitable applications of core technologies that form its principal focus in the discourse, along with skilled 'knowledge labourers' who can contribute to the implementation and utilization of profitable technologies. Perhaps the final sentence of the excerpt above underscores best the neoliberal emphasis of this discourse: tertiary education systems are under pressure to "contribute to economic growth", that is, to be reconfigured as more active fuel for knowledge capitalism.

In this way a more discrete policy platform emerges, one that, while based in somewhat slippery yet effusive rhetoric, is in reality quite prescriptive. In a press release accompanying the release of the 2008 report from which the above excerpts are taken entitled "Be more purposeful in guiding tertiary education, OECD tells governments", the first mentioned recommendation centers on 'goals': "...Ensure that tertiary education contributes to economic and social objectives: foster links to employers, communities and labour markets; promote effective university-industry links for research and innovation." 'Innovation' is a term that runs synonymously with 'knowledge economy' in this context: universities are consistently exhorted to become partners in 'networks of innovation', helping to drive national competitiveness through their 'contributions'. Once this leap is worked out, the question of better university-industry linkages ('getting knowledge products to market') becomes a technical exercise.

Canada, particularly under the Federal Conservative governments led by Prime Minister Stephen Harper, has enthusiastically embraced the view of universities encapsulated in the vague cheerleading for the knowledge economy that is pervasive now in OECD discourse. In 2007, the Harper government released a report entitled 'Mobilizing Science and Technology to Canada's Advantage' that represents neoliberal knowledge economy discourse well for the Canadian context. In this document the government enumerates what the demands of universities should be to realize their potential to better contribute to the economy as per OECD vision. The strategy begins with three areas for 'advantage'

The Government of Canada will foster three distinct Canadian S&T advantages: an Entrepreneurial Advantage, a Knowledge Advantage, and a People Advantage:

- Canada must translate knowledge into commercial applications that generate wealth for Canadians and support the quality of life we all want in order to create an **Entrepreneurial Advantage**.
- Canadians must be positioned at the leading edge of the important developments that generate health, environmental, societal, and economic benefits in order to create a **Knowledge Advantage**.
- Canada must be a magnet for the highly skilled people we need to thrive in the modern global economy with the best-educated, most-skilled, and most flexible workforce in the world in order to create a **People Advantage**.
(Government of Canada, 2007, p. 11).

The first two categories relate directly to prescriptions and plans for 'steering' higher education more appropriately to realize the goal of 'mobilizing science and technology to Canada's advantage'. In a section immediately following this one, the report goes on to detail what the implications are for working toward these 'advantages' in terms of universities (italics added):

Promoting World-Class Excellence. The Government of Canada will ensure that its policies and programs inspire and assist Canadians to perform at world-class levels of scientific and technological excellence. *The government will foster an environment of healthy competition to ensure that funding-supports the best ideas.*

Focusing on Priorities. The Government of Canada will continue to play an important role in supporting basic research across a broad spectrum of science. *To enhance our success, we will also be more focused and strategic— targeting more basic and applied research in areas of strength and opportunity.*

Encouraging Partnerships. *The Government of Canada will support S&T collaborations involving the business, academic, and public sectors, at home and abroad. Partnerships are essential to lever Canadian efforts into worldclass successes and to accelerate the pace of discovery and commercialization in Canada.* Through partnerships, the unique capabilities, interests, and resources of various and varied stakeholders can be brought together to deliver better outcomes (Government of Canada, 2007, p. 11).

Of particular interest in this excerpt is the mention of "targeting more basic and applied research in areas of strength and opportunity". A few pages on, the report details some of these areas, enunciated as "Environmental science and technologies", "Natural resources and energy", "Health and related life sciences and technologies", and "Information and communications technologies" (Government of Canada, 2007, p. 13). These areas capture well the key focus areas of computer technology and biotechnology that are purportedly essential to the success of a knowledge economy. On page 16 the report credits the OECD as the sole international organization that has made a strong contribution in terms of "ideas" toward articulating recommendations. The phrases "success in the global economy" and "competing in the global economy" are used repeatedly, and are consistent threads through neoliberal discourse for education in Canada, having been wielded heavily by the

Harris and Eves governments in Ontario in the 1990s and ubiquitously, it seems, in public policy across the world as neoliberalism has marched on.

Ramping up the rhetoric somewhat, the report speaks of "fierce" competition in the global economy as a reason for 'stepping up' Canada's advantage in supporting the "best ideas": "In today's fiercely competitive global economy, merely being good is not good enough" (Government of Canada, 2007, p. 46). Will it be surprising to discover that the 'best ideas' are those that are most closely aligned with the objectives set out by the government, and attached to accountability and "steering" mechanisms that ensure that the most profitable and "valuable" research comes to market? The report goes on to look at potential mechanisms of accountability to ensure "value for money" (p. 47). Quite interestingly, some numbers are then crunched: $300 million is allocated for the traditional granting councils (which themselves have begun to be more aligned to knowledge economy interests and discourses, though this phenomenon is outside the scope of this paper), while $400 million is allocated to the Canadian Foundation for Innovation (CFI), a new agency that better embodies, one might say, the core principles at work in the push of the Harper government's science and technology strategy.

On the CFI's website, one can do a search of awarded grants at all Canadian universities[9]. I took the opportunity to look at a few institutions: Queen's being one, as this is the institution where I am housed presently, and I am undertaking my SSHRC-funded postdoctoral research here (mentioned previously). It is plain to see through searching the CFI's online database that the results one obtains concerning funded projects are in fact, aligned closely with the "areas of strength and opportunity" that the government targets, and that form (according to the OECD and others) the basis for a sound knowledge economy. This is an interesting twist, though: this 'targeted funding' mechanism outstrips allocations to the traditional granting councils, thus effectively prioritizing research that is aligned to national objectives and interests... fulfilling nicely the prescriptions of the OECD and their encouragement of governments to 'steer' higher education to fit national interests and objectives – particularly economic ones.

At this point it is interesting, and germane, to highlight two different responses to the government's clarion call for aligning universities to 'knowledge capitalism', in the context of working toward some criticism of this direction for higher education, and along with it some criticism of our government's goals and objectives. First, the Association of Faculties of Medicine of Canada (AFMC) had some interesting feedback, based on the need for balance, also voiced in strong language:

A balance must be struck between the funding of basic and applied research, both of which are essential in order to achieve the government's goals. While the latter is most obviously tied to the commercialization agenda, it cannot be forgotten that great discoveries and innovations also stem from investigator-driven, basic research. It is essential that as we increase the targeted nature of our research funding enterprise that we do not do so at our own peril (AFMC, 2007).

In medicine and pharmacology, the social consequences of marketization and the political and ethical implications of 'steering' the most profitable medicines to market are palpable, as evidenced by Canadian controversies in this area (Healy, 2008; Olivieri, 2000). Desirable social and economic objectives become conflated under a neoliberal imperative for the knowledge economy: what is 'good' for economic growth and profitability, is therefore 'good' for the people of Canada. However, there is no clear connection between these two assertions. Indeed, continuing the status quo of corporate-dominated pharmacological research helps perpetuate structures of inequity regarding access to, and development of medicines that are out of reach of the word's majority that may need critical medicines. If national objectives are myopically focused on economic criteria and benchmarks, any sense of how medicine ought to serve a public good is fundamentally blurred. I am not attempting to put words in the AFMC's collective mouth here, but rather making an observation that is consistent with their reaction.

We may contrast this note of sobriety with the rather more desperate and somewhat interesting reaction of the Canadian Federation of Humanities and Social Sciences (CFHSS). In their brief to 2008 pre-federal budget consultations, the CFHSS both embraced the discourse the government offered (along with its premises) and expressed dismay over the lack of attention given to social sciences and humanities in the government's 'strategy' for the knowledge economy:

> The government's 2007 "Mobilizing Science and Technology to Canada's Advantage" is the strategy by which funding decisions for research and post-secondary education in Canada are made. It is quite striking to note that the humanities and social sciences are largely unmentioned in the document. Yet, the strategy itself could not even begin to exist without the underpinning of various SSH disciplines. Our goal with this brief is to make this underpinning explicit. The social sciences and humanities have been compared in the past to the air around us: invisible, essential and so ubiquitous that we seldom stop to think about its importance, until it is removed. Investing in the humanities and social sciences is crucial to the success of the Science and Technology strategy, and to Canada's economy and social success. (CFHSS, 2008, p. 1).

Elsewhere the CFHSS notes that of $9.2 billion invested in postsecondary education since 1998, about 10% has gone to fund the social sciences and humanities (CFHSS, 2009). The title of the organization's brief to the pre-budget consultation is 'Mobilizing the Humanities and Social Sciences to Canada's Advantage'. In the conclusion of its brief, the CFHSS attempts again to reiterate and cloak itself in the government's assumptions and premises:

> The federal government has quite rightly recognized the advantages that can be created by encouraging an environment in which innovation can flourish. Canada's economic and social future relies as much on its human sciences as it does on its natural, engineering and health sciences. Success involves human potential and human excellence, and development of skills and knowledge founded in the humanities and social sciences is crucial for Canada's success. By investing in targeted research, the government has indicated

areas of research in need of immediate attention, and for which immediate return on investment is expected. To complement this strategy, we urge the government to champion basic research just as forcefully, as it forms the backbone of Canada's innovative potential in the future (CFHSS, 2008, p. 5).

The CFHSS' response is a good example of its implication in the neoliberal governmentality flowing from knowledge economy discourse in Canada. By voluntarily reacting in a way that reifies the hegemonic discourse and gives it legitimacy, the organization itself enacts a form of power/knowledge, in Foucault's terms, that is the discourse of neoliberalism and the knowledge economy as it applies to universities. Employing the language of this discourse to attempt to justify the role of humanities and social sciences comprises an effective form of governmentality, or governing at a distance. The discourse is fundamentally one-dimensional in that it subsumes all of the functions and goals of universities to those that contribute to the national [economic] interest, and aims to configure the place of universities in Canadian society in this light. Of course, the CFHSS is but one player in such an observable pattern; one need only look at the speeches of prominent university presidents such as Toronto's David Naylor exhorting change to fit into the knowledge economy (Naylor, 2008), for other salient examples. More insidiously, with declining shares of operating expenditures from provincial and federal governments, universities have responded consistently in policy terms by attempting to burden students more with the 'cost-sharing' that the OECD readily recommends as a sustainable financing mechanism for the tertiary education sector, along with compliant and cheerleading neoliberal think tanks in Canada, such as the C.D Howe institute (Laidler, 2002). Declining shares of such expenditures also privileges external research funding, leading to increased entrepreneurialism and competition among faculty of increasingly scarce and targeted funding. At the same time, the knowledge that is the stock-and-trade of academics is increasingly subject to market forces and pressures, with the most prestigious journals operating on capitalist bases, subscriptions and publication prices outrageous and inaccessible to most.Faculty are increasingly viewed as microeconomic fuel into knowledge capitalism where universities are macroeconomic fuel: our work constantly reiterated as 'intellectual property' and our contributions as 'knowledge products' and com-modities, further reifying the neoliberal discourse for education.

In these ways, Foucault's observation that knowledge and discourse come to play as important a role as capital in the exercise of power are prescient:

We live in a social universe in which the formation, circulation, and utilization of knowledge presents a fundamental problem. If the accumulation of capital has been an essential feature of our society, the accumulation of knowledge has not been any less so. Now, the exercise, production, and accumulation of this knowledge cannot be dissociated from the mechanisms of power [...] (Foucault, 1991, p. 165).

As touched upon above, I would characterize the two poles (knowledge/capital, discursive/material) as in a dialectic, reinforcing one another in reproducing the still-ascendant neoliberal hegemony in social and economic policy. In Canada's case, through a compliant and enthusiastic federal government under Harper, increased pressure is actively sought to bear upon universities to be accountable for the national economic interests that would see only the 'best' (read 'most profitable') ideas brought to market as quickly as possible, thus positioning Canada to 'better compete in the global economy'. Canadian universities under knowledge capitalism are beholden to the wishes of industry as interpreted by government, illustrating well Schugurensky's idea of 'heteronomy' (2002; 1999).

CONCLUSIONS

Many have observed the trend of the growing direction of universities by external, marked-tied agendas and bemoaned the erosion of the notion of the university as a place for the public good, accessible to all on the basis of merit. In the disciplines that are closest to market, criticism has centered on the drift toward allowing the market to shape research priorities to an unprecedented and disturbing degree. The shift to academic capitalism has been swift, and substantial. Those of us not close to market continue to bear a disproportionate burden of the efficiency-related restructuring and funding cuts that aim to whittle down university work until the 'best ideas' remain.

Critical reaction has been equally swift and substantial. Axelrod's characterization of the current political economy and tensions within universities as a 'clash of values' is an interesting one (2002). The vision of a comprehensive research university rooted in the foundation of a liberal education, beset by the demands of the global marketplace has been proffered as a means for understanding current trends. Perhaps reality is somewhat more complex in the Foucauldian sense; many university administrations and some faculty have in fact embraced the drift toward market, and its concomitant displacing of financial burdens further onto students, with privatization and 'steering' further introduced into financing mechanisms for research. Lewis (2008) as well as Sit (2008) observe that taken together, the neoliberal imperative for Canadian universities constitutes an attempt to reconfigure universities and the work done in them as a set of private goods, rather than the public goods we have assumed them to be. This type of mission is consistent with neoliberalism in general: the shaping of society after the market, as a marketplace of private competitors vying for private goods, for private gain.

The purpose of universities in this type of framework is clear, and captured well in the Harper government's strategy paper: they are, first and most importantly, contributors to economic growth. There is a vision, albeit a shallow, economically reductionist vision, of responsibility for the university embodied in the neoliberal knowledge economy discourse. The responsibility of universities under this discourse is to fuel knowledge capitalism, to contribute to national success, to better position Canadian capitalism on the global capitalist stage. What other visions of responsibility can we bring to the table to compete with this vision? By acting as a forum where competing truth claims and forms of knowledge are debated, questioned, and innovated, universities can fulfill a responsibility to society to act as crucibles of democracy – without question, reflection, innovation and critique societies are stagnant, ossified. Universities can offer the hope of renewal and a vision that extends beyond the status quo and to new horizons. Just what new horizons lay in store is always up for debate. To this end, it is vitally necessary that the full range of standpoints be given a chance to be nurtured and encouraged toward allowing the chance for deliberation, choice and democracy to flourish.

Rather than acquiesce to the continuing transformation of universities into the fuel for knowledge capitalism, we can explore different ways to do academic work that are not subject to the market and its demands. Calls for forms and practices of 'knowledge socialism' of various kinds – open access publishing, public databases and knowledge sharing – have begun to emerge recently to be juxtaposed against the imperatives of neoliberalism for universities and scholarly work. As faculty and students, we have the choice to resist these types of transformations and work to enunciate our own view and alternatives of what universities should be, and who they should be accountable to. Will universities fulfil the term that Weber ascribed to parts of them as 'state capitalist enterprises' (Weber, 1946), functional apparatuses within the wider capitalist system, or will they be something else? As global capitalism turns to the universities and attempts to pressure them to become molded to suit the purposes of capital accumulation, counter-hegemonic initiatives such as the World Education Forum[10] attempt to push in the opposite direction, affirming universities as vital parts of the social (or civil) commons (McMurtry, 1999), spaces that ought not be subject to the whims of capitalism or transmuted into forms of private property and private goods. These types of deep questions have the power to create spaces for questioning about just what kind of economy we want, and strategies about how to subject our economies to democratic scrutiny, toward making our societies socially and ecologically sustainable and equitable. But of course, these tasks and responsibilities cannot lie at the feet of universities per se, but with the people that constitute them, and with the people in general.

NOTES

[1] While this work is dedicated to an elucidation of the thesis' working conception of neoliberalism, references to Marx, as well as 'Marxism' and 'neo-Marxism' will resurface throughout the subsequent discussion, as well as in analytical sections of the thesis. For the purposes of this work, 'Marx-inspired' denotes a general reference relating to strands of thought and research drawing upon Marx's work as a core term of reference in some way. This type of working definition encompasses both 'Marxism' and 'neo-Marxism'. In contemporary scholarship, both of these latter terms are frequently used to denote scholarly work that draws upon aspects of Marx's thought, while not necessarily attempting to ascribe validity to his work taken as a whole. With this point in mind, this thesis pinpoints 'Marxism' as referring to contemporary work that draws upon aspects of Marx's theories and interpretations for use in contemporary research, while 'neo-Marxism' is understood here as representing contemporary work that also draws upon such aspects, but also adapts and expands aspects of Marx's thought, as well as inventing new strands of theory that relate to, but do not directly 'reproduce', the thrusts of Marx's original theorizing. Leonardo (2004) documents these differences in educational research by juxtaposing 'orthodox' Marxist educational research ('Marxism', e.g. in the work of Bowles and Gintis, 1976) with neo-Marxist lines of such research, represented in the work of scholars such as Bourdieu (Bourdieu & Passeron, 1990).

[2]   John McMurtry (1998) takes a related position with respect to conflicting conceptions of 'freedom' in capitalist society.

[3]   These federal transfer cuts to the provinces, estimated at approximately $5 billion by 1995, are discussed both by Fisher & Rubenson (2000), as well as the Canadian Association of University Teachers (CAUT, 1999).

[4]   The GATS is currently being negotiated by WTO member countries and is due to be ratified by 2005, although the process has encountered significant setbacks as recent rounds of WTO negotiations have been cut short due to several factors.

[5]   See Quah's writings on the topic: http://econ.lse.ac.uk/~dquah/tweirl0.html

[6]   In a critical sense, finance capital has become increasingly disarticulated from the productive economy, though it still rests on it; a fact well attested to in the ongoing global capitalist crisis underway as I write in January 2009.

[7]   The two tables from which these points are excerpted can be found at the end of this paper at 'Appendix 2'.

[8]   The author cited in this excerpt, Jamil Salmi (Salmi 2000; 2009), is, according to his website description, "coordinator of the World Bank's network of tertiary education professionals" (this World Bank page can be found easily through an internet search). World Bank discourse regarding tertiary education is closely aligned with the OECD's, particularly in the Bank's recent enthusiasm around the potential of 'knowledge-economy'-oriented universities in sub-Saharan Africa; enthusiasm which needs tempering from the Bank's long history of structurally disempowering meaningful development in that part of the world (Bond, 2006). Proper critical treatment of World Bank discourse requires a separate paper. For his part, Salmi employs strikingly similar discourse to the OECD's in a 2007 paper entitled 'the challenge of establishing world-class universities':
Preoccupations about university rankings reflect the general recognition that economic growth and global competitiveness are increasingly driven by knowledge, and that universities can play a key role in that context. Indeed, rapid advances in science and technology across a wide range of areas from information and communication technologies (ICTs) to biotechnology to new materials provide great potential for countries to accelerate and strengthen their economic development. The application of knowledge results in more efficient ways of producing goods and services and delivering them more effectively and at lower costs to a greater number of people (Salmi, 2007, p. 1).

[9]   http://www2.innovation.ca/pls/fci/fcienrep.base

[10]   http://www.forummundialeducacao.org/article265.html

REFERENCES

Association of Faculties of Medicine of Canada (AFMC). (2007). *Mobilizing science and technology to Canada's advantage: A response by the association of faculties of medicine of Canada*. Ottawa, ON: The Author. Retrieved January, 2009, from http://www.afmc.ca/pdf/pdf_2007_st_release_en.pdf

Axelrod, P. (2002). *Values in conflict: The University, the marketplace, and the trials of liberal education*. McGill-Queen's University Press.

Ball, S. (1990). Introducing monsieur Foucault. In S. Ball (Ed.), *Foucault and education: Disciplines and knowledge*. London: Routledge.

Bocking, S. (2006). Big business on campus. *Alternatives Journal, 32*(2), 28.

Bourdieu, P., & Passeron, J.-C. (1990). *Reproduction*. London: Sage.

Bowles, S., & Gintis, H. (1976). *Schooling in capitalist America: Educational reform and the contradictions of economic life*. New York: Basic Books.

Buchanan, J. M., & Tullock, G. (1962). *The calculus of consent: Logical foundations of constitutional democracy*. University of Michigan Press.

Becker, G. (1964). *Human capital; A theoretical and empirical analysis, with special reference to education*. New York: National Bureau of Economic Research/Columbia University Press.

Bratich, J., Packer, J., & McCarthy, C. (2003). Governing the present. In J. Bratich, J. Packer, & C. McCarthy (Eds.), *Foucault, cultural studies, and governmentality* (pp. 3–21). Albany, NY: SUNY Press.

Canaan, J., & Shumar, W. (Eds.). (2008). *Structure and agency in the neoliberal university.* New York: Routledge.

Canadian Council for International Co-Operation (CCIC). (2001). *Putting poverty on the trade agenda.* Ottawa, ON: Canadian Council for International Co-Operation.

Golfman, N. (2008). *Brief to the house of commons standing committee on finance: Mobilizing the humanities and social sciences to Canada's advantage.* Ottawa, ON: Canadian Federation of Humanities and Social Sciences. Retrieved January 2009, from http://www.fedcan.ca/english/pdf/publications/FinanceBrief2008_E.pdf

Doherty-Delorme, D., & Shaker, E. (2000). What should we spend on education? Highlights from the Year 2000 Alternative Federal Budget and the Ontario Alternative Budget. Retrieved January 2009, from http://www.policyalternatives.ca/eduproj/ososaltbudgets.html

Canadian Federation of Humanities and Social Sciences (CFHSS). (2009). *Research funding.* Retrieved January 2009, from http://www.fedcan.ca/english/advocacy/funding/

Drucker, P. (1969). *The age of discontinuity: Guidelines to our changing society.* New York: Harper & Row.

Drucker, P. (1998). From capitalism to knowledge society. In D. Neef (Ed.), *The knowledge economy.* Woburn, MA: Butterworth.

Du Gay, P. (2000). Representing 'globalization': Notes on the discursive orderings of economic life. In P. Gilroy, L. Grossberg, & A. McRobbie (Eds.), *Without guarantees: In honour of Stuart Hall.* London and New York: Verso.

Du Gay, P. (1997). Organizing identity: Making people up at work. In P. Du Gay (Ed.), *Production of culture/cultures of production.* London: Sage.

Etzkowitz, H., & Leydesdorff, L. A. (Eds.). (1997). *Universities and the global knowledge economy: A triple helix of university-industry-government relations.* London: Pinter.

Fairclough, N. (1995). *Critical discourse analysis: The critical study of language.* London and New York: Longman.

Fisher, D., & Atkinson-Grosjean, J. (2002). Brokers on the boundary: Academy-industry liaison in Canadian universities. *Higher Education, 44,* 449–467.

Fisher, D., & Rubenson, K. (2000). The changing political economy: The private and public lives of Canadian universities. In J. Currie & J. Newson (Eds.), *Universities and globalization: Critical perspectives* (pp. 77–98). London: Sage.

Friedman, M. (1963). *Capitalism and freedom.* Chicago: University of Chicago Press.

Friedrich, C. (1955). The political thought of neo-liberalism. *The American Political Science Review, 49*(2), 509–525.

Foucault, M. (1991). Governmentality. In G. Burchell, C. Gordon, & P. Miller (Eds.), *The Foucault effect: Studies in governmental rationality* (pp. 87–104). London: Harvester Wheatsheaf.

Foucault, M. (1983). The subject and power. In L. Dreyfus & P. Rainbow (Eds.), *Michel Foucault: Beyond structuralism and hermeneutics.* Chicago: University of Chicago Press.

Foucault, M. (1980). *Power/knowledge: Selected interviews and other writings 1972–1977* (C. Gordon, Ed.). Brighton, Brighton and Hove: Harvester.

George, S. (1999). *A short history of neoliberalism.* Paper presented at the conference on Economic Sovereignty in a Globalising World. Retrieved September, 2003 from http://www.globalpolicy.org/globaliz/econ/histneol.htm

Giroux, H. A. (2007). *The university in chains: Confronting the military-industrial-academic complex.* Boulder, CO: Paradigm Publishers.

Gordon, C. (1991). Governmental rationality: An introduction. In G. Burchell, C. Gordon, & P. Miller (Eds.), *The Foucault effect: Studies in governmental rationality* (pp. 1–52). London: Harvester Wheatsheaf.

Gould, E. (2003). *The university in a corporate culture*. New Haven, CT: Yale University Press.

Government of Canada. (2007). *Mobilizing science and technology to Canada's advantage*. Ottawa, ON: Industry Canada.

Grieshaber-Otto, J., & Sanger, M. (2002). *Perilous lessons: The impact of the WTO services agreement (GATS) on Canada's public education system*. Ottawa, ON: Canadian Centre for Policy Alternatives.

Harvey, D. (2005). *A brief history of neoliberalism*. Oxford, UK: University Press.

Hayes, D., & Wynyard, R. (2002). *The McDonaldization of higher education*. Westport, CT: Bergin & Garvey.

Healy, D. (2008). Academic stalking and brand fascism. In J. Turk (Ed.), *Universities in crisis: How politics, special interests and corporatization threaten academic integrity*. Toronto, ON: Lorimer.

Ibarra-Colado, E. (2007). Future University in present times: Autonomy, governance and the entrepreneurial university. *Management Revue, 18*(2), 117.

Jones, G. A., McCarney, P. L., & Skolnik, M. L. (2005). Introduction. In The Authors (Eds.), *Creating knowledge, strengthening nations: The changing role of higher education*. Toronto, ON: University of Toronto Press.

Laidler, D. (Ed.). (2002). *Renovating the Ivory Tower: Canadian universities and the knowledge economy*. Toronto, ON: CD Howe Institute.

Lemke, T. (2001). 'The birth of bio-politics': Michel Foucault's lecture at the Collège de France on neo-liberal governmentality. *Economy and Society, 30*(2), 190–207.

Lemke, T. (2000, September 21–24). *Foucault, governmentality, and critique*. Paper presented at the Rethinking Marxism Conference, University of Amherst (MA).

Leonardo, Z. (2004). The unhappy marriage between Marxism and race critique: Political economy and the production of racialized knowledge. *Policy Futures in Education, 2*(3/4).

Levidow, L. (2000). Marketizing higher education: Neoliberal strategies and counter-strategies. *Cultural Logic, 4*(1).

Lewis, M. (2008). Public good or private value. In J. Canaan & W. Shumar (Eds.), *Structure and agency in the neoliberal university*. New York: Routledge.

Lynch, K. (2006). Neo-liberalism and marketisation: The implications for higher education. *European Educational Research Journal, 5*(1), 1–17.

Lynskey, M. (2005). Editorial: Moving beyond metaphors: University-industry collaboration in biotechnology. *Journal of Commercial Biotechnology, 11*(4), 301.

Marcuse, H. (1968). *One-dimensional man*. Boston, MA: Beacon.

McCarthy, C. (1998). Chapter four: Contradictions of experience: Race, power, and inequality in schooling. In The Author (Ed.), *The uses of culture: Education and the limits of ethnic affiliation*. New York: Routledge.

McCarthy, C., & Dimitriadis, G. (2000). Governmentality and the sociology of education: Media, educational policy and the politics of resentment. *British Journal of Sociology of Education, 21*(2), 169–185.

McLaren, P., & Farahmandpur, R. (2002). Breaking signifying chains: A Marxist position on postmodernism. In D. Hill, P. McLaren, M. Cole, & G. Rikowski (Eds.), *Marxism against postmodernism in educational theory* (pp. 35–66). Lanham, MD: Lexington.

McLellan, D. (1977). *Karl Marx: Selected writings*. Oxford, UK: Oxford University Press.

McMurtry, J. (1999). *The cancer stage of capitalism*. London: Pluto.

Morley, D., & Kuan-Hsing, C. (1996). Introduction. In D. Morley & C. Kuan-Hsing (Eds.), *Stuart Hall: Critical dialogues in cultural studies*. London: Routledge.

Naylor, D. (2008, July 24). Building an economy based on innovation. *The Globe and Mail*, A.15.

Newson, J. (1998). The corporate-linked university: From social project to market force. *Canadian Journal of Communication, 23*(1), 107–124.

Olivieri, N. (2000). When money and truth collide. In J. Turk (Ed.), *The corporate campus: commercialization and the dangers to Canada's colleges and universities* (pp. 53–62). Toronto, ON: Lorimer.

Olssen, M., & Peters, M. (2005). Neoliberalism, higher education and the knowledge economy: From the free market to knowledge capitalism. *Journal of Education Policy, 20*(3), 313–345.

Pannu, R. S. (1996). Neoliberal project of globalization: Prospects for democratization of education. *The Alberta Journal of Educational Research, 62*(2), 87–101.

Peters, M. (2001a). Education, enterprise culture and the entrepreneurial self: A Foucauldian perspective. *Journal of Educational Enquiry, 2*(2), 58–71.

Peters, M. (2001b). *Poststructuralism, Marxism, and neoliberalism: Between theory and politics.* Lanham, MD: Rowman & Littlefield.

Peters, M. (2001b). Neoliberalism. In *The Internet Encyclopaedia of Philosophy of Education.* Retrieved January 2009, from, http://www.ffst.hr/ENCYCLOPAEDIA/doku.php?id=neoliberalism

Peters, M., & Besley, A. C. (2006). *Building knowledge cultures: Education and development in the age of knowledge capitalism.* Lanham, MD: Rowman & Littlefield.

Peters, M., Marshall, J., & Fitzsimmons, P. (2000). Managerialism and educational policy in a global context: Foucault, neoliberalism, and the doctrine of self-management. In N. Burbules & C. Torres (Eds.), *Globalization and education: Critical perspectives* (pp. 109–132). New York: Routledge.

Polanyi, K. (1957). *The great transformation.* Boston, MA: Beacon.

Popkewitz, T. (1999). Introduction. In T. Popkewitz & L. Fendler (Eds.), *Critical theories in education: Changing terrains of knowledge and politics.* London: Routledge.

Porter, P., & Vidovich, L. (2000). Globalization and higher education policy. *Educational Theory, 50*(4), 449–465.

Rikowski, G. (2002). Prelude: Marxist educational theory after postmodernism. In D. Hill, P. McLaren, M. Cole, & G. Rikowski (Eds.), *Marxism against postmodernism in educational theory* (pp. 15–32). Lanham, MD: Lexington.

Robertson, S., Bonal, X., & Dale, R. (2002). GATS and the education service industry: The politics of scale and global re-territorialization. *Comparative Education Review, 46*(3), 472–496.

Salmi, J. (2009). *World class universities. Directions in development series.* Washington, DC: The World Bank.

Salmi, J. (2000). *Tertiary education in the twenty-first century: Challenges and opportunities.* LCSHD Paper Series, the World Bank, Washington.

Sauvé, P. (2002). *Trade, education and the GATS: What's in, what's out, what's all the fuss about?* Paper presented to the OECD/U.S. Forum on Trade in Educational Services, May 23–24. Retrieved September 2002, from http://www.oecd.org/pdf/M00029000/M00029613.pdf

Schugurensky, D., & Davidson-Harden, A. (2003). From Cordoba to Washington: WTO/GATS and Latin American education. *Globalisation, Societies & Education, 1*(3).

Schugurensky, D. (2000). Syncretic discourses, hegemony building and educational reform. *Education and Society, 18*(2), 75–94.

Schugurensky, D. (1999). Higher education restructuring in the era of globalization: Towards a heteronomous model? In R. Arnove & C. A. Torres (Eds.), *Comparative education: The dialectic of the global and the local* (pp. 283–304). Lanham, MD: Rowman and Littlefield.

Shiva, V. (1997). *Biopiracy : The plunder of nature and knowledge.* Toronto, ON: Between The Lines.

Shiva, V. (2001). *Protect or plunder?: Understanding intellectual property rights.* London: Zed.

Sit, V. (2008). The erosion of the university as a public sphere. *Education Canada,* fall issue.

Slaughter, S., Archerd, C. J., & Campbell, T. I. D. (2004). Boundaries and quandaries: How professors negotiate market relations. *Review of Higher Education, 28*(1), 129–165.

Slaughter, S. (2000). National higher education policies in a global economy. In J. Currie & J. Newson (Eds.), *Universities and globalization: Critical perspectives* (pp. 45–70). London: Sage.

Slaughter, S., & Leslie, L. (1997). *Academic capitalism: Politics, policies and the entrepreneurial university.* Baltimore: John Hopkins University Press.

Smith, D. (1999). *Writing the social: Critique, theory and investigations*. Toronto, ON: University of Toronto Press.

Smith, D. (1990). *The conceptual practices of power: A feminist sociology*. Toronto, ON: The University of Toronto Press.

Smith, K. (2002). *What is the 'knowledge economy'? Knowledge intensive industries and distributed knowledge bases*. United Nations University/UN Institute for New Technologies discussion paper. Retrieved January 2009, from http://www.intech.unu.edu/publications/discussion-papers/2002-6.pdf

Statistics Canada. (2003, August 12). University Tuition Fees. *The Daily*.

Taylor, S., Rizvi, F., Lingard, B., & Henry, M. (1997). *Educational policy and the politics of change*. London: Routledge.

Teeple, G. (2000). *Globalization and the decline of social reform*. Aurora: Garamond.

Turk, J. (Ed.). (2000). *The corporate campus: Commercialization and the dangers to Canada's colleges and universities*. Toronto, ON: Lorimer.

Vallas, S., & Kleinman, D. (2008). Contradiction, convergence and the knowledge economy: The confluence of academic and commercial biotechnology. *Socio—Economic Review, 6*(2), 283.

Weber, M. (1946). Science as a vocation. In H. Gerth & C. Mills (Eds.), *From Max Weber: Essays in sociology* (pp. 129–156). New York: Oxford University Press.

APPENDIX 1: Table 1 from peters, 2001b on Neoliberal Governmentality (peters, 2001b, pp. 21–22)

Table 1 Elements of Neoliberal Governmentality

1. **Classical liberalism as a *critique of state reason*.** A political doctrine concerning the self-limiting state where the limits of government are understood to be related to the limits of state reason (i.e., its power to know) thus becoming a permanent critique of the activity of rule and government.

2. ***Natural* versus *contrived* forms of the market.** Hayek's notion of natural laws based on spontaneously ordered institutions in the physical (crystals, galaxies) and social (morality, language, market) worlds has been replaced with an emphasis on the market as an artifact or culturally derived form and (growing out of the catallaxy approach) a *constitutional* perspective that focuses on the judicio-legal rules governing the framework within which the game of enterprise is played.

3. **The politics-as-exchange innovation of Public Choice theory ("the marketization of the state").** The extension of Hayek's spontaneous order conception (catallactics) of the institution of the market beyond simple exchange to complex exchange and finally to *all processes of voluntary agreement* among persons.

4. **The relation between government and self-government.** Liberalism as a doctrine that positively requires that individuals be free in order to govern. Government is, therefore, conceived as the community of free, autonomous, self-regulating individuals. It is a form of government that leads to the "responsibilization" of individuals as moral agents based upon the neoliberal revival of *homo economicus* (premised on assumptions of individuality, rationality, and self-interest) as an all-embracing redescription of the social as a form of the economic.

5. **A new relation between government and management.** The rise of the new managerialism and so-called "New Public Management" that enacts the shift from *policy* and *administration* to *management*, with the emulation of private sector management styles, the emphasis on "freedom to manage," and the promotion of "self-managing" (i.e., quasi-autonomous) individuals and entities.

6. **A "degovernmentalization" of the state (considered as a positive technique of government).** Government takes place "through" the market, including promotion of consumer-driven forms of social provision (health, education, welfare) involving "contracting out," the development of quasi-markets for public services and privatization.

7. **The promotion of a new relationship between government and knowledge.** "Government at a distance" developed through relations of forms of expertise (expert systems) and politics, accompanied by the development of new forms of social accounting that are responsible for an *actuarial rationality*. Referendums and intensive opinion polling have been made possible through the new information and computing technologies, and there is privatization and individualization of "risk management," together with the development of new forms of prudentialism.

8. **An economic theory of democracy ("the marketization of democracy").** There is an emerging structural parallel between economic and political systems—political parties have become entrepreneurs in a vote-seeking political marketplace, professional media consultants use policies to sell candidates as image products, voters have become passive individual consumers. In short, democracy has become commodified at the cost of the project of political liberalism, and the state has become subordinated to the market.

9. **The replacement of "community" for "the social."** The decentralization, "devolution," and delegation of power/authority/responsibility from the center to the region,

the local institution, and the "community," with the development of new forms of "social capital" and a greater interpenetration of public and private spheres.

10. **Cultural reconstruction as deliberate policy goal ("the marketization of 'the social' ").** The development of an "enterprise society" as a deliberate policy goal involving the privatization of the public sector, the development of quasi-markets, marketization of education and health, and an emphasis on a national curriculum of competition and enterprise.

11. **Low ecological consciousness.** The emerging concept of "green capitalism" and "green consumerism" accompanied by a linear as opposed to an ecological modernization. Also evidenced in "no limits to growth" and the adoption of market solutions to ecological problems.

12. **Promotion of the neoliberal paradigm of globalization.** World economic integration promoted by the International Monetary Fund (IMF), World Bank (WB), and World Trade Organization (WTO) based on a concept of "free trade" and enacted in regional and international trade agreements that place no regulatory controls on global capital.

Appendix 2: Excerpted tables from *Tertiary education for the knowledge society*

16 – EXECUTIVE SUMMARY

Table 1. Main challenges in tertiary education

Domain	Main challenges
Steering tertiary education	Articulating clearly the nation's expectations of the tertiary education system
	Aligning priorities of individual institutions with the nation's economic and social goals
	Creating coherent systems of tertiary education
	Finding the proper balance between governmental steering and institutional autonomy
	Developing institutional governance arrangements to respond to external expectations
Funding tertiary education	Ensuring the long-term financial sustainability of tertiary education
	Devising a funding strategy consistent with the goals of the tertiary education system
	Using public funds efficiently
Quality of tertiary education	Developing quality assurance mechanisms for accountability and improvement
	Generating a culture of quality and transparency
	Adapting quality assurance to diversity of offerings
Equity in tertiary education	Ensuring equality of opportunities
	Devising cost-sharing arrangements which do not harm equity of access
	Improving the participation of the least represented groups
The role of tertiary education in research and innovation	Fostering research excellence and its relevance
	Building links with other research organisations, the private sector and industry
	Improving the ability of tertiary education to disseminate the knowledge it creates
The academic career	Ensuring an adequate supply of academics
	Increasing flexibility in the management of human resources
	Helping academics to cope with the new demands
Links with the labour market	Including labour market perspectives and actors in tertiary education policy
	Ensuring the responsiveness of institutions to graduate labour market outcomes
	Providing study opportunities for flexible, work-oriented study
Internationalisation of tertiary education	Designing a comprehensive internationalisation strategy in accordance with country's needs
	Ensuring quality across borders
	Enhancing the international comparability of tertiary education

Table 2. Main Policy Directions

Policy Objective	Main policy directions
Steering tertiary education: setting the right course	Develop a coherent strategic vision for tertiary education
	Establish sound instruments for steering tertiary education
	Ensure the coherence of the tertiary education system with extensive diversification
	Build system linkages
	Strengthen the ability of institutions to align with the national tertiary education strategy
	Build consensus over tertiary education policy
Matching funding strategies with national priorities	Develop a funding strategy that facilitates the contribution of the tertiary system to society and the economy
	Use cost-sharing between the State and students as the principle to shape the funding of tertiary education
	Publicly subsidise tertiary programmes in relation to the benefits they bring to society
	Make institutional funding for instruction formula-driven, related to both input and output indicators and including strategically targeted components
	Improve cost-effectiveness
	Back the overall funding approach with a comprehensive student support system
Assuring and improving quality	Design a quality assurance framework consistent with the goals of tertiary education
	Develop a strong quality culture in the system and put more stress on internal quality assurance mechanisms
	Commit external quality assurance to an advisory role as the system gains maturity but retain strong external components in certain contexts
	Align quality assurance processes to the particular profile of TEIs
	Avoid fragmentation of the quality assurance organisational structure
Achieving Equity	Assess extent and origin of equity issues
	Strengthen the integration of planning between secondary and tertiary education systems
	Consider positive discrimination policies for particular groups whose prior educational disadvantage is well identified
	Provide incentives for TEIs to widen participation and provide extra support for students from disadvantaged backgrounds
Enhancing the role of tertiary education in research and innovation	Improve knowledge diffusion rather than strengthening commercialisation via stronger IPRs
	Improve and widen channels of interaction and encourage inter-institutional collaboration
	Use the tertiary education sector to foster the internationalisation of R&D
	Broaden the criteria used in research assessments
	Ensure the shift towards project-based funding is monitored and provide a mix of funding mechanisms
Academic career: adapting to change	Give institutions ample autonomy over the management of human resources
	Reconcile academic freedom with institutions' contributions to society
	Improve the entrance conditions of young academics
	Develop mechanisms to support the work of academics
Strengthening ties with the labour market	Coordinate labour market and education policies
	Improve data and analysis about graduate labour market outcomes
	Strengthen career services at secondary and tertiary educational levels
	Enhance provision with a labour market orientation
	Include labour market perspectives and actors in policy development and institutional governance
Shaping internationalisation strategies in the national context	Develop a national strategy and comprehensive policy framework for internationalisation
	Improve national policy coordination
	Encourage TEIs to become proactive actors of internationalisation
	Create structures to promote the national tertiary education system
	Develop on-campus internationalisation
Implementing tertiary education policy	Establish ad-hoc independent committees to initiate tertiary education reforms and involve stakeholders
	Allow for bottom-up policy initiatives to be developed into proposals by independent committees
	Recognise the different views of stakeholders through iterative policy development
	Favour incremental reforms over comprehensive overhauls unless there is wide public support for change

Adam Davidson-Harden
Queen's University
Canada

BERNADETTE BAKER

17. GOVERNING THE INVISIBLE: PSYCHICAL
SCIENCE AND CONDITIONS OF PROOF

Theoretico-experimental sciences are distinguished by the practice of making their version of "reason" depend on the power to "give reasons" for or to explain phenomena. This version of reason thus presumes the power of predicting outcomes, of controlling in order to replicate, or purifying to insure the implication of a theory – the power, in sum, to make a phenomenon "admit" its truth (Chertok&Stengers, 1989/1992, p. xvi).

Richard Hodgson died suddenly upon December 20th, 1905. On December 28th a message purporting to come from him was delivered in a trance of Mrs. Piper's, and she has hardly held a sitting since then without some manifestation of what professed to be Hodgson's spirit taking place. Hodgson had often during his lifetime laughingly said that if he ever passed over and Mrs. Piper was still officiating here below, he would "control" her better than she had ever yet been controlled in her trances, because he was so thoroughly familiar with the difficulties and conditions on this side. Indeed he was; so that this would seem prima facie a particularly happy conjunction of "spirit" with medium by which to test the question of spirit-return (James, 1909a/ 1986, p. 253).

So opens William James' (1909a) "Report on Mrs. Piper's Hodgson-Control" (hereafter the *Report*).[1] This chapter springboards from a series of events around Hodgson's death and James' analysis of it. It locates psychical research's effort to become a science and turn the ghost into an object of study as a prism through which several mesmerizing and astigmatizing horizons pass at the turn of the twentieth century – the interpenetration of a new logics of perception with the formation of rationalities in (social) sciences with the fabulation of nation and West. These horizons continue to haunt the production of World today with their leaky yet not insipid tenacity. They form a braid through this analysis without organizing it discretely, for it is via the very defiance and problematization of clarity and of borders that Hodgson could be studied, James involved, sciences separated, nations formed and invaded, and the limits of the West claimed and tested.

There have already been significant critiques of the formation of scientific disciplines 'in' the West and how the formation of 'the West' and 'scientific disciplines' followed the flag:

M.A. Peters et al. (eds.), Govermentality Studies in Education, 303–340.

During the last three decades, historians of science have come increasingly to appreciate the role of science and technology in the making of nations, and in the development of world systems in trade and commerce. For centuries, knowledge has been a companion of commerce and both have followed the flag....Both pursuits drove international rivalry in voyages of discovery and exploration. Both also served a growing European interest in establishing colonies, whether by conquest, trade, or settlement (MacLeod, 2000, p. 1).

Appeals to rationality-as-procedural more broadly, and the formation of Western sciences more specifically could be seen, under this equation, as instances or parts of (multiple) colonizing enterprises and impulses, interpenetrating the "whether by conquest, trade, or settlement" of colony-establishment. As MacLeod notes, however, the focus has largely been on disciplines such as geophysics, meteorology, and astronomy and on nations in Europe. The social, natural history, and life sciences have only recently been studied as everyday companions of colonial enterprise and the instability of nation or territory as a unit of analysis has but just arisen to the fore.

The problem of universalizing and essentializing in postcolonial critiques such as colonizer, colonized, West, East, North, South, European, nation, and so forth has already been raised, even if simultaneously and overtly deployed as an opening strategy.[2] The availability of distinctions, of science from spirituality from philosophy, of nations from each other, and the complication of what constitutes rationality dovetails directly into the dilemma that James faced in conducting psychical research. The labor he performed around Hodgson's passing over in preparing the *Report*, was on the one hand, already implicitly structured around such divisions. He overtly participates across his writing in the definitional process that distinguishes reason from science from philosophy from religion and delineates via his participation in the Anti-imperialism League the kind of America that he would like to see in the twentieth century (reputedly exclaiming "God damn the US for its vile conduct in the Philippine Isles!"). On the other hand, the need for definition and delineation suggests that distinct entities had never quite formed or stabilized sufficiently for the boundaries to be shared and unspoken. This is part of a broader problematic and paradox in which James participated: the formalization of a heterotopic spectrum of rationality that would seemingly become the mark of an independent nation and of the West[3] - the belief that rationality was required to produce knowledge and the simultaneous belief that the unifying appeal to rationality could be ruptured and/or not be fully accounted for through the term science.

Abraham (2006, p. 211) notes the circularity and the slippage that appeal to the moderness of science has had:

Modernity, nation, and later, state all pass through and are interpellated in the institutions and cultures of modern western science. However, colonial and later postcolonial science was always a contradictory formation. Though science presents itself as universal knowledge, it is never able to do so unambiguously in a location distant from its putative origins in Western Europe. Science's conjoint history with colonial and imperial power implies a constant representation of its condition in order to pass as universal knowledge in the colony.

The constant representation takes place within the prior presumption of a civilizational lack in the colonies:

Science and technology is, in a material and cultural sense, central to postcolonial visions of third world states and anti-colonial movements because of its role in reinforcing colonial and neo-colonial dominance, because the practical realization of modernity came about foremost through technological transformation, and because it appears unambiguously to mark the (missing) modern, an assumed absence that was at the heart of the colonial project (Abraham, 2006, p. 211).

Abraham's concern with the biophysical laboratory sciences underscores via its absencing of social sciences, the paradoxical formation of a heterotopic spectrum of rationality: within the emergent empire-building of the United States (US), there was a presumption of lack and constant representation of 'social science's' condition in order to pass as universal knowledge. The impurity impugned to the colonies was also impugned in unique ways to the soft or feminine sciences. Chertok and Stengers argue that because "the infant's relation with its caretakers are already characterized by what we should recognize as a form of suggestion" that the social sciences which focused on human relations could not so readily make a phenomenon admit its truth via a purification process: "suggestion puts 'truth' in question, that is, it problematizes the possibility of constructing a theory on the basis of experiment or experience. Suggestion is impure; it is the uncontrollable par excellence" (Chertok&Stengers, 1989/1992, pp. xvi–xvii).

The 'human relations' to which James attends in his writings are multifarious. For instance, he overtly positions America as lower than Europe, psychical research as more problematic than other kinds of science, and elevates 'the West' over 'the Oriental.' The interplay of effects – insecurity, liminality, and superiority – make the work done in the name of psychical science a fascinating and significant site of border-makings, attempted crossings, seepage, and apparent ambiguity, leading to multiple, creative attempts to identify the not-so-"motionless structure" that "does not resolve the ambiguity, but determines it" (Foucault 1961/1965, p. xii).

Psychical science as James and his contemporaries referred to it (today, parapsychology) became an incitement to discourse in the second half of the nineteenth century in the US – reported on widely in newspapers, as well as being the subject of many journal articles, conference proceedings, monographs, novels, and official, bureaucratic investigations. The research undertaken as psychical was integral to the very project of constituting the sciences, organizing the domains of different disciplines, and conjointly reinforcing and rupturing the spectrum of rationalities permitted within the elaboration of ethico-redemptive sciences, their (self)critique, and their distinction from the theoretico-experimental sciences.[4]

James' wrestling with psychical science and the validity of the ghost operated in terms of both unifying and rupturing existing codifications that had earned the label of rationality and that appeared as the application of human reason to the ordering of social affairs. By considering the production of scientific objects and sciences within a milieu in which existing codifications were already being debated, then, in which potentially "new" objects were considered invisible to the sighted, naked eye, and in a situation where contemporaries overtly argued that they had no previous models for understanding the events encountered several of Foucault's earlier and later concerns are brought into contact. This includes the way in which discourse produces its objects, such as characterized across disciplines in *The Order of Things*, his brief excursus into governmentality, and the theorization of biopower, particularly here as "to make live and to let die." Through an examination of debates over the formation of psychical science and whether the ghost exists and can be treated as a scientific object, I offer a re-reading or perhaps re-deployment of the connection between science, governmentality, and biopower.

In the oft-quoted chapter on the middle term Foucault posits that characteristic of the sixteenth-century were certain questions "How to govern oneself, how to be governed, how to become the best possible governor" which lie at the crossroads of two processes in Europe "the establishment of the great territorial, administrative, and colonial states; and a totally different movement that, with the Reformation and Counter-reformation, raises the issue of how one must be spiritually ruled and led on this earth in order to achieve eternal salvation" – a double movement of state centralization on the one hand and dispersion and religious dissidence on the other (Foucault, 2000a, pp. 201–02). I suggest indirectly here that Foucault's briefly-elaborated yet richly-textured notion of governmentality structured around tendencies that he conjures as distinct if not oppositional and whose intersection poses the problematic of government in general with a peculiar intensity is both a necessary and inadequate vector for approaching the formation and fabric of social sciences in the US, and in this case psychical science. More significantly, I consider how such a science was imbricated in the reformation of an Apollonian eye, even and especially in regard to the invisible, and how integral this was not simply to empire-building in US foreign policy which was underway by the late nineteenth century, but to the elaboration of what could, arbitrarily, constitute the West.

Such a project retains interest for the field of curriculum studies in which I am institutionally located on at least three grounds which I do not elaborate here but which comport the investigative focus[5]: first, James' *Talks to Teachers on Psychology: and to Student's on Some of Life's Ideals* (1899/1915) was for thirty years the single most popular textbook on education in the United States as judged by reprints – its definitions of psychology, philosophy, education, and the normal mind cannot be separated from investigations into phenomena now called psychical, or from James' elaboration of those phenomena in a separate and contemporaneous set of lectures on exceptional mental states. I look here not so much at the canonical texts on psychology, teaching, and exceptionality, but more so at those documents which to this point in education have not been studied and taken seriously at all – first, James' psychical research and specifically his analysis of spirit-return. Second, James located psychical science, such as the investigation of telepathy, spirit-return, and seership as a branch of education, a positioning that is met today sometimes with shock and disbelief and which indexes the territorial politics of the separation of sciences – for if education prides itself on being overtly obsessed with mind, then out of the breadth of historical possibilities which versions of mind and what "practices" have become confined within its purview? Third, James' fascination with mediumship suggests a new orientation to biopower rarely explored – that which focuses on the "to make live" - longer and beyond the grave – part rather than on the "to make die" which has been overwhelmingly the concern of sociological uptakes of Foucault. To that end, the chapter lies in the middle of a potent brew – that volatile cocktail that drew the formation and separation of religions, sciences, and nations into new formattings of Life, of Death, and of the visible now claimed as occidental.

It goes almost without saying that the aim here is neither to elevate nor to pillory James. Rather, James, as for Freud, Durkheim, Jung, and Saussure, among many, was caught up in a complicated process of theorizing consciousness amid an analytical shift from privileging the placement of an object with an essence in absolute space into a strategy that favored the primacy of relations. Professor at Harvard University and popularizer of those seemingly quintessential American terms *self-esteem*, *stream of consciousness*, and *pragmatism*, James was also at one point president of the American Society for Psychical Research (ASPR), which, like the American Psychological Association, he helped to found. Richard Hodgson was secretary and treasurer of the ASPR when he passed over suddenly playing handball in New York in his early 50s. He and James were also founding members of the American Anthropological Association and in their correspondence referred to each other as best friends. Much of their professional interaction circled around the spirit-return thesis and its veridicality. After graduating with a Masters degree from the University of Melbourne, Hodgson obtained a law degree at Cambridge University and became involved with the newly-formed Cambridge-based Society for Psychical Research (SPR), earning a reputation as a psychic detective, an anti-spiritualist, and a fraud-buster who exposed mediums, clairvoyants, or prophets (in one case the claims of Madame Blavatsky – his most famous debunking). Hodgson was called upon in many such investigations and elaborated the devices and illusions used. After being asked to help the ASPR in New York, he moved there and became caught up in a project that would consume him until 1905 and apparently beyond. He was introduced to Leonora Piper, who had come to the attention of the ASPR through William James' wife, Alice, for her mediumship and other 'psychic' demonstrations. James encouraged Piper to focus exclusively on mediumship and this became the site of subsequent investigations. She was taken across the Atlantic and tested extensively by the members of the Cambridge-based SPR and after passing all the contemporary fraud-detection tests of those involved, was eventually paid a retainer for her services by the ASPR.

Piper explained in a newspaper article that she had no memory when she came out of trance of what had happened in it or what she had said and thus could not subsequently verify or deny the spiritist thesis. This was taken as a vote against spiritism and an instance of fraud to which the ASPR had to respond. The 'survivalist' belief – that consciousness, mind, soul, and/or Life extended beyond the grave – entertained both the popular reading public and very high status academics – an unusual combination of audience. Piper was, then, caught in the midst of one of the most controversial and titillating topics of the time and subjected to one of the longest-lasting formal investigations into "personal morality" within the US to that point.

Hodgson tracked Piper and her husband for over ten years, both personally and using other private detectives to follow and scrutinize them, trying to detect character flaws and marks of deception. Piper was eventually described as of humble background and of upright morals and standing. After over a decade of analysis Hodgson wrote what became known as his Confession of Faith, a long, multilayered article in the 1898 Journal of the ASPR drawing on transcripts from her trance sessions and years of tracking. Hodgson goes through all the available explanations for what he has observed, weighing their merits and limits in legalistic, cross-witnessing fashion. He concludes that he now believes in spiritism because he can find no other explanation that fits better for what Mrs. Piper does and reveals.

The 'spirits' whom Piper were said to channel across the years had various names and were called, tellingly, controls, i.e., the spirit who was in control of any others trying to get through from the other side and/or speaking and/or writing through the channel that Piper was taken to represent. The controls are spoken about in the archival documents as who, not as that or which, in the grammar and style one would speak about the embodied living. The first repetitive control was known as Phinuit, presented as a highly entertaining Frenchman whose accent and sense of humor were often remarked upon by sitters (observers who were allowed into the trance setting and who often subsequently wrote up their impressions). The Phinuit-control lasted for several years across the 1890s. A second control appeared after Phinuit. It was called the Imperator-band, believed by some members of the ASPR to be former members of the SPR who had passed over, with the dominant personality being called Rector and considered by some to be Frederick Myers, an SPR founder. Rector was like the director – he would determine whom of the others could come through and when.

Within this broth of debates over spiritism, controls, psychic detectives, transcripts, and sittings, then, Hodgson's Confession of Faith was not taken lightly. He had changed teams as it were – the famous exposer of fraud had met his limit in Piper's trance state. Undoubtedly, her depiction as white, feminine, chaste, and married contributed to the perception of purity and authenticity around her performances, as well as her husband's testimony regarding her condition at different points. After his Confession, Hodgson explains in his further writings how Rector had told him that "the Piper-organism" was very delicate and in a bad condition from being studied too much. From that point on, Hodgson stresses that he put into place every recommendation that Rector gave, especially that which involved limiting the number of sittings and the number of new sitters in each session. He argued in some of his last writings that Rector's recommendations had been the best thing to follow for both Piper and himself, and explained how he, like other sitters, sometimes consulted Rector for personal advice.

Finally, William James notes that Hodgson jokingly agreed with him that whoever should pass over first ought to try to return through Piper to clarify once and for all the spiritist thesis. Eight days after his heart attack, Leonora Piper got a call. James explains the transcripts that he reviews in the *Report* are from the American sittings collated from December 28, 1905 to January 1st, 1908. The Imperator-band, with Rector in charge, was considered the control when William and sometimes Alice attended the Piper-Hodgson sittings. 'Hodgson' was described as eventually speaking in his own name without the conduit of Rector, with his name suspended in quotes in the transcript to indicate uncertainty over the status. James wrote up his review of the transcripts at the same time as his thoughts on pragmatism, radical empiricism, and pluralism. They were published a year before James passed over, at which point another series of claims regarding James being channeled were set off up until 1930.

Although James is an iconic and enigmatic figure in US history of social science today, there is very little sustained analysis of this series of events in mainstream disciplines. The silences, delays, and lesser-knowns around his work suggest something of their appropriateness for an historical retrieval and allude to the epistemological structures that must have initially buried them. In sections one and two the work that James does upon the transcripts is the focus, moving from consideration of a trans-Atlantic history of subject-object perception, consciousness, and a visible/invisible problematic, into the differential meanings of science in France, where James drew many of his primary documents from, relative to the US at the turn of the twentieth century.[6] Here, mind sciences and the 'discovery of the unconscious' are the site of analysis, with James' unpacking of the Hodgson sitting transcripts illustrative of the realignment of veridicality in the 'psychical' realm. In sectionsthree and four, I consider the kinds of work James does upon himself in a mode of what Foucault calls Western spirituality and its relationship to shifting conceptualization of rationality and the mystical, examining the stakes in the spirit-return thesis in terms of nation-formation with biopower as its mode of operation.

Together, these layers enable a different orientation to the question of why it would matter whether there was such a thing as a ghost, opening onto all the problems of borders, territoriality, porousness, intersubjectivity, and suggestibility of the ethico-redemptive sciences and their inscription as Western. Such apparent ambiguity, unique models of causality, and of invisible objects threatened the neat packaging of theoretico-experimental sciences, their formation of a finite, this-worldly horizon, and the enforceability of boundaries around such entities as geopolitical territories, religions, and selves. Moreover, the reinforcement of a West/Orient division upon which James comments directly is put at stake. This accounts in part for how the marginal position of psychical science can be understood beyond the usual framing – less in relation to other sciences and their mastery of empirical conditions of proof, and more in relation to onto-theo-philosophical regionalism in which "the mystical" comes to be redefined, separated from science, from literature, and from the West, while operating from "within" as a necessary yet subordinate, constitutively unstable node in the new logics of perception.

SUBJECT-OBJECT AND CONSCIOUSNESS: NEW LOGICS OF PERCEPTION

James explains against backdrop of much earlier involvement with Piper in his career that until the Spring of 1906 he had no sittings with her for nine years but kept up with records in the ASPR. Upon reports of Hodgson being channeled, James attends some of the sittings. The transcripts produced are taken not as evidentiary but as that which must be analyzed for incidences and events that could be seen as evidentiary, as good test cases, for deciding upon the spirit-return thesis. The second-order normativity embodied in the approach – that there are conditions of proof for what can count as conditions of proof – places most of the transcribed sessions outside of detailed focus. Some remain, however, in the *Report* for instructive purposes. For instance:

RH: Did you get my messages?[7]

WJ: I got some messages about you are going to convert me.

RH: Did you hear about that argument that I had? You asked me what I had been doing all those years, and what it amounted to. [R. H. had already sent me, through other sitters, messages about my little faith – W.J.]

WJ: Yes.

RH: Well it amounted to this, – that I have learned by experience that there is more truth than error in what I have been studying.

WJ: Good!

RH: I am so delighted to see you to-day that words fail me.

WJ: Well, Hodgson, take your time, don't be nervous.

RH: No. Well, I think I could ask the same of you! Well, now, tell me, - I am very much interested in what is going on in the society, and [Frederick] Myers [Frederick] and I are also interested in what is going on in the society over here. You understand that we have to have a medium on this side while you have a medium on your side, and through the two we communicate with you.

WJ: And your medium is who?

RH: We have a medium on this side. It is a lady. I don't think she is known to you.

WJ: You don't mean Rector? [another control who appears through Mrs. Piper]

RH: No, not at all. It is —— do you remember a medium whom we called Prudens?

WJ: Yes.

RH: Prudens is a great help. Through Prudens we accomplish a great deal. Speak to me, William. Ask me anything. What I want to know first of all is about the society [ASPR]. I am sorry that it could not go on.

WJ: There was nobody to take your place (p. 324).

In a later moment, Alice James sits with William for one of the sessions and poses her own questions.

WJ: Hodgson, what are you doing apart from Mrs. Piper?

RH: Why, I am working with the society, William, trying to reach other lights, trying to communicate, trying to get in touch with you all.

WJ: Why can't you tell me more about the other life?

RH: That is part of my work. I intend to give you a better idea of this life than has ever been given.

WJ: I hope so.

AJ: Hodgson, do you live as we do, as men do?

RH: What does she say?

WJ: Do you live as men do?

AJ: Do you wear clothing and live in houses?

RH: Oh yes, houses, but not clothing. No, that is absurd. Just wait a moment, I am going to get out.

WJ: You will come back again?

RH: Yes.

Rector: He has to go out and get his breath. (p. 330)

Besides the entertaining content, especially if one considers why clothing would be any more absurd than housing "on the other side," the "non-selected" transcripts are important to consider here for at least two reasons. First, the nature of Alice and William's questions indicate something rather vague but significant about the common-sensical role of the visible and invisible in truth-production – they gesture toward the different conditions of objectification and unique pathways to science-formation already aggravating the disconnect between the biophysical and social sciences. While the role of what are now called the senses in epistemology, and especially the eyes, is often attributed to North Africa, especially Egyptian cosmology, modified by Aristotle, whose preservation and reinterpretation as text is then attributed to Islamic scholars and Celtic monks, and thereby reintroduced into medieval Latin Europe where Aristotelianism flourishes among the Scholastics, the difficulty of 'looking backwards'" as though a continuous line has been in place is as Foucault noted part of the problem – and expectation – of a modern episteme, where single origin is sought and continuous history required, where the notion of continuity is protected and located in the conscious, human subject.

As Clark (2007) has recently pointed out 'ocularcentrism' has been on the defensive for more than a century, with Foucault's work an essential component, in addition to many others:

> Mirroring, imaging, and anamorphosis were all part of the reconceptualizing of vision that was fundamental to the psychoanalytical theories of Jacques Lacan. Richard Rorty's influential assault on modern philosophy was built, likewise, on undermining its dependence on the mind as the 'mirror' of nature. Above all, perhaps, thanks to developments in art history, visual anthropology, and visual hermeneutics we now take for granted the constructed nature of vision and the extent to which visual perception and visual meaning are fused (p. 9).

This fusing, especially of optical theory with cognitive philosophy Clark attributes in part to the pivotal role of the tenth- to eleventh-century Islamic scholar, Alhazen who characterizes vision as transmission of image or picture through the optic nerve to the brain – a belief infused into medieval and early modern thought. A shift from attempts to make linear perspective equivalent to vision to the idea that vision itself was pictorial was facilitated by the idea of a point-by-point mapping onto the eye of rays of lights transmitted from objects along a "visual pyramid." Alhazen suggested that after leaving the object as a mosaic of visible color and light the custodial power of the optic nerve preserved the picture with perfect integral order to reach the forefront of the brain intact (p. 16). Key here, and for understanding what permits Jamesian versions of associationist psychology and sequencing is the cosmological assumption that drives the process of attribution "That the entire process was dictated by causal demands that made each form in the sequence a cause of its successor and an effect of its antecedent also helped to ensure that the picture of reality occurring in the brain was veridical" (p. 16). Perceptual certitude becomes assured because categories or species are taken as natural signs of their objects, making the external object, the species, and the mental representation of it ontologically continuous (p. 34). The integrity and coherence of the image between object and brain was taken as a radical new line of thought in which it was postulated that if things external to us "are able to reproduce their essential qualities in our senses and minds, then the content of the mind is assuredly objective" (p. 16).

Even if, then, "ocularcentrism" is dubiously flattened out as a singular historical category and rendered backwards as that which links medieval and early modern 'sciences,' the task for James is not the same as for Alhazen, Galileo Galilei, or Sir Isaac Newton. In postulating gravity as an invisible force that brings a discrete apple into contact with a discrete ground surface the question was not whether there was such a thing as apple or earth but rather what mediates their contact. For James, the first question arises at the level of legitimacy of the object, not simply of relations between a priori objects. Moreover, the discourse of visuality and its role in veridicality has changed dramatically by the twentieth century – confidence in the integrity of mental representation, its neutrality, has waned, while the mechanism of sight's formation has been transformed. Compounding this is, for James, the possibility of non-discreteness – a "spirit" either speaking through, inhabiting, being channeled, interpenetrating, or co-mingling with a subject already positioned as "medium" and "in a trance state" complicates any search for mechanical explanation if the object is legitimated – what would one say was Leonora Piper's "self" in such a circumstance? How would the medium that Hodgson claims to make use of on the other side be verified and tested? Where would the discrete locus of origin, and if not origin then cause, for the communication be placed?[8]

Second, the extracts lend consideration to how such exchanges became transcripts at all that James could subject to analysis as objects, how the production of the dialogue and its unpacking becomes taken-for-granted as a research task, focus of study, and site of testimony. In pursuing this possibility of how the stage becomes set for James to enter in upon such a task, the distantiation of subject-object and allied notions of consciousness are necessary to unfold as integral, at least as James proffered, to the limits of the West.

Foucault does of course devote much of his career to the historicization of subject-object and the problematization of consciousness as s guide to writing history. I want to follow the route laid by some contemporary parapsychological research, however, because of the discourse networks to which James felt he was tied in deciding upon the legitimacy of an object qua object and because the location of the 'para' and the 'psychical' held and hold a paradoxical yet inciting relation to the versions of rationality that James must cling to in approaching the transcripts if he is to avoid being positioned as mad, mystical, occultist, or lacking in rigor by a broader public imagined as the audience.

In "Melting Boundaries: Subjectivity and Intersubjectivity in the Light of Parapsychologial Data" Walach, Schmidt, Schneider, Seiter, &Bösch (2002) set a date for the transformation that bequeaths modern science a set of assumptions about space, time, and observation: 1336. Here, they argue that Francesco Petrarca, who some count among the inaugurators of the Renaissance, wrote a letter to his teacher and friend, the Augustinian monk Dionigi Roberti daBorgo San Sepolcro, in which he described his experience when climbing Mt. Ventoux at the outskirts of the Alps near Avignon. In a rather grandiose gesture, his description of the splendor and thrill of seeing a landscape from a distance as opposed to being immersed in it is positioned in the following way:

> And for the first time in recorded Western history, an individual conscious subject became aware of perspective of distance and thereby of space and time. This experience and its publication marked the beginning of the modern concept of space. It made possible the concept and practice of perspective in painting and thereby marks one of the most prominent and least questioned presupposition of the modern way of seeing and understanding the world, ourselves and others: that we as subjective observers are distant from what we observe, from other observers, and from the world. It marks what later came to be called the separation of subject-object, and this separation presupposes a conscious understanding and a concept of space. Petrarca's experience is a milestone for both, and from this experience the rise of modern consciousness, or what Gebser (1985) calls the perspectivistic or mental structure of consciousness, began (pp. 72–73).

While the single origin that such an account encourages is questionable, it is important to underscore the latter of two presuppositions that Walach et al raise through this vignette. They argue that the Petrarca experience indicates not only that the foremost and most important tacit presupposition is that the observer and the observed, subject and object are distant, but that with this presupposition comes the belief that subject and object *do not directly influence each other*. They note the follow-through of this presupposition – that in the jargon of modern physics, the locality thesis asserts that all causes are local, and non-local, distant causes thus become a scientifically obscene notion. In more contemporary terms, Petrarca's experience would be theorized, contra Alhazen, through photons: Petrarca could see the distant landscape as distant because photons are carried from the object of perception to the perceiving subject where they cause a complex perceptual image to arise:

> Were it not for the many photons traveling the distance, we could not see at all. Thus, the cause for our seeing objects are not the objects themselves, but

the photons, which, locally in our retina, cause a perceptual image, which by our brains is structured into a percept of the object. Distance, then, has become some general objective category with Petrarca's experience, and a lot of scientific thought and effort is poured into the question, how causes can bridge distances (p. 73).

Walach et al argue that time also becomes a new element here. It is not as for St. Augustine, for instance, a category of the soul, of inner experience. Rather, time also becomes something external, and inextricably connected with space – the traveling photons take time to cross the distance hypothesized as a gap, marking absolute time. In contemporary theories, nothing is supposed to be faster than light,

and thus light, or in other words, electromagnetic signals, mark the boundaries of the time arrow as well as of the space which can be bridged by it. Time and space, then, are seen as something absolute, outside of our consciousness, rather categorical, absolute presuppositions in the same sense as Aristotle or Kant used the notion of 'category', outside of which we cannot perceive, exist, think, let alone gather knowledge (p. 73).

Walach et al contend further that the concept of Nature and Universe that eventuates, for example, via Descartes and then Newton, is prepared for through dualisms that continue to assume space and time as objective phenomena. The Cartesian distinction between matter ('extended thing – *res extensa*'') and mind or consciousness ('thinking thing – *res cogitans*') assumes matter as already involving an implicit concept of absolute external space such that Newton's codification was only a prolongation and logical extrapolation of Descartes' concept of matter. "Thinking things" are characterized by having or producing thoughts "which are not in a specific place or localizable, but thoughts come in sequences. Therefore, time is intricately connected with the life of the mind, or, in other words, time is the mode of the mind" (pp. 73–74). Contra the scholastics, then, Descartes' intro-duces a split of kind and substance between matter and mind – mind and matter are not two aspects of one substance but categorically different, marking unique realms of being. While Walach et al do not consider the later writings of Descartes such as the *Passions* in which the interpenetration between the realms is more tantalizingly gestured at, the structural separation is what makes the claim to interpenetration recognizable in the first place. Moreover, they argue that, via Newton, Petrarca's experience is made into a kind of scientific law. Absolute space is posited as something, and a something in which things are ordered, placed and stowed away.[9] Relations between things became secondary to this placement of objects in absolute space so in analytical terms objects become primary and relations between objects follow. In the process of these calcifications, the very act of 'experiencing' becomes redefined:

A subject experiencing space and matter and objects as distant and outside of itself cannot but take this act of experiencing as something different from the object. Thus, positing material objects out there in an absolute space, which Petrarca did implicitly, and Descartes and later Newton, did explicitly so, is tantamount to positing mind or consciousness as something completely different from material objects (p. 74).

As founding assumptions within shifting conceptualizations of rationality and the new procedural relation between knowledge, truth, and right, such themes explicitly guided the appeal to rigorous methods or implicitly inhered in them. As Walach et al note:

This dualism between matter and mind has since haunted modern science. While science proper just strode along the path delineated by Newton, regarding only material objects sitting in absolute space and disregarding consciousness, the humanities have ever more tried to adopt the effective methods of natural science to understand consciousness. The irony and dialectics of that process is that the very philosophy Descartes used to find a firm foundation for science and consciousness at the same time, seems to eradicate exactly the foundation from which the whole process starts: mind and consciousness as a separate ontological substance or category.... But even if modern scientists often do not reflect on those presuppositions of their work and do not take a definite stance, or adhere to a vague and implicit materialism in their work, the methodological dualism introduced by Descartes is still the necessary precondition even of the hardest science, namely physics. Physics always presupposes some conscious observer, who in the equation of physics, is outside of the system itself (2002, p. 74).

The spatiotemporal definition of a subject-object distinction and the allied sequence, human – mind – consciousness – rational-thought-that-is-procedural, which delimits humanity in new ways and finds a special role for something called the self, launches somewhat discrete pathways of investigation in post-Cartesian epistemologies. The consistency of self-presence and world becomes shattered. But just how shattered remains a question, for the limits are set in advance once space, time, and objects are regularized as external and given.[10] In the hard sciences,

Consciousness itself is normally either not directly addressed as a problem, or presupposed in a kind of methodological, if not ontological, dualism. But it is certainly not to interact with matter across space and time in any direct way. This is prohibited by the principle of locality, which means that only contiguous causes which take time and bridge space, can wield effects.... Thus the modern concept of time and space places things and living participants...into space, constructs external relations with each other, and poses limits on contact and communication. (Walach et al., 2002, p. 74)

James' psychical research contested at a certain level the limits on contact and communication, covering such topics as telepathy, automatic writing, raps, hypnosis, mediumship, mental healing, and New Thought. Psychical researchers in the nineteenth century certainly described themselves as working on a frontier, at the limits of science at that point. Space and time are often invoked as both necessarily objective yet challengeable in face of "data" for which no ready explanations appear. For contemporary parapsychological researchers as for James this gestures toward a new order of things that modern science cannot yet grasp.

> From a modern scientific point of view, it is not possible to have communications from the future, since time has to evolve and the future is not yet present and determined. It is not possible to directly communicate with someone who is separated from oneself by distance, without having a technical device, like a phone or a cell phone, which again uses electromagnetic signals that take time to travel. And it is not really possible that a thinking thing, a mind, affects a categorically different thing, like a material body, without any intermediate causes, by using one's body and the ways of signaling, acting and perception provided by our physiology. This is, incidentally, why the mind-body problem is haunting modern science, and most researchers tend to avoid it or take a shortcut by subscribing more or less bluntly to a materialist and reductionist approach, making consciousness a kind of result, emerging property or epiphenomenon of, material processes, if not simply identical with them. This situation is the reason why parapsychology is both a non-science from the modern scientific point of view and shunned by most respected researchers, and at the same time important for mainstream science. For the results of parapsychological research can teach us a lot about the question, whether those presuppositions of modern science [space, time, subjectivity, etc] are indeed correct, or whether we need altogether an expanded, if not different approach. (Walach et al., 2002, p. 74–75).

It is crucial to recognize the central theme or umbrella under which psychical phenomena became viewed as psychical – telepathy, clairvoyance, and mediumship were for James instances of research on *consciousness* and fundamentally attached to what he called exceptional mental states. Consciousness remains his concern for twenty-five years and the investigations are bound by at least two trajectories – his elaboration of an associationist, sensationist, and adaptationist psychology of normal human development in which the stream of consciousness is the central explanatory figure that unites the diversity of stimuli, and related, his rewriting of exceptional mental states.

In both strands, James' schemata admit of Soul but remain open to its origin, uncertain of the source being a single creator or something else. In addition, both tributaries of his investigations into mind pivot on consciousness as a given feature. Like much analysis that becomes attributed to the West, an "always-already" thing has to be asserted – for Foucault, one cannot be outside of power's "field of force," for Derrida, there is no outside to "text," and for James at the turn of the twentieth century consciousness was always already going on. It is not insignificant or coincidental, then, that something called consciousness can be the thing that is always already going on in sciences of mind that James encounters and elaborates: "Now the *immediate* fact which psychology, the science of mind, has to study is also the most general fact. It is the fact that in each of us, when awake (and often when asleep), *some kind of consciousness is always going on*. There is a stream, a succession of states, or waves, or fields (or whatever you please to call them), of knowledge, of feeling, of desire, of deliberation, etc., that constantly pass and repass, and that constitute our inner life (p. 15)."The "first general fact" is "We thus have *fields of consciousness*" and the "second general fact" is "that the concrete fields are always complex" (p. 17). Consciousness was, in turn, understood through the dynamics of proximity-impression and focus/margin. Because some kind of consciousness *is always going on* the proximity of any thing means it can (somehow) leave impressions, get "in" there even if one remains unaware that something "got in."In his "Confidences of a 'Psychical Researcher,'" for instance, James asserts: "The next thing I wish to go on record for is *the presence*, in the midst of all the humbug, *of really supernormal knowledge*. By this I mean knowledge that cannot be traced to the ordinary sources of information – the senses namely, of the automatist" (1909b, p. 372).

James' investigation into spirit-return plays out, then, within the mind-consciousness-self conflation and triangulation of human specificity, which is elaborated in the formation of mind sciences. His analysis of the transcripts embodies not just the heritage of the subject-object distinction and of consciousness as of primary concern to what is now called Western philosophy, sciences, and spirituality (discussed below) but becomes embedded in the very conditions of proof for selecting evidential instances from the transcripts. James explains, for example, how the *Report* focuses on four incidents that through the transcripts presented the most difficulty for "shooting down" the spirit-return thesis: "My best plan will be to cull a few of the best veridical communications, and discuss them singly, from the point of view of the alternatives of explanation" (1909a, p. 263). These stand out as test cases or incidences because James explains they have been judged as "veridical communications," which means there has been a corroboration of the information revealed in the sittings and that information was considered to have been very exclusive, previously known to only a small number of persons or just one person. The *conscious awareness* of the sitters of an exclusive knowledge, then, determines their appropriateness. The incidents are treated under separate subheadings and labeled as follow:
- The Ring Incident – p. 263
- The Nigger-Talk Case [*sic*] – p. 268
- The Huldah Episode – p. 270
- The Pecuniary Messages – p. 276

The four incidents treated in Part 1 are listed in advance and the criteria by which such incidents were to be analyzed for testing the spirit-return thesis are laid out. They are then divided into two categories with seven total explanations available beside the spirit-return thesis itself: five naturalist explanations and two supernaturalist or mystical which appear to be classified so because the audit trail in numbers 6 and 7 remains invisible, delimiting the possibility for corroboration via externalization in an artefact:

Sources other than R. H's surviving spirit for the veridical communications from the Hodgson-control may be enumerated as follows:

- Lucky chance-hits.
- Common gossip
- Indications unwarily furnished by the sitters.
- Information received from the living R. H., or others, at sittings, and kept in Mrs. Piper's trance-memory, but out of reach of her waking consciousness.
- Telepathy
- Access to some cosmic reservoir, where the memory of all mundane facts is stored and grouped around personal centres of association. (p. 255)

If any of the first five could be the explanation for the contents of the transcripts that were corroborated as 'accurate' then the spiritist thesis does not have 'knock-down' or independent proof. If that is not the case, then the last two supernatural explanations have to be compared to the spiritist thesis as a third possible supernatural explanation that would be weighed. James explains it thus: "It is obvious that no mystical explanation ought to be invoked so long as any natural one remains at all plausible. Only after the first five explanations have been made to appear improbable, is it time for the telepathy-theory and the cosmic-reservoir theory to be compared with the theory of R. H.'s surviving spirit" (p. 255).

The possibilities for explanation and their hierarchy expose the difficulties of taking the corporeal (i.e., how the body was studied in the linking of icon and words, surfaces and depths) as the model for a psychic realm where invisibility prevented the object of study from being iconicized via drawing, painting, or photography, leaving only words. The corporeal model for verification forms the basis for James' review, however, even as he changes the trajectory for knowledge-production around it. That is, in the biophysical sciences, the patterns of 'see and corroborate,' i.e., social consensus around what was viewed, founded the notion of reproducibility that made knowledge appear free-floating, ejected from body, and the observer as He who sees without being seen. The strategies of cause-effect became disarticulated from the doer with the predictive potential of the biophysical sciences cemented in this traveling ability – manipulating a variable to produce an effect agreed upon as an effect and as having only one cause. The predictive potential reinforces a perception that 'scientific method' in biophysical sciences works, it has a grip on 'reality' because clearly, whatever is manipulated produces the same outcome across laboratory sites – 'somehow' it just works. The transportation of such a model to investigations in a realm called psychic in part because of the invisibility issue meets its limits more immediately. Verbal corroboration is considered the only available strategy, exposing in an immediate way all the effort that had already been put into the social consensus formed around laboratory sciences.

That is, the social consensus-making that takes place in all the activities that claim the label of science becomes most exposed here because of the already-forged relation of the observer to the observed in dominant discourses of truth-production and the model of visuality in place – in mediumship studies, there is no 'visual' object apparently outside of 'body' that would enable an apparent escape from the privacy and subjectivity attributed to introspection, of the personal as an uncorroborated site. The corporeal does model, however, the hierarchy of possible explanations and conditions of proof in James' analysis in order for the verdict to appear as weighed, as corroborated outside of body, as more public, and as non-phenomenological. In the end, the breakdown of the transcripts suggest to James not that the model for vision and condition of proof is inadequate to the specificity of the subject-matter but that the subject-matter does not exist.

Once three-dimensional space, linear time, and consciousness-as-awareness (e.g., the conscious awareness of the sitters regarding what they have and have not told others) are taken-for-granted as measures within method and conditions of proof, other things become almost impossible to conceive. This is, at least, something of the verdict about the milieu which James helped both to forge and in which he found himself floundering in regard to the formation of a psychical science: "This is why I personally am as yet neither a convinced believer in parasitic demons, nor a spiritist, nor a scientist, but still remain a psychical researcher waiting for more facts before concluding." He argues that on the basis of such research the very nature of science will change: "Hardly, as yet, has the surface of facts called 'psychic' begun to be scratched for scientific purposes. It is through following these facts, I am persuaded, that the greatest scientific conquests of the coming generation will be achieved" (James, 1909b, p. 342). For Chertok and Stengers (1989), however, the conundrum and the contribution of social sciences lies more broadly in the problem that heart posed to reason, and crucially, the role that suggestibility played in muddying the isolation of variables and smooth causal narratives.

A HETEROTOPIC SPECTRUM OF RATIONALITY? CONCEPTIONS OF SCIENCE IN THE MIND SCIENCES

The greatness of psychoanalysis resides, we believe, in the fact that its failure forces us to pose the problem of "reason" itself, and more precisely, the problem of the model of rationality guiding modern sciences. (Chertok& Stengers, 1989/1992, p. viii)

James' struggle with a notion of spirit conjured in regard to a subject-object dualism meets its limit in Hodgson's controversial return. Its limit has less to do with what is subject and what is object, what is visible and what invisible, however, than with the conceptualization of rationality. Because of the substance of what one encounters in James, i.e, often a critique of 'science' and yet an upholding of 'reason,' the difficulty that the terms *rationality*, *rationalities*, and *reason* pose in regard to his writings and how to navigate their appearance needs to be attended to. As noted in the introduction, there have already been important critiques of how broad appropriations of Cartesian rationality have been implicated in the formation of specific scientific disciplines in the West (Dear, 1995; Foucault, 1972), and how the formation of the West and scientific disciplines followed the flag. James is usually read in regard to a religion/science dualism – initially he tries to reconcile it and later he gives up, rejecting both as categories as he works through the distinctions between pragmatism, radical empiricism, and pluralism before his passing over. What I am interested in here and the following section is not trying to get closer and closer to the action of subjectivity in James but rather the discourse networks in which belief in a broader science/religion dualism could form and in which the separation of strategies of reasoning, including nationalization, populational, and professional, took a particular turn. Once ontology and epistemology are considered discrete and domains of knowledge are spatialized, 'data' can arise, in an apparent return of the repressed, taunting the investigator with its ambiguity.

In their analysis of the formation of mind sciences in France and the US, for instance, Chertok and Stengers (1989) argue that psychoanalytic theory and practice at the turn of the twentieth century "does not simply reproduce the model of other rational practices. The 'heart' to which psychoanalysis addresses itself is not conceived in such a way as to guarantee a science resembling other sciences (by contrast to the role 'behavior' plays in experimental psychology, for example)." Rather, two differences mark the uniqueness, differences that circulate profoundly through James' consideration of psychical research, exceptional mental states, and his struggle to disarticulate explanations from what he called the occult, while criticizing the limitations of a reasoning process that he called science.

First, one objective was to create a practice that would render intelligible the obstacle 'heart' poses to the efforts of 'reason.' A second objective was to create a practice that would *not* be limited to making 'heart' an object of science, like any other, only more complex. Consideration of certain states as mental and as exceptional, for instance, move back and forward between these possibilities. Such possibilities were structured as such partly by debate over animal magnetism, mesmerism and hypnosis. As Chertok and Stengers (1989) argue "the critique of scientific reason to which the failure of psychoanalysis leads us...has as its correlate the problem of hypnosis" (p. ix).

The precursor of late nineteenth century clinical and laboratory studies in hypnosis were called mesmerism and/or animal magnetism and took place in homes, town halls, university lecture rooms, hospitals, schools, gardens, and popular theaters. Animal magnetism was a theory of a universal fluid passing through and connecting all bodies, animate or animate, planetary and extraplanetary, elaborated by Franz Anton Mesmer in the late 1780s – an explanation that Mesmer called *scientific* and *natural*, i.e., he did not classify it as supernatural causation. As an etiology of the universe it was (yet another) version of monism: one explanation, one diagnosis, one cure – unblock the fluid's flow (which has to be understood less as wet and more like energy) and restore to health the patient, animal, tree, or object (Mesmer claimed at one point to have magnetized the sun) that was suffering. In patients, the process often began by making passes of the hands over the body of the reclining patient, inducing relaxation, and then inciting a "crisis" in which convulsions, laughter, screaming, etc, assisted in the unblocking. Two official investigations in France in the late 1700s, one led by Benjamin Franklin, debunked the practice as an independent therapy and argued no such fluid existed. A third in the 1820s argued that inexplicable effects, including the ability of epileptic patients in trance states to predict the exact date, minute, and severity of their next fit, were occurring and refused to enter in upon the question of a universal fluid's existence. It was not until the 1830s that such debates were reopened in the United States on the basis of the third report. When commentators who labelled themselves as Professors of Mesmerism or of Animal Magnetism arrived on the east coast, they repeatedly noted that no one seemed to have heard of the practice or the terms animal magnetism or mesmerism before – the late eighteenth century debates involving Franklin and other high profile characters had disappeared from popular discussion (Baker, 2007b).

Winter has noted of Victorian Britain a pattern that erupted also in the US: the impact of traveling mesmerists in the mid-century decades shows how little consensus there was about what constituted a legitimate practice of truth-production. In the later part of the nineteenth century, important changes took place in the authoritative status of the sciences. By 1870 new disciplinary divisions had crystallized, brought on by reform in university education and the new laboratories, leaving less space for the lines of inquiry that mesmerism had earlier suggested. Winter (1998, p. 3) argues that as experimenters asked each other how a particular trial was to be conducted and evaluated, they confronted the larger question of who could pronounce upon *any* controversy. It was vital to determine whether someone was in an altered state (and why), because issues of much greater significance hung in the balance. By 1900, the observability of the effects was less in question, but their significance was another matter, because whatever conclusions one drew would involve ascriptions of relative social and moral standing. As James noted, it was largely on the basis of the criminal threats perceived around the abuse of mesmerism that the proposed reduction of its practice to medical doctors with a diploma was forwarded.

James' reference across his writing to the mystics and the scientifics, in which he recounts this travel from disreputable obscurity ('animal magnetism') to scientific status ('hypnotic suggestion') captures well the sentiment of many mental healing movements in the US at the time and the tensed relation they held to chemical medicine – a relation that became even more strained after the refinement of several chemical anaesthetics which displaced the use of hypnosis to achieve anaesthesia for surgery and dentistry. In his lectures on exceptional mental states, recomposed by Eugene Taylor, James argued that hypnotism had been rediscovered since Mesmer and denied by scientists:

> It was the theory of suggestion, however, that finally robbed hypnotism of its former marvel. Mesmer's theory of a universal fluid through all of nature, later theories that it was the will of the strong over the weak – all these explanations are now exploded (James, 1986, p. 25).

James defined hypnosis as possibly only partial sleep, as not requiring a strong will of the hypnotizer because you need only to suggest an idea that the mind grips. The subject's mind is hypnotized only in the passage from waking to sleeping state, hence we all go through this passage at least twice a day – the hypnagogic state. The idea is to prevent the subject from deep sleep and to catch them on the way, for then they will immediately act upon an idea. James argued further, in a redefinition of what animal magnetism was, that

Everything depends on the subject allowing himself to be entranced and hardly anything on the operator, except that he must engender the subject's trust and be able to fix attention on the relaxed condition (p. 25).

Suggestibility, James argued, is the main symptom of hypnosis and is identifiable where the intrusion into the mind of an idea is at first met with opposition by the person, then accepted uncritically, and realized unreflectively, almost automatically. In turn, this means vividness and motor efficacy, the former producing intense emotional excitement that banishes all other ideas and creates a state of monoideism and the latter referring to the ease with which the idea can then be translated into muscular activity – an increase in the reflex excitability: "This is unquestionably the true explanation" concludes James. This countered Hippolyte Bernheim's Nancy school theory where it was argued that there was no such thing as a hypnoidstate, rather, hypnosis was due to suggestibility alone. James argues, however, that it was a genuinely peculiar state, carrying increased suggestibility in its train. The fall of the threshold of consciousness enabled a single idea to be implanted and motor activity to follow but only when this opening of doors to the subliminal had taken place. Even in states that are similar, such as crowd-induced excitement or when remarkable feats are performed thought impossible before, the result he explains is caused by the narrowing of the field of consciousness that permits the suggestibility to take hold.

Winter (1998) has noted in regard to similar debates over mesmerism that the existence of a scientific or medical orthodoxy must not be presupposed; the very constitution of this orthodoxy was at issue. Definitions of science across the mid- to late nineteenth century were malleable and there was no agreement on what could be said about natural law, nor was it obvious when, where, and how one could say it – only in retrospect would it be possible to portray the new mental physiologies developed as unambiguously different from and opposed to mesmerism. Chertok and Stengers concur in regard to the pivotal role animal magnetism played in the very formation of sciences as sciences:

Animal magnetism is inseparable from the project of constituting a science. Similarly, hypnosis, which succeeded magnetism, activated a relation *purified* of any belief in a supernatural causality; it had as its goal to explain what pre-viously had appeared supernatural in terms of scientific knowledge, to discover the scientific truth beyond trances, ecstasies, possession, thaumaturgical prodigies, etc. Nevertheless, both hypnosis and magnetism have had troubled relation with scientific reason. The practical invention of the hypnotic relation, which endeavors to submit "heart' to a rational reading, has had the effect of providing a privileged terrain where "heart" and scientific reason confront each other, a terrain where proclamations of rational conquest alternate with admissions of defeat. (1989/1992, p. x)

Animal magnetism seems, then, an important fulcrum upon which the separation of sciences and the formulation of what could constitute an investigative approach turned. It is not surprising that debates over such phenomena appear across a range of emergent biophysical, humanities, and social science fields in the late nineteenth century, because they raised the question of human/nonhuman distinctions, of cause, effect, proximity, and distance, and significantly, of subject- or object-closure. James' *Report*, "Confidences," and lectures on exceptional mental states, "where proclamations of rational conquest alternate with admissions of defeat" illustrate how the "rationalities" of many social sciences including and beyond psychoanalytics that were dedicated to "heart" obtained a "feel" that is still recognizable today, navigating new pathways of truth-production in desperate attempts to find causality for objects that did not seem to remain stable or retain the same features in the process of studying them. The apparent problem of interpenetration, intersubjectivity, and/or non-closure between researcher and researched, would not go away.

> To the extent that hypnosis has indeed become (principally in the United States) a phenomenon subject to experimental research, the controversies surrounding that research teach us less about hypnosis itself than about the *price* the experimental ideal requires a phenomenon to pay if it is to become an object of study. And it is not a matter of hypnosis being incapable of paying the price, but rather of that payment making the hypnotic relation not a scientific object but instead a deceptive mirror where the very ambition to submit it to science is reflected. In that respect, we believe that the French attitude toward hypnosis – the "irrational" character the French attribute simultaneously to hypnosis and to interest in it – uncovers a question left in the shadows of the American attitude that hypnosis in "normal." Can rationality be defined by a standard pertaining to the phenomenon to be studied and not to those who study it? Can the operation of purification, of creating the experimental setting, be conceived as "right" of reason? (1989/1992, p. xiii; original emphasis)

A nexus, construed as a problem, in which cause-effect, visibility, and 'proper character' of the researcher who reflexively moves between 'heart' and 'reason' begins to compose the domain of the social sciences in the US. Suggestibility becomes a problem under such an apparent spatialization:

> The question of suggestion always arises when 'heart' and 'reason' are no longer conceived as being in opposition, when 'heart' is no longer considered an obstacle to the legitimate power of (theoretico-experimental) reason (Chertok&Stengers, 1989/1992, p. xvi–xvii).

The obstacle and the manner of composition was different elsewhere. In asking "What can hypnosis, which has been condemned as a disappointing therapeutic instrument, teach us about the ideal guiding Freud in the creation of psychoanalysis?" (p. xii), Chertok and Stengers elaborate how unique understandings of science emerge on different sides of the Atlantic. They argue, for instance, that in a long tradition as marked by philosophers such as Bachelard, 'scientific reason' in France has not at all been understood as empirical but instead understood on the basis of the power of the 'concepts' it creates, where the use of the term concept excludes ideology, professional interests, and individual psychology. For this reason, French epistemology came to identify the creation of psychoanalysis with a rupture: the epistemological value of the Freudian *concept* of the unconscious is based on this difference from the aggregate of knowledge preceding it. The difference that Freud's American heirs invoked creates a new representation of the relations between heart and reason, however. Through all its mutations in the US, the psychoanalytic unconscious is marked by one constant:

It is always linked with the theme of 'truth,' and more precisely 'resistance to truth,' taking 'truth' here to refer to the painful but uniquely effective pathway toward a 'cure.' 'Heart,' in the sense of an obstacle refusing to submit to the reasons of reason, is therefore central to the Freudian conception of the human psyche. But the relation in the US heirs between 'heart' and 'reason' is no longer this traditional relation (1989/1992, pp. xiii–xiv).

The shifting foci in James' writings might be read this way (although see below) - his earlier career focused on the effort to allocate distinct, complementary, and con-tributory realms for science and Protestantism (e.g., *Principles of Psychology*), into his later one, the effort to demonstrate how reason emerges from intuitive foundations (heart) (e.g., *Varieties of Religious Experience*) – illustrating how the pathways to truth were reconfigured in the new relation. Nevertheless, the relations of heart and reason are conceived in such a way as to preserve the possibility of deciding upon a *theory* – pragmatism, radical empiricism, and pluralism in James' case – in which the corporeal, conjured as the practical and the visible, holds the card for the final verdict, modeling as well the verification processes in the psychical realms that prohibited the legitimation of Richard Hodgson's spirit and more broadly the ghost as object. The theory-building of mind sciences in the US cannot be separated, however, from Protestant doxology which gave shape to the matter of heart and the version of reason that starts to sound acceptable *as* a theory. It is here that Foucault's differentiation of sixteenth century tributaries – state-formation and how to be spiritually led – needs to be modified to account for an 'interpenetration' in US mind 'sciences' that never relied upon totalizing dis-tinctions between religion, nation, and science in the first place and that helps account for the differences to which Chertok and Stenger's point.

WESTERN SPIRITUALITY, PHILOSOPHY, AND SCIENCE: BIOPOWER AND 'THE MYSTICAL' IN THE NEW WORLD

For twenty-five years I have been in touch with the literature of psychical research and have had acquaintance with numerous "researchers." I have also spent a good many hours (although far fewer than I ought to have spent) in witnessing (or trying to witness) phenomena. Yet I am theoretically no further along that I was at the beginning; and I confess that at times I have been tempted to believe that the creator has eternally intended this department of nature to remain baffling, to prompt our curiosities and hopes and suspicions all in equal measure, so that although ghosts, and clairvoyances, and raps and messages from spirits, are always seeming to exist and can never be fully explained away, they also can never be susceptible of full corroboration. (James, 1909b, pp. 361–62)

It is not until the twentieth century that a category called World Religions comes into existence and it is across the nineteenth century that the previous taxonomic quadratic structure for defining nations and peoples – Christians, Jews, Moslems, and Others (often called heathens, pagans, and idolators) was modified (Masuzawa, 2005). Masuzawa argues that the modification concerned the reworking of the boundaries of the West through an Indo-Aryan turn that was accompanied by the Semiticization of Judaism and Islam and a German interest in Sanskrit. The Christian West needed to create a new, bleaching narrative about origins and at the intersection of comparative philology and comparative religion it was found(ed). In his genealogy of the terms religion and mysticism, King (2005) makes a similar point – that the labeling of Christianity as a *religion* that attempts to dominate especially through the medieval period meant that Christianity had become the reference point for what constitutes a religion. *Religio* as tradition and as 'to close' (such as to close eyes and ears for revelation or to close into secret initiations) in ancient Rome was transformed into *religio* as 'to bind' in the medieval period – to a set text, a series of rituals, and presumption of shared beliefs that could be referred to systemically. That religion could become distinct at all, separated from other possibilities and treated as a category rather than as way of life suggests not a disciplining of Christianity for King but a move into a new colonizing mode of occupying the point of reference, for organizing all comparisons. While Masuzawa sees secularization as a torsion within Christianity which masks European universalism in the language of pluralism, King argues that secularization arises out of a public/private division in which the domination of the index of what counts as a religion is placed in association with the private, the irrational, the mystical, and the feminine. Hence, even when or where Christianity is pushed to the side, it still dominates the criterion for determining what counts as public and what private. For King, the nations that form the area known in the nineteenth century as Europe were dependent in part upon prior obsession with religious homogeneity – the belief in a shared essence emerges around "to bind" and especially but not only around Protestant and Catholic versions of what it meant to bind. It was religious particularity as viewed through a Christian theological template that enabled the idea that nations could operate as enforced groupings with constitutional boundaries. With the Enlightenment, King argues, the mystical becomes redefined and ejected within the messy intersection of religion-nation-rationality, as something that is separate from science and literature, attributed to the East, to the invisible, to the personal, to that which cannot be publicly corroborated. At the same time, King suggests, the mystical becomes that which is already existing within the West's story about itself, repressed as pagan or occult – the mystical as the unconscious of the West, the unknowable and unfaceable alterity within and without.

It is at this point that the outline of processes suggestive of the colonizing and/or imperial might be glimpsed beyond the territoriality of the *geo-*, not just via attention to what constituted science that erupted, for instance, within the formation of laboratories in university and clinical settings, and not just via attention to the kinds of subject-matter elevated or the conditions of proof invoked. That is, such contours also took shape, and required, a kind of *subject who could be produced in the new relationship to truth* that practices now called the social sciences promulgated.

In *The Hermeneutics of the Subject* (1981/2005) Foucault lays out among other things how notions of conversion become elaborated and transformed, how there is an important and constant presence of an image of the return to the self that marks conversion and its relationship to knowing. The micro-strategies of conversion and this relationship to knowing are apparent in Hellenistic and Roman thought while the relation of return is refigured in early and later Christian thought, including how self withdraws from its surrounds, how self flees from self, how self splits from self to be under it's own eyes, etc. He maps, then, a shift from Platonic *epistrophe* (first turning away from appearances, second, taking stock of oneself by acknowledging ignorance, and third, using this reversion to the self, which leads to recollection, to return to the homeland of essences, truth and Being), to Christian *metanoia* (organized around self-renunciation, the sudden, dramatic change to one's being, and living a life without error and regrets), to a third way in which "turning your gaze on yourself" and "knowing yourself" became established within the general theme of conversion as turning away from distraction to clear a space around the self, to think of the relation between self and aim, to a fourth in which one is taking oneself as an object of knowledge, an object of analysis, decipherment, and reflection. The turning back of the gaze on oneself has taken different forms, then, some of which become elaborated and some more or less lost. Descartes' version of self-gazing exemplifies this complexity. The Cartesian approach had referred to knowledge of the self as a form of consciousness and

> What's more, by putting the self-evidence of the subject's own existence at the very source of access to being, this knowledge of oneself (no longer in the form of the test of self-evidence, but in the form of the impossibility of doubting my existence as a subject) made the 'know yourself' into a fundamental means of access to truth…But if the Cartesian approach thus requalified the *gnothiseauton*, for reasons that are fairly easy to isolate, at the same time – and I want to stress this – it played a major part in discrediting the principle of care of the self and in excluding it from the field of modern philosophical thought (Foucault, 1981/2005, p. 14).

This separation underwrites the distinctions between what Foucault calls Western philosophy, science, and spirituality. Philosophy was

> The form of thought that asks, not of course what is true and what is false, but what determines that there is and can be truth and falsehood and whether or not we can separate the true *and* the false. We will call 'philosophy' the form of thought that asks what it is that enables the subject to have access to the truth which attempts to determine the conditions and limits of the subject's access to the truth (p. 15).

What he next lays out are the dimensions of spirituality in its split from philosophy and science, a sheering that I suggest here never quite took place in the formation of social sciences in the US and in particular psychical science, for such practices built their pathways to truth via the necessity of the conversion of the subject:

> If we call this 'philosophy,' then I think we could call 'spirituality' the search, practice, and experience through which the subject carries out the necessary transformations on himself in order to have access to the truth. We will call 'spirituality' then the set of these researches, practices, and experiences, which may be purifications, ascetic exercises, renunciations, conversions of looking, modifications of existence, etc., which are, not for knowledge but for the subject, for the subject's very being, the price to be paid for access to the truth (p. 15).

Foucault argues that spirituality, as it appears in the West at least, has three characteristics. First,

> Spirituality postulates that truth is never given to the subject by right....It postulates that for the subject to have right of access to the truth he must be changed, transformed, shifted, and become, to some extent and up to a certain point, other than himself. The truth is only given to the subject at a price that brings the subject's being into play. For as he is, the subject is not capable of truth. I think that this is the simplest but most fundamental formula by which spirituality can be defined. (p. 15)

This establishes the grounds for doing the work on the subject that is deemed necessary for the subject to be a knowing one. This work involves two kinds – *eros* and *askesis*.

> It follows from this point of view there can be no truth without a conversion or a transformation of the subject. This conversion, this transformation of the subject – and this will be the second major aspect of spirituality – may take place in different forms. Very roughly we can say (and this is again a very schematic survey) that this conversion may take place in the form of a movement that removes the subject from his current status and condition (either an ascending movement of the subject himself, or else a movement by which the truth comes to him and enlightens him). Again, quite conventionally, let us call this movement, in either of its directions, the movement of *eros* (love). Another major form through which the subject can and must transform himself in order to have access to the truth is a kind of work. This is a work of the self on the self, an elaboration of the self by the self, a progressive transformation of the self by the self for which one takes responsibility in a long labor of ascesis (*askesis*). Eros and askesis are, I think, the two major forms in Western spirituality for conceptualizing the modalities by which the subject must be transformed in order finally to become capable of truth. (p. 15)

Last, the truth-effects have to become visible in the subject and understood as caused by the work the subject did to prepare for the transformation or conversion that gave access to truth:

> Finally, spirituality postulates that once access to the truth has really been opened up, it produces effects that are of course, the consequence of the spiritual approach taken in order to achieve this, but which at the same time are something quite different and much more: effects which I will call 'rebound' ('de retour'), effects of the truth on the subject. For spirituality, the truth is not just what is given to the subject, as reward for the act of knowledge as it were…(I)n the truth and in access to the truth, there is something that fulfills the subject himself, which fulfills or transfigures his very being….I think we can say that in and of itself as an act of knowledge it could never give access to the truth unless it was prepared, accompanied, doubled, and completed by a certain transformation of the subject; not of the individual, but of the subject himself in his being as subject (p. 16).

The triadic patterning of the subject can be seen in James' approach to the transcripts and the formation of psychical science, and insofar as such an approach required a conversion of the subject spirituality, science, and philosophy remain difficult to disaggregate. The patterning of the subject suggests something less about divisions between disciplines, then, and something more about a different kind of regionalism. The kind of rationality that suits the term *rigorous* in the transcript analysis, for example, is already a version of Protestant interpretive strategies, the legacy of idealist philosophy, and of *Bildung* pedagogy, where intersubjectivity is the precondition for subjectivity. The difficulty of using the categories to problematize the categorizations is compounded by a further noticeability – the existence of a spirit is not conflatable with spirituality for James. Rather, the entire approach to the transcripts and the question of spirit-return might simply be cast as part of the formation of 'Western' and the limits of Occidental thought on thought, but in a different form than what Foucault attributes to the onto-epistemological divisions drawn mainly from Enlightenment, revolutionary, and modern experiences on the European continent. This becomes 'evident,' for instance, in James' discussion of what Rector of the Imperator-band could be if not a spirit and in his treatment of the most vexing of the incidents for him, the pecuniary messages. In regard to the former, James explains that Rector was mostly in control of Piper during the Hodgson sittings, laying out his position in regard to who or what Rector was (p. 254).

> Dr. Hodgson was disposed to admit the claim of reality of Rector and of the whole Imperator-Band of which he is a member, while I have rather favored the idea of their all being dream creations of Mrs. Piper, probably having no existence except when she is in trance, but consolidated repetition into personalities consistent enough to play their several roles. Such at least is the dramatic impression which my acquaintance with the sittings has left on my mind. I can see no contradiction between Rector's being on the one hand an improvised

creature of this sort, and his being on the other hand the extraordinarily impressive personality which he unquestionably is. (1909a, p. 254)

The question arises, though, as to *how* – if this be so, *how* is it that Piper can do this?

> As I conceive the matter, it is on this mass of secondary and automatic personality of which of late years Rector has been the centre, and which forms the steady background of Mrs. Piper's trances, that the supernormal knowledge which she unquestionably displays is flashed. Flashed, grafted, inserted – use what word you will – the trance-automatism is at any rate the intermediating condition, the supernormal knowledge comes as if from beyond, and the automatism uses its own forms in delivering it to the sitter. The most habitual form is to say that it comes from the spirit of a departed friend. The earliest messages from "Hodgson" have been communicated by "Rector," but he soon spoke in his own name, and the only question which I shall consider in this paper is this: *Are there any unmistakable indications in the messages in question that something that we may call the "spirit" of Hodgson was probably really there?* We need not refine yet upon what the word "spirit" means and on what spirits are and can do. We can leave the meaning of the word provisionally very indeterminate, – the vague popular notion of what a spirit is is enough to begin with. (1909a, pp. 254–55)

What becomes noticeable is not so much internal distinctions such as spirituality, philosophy, and science but the conditions of proof – work of the subject upon self, the shift into another state, the confessional and testimony, *eros* and *askesis*, the subject-object distinction, consciousness, conversion of looking, access to truth – the intersection that Foucault argued belonged to "that field in which the questions of the *human being, consciousness, origin*, and *the subject* emerge, mingle, and separate off," a field where "it would probably not be incorrect to say that the problem of structure arose there, too" (Foucault, 1972, p. 16; emphasis added). Here resides, then, the nodal point of a logocentrism of argument-building ('rationalism') formulated within the limits of discourse that make 'the West' recognizable as such and applied to a topic that James felt he had no intellectual heritage for disentangling, i.e., how to turn a 'spirit' into a 'scientific' object.

Caught between analytical priorities of object and structure, of essence and the primacy of relations, James thus weaves between adjacent rationalities, leaving one version only able to end up in another in order to problematize the former. It is almost as though the Motherland (theoretico-experimental scientific rationality) as imitated unsuccessfully by the colony (ethico-redemptive scientific rationality) allows nothing outside of it's Self, requiring for respect and recognition an emulation sure to fail which returns to elevate the origin as pure and proper.

The 'feeling' upon reading the *Report* is that James seems desperate to preserve a reputation as measured and rational and to foreclose the spiritist thesis while deep down holding to it or at least to its hope. This is the impression Hodgson had of him that he wrote about in a letter to a friend – that James had never to Hodgson's knowledge admitted publicly belief in spiritism but that he, Hodgson, thinks James privately adheres to the belief.

How one gets that 'feeling' upon reading the *Report* or makes such a call, however, was and is a central part of the dilemma under discussion and that James directly engages and confronts. His willingness to admit his fluctuation around what he called "the reality-feeling" when in a sitting with Piper and when reading over the transcript later is indicative of two new scientific objects in the (almost) making – the ghost *and* the social scientist.

> This was the shape in which I myself left the matter in my recent preliminary report. I said that spirit-return was not proved by the Hodgson-control material, taken by itself, but that this adverse conclusion might possibly be reversed if the limited material were read in the light of the total mass of cognate phenomena. To say this is to say that the proof still baffles one. It still baffles me, I have to confess; but whether my subjective insufficiency or the objective insufficiency (as yet) of our evidence be most to blame for this, must be decided by others. (1909a, p. 282)

For some of his colleagues in the ASPR, invisible did not mean untrue or non-existent, nor did it mean not amenable to scientific rationality. For James, the externally visual had to play a part in the confirmation, in the conditions of proof, despite his deep commitment to introspection. The transcripts, then, became the key visual object to which the researcher could return, the ejected-from-body site of calculation in the apparent absence of any other pivot point around which viewers could gather and point to, agreeing about the work they had already done upon themselves. Naturalist explanations and scientific logic as James called it fundamentally required mechanical or chemical causation and for the motion to be captured somehow in a visible object:

> One who takes part in a good sitting has usually a far livelier sense, both of the reality and of the importance of the communication, than one who merely reads the record. Active relations with a thing are required to bring the reality of it home to us, and in a trance-talk the sitter actively co-operates. When you find your questions answered and your allusions understood; when allusions are made that you think you understand, and your thoughts are met by anticipation, denial, or corroboration; when you have approved, applauded, or exchanged banter, or thankfully listened to advice that you believe in; it is difficult not to take away an impression of having encountered something sincere in the way of a social phenomenon. The whole talk gets warmed with your own warmth, and takes on the reality of your own part in it; its confusions and defects you charge to the imperfect conditions, while you credit the successes to the genuineness of the communicating spirit. Most of us also, when sitters, react more, prick our ears more, to the successful parts of the communication. Those consequently loom more in our memory, and give the key to our dramatic interpretation of the phenomenon. But a sitting that thus seemed important at the time may greatly shrink in value on a cold re-reading;

and if read by a non-participant, it may seem thin and almost insignificant. (1909a, p. 281)

One of the many questions that James' reflections here draws one into, then, pertains to how boundaries form around conferring reality in one direction and not another, and to what extent the emergent (and contemporary) social sciences might be suggestive of 'softer, gentler' forms of colonizing and/or imperial processes that often escape the focus of studies directed at war, the biophysical sciences and technology, and their relation to accumulation (Macleod, 2000). In his critique of Tolstoi's 'Oriental pessimism' and elevation of 'our Western commonsense' in *Talks to Teachers*, for instance, James argues that it is the belief in *both* the importance of outer appearances and a spiritual world that succeeds in the real understanding of things. The regionalization is a priori and remains so across much of the twentieth century. What remains unclear in Foucault's early lectures of *The Hermeneutics of the Subject* is how the outcome is used as the tool, how Foucault's reference to the Western in Western spirituality, science, and philosophy becomes recognizable as Western and why texts from ancient Greece set the temporo-epistemic limits on the analysis. Where the arbitrary border between West and rest, and repetitively West and East, gets laid seems to remain part of 'the unconscious of history' in the *Hermeneutics* lectures, while distinctions between France and the US can be confidently attended to in texts such as Chertok and Stenger's.

The urge to distinguish, the processes of perception, and distantiation are, however, a part of the problematic being approached. It is here that one is able to more fully elaborate what might have been at stake in the rationalization of the mystical as personal and as excess, that is, the new versions of biopower upon which nation-formation in the so-called New World relied. The human-mind-consciousness-rational-thought-that-is-procedural equation, which is given new dimensions and modes of operation across James' writings, facilitates a non-total shift in the definition of 'our Western commonsense', that from acquiring more apparently '"material' geopolitical territories, which he protests as anti-imperialism, to the exploration of the final two, unchartered frontiers of the nineteenth century – the conscious/unconscious border and the life/death border – the seemingly last available 'spaces' of conquest and expansion made available now to perception and governance.

The link to Foucault's understanding of biopower becomes more obvious and more crucial at this point, then: what is given in seeing, the pre-coded eye, is now largely instrumental –James as for his contemporaries, argues that physical form suggests inner virtue which in turn determines what one is fitted for. The body especially acts as a slate for *étatisation*, "the extension and intensification of micro-powers, in the guise of an unrestricted state control" (Foucault, 1976/1978, p. 149–150). Here, one would not envisage

A 'history of mentalities' that would take account of bodies only through the manner in which they have been perceived and given meaning and value; but a 'history of bodies' and the manner in which what is most material and most vital in them has been invested (Foucault, 1976/1978, p. 152).

A common argument in political philosophy about physical form relates racism and state-formation. Here, the creation of nation-states, standing armies, and police forces are posited as structures and then racism follows as an arbitrary grouping strategy specific to each context for maintenance of bourgeois privilege within those structures. Foucault's reversal of this account is key. The specificity attributed the human and the sequencing within a hierarchical chain of being is the normalizing move that precedes and enables nation-state formation – that is, to reduce it, racism makes nationalism possible, and racism took shape ("racism in its modern, 'biologizing,' statist form") when an analytics of sexuality and symbolics of blood, initially distinct regimes of power, merged, fabricating and lodging the practice of sexual intercourse *not as the anchor but as a manifestation within* the discourse of sexuality, eugenics, and populational management. Biopower, as techniques of populational management infused and supported by forms of disciplinary power that emerge in the late eighteenth century for Foucault, is not a monolithic causal explanation, however, but a series of strategies and tactics "in accordance with the development of modern technologies of power that take life as their objective" (Foucault, 1976/1978, p. 152).

By the turn of the twentieth century, the forms of biopower that emerged to refigure 'nation' and 'race' on a now-'global' surface had shifted. They were concerned as Foucault argued about nation-formation in Europe with the purity of blood and in regard "to make live and to let die." Quite often in sociological uptakes of Foucault, the focus has been on the latter, eradication as part of official and unofficial policies such as 'removal' of Native Americans from traditional lands, eugenic-based sterilization programs of babies with disabilities, lynchings of African Americans which reached their peak in the 1890s in the US, organized war, and the death penalty. Mendieta asks, for instance, "In so far as biopolitics is the management of life, how does it make die, how does it kill?" (Mendieta, 2002, p.7). Drawing on Foucault's lectures he argues that

> Foucault's answer is that in order to reclaim death, to be able to inflict death on its subjects, its living beings, biopower must make use of racism; more precisely, racism intervenes here to grant access to death...the political rationality of biopower is deployed over a population, which is understood as a continuum of life.

The focus on the continuum of life places the structures of racialized worldviews and hence of racism into close proximity with putting to death:

> This is where racism intervenes, not from without, exogenously, but from within, constitutively. For the emergence of biopower as the form of a new form of political rationality, entails the inscription within the very logic of the modern state the logic of racism. For racism grants...[quoting Foucault] "the conditions for putting to death in a society of normalization. Where there is a society of normalization, where there is a power that is, in all of its surface and in first instance, and first line, a bio-power, racism is indispensible as a condition to be able to put to death someone, in order to be able to put to death others. The homicidal function of the state, to the degree that the state

functions on the modality of this bio-power, can only be assured by racism. (Foucault 1977, p. 227)" (Mendieta, 2002, p. 7)

The operation of biopower, backgrounded by a long history of war, thus made possible a new turn in regard to nation-building. Mendieta argues that the war of peoples, a war against invaders, imperial colonizers, turned into a war of races, which then turned into a war of classes, and then by the late nineteenth century turned into the war of a race, a biological unit, against its polluters and threats:

> Racism is the means by which bourgeois political power, biopower, re-kindles the fires of war within civil society. Racism normalizes and medicalizes war...Racism makes the killing of the other, of others, an everyday occurrence by internalizing and normalizing the war of society against its enemies. To protect society entails we be ready to kill its threats, its foes, and if we understand society as a unity of life, as a continuum of life, then these threat and foes are biological in nature (Mendieta, 2002, p. 8).

It is important to place the analysis of Hodgson's potential return within this process of nation-building, what Sylvia Wynter (1995) calls in the US the shift from the spirit to the flesh, from religion to Race as the main principle of identity and difference, and against the emphasis on 'to let die' because so rarely has biopower been understood in terms of new and intensified attention to paranormal phenomena at the turn of twentieth century, on the 'to make live' (longer or again) part that emerged and that attention to a conscious/unconscious problematic facilitated. That is, the focus on the continuation of life, on 'the other end' of the spectrum, suggests something in addition to the denigration of African Americans that the second incident in the *Report* raises overtly, and which James treats hurriedly. The reinscription and continuous elevation of whiteness arises not just as part of a continuum of life that eugenics, social hygiene, etc attended to, but also in the territorialization of after-life, as the ultimate proof of pre-destination and supremacy – the ability to keep on going, keep influencing, keep sequencing the system. Thus, the linking of nation-building to not just race-management but to life-management becomes possible from multiple angles, from bio- and thanatopolitics:

> If we understand racism to be about the management of life by creating a caesura in the living body of the population, which requires an urgent and exceptional vigilance, one that might call for an emergency and extreme measure, namely that of putting to death the now internalized threat; if, in other words, we understand racism as the normalization of the state of emergency against a biological threat, then we must seek to understand those institutions that normalize the mechanisms for dealing with racial threats (Mendieta, 2002, p. 9).

A state of emergency and of exceptionalism works in the other direction in the *Report*, but in different ways for James, not simply as biological threat, but as threat to the contours of governance that had been so dedicated previously to elevating the corporeal and the visible. These were the anchors of phenotypical difference, of deciding outer place, of allocating race among other 'populational categories,' these were the variables for determining that life was functional and adaptationist, that is, evolutionary, of proving that senses were given for survival, and that "higher" psychic faculties like telepathy and clairvoyance were only unfolded in the highest group, that is, within the developmental trajectory of a mostly sane whiteness, in the 'superior reasoning power' of Man, the faithful and/ or lapsed Protestant – the all-seeing, transcendent eye claimed for and as 'the West.'

The bases and contours of processes that appear colonizing and/or imperial thus take shape not simply through how a color-coded infant learns to think in early life, but how the adult might think on in the after-life – the willingess of whiteness, masculinity, and Protestant devotion, for instance, to be available in apparent absentia, to return as sage and prophet with even more knowledge than before. Far from being a window that made one open to new theories of Life or theses of reincarnation, the *Report's* distancing of spirit-return and its leaving for others to resolve indexes both the difficulty of taking corporeal models into the "psychic" realm once graphed and divided around a visible/invisible dichotomy indebted to structure/function, as well as the instability of commitments within Protestant expertism to the question of just what should be "known" or made available to a public positioned as beneath and graphed and coded around a primitive/civilized dichotomy.

CONCLUSION

The above has drawn Foucault's analysis of science, governmentality, and biopower into conversation in ways that exceed their initial concerns and has necessarily been oriented toward a different understanding of the political that is not reducible to the prerogatives of political philosophy:

> Political theory has to attend to the emergence of political rationality in terms not of its rationality, or claims to reason, but in terms of modalities of operation. Behind political rationality does not stand reason, or rather, reason is not the alibi of political rationality; instead, political rationality has to do with the horizon of its enactment" (Mendieta, 2002, p. 6).

Such horizons of enactment can be brought into view in different ways, for example by focusing traditionally on men killing each other in wars, tracking the flow of money, mapping the spread of technical inventions, mounting continuous critiques of neoliberalism, identifying the effects of power in new institutions, etc. I have taken the liberty here of considering that which more silently failed – the formation of psychical science as a legitimate research pursuit and the subsequent burial that nonetheless made it useful for bringing such now-traditional foci to the fore as the 'serious sites' for pursuits such as political philosophy.

Psychical science as examined through the endeavors in which James participated was an incitement to discourse that enabled at least three horizons of enactment to crystallize (which is not the same as making them clear): a religion-science-nation-West nexus in which were enfolded onto-theo-philosophical regionalism, the rationalities of social science, and a new logics of perception. At least three aspects of these horizons are important to underscore here. First, in a modern episteme and its search for origin, life/death dualism in particular becomes a commonsensical characteristic of 'the West' amid a scientific emphasis on rationalizable, this-worldly, finite causations – a dualism that James seriously questioned. The implicit link between science, governmentality, and biopower becomes clearer regardless of for or against– for the way in which discourse produces its objects as amenable to scientific analysis is tied to the pressure on Life as an objectifiable continuum that must be governed and managed for the overall health of 'the social organism.' The role of an unconscious can, then, be fairly well limited by the boundaries set within such a cosmological structure:

> In Western psychology...I think that there may be a tendency to over-emphasize the role of the unconscious in looking for the source of one's problems. I think that this stems from some basic assumptions that Western psychology starts with: for instance, it does not accept the idea of imprints being carried over from a past life. And at the same time there is an assumption that everything must be accounted for within this lifetime. So, when you can't explain what is causing certain behaviors or problems, the tendency is to always attribute it to the unconscious. It's a bit like you've lost something and you decide that the object is in this room. And once you have decided this, then you've already fixed your parameters, you've precluded the possibility of its being outside the room or in another room. So you keep on searching, but you are not finding it, yet you continue to assume that it is still hidden somewhere in the room. (HH Dalai Lama & Cutler, 1998, p. 7)

Second, the advent and controversies of psychical research, conditions of proof, and their allied discourses of vision as approached through this portrayal of Jamesian curiosity further demonstrate how the internal, in the double sense of both introspection and domestically, and external, in the double sense of an immediate exterior that subjectifies a child and transnationally, were each other's 'environment' for the 'systems' formulated, reciprocally linked into relations of intensification rather than opposition (Luhmann, 1985/1995). They fueled in an incidental or less direct way the pursuit of certainty, control, and perfection via the social sciences that would in part re-authorize a category or ordering called the West and its gradation of the world on a developmental scale. Elaborating such entanglements from a position that cannot completely and confidently articulate (and disarticulate) what the exclusively American part of this Western is or was at the time and what definitively constitutes the anti-imperial and/or postcolonial[11] (e.g., the temporal, the dispositional, the epistemological, the poetical, etc) always runs the risk of displeasing where habits of reading have relied upon entification rather than seepage. Yet, it is so very much the idea (fear? fascination?) of seepage from one maybe-entity into another that James and his colleagues in the ASPR investigated in all seriousness and with incredible diligence.

Third, the restrictions on knowledge-production at the turn of the twentieth century allowed sciences not only to professionalize but to do work for each other. The incitement to discourse especially that provided by the "discovery of the unconscious" enabled territories to be drawn around expansive and multiple conceptions of mind – in light of the excess that "psychical" came to represent academic fields worked out their respective and messy domains of obligation, roughly psychology to habit, behavior, and belief; medicine to diagnosis and correction; education to imitation and emulation; and parapsychology to 'extra'ordinary phenomena and psychic energy. These patterns continue today: The confinement of rationality and restriction on knowledge-production position curiosity in instrumental ways and with dual effects – a proliferation of curiosity emerges seeking affirmation as rational, and, a restriction on what can be imagined as real arises: one must believe there are a priori boundaries and borders, that only by crossing them can one know something (for the opposite, that of borderlessness, is automatically imagined as either some kind of homogenization/colonization in disguise or romantic transcendentalism), that there is such a thing as the human, that societies exist, that the most important if not only thing to look at is 'relations' between humans, and that the word power must be used somewhere in the fray to explain it all – a conceptual linkage and humanist pattern that Foucault historicizes but that much uptake of his governmentality thesis remains wedded to as given.

Psychical science, at the point of being named as such in the late nineteenth century, held a relation of intimate alterity to other emergent social sciences such as psychology, anthropology, and education. The points of overlap and separation between such sciences, then, remain an apt site for considering the politics of object-formation and conditions of proof, the (un)acceptable pathways to truth-production – in short, a heterotopic spectrum of rationalities in the (non)making that was never just about such sciences but the very composition of World. Beloff (1997) argues that this is a longer-standing pattern than might be presupposed – since the Scientific Revolution on the European continent, parapsychology has fallen outside the enclave of science, for such an event constitutes the scission that enables the 'para' to form. He defines parapsychology as challenging the mechanistic and reductionist implications of 'official science' by reaffirming the autonomy of mind, noting that such researchers are often accused of magical thinking. But magical thinking, he argues, differs in the manner of treatment of evidence. Parapsychology, unlike magic, must be open to the rejection of a hypothesis if it is to be taken seriously. This aligns it in the present with science as opposed to magic or pseudo-science, and in a reverse direction, rewrites its past. Beloff (1997, p. 15) notes, however, that in the challenges that parapsychological research has raised "the basic materialist assumption that the universe or physical world is a closed system, impervious to anything falling outside the domain of space-time events has never been renounced."

Beloff's historical survey of parapsychological studies notes further that none of the events of parapsychology which purport to cast doubt on this tenet has so far succeeded in upsetting it, "not, at any rate, in the eyes of the arbiters of official science." The result, outside quantum studies, has not been an open investigation but rather the reduction of 'new' evidence to the same conceptual, a priori template, 'an uneasy stalemate unsatisfactory to all concerned remains the case,' implying the (im)possibility of (another) narrative that might be lost: "It would be an unforgivable failure of nerve to call a halt to further efforts to come to grips with such [parapsychological] phenomena" and "The fact that opinions differ should never be an excuse for not expressing an opinion. One needs also to remember that skepticism is not necessarily a badge of tough-mindedness: it may equally be a sign of intellectual cowardice" (1997, p. xiv). As such, he suggests that the question of whether "mentalist abilities transcend a physicalist explanation" should be kept open. Moreover, amid the debate over whether things that appear as historical oddities should be ignored or examined he argues that it is vital to include cases that have no contemporary counterparts.

Beloff seems to suggest that parapsychology is the alterity by which 'official science' colonizes and reconstitutes itself as authoritative, especially via absorption – only when something becomes similar enough can it be recognized as different, as variation of a theme and deviation from a silent norm. Thus, whatever parapsychology would prove in 'empirical' and reproducible terms as perceivable and publicly corroborated would no longer belong to the domain of parapsychology. The results would be normalized and included within an expanded definition of the science of nature. Because of the historical malignment of parapsychological research, the rigor put into organizing and ensuring experimental controls in laboratory-based studies is immense. This has generated new efforts to theorize cause-effect, to undo the locality thesis, and to contest, from within as it were, the limits of scientific rationality in biophysical sciences and the new logics of perception formed in/as the social sciences at the turn of the twentieth century that presume linear, proximate causes as the most probable explanation for all events.

The point is not which view is correct, nor the elevation of parapsychological research. Nor is it to suggest that the interpenetration of a new logic of perception with rationalities of social science with the fabulation of nation and West is a matrix or event that simply falls from the sky, even if it involves it, or could have happened just anywhere. Nor is the goal to claim an "outsideness" from that which is here raised: The analysis, that is, encounters the historical conditions that make its sections and its turn possible, deploying a rationality, reflexivity, suggestiveness – strategies that are not substituting an alternative form, nor cutting across geometrical figures left uncontested in their shape. The remoralization or restoration of morality has not, then, been the aim. Rather, James' investigation into the spirit-return thesis at the moment of a new but submerged field's formation gives different content to one of Foucault's most profound questions in *Histoire de la Folie* that few critics of scientific rationality or of hyper-reflexivity ever take on directly or poetically: "Where can an interrogation lead us that does not follow reason in its horizontal course, but seeks to retrace in time that constant verticality which confronts European culture with what it is not, establishes its range by its own derangement?" (Foucault, 1961/1988, p. xi).

James' psychical research can perhaps now be seen as the embodiment of a response in the US, of where an interrogation can lead post-scission, once a mad-reason nexus has already made its mark, illustrating not the essence or identity of perception, rationality, America, Europe, Foucault's 'us,' or a chimerical, yet still-has-to-be-dealt-with West, but the difficulties of a 'realm' that defies the concern for quiddity - a confrontation beneath the language of reason, posed as a spirit in the sky:

> What realm do we enter which is neither history or knowledge, nor history itself; which is controlled neither by the teleology of truth nor the rational sequence of causes, since causes have value and meaning only beyond the division? A realm, no doubt, where what is in question is the limits rather than the identity of a culture (Foucault, 1961/1965, p. xi).

NOTES

[1] As elsewhere (see Baker, 2001), I do not use the possessive here such as James' and Jamesian to indicate individualization, blame, origin, or ownership. Readers familiar with Foucault's critique of authorship, the book, and especially of the oeuvre should be familiar with such caveats and their rationale. The problem of writing – attributions to a subject of a sentence such as Foucault, I, James, etc – always raises its head in the form of re-entry in such explanations, however.

[2] For examples of this strategy and reflexivity in regard to it see Anderson, 2002 and Chakrabarty, 2000.

[3] Foucault makes this argument in the opening of *Histoire de la Folie*, that the formation of a mad-reason nexus participates in the where and when of the West.

[4] I use ethico-redemptive sciences as per Chertok and Stengers to refer to social sciences and humanities (the human sciences) and theoretico-experimental sciences to refer to biophysical sciences.

[5] Before turning to the impossible ambitiousness of such a project I want to say a brief word here about the field of curriculum studies. Curriculum studies operates as the cultural studies of education, an interdisciplinary site in which the often zealously-guarded encampments of theoretical divisions in other disciplines are known but ignored and/or redeployed. Because education is both a discipline and preparation for a profession it is bound by nationalisms, history, and by law in ways that other disciplines sometimes are not. In the separation of sciences, the unconscious, and "its" formative role in the delineation of academic domains education's reduction to concerns over compulsory or enforced schooling acts as a kind of unconscious for other disciplines, enabling the "What to do with the kids?" questions to be avoided and shifting focus, for instance, to relations between "adult" rational actors (rethinking "the subject"), almost obsessively and infinitely so. I have discussed the limitations of political philosophical rethinkings of the subject in regard to "the child" in Baker (2001), which opens different analytical possibilities that the debate between structuralism and "post" approaches have foreclosed or ignored, and I have laid out in Baker (2007a) in regard to anglophone receptions of Foucault how the persistence of the subject is part of the limit, and repetition, of Occidentalist thought.

[6] As the discussion will indicate the naming of nations is part of the problem of border. For analytical purposes here I refer to *in* France and *in* the United States, but the entification problematic exceeds this rhetorical device.

[7] RH = "Richard Hodgson"; WJ = William James; AJ = Alice James.

[8] James popularizes Peirce's term pragmatism. Jamesian pragmatism disarticulates origin from cause. See James (1907).

[9] I have argued that Newton inferred the presence of absolute space rather than assumed it, which is Walach et al's position. For a discussion of his *Principia* in relation to theories of power and force and their implications for political philosophy and education see Baker (2001).

[10] By given I mean this: that space, time, and object may not always be theorized in the same way but like the terms *power* and *force* today in the social sciences they always have to be mentioned, invoked, assumed, or dealt with *as* the very idea of analysis.

[11] See Anderson's (2002) discussion of distinction between anti-colonial and anti-imperial approaches, postcolonial theory, and historical anthropologies of modernity.

REFERENCES

Abraham, I. (2006). The contradictory spaces of postcolonial techno-science. *Economic and Political Weekly*, 210–217.

Anderson, W. (2002). Postcolonial technoscience. *Social Studies of Science, 32*, 643–658.

Baker, B. (2007a). Hypnotic inductions: On the persistence of the subject. *Foucault Studies, 4*, 127–148.

Baker, B. (2007b). Animal magnetism and curriculum history. *Curriculum Inquiry, 37*(2), 123–158.

Baker, B. M. (2001). *In perpetual motion: Theories of power, educational history, and the child* (Vol. 14). New York: Peter Lang.

Beloff, J. (1997). *Parapsychology: A concise history*. New York: Palgrave Macmillan.

Bynum, E. B. (1999). *The African unconscious: Roots of ancient mysticism and modern psychology*. New York: Teachers College Press.

Chertok, L., & Stengers, I. (1989/1992). *A critique of psychoanalytic reason: Hypnosis as a scientific problem from Lavoisier to Lacan*. Stanford, CA: Stanford University Press.

Clark, S. (2007). *Vanities of the eye: Vision in early modern European culture*. Oxford, UK: Oxford University Press.

Dear, P. R. (1995). *Discipline and experience: The mathematical way in the scientific revolution*. Chicago: University of Chicago Press.

Ellenberger, H. (1970). *The discovery of the unconscious: The history and evolution of dynamic psychiatry*. New York: Basic Books Publishers, Inc.

Foucault, M. (2001/2005). *The hermeneutics of the subject: Lectures at the Collège de France 1981–1982*. New York: Palgrave Macmillan.

Foucault, M. (2000a). Governmentality. In J. D. Faubion (Ed.), *Essential works of Foucault, 1954–1984: Power* (Vol. 3, pp. 201–202). New York: The New Press.

Foucault, M. (1976/1978). *The history of sexuality: An introduction* (Vol. I). New York: Vintage Books.

Foucault, M. (1966/1973). *The order of things: An archaeology of the human sciences*. New York: Vintage Books.

Foucault, M. (1961/1988). *Madness and civilization: A history of insanity in the age of reason*. New York: Vintage Books.

His Holiness the Dalai Lama, & Cutler, H. (1998). *The art of happiness*. New York: Riverhead Books.

James, W. (1909a/1986). Report on Mrs. Piper's Hodgson-control. In G. Murphy & R. O. Ballou (Eds.), *The works of William James: Essays in psychical research* (pp. 253–260). Cambridge, MA: Harvard University Press.

James, W. (1909b/1986). Confidences of a "psychical researcher." In G. Murphy & R. O. Ballou (Eds.), *The works of William James: Essays in psychical research* (pp. 361–375). Cambridge, MA: Harvard University Press.

James, W. (1907). *Pragmatism: A new name for some old ways of thinking. Popular lectures on philosophy series*. New York: The Riverside Press.

James, W. (1902/2007). *Varieties of religious experience*. Charleston, SC: Bibliobazaar.

James, W. (1899/1915). *Talks to teachers on psychology and to students on some of life's ideals*. New York: H. Holt.

James, W. (1890/1923). *The principles of psychology* (Vol. 1). New York: Henry Holt & Co.

King, R. (2005). *Orientalism and religion: Postcolonial theory, India, and "the mystic East"*. London: Routledge.

Luhmann, N. (1985/1995). *Social systems* (J. John Bednarz, with Dirk Baecker, Trans.). Stanford, CA: Stanford University Press.

MacLeod, R. (Ed.). (2000). *Nature and empire: Science and the colonial enterprise: Vol. 15. Osiris.* Chicago: History of Science Society, Inc.

Masuzawa, T. (2005). *The invention of world religions or, how European universalism was preserved in the language of pluralism.* Chicago: University of Chicago Press.

Mendieta, E. (2002). *"To make live and to let die": Foucault on racism.* Paper presented to the Foucault Circle, APA Central Division Meeting.

romanticism and the science of the mind. New York: Cambridge University Press.

Spivak, G. C. (2000). *A critique of postcolonial reason: Toward a history of the vanishing present.* Cambridge, MA: Harvard University Press.

Taylor, E. (1986). *William James on exceptional mental states: The 1896 Lowell Lectures.* Amherst, MA: The University of Massachusetts Press.

Walach, H., Schmidt, S., Schneider, R., Seiter, C., & Bösch, H. (2002). Melting boundaries: Subjectivity and intersubjectivity in the light of parapsychological data. *European Journal of Parapsychology, 17,* 72–96.

Winter, A. (1998). *Mesmerized: Powers of mind in Victorian Britain.* Chicago: The University of Chicago Press.

LEW ZIPIN AND MARIE BRENNAN

18. ANALYSING SECONDARY SCHOOL STRATEGIES IN CHANGING TIMES: THE INSIGHTS AND GAPS OF A GOVERNMENTALITY LENS

GOVERNMENTALITY ANALYTICS – A FOUCAULDIAN EXCITEMENT

In English-speaking academia, Foucault's work has arrived among critical educationalists – those who focus analytically on *power* in schooling – in three significant waves. In the early 1980s, came the genealogy *Discipline and Punish* (1977), inciting critical vision of schools as exemplars of time/space microphysics, panoptic surveillance and other disciplinary institutional mechanisms[1]. Shortly after, *History of Sexuality Vol 1* (1979) brought further concepts for analysing schools as sites of biopower that regulates lives and constitutes identities through confessional pedagogies and other pastoral discursive practices. Trickling into translation since the early 1990s, but gathering pace recently, Foucault's govern-mentality lectures (1991; 1997) are stimulating new inquiries into how pedagogic constitution of educated subjects, at the micro level of classrooms, links to macro-scale formations of state rationales for governing the conduct of conduct of social activities and resources in targeting economic and other security needs of populations.

As with many ground-breaking fields of academic enterprise, those who identify with Foucauldian analytics tend to define their methodo-logics in terms of analytic gains *vis a vis* older approaches they consider theirs to supersede. At the same time, they enter into and provoke debates about what conceptual tools offer what explanatory virtues for understanding operations of power upon, within and through social institutions. Indeed, what some had critiqued as a major gap in Foucauldian analytics – that its stress on dispersed and capillary micro-power mechanisms explained little about power at more macro levels of state and political economy – seems in vital ways addressed by Foucault's attention to liberalism as a governmental rationality, and to historic shifts from classical to neo-liberal regimes of policy and practice. In varied domains of socio-political study, including education (as this volume reflects), many are applying a governmentality lens to diverse and widening phenomena, generating a fertile field of investigation into how social conduct is governed – through what programs, techniques and rationalities – in trajectories from historic pasts into presents and verging futures.

We believe a governmentality lens offers much that is insightful and needed, including challenges to the assumptions of prior critical analytic traditions. At the same time, we see need to interrogate some of the departures, and the reasoning

M.A. Peters et al. (eds.), Governmentality Studies in Education, 341–354.

behind them that Foucault and his followers have championed; for example, Dean (1999):

> The study of governmentality is continuous with [prior critical] framework[s] in that it regards the exercise of power and authority as anything but self-evident and in need of considerable analytical resources. It does, however, break with many of the characteristic assumptions of theories of the state, such as problems of legitimacy, the notion of ideology, and the questions of the possession and source of power. (p. 9)

In what follows we weigh gains but also costs of such breaks for explanatory power in critical analysis of schooling. To begin, we apply a governmentality lens – particularly its ways of treating human capital as a neoliberal rationale – to a phenomenon in our Australian home state of South Australia: rising numbers of part-time students in the final two years of high school. Extending from this we consider the viability of breaking from questions of (1) state legitimacy and ideology, and (2) who possesses power in relation to whom, as problematics for analysis.

Human Capital (govern)Mentalities in Policy/Institutional Assemblages

In Foucault's analysis, as has been noted (Lemke, 2001; Dean, 1999; Gordon, 1991), a key principle of liberal political rationality is that government continually must critique itself to ensure that it furthers individual and collective liberty. In economic terms this meant, for classic liberalism, that government should limit its extensions into social domains so as not to interfere with but to respect the form of the market (Lemke, 2001, p. 198). In contrast, *neo*liberalism exalts "market freedom" as a principle that government must not just respect but actively foster by functioning as "a kind of permanent economic tribunal" (Foucault, 1979, quoted by Lemke, 2001, p. 198). Thus, "government itself becomes a sort of enterprise whose task it is to … invent market-shaped systems of action for individuals, groups and institutions" (ibid, p. 197).

This proactive impetus to market-motivate social conduct can be seen in government policies urging development of *human capital*: a concept put into political play in the 1960s by Chicago School economists, most notably Becker (1964). Human capital rationalities incite people to think of themselves as having capacities – both "inborn physical-genetic predispositions, and the entirety of skills … acquired as the result of 'investments' in … education, training and also love, affection, etc" (Lemke 2001, p. 199) – that are marketable in economic and social-cultural domains. Such ways of thinking thus operate as govern*mentalities* in the eminently Foucauldian sense of linking policy/institutional regimes for governing populations with individual inculcation of self-regulatory subjective norms. In economic terms, people are stimulated to shift their orientations to labour markets, notes Lemke (2001, p. 199):

No longer [as] employees dependent on a company with only their labour power to sell, but bearing a special type of capital ... not like other forms, for the ability, skill and knowledge cannot be separated from the person who possesses them.

In parlaying their *humanly embodied* capital, people presumably can and ought to act in society as "autonomous entrepreneurs with full responsibility for their own investment decisions" (ibid., p. 199), who pursue lifelong learning – not just in formal schooling but through experiences in work and life-style domains – in order continually to expand their powers of human capital (Simons, 2007).

As Dean and Hindess (1998, p. 7) advise, Foucault saw government "as a complex activity ... viewed [not] simply as the expression ... of political or economic theories" but as "an inventive, strategic, technical and artful set of 'assemblages' fashioned from diverse elements, put together in novel and specific ways" (p. 8). Within such assemblages, rationales like human capital are effective only in the ways and degrees to which they articulate with material techniques and strategies "associated with the exercise of various kinds of authority" (ibid., p. 7). Indeed, such exertions of authority extend and assemble across a far more diverse terrain than just agencies of the state. To understand formations, cohesions and transmutations of governmental assemblages, we do need to look at loci of state action through which discourses promoting mentalities such as human capital circulate; but we must also look across multiple institutional and lived sites where mentalities are more tacitly taken up and put to work by actors in specific contexts.

In Australia as other western nations, an ascendant neoliberal policy climate has seen much enunciation – from international bodies, national and state governments, business organisations, media and other venues – of economic rationales stressing schools as producers of human capital to secure national growth and individual job prospects. After percolating for a few decades, such discourses reached crescendos following 1981 and 1991 recessions, from which decent job prospects, especially for *young* workers, significantly and lastingly declined. Government reports (Carmichael, 1992; Mayer, 1992), media and union voices began stressing high school completion and further education in relation to employment skills. Categories of national statistical collection altered in telling ways: whereas youth – signifying pre-working young adults – previously meant ages 12-18, a later youth stage, ages 19-25, has since been added. Associated discourses normalise notions that more qualifications and contractual early work experiences are needed for adult work readiness in new knowledge economies. Policies to increase school retention have been accompanied by tactical mechanisms such as new forms of senior school certificate that include VET subjects. More recently some states have introduced legislation increasing the compulsory schooling age.

Such policy/populist mediations entwine a melange of mentalities – pathways from school to work; balancing academic, work and life activities; workplace experience; flexible competencies; lifelong learning; human capital – that circulate as resources feeding into identity and strategy formations among young people, teachers, parents and others. Ministries of Education are important catalytic agents in this process, working to make diverse discursive and practical threads more or less cohesive with an overarching neoliberal reasoning. Other government agencies are also interactively involved: in South Australia, a whole of government approach to increasing school retention makes policy workers in each area of government responsible for weaving their own Ministers portfolio concerns into addressing the problem of educational retention – i.e. keeping more students in schools to graduation in year twelve through the promise of building their human capital. Government itself, then, can be understood as a complex assemblage of diverse assemblers.

Seen through a Foucauldian lens, however, government Ministries more importantly are sites where much broader governmentalisation processes act upon the state (rather than vice versa; see Dean, 1999). Education policy workers thus weave discourses and techniques circulating from multiple sites: other government agencies, industry bodies, international policy documents and more. Not least are institutional settings where people in everyday life put such resources to work. In this vein, we emphasise that mixes and new emergences of reason and tactic arise not only in venues of 'government' *per se*, but in schools, workplaces and other locations where learners take up and assemble both discursive and practical-technical resources. Approximately 80% of high school students participate in the casual labour market from year 9 at school, appropriating and developing rationales and practices, across school and work venues, of CV; portfolio; demonstrations of flexibility, competencies and teamwork capacities; and more. The complex assemblages by which human capital is pursued are part-and-parcel of what Rose (1999) and others see as the *pedagogisation* of everyday life, linking diverse spaces of academic, work and life-style strategies by which learners come to sense themselves, says Lemke (cited above), as autonomous entrepreneurs with full responsibility for their own investment decisions.

Human Capital (govern)Mentalities in Senior Secondary School Strategies

In a research project in South Australia, human capital mentalities could be seen within a growing trend toward part-time study in senior secondary years (Ramsay, 2004; Brennan et al., 2007)[2]. While most schools persisted in dominant institutional constructions of normal students as full-time in an age-cohort progression – reinforced by timetabling and other practices – the study found perhaps half of students doing years 11 and 12 part-time. Part-time strategies showed an emergent variety, depending on school and student contexts, with staff and students stating a range of time-balancing reasons:
- working in family business/farm or to support their/family financial needs;
- caring for child (one's own or others), sibling, parent, grandparent;
- reducing stresses of disability or physical/mental health needs ;
- returning to school to try again while balancing adult life demands;
- managing risks of failing out of school altogether;
- allowing other school activities, e.g. sport teams, music;
- spreading the load over three or more years rather than two;
- increasing tertiary entrance scores.

In focus groups and surveys, both full- and part-time students stated needs to gain school certificates to position themselves for future education/work pathways. Some echoed policy rhetoric of international NGOs (e.g. deLors, 1996), national/ state governments and business organisations (e.g. BCA, 2007). Discourses of investment in building study and work capacities were prevalent, with needs to 'open doors to better futures' perhaps more pronounced by those with lower expectations of *academic* success, often joined to self-blame for not having been 'better' students. Still, young people working on family farms, caring for children, etc, articulated then-versus-now senses of increased options; indeed, one third of part-time students claimed that without part-time options they would not be in school at all, indicating the importance of new modes of managing oneself across diverse institutions and times of life. In schools, correspondingly, an emergent new norm of the flexible student was discernable: one who can maximize future options in work, education, training and life through a balance of activities during school years: work, community service, child/family care, academic and vocational subjects.

Such mobile transactions between home, work, school and other institutional locations, in ways and degrees not seen before, suggests that rationales and tactics of educational self-investment derive from, and (re)assemble in, diverse points of emergence. Moreover, new strategic inventions are not simply top-down, but emerge to real extent among young people themselves. We note that the phenomenon of part-time study, and strategies and mentalities associated with it, took little impetus from agencies and instruments of government *per se*. Rather, students and schools – encountering exigencies of historic time and place in concretely lived sites – started 'doing' part-time, in the process finding leeway for it within policy regimes. We suggest that a complex climate of shifting socio-economic and cultural possibilities and constraints opens room for such inventions, included intersecting policy initiatives from diverse quarters: e.g. new options to add VET courses from Technical and Further Education colleges to school subject portfolios; or new options for young mothers and other drop outs to keep government funding by pursuing a qualification, rather than be treated as an undeserving welfare case. Still, conjunctions of policy and other forces do not simply drive strategies of students, school staff, parents, peers and others involved, but, entering into their lived sites, serve as resources for strategic action.

Within this shifting normativity of senior secondary schooling, long-standing tactics of middle class students continued – e.g. repeating subjects to maximize tertiary entrance scores, and starting early to lower the load and maximize high scores – but these now articulated with discourses of human capital, entailing calculations of opportunity and risk, aiming to maximize relative advantage for tertiary entrance *vis a vis* other students. Thus, older practices for gaining relative advantage readily transmuted in grafting onto newer mentalities of flexibility and self-responsibility, as re-shaped by conditions in which particularly situated students are immersed.

In sum, a governmentality lens opens analytic insight into how ensembles of reason and tactic, running across lives of secondary students, are by no means simply ideological (or discursive), nor confined to a single domain of schooling, nor derived top-down from a state, capitalism or other central locus. They assemble from multiple sites and vectors, including emergences from ground levels of strategic practice, calculation and sense-making among school, family and other situated actors coping with life conditions – which policy-makers may only later recognise and articulate as enterprising pursuits of human capital. Assemblages of practice, technique and mentality thus govern social conduct in transacting between government proper – itself a complex set of ensembles – and people inhabiting diverse loci and layers of *lived* institutional regimen. But what about *differences* among people in terms of *powers* to access and make strategic use of the discursive, technical and practical resources of governmental regimes?

Questions of the Possession and Source of Power

As quoted earlier, Dean places governmentality analysis as continuous with prior critical frameworks in its concern with the exercise of power and authority, while breaking from prior concerns with (1) questions of the possession and source of power; and (2) problems of legitimacy [and] the notion of ideology. In this and the next section we interpret these breaks in terms of what conceptions of power animate governmentality analytics and the consequences for what is/is not made investigable.

According to Gordon (1991), Foucault saw Western liberal/neoliberal societies to tend towards a form of political sovereignty which would be a government of all and of each, and whose concerns would be at once to "totalize" and to "individualize" (p. 3). In like vein, Lemke (2001) cites Foucault as noting that the enterprise mode of conduct obeys the principle of "equal inequality for all" (p. 195). These statements suggest an historic trend toward micro-dispersion of power relations, away from socially broad and steep inequalities; and it is unclear if Foucault saw this as a (neo)liberal *idea* of the changing shape of social power, and/or as an actual *material*-historical development. In any event, conceptual de-emphasis on seeing social space as inter-leaved with deep-structural power asymmetries is indicated in Foucault's propositions, in *History of Sexuality Vol. 1* (1979), about what power is and is not. We quote a few choice statements:

> [P]ower must be understood in the first instance as the multiplicity of force relations immanent in the sphere in which they operate ... which, by virtue of their inequality, constantly engender states of power, but the latter are always local and unstable (Foucault. 1979, p. 92–93).

> Power is not something that is acquired, seized or shared, something that one holds on to or allows to slip away; power is exercised from innumerable points in the interplay of nonegalitarian and mobile relations (p. 94).

> Power comes from below; that is, there is no binary and all-encompassing opposition ... at the root of power relations, and serving as a general matrix ... [T]he relationality of power is characterized by tactics (pp. 94–95).

Are there no great radical ruptures, massive binary divisions then? Occasionally, yes. But most often one is dealing with mobile and transitory points of [power and] resistance, producing cleavages in society that shift about, fracturing unities and effecting regroupings (p. 96).

Foucault views power as *relational*: i.e. inequalities inhere in *relations* among different elements, not in the *elements* themselves. In this sense, power cannot be acquired, seized or held – i.e. possessed – by the elements, be they individuals, social groups, agencies of state, etc. While a relational view also typifies critical traditions such as feminisms, anti-racisms and Marxisms, these emphasise how power inequalities sediment historically along axes of relative position: e.g. male in relation to female, white relative to ethnic others, or positions of wealth and status relative to those with weak stores of economic and cultural capital. Power thus could be seen as possessed in the sense of positional goods that can be leveraged strategically. In contrast, while Foucault accepts that massive relational asymmetries can occur as what he calls 'states of power', he insists that such 'states' are secondary orders of 'relationality' that do not warrant analytic focus, as against a more primary 'first instance' of power as 'force relations.' It is in the vigour of this counter-emphasis that we find a decisive analytic break from questions of who possesses power relative to whom. Foucault allows that, occasionally, yes, *macro*-relational (op)positions do appear in history; but he promptly warns us off from seeing this as often the case. He insists that force relations are too radically multiple and mobile – on a *micro*-scale of points in tactical interplay – for consolidated positional amassments of power to be anything but transitory, unstable, epiphenomenal occasions in social history.

Foucault's historical research is more structuralist than this vision of the ephemerality of states of power might suggest. He discerns power formations – such as 'disciplinary institutions' – of significant extent across social space and duration over historic time. Yet his genealogies do not analyse savage inequalities (Kozol, 1991) of macro-relational power, but focus on a 'relationality ... characterized by *tactics*' (Lemke, quoted above) and by a micro-physical mechanics in "[t]he way power [is] exercised – concretely and in detail ... its techniques" (Foucault, 1980, p. 58). Prisons, as researched by Foucault, display panoptical towers and other technologies of time-space surveillance. They do not show poorer and more marginal inhabitants relative to the general population, let alone to those in government or other sites of authority to legislate and build panopticons.

How does such emphasis on micro-tactical *as against* macro-positional force relations apply to analysis of neoliberal or other political economic formations? Both Gordon (1991) and Lemke (2001) note Foucault's appreciation of the post-WW2 German *Ordo*-liberals for conceiving capitalism as specific forms of market relations, practices and techniques that arise historically with no basis in human nature. Hence, forms of capitalism are specific and variable effects, not general and fixed causes, of social-historical processes, and can work for good or ill depending on contingencies that require vigilant and creative political attention. "What is called capitalism," is thus "not the product of a pure economic process and historical capitalism cannot be derived from a "'logic of capital'". Indeed, "there is no logic to capital, but only contingent assemblages comprising any number of economic and [non-economic] institutional variables" that converge and shift "in a field of possibilities" (Lemke, 2001, p. 194).

We agree that there is no 'logic of capital' inhering in a natural substrate outside history; but this does not mean there can be no logics of long, deeply institutionalised *historical* duree that define *capitalist* as against other variant market forms. To meaningfully call an assemblage of political-economic processes capitalist, we argue, connotes alogic of *uneven accumulation* of powerful investment leverage, with stratifying effects of savage inequality well beyond what could reasonably be described as equal inequality for all. However, it is precisely an *accumulation* logic of power, we argue, that Foucault renders unfeasible in his above-quoted assertions of what power is and is not.

With Bourdieu (1984), we take 'capital' to indicate accumulations of more diverse qualities of power than just economic, including cultural, social and other species, parlayed in varied domains of institutional market. While we lack textual space to give due elaboration to a Bourdieu's conception of capital, we emphasise that, like a Foucauldian concept of governmentalities, Bourdieu's cultural and other modes of capital bridge across the coded rationalities of institutions and the subjectively embodied dispositions (or *habitus*) of individuals. However, in Bourdieu's framework both the institutional encodings and the subjective embodiments, while contingent and shifting, are more deeply self-inhabiting and (ac)cumulative, and hence power-conservational (or reproductive), than Foucault's fluid interplay of 'points.'

Looking again at senior secondary school strategies, we ask whether a governmentality lens sheds sufficient light into what is at stake in the power gambits of part-time tactics. In some schools of more elite clientele, with academic focus on subjects that count in tertiary entrance scores (Teese, 2000), staff and students come up with part-time strategies to increase competitive access to prestigious university programs. This contrasts with schools of more working-middle clientele, which typically have not formally supported part-time options, and where we heard some students and staff speak disparagingly about part-time study, seeing it as a last-resort move that might grease the slippery slide out of school. It would be an analytic omission, we argue, not to see significance in the statistic that most students who engage part-time are from families/regions the school system recognises as 'disadvantaged' (Ramsay, 2004); and it was in these schools where we heard rationales about holding onto the promise that a bit more schooling might translate to a bit more human capital, which might parlay into future work that, hopefully, is a bit above bottom-feeding levels in increasingly tenuous job pools. Notably, the 'less advantaged' tend to 'cash in' weakly on positional goods of school credentials, just as in decades prior to the current prominence of human capital rationalities.

Students of diverse social positioning do enter into, embody, and are incited to strategic action by assemblages of human capital and associated discursive and practical resources. A governmentality lens helps us see how the 'game' of schooling has changed for many senior secondary students, entailing new norms of 'the good student', in which not only the elite may benefit from techniques such as education-to-work portfolios, etc. But the definitions of power that animate a governmentality lens – and especially its stipulations on how we must *not* conceive power – inhibit analytic insight into how differently positioned students enter governmental assemblages with unequal inheritances of *deeply* embodied dispositional resources for *conserving and accumulating* capital – including more and less powerful strategies of human capital embodiment – in high-stakes games of school, work and other institutional competitions.

Dean (1999) argues that to focus on who possesses power, relative to whom, assumes notions of power as "a zero-sum game played within an *a priori* structural distribution, rather than the (mobile and open) resultant of the loose and changing assemblage of governmental techniques, practices and rationalities" (p. 29). Although we find the zero-sum ascription cartoonish, we see no error in recognising that an historically sedimented logic of *uneven* capital *accumulation* tends toward institutional 'games' by which relative winning for some entails relative losing for others. We dispute the suggestion that analytic attention to macro-relational distributions need assume these as *a priori*; Bourdieu, among others, sees distributional structures as continually formed and transformed historically, if not with the rapidity of Foucault's hugely unstable states.

We worry about the Foucauldian tendency, in its one-sided stress on micro-points of fluid force relation, to vaunt the "productive aspect of power" (Foucault, 1980, p. 60) in ways that reduce historic accumulations of weighty inequality to unbearably light occasions unworthy of analysis. We suggest that too great a *degree* of emphasis on mobile, open, loose and changing assemblages can slip into odd accord with neoliberal promises of human capital as an indefinitely expandable (and self-responsible) solution for people struggling with hard times. This brings us to the question of whether/how rationalities such as human capital may serve legitimating and ideological functions.

PROBLEMS OF LEGITIMACY AND IDEOLOGY

In Foucault's studies of bio-politics, notes Dean (1999), historic processes of nation-state formation entailed "recognition by the state that the health, happiness, wealth and welfare of its population were among the key objectives of its rule" (p. 24). In addressing such problematics, there emerged "regimes of practices of government, with particular techniques, language, grids of analysis and evaluation, forms of knowledge and expertise" (p. 28), resulting in a "complexity of the relations between the institutions that constitute the state" (p. 24). In contrast to this complex vision of the composition and relations of government, "social scientific theories of the state", argues Dean, "assume [a simplistic] unity when they typically seek to discover the source of the states power, who holds it, and the basis of its legitimacy" (p. 24). Hence "[a]n analytics of government brackets out such questions not simply because they are stale, tiresome, unproductive and repetitive", but in order to "focus on 'how' questions, such as how different locales are constituted as authoritative and powerful, how different agents are assembled with specific powers, and how different domains are constituted as governable and administrable" (p. 29).

We challenge the claim that a simplistic unity of state formation is assumed in attending to how different social fractions enact leverage on and within state institutions, and how leverages that gain sway are legitimated. Indeed, we argue that they arise out of the very phenomena on which governmentality analytics focuses. The health, happiness, wealth and welfare needs among populations are by no means simple to address. Efforts by state agencies run up against constraints and contradictions that thwart capacities of their techniques, language, expertise, evaluation grids, etc to satisfy all social fractions; and often, significant population portions register dissatisfaction. While a governmentality lens appreciates this dimension of complexity around which governmental assemblages build, it obviates the systemic differences and power differentials within populations – including divergent demands from diverse social fractions – that add both complexity and emotive intensity to pressures on government agencies to come up with tactics and state reasons representing solutions. When possibilities of reasonable solution are in these ways taxed, government impulses build towards political/populist efforts at deflection and finesse, e.g. by re-defining complex struggles of people in simplistic ways. Such *legitimation tactics* are themselves highly complex processes; and so attending to them contributes to appreciating the complexities of governmental assemblages.

We argue that the sorts of intensified complexities that provoke legitimation tactics are much associated with neoliberal rationalities pervading Australian government, media, business and wider discourse in the past few decades. In the collapse of post-World War II policy regimes that made concerted efforts to keep distribution more-or-less around a working-middle (Pusey, 2003), Australia has seen radically new degrees, mechanisms and forms of social stratification. To put it simply (lacking space for complex portrayal), we might say that a rough equal inequality for all has morphed into steepening stratification in a context of global shifts in how large-scale capital interacts with workforces. There has been consequent large-scale decline in both industrial and service jobs of decent pay, conditions and future career security for young people who in Australia could previously gain such work without schooling beyond year 10; and only small growth in upwardly mobile work for which year 12 completion and further degrees are the passport for entry.

This has presented the governing of education, and especially secondary education, with what we will call *exquisite tensions*. We lack space to go into the detail this deserves; but the crux of the matter is that governments respond to simultaneous and contradictory pressures for (1) meeting increased demands from families in powerful positions or with upwardly mobile aspirations to institute competitive sorting and selecting, by means such as gifted and talented academic curriculum in which a small portion of students wins the game of cultural capital competition, relative to many vocational others; and (2) keeping the latter in school longer, either by more engaging curriculum and/or the promise of increasing their human capital for new knowledge/service economies. (The latter is far more typical, since many factors work against development and use of seriously engaging curriculum for less advantaged learners.)

As found in the part-time study, many students incorporate human capital rationalities – the new commonsense – in their strategic thinking and acting. Yet many at the same time sense the simplistic limitations of the human capital promise, stacked against their complex lives. Inter-generational poverty and unemployment, and lack of jobs accessible to them and their families, cast doubt on the message that investment in educational credentials will change their future prospects. As well, the continuing rigidity of the school structure – its authoritarian practices; its curriculum perceived as at once irrelevant and impugning their intelligence – are often stronger affective drivers away from school than any persuasiveness of human capital promises to keep them in. Although the human capital push by governments from the early 1980s saw retention rates in high schools rise from 30% to 79% completion nationwide, retention since 1991 has declined as students who feel themselves outcasts on the inside (Bourdieu & Champagne, 1999) vote with their feet. Yet, as the part-time study found, students are variously hanging on, buying in and making do through many strategies, with different degrees of success.

Such manifestations of exquisite tension inject acute challenges into govern-mentality ensembles. School systems across Australia have been experimenting with mixtures of curriculum reform, with mixed success, in trying both to enable winners to win, and prevent others from feeling like losers. Multiplied efforts of state agencies to manage the conduct of conduct in application to such problems come up against the difficulty of solutions that satisfy sufficient numbers and range of social-positional needs and hopes. Mobilisation of rationalities such as human capital then take on functions not simply of addressing welfare and security needs of populations by means of practices that link education and work, but also of solving governmental agencies own problems of legitimacy. Thus, governmental address to such problematics does not just incite multiplications of techniques and rationalities to induce young people's participation – as within a governmentality purview for analysis – but also incites legitimation problems for governments – which seem precluded from a governmentality lens.

From a Foucauldian perspective, governmental rationalities can be declined by individuals and social fractions, yet still exert normative effects. But when significant blocs of population act in ways showing that they are not rationally persuaded, this poses problems for government of a different order than fits into a governmentality perspective. If critical analysis omits struggles by elements of government to affirm and defend their legitimacy, we fail to see all that is at stake for governments in the directions taken to organise the conduct of conduct of young people. When governing agencies run up against the limits of their problem-solving capacities, the political survival of what they think of as their government – the sites of their careers and professional identities – is open to question, and a different set of activities comes into play. Impetus develops to finessing complex underpinning conditions of peoples life struggles that governing authorities do not sense themselves having wherewithal to solve and thus are not inclined to articulate in their actual complexity, even to themselves. Specific state actors and agencies, often linked to popular media – but also to business organisations, charities, etc – heighten efforts to win consent in a Gramscian sense (1971), through tactics that generate production of policies, programs, populist initiatives and public discourses feeding into ensembles of what we would dare to call an ideological kind. It would be important to include rather than preclude such processes in analyses focused on complex formations and transformations of governmental assemblages.

In the current context of exquisite tensions, rhetorical deployment of human capital rationalities, and associated discourses such as lifelong learning, come to serve a most *ideo*logical function: i.e. *simplistically* redefining difficult-to-solve complexities that underpin struggles in peoples' lives. Such discourses do indeed incite peoples conduct; but this includes ideo-logically *mis*-directing their conduct through simplifications that obscure the complex conditions of their changing standards of living, e.g. by reducing these to matters of literacy and numeracy needed for knowledge-economy jobs, thus over-promoting an actually tenuous, if (ideo) logically reasonable, link between school literacies, job growth and work readiness.

Notably, such simplification processes entail highly complex techniques and tactics of think-tanking, alliance-building, mediating and more, striving to create appearances of government as legitimately able to lead and solve problems in ways politically responsive to often contradictory expressions of need and aspiration from diverse social fractions with differential powers. Such complexities multiply unintended consequences, adding further to the range of challenges and efforts that apparatuses of legitimation face. We thus argue that governmentality analysts who dismiss ideology critique as too simplistic ironically reduce the complexity of their own insights by not attending to highly complex processes of ideological legitimation.

CONCLUSION

Our argument is certainly not that taking up governmentality analytics is a wrong turn; we find it to offer significant insight into current educational phenomena such as part-time strategies of South Australian senior secondary students. We do argue that, if the breaks often stipulated as making this lens distinctive are too adamantly exerted in the name of a more complex analysis, this can, ironically, be dangerous to more fully nuanced understanding of social-educational phenomena. Tendencies develop to dismiss so-called wrong turns of prior critical approaches by reducing these too simplistic caricatures, thus failing to recognise newer sophistications within older traditions (some of which have been precipitated by Foucauldian challenges).

In this light, we want to observe, from wider reading into governmentality literature than cited in this chapter, that governmentality analysts do not all avoid considering how gender, race, class and other macro-relational inequalities might be implicated in the power ensembles they research. However, we find these attentions typically to be glancing and hedged, often qualified by theorising states of macro-power from Foucauldian micro-force relations, with stress on the analytic pre-eminence of the latter. We also find that analyses of rationalities such as human capital, lifelong learning, etc, do not entirely avoid a sense that these are suspect in their promises, inducing negative effects in peoples' lives. However, this sense of critical suspicion is typically insinuated more than stated, through sardonic tones that mute connotations of ethical reproval, often accompanied by reminders that power is not basically oppressive but more significantly productive. (See Rose 1999 as an illustrative case. We hasten to add that his work offers much rich genealogical analysis of governmentalities under recent public management.)

We want to encourage these tenuous gestures by governmentality analysts into a more forthright rapprochement with attention to macro-power relations, and to ideological legitimation tactics, from which they work so hard to break. We argue that reasonable empirical assessment of extant and emerging conditions of our times would recognise that savage power inequalities, and populist/political tactics of ideological finesse, are salient – indeed, both have intensified in Australia over the past few decades. At the same time, the challenges of Foucault's bold experiments in thinking differently have pushed many – who are not simply ready to accept his breaks – to analyse power more complexly, with greater care not to read off reductively from overly presumed and generalised structures, nor to assume essentialist bases for power inequalities. We agree that Foucault's work has breathed vital excitements into critical studies of social-institutional power. Yet these winds of change are now 25-30 years old; and we suggest it is time to re-think whether Foucault's departures are purely tenable. In approaching critically the shifting and emerging complexities of current times and verging futures, we advocate bringing the nuanced assemblage analytics of governmentality studies into productive connection with sophisticated neo-structural and ideology critique modes of analysis.

NOTES

[1]   While Foucault's 'archaeological' studies of scientific knowledge preceded *Discipline and Punish*, these were mainly read afterwards and had less significant influence in critical studies of education.

[2]   We acknowledge the Australian Research Council funded Linkage Project *Pathways or Cul-de-sacs: the causes, impact and implications of senior secondary part-time study*, 2005-2007 (# LPO455760) conducted 2005-2007 with three Chief Investigators: Prof Eleanor Ramsay, Prof Marie Brennan and Prof Alison Mackinnon from the University of South Australia, with Partner Investigators from the Department of Education and Children's Services: Wendy Engliss; Judith Lydeamore, Tanya Rogers, Bev Rogers (at different times); the Premier's Social Inclusion Unit, Dr Jan Patterson; and the state senior secondary curriculum authority, SSABSA: Dr Jan Keightley, then Dr Paul Kilvert. Research assistants Lynette Arnold, Katherine Hodgetts and Kirrilly Thompson, and the PhD student attached to the project, Rochelle Woodley-Baker, have also made active contributions which Marie Brennan acknowledges with thanks.

REFERENCES

Becker, G. (1964/*1993*). Human capital: A theoretical and empirical analysis, with special reference to education *(3rd ed.)*. Chicago: University of Chicago Press.

Bourdieu, P. (1984). *Distinction: A social critique of the judgement of taste* (R. Nice, Trans.). Cambridge, MA: Harvard University Press.

Bourdieu, P., & Champagne, P. (1999). Outcasts on the inside. In P. Bourdieu et al. (Eds.), *Weight of the world: Social suffering in contemporary society* (pp. 421–426). Oxford, UK: Polity Press.

Brennan, M., Ramsay, E., & Mackinnon, A. (2007, September). *Patterns in part-time participation: narratives of investment in school completion.* Paper presented at the British Educational Research Association conference, Institute of Education, London.

Business Council of Australia (BCA). (2007). *Restoring our edge in education.* Retrieved from http://www.bca.com.au/Content/101189.aspx

Carmichael, L. (1992). *The Australian vocational training system.* Canberra, ACT: National Board of Employment, Education and Training.

Dean, M., & Hindess, B. (1998). Introduction: Government, liberalism, society. In M. Dean & B. Hindess (Eds.), *Governing Australia: Studies in contemporary rationalities of government* (pp. 1–19). Cambridge, UK: Cambridge University Press.

Dean, M. (1999). *Governmentality: Power and rule in modern society.* London: Sage.

Dean, M. (2007). *Governing societies: Political perspectives on domestic and international rule.* Maidenhead, UK: Open University Press.

deLors, J. (1996). *Learning: The treasure within.* Paris: UNESCO.

Dusseldorp Skills Forum. (2007). *It's crunch time: Raising youth engagement and attainment.* Australian Industry Group and Dusseldorp Skills Forum. Retrieved from www.dsf.org.au

Foucault, M. (1977). *Discipline and punish: The birth of the prison* (A. Sheridan, Trans.). London: Penguin.

Foucault, M. (1979). *The history of sexuality, Volume 1: An introduction* (R. Hurley, Trans.). New York: Pantheon.

Foucault, M. (1980). Truth and power. In C. Gordon (Ed.), *Power/knowledge: Selected interviews and other writings 1972–1977.* New York: Pantheon Books.

Foucault, M. (1991). Governmentality (R. Braidotti, Trans. & C. Gordon, Rev.). In G. Burchell, C. Gordon, & P. Miller (Eds.), *The Foucault effect: Studies in governmentality* (pp. 87–104). Hemel Hempstead, Hertfordshire: Harvester Wheatsheaf.

Foucault, M. (1997). Security, territory, and population. In M. Foucault (Ed.), *Ethics, subjectivity and truth* (P. Rabinow, Ed., pp. 67–71). New York: The New Press.

Gramsci, A. (1971). *Selections from the prison notebooks* (Q. Hoare & G. K. Smith, Ed. and Trans.). New York: International Publishers.

Gordon, C. (1991). Governmental rationality: an introduction. In G. Burchell, C. Gordon, & P. Miller (Eds.), *The Foucault effect: Studies in governmentality* (pp. 1–51). Hemel Hempstead, Hertfordshire: Harvester Wheatsheaf.

Kozol, J. (1991). *Savage inequalities: Children in America's schools.* New York: Crown Publications.

Lemke, T. (2001). The birth of Bio-Politics: Michel Foucault's Lecture at the College de France on Neo-Liberal governmentality. *Economy & Society, 30*(2), 190–207.

Mayer Committee. (1992). *Employment-related key competencies: A proposal for consultation.* Melbourne, Victoria: Mayer Committee.

Pusey, M. (2003). *Experience of Middle Australia: The dark side of economic reform.* Port Melbourne, Victoria: Cambridge University Press.

Ramsay, E. (2004). Life-wide learning and part-time senior secondary study: An exploration of the causes, educational impact and implications of the trend towards part-time senior secondary study in Australian public schools. *International Journal of Learning.*

Rose, N. (1999). *Powers of freedom: Reframing political thought.* Cambridge, UK: Cambridge University Press.

Simons, M., & Masschelein, J. (2008). The governmentalization of learning and the assemblage of a learning apparatus. *Educational Theory.*

Teese, R. (2000). *Academic success and social power: Examinations and inequity.* Melbourne, Victoria: Melbourne University Press.

Lew Zippin & Marie Brennan
University of South Australia
Adelaide

LINDA J. GRAHAM

19. THE SPECIAL BRANCH: GOVERNING MENTALITIES THROUGH ALTERNATIVE-SITE PLACEMENT

INTRODUCTION

> … one should try to locate power at the extreme points of its exercise, where it is always less legal in character. (Foucault, 1980, p. 97)

Studies of schooling practices as techniques deriving from a particular art of governing that Foucault (2003b) called 'governmentality' have shown how psychopathologising discourses work to construct particular student-subjects and legitimise various practices of exclusion (Graham, 2007b). Here I extend this work to consider the use of alternative-site placement as an intensification in response to governmentality being put 'at risk'. Governing 'at a distance' conjures an illusion of individual freedom which relies on the production of subjects who 'choose' to make choices that are consistent with the aspirations of government. In this chapter, it is argued that the designation of a child as 'disorderly' legitimises the intrusion of state into the private domain of the family via the Trojan horse of early intervention. This is enabled by the psy-sciences, whose technologies and aims amount to the moral retraining of 'improper' future-citizens who, in choosing to choose otherwise, threaten to make visible invisible relations of power. Alternative-site placement in special schools running intensive behaviour modification programs allows for a 'redoubled insistence' (Ewald, 1992) of those norms and limits that a 'disorderly' child threatens to transgress.

Alternative-site placement is used in a number of ways and in numerous contexts. This analysis focuses on one site in Queensland specialising in intensive behaviour modification programs. The stated intent of such modes of alternative schooling is to rehabilitate and reintegrate children with challenging behaviour back into mainstream primary schools. Of particular interest here are the technologies of "choice" used in this particular school and the use of practices that claim to draw on the Glasserian model of *Choice Theory*. William Glasser (1998) believed that children act disruptively when schools fail to meet a child's basic needs. In modern democratic societies it is assumed that the most fundamental need of security (shelter, clothing, food etc) is met. Beyond this, Glasser maintains that children desire and act in ways to achieve other fundamental human needs, which he categorised as:

M.A. Peters et al. (eds.), Govermentality Studies in Education, 355–368.

freedom independence, trust, autonomy and their own "space";

fun stimulating curriculum, active learning environments and other opportunities for pleasure and enjoyment;

power the experience of achievement, feeling worthwhile, some sense of control of self and environment and the opportunity to excel; and

love to be understood, the chance to fit in with groups, to not be bullied, teased or oppressed.

Glasser's (1998) Choice Theory is premised on the idea that a person's every action is organised towards meeting these needs. Disruptive behaviour is viewed then as behaviour directed towards the achievement of something that will satisfy the child's desire for freedom, fun, power or love, but the action used to achieve those ends may or may not be the most effective. Choice Theory aims to work on recognising which need the individual may be trying to achieve and whether the behaviour in question realises that end. The logical thought process used is: "What do you want?" "What are you doing to get what you want?" "Is it working?"

Behaviour management practices said to be modelled on Glasserian principles are commonly found in Australian schools. The distance however between theory and practice is highly problematic, as is the incorporation of coercive practices from behaviourism – some of which are in fundamental opposition to Glasserian principles (Glasser, 1990). The amalgamation of practices of school and classroom discipline originating from disparate epistemological bases results in things "being done" but, at the same time, there appears to be insufficient theoretical understanding of the underlying epistemological premises of Glasserian ideas. Therefore, *nothing actually changes* and instead Glasser's work comes to used as a psychological tool to coerce children into submitting to undemocratic rules and inflexible models of schooling. Despite many efforts to make schooling more equitable and more inclusive, recent research (Luke et al., 2006; Graham, 2007, forthcoming) shows that systems of education still recognise and reward particular cultural groups, their structural and academic demands are consistent with a particular habitus, and those whose characteristics align with contemporary cultural and educational norms succeed more often than those whose do not. There are programs in schools that aim to support children who experience difficulty with learning, however, they typically focus on the narrow areas of numeracy and literacy and peter out after the early years. This occurs in spite of research that shows not only the existence of a fourth/fifth grade 'slump' but also that the 'cognitive architecture' of the academic curriculum functions to shut out all but the most able or advantaged students (see Teese, 2000; Teese & Polesel, 2003). Under the guise of inclusion, support programs together with assessment practices used to ascertain eligibility 'work to refine schooling as a field of application for disciplinary power' (Graham & Slee, 2007, in press).

The resulting differentiation, categorisation and spatialisation of 'different' school children is assisted by psychopathologising discourses which produce "'disorderly' children by speaking about particular behaviours within a clinical sub-text that defines recognisable objects for professional scrutiny (Graham, 2007a). Objectification acts as a locating device; a mechanism of visibility (Deleuze, 1992; Ewald, 1992) that formulates how a "group is seen or known as a problem" (Scheurich, 1997, p. 107). Once constituted as an object of a particular sort, individuals can be dispersed into disciplinary spaces within a "grid of social regularity" (Scheurich, 1997, p. 98) and from there, become subject to particular discourses and practices that result in what Butler (1997, p. 358–359) describes as, "the 'on-going' subjugation that is the very operation of interpellation, that (continually repeated) action of discourse by which subjects are formed in subjugation." In other words through the process of objectification, individuals not only come to occupy *spaces* in the social hierarchy but, through their continual subjugation, come to know and accept their *place*.

It is no accident then that psychological discourse has as its object the recalcitrant, the disordered and the unruly. The normative project engendered towards the production and maintenance of a "sovereignty of the good" (see Graham, 2007, early online) culminates in the perpetual reinvestment of disciplinary power through techniques of normalisation which manifest in notions of the self-governing individual (Marshall, 1997) and the self-regulated learner (Popkewitz, 2001). This modern art of governing that Foucault (2003b) called "governmentality" is effectively operationalised by the psy-sciences and can be characterised by its focus on the individual and preoccupation with governing the soul (Rose, 1990).

In their effort to (re)claim the unreasoned however, psychological discourses that speak to self-regulation and reason disseminate universalising theories of cognition and development that exclude through "systems of recognition, divisions, and distinctions that construct reason and 'the reasonable person'" (Popkewitz, 2001, p. 336). Whilst psychological techniques aim to bring about the seemingly voluntary management of the self by the self in order to prevent "the weakening of discipline and the relaxation of morals" (Foucault, 1988, p. 59), at the same time there occurs a moral requalification of the subject where the demarcation of 'good' and 'bad' choices works to constitute 'good' and 'bad' choosers. Such constructions of the individual subject are dependent upon the discourse of the human sciences, particularly the appeal to reason and the ability to choose *reasonably*. 'Bad choosers' end up referred to and become the domain of those same fields of knowledge: medicine, psychology and special education (Graham, 2007).

Ironically but also tragically, what Glasser argues disruptive children most desire is precisely what is denied to them through the amalgamation of "choice theory" into generic school behaviour management practices.Such "identikit" models, informed by any number of psychological, psychoanalytical and/or psychobiological theories, play out everyday in the local primary classroom. As shown in this ethnography of the 'special' special school, the (mis)use of such practices results in the rearticulation and reworking of those needs, while the institution of the school continues to fail to respond to children's needs. In this way these children, their needs and what little voice they express through 'legitimate' means – for example, by nominating freedom, fun, power or love on their time-away reflection sheets – are rendered subordinate to the imperative of 'institutional equilibrium' (Slee, 2000).

This is contrary to Glasserian ideals however. Glasser (1969) was a keen educational reformist and argued that discipline problems in schools resulted mainly from boredom. He maintained that in the face of disruptive behaviour, schools and teaching must change in order to better satisfy the child's needs in the areas of freedom, fun, power and love. In this chapter, I make the argument that schools and teachers fail to understand the significance of these in the life of the child and warn that when children are given false choices – between, for example, subordination/domination unconvincingly packaged as compliance/discipline – they are effectively given no choice at all. What this does however, is make visible the illusion of freedom and autonomy upon which neoliberal forms of government depend. Articulating the difference between the autonomous individual who can decide for themself and, what he describes as the "autonomous chooser" imbued with "a faculty of choice", James Marshall (2001, p. 295) outlines the character of the neo-liberalised subject who is enabled simply to choose between choices allocated and approved by others. The object of alternative-site placement becomes the "child who chooses otherwise" (Graham, 2007, p. 13), because he/she not only resists authority but, more fundamentally, threatens to expose the falsity and rhetoric of 'choice.'

THE SPECIAL BRANCH

A series of ethnographic narratives from doctoral research conducted in 2004 are offered as vignettes that each explore the themes of freedom, fun, power and love and how these concepts play out in disciplinary ways at the scene of the school – especially at those extreme points where power and control is most contested (Foucault, 1980). Alternative placement centres and 'special' special schools operate at these margins, under the shadow of traditional schooling. Their stated objective is to rehabilitate children labelled as deviant, disruptive and disturbed with the aim of reintegration, however, it can be argued that the aim of the 'special branch' is far wider and higher in scope and interest than the mere local primary.

Using a lens informed by Foucault's (2003b) notion of governmentality, I examine these vignettes as events in which children, whose behaviour threatens to make visible invisible relations of power, are subjected to an intensification of disciplinary practice; a 'redoubled insistence' (Ewald, 1992) of those norms and limits that a "disorderly" child threatens to transgress. I argue that it is those norms and limits – structured by dominant social, cultural and political forces constituting the 'sovereignty of the good' – that ultimately take precedence. The child and his/her needs and desires remain subordinate to a status quo that came into being long before they arrived and which will, if current practices remain unchallenged, prevail long after their removal from the school.

"Freedom"

A television monitor is suspended from the ceiling above the staff room door. It is clearly visible from the front stairs of the administration building, where the researcher waits for a meeting with the principal. The screen shows a male child, about 8 years of age, sitting huddled in a corner of an empty room with his head in his hands. The windows have external steel grills and the floor is bare linoleum. A teacher emerges from the staff room and follows my stare to the screen. She shrugs and says brusquely, "Don't worry, you'll get used to it".

In Glasser's theory, freedom is not characterised as the ability to do whatever one wants but to have enough autonomy to be able to feel as if one has control over one's life and self. In his writings on education, Glasser (1969; 1990) argues that schools should be organised democratically and that basic student needs should be reflected in curriculum offerings, pedagogy and school culture. In the tradition of Dewey and Spady, he repeatedly states that coercive systems produce disruptive, resistant behaviour and that cooperative inquiry-based learning models with enthusiastic teachers who lead, rather than command their students will experience more success. Curiously, these insights seem to have been relatively neglected in the take-up of Glasserian principles, particularly as teachers face increased accountability measures that result in their dispensing "low-quality, standardised, fragmented" (Glasser, 1990, p. 22) information packaged as measurable academic knowledge.

In this particular alternative-site, Glasser's (1965) original Reality Therapy techniques inform behaviour management practice. Following his later reworking of Reality Therapy as Choice Theory, the emphasis is on individual responsibility and choice. Behaviour is viewed as action directed towards the achievement of a goal but importantly, the behaviour itself is seen as independently chosen. In the 'special' school, particular behaviours are interpreted as appropriate and some inappropriate and the aim is to get the child to recognise which behaviours are more likely to get the result they desire and keep them out of trouble. Inappropriate behaviours are followed with a series of consequences called 'time-away' of which there are three stages:

Stage 1: move to an allocated spot on the periphery of the classroom.

Stage 2: relocate to a desk in a neighbouring classroom.

Stage 3: go to the "safe" room (described in the above vignette).

At each stage the child is to remove themselves quietly and by their own volition. If not, they move to the next stage. Time-away is not intended as punishment. Instead it is meant to provide the child with a period of quiet reflection in which they are asked to consider what it was that they were trying to achieve, what they did towards that end and whether it was successful. A debrief takes place with a teacher or aide and the child is required to consider whether the choice they made was the right one and what alternative choices they could have made to bring about a more successful result. 'Success' is understood by the school as remaining in class and being included in schooling activities, although to the student success could be viewed as escaping from them.

During the time-away period, the student is given a sheet to fill out:

What Happened?	What did I do?	What happened next? (Consequences)	What will I do next time?
▪ In the classroom ▪ In the playground ▪ Eating ▪ Under the building	▪ Kicked ▪ Pushed ▪ Punched ▪ _____ ▪ _____	Then I got: ▪ Time away ▪ Stage 2 ▪ Stage 3	▪ Follow instructions ▪ Keep hands and feet to myself ▪ Respect others
I was _____ _____ _____ _____ _____ _____	I was _____ _____ What did I think? _____ _____	What did I need? LOVE POWER FREEDOM FUN	I will _____ _____ _____ _I will think...._

Problematically, what the child expresses on this sheet is not taken into account in a manner consistent with Glasser's conception of 'working on the system.'

'Randle'[1] completed a great many of these sheets during his six month enrolment at the special school. For the question: *What did I think?* Randle answered most of the time: "Angry". More often than not, this was coupled with "School sucks!" which alternated with "Bored". In response to the question: *What did I need?* Randle circled "Freedom" twenty-one times.

"Fun"

Eight boys ranging from 7 to 10 years sit in a circle on the floor. The music teacher, young and buxom, tries to engage them in a game often played in preschools. "Markie"[2] is tapped on the head. Giggling he skips around the circle to the music and then taps the teacher on the head, rushing to sit in her newly vacated spot. She smiles ruefully and continues the game, tapping another boy's head and racing to his vacated place. When it is his turn to do the same he looks across to Markie and giggles, skipping around the circle to again tap the teacher on the head. She pulls herself from the ground – mouth hardening and breasts heaving – to run the circle again. The young boys fall about laughing.

Glasser (1969; 1990) acknowledges that children may choose a behaviour to achieve an end so desired that its importance (in the child's perspective) overrides the possible consequences. The example he uses is that to escape excruciating boredom, a person may elect to walk out of a classroom having decided that the likely consequence is less painful than being subjected to mind-numbing fact memorisation. I argue that this is the part of Glasser's work that has been neglected and instead schooling systems are using his principles (as well as those of others) to 'work on the students, not on the system' (Glasser, 1990, p. 49).

For example, on other reflection sheets, to the question: *What did I need?* Randle circled "Fun" a total of twenty times. The institutional response was not to consider what need-satisfying changes (environmental, pedagogical or curricular) could be implemented to better engage him – instead the system and all its shortcomings remained unexamined and Randle was encouraged to change not only his actions but also what he *thinks*. Glasser notes that people seem surprised that fun is a basic human need, but argues strongly that children learn and grow in motivation when they experience fun. The problem is that when fun is non-existent due to boring, irrelevant curriculum or stale, authoritarian pedagogical styles, children may create it for themselves. Contrary to Glasser's theory however, these children are then punished for need-satisfying behaviour – behaviour which could be used as an indicator of where the system's failures lie.

"Power"

> The music lesson ends abruptly and the desks are pulled back into line. There are eight young boys in the glass, ranging from Grade 3 to Grade 5. Their desks form two neat lines of four across. As the boys sit down, the adults take up their positions. The two teachers place themselves at the front and rear of the classroom with the younger teacher at the head. The senior teacher stands watching the boys from behind. The two teacher aides move to either side of the two short rows of desks. As lessons begin the female aide stares listlessly at the carpet, while the male stifles a yawn.

Architectural arrangement of the classroom is cited in most pre-service teacher textbooks featuring behaviour management. A chapter titled "Managing Behaviour and Classrooms" in one such text used in pre-service teacher education in some Australian universities offers examples of many different styles, models and theories, including Glasser's (Krause et al., 2003). Frederic Jones' model of interventionist teaching based on operant-conditioning principles is also provided. This includes a diagram of classroom layout which optimises opportunities for teacher's to enact Jones' interventionist steps. The architectural distribution of desks is meant to leave room for a teacher to be able to walk around the desks and more easily use the "proximity" technique. This is where the teacher uses physical proximity (i.e. placing hands on the student's desk on either side of the students work), eye and body contact to "maintain students engagement" (Krause et al., 2003, p. 382). Not only does the placement of the boy's desks at the 'special'

special school optimise this but the placement of extra staff enhances the panoptic quality of classroom surveillance.

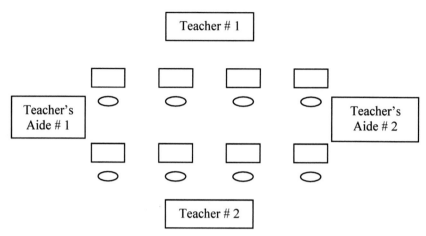

The students are surrounded – watched from every direction – even from behind. They cannot do anything without being seen. Not surprisingly under these conditions on his reflection sheets following time-away, Randle responds to the question, "What did I need?" by circling "Power" 46 times. This is more than double the amount that he marks any of the others. Interestingly, despite the enduring belief that disruptive, disordered and disturbed behaviour originates from a child desperate for attention that he/she doesn't get at home, Randle never even circles "Love" once.

"Love"

Markie seems to miss parts of the teacher's instructions and fails to complete tasks exactly as told. When instructed to put his song sheet at the back of his music folder and place it in the brown tray, he fails to put it in the *back* of the folder and instead puts it in the front. When challenged to recite what he was meant to do by the male aide closest to him, he replies "I dunno!" Markie is sent to Stage 1 time-away. He sighs and walks to the single desk in the rear corner. The senior teacher at the rear moves closer to him.

***

After 10 minutes, Markie is allowed to return to his desk. The female aide has stopped studying the carpet and is now watching him intently. While working on a maths problem, Markie concentrates hard but starts to tap his pencil (noiselessly) on his desk. The male aide moves behind and issues a warning. Markie shifts about on his chair and runs his hand through his hair. He looks frustrated. The male aide starts to lean over him, at which point Markie puts his hands in the air saying "Alright!" For this, he is sent to Stage

2 time-away in the empty classroom next door. Markie is taken into this room by the senior teacher at the rear. The door closes.

The Special Branch exists for a reason. Children whose actions endanger other children place schools in a difficult situation. Whilst schooling systems in Australia have embraced the idea of an inclusive education system, it is argued that this must be balanced with the need for safety. Education policy reflects the tension between these two ideals, where discourses of inclusion exist alongside and are cut across by discourses of risk. But do 'special' special schools exist only for violent students who endanger others? Or do referring schools also use alternative-site placement centres as a 'too hard basket'?

Randle's main reasons for getting into trouble at school were coded as "Not Respecting Others" and/or "Not Respecting Property". He was described by referring teachers as "extremely revengeful" and his stay at the special school was intended to help him to find other ways of dealing with anger so that he would not be a danger to other children. This is fair enough. However, Randle had not always been so aggressive and whilst he was enrolled in the "special" school, it came to light that 10 year old Randle had experienced severe language delay since beginning school at the age of 6. Instead of following this up as the potential source of his anger and frustration, each successive school he attended suggested that he had ADHD and referred his mother to Child & Youth Mental Health Services. Even though the resident psychiatrist agreed with his mother that Randle did not have ADHD, the queries persisted from school to school – as did the referrals.

Problematically, even when it was established during his stay at the special school that Randle qualified as speech/language impaired by a visiting speech pathologist, Child Youth & Mental Health Services were again consulted about the possibility of ADHD, Oppositional Defiance Disorder and/or Conduct Disorder. In Randle's case, it appears the celebrity status of "disruptive behaviour disorder" and the promise of a pharmaceutical fix, eclipsed the quiet but debilitating effects of severe language difficulties which often manifest in behaviours identical to the DSM-IV diagnostic criteria for behaviour disorder (Bishop, 1989; Augustine & Damico, 1995).

Markie on the other hand was not violent or aggressive, although he *was* irrepressible, cheeky and bright. He also had a habit of forgetting what he was meant to be doing. Markie's main reasons for attracting attention at the special school were coded as "Not Following Instructions". This incidentally can also be due to problems with receptive language ability. During the class time observed, Markie was the only student to get in trouble. But the reasons for it were minor. In the case of Markie, the role of the 'special' special school appeared to be to get Markie to subordinate his needs to the needs of the system; to learn how to submit to boredom, sit still to complete worksheets, to engage with curriculum that was beneath his intellect and to respond automatically to authority. Markie had obvious difficulty in doing this and his frustration and growing anger was evident. Here the "special" special school was operating against Glasserian principles by engaging in coercive practices that Glasser argues *produce* resistance in the form of disruptive behaviour.

Whilst the stories of Randle and Markie give us some idea of how alternative-site placement centres may be used to correct the mistakes made by referring schools who may lack the time, ability and/or inclination to successfully address these kinds of problems themselves; at another level, it must be asked: does modern disciplinary society use alternative-placement centres to maintain a sociopolitical centre 'at risk' of collapse under the mounting pressure of diversity?

Governmentality through techniques that Foucault calls discipline-normalisation (2003a) results not in total exclusion but in a forced and ever more strange inclusion, a process which perpetually reinvents both centre and margin (Graham & Slee, 2007). The illusory interiority of centred-ness comes under increasing strain from vocal minority groups who challenge its authenticity by "identifying the margins as their own centre" (Bottrell, 2006, p. 9). For example in relation to marginalised young people in Glebe, an inner city area of Sydney, Bottrell (2006, p. 9) writes:

> …conformities to neighbourhood values and illicit activities are interpreted as resistances by others. However, the young people want to be able to define themselves and not be limited by others' stereotypes. Claiming their place in terms of specific groups, values and norms, different from what "others" regard as appropriate or legitimate, may be read as an inversion of the privilege relations of centre and margins.

The current backlash against multiculturalism in Australia, mandatory detention centres and the Cronulla 'race riots' where 5,000 young white Australians 'reclaimed the beaches' is an overt example of what happens when the centre pushes back. More insidiously, the use of alternative-sites in which to house and retrain resistant, disruptive school children is an example of the other work done in the name of schooling – one that achieves the same centric end. Through such use of ignoble practices that occur on "the underside of the law" (Foucault, 1976, p. 93f in Marshall, 2001, p. 35), schools serve to construct a naturalised sociopolitical centre. This "sovereignty of the good" is maintained via the normalising institution of schooling, which is itself backed up by the "special branch" constituted by "other programs" and "alternative sites" (Education Queensland, 2001, p. 4; Bouhours et al., 2003; MCEETYA, 2005). This is where 'inclusion' comes to be subsumed within the traditional role of special education, which Armstrong (2005) describes as, "containing troublesome individuals and depoliticising educational failure through the technologies of measurement and exclusion" (Armstrong, 2005, p. 147). Special education, argues Armstrong (2005, p. 147), "constructs the role of inclusion as a disciplinary force, regulating the lives of those disabled by their lack of utilitarian value to the interests of an individualised society."

Despite the benevolence in the move to include children and youth 'at risk', the emphasis on regulating risk is not purely and simply directed at saving young people even from themselves. More fundamentally, the emphasis is about saving the social order established by the good from the destructive, disorderly influence of the bad. The twin-faces of risk then are about risk *to* the individual and risk posed *by* the individual, and it is the latter that wins more attention in public and social policy; although this is subtle and usually overlaid by the rhetoric of risk to the individual. Importantly however, the discourse of the individual 'at risk' (of school failure, drug ab/use, or any other misadventure) is used to legitimise the intrusion of state into the private domain; that is, in modern liberal democracies that have embraced neo-liberalism (ostensibly as a reaction to the inefficiencies of 'big government' but in reality as a means to reduce the role of the state in the welfare of its citizens), the discursive construction of 'risk' is used to enforce rule and a certain sense of order through increased legislation and regulation. Should that fail, 'risk' is used to justify the subordination of individual liberty itself.

Evidence suggests that market-based systems informed by a neoliberal rationality, which leave education systems uninsulated by active social investment and a healthy social fabric, place inordinate strain on teachers, schools, parents and communities (Graham, 2007). Inadequate safety nets leave gaping holes leading to social closure and lives spent in the constant shadow of stress, insecurity, low self-esteem, increased risk of depression, suicide, substance abuse, low intergenerational mobility, welfare-dependency and general despair. But rather than investigating the moral deprivation inherent to modern neoliberal rationalities of government, regulation of risk that may be posed by "at risk" individuals from 'risky' groups is operationalised through disciplinary institutions of which the school is only one. For 'risky' individuals unprotected by minor status, the justice system operates as another. In this context however, Armstrong (2006, p. 276) argues that:

> Fear leads to demands for authoritarian solutions, such as imprisonment. By contrast, it might be argued that a more 'hopeful' perspective is reflected in early intervention programmes aimed at supporting children, families, schools and communities who are seen to be 'at risk' or dysfunctional. Yet a belief in the possibility of an accurate calculation of risk is perhaps always an illusion, a naïve philosophy of hope located in beliefs about the redemption of individuals rather than in a critique of the society in which we live.

Arguably however, the school is increasingly important in the workings of governmentality, particularly because of its role in the development of the 'reasonable' future-citizen – one which is purposefully aligned with a particular reason of state (Popkewitz & Lindblad, 2000; Peters, 2005). As an extension of the schoolroom which 'provides the necessary field in which to make visible the specifics of conduct and educational attainment' (Laurence, forthcoming), 'inclusive' schooling allows the state greater reach into the private domain of the family, particularly through the Trojan horse of early intervention. The argument goes that the earlier the child's special needs are addressed, the better chance they have of catching up to 'normal' children. Perhaps this is why the 'special' special school only enrols primary aged children - by the time they hit high school, it is presumed that they are too far gone to change and other measures and other institutions come into play at that point. But the question must be asked: too-far-gone, in what way?

In physically endangering other children, Randle personified 'risk'. But to whom did Markie pose risk? It could be argued that in finding the structures and learning environment of schooling difficult to adjust to, Markie posed a risk to himself through school failure and the social closure that often results (Barry, 2005). It could also be argued however, that Markie posed a risk to the system because his inability to silently conform to the demands of schooling threatened to expose the arbitrary nature of those demands. In addition, the challenge posed by Markie's inability to conform threatened to make visible invisible relations of power, placing governmentality itself 'at risk'. As he struggled, he met the normative mechanisms of the system. Rather than absorbing the shock of difference, which is what an inclusive system is supposed to do, the system opposes it and attempts to overpower through the use of the 'special branch' and a 'redoubled insistence' (Ewald, 1992) of the norms and limits upon which the system of schooling and the rationality of disciplinary society rely.

CONCLUSION

Behaviour management practices said to be modelled on Glasserian principles are commonly found in Australian schools but, the disconnection between theory and practice is highly problematic. The amalgamation of practices of school and classroom discipline originating from disparate epistemological bases results in things 'being done' but, at the same time, there appears to be insufficient theoretical understanding of the underlying premises of Glasserian ideas. Therefore, nothing actually changes and instead Glasser's work is used as a psychological tool to coerce children into submitting to undemocratic rules and inflexible models of schooling.

Paradoxically then, Glasser's notion of 'choice' is rearticulated and the child is coerced into 'choosing' to do what he is *told* to do or face the consequences of making a "bad" choice. This is actually non-choice masquerading as 'choice' but the rearticulation of submission/resistance as 'good/bad' choices means that children can be characterised as not only responsible for their actions but inflexible, undemocratic schooling structures and practices become naturalised and as such, escape critical attention. The focus on the responsibility of the child therefore works to relinquish the school's responsibility to respond to their needs. In addition, the needs of the disruptive, resistant child come to be reconfigured as 'special needs,' which require the analysis and attention of the experts of abnormality and soldiers of governmentality: guidance officers, counsellors, psychologists, psychiatrists and paediatricians.

NOTES

[1] "Randle" is a pseudonym for a Grade Three boy who attended the special school during the research period.
[2] "Markie" is a pseudonym for a Grade Four boy who attended the special school and was in class during the observed period.

REFERENCES

(2001). Defining students with disabilities in Queensland State schools: Discussion stimulus paper (August 2001). *Discussion Stimulus Paper (August 2001)*. Education and Queensland. Brisbane, Queensland: Education Queensland.

Armstrong, D. (2005). Reinventing "inclusion": New labour and the cultural politics of special education. *Oxford Review of Education, 31*(1), 135–151.

Armstrong, D. (2006). Becoming criminal: The cultural politics of risk. *International Journal of Inclusive Education, 10*(2–3), 265–278.

Augustine, L. E., & Damico, J. S. (1995). Attention deficit hyperactivity disorder: The scope of the problem. *Seminars in Speech and Language, 16*(4), 242–257.

Barry, B. (2005). *Why social justice matters*. Cambridge, UK: Polity Press.

Bishop, D. V. M. (1989). Autism, asperger's syndrome and semantic pragmatic disorder: Where are the boundaries? *British Journal of Disorders of Communication, 24*, 107–121.

Bottrell, D. (2006). "You can't be walking around on tippytoes": Resistance, resilience and social identities. *Different Futures Conference*. Glasgow, Lanarkshire: University of Strathclyde.

Bouhours, T., Bryer, F., & Fleming, S. (2003). Exclusion of primary school students: Archival analysis of school records over a 30-year period. In B. Bartlett, F. Bryer, & D. Roebuck (Eds.), *Re-imagining practice—Researching change* (pp. 102–114). Brisbane, Queensland: School of Cognition, Language and Special Education, Griffith University..

Butler, J. (1997). Sovereign performatives in the contemporary scene of utterance. *Critical Inquiry, 23*(2), 350–377.

Deleuze, G. (1992). What is a dispositif? In T. J. Armstrong (Eds.), *Michel Foucault: Philosopher* (pp. 159–168). New York: Harvester Wheatsheaf.

Ewald, F. (1992). A power without an exterior. In T. J. Armstrong (Eds.), *Michel Foucault: Philosopher* (pp. 169–175). New York: Harvester Wheatsheaf.

Foucault, M. (1980). Two lectures. In C. Gordon (Ed.), *Power/knowledge: Selected interviews & other writings 1972–1977* (pp. 78–108). New York: Pantheon Books.

Foucault, M. (1988). *Madness and civilization: A history of insanity in the age of unreason*. New York: Vintage Books.

Foucault, M. (2003a). *Abnormal: Lectures at the College de France 1974–1975*. London: Verso.

Foucault, M. (2003b). Governmentality. In P. Rabinow & N. Rose (Eds.), *The essential Foucault: Selections from the essential works of Foucault, 1954–1984*. New York: The New Press.

Glasser, W. (1965). *Reality therapy: A new approach to psychiatry*. New York: Harper & Row.

Glasser, W. (1969). *Schools without failure*. New York: Harper & Row.

Glasser, W. (1990). *The quality school: Managing students without Coercion*. New York: HarperCollins.

Glasser, W. (1998). *Choice theory: A new psychology of personal freedom*. New York: HarperCollinsPublishers.

Graham, L. J. (2007a). Out of sight, out of mind/out of mind, out of site: Schooling and attention deficit hyperactivity disorder. *International Journal of Qualitative Studies in Education*.

Graham, L. J. (2007b). *Schooling attention deficit hyperactivity disorders: Educational systems of formation and the "behaviourally disordered" school child*. Centre for Learning Innovation, Faculty of Education. Queensland University of Technology: Brisbane. Unpublished Doctor of Philosophy Thesis.

Graham, L. J. (2007). (Re)Visioning the Centre: Education reform and the 'ideal' citizen of the future. *Educational Philosophy and Theory*.

Graham, L. J. (2007). Towards equity in the futures market: Curriculum as a condition of access. *Policy Futures in Education*.

Graham, L. J., & Slee, R. (2007). An illusory interiority: Interrogating the discourse/s of inclusion. *Educational Philosophy and Theory*.

Krause, K.-L., Bochner, S., & Duchesne, S. (2003). *Educational psychology: For learning and teaching*. Melbourne, Victoria: Thomson.

Luke, A., Graham, L. J., Sanderson, D., Voncina, V., & Weir, K. (2006). *Curriculum and equity: A review of the international research*. Adelaide, SA: Department of Education and Community Services.

Marshall, J. D. (1997). Michel Foucault: Problematising the individual and constituting 'the' self. *Educational Philosophy and Theory, 29*(1), 32–49.

Marshall, J. D. (2001). Varieties of neo-liberalism: A foucaultian perspective. *Educational Philosophy and Theory, 33*(3 & 4), 293–304.

MCEETYA. (2005). *Initiatives targeting recommendation 21: Queensland—alternative schooling provision*. Melbourne, Victoria: Curriculum Corporation. Retrieved from www.mceetya.edu.au/stepping/projects/21

Peters, M. (2005). Education, post-structuralism and the politics of difference. *Policy Futures in Education, 3*(4), 436–445.

Popkewitz, T., & Lindblad, S. (2000). Educational governance and social inclusion and exclusion: Some conceptual difficulties and problematics in policy and research. *Discourse: studies in the cultural politics of education, 21*(1), 5–44.

Popkewitz, T. S. (2001). Dewey and Vygotsky: Ideas in historical spaces. In T. S. Popkewitz, B. M. Franklin, & M. A. Pereyra (Eds.), *Cultural history and education: Critical essays on knowledge and schooling*. New York: RoutledgeFarmer.

Rose, N. (1990). *Governing the soul: The shaping of the private self*. London: Routledge.

Scheurich, J. J. (1997). *Research method in the postmodern*. London: Falmer Press.

Slee, R. (2000). Keynote address: Talking back to power: The politics of educational exclusion. *International Special Education Congress: Including the Excluded*. University of Manchester. Retrieved July 24–28, 2000, from http://www.isec2000.org.uk/abstracts/keynotes/slee.html

Teese, R. (2000). *Academic success and social power: Examinations and inequality*. Melbourne, Victoria: Melbourne University Press.

Teese, R., & Polesel, J. (2003). *Undemocratic schooling: Equity and quality in mass secondary education in Australia*. Carlton: Melbourne University Publishing.

Linda J. Graham
Macquarie University
Sydney
Australia

JAMES WONG

20. GROWING DENDRITES: BRAIN-BASED LEARNING, GOVERNMENTALITY AND WAYS OF BEING A PERSON

INTRODUCTION

My chapter examines the recent development in education practice at the elementary and secondary school level involving brain-based learning from a Foucauldian perspective. In this paper, I draw out the connection between brain-based learning and what Foucault calls "governmentality," a way of governing populations by focusing on their welfare and improving their condition. Foucault argues such governing requires the development of bodies of knowledge on various features of individuals' behavior, which though aimed at benefiting individuals are inextricably intertwined with ways to discipline those same individuals. I examine how brain-based learning initiatives, with their recommendations for new learning and teaching competencies, could potentially mould the behavior of not only children but their teachers and care-providers as well. Yet, I argue that the connection of brain-based learning to discipline is but one aspect of knowledge gained through research on the brain and learning. Following philosopher Ian Hacking, I contend that such knowledge opens up possibilities of new ways of being a person. Our perceptions of learners and educators, as well as their perceptions of themselves, are shaped by the ways in which they are categorized based on knowledge gain through such research, what Hacking calls "human kinds" (Hacking, 1996).

WHAT IS BRAIN-BASED LEARNING?

The term 'brain-based learning' may appear, at first blush, to state the obvious: isn't the brain centrally involved in learning? Yet interest in brain-based learning has intensified in recent years witnessed by the flood of articles and books published on the connection between brain research and education. For example, between 1998 and 2000, the education journal Educational Leadership published a series of articles on the impact of advances in brain research on teaching. Following President Bush's declaration that the 1990s was the "decade of the brain," various authors hoped that advances in brain research would usher in a decade of enlightened education initiatives in the first decade of the 21st Century (Wolfe and Brandt, 1998). One enthusiast writes,

M.A. Peters et al. (eds.), Govermentality Studies in Education, 369–377.
© 2009 Sense Publishers. All rights reserved.

> Stimulated by research in cognitive science a new view of learning draws its strength from cognitive neuroscience, cognitive psychology and artificial intelligence. The new conception has a direct bearing on … how we develop curriculums [sic.] and teach all subjects most effectively (Lowrey, 1998, p. 27).

The mention of cognitive neuroscience, cognitive psychology and artificial intelligence in conjunction with the new conception of learning triggers extra-logical connotations. Nonetheless, developing curricula is a lofty, but highly ambiguous claim. Does it mean that research in neurosciences will determine the content to be taught and how at a particular age? Say, addition is best taught at age seven in conjunction with music education, that of Telemann or Beck for example. Now that would be a significant achievement. Or, does developing curricula mean something much more modest, such as research in neuroscience enables educators to "understand what fosters learning" (Lowrey, 1998, p. 27)? For instance, brain research can show what classroom practices are counter-productive to learning. That too would be an achievement.

If we were hoping for disambiguation from the writings on brain-based learning, we would be sorely disappointed, for there is a wide range of claims from flights of fancy to guarded statements. For example, one author tells us that brain-based learning consists of three central ideas:
– Learners construct understanding for themselves;
– To understand is to know relationships;
– Knowing relations depends on having prior knowledge (Lowrey, 1998, p. 26).

The author then explains the three ideas by way of how the brain makes connections between neurons. These connections organise "words, objects, events and relationships in successively interwoven layers of categories" (Lowrey, 1998, p. 26). The author, however, does not tell us the connection between neural events and learning. It is as if there is a straight forward connection between the two.

However, there are also some quite cautious claims about how brain research validates effective classroom practices (Wolfe, 1998). Presumably this is what is meant by the claim made by one Board of Education in the Greater Toronto Area who has jumped on the brain-based learning band wagon. On its website, the York Regional District School Board tells us that brain-based learning "is what is sounds like, the alignment of teaching with the way in which [the brain] learns best" (YRDSB website).

So what is brain-based learning? Several findings in neurophysiology appear to underlie the motley of claims. There is the suggestion that there are critical periods of learning in the early years. Writers point to recent brain research indicating that synaptogenesis, the connection between brain cells (neurons), are rapidly generated until age three. After which the number of connections reach equilibrium between new growth and 'pruning' of some connections until age twelve. The number of connections then levels off in late teens to adult levels (Greenleaf, 1999, p. 83). Such connections, called dendrites, are the result of exposure to new experiences through the senses. Connected to the findings about dendrites, there is often the suggestion of the importance of an enriched environment in which the connections between brain cells are fostered. The challenge to educators, according to one author, is to determine "what constitutes an enriched environment," for educators are "either growing dendrites or letting them wither and die" (Wolfe and Brandt, 1998). However, recent research tells us that the brain is exceedingly plastic and that dendrites can grow at any age. So the risk of losing connections between neurons has taken on more urgency, for growing dendrites is a life-long process. Individuals are implored to exercise their brains or lose their dendrites!

Brain-based learning enthusiasts also note the importance of the role emotions play in learning. They point out that recent research in memory show the importance of motivation and patterning on organising information into categories. It has been suggested that neurotransmitters are released on noteworthy occasions "which 'tag' the event with special significance and give it prominence in the meaning pathways" (Weiss, 2000, p. 24). Another way in which emotions play an important role centres on the learning environment. If the setting is perceived to be threatening, researchers claim that the fight-or-flight instinct will be triggered in students. Once the instinct is activated, adrenalin is released by the hypothalamus, pituitary and adrenal glands inhibiting higher cognitive processes (Dwyer, 2001. p. 312). On the other hand, researchers also note that appropriate stress allow connections to be made between "the thalamus, hippocampus and cortex (where stored memories are housed and high level thinking takes place)" (Weiss, 2000, p. 23).

WHAT TO MAKE OF BRAIN-BASED LEARNING?

I contend that these recent findings about neural processes support what educators have known about learning activities all along. Educators already know that learners fare well in a non-threatening environment which offers appropriate challenges; that individuals learn the subject matter if they are motivated and if they have previous background knowledge and experience which allows them to relate to the new information. But this is just old wine in new bottles.

As Andrew Davis has recently pointed out supporters of brain-based learning appear to have committed a category mistake in using scientific discourse to justify our ordinary folk psychological understanding of learning (Davis, 2004). For instance, one tenet accepted by advocates of brain-based learning is that the brain is a social brain. But how is the brain social? We know, for example, an infant's brain weighs about 300 grams, while an adult brain weighs about 1300 grams (Hacking, 2005). It is walnut-shaped and roughly the size of a coconut. But none of this has anything to do with the brain being social. Indeed, the brain isn't social at all; human beings are. Furthermore, we can understand claims such as 'to understand is to know relations' and 'knowing relationships depends on prior knowledge' without referring to any discourse involving neurons, the hypothalamus and adrenaline. It is a conceptual point, for instance, that to understand double integrals requires a person to first know something about differential calculus. Reference to neurotransmitters and the like would appear to be besides the point for understanding the claim 'knowing relationships depends on prior knowledge' (Davis, 2004, p. 26). No doubt claims such as "our bodies have high-low cycles of about 90-110 minutes. At the top of the cycle, we are more attentive than at the bottom" are useful to educators (Weiss, 2003, p. 22, cf. Dwyer 2001, pp. 314–315). However, readers are left in the dark as to what neural processes are involved with claims such as "higher order thinking synthesize information and integrate it to come up with new ideas" (Weiss, 2003, p. 23). Such claims are not correlated with any specific findings about brain or neurochemical processes, such as connections between neurons. That is a matter of empirical research, not arm-chair theorising.

Despite warnings against brain research offering a 'magic bullet' for educators, perhaps the hope is that neurosciences will tell us what the relationship is between neurochemical processes and learning. The link between brain processes and brain function and education is, after all, quite seductive. It is tempting to think that if we know enough about neurophysiology then we can tailor classroom practices to maximize learning. However, any such relation presupposes a simplistic, reductionist account of philosophy of mind. For, we are tempted to draw the inference that when a neural process is correlated with a certain episode of learning, then there is a specific correlation between that neural process and learning. Classroom practices could then be aligned with such findings, based on an assumption of an identity between a brain state and learning. However that suggestion would appear to fly in the face of the acknowledged plasticity of mind, with its suggestion of the multiple realizability of brain function (Graham, 1998).

WHY BRAIN-BASED LEARNING—GOVERNMENTALITY?

A convergence of factors led to the emergence of the enthusiasm for brain-based learning. First the idea that children develop is by now a commonplace. But the idea of childhood development is recent, perhaps only 200 years old beginning with various anthropometric studies carried out in the first half of the nineteenth century (Wong, 2003). It now organises an entire system of child-rearing and child-caring practices. Norms have been established gauging children's physical, cognitive and even emotional growth. There are now even age-appropriate toys and games, all geared towards children's development. Given the current discourse of child development, parents are perhaps concerned about how their children develop. They would be anxious if their children were to lag behind. Lagging behind would suggest their child were sub-normal with all the extra-logical connotations of that label. Some would also want to help their children excel, to be better than the norm. Normal means average and why settle for that (Hacking 1999). There is a market for bettering performance, and toy and game makers have caught on. For example, Nintendo has developed a game, the Big Brain Academy: Wii Degree, which claim to improve players' brain scores. The game tests players on work through fifteen activities in five categories. The tests are graded and players are assigned a brain score. For about $50, an individual can purchase the game and by playing improve her brain score. Of course, whether or not playing these games actually makes a person smarter is another matter. Nintendo makes no such promises.

With the popularisation of neuroscientific research and the current talk of a 'knowledge economy' and creative 'knowledge workers' (Nadesan, 2002; Wall, 2004), parents may feel added urgency in attending to information from recent brain research. They are told repeatedly of the importance of the early years for brain development and the consequences in later years if the opportunity were missed. Some parents have incorporated such information into their repertoire of concerns. For example, John Bruer, a critic of the brain-based learning, cites a case in which a mother asked an experienced grade five teacher what she was doing to take advantage of her daughter's windows of opportunity for learning before they closed. The meeting between parent and teacher ended badly because the teacher could not answer the parent's questions since she did not follow research on synaptogenesis. The parent left dissatisfied and the teacher upset (Bruer, 1999).

Governments too take such knowledge seriously. Foucault claims that since the eighteenth century there emerged a new way by which individuals are governed, what he calls 'governmentality.' Two features of governmentality are:

1. The ensemble formed by the institutions, procedures, analyses, and reflec-tions, the calculations and tactics that allow the exercise of this very specific albeit complex form of power which has its target population, as its principal form of knowledge political economy, and as its essential technical means apparatuses of security.

2. "[The tendency] of this type of power—which may be termed 'govern-ment'—resulting, on the one hand, in the formation of a whole series of specific governmental apparatuses, and, on the other, in the development of a whole complex of knowledges" (Foucault 1994a, p. 220).

Such bodies of knowledge are deployed in "administering the welfare of the population, to improve its condition, wealth, longevity and health" (Foucault, 1994a, p. 217). For example, the province of Ontario has initiated plans to set up a network of Early Years Centres—around 100 by last count (Wall, 2004, p. 42). The plan for these centres grew out of a 1999 study of the early years commissioned by the province. The study offered advice to help parents understand and promote all facets—physical, intellectual and emotional—of their children's development. One recurring theme in the study is the centrality of brain development before age five and its importance for children's later success.

Schools have also taken brain research to heart. For example, the York Regional District School Board offers its teachers a resource called "Instructional Intelligence," in which brain-compatible learning is a central component. One book cited in the document tells its readers that brain research is "the hot area of professional development" (Bennett and Rolheiser, 2001, p. 368). The authors list eleven key ideas of brain research for educators. Some of these ideas echo claims discussed above, such as "the brain is plastic," "there are specific windows of opportunities for some experiences to be 'wired' otherwise those wires get pruned," and "brains [at least those of laboratory rats] that live in enriched environments have 40% more neuron connections than those that live in bland environments" (Bennett and Rolheiser 2001, pp. 368–369).

The authors of a recent article urged principals to "establish policies to support" recent research in the neurosciences (Nunnelley *et al.*, 2003, p. 54). If the brain functions best with patterning, so be it. Principals should tailor the scheduling of classes to match the findings from such research, such as allowing teachers more time to show students connections between the topic and real-life concerns (ibid.). Principals are to promote professional development for the staff to understand brain-based learning so that they can "develop their own meaningful mental schema of the brain, to assimilate research and then use its findings" (Nunnelly *et al.*, 2003, p. 49). The authors advocate the establishment of a "learning community" in which staff are encouraged to work collaboratively to implement various techniques for those interested in trying them, including working with a teaching mentor as well as having in-class observations by a peer coach. The authors also emphasized the need to align brain-based learning strategies with standards. Principals are to enlist strategies such as classroom observations, hallway walks, periodic review of lesson plans, as well as gathering data from the entire school to see if brain-based instruction actually improves student outcomes because "no time can be wasted" with students (Nunnelly *et al.*, 2003, pp. 54 & 57).

GOVERNMENTALITY AND SUBJECTIVITY—LOOPING EFFECTS

With brain-based learning, we see how the discourse of science is wedded to disciplinary matrix in which individuals—administrators, teachers and students—are moulded into specific subjectivities, ways to be administrators, teachers and students. Foucault tells us that,

> This form of power ... categorizes the individual ... attaches him to his own identity, imposes a law of truth on him that he must recognize and others have to recognize in him (Foucault, 1994b, p. 331).

He adds that "the struggle against the forms of subjection ... is becoming more and more important" and that new forms of subjectivities need to be promoted "through the refusal of [the] kind of individuality that has been imposed on us" (Foucault, 1994b, pp. 331–2 & 336).

One way the struggle against the imposition of subjectivity is by way of the interaction between individuals and the group or category under which they are classified, what Ian Hacking describes as the "looping effect of human kinds" (Hacking, 1996). In contrast to "natural kinds," say swamp gas, Hacking calls categories by which individuals are classed "human kinds." Human kinds differ from natural kinds in at least one important aspect. With our example of swamp gas, it is obvious that it makes no difference to swamp gas molecules what anyone thinks of them. They don't care if we hold them responsible for the foul stench. Yet how people are classified may have a tremendous impact on them. Further, the difference it makes to those classified in a particular way may bring about a change in the classification. Because individuals can act in response to how they are classified, human kinds may thus exhibit a feedback cycle that natural kinds may not.

To focus our thinking about looping effects, consider the category 'homosexual.' Homosexuals, as a kind of person, may seem to have been with us always. But as Foucault and others have argued, while there has always been same-sex sexual activity, the idea of homosexuals as a kind of person with a distinctive set of properties only emerged in the nineteenth century, thanks to the proliferation of discourses by various self-styled experts on sexuality. Only then did the homosexual become a 'relevant' kind, often portrayed as deviant and abnormal. Foucault tells us,

> As defined by ancient civil or canonical codes, sodomy was a category of forbidden acts; their perpetrator was nothing more than the juridical subject of them. The nineteenth-century homosexual became a personage ... a type of life, a life form ... with an indiscreet anatomy and possibly a mysterious physiology. ... The sodomite had been a temporary aberration; the homosexual was now a species (Foucault, 1979, p. 43).

Foucault's historical claims are not uncontroversial, but, regardless of one's position on when the kind 'homosexual' originated, we should at least be able to agree that it has undergone further changes. This has occurred, at least in part, as a consequence of looping effects. Those classified as homosexual, hence deviant and abnormal, rebelled against such categorization. They have succeeded in some measure to take control of the category for themselves. Instead of 'homosexual', they are now 'gay', 'lesbian' or 'queer' (Wong, 2002, p. 457).

As the examples of the confrontation between the parent and the grade-five teacher and the establishment of Early Years Centres in Ontario remind us, it would appear that teachers and childcare providers are expected to have absorbed the recent findings of neuroscientific research and incorporated them into their classroom practices. The subjectivities of teachers and other childcare providers are moulded in part by the discourse of brain research. Failure to do so may mean a person no longer falls under the category of a good teacher or parent or childcare provider. However individuals may respond to such negative categorization of themselves. Teachers or principals may challenge the easy and simplistic link between the discourse of brain research and classroom practice. They may offer alternative explanations for effective classroom practices. For example, there may be very good pedagogical reasons to break down a lesson into smaller parts and to relate each part to everyday concerns of students, but these reasons may be understood in simple folk psychology terms and will not have anything to do with neurophysiology.

CONCLUSION

If the discussion on governmentality is connected to the theme of control, the discussion of looping effects hints at the possibility of the ability of individuals participating in steering their own lives. Of course, not every attempt at resistance automatically succeeds. This is because there is an inescapable collaborative element to loop. At the very least, the desired changes to a classification must be generally accepted. For example, many members of extremist groups no doubt want to change how their particular classification is conceived, but no such think is likely to happen. This is because, even if they are prepared to claim their views have positive value, almost no one else is prepared to agree. Hence, a loop that results in a positive conception of such individuals is unlikely to take place. Conversely, a significant portion of the community was willing to accept the claim that lives of homosexuals are valuable ones, so loops that resulted in a more positive conception of homosexuals were able to take place. What's more, people's willingness to accept some changes and not others may alter the trajectory of particular loops (Wong and Latus, 2003). In the case of brain-based learning, perhaps what is needed is the positive valuation of what educators already know about teaching practices in order for the category of 'teacher' not to reflect disciplinary features.

REFERENCES

Bennett, B., & Rolheiser, C. (2001). *Beyond monet: Artful science of instructional integration*. Toronto, ON: Bookation Inc.

Bruer, J. T. (1999, May). In search of brain-based education. *Phi Delta Kappan, 80*, 649–657.

Davis, A. (2004). The credentials of brain-based learning. *Journal of Philosophy of Education, 38*(1), 21–35.

Dwyer, B. (2001). Successful training strategies for the twenty-first century: Using recent research on learning to provide effective training strategies. *International Journal of Educational Management, 15*(6), 312–318.

Foucault, M. (1979). *The history of sexuality* (Vol. I, Robert Hurley Trans.). New York: Vintage Books.

Foucault, M. (1994a). Governmentality. In J. D. Faubion (Ed.), *Essential works, Vol. 3: Power* (pp. 201–222). New York: The New Press.

Foucault, M. (1994b). The subject and power. In J. D. Faubion (Ed.), *Essential works, Vol. 3: Power* (pp. 326–348). New York: The New Press.

Graham, G. (1998). *Philosophy of mind: An introduction* (2nd ed.). Oxford, UK: Basil Blackwell.

Greenleaf, R. K. (1999, September). It's never too late! What neuroscience has to offer high schools. *NASSP Bulletin*, 81–89.

Hacking, I. (1996). The looping effects of human kinds. In D. Sperber, D. Premack, & A. J. Premack (Eds.), *Causal cognition: A multidisciplinary approach* (pp. 351–394).

Hacking, I. (1999). *The taming of chance*. Cambridge, UK: Cambridge University Press.

Hacking, I. (2005). Get knitting. *London Review of Books, 27*(16).

Lowrey, L. (1998, November). How new science curriculums reflect brain research. *Educational Leadership, 56*, 26–30.

Nadesan, M. H. (2002). Engineering the entrepreneural infant: Brain science, infant development toys, and governmentality. *Cultural Studies, 16*(3), 401–432.

Nunnelley, J., Whaley, J., Mull, R., & Hott, G. (2003, December). Brain compatible secondary schools: The visionary principal's role. *NASSP Bulletin*, 48–59.

Wall, G. (2004). Is your child's brain potential maximized? Mothering in the age of new brain research. *Atlantis, 28*(2), 41–49.

Weiss, R. P. (2000). Brain-based learning. *Training & Development, 54*(7), 20–24.

Wolfe, P. (1998, November). Revisiting effective teaching. *Educational Leadership*, 61–63.

Wolfe, P., & Brandt, R. (1998). What do we know from brain research? *Educational Leadership, 56*, 8–13.

Wong, J. (2002). What's in a name? An examination of social identities. *Journal for the Theory of Social Behaviour, 32*(4), 451–463.

Wong, J. (2003). Can power produce knowledge? Reconsidering the relationship of power to knowledge. *The Southern Journal of Philosophy*, *XLI*, 105–123.

Wong, J., & Latus, A. (2003). Fraser and the politics of identity: Human kinds and transformative remedies. *Philosophia*, *31*(1–2), 205–219.

York Region District School Board. Instructional Intelligence. Retrieved May 1, 2006, from <www.ydrsb.edu.on.ca>

James Wong

MAJIA NADESAN

21. GOVERNING AUTISM: NEOLIBERALISM, RISK, AND TECHNOLOGIES OF THE SELF

In 2007, the Center for Disease Control (CDC) reported that autism spectrum disorders now affect 1 in 150 children (CDC, 2007). The Harvard School of Public Health estimates the cost of care for a person with autism at $3.2 million over a lifetime with the care of all persons with autism estimated at $35 billion per year (Kantrowitz & Scelfo, 2006). Parents, educators, medical professionals, and state sponsored social service providers demand that autism's social and economic costs be addressed and managed. Managing the social and economic risks posed by autism presents significant challenges and opportunities within neoliberal rationalities of government.

Neoliberal governmentality entails dismantling and/or privatizing state apparatuses advocating "a return to a technology of 'frugal government'" (Foucault, 1997, p. 78). Those state entities that continue to exist under neoliberalism must adopt regimes of accountability emphasizing measurable and calculable outcomes. Moreover, as articulated by Foucault (1997) in "The Birth of Biopolitics," the American style neoliberalism associated with the Chicago School seeks "to extend the rationality of the market, the schemes of analysis it proposes, and the decision making criteria it suggests to areas that are not exclusively or primarily economic" (p. 79). In particular, neoliberal governmentalities increasingly govern the problem space of biological life.

Neoliberal government of biological life aims to reduce the health costs associated with population by shifting costs and risks to responsibilized individuals. Individuals are exhorted to adopt personal technologies of the self that reduce their health risks; simultaneously, they are forced to assume economic costs as employers shed responsibility for underwriting employees' health. Concomitantly, investigation and engineering of biological health is primarily pursued, or financed, by entrepreneurial market agents as demonstrated by the fact that by 2005, at least 18.5% of human genes were covered by private U.S. patents (Westphal, 2005).

Autism is a problem space governed by diverse technologies of power but this space is increasingly understood and managed within neoliberal strategies of government (Nadesan, 2005). Formulations of autism within neoliberal govern-mentalities can be demonstrated by three related trends. The first trend concerns the formulation of autism as a bio-genetic disorder best managed through genetic, pharmacological and neurological government. In this context, autism constitutes an opportunity space for marketized biopolitical authorities. In contrast, the second trend concerns constitutions of autism within the space of population, wherein

M.A. Peters et al. (eds.), Govermentality Studies in Education, 379–394.

autism treatment and prevention regimes are pursued by anxious parents. Parents' pursuits of autism treatment and prevention illustrate personalized technologies of the self because parents must become expert on their children's disorders in order to evaluate the privatized marketplace of autism treatments, which are oddly detached from 'legitimate' biopolitical expertise. Rather than exploring these treatments in detail, I focus on parents' mobilization around vaccinations as an autism prevention strategy. Finally, the third trend addresses some disturbing practices in the institutional disciplining of autistic children as public schools grapple with their special needs in the context of neoliberal regimes of accountability and funding.

Accordingly, this chapter explores how autism is governed through genetic and neurological discourses of life. It then contrasts these approaches with those governmental strategies adopted by parents of autistic children and public school personnel, emphasizing domestic technologies of the self and institutional disciplinary strategies.

BIO-GENETIC GOVERNMENT

Martha Herbert (2005) suggested that distinct approaches to autism exist today; the first approaches autism as a strongly genetic, "*brain based*" disorder (my italics, p. 355) while the second approach views autism as a *systemic* disorder conferred by genetic susceptibility but extensively modulated by, and responsive to, environmental phenomena. Although both approaches view autism within 'genetic' frameworks of understanding and are commensurable with market-based management, the latter (systemic approach) stresses contingency and openness while the former (brain-based approach) tends to view autistic brains as irreparably damaged. The pessimism of the 'brain-based' approach does not preclude bio-medical interventions but strongly emphasizes pharmacological management, rather than treatment of, autistic symptoms.

Comparative analysis of these two approaches points to the shift from the certainty of Mendelian genetics to the genetic contingencies of genomics (see Petersen & Bunton, 2002). The brain-based approach rests in the Mendelian premise that genetic states are directly linked to behavioral/cognitive states, as mediated through brains tastes. Thus, Mendelian genetics views genes as agentive first principles that govern other neurological and behavioral states. In contrast, genomic science emphasizes the loose coupling across gene, brain, and behavioral/ cognitive states and sees genes as modulated contingencies contributing to probabilistically calculated risks.

Contemporary researchers working on genetics and neuroscience understand the importance and implications of genomic contingency. However, private and public research dollars tend to support studies that identify specific causal pathways that can be subject to biomedical government, particularly through development of commercial products. Neoliberal strategies of genetic government thus favor Mendelian representational frameworks and/or intervention strategies.

Robin Bunton and Alan Petersen coined the phrase "genetic government" to refer to how genetic technologies and envisioned changes impact individual bodies (i.e., through treatment protocols), social communities, and political and economic environments (2005, p. 1). Regimes of genetic government shift across time, reflecting changing epistemic fields and technologies, illustrated by the ontological shift from Mendelian genetics to genomics. But, the narrow laboratory focus of genetic research, a legacy bequeathed by a century of investigative practices, constrains understandings of the contingencies that shape genetic expressions while marketized imperatives shape genetic research objectives and product development. Material apparatuses therefore profoundly shape how autism is subject to genetic and also neurological government, as will be discussed below.

GENETIC GOVERNMENT

Let us begin with the operating practices characteristic of genetic research. Lily Kay (1993) in *The Molecular Vision of Life* traces American efforts to govern life at the genetic level to the Rockefeller Foundation's funding of "molecular biology" in the 1930s. Kay identified characteristic features of this emerging field that would shape the problem space of investigation across much of the twentieth century:

- The new biology emerging in the 1930s would focus on the "unity of life phenomena common to all organisms" (p. 4).
- Phenomena would be approached at their most minimalist levels leading to employment of bacteria and viruses as probes and models.
- Research aimed at discovering "physicochemical laws governing vital phenomena" that were cleaved from host organisms, leading to an almost exclusive focus on "mechanisms of upward causation, ignoring the explanatory role of downward causation" (p. 5).
- Research defined the locus of life phenomena primarily at regions between 10^-6 and 10^-7 cm, requiring an "imposing technological landscape" of microscopes, ultracentrifuges, x-ray diffraction, etc. (p. 5).
- "Research problems were often defined by the instruments designed to examine them" (p. 5).

This relatively narrow focus of investigation and analysis tended to exclude synergistic and environmental effects as life was distilled as information through abstraction of genetic sequence data. The cybernetic, self-replicating gene served as the locus for life and as an integral component of the Cold War "knowledge-power nexus" (Gottweis, 1998, p. 53). Genetic research promised economic returns on commercially-applicable innovations in health and agriculture and, simultaneously, promised to maximize the health of the population.

For much of the twentieth century, expert laboratory authorities pursued Mendelian models of genetics inheritance positing relatively singular and direct relationship between gene alleles and phenotypic traits. In the context of Mendelian genetics, gene alleles are believed to directly shape phenotypic expressions by governing protein production such that:

Gene allele ▶ protein (e.g., affecting eye color) ▶ phenotypic trait (e.g., eye color)

Discovery of the molecular form of DNA suggested that deletions or substitutions of one of DNA's four nitrogen bases—Adenine (A), Guanine (G), Cytosine (C), or Thymine (T)—explained variations of genetic inheritance. Deletions or mutations in gene sequences were understood as "causing" diseases.[1]

Researchers pursuing the genetic origins of autism used technologies such as linkage analysis to identify genetic deletions or mutations that could be associated with the disease. Linkage analysis looks at related individuals to determine whether they share the same chromosomal interval or, more specifically, allele(s) for targeted DNA markers, and therefore assumes that shared intervals/alleles are somehow responsible for, or linked to, a given phenotypic characteristic (e.g., disease diagnosis or trait) without necessarily understanding how the alleles are expressed (ibid). Linkage analysis has been used to study families with more than one autistic member to identify suspect alleles. Researchers often scan DNA regions that have previously been linked to other related disorders in order to narrow their research scope. Chromosomal regions 2q, 7q, 16q, have been identified as suspect regions for autism susceptibility gene errors or alleles (Monaco & Bailey, 2001). Regions on the X chromosome and on chromosomes 2, 3, 15, 19, and 22 have also been implicated as playing a role in autism's development (Shao et al., 2002; Travis, 2003).

But findings derived from linkage analysis also problematized the Mendelian model of genetic inheritance. Family members of autistic individuals occasionally exhibited the same genetic variations yet did not suffer from or exhibit autistic traits. The presence of targeted gene alleles does not necessarily predict or explain the disorder. Researchers concluded that the diversity of the autism phenotype explained some of the variability found across research studies but they were also forced to recognize that autism was probably produced by a wide variety of genetic and environmental contingencies that synergistically modulated genetic risks.

This type of thinking ushered in contemporary strategies for genetic research on autism, strategies premised in models of genetic risk that have been calculated at the level of population (Petersen & Bunton, 2002). Genomic analysis involves calculations of genetic risk derived from analyses of aggregate populations. Genomic analysis differs from earlier forms of focused genetic analysis because it scans entire genomes for SNPs linked to disease susceptibility using new representational and computing technologies. Genomic analysis therefore allows researchers to identify a range of single base substitutions (SNPs) or mutations of nucleotides that are statistically correlated with a disease. A drawback of genomic analysis is spurious correlation (Cardon & Palmer, 2003). Moreover, genomic calculations of correlation do not imply genetic determinism: rather, they suggest 'risk' or susceptibility.

While genomic approaches to autism emphasizing genetic risks and epigenetic ('post-translation') processes offer the most viable framework for understanding the complex autism phenotype (Klauck, 2006), they also complicate development of marketable products. Consequently, the genomic complexities of psychiatric government (Insel & Collins, 2003) may be swept aside in the push for commercial commodities: under neoliberal regimes of marketization and public accountability, funding dollars tend to chase marketable outcomes.

TGen's operating practices illustrate how genomic science is subject to neoliberal market imperatives. In 2006, the Translational Genomics Research Institute (TGen), a privatized research entity operating in collaboration with Arizona State University, received 10 million in state funding to pursue a large study of autism using genomic analysis. Although partially funded with state funds, this study aimed to use its initial capital investment by the state to "raise $50 million in private and public funds to develop autism-related drugs" (Snyder, 2006, p. B1). The study also sought to develop a pre-natal autism test that would predict autism risks.

TGen's research aims, technologies, and strategies illustrate neoliberal genetic government in several ways. First, although TGen is partially funded by state apparatuses, its funding strategies aim primarily to secure private investment. Second, TGen approaches genomic analysis of autism risk using a market-based approach that aims ultimately at developing commercial products including an autism susceptibility test and autism-related drugs. TGen authorities view development of autism drugs as contingent upon identification of distinct autism sub-groups using genomic screening. Researchers hope to identify specific gene alleles within sub-groups that cause cascading genetic effects. Identification of such alleles would point to possible bio-chemical or engineering interventions that could be marketed. But this research and market strategy re-introduces more linear and mechanistic Mendelian frameworks of genetic understanding and government that may ultimately prove unproductive commercially.

TGen's efforts to develop an autism susceptibility test may be more productive commercially than drugs because such a test would simply calculate autism risk based on identification of the presence of alleles known to confer risk. A pre-natal autism susceptibility test would have the effect of shifting autism risks to privatized individuals. Parents would have the opportunity and responsibility to 'choose' whether to 'have' a potentially autistic baby. Because the test could only offer probabilistic estimates, this choice would be marked by uncertainty, weighed by fear. Parental fears about having an autistic child are no doubt amplified by media sensationalism surrounding the disorder and economic calculations of costs for families associated with caring for autistic children.

TGen is not alone in its efforts to leverage autism risks for market gain. But given the complexities surrounding genetic government of autism, research currently aims to better understand how gene states govern neurological states. Neurological investigations of autism need not be vested in a particular genetic framework of understanding. However, Mendelian models of genetic government presuppose linear formulations of relationships across gene states, brain states, and behavioral/ cognitive states and therefore are particularly appealing for enterprising agents pursuing autism's pharmacological government.

NEUROLOGICAL GOVERNMENT

Biopolitical authorities have for centuries sought to peer into the inner realms of the brain using pathology studies of deceased individuals. But technological advances promise new strategies for rendering the living brain's hidden anatomy and chemistry visible.

Uttal (2001) describes 3 contemporary technologies, beginning with the electro-encephalogram (EEG), which represents electrical activity in the living brain. The EEG reliably detects tumors, lesions, gross anatomical brain abnormalities. EEG technologies have been used to try and correlate cognitive processes with the localization of electrical activity in the brain by addressing "evoked brain potentials" (EVBPs), although clear successes have been limited to establishing relations between "cortical activity and particular stimulus or behavior measures" (e.g., eye movements) (Uttal, 2001, p. 56). More sophisticated and nuanced technologies such as computer-aided X-Ray tomography and CAT scans create three-dimensional anatomical representations. In contrast, positron emission tomography (PET) and magnetic resonance imaging (MRI) address metabolic processes. PET entails introducing a radioactive substance into the body, using the energy emitted in its decay as the means for creating a three-dimension image of the brain (Uttal, 2001). PET scans enable insight into the brain's metabolism of particular substances, as well as blood flow into a particular brain region; although, it remains unclear whether the site of the greatest metabolic activity (as measured by the PET scan) is necessarily the site for the operation of a cognitive process. MRI uses both magnetism and radio frequencies, to make (computer-mediated) three-dimensional representations of scanned tissues based in the magnetic resonance of protons. Application of MRIs to functional brain activation is called functional magnetic resonance imaging (fMRI), which studies the activity of haemoglobin in response to oxygen demand (Uttal 2001). Changes in blood oxygen level are believed to be causally related to variations in neural activity at the respective site.

The fantasy of rendering the living brain visible seems to have been achieved, at first glance. More careful investigation of these brain imaging technologies reveals layers of contingency and uncertainty. Uncertainty and contingency problematize the project of neurological government.

First, contrary to the biopolitical fantasy of neurological government, brain imaging technologies offer highly conditional findings. The images produced by these technologies are not transparent representations of easily discernable, universal characteristics (e.g., see Carey, 2005). Technological limitations are inherent in the generation of these images and their results must be *interpreted* (Dumit, 2004; McGonigle et al., 2000; Parker-Pope, 2003; Raz et al., 2005; Uttal, 2001; Wolpe, Foster, & Langleben, 2005). Although new imaging technologies suggest increased electrical or metabolic activity in certain brain regions in response to laboratory-invoked stimuli, this activity is difficult to interpret in terms of its significance and its relevance with respect to the *operation of the brain as a whole* (Uttal, 2001). More profoundly, data generated from contemporary representational technologies are not transparent; data are produced through complex digital transformations that shape understandings. The "technological fix" for handling large samples of neurological data has profound epistemological and ontological consequences (Beaulieu, 2001, p. 668) including informatic abstraction, standardization, normaliz-tion and the quantification of variability from standardized norms. The people who read brain scans are required to make sense of statistically generated variations from imagined means.

Where do neurological means come from? How are the characteristic anatomical and metabolic characteristics of 'normal' brains discerned? Who decides what kinds of variations are abnormal? What factors condition determination of risky or dangerous variations? These questions and their answers point to contemporary psychiatric problematics of neurological government (Peterson, 2003). One current study illustrates how research approaches identification of normal brains using MRI data:

> About 400 health newborns to teenagers, recruited from healthy families, are having periodic MRI cans of their brains as they grow up. They also get a battery of age-linked tests of such abilities as IQ language skills and memory. The project is funded by the National Institutes of Health. The MRI images measure how different parts of the brain grow and reorganize throughout childhood. Overlap them with the children's shifting behavioral and intellectual abilities at each age, and scientists expect to produce a long-sought map of normal brain development in children representative of the diverse U.S. U.S. population. (Researchers Learning, 2007, p. A19)

Researchers recognize that brains change across development so this study promises to provide neurological norms for distinct development stages, expanding Arnold Gessell's typology of development stages to embrace neurological normality.

Anatomical, metabolic, and neurochemical norms could be used as baselines against which to measure the neurological differences of children referred for odd or delayed development. On the one hand, childhood referrals are motivated by an economy of hope and the desire to manage autism risks but on the other hand they open up the possibility for new kinds of surveillance and labeling premised in problematic methodologies and ontologies.

Neurological norms may very well be idealizations that lack (generalizable) material existence, particularly if brain development and metabolism are subject to myriad environmental influences. Imagined means may obscure the adaptive and experiential realities of neurological variation and may complicate any direct correspondences across gene, brain, and behavioral/cognitive states (e.g., see Fisher, 2006; Schwartz & Begley, 2003). How could researchers discern whether a given variation is linked to the observed behavioral or developmental phenomena when the relationship between neural states and mental/behavioral states is so fundamentally unclear and potentially contingent? Consequently, efforts to "fix" brains outside operative means may harm as well as help.

Current efforts to manage autistic symptoms point to the complexities and dangers of neurological government. Currently, psychiatric drugs do not "treat" autism; rather, drugs manage troubling symptoms. Commonly used and approved drugs for autism such as Risperdal target the (believed) unruly biochemistry of the autistic brain, seeking to govern biogenic amines such as dopamine ("Johnson," 2006). But the relationship between neurochemistry and behavior remains unclear. Furthermore, psychiatric drugs typically lack the capacity of "targeted government"

(Valverde & Mopas, 2004, p. 232) in that they have unknown "downstream" effects that extend beyond the neurochemistry targeted for government. Consequently, psychiatric drugs often have a significant array of unwanted side-effects that can be as troubling as the symptoms that the drugs were employed to manage, including excessive sleepiness and weight-gain. Parents considering one commonly used autism drug, for example, face the potential for their children to be transformed into corpulent zombies.

Although drugs that actually treat autism neurochemically would be widely welcomed, the prospects for their development are uncertain. As genomic science recognizes, autistic symptoms are mediated by complex genetic and molecular synergies. Consequently, it is unclear whether people with autism bear the same unruly neurochemistry. It is unclear how neurochemistry shapes behavioral or cognitive predispositions. And it is unclear how neurochemistry is itself shaped by gene alleles amendable to identification and manipulation. Autism is a problem-space lacking clear demarcation and therefore problematizes development of clear-cut strategies for government.

To this date, genetic and neurological government of autism have together failed to produce products for desperate parents hoping to help their autistic children. While research dollars circulate extensively, they circulate within a public-private research apparatus with few links to the privatized lives of autistic families. State and market genetic/neurological government are largely unconnected to the lives and needs of autistic population. Promises of autistic drugs and effective autistic treatments suggest future strategies for risk-management but have no application or relevance for contemporary autistic lives.

GOVERNING AUTISM: TECHNOLOGIES OF THE SELF

Most private health insurance in the U.S. does not cover autism treatments such as occupational and speech therapy (Hadi, 2007). Parents of autistic children are referred to state agencies such as state departments of economic security. States vary widely in eligibility requirements for, and extent of, services. Desperate parents, mobilized by fear and hope, turn to a wide range of private authorities for guidance and treatment (see Nadesan, 2005). More traditional biopolitical authorities, such as psychiatrists and pediatricians, tend to adopt the gene based genetic model and therefore offer pharmaceutical agents as the primary technology for suppressing troubling autistic behaviors. But parents often find pharmacological government disappointing because of significant side effects and the drugs lack of curative properties. Parents subsequently adopt a wide range of behavioral, cognitive, and 'alternative' bio-medical approaches loosely grounded in the systemic approach of autism susceptibility (e.g., see Shaw, 1998). Parental efforts to 'save' their children illustrate personalized and often market-based technologies of the self as well as pointing to very historical conditions of understandings of childhood (see Aries, 1992; Nadesan, 2002, 2005).

Parents of children diagnosed as autistic often describe themselves as autism experts. Their expertise rests in their extensive and often Internet-based research of bio-medical investigation and treatment of autism as much as it does their everyday experiences with their children. Parents typically embrace the systemic approach to autism susceptibility because it stands as more open to the role of environmental influences, suggesting a viable space for parental remediation. Parents mobilized to save vulnerable and innocent children target a wide range of environmental agents believed to amplify or moderate genetically conferred risk and susceptibility including but not limited to vaccinations, dietary factors, and behavioral-cognitive therapies (see Nadesan, 2005). Given limitations of space, I focus only on vaccinations as debates surrounding vaccination practices illustrate parental technologies of the self, biosociality, and antagonistic formulations of individual and societal risk management.

In the first half of the twentieth century, vaccinations were mandated by the pastoral social-welfare state to protect the population: vaccinations were an important security technology and are regarded as among the most cost-effective and widely used public health interventions (Hodge & Gostin, 2001/2002). Today, vaccination manufacturing and development in the U.S. typically is pursued by private market based entities but companies are offered a wide range of legal protections from law suits stemming from vaccination injuries. Claims of vaccination injury must go before a special vaccination court for adjudication (Offit, 2005). Vaccinations have been effective as a security technology in that they have eliminated and/or significantly reduced incidences of childhood diseases, particularly polio, diphtheria, measles, mumps, rubella, among others.

However, a wide array of individuals acting outside of market and state apparatuses contend that vaccinations produce risks for specific individuals with biological susceptibilities. Vaccination dissidents, as they shall be referred to, rarely question vaccinations' capacities to secure aggregate populations. Rather, dissidents elevate the significance of discrete individuals who may be harmed by technologies that secure the larger population. The systemic model of genetic susceptibility offers dissidents a specific explanatory mechanism for explaining the seeming contradiction between aggregate gains and individual harms.

State and market authorities have responded to dissidents' claims with study after study purportedly conclusively demonstrating no adverse effects from vaccinations (both from active and inactive ingredients, such as methyl mercury). Vaccine proponents can dismiss dissidents' claims because of the difficulty in conclusively establishing side-effects (Dew, 1999). Most recently, the debate between 'legitimate' biopolitical authorities and vaccination dissidents was demonstrated by a study published in *Pediatrics* (D'Souza, Fombonne & Ward, 2006) that was subsequently deconstructed in the *Autism Research Review*, a quarterly autism advocacy journal that summarizes autism research results ("New Findings," 2007). Given the difficulties in proving direct links between vaccinations and autism based on individual cases, autism advocates have turned to mining aggregate data for statistical correlations. In 2007, survey results produced by SurveyUSA but commissioned by an autism advocacy organization, Generation Rescue, suggested that vaccinated boys are 155% more likely to have neurological disorders than unvaccinated peers (Olmsted, 2007). Generation Rescue publicized the results in full-page newspaper ads.

The ceaseless debate between biopolitical authorities and biopolitical dissidents on the safety and security risks of vaccinations is in part fueled by the very uncertainty and environmental openness of contemporary genomic findings.[2] Diet, stress, random radiation, lead, mercury, etc. are implicated as potential dangers to the developing person in an age of heightened anxiety about personhood (Dunant & Porter, 1996). It is therefore not surprising that those who bear the greatest risks posed by disabled children—that is, parents—are mobilized politically to identify factors that increase autism risk, and vaccinations, as state mandated protocols with established risks, are ready targets for political action.

The debate about the relationship between autism and vaccinations illustrates the cultural power of what Rabinow (1996) has described as 'biosociality.' Autism advocates are united by their perception of a common biology. Advocates need not possess the common biology. Bonds of love and friendship also link those who stand united within a common frame of biosociality (see Rose, 2007). Autism advocates have become very powerful in lobbying state actors and in mobilizing public concern over rising autism diagnoses. Autism advocacy led to a special session before the U.S vaccination court in the spring of 2007 (Debate, 2007).

Public health authorities tend to regard autism dissidents as posing new risks to national health and fret publicly over declining vaccination rates. Biomedical authorities who support the possibility of autism risks from vaccinations face professional reprisals. In Britain, a London doctor whose research suggested a link between autism and the combined measles, mumps, and rubella vaccine faces charges of professional misconduct stemming from his research practices. A council, which regulates doctors in Britain, will consider whether the doctor in question violated ethical practices during his study of young children including advising solicitors representing children who claimed to have suffered from the MMR vaccine and collecting blood samples during a birthday party "without proper ethical approval" (Doctor, 2007, p. B4).

Anecdotal experiences suggest that parents who express vaccination concerns to their pediatricians are also subject to sanctions. Parental efforts to secure alternative vaccination schedules for children that minimize multiple injections are regarded with skepticism and parents are sometimes harassed by health care providers who see alternative protocols as endangering both children and the nation's health. Vaccinations have become a fundamental point of conflict between officials who shepherd the public's health and individuals who view their children as 'at risk' by widely practiced and mandated health technologies.

At a more general level, health care officials occasionally express concern over, and frustration with, the activist efforts and therapeutic requests/demands of parents with autistic children. In 2004, *Pediatrics*, the official journal of the American Academy of Pediatrics, published a special section addressing "difficult parents" exemplified by the mother of a child diagnosed with the autism spectrum disorder of Asperger's syndrome (Stein, Jellinke, & Wells, 2004, p. 1492). The article, and subsequent responses by other clinicians, represented such parents as demanding, "rigid" (p. 1493), and "disruptive" (1494). While there can be little doubt that some parents occasionally or always act as so characterized, their efforts must be construed within a cultural milieu that holds them responsible for their children's care and outcomes, and this responsibilization tends to overcome genetic fatalism and traditional expressions of 'respect' and deference to biopolitical authorities.

Accordingly, activist efforts to govern rising rates of autism are matched by individualized technologies of the self pursued by parents to recover or help treat autistic children. Parental efforts to secure desired treatments for children meet resistance from health care officials who are unfamiliar with treatment protocols or perceive them to be risky and/or experimental. In the face of professional reluctance, parents may turn to the market of 'alternative' autism treatments, which further radicalizes their advocacy in the imagination of mainstream health care providers.

In sum, parental technologies of the self aimed at securing their children's health and reducing autism risks to susceptible individuals confront professional protocols based in aggregate formulations of health and risk management. The conflict between formulations of individual and aggregate needs is perhaps more pronounced in the context of public schooling.

GOVERNING AUTISM: DISCIPLINARY POWER

Public school teachers stand unprepared for understanding and responding to the needs of the vast numbers of "autistic" children mainstreamed into their classrooms (Tomsho, 2007) and public schools have been accused by the Department of Education of failing to meet their legal obligations to special needs children (Zuckerbrod, 2007). Mainstreaming is legally mandated in the U.S. by the 1975 Individual with Disabilities Education Act, which stipulates that children be placed in the least restrictive educational environments. But state funding often does not provide adequate resources for supporting disabled students mainstreamed into regular classrooms. Moreover, teachers facing already crowded classrooms typically have little to no educational or skills preparation for dealing with the vast array of special needs they confront. Overwhelmed by the needs of typical students, and unprepared for dealing with those with 'special needs,' teachers and school administrators occasionally resort to overt disciplinary methods to constrain 'out-of-control' disabled children including physical restraints and seclusion rooms.

In 2007, Colorado's federally funded disability office claimed that a Colorado Springs-area school abused disabled autistic students by allowing them to "beat themselves bloody while being held in seclusion rooms" (Tomsho, 2007, p. A12). One autism advocacy organization, AUTCOM, the Autism National Committee, reported in 1999 that between 50 and 150 children die each year during or immediately after use of physical restraints. Expressed concerns about the use of physical restraints and enforced seclusion are found widely across autism advocacy web pages and in 2007 the Autism Society of America featured a special session at its annual conference dedicated to elimination of physical restraints (Our journey, 2007).

For readers unfamiliar with autism the spectacle of manacled, physically secluded children strains the liberal imagination. How could it be that autistic children are treated in this fashion given a wider cultural milieu that increasingly discourages the corporeal disciplining of children?

Autism spectrum children typically have low anxiety thresholds and are readily stressed by the stimuli of regular classrooms. Even high functioning autistic children exhibit difficulties following oral instructions and may lack understanding of expectations even when they possess the intellectual capacities for executing assignments. Stress leads to preservative activities that are often regarded as disruptive and bizarre by classmates and teachers. The subsequent pattern of escalation stemming from teachers efforts to stop unwanted behavior readily culminates in staff efforts to physically remove the offending student from the classroom. Autistic children typically cannot tolerate any kind of physical restraint due to their sensory sensitivity and become highly unmanageable. Shackled or secluded, stressed autistic children often resort to self-injurious behavior.

The autistic child is not locked in a solipsistic psychological universe but has significant difficulty developing cultural disciplines and technologies of the self characteristic of "normal" children. Consequently, they are perceived as ungovernable. Their ungovernable may trigger disciplinary reprisals by pedagogical, parental, and other authorities.

Foucault (2006) argued in *Psychiatric Power* that nineteenth century biopolitical efforts to govern the insane (or "idiot") aimed primarily at rendering them "docile and submissive" (p. 22). To illustrate this objective, Foucault described how Edouard Seguin (1812–1880), approached "idiot children" using "moral treatment" aimed at conquering their "monarchical will," (cited in Foucault, 2006, p. 215). Seguin held that these children's refusal to submit to parental authority and to integrate within a system should be combated with absolute pedagogical mastery enforced by the impeccable corporeality of the teacher's body (p. 216).

Nineteenth century pedagogical practices clearly differ significantly from those widely practiced in western nations at the beginning of the twenty-first century. However, the seemingly obstinate and ungovernable will of autism-spectrum children may, at times, overcome pastoral pedagogical imperatives. Frustrated and overwhelmed teachers, aids, and others (including parents) may resort to totalizing disciplines to control the corporeality of the seemingly ungovernable autistic child.

Even teachers who struggle to understand and adapt to special children's needs face conflicting imperatives as neoliberal rationalities increasingly govern their evaluation by administrative officials. In the U.S. there is considerable popular support for linking teacher compensation to standardized test scores. This type of "reward" system is viewed as instilling pedagogical accountability and provides the type of standardized and quantifiable measures preferred by neoliberal calculi of value. Inclusion of special needs children in regular classrooms can lower class averages on test scores (they are not factored out). Additionally, teacher efforts to adjust classroom curriculum to those with the greatest learning challenges may incur calculative costs for the highest achievers. Inclusion of autistic children in regular classrooms may therefore be perceived by parents and educators alike as posing risks to aggregate educational outcomes.

Pedagogical government of autistic children is rendered more complicated by parents' willingness to pursue legal means to maximize their children's educational opportunities. The liberal democratic ethos of individual rights and responsibilities is enforced by cultural supports and juridico-legal apparatuses. Parent efforts to pursue legal recourse are facilitated by a wide array of activist networks who provide background information on relevant legal statutes while offer socio-emotional support. However, legal-juridical and cultural autism advocacy efforts increasingly confront opposition from school administrators resisting special education costs, from teachers lacking support for mainstreaming, and from the parents of 'normal' children who fear that mainstreaming dilutes educational quality. More broadly, autism advocacy confronts heightened popular suspicion about the potential dangers posed by those whose mentalities stray from optimal norms.

FROM DANGEROUSNESS TO DESERVING, FROM AT-RISK TO HIGH RISK

The nineteenth century apparition of the 'feeble-minded' child, which posed risk to the biological health of the national race, was replaced over the twentieth century with the special needs child deserving of, and legally entitled to, public succor. The special needs child is understood as vulnerable, at-risk for future dependency and requires risk-management in order to minimize future costs while maximizing opportunities for self-actualization.

But the image of the at-risk child deserving of special protections and care is confronted by an emerging formulation of risky individuals based in bio-genetic formulations and construed within public health models of risk management (see Rose, 2007). Childhood-onset autism spectrum disorders have been linked to adult criminology (see Anckarsäter, 2005; Johansson, Kerr, & Andershed, 2005; Soderstrom et al., 2004). Although links drawn between autistic spectrum disorders and violent crime no doubt confound environmental effects (e.g., post-traumatic stress from child abuse) with innate neurological differences (autistic communication deficits), the idea that criminal predispositions can be explained by biologically based personality characteristics has enthralled biopolitical authorities since the mid nineteenth century (Foucault, 2003). In the wake of the Virginia Tech shooting of students in the spring of 2007, psychiatric authorities are under increased public scrutiny for their role in protecting public safety through the identification and monitoring of risky individuals.

Renewed efforts to biologize crime and dangerous personality traits (see Nadesan, in press) coupled with anxiety about public safety may undermine the mid to late twentieth century formulation of the autistic child as innocent, vulnerable, and in need of special protections. The "at risk" autistic child, particularly the "high-functioning" autistic child, may be replaced by a formulation of the dangerous, "risky" autistic child afflicted by an aggressive neurochemistry (e.g., dopamine levels) (e.g., see Talan, 2005). The dangerous child of the late nineteenth century (see McCallum, 2001) reappears, albeit clothed in new psychiatric and genomic vocabularies.

Autism advocates will have to work diligently to combat popularization of this specter of the dangerous autism-spectrum child. Advocacy efforts may be challenged by the convenience of this formulation for educational authorities and public health and safety officials who must meet public demands that they demonstrate pre-emptive strategies for crime prevention. In effect, genomic and neurochemical formulations of risk, when applied to the autistic individual, may have the effect of ushering in technologies of surveillance and control that undermine liberal protections and rights.

In conclusion, neoliberal market imperatives that have driven efforts to establish direct links between and across genes, neurochemical states, and behaviors may have significant illiberal effects for those targeted as dangerous and risky. People with autism, who are by definition odd socially, may be vulnerable to new regimes of control and discipline that promise targeted government (Valverde & Mopas, 2004, p. 232) of risky individuals.

NOTES

[1] Humans vary in their DNA sequences by about 0.1% (i.e., people share 99.9% of the same DNA sequences). Of the 0.1% difference, over 80% are single base substitutions of nucleotides (SNPs) that are found in 1% or more of the population. The remaining variations are regarded as mutations (Cambridge Healthtech Institute, 2006). SNPs are the most frequent form of polymorphism in the genome.

[2] For an excellent analysis of vaccine safety debates, see Dew (1999).

REFERENCES

Anckarsäter, H. S. (2005). Clinical neuropsychiatric symptoms in perpetrators of severe crimes against persons. *Nordic Journal of Psychiatry, 59*(4), 246–252.

Aries, P. (1962). *Centuries of childhood: A social history of family life* (R. Baldick, Trans.). New York: Vintage Books.

AUTCOM. (1999). *Position on restraints*. Retrieved August 7, 2007, from http://www.autcom.org/articles/Position4.html

Beaulieu, A. (2001). Voxels in the brain: Neuroscience, informatics and changing notions of objectivity. *Social Studies of Science, 31*, 635–680.

Bunton, R., & Petersen, A. (2005). *Genetic government: Health, risk and ethics in the biotech era*. New York: Routledge.

Cambridge Heathtech Institute. (2006). *Genomic glossary*. Retrieved July 6, 2007, from http://www.genomicglossaries.com/content/gene_def.asp

Cardon, L. R., & Palmer, L. J. (2003). Population stratification and spurious allelic association. *The Lancet, 361*, 598–604.

Carey, B. (2005, October 18). Can brain scans see depression? *The New York Times*. Retrieved October 18, 2005, from http://www.nytimes.com/2005/10/18/health/psychology/18imag.html?th=&emc=th&page

CDC: 1 in 150 children has autism spectrum disorder. (2007). *Autism Research Review, 21*(1), 1.

D'Souza, Y., Fombonne, E., & Ward, B. J. (2006). No evidence of persisting measles virus in peripheral blood mononuclear cells from children with autism spectrum disorder. *Pediatrics, 118*, 1664–1675.

Debate over vaccine's role in autism heads to a court. (2007, June 11). *The Wall Street Journal*, B7.

Dew, K. (1999). Epidemics, panic and power: Representations of measles and measles vaccines. *Health, 3*(4), 379–398.

Doctor faces hearing over autism claim. (2007, July 16). *The Wall Street Journal* B4.

Dumit, J. (2004). *Picturing personhood: Brain scans and biomedical identity*. Princeton, NJ: Princeton University Press.

Dunant, S., & Porter, R. (1996). *The age of anxiety*. London: Virago.

Fisher, S. E. (2006). Tangled webs: Tracing the connections between genes and cognition. *Cognition, 101*, 270–297.

Foucault, M. (1997). The birth of biopolitics. In P. Rabinow (Ed.), *Ethics, subjectivity and truth* (pp. 73–85). New York: The New Press.

Foucault, M. (2003). *Abnormal: Lectures at the Collège de France 1974–1970* (V. Marchetti, A. Salomoni, Eds., & G. Burchell, Trans.). New York: Picador.

Foucault, M. (2006). *Psychiatric power: Lectures at the Collège de France 1973–1974* (J. Lagrange, Ed. & G. Burchell, Trans.). Houndsmill: Palgrave.

Gottweis, H. (1998). *Governing molecules: The discursive politics of genetic engineering in Europe and the United States*. Cambridge, MA: The MIT Press.

Hadi. (2007, February 4). Family finances: Financing the care of a disabled child. *The Wall Street Journal*, A2.

Herbert, M. R. (2005). Autism: A brain disorder, or disorder that affects the brain? *Clinical Neuropsychiatry, 2*(6), 354–379.

Hodge, J. G., & Gostin, L. O. (2001/2002). School vaccination requirements; historical, social and legal perspectives. *Kentucky Law Journal, 90*(4), 831–390.

Insel, T. R., & Collins, F. S. (2003). Psychiatry in the genomics era. *American Journal of Psychiatry, 160*, 616–620.

Johansson, P., Kerr, M., & Andershed, H. (2005). Linking adult psychopathology with childhood hyperactivity-impulsivity-attention problems and conduct problems through retrospective self-reports. *Journal of Personality Disorders, 19*(1), 94–101.

Johnson & Johnson: Risperdal approval is expanded to include childhood autism. (2006, October 9). *The Wall Street Journal*, B2.

Kay, L. E. (1993). *The molecular vision of life: Caltech, the Rockefeller Foundation and the rise of the new biology*. Oxford, UK: Oxford University Press.

Kantrowittz, B., & Scelfo, J. (2006, November 27). What happens when they hrow up? *Newsweek, CXVLIII*(22), 46–53.

Klauck, S. M. (2006). Genetics of autism spectrum disorder. *European Journal of Human Genetics, 14*, 714–720.

McCallum, D. (2001). *Personality and dangerousness: Genealogies of antisocial personality disorder*. Cambridge, UK: Cambridge University Press.

McGonigle, D. J., Howseman, A. M., Athwal, B. S., Friston, K. J., Frackowiak, R. S. J., & Holmes, A. P. (2000). Variability in fMRI: An examination of intersession differences. *NeuroImage, 11*, 708–734.

Monaco, A. P., & Bailey, A. J. (2001). The search for susceptibility genes. *Lancet, 358*(3), s3.

Nadesan, M. (2002). Engineering the entrepreneurial infant: Brain science, infant development toys, and governmentality. *Cultural Studies, 16*(3), 401–432.

Nadesan, M. H. (2005). *Constructing autism: Unravelling the "truth" and understanding the social*. London: Routledge.

Nadesan, M. H. (in press). *Governmentality, biopower, and everyday life*. New York: Routledge.

New findings show major flaws in Flombonne study clearing vaccines. (2007). *Autism Research Review, 21*(1), 1.

Offit, P. A. (2005, December 1). Lawsuits won't stop pandemics. *The Wall Street Journal*, A16.

Olmsted, D. (2007). The age of autism: Study sees vaccine risk. ScienceDaily. Retrieved July 10, 2007, from http://www.sciencedaily.com/upi/index.php?feed=Science&article=UPI-1-20070626-16403000-bc-ageofautism.xml.

Our journey to eliminate the use of physical restraint. (2007, July 11–14). Symposium conducted at the Autism's Society of America's 38th Annual Conference. Scottsdale, AZ. Retrieved August 11, 2007, from http://asa.confex.com/asa/2007/techprogram/S2970.HTM

Parker-Pope, T. (2003, February 18). Warning your MRI may be out of focus: Why scans often miss what's wrong. *The Wall Street Journal*, D1.

Petersen, A., & Bunton, R. (2002). *The new genetics and the public's health*. London: Routledge.

Peterson, B. (2003). Conceptual, methodological, and statistical challenges in brain imaging studies of developmentally based psychopathologies. *Development and Psychopathology, 15*, 811–832.

Rabinow, P. (1996). *Essays on the anthropology of reason*. Princeton, NJ: Princeton University Press.

Raz, A., Lieber, B., Soliman, F., Buhle, J., Posner, J., Peterson, B. S., et al. (2005). Ecological nuances in functional magnetic resonance imaging (fMRI): Psychological stressors, posture, and hydrostatics. *Neuro Image, 25*(1), 1–7.

Researchers learning how young brains grow. (2007, May 19). *The Arizona Republic*, A19.

Rose, N. (2007). *The politics of life itself*. Princeton, NJ: Princeton University Press.

Schwartz, J. M., & Begley, S. (2003). *The mind and the brain: Neuroplasticity and the power of mental force*. New York: Harper.

Shao, Y., et al. (2002). Genomic screen and follow-up analysis for autistic disorder. *American Journal of Medical Genetics, 114*, 99–105.

Shaw, W. (1998). *Biological treatments for autism and PDD*. Overland Park, KS: Great Plains Laboratory.

Snyder, J. (2006, July 25). State dollars jump-start autism research. *The Arizona Republic*, B1.

Soderstrom, H., Sjodin, A., Carlstedt, A., & Forsman, A. (2004). Adult psychopathic personality with childhood-onset hyperactivity and conduct disorder: A central problem constellation in forensic psychiatry. *Psychiatry Research, 121*(3), 271–280.

Steiln, M. T., Jellinek, M. S., & Wells, R. D. (2004). The difficult parent: A reflective pediatrician's response. *Pediatrics, 114*, 1492–1495.

Talan, J. (2005). Cooling hot aggression. *Scientific American Mind, 16*(2). Retrieved August 2, 2007, from http://www.sciam.com/article.cfm?articleID=0001D3B6-614F-128A-9DD683414B7F0000& sc= 1100322

Tomsho, R. (2007, July 9). When discipline starts a fight; pressured to handle disabled children, a school tries restraints, "Isabel's office". *The Wall Street Journal*, A1.

Travis, J. (2003). Autism advance. *Science News, 163*(14), 212–213.

Uttal, W. R. (2001). *The new phrenology: The limits of localizing cognitive processes in the brain*. Boston, MA: MIT Press.

Valverde, M., & Mopas, M. (2004). Insecurity and the dream of targeted government. In W. Larner & W. Walters (Eds.), *Global governmentality* (pp. 232–250). New York: Routledge.

Westphal, S. P. (2005, October 14). Human gene patents 'surprisingly high' a new study shows. *The Wall Street Journal*, B1.

Wolpe, P. R., Foster, K. R., & Langleben, D. D. (2005). Emerging neurotechnologies for lie-detection: promises and perils. *The American Journal of Bioethics, 5*(2), 39–49.

Zuckerbrod, N. (2007, June 20). *Education Department says states aren't meeting special-ed law's requirements. Bridges4kids*. Retrieved August 8, 2007, from http://www.bridges4kids.org/articles/6-07/AP6-20-07.html

Majia Nadesan

III. FOUCAULT, EDUCATION AND GOVERNMENTALITY: EUROPEAN PERSPECTIVES

SUSANNE MARIA WEBER AND SUSANNE MAURER

22. THE ART OF BEING GOVERNED LESS

Educational Science in Germany and Governmentality

Governing people: that used to mean, taking them by the hand, leading them to their salvation – aided by a detailed technology of management that implied a lot of knowledge: knowledge about the managed individual; knowledge about the truth the individual is led to… (Foucault, 1992, p. 50).

The Foucauldian perspective on power and knowledge is highly relevant in educational science, as Klaus Mollenhauer confirmed in the late 1970s (Krüger, 1999). Yet, over a long period of time educational science in Germany seemed to have quite an ambivalent relationship to this highly creative, critical political philosopher. Ludwig Pongratz remarked (1989) that Foucault's reception, or lack of it, was characterized mostly by rejection and skepticism, that the impact of his analysis was much too little appreciated and that it was employed not nearly enough in the critical analysis of educational knowledge. This seems to be changing. 'Power' has not only been a topic explicitly addressed in the context of the Convention of the German Association of Educational Science (DGfE) in 2006, but the last few years have also seen a number of publications that emphasize Foucault's usefulness for educational science. Similar to Axel Honneth's (2003) prediction about the changes in social sciences, Nicole Balzer (2004) confirms that the overall discussions in educational science are becoming more productive.

With the term *gouvernementalité*, Michel Foucault added "a new dimension to his power analysis that made it possible to analyze power relations under a perspective of 'leadership,' separating it equally from the model of law and of war" (Lemke et al., 2000, p. 8). Thomas Lemke, Ulrich Bröckling and Susanne Krasmann see the term's innovative power mainly in its "hinge function": government can now be described as a "connecting link between strategic power relations and states of governance" (ibid.) and Foucault draws a sharper distinction than before between governance and power. The term of government also mediates between power and subjectivity, and last but not least it offers "an important analytical tool for the investigation of the power-knowledge complexes that Foucault has so frequently underlined" (Lemke et al., 2000, p. 8). In his works on governmentality Foucault (2004a; 2004b) analyzes power-knowledge in a context of government, normalization and subjectivation by focusing on the art of government. Foucault's term 'government' does not refer to the state's power of government but to that of

M.A. Peters et al. (eds.), Govermentality Studies in Education, 397–414.

leading people in a sense of guidance, control, and management. This implied guidance here is both autonomous as well as heteronomous:

> The point of contact, where the form of the individuals' guidance by others is tied up with their self-guidance can be called government, in my opinion. In the wider sense of the word, government is not a way of forcing people to do what those in government want; much rather it is a steadily shifting balance with additions and conflicts between techniques that ensure force, and processes by which the self construes and modifies itself (Foucault, 1993, quoted by Lemke et al., 2000, p. 29).

So government refers to the "(self-)production" of subjectivity, and to the "invention and promotion of self-technologies that can be tied to objectives of government" (ibid.). The analysis of governmentality distinguishes self-constitution from the ulterior constitution of technologies and aims at analyzing the inter-dependence between the two technological forms – technologies of government and technologies of the self. Discussions of problems define a political-epistemo-logical space or the "space of opportunity" (Foucault 1987, p. 255, quoted by Lemke et al., 2000, p. 20) thus focusing on the knowledge inherent in the practices, the systematization and rationalization of pragmatic leadership. The way rationality is used here has to be seen in reference to "historical practices in whose context strategies of perception and of assessment are generated. So it does not imply a normative evaluation but mostly has a relational significance" (ibid.).

Governmental practices can depart from the body, organism or discipline just as well as from the wishes and the will of the subjects. They can derive their effect from the population as a whole, as normalizing knowledge, regulating the 'normal' and 'abnormal' along degrees of normality. The governmental knowledge that is employed here does not bounce off the subjects but has an effect as subjectifying practice – "the power relations run through the inner body" (Foucault, 1978).

Foucault replaces simple juxtapositions of force and freedom, or consensus and violence with a "reflective mode of government as 'leading the leadership'" (Lemke et al., 2000, p. 27):

> A term like 'leading' may be particularly appropriate to describe the specific character of power relationships because of its double meaning: 'leading' can be the 'leadership' over others (...) or the way to behave in a more or less open field of possibilities where you 'lead your life' (Foucault, 1987, quoted by Lemke et al., 2000, p. 27 et seq.).

Both aspects have strong ties to educational lines of questioning and practices as the essays in this collection exemplify. In Germany Lemke et al. (2000) have introduced governmental ways of thinking to diagnose the present – into the analysis of power-knowledge complexes in a context of new models for leading one's life, as total mobilization of the subjects of institutional strategies. They analyze the relationship between subjectivation processes, the technology of the self and the development of possible forms of governance.

This collection has been born out of an interest in tying the questions generated by a governmentality perspective in the Foucauldian tradition, to thinking and research in the field of educational science. The background and horizon that all contributions share, is their interest in the possibilities of criticism of current social conditions and developments. But what can science, and particularly educational science's line of questioning, contribute to the development of a culture of criticism?

WHAT IS CRITICISM?

Foucault's work is situated in a context of perspectives that carry the question of power into educational fields of action, thus counteracting educational science's obliviousness of power. It is committed to a critical perception of science (Masschelein et al., 2004). From Foucault's point of view, the potential of criticism is "that it tirelessly forms itself, continues and reforms itself anew again and again" (Foucault 1992, p. 8). Foucault describes criticism as an *attitude*, as "a particular way of thinking, of saying, also of acting, a particular relationship to that which exists, to that which one knows, to that which one does, a relationship to society, to culture, a relationship also to others – something you could call the attitude of criticism" (ibid.). His *history of criticism* starts with the Christian pastoral, continuing with the multiplication of arts and institutions of government. "All controversy over the pastoral in the second half of the Middle Ages has prepared the way for the Reformation and was the historical threshold, so to speak, on which that critical attitude developed" (ibid.).

A critical attitude forms the opposite number to the arts of government, "at the same time their partner and their opponent" – the cultural form of a moral and political attitude, a way of thinking, an "art of being less governed" (ibid., p. 12). The place where criticism is forged then is primarily "the bundle of relationships between power, truth and the subject." For Foucault, criticism is a movement in which the subject demands the right "to try and discover the power effects in truth and the truth effects in power."

Criticism as the art of "reflective disobedience" and of "self-determined un-bondage" within the games of the truth politics takes on the function of de-subjugation (ibid., p. 15). It continues the enlightenment understanding that opposes immaturity and a lack of decisiveness and courage. *Sapere aude*[1] is the critical attitude. Direct and on the surface of visible transformations, it is important to "analyze the relationship between power, truth and the subject." For Foucault, the question, "What is criticism?" turns into that of "What is enlightenment?" (Foucault, 1992). With this, Foucault places himself in the enlightenment's critical tradition of thinking. The central element of the critical attitude has to be "especially the questioning of knowledge about its own limitations and dead-ends, which it encounters during its initial and concrete execution" (ibid., p. 43). Unlike Kant he emphasizes that criticism is not a "test of legitimacy," that it is rather about finding the linking points of elements of force and of knowledge (Schäfer, 2004, p. 162):

First of all it takes courage, in dealing with knowledge and perception, to recognize what is there to recognize. That is the radicalism and, for Kant, the universalism of his endeavor (Foucault, 1992, p. 59).

While the critically oriented, social science perspectives, in a quasi materialistic way assume institutional and personal power structures whose ideological shaping has to be unmasked. Foucault's discourse analysis starts out from power as power-knowledge. The fully developed hegemonic forms are not pre-existent, but they are, rather permanently actualized results and processes of a specific rationalizing practice. This could be one of the reasons why the German audience could not readily embrace Foucauldian thinking.

CRITICAL EDUCATIONAL SCIENCE

Observation of the pluralistic field of a 'critical educational science' can follow the core terms of emancipation and *Mündigkeit* (Self-Ownership; Self-Accountability; see Maurer, 2001). Heinz-Hermann Krüger (1999) exemplifies what a critical educational science wants by pointing out authors like Herwig Blankertz, Wolfgang Klafki and Klaus Mollenhauer, who demanded social theoretical perspectives for an education that was at the time still oriented towards social sciences (Krüger, 1999). In 1968 Mollenhauer held the position that education and knowledge have to find their raison d'être in the *Mündigkeit* of the individual. Knowledge in the educational sciences is guided by the interest in emancipation (ibid.). According to Krüger, during the 1970s, Mollenhauer and Klafki's postulate of emancipation was increasingly grounded in the discourse theory of Jürgen Habermas. The project of a consensus in keeping with reason was oriented on the idea of oppression-free communication. Krüger regards critical educational science as "attempting, on a level of theoretical definitions, to view pedagogical action as a social practice determined by its history and attempting to formulate the interdependency of the respective educational systems and the structure of their societies" (ibid., p. 165). Education and society are dialectically linked and, in the 1970s and 1980s, research mostly follows an ideology-critical methical design. The programmatic character that criticism gains in this way quickly lead us to the question, to what degree is the enlightenment capable of enlightening us about itself? Is criticism itself not subject to that which it criticizes?

Christiane Thompson points out the problem posed by the claim of criticism as expressed in the postulate of emancipation (2004). She sees the contradictions of the 1980s critical educational sciences as rooted mainly in the trust that is put into an emphatic term of emancipation. A critical pedagogy working with the distinction between ideology and truth and with the assumption of power-free knowledge is blind to the fact that the emancipation discourse itself is already tied to something powerful. Confessional compulsions can curb the free range of deliberation, and it might become impossible to question emancipation and *Mündigkeit* as idealistic and idealized programs, as to their position within the discourse and to their subjectifying practice. This would preclude consideration of self-responsibility as an option for personnel management practice (Weber, 1998; Liesner, 2004).

From a Foucauldian perspective, the antagonistic pairing of *Mündigkeit* and immaturity, autonomy and heteronomy, the contrasting of self-determination and heteronomy, of freedom and power have to be understood as reductive. The intimate interdependency of knowledge and power would rather have to be uncovered in a genealogical-archeological fashion, in the form of constellations. Criticism then does not rely on the differentiation of "legitimacy" and "illegitimacy," of "truth" and "ideology" but on the "fracture lines" in the emergence of an accepted system of power-knowledge (Thompson, 2004 p. 47). It is particularly these fractures and contingencies within the power-knowledge ensembles that mark the possibilities for course corrections and change. In this changing field of discussion and of discursive struggle, criticism also becomes a strategy that builds its bases and participates in the game of truth and power (Thompson, 2004). The objective is not so much to become the source of social change but to make changes and shifts accessible as processes of experience, as "borderline experiences that pull the subject away from itself (...)" (Foucault, 1996, p. 27, quoted by Thompson, 2004, p. 53). Criticism is no longer a pure model of knowledge but a critical attitude and the art of "not being governed in this way and at this price" (Foucault, 1992, p. 12).

EDUCATIONAL SCIENCE BETWEEN AFFIRMATION AND CRITICISM

In a 1991 supplement of the *Zeitschrift für Pädagogik*, Jürgen Oelkers and Heinz Tenorth demand that pedagogical knowledge itself should be opened up to analysis and scrutiny. Places and systems for the generation and utilization of pedagogical knowledge, its functions, the patterns and instances of affirmation, the characteristics that define the structure of pedagogical knowledge, the themes that make it possible to distinguish this object from others, as well as the different kinds of knowledge should be analyzed. Jochen Kade (1989; 1997; 2003) continues in this vein when he poses questions about the different kinds and conditions of pedagogical action and its reconstruction, about the shape of the pedagogical element in a time of reflective modernism. Under a perspective of uncertainty the fields of action become equivocal (Helsper et al., 2003). As part of new pedagogical arrangements, one can discover "dynamic mixtures of certainty and uncertainty, knowledge and non-knowledge" that are more characteristic than "unequivocal orientations and stable patterns of action" (ibid., p. 18).

The pedagogical suffers a loss of unequivocal determination, in many ways finding itself on unsteady ground. Clear borders slip out of focus and new interconnections as well as new limitations become visible. The pedagogical then has to be analyzed in fields whose structures are full of contradictions and which become "the problem and marker of pedagogically oriented design and of reflection in educational science" (ibid., p. 8). Is the reflexivity of educational science now becoming the silver bullet for today's critical analysis of the status of the pedagogical?

According to Michael Wimmer (1996), the 'universalization of the pedagogical' – the shift from a position where professional pedagogues consider their actions, tasks and functions as specifically connected to certain fields, towards an attitude that has become generalized, universal, beyond the need for rationalization – has not only delegitimized the self-description of social and educational professions, but has also left its traces in pedagogy's system of reflection, in educational science. As part of the process of differentiation and interconnection of numerous social areas, the pedagogical *habitus* now encodes modes of thinking, of experience and of action as its natural area of activity, which creates specific rifts within the educational science discourse (Wimmer, 1996). In this context Michael Winkler (1999) holds that pedagogy, which has always been reflective, gains a central position in modern societies by "discarding its institutional, practical-operative dimension and limiting itself to reflexivity. *Pedagogy today primarily appears as reflexive pedagogy, and can today only be reflexive pedagogy*" (Winkler, 1999, p. 272; italics in the original). But reflexivity does not at all promote the process of critical affirmation. "The opposite is true: as reflective, pedagogy can only prevail at the price of social affirmativeness which obviously drains the critical potential it might still have" (ibid.). Winkler points out that a reflective educational science finds itself right in the middle of the "field of social availability" – and escape from these processes of social availability, reaching deeply into reflection, is not easily accomplished (Winkler, 1999, p. 297).

So it is in the middle of the field of social availability where we find pedagogical practices and pedagogical knowledge committed to an emancipatory discourse. Here uncertainty becomes a resource and the principle of the researching practice of the hypothetical and experimental, and learning approach to information in society becomes a general mode of action (Weingart, 2001). Such productive practices of uncertainty are embedded in processes of communicative rationalization (Ulrich, 1990). Deleuze regards this as the work of the control society that does not operate by disciplining and inclusion but by continuous control and immediate communication (Deleuze, 1993a). In control societies, ultra-fast forms of control in a liberal guise are introduced that are "just as efficient as the most rigid enclosures." The "school regime" demands forms of continuous control in an open environment and the influence of permanent further learning, the establishment of the "company" on all levels of the educational and vocational training system (Deleuze, 1993b, p. 261). That is why Deleuze no longer acknowledges any utopian potential in the "free association of free individuals" in the marketplace of the communication society. "In capitalism there is only one universal language – the market" (ibid., p. 247). There is no reason for either fear or hope, "only for searching new weapons" (ibid., p. 256). The search for "new weapons" takes place inside a tradition of giving voice to the polyphonic ensemble of criticism.

CRITICISM AS A 'POLYPHONIC ENSEMBLE' – INTERPRETATIONS AND RECEPTIONS OF FOUCAULT

Criticism is not confined within the borders of disciplines. Lines of reception in social as well as educational sciences are pluralistic. They offer a diversity of inspirational potential and of possible interfaces for critical thinking. It is in this sense that we will try to sketch, with the following overview of different receptions, possibilities of building connections to Foucault's perspective of criticism. We do not intend to play 'correct' receptions off against 'false' ones but follow Foucault in seeing criticism as a 'polyphonic ensemble.'

'A figure of Discursivity'

Michael Peters (2004) reminds us that there is no text without a reader – that the reader construes the text actively while reading. How we read and what we receive depends on historical constellations, cultural discourses and acceptabilities. Some circles of readers take a critical view of poststructuralist thinking, others a more positive one. In some places Foucault is subsumed into literary studies rather than philosophy. Against this background, Peters urges us to focus more on the cultural context of reception instead of ideologically (or ideology-critical) laboring over 'truths.' Still he draws a line of division between his own position on Foucault and one where 'anything goes'. Even though there cannot be one reception of Foucault, interpretations can still be bad, faulty or distorted. Against the "bitter antagonism of the 1980's" he promotes on the whole a creative, theoretically differentiated and reflective style of critical contemplation. Foucault and his work are to be opened up to multiple interpretations. But Foucault, Peters (2004, p. 197) says is often worn out and mistreated as "Mr. Elastic Man" – especially because he extended the invitation to use his 'tool-box of criticism' for a wide variety of critical intentions. To Peters, Foucault is a "figure of discursivity,"– time and again reformulating and discursively developing his own project (of knowledge). Peters points out the existence of a variety of readings of Foucault in an Anglophone context. So Stephen Ball can enlist him as a critical ethno-sociologist and Tina Besley as a Nietzschean genealogist, both using him productively in their respective works. To Bernadette Baker, he is an historian of thought systems, to Mark Olssen a historical materialist and democrat, to Tom Popkewitz and Marie Brennan he is a social-epistemologist, and to Sue Middleton a crypto-feminist. Michael Peters describes his own approach as post-structuralist.

The reception of Foucault apparently changes according to national and cultural contexts, to readership, generation and gender. The categorizations and headings that are found in the respective disciplinary and interdisciplinary discursive spaces also differ, mirroring in each case the cultural and scientific contexts. For this reason, Peters says (2004), the reception has to be chronicled differently for different countries, places and disciplines. Tying reception to a cultural context would also include the chance to avoid ideological calcification.

Beyond Hagiography and Transfiguration – Foucault's Reception in Educational Science in German-speaking Countries

In German-speaking countries, 'Foucault's toolbox' has been put to use in quite different ways as well. Norbert Ricken and Markus Rieger-Ladich share the view that the different pedagogical readings of Foucault try to test his inspirational potential and that they keep "beyond hagiography and transfiguration" (Ricken & Rieger-Ladich, 2004, p. 9). Nicole Balzer (2004) sees reading Foucault in educational science in German-speaking countries as still being caught up in oppositional definitions such as freedom vs. power, autonomy vs. heteronomy, self-determination vs. determination by outside forces (ibid., p. 16). But lately the frame of reception has widened analyzing increasingly – beyond dichotomous thinking patterns – intermittent gaps, transitions, and interweavement. The pheno-menon of power is now less understood as repressive or descriptive, and Foucault's central terms power, knowledge and subjectivity are less and less discussed as separate categories but rather in their interdependence.

To adequately construct Foucault's reception would require extensive research, but three axes of reception as follows, can serve as guiding lines. One axis is an institution-analytical axis, where we find meso- and macro-theoretical works that use an institution and repression critique. This line reconstructs the increasing prevalence of state-like structures throughout society or social politics as social control, in macro-analyses that follow a design critical of state and ideology. A second axis of reception lies between genealogy and educational aspirations, between the pathos of the education discourse and an archaeology of the pedagogical gaze that Käte Meyer-Drawe demanded (1996). The pathos of the formula of the authentic self and the demand of subject formation gets relativized as self-constitution or is entirely called into question. Throwing a critical light on the illusion of autonomy and not setting the pedagogical *outside* the discourse has been a great challenge of the past and one that the educational science discussion exposes itself to more and more readily. Reinhard Hörster (1993) uses Foucault productively for regional material analyses while Helmut Forneck and Daniel Wrana (2005) push for the analysis of the subjectifying power in power-knowledge complexes. This places a third axis of reception between a knowledge-sociological view of pedagogical settings and material, methodically designed, discourse analyses (Hörster, 2003). Overall, the focus within theory debates in educational science shifts away from a programmatic stance towards a reflective one (which may also be critically reflexive). It moves from emphasis and pathos to an analytically minded self understanding; from a simple disciplinary perspective towards the question of power-knowledge-relations; from the static institutional setting to the dynamic discursive field; from subject and interaction centeredness towards the complexity of non-subjective but intentional discourses and the multi-level analyses of real, reflective and discursive relationships.

There are numerous possible interfaces, connecting lines and discursive ties between pedagogical power-knowledge and other forms of knowledge. Where Foucault analyzed medicine, the judicial system, psychiatry and sexuality, today the rationalizations that emerge at other surfaces are also considered (e.g. in the economy, in genetic and reproductive technology, the media etc). The central point is always to 'say what is' with critical intentions and to analyze the mode or the how of the creation of validity criteria for truth.

THE CRITICAL POTENTIAL OF INSIGHT BETWEEN SOCIAL AND DISCURSIVE CONSTRUCTIVISM

Reinhard Hörster (1993) brings to our attention the differences between social and discursive constructivism. In opposition to a social scientific approach – one that has society as its point of reference – discursive constructivism follows an epistemological perspective in the sense of a political philosophy. According to Hörster, a research approach which makes productive use of discourse analysis methodology is not determined by social theory or sociology of governance and is not just about cognitive strategies of social integration. Neither does such research aim to analyze concepts and their implementation or to evaluate them normatively. A discourse analysis approach does not deal with symbolic action or criticism of institutions. Instead it analyzes power-knowledge, not the marginal unit of the institution:

> Criticism of the power over the mentally ill or the lunatics cannot be limited to the psychiatric institutions: and those who question the punishing power cannot be satisfied with denouncing the prison as a total institution. The question is: How are such power relations rationalized? Asking this question is the only way to prevent other institutions from taking their place with the same goals and the same effects (Foucault, 1988, p. 66).

The issue here is the effects of productive power on discursive modalities of utterance. This analysis takes place on a different level to the analysis of 'social realities' by means of social scientific concepts – it analyzes the creation of validity criteria for truth within a process. In such an approach, terms are not defined a priori, neither are they pre-existent. But discursive practice has social scientific relevance since it deals with the problems of social regulation (Hörster, 1993).

The epistemological perspective that is emphasized here analyzes knowledge as power-knowledge as a 'commanding and ordering knowledge,' that can utilize specific ways of rationalization in the social discursive space.

Following Reinhard Hörster (1993), we can discuss those dimensions which are relevant for *methodical* approaches, to clarify which questions can be addressed with discourse analysis, constructivism and which ones with social scientific constructivism. Early on, Klaus Mollenhauer (1979) recommended that educational science pay attention to Foucault's methods. This recommendation is still valid today, but as Hans-Christoph Koller and Jenny Lüders (2004) show Foucault is still being recognized and read with more attention to content and terms than to method. The latter is more prevalent in other disciplines e.g., in literary studies, history, sociology or political science. Overall the term discourse analysis is being used fuzzily and is based on different theoretical and methodological convictions.

Epistemology or Social Criticism?

Foucault's discourse analysis aims to analyze orders of knowledge and power relations. When he uses the term discourse he refers to the "discursive practice" of a rule-guided production of statements and the system of order itself that is established by these rules (Koller & Lüders, 2004, p. 60). By knowledge Foucault means all "procedures and effects of insight," which "are acceptable at a certain moment in a certain area. Secondly, the term power is used, which covers many individual, definable and defined mechanisms that seem to be capable of inducing behavior or discourses" (Foucault, 1992, p. 32).

Beyond the legitimization or hierarchization of values, the terms knowledge and power have a methodological function here – they are "just an analytical grid" (ibid., p. 33) that has to be kept unified "because nothing can be presented as an element of knowledge if it does not conform to a system of specific rules and restrictions," and nothing can work as a mechanism of power "if it is not unfolded in procedures and relations of means and ends which are rooted in knowledge systems." So we are talking about the "power-knowledge nexus" that lets us estimate the "acceptability of a system" (ibid.).

Sociology of knowledge approaches on the other hand deal with the social production of knowledge, with society itself acting as its point of reference. The social scientific as well as the discourse analysis perspectives are based on a fundamentally deconstructivist position, presupposing orders that are created by discourses. A social scientific discourse analysis "attempts to reconstruct processes of social constitution, objectivation, communication and legitimization of structures of meaning, on a level of institutions, organizations and collective actors and to analyze the social effects of these processes" (Keller, 1997, p. 319). A discourse analysis reading from a sociological position thus finds its place within the "paradigmatic framework of hermeneutically oriented social science" and as a "constructivistically oriented approach to the analysis of objectified systems of meaning, their historically determined genesis, their discourse-internal and external functions in the social context" (ibid., p. 329).

Foucault is concerned with discourse knowledge as epistemological knowledge, which (as has become clear to Hörster) –gains social scientific relevance. Foucault does not see himself as a sociologist (as say Pierre Bourdieu) but as a 'contemporary philosopher': "I am trying to say what we are today, and what it means now to say what we are saying. This digging underneath our own feet has characterized contemporary thinking since Nietzsche, and in this sense I can call myself a philosopher" (Foucault, 1992, p. 33).

From a discourse analysis perspective Foucault differentiates the levels of real, reflective and discursive relationships that are loosely connected to, but can also disengage from each other. Referring back to power-knowledge in an epistemological sense then means trying to detect 'constructions of the third order.' Discourse analysis as described in the *Archaeology of Knowledge* (Foucault, 1981) is to be used for research into the objects of discourse, the rules of formation for a discourse's modalities of utterance, and a discourse's terms and strategies (Koller & Lüders, 2004, p. 60 et seq.) Discourse analysis now can take a genealogical and/or a critical direction. The critical direction follows the principle of "reversal" (ibid., p. 65) and 'unmasks' contingent results of historical processes. The genealogical direction, on the other hand endeavors to find out how knowledge has been constituted. Genealogy means digging through archives, it is also a kind of parodistic destruction, an "anti-science" with analytical strength (Foucault, 2001,

p. 23). Discourse analysis also relies on understanding the constitution of knowledge in time and space. Knowledge is not reconstructed as lying 'outside of power' but recognizes the emergence of institutional structures and power effects, their underlying forms of statements and formative rules and the social practices tied to them (Keller, 2003b, p. 204). Its point of departure and reference is always society, not political philosophy or the social field or epistemology.

When the many options of Foucault's 'tool-box' are used critically different kinds of procedures and of reflection can be productively employed to detect and follow the traces that 'educational knowledge' generates. Foucault's understanding of criticism is not juridically, but generatively oriented, and this strengthens his analytical, transformative position.

> I can't help thinking of a criticism that does not try to judge but that helps a piece of work, a book, a sentence, an idea to become a reality; it would light torches, see the grass grow, listen to the wind, would catch the foam in flight and make it dance. It does not pile judgment on judgement but gathers as many signs of existence as possible. (Foucault, 1980, quoted by Mazumdar, 1998, p. 88).

The implementation of the contents of Foucault's concept of governmentality in the educational sciences as well as the methodical application of discourse analysis for the analysis of pedagogical power-knowledge is certainly still at the beginning – one of many beginnings that are necessary to advance critical thinking. We thus take our place in the line of those trying "to find out if it is possible to constitute new politics of truth" (Foucault, 1978, p. 54).

The individual contributions to this collection analyze different pedagogical fields and interface points in terms of the modes of (self and external) government and the disciplinary and normalizing practices, and the ways of subjectivation connected to them. The 'objects' emerge on different surfaces enabling them to be more easily observed. The different criteria of these objects, how they are formed, what modalities of utterance (how, for example, terms are formed and the relations they have to the strategies of the discourse), what techniques the strategies use, which patterns of subjectivation and subject positions are generated in the process – all this provides a large field for testing and employing Foucault's 'tool-box.'

"DIGGING UNDERNEATH OUR FEET" WITH FOUCAULT'S TOOL-BOX

The dimensions of Foucauldian analysis are structured by central terms. It is the relationship between governing, the strategies and tactics of normalization and disciplining in relation to subjectivation which is analyzed by governmentality. First, the very object of analysis is 'rationality.' Second, are the 'strategies' that comprise it and third, the respective 'tactics' and techniques of governing. Another dimension of analysis comprises the positions and 'patterns of subjectivation' that go with educational power-knowledge (Foucault, 1981, p. 9). With different analytical levels creating a polyphony of critical thought, a governmentality perspective is fruitful for the educational sciences.

The desire to find new types of rationality and their various effects is what Foucault expresses in his *Archaeology of Knowledge* (Foucault, 1981). Another focus is on the 'strategies' by which rationalities can be understood within a power-knowledge apparatus. Discourses provide "space for certain organizations of terms, certain regroupings of objects, certain types of statements. ... conventionally these themes and theories would be called 'strategies.' The problem that remains is to know how they are distributed throughout history" (Foucault, 1981, p. 94). In this we separate discursive formations and systems, the amount of objects and the formation of objects. Foucault suggests defining the "breaking-points of discourses," the "specific instances of decision-making," the "economy of the discursive constellation" and the formative system of strategic choice that the discursive formation occupies.

A further area concerns the practices and tactics of government that are embedded in strategies, actualizing them and contributing to the process of maintenance and transformation of the discourse. The discourse practices follow a specific rationality, they are embedded in a discursive space that is regulated by rules and that emphasizes and privileges specific patterns instead of others.

Archaeology is not ordered by the sovereign shape of the work; it does not attempt to catch the moment where the latter has pulled itself away from the anonymous horizon. It does not want to rediscover that mysterious point where the individual and the social turn one into the other. It is neither psychology nor sociology, nor general anthropology of creation. The work is no pertinent excerpt for it, even if it was to be rearranged in a global context or in a grid of the causalities that support it. Archaeology defines types and rules of discursive practices that traverse individual works, without missing a thing but sometimes only ruling part of them. The instance of a creative subject as *raison d'être* of a piece of work and as a principle of its unity is alien to archaeology (Foucault, 1981, p. 199).

This approach represents a perspective of dynamic discourse constellations that Foucault encourages. Generally Foucault assumes the materialization of discourses in and as practices (Foucault, 1981, p. 74). A discursive formation

Does not play the role of a figure stopping time, freezing it for decades or centuries; it determines a regularity typical for temporal processes; it further determines the articulation principle between a series of discursive events and other series of events, of transformations, of changes and processes, it is not a form without time but a scheme of correspondence between a number of temporal series (Foucault, 1981, p. 109).

The governmentality perspective is systematically accompanied by the dimension of subjectivation. The focus is put on the analysis of subject constitution, subjectivation and subject positions. Here, a lot of connections exist with the analysis of discursive formations:

Positions of the subject are also defined by the situation that it can occupy relative to different areas or groups of objects, according to its possibilities: it is an enquiring subject with a certain grid of more or less explicit questions, and subject as listener according to a certain program of information; it is a contemplating subject with a board full of characteristic traits, and subject as note-taker according to a descriptive type. ... To these situations of perception we have to add positions that the subject can inhabit in an information network (in theoretical education or in hospital pedagogy; in a system of oral communication or one of written documentation; as sender and receiver of observations, reports, statistical facts, general theoretical assumptions, of plans and decisions) (Foucault, 1981, p. 78 et seq.).

The potential of governmentality for analysis, theory formation and criticism in educational science is evident. Such an analytical perspective does not place pedagogical knowledge outside of the power-knowledge complexes in discourse constellations but looks at its positioning and functioning inside the discourse. Analyzing pedagogical knowledge as power-knowledge goes one step further on the road that Käte Meyer-Drawe (1996) pointed to when she promoted an archaeology of the pedagogical gaze. Especially in today's uncertain times where 'hard' and 'soft' technologies merge, where power-knowledge involves disciplining as well as normalizing, where generative and control strategies unite to increase performance, it is impossible to conceptualize and analyze the generalization of the economic form, like Lemke, Krasmann & Bröckling (2000) put it, without pedagogical power-knowledge. An analytical perspective that calls itself critical is aware of its own place in the discourse – it is analytically reflective in the sense that it is aware of the unsteady ground, as Foucault called it and on which we are standing, it is politically reflective in the sense that it has the courage 'to dig underneath its own feet.'

CHAPTERS IN THIS SECTION

Fabian Kessl points out the relevance of research on governmentality as an analysis of power for social work (and social policy) studies. In his chapter he states that such an approach is not only helpful, but systematically required for social work studies, because more adequate analytical instruments are needed to reconstruct and interpret the fundamental shift in the current transformation of 'the Social'. The former nation and welfare states – which are the contexts of social work as we know it since the 19th century – are in flux leading to an emergence of post-welfare and post-nation states. Studies on governmentality can offer an appropriate analytical basis for a new type of policy studies concerning these transformation processes. The state-of-the-art of German governmentality studies in social work is indicated in this chapter. The discussion involves some main objections raised against the governmentality approach including the allegation of assuming a concept of totalizing power, that of reducing its observations on political programs and an ambiguous analytical point of view.

Ute Karl focuses on changes concerning discourses, which deal with the elderly, In her chapter she shows that the classification of a part of the population as 'older people', 'senior citizens', 'young elderly', 'oldest old' etc. is a power related construction. Using governmentality, Karl brings into focus the specific measures of leading and steering those parts of the population, which are not based on coercion or general laws. These measures are directed at the subjectivity of individuals and influence the technologies of self-regulation, of self-government, and of the conduct of life. Ute Karl wants to show that the neoliberal rationale can be found more and more in the role models of age and ageing: The individual is made responsible for the well-being, taking care is a matter of private responsibility, and self-concept and self-management are prominent issues in the educational work with old people. At the same time it is intended to encourage people in community building and to lead the individual, without coercion, to a socially useful behaviour.

Susanne Maria Weber discusses participatory pedagogical learning practices and transformation which can be found in all social fields of action. These practices give insight into an educational rationality which takes place in the context of organizational transformation. Historically, one can start from the organizational practice of a reform experiment in pedagogy and basic democracy experiment, the children's home *Kinderheim Baumgarten*, which was established by Siegfried Bernfeld, a Jewish socialist activist and educator in the 1920's. The procedural norm or creation of order does not follow a rigid trajectory, unlike the the *Kinderheim*-practices. It works with variable creativity. Weber discusses Bernfeld's attempt to create a school community as experimental democracy in the horizon of the actual subjectivating practices of creative productivity.

Daniel Wrana discusses the Copernican turn in the use of pedagogic means, as represented by the concept of informal, self-guided learning. The associated economics of continuing education goes deeper than the organization since it affects the learning adults themselves. This is an economics of continuing education in that the individuals are oriented towards increasing wealth, but at the same time, it is a pedagogizing in that all individuals within society are subjected to an imperative of permanent flexibility, an advancing of the self, of one's strengths and activities. What is new about this pedagogic form, however, is that a profession is no longer responsible; instead, every individual must take over the responsibility for their own formation – creating an entrepreneurial self. The new counterweight to freedom is not a norm, but a form, he argues, and one that assumes the subject's reference to itself. Wrana shows this by referring to two theories that play a central role in this new arrangement – metacognition theory and human capital theory.

Hermann J. Forneck's analysis also deals with adult education and highlights the changing relationship between adult education providers and adult education recipients, emanating from an adjustment in the structure of the full-time personnel in further education. He focuses on a specific type of relationship between further education providers and participants, which he identifies and analyzes as a 'secular pastorate'. In contrast to this pastoral relationship, Forneck examines the new form of provider-participant relationship and finally states that entirely new strategic relations are emerging.

Thomas Höhne and Bruno Schreck trace transformations of knowledge from its more classical curricular appearances to its modularized forms, thus giving a theoretical account of these transformations from the perspective of governmentality. They discuss their findings in light of the issue of structural transformations of the university in the neoliberal context. Modularization, they argue, is an indicator for tendencies to restructure knowledge in a Tayloristic manner. Modularization also represents the commodification of knowledge since by this very process, knowledge becomes part of a structure of economic exchange, and its value is only acknowledged in terms of its status as an object of that exchange. The modularized production of knowledge can no longer be accounted for in terms of the classical form of critique of rationalism as it is presented in the "Dialectic of Enlightenment".

Andrea Liesner reflects on the proposed introduction of the 'Teaching Points model' within the framework of the Bologna process – that ongoing transformation of European higher education landscapes characterized by elements, which can be identified as part of a governmental regime. In her short comment she raises the following question: If the explicit distance of numerous governmentality studies towards approaches dedicated to a critique of ideology and the critique of capitalism does not imply a too hermetic perspective, is Foucault's "Critique of Liberations" being transformed into "Liberation from Critique" (Messerschmidt, 2007)?

NOTES

[1]   *Sapere aude* – "Dare to know" or "Dare to be wise" is found in Immanuel Kant's essay *What is Enlightenment?*

REFERENCES

Balzer, N. (2004). Von der Schwierigkeit, nicht oppositional zu denken. Linien der Foucault-Rezeption in der deutschsprachigen Erziehungswissenschaft. In N. Ricken & M. Rieger-Ladich (Eds.), *Michel Foucault. Pädagogische Lektüren* (pp. 15–35). Wiesbaden: VS Verlag für Sozialwissenschaften.

Benhabib, S. (1992). *Kritik, Norm und Utopie. Die normativen Grundlagen der Kritischen Theorie.* Frankfurt/M: Fischer.

Bröckling, U. (2000). Totale Mobilmachung. Menschenführung im Qualitäts- und Selbstmanagement. In U. Bröckling, S. Krasmann, & T. Lemke (Eds.), *Gouvernementalität der Gegenwart. Studien zur Ökonomisierung des Sozialen* (pp. 131–167). Frankfurt/M: Suhrkamp.

Bröckling, U., Krasmann, S., & Lemke, T. (Eds.). (2000). *Gouvernementalität der Gegenwart. Studien zur Ökonomisierung des Sozialen.* Frankfurt/M: Suhrkamp.

Bröckling, U., Krasmann, S., & Lemke, T. (Eds.). (2004). *Glossar der Gegenwart.* Frankfurt/M: Suhrkamp.

Combe, A., & Helsper, W. (Eds.). (1996). *Pädagogische Professionalität. Untersuchungen zum Typus pädagogischen Handelns.* Frankfurt/M: Suhrkamp.

Deleuze, G. (Ed.). (1993). *Unterhandlungen. 1972–1990.* Frankfurt/M: Suhrkamp.

Deleuze, G. (1993a). Kontrolle und Werden. In G. Deleuze (Ed.), *Unterhandlungen. 1972–1990* (pp. 243–253). Frankfurt/M: Suhrkamp.

Deleuze, G. (1993b). Postscriptum über die Kontrollgesellschaften. In G. Deleuze (Ed.), *Unterhandlungen 1972–1990* (pp. 254–262). Frankfurt/M: Suhrkamp.

Dzierzbicka, A., & Sattler, E. (2004). Entlassung in die Autonomie. Spielarten des Selbstmanagements. In L. Pongratz, A. Ludwig, M. Wimmer, W. Nieke, & J. Masschelein (Eds.), *Nach Foucault. Diskurs- und machtanalytische Perspektiven der Pädagogik* (pp. 114–133). Wiesbaden: VS Verlag für Sozialwissenschaften.

Foucault, M. (1978). Die Machtverhältnisse durchziehen das Körperinnere. Gespräch mit Lucette Finas. In M. Foucault (Ed.), *Dispositive der Macht. Michel Foucault über Sexualität, Wissen und Wahrheit* (pp. 104–117). Berlin: Merve.

Foucault, M. (1981). *Archäologie des Wissens*. Frankfurt/M: Suhrkamp.

Foucault, M. (1987). *Dispositive der Macht. Michel Foucault über Sexualität, Wissen und Wahrheit*. Berlin: Merve.

Foucault, M. (1988). Für eine Kritik der politischen Vernunft. In Sommer (Ed.), *Lettre international* (pp. 58–66).Berlin.

Foucault, M. (1992). *Was ist Kritik?* Berlin: Merve.

Foucault, M. (1993). *Technologien des Selbst*. Frankfurt/M: Suhrkamp.

Foucault, M. (1996). *Der Mensch ist ein Erfahrungstier. Gespräch mit Ducio Trombadori*. Frankfurt/M: Suhrkamp.

Foucault, M. (2000). Die Gouvernementalität. In U. Bröckling, S. Krasmann, & T. Lemke (Eds.), *Gouvernementalität der Gegenwart. Studien zur Ökonomisierung des Sozialen* (pp. 41–67). Frankfurt/M: Suhrkamp.

Foucault, M. (2001). *In Verteidigung der Gesellschaft*. Frankfurt/M: Suhrkamp.

Foucault, M. (2004a). *Geschichte der Gouvernementalität. Band I. Sicherheit, Territorium, Bevölkerung*. Frankfurt/M: Suhrkamp.

Foucault, M. (2004b). *Geschichte der Gouvernementalität. Band II. Die Geburt der Biopolitik*. Frankfurt/M: Suhrkamp.

Foucault, M. (2005). *Die Heterotopien. Der utopische Körper*. Frankfurt/M: Suhrkamp.

Forneck, H., & Wrana, D. (2005). *Ein parzelliertes Feld*. Bielefeld: Bertelsmann.

Gamm, G. (Ed.). (1985). *Angesichts objektiver Verblendung. Über die Paradoxien Kritischer Theorie*. Tübingen: Konkursbuchverlag.

Helsper, W., Hörster, R., & Kade, J. (2003a). *Ungewissheit. Pädagogische Felder im Modernisierungsprozess*. Weilerswist: Velbrück Wissenschaft.

Hörster, R. (1993). *Normale Regulierung der Delinquenz und Sozialpädagogik. Methodologische Überlegungen zur Analyse einer diskursiven Praxis in pädagogischer Absicht*. Frankfurt/M. (habilitation manuscript)

Hörster, R. (2003). Fallverstehen. Zur Entwicklung kasuistischer Produktivität in der Sozialpädagogik. In W. Helsper et al. (Eds.), *Ungewissheit. Pädagogische Felder im Modernisierungsprozess* (pp. 318–344). Weilerswist: Velbrück Wissenschaft.

Honneth, A. (2003). Foucault und die Humanwissenschaften. Zwischenbilanz einer Rezeption. In A. Honneth & M. Saar (Eds.), *Michel Foucault. Zwischenbilanz einer Rezeption. Frankfurter Foucault-Konferenz 2001* (pp. 15–26). Frankfurt/M: Suhrkamp.

Kade, J. (1989). Universalisierung und Individualisierung der Erwachsenenbildung. Über den Wandel eines pädagogischen Arbeitsfeldes im Kontext gesellschaftlicher Modernisierung. *Zeitschrift für Pädagogik, 35*, 789–808.

Kade, J. (1997). Entgrenzung und Entstrukturierung. Zum Wandel der Erwachsenenbildung in der Moderne. In K. Derichs-Kunstmann et al. (Eds.), *Enttraditionalisierung der Erwachsenenbildung* (pp. 13–31). Frankfurt/M: Deutsches Institut für Erwachsenenbildung.

Kade, J. (2003). Wissen—Umgang mit Wissen—Nichtwissen. Über die Zukunft pädagogischer Kommunikation. In I. Gogolin & R. Tippelt (Eds.), *Innovation durch Bildung. Beiträge zum 18. Kongress der Deutschen Gesellschaft für Erziehungswissenschaft* (pp. 89–108). Opladen: Leske & Budrich.

Keller, R., Hirseland, A., Schneider, W., & Viehöver, W. (Eds.). (2003a). *Handbuch Sozialwissenschaftliche Diskursanalyse. Bd. 1. Theorien und Methoden*. Opladen: Leske & Budrich.

Keller, R., Hirseland, A., Schneider, W., & Viehöver, W. (Eds.). (2003b). Handbuch Sozialwissenschaftliche Diskursanalyse. In *Handbuch Sozialwissenschaftliche Diskursanalyse. Bd. 2. Forschungspraxis*. Opladen: Leske & Budrich.

Keller, R. (1997). Diskursanalyse. In R. Hitzler & A. Honer (Eds.), *Sozialwissenschaftliche Hermeneutik. Eine Einführung* (pp. 309–335). Opladen: Leske & Budrich.

Koller, H.-C., & Lüders, J. (2004). Möglichkeiten und Grenzen der Foucaultschen Diskursanalyse. In N. Ricken & M. Rieger-Ladich (Eds.), *Michel Foucault. Pädagogische Lektüren* (pp. 57–76). Wiesbaden: VS Verlag für Sozialwissenschaften.

Krüger, H.-H. (1999). Entwicklungslinien und aktuelle Perspektiven einer Kritischen Erziehungswissenschaft. In H. Sünker & H. H. Krüger (Eds.), *Kritische Erziehungswissenschaft am Neubeginn?* (pp. 162–183). Frankfurt/M: Suhrkamp.

Lemke, T. (1997). *Eine Kritik der politischen Vernunft. Foucaults Analyse der modernen Gouvernementalität.* Berlin and Hamburg: Argument.

Lemke, T. (2000). Neoliberalismus, Staat und Selbsttechnologien. Ein kritischer Überblick über die governmentality studies. *Politische Vierteljahreszeitschrift, 41*(1), 31–47.

Lemke, T., Krasmann, S., & Bröckling, U. (2000). Gouvernementalität, Neoliberalismus und Selbsttechnologien. Eine Einleitung. In U. Bröckling, S. Krasmann, & T. Lemke (Eds.), *Gouvernementalität der Gegenwart. Studien zur Ökonomisierung des Sozialen* (pp. 7–40). Frankfurt/M: Suhrkamp.

Liesner, A. (2004). Von kleinen Herren und großen Knechten. Gouvernementalitätstheoretische Anmerkungen zum Selbständigkeitskult in Politik und Pädagogik. In N. Ricken & M. Rieger-Ladich (Eds.), *Michel Foucault. Pädagogische Lektüren* (pp. 285–300). Wiesbaden: VS Verlag für Sozialwissenschaften.

Masschelein, J., Quaghebeur, K., & Simons, M. (2004). Das Ethos kritischer Forschung. In L. Pongratz, A. Ludwig, M. Wimmer, W. Nieke, & J. Masschelein (Eds.), *Nach Foucault. Diskurs- und machtanalytische Perspektiven der Pädagogik* (pp. 9–29). Wiesbaden: VS Verlag für Sozialwissenschaften.

Maurer, S. (2001). Emanzipation. In H. U. Otto & H. Thiersch (Eds.), *Handbuch Sozialarbeit/ Sozialpädagogik* (pp. 373–384). Neuwied: Luchterhand.

McLaren, P. (1999). Kritische Erziehungswissenschaft im Zeitalter der Globalisierung. In H. Sünker & H. H. Krüger (Eds.), *Kritische Erziehungswissenschaft am Neubeginn?* (pp. 10–34). Frankfurt/M: Suhrkamp.

Messerschmidt, A. (2007). Von der Kritik der Befreiungen zur Befreiung von Kritik? Erkundungen zu Bildungsprozessen nach Foucault. *Pädagogische Korrespondenz, 36*(2), 44–59.

Meyer-Drawe, K. (1996). Versuch einer Archäologie des pädagogischen Blicks. *Zeitschrift für Pädagogik, 42*, 655–664.

Mollenhauer, K. (1979). "Dies ist keine Pfeife". Ein etwas irritierter Versuch, sich Foucault zu nähern. *PÄD extra. Magazin für Erziehung, Wissenschaft und Politik*, Heft *1*, 63–65.

Oelkers, J., & Tenorth, H.-E. (Eds.). (1991a). *Pädagogisches Wissen.* Sonderheft der Zeitschrift für Pädagogik. 27. Beiheft. Weinheim and Basel: Beltz.

Oelkers, J., & Tenorth, H.-E. (1991b). Pädagogisches Wissen als Orientierung und Problem. In J. Oelkers & H.-E. Tenorth (Eds.), (1991a). *Pädagogisches Wissen* (pp. 13–35). Sonderheft der Zeitschrift für Pädagogik. 27. Beiheft. Weinheim and Basel: Beltz.

Peters, M. (2004). Why Foucault? New directions in Anglo-American educational research. In L. Pongratz, A. Ludwig, M. Wimmer, W. Nieke, & J. Masschelein (Eds.), *Nach Foucault. Diskurs- und machtanalytische Perspektiven der Pädagogik* (pp. 185–219). Wiesbaden: VS Verlag für Sozialwissenschaften.

Pieper, M., & Gutiérez Rodriguez, E. (Eds.). (2004). *Gouvernementalität. Ein sozialwissenschaftliches Konzept im Anschluss an Foucault.* Frankfurt/M. and New York: Campus.

Pongratz, L. (1989). *Pädagogik im Prozess der Moderne. Studien zur Sozial- und Theoriegeschichte der Schule.* Weinheim: Deutscher Studien Verlag.

Pongratz, L. A., Wimmer, M., Nieke, W., & Masschelein, J. (Eds.). (2004). *Nach Foucault. Diskurs- und machtanalytische Perspektiven der Pädagogik.* Wiesbaden: VS Verlag für Sozialwissenschaften.

Ricken, N., & Rieger-Ladich, M. (Eds.). (2004a). *Michel Foucault. Pädagogische Lektüren*. Wiesbaden: VS Verlag für Sozialwissenschaften.

Ricken, N., & Rieger-Ladich, M. (2004b). Michel Foucault. Pädagogische Lektüren. Eine Einleitung. In N. Ricken & M. Rieger-Ladich (Eds.), *Michel Foucault. Pädagogische Lektüren* (pp. 7–13). Wiesbaden: VS Verlag für Sozialwissenschaften.

Schmitz, G. (2004). Auswahlbibliographie zur Michel Foucault Rezeption. In N. Ricken & M. Rieger-Ladich (Eds.), *Michel Foucault. Pädagogische Lektüren* (pp. 303–310). Wiesbaden: VS Verlag für Sozialwissenschaften.

Sennelart, M. (Ed.). (2004a). *Michel Foucault. Geschichte der Gouvernementalität. Bd. I*. Frankfurt/M: Suhrkamp.

Sennelart, M. (2004b). Situierung der Vorlesungen. In M. Sennelart (Ed.), *(2004a). Michel Foucault. Geschichte der Gouvernementalität. Bd. I* (pp. 445–489). Frankfurt/M: Suhrkamp.

Thompson, C. (2004). Diesseits von Authentizität und Emanzipation. Verschiebungen kritischer Erziehungswissenschaft zu einer "kritischen Ontologie der Gegenwart". In N. Ricken & M. Rieger-Ladich (Eds.), *Michel Foucault. Pädagogische Lektüren* (pp. 39–56). Wiesbaden: VS Verlag für Sozialwissenschaften.

Ulrich, P. (1990). Kommunikative Rationalisierung – ein neuer Rationalisierungstyp jenseits der technikgestützten Systemsteuerung. In R. Rock, P. Ulrich, & F. Witt (Eds.), *Strukturwandel der Dienstleistungsrationalisierung* (pp. 237–270). Frankfurt/M and New York: Campus.

Weingart, P. (2001). *Die Stunde der Wahrheit? Zum Verhältnis der Wissenschaft zu Politik, Wirtschaft und Medien in der Wissensgesellschaft*. Weilerswist: Velbrück Wissenschaft.

Winkler, M. (1999). Reflexive Pädagogik. In H. Sünker & H. H. Krüger (Eds.), *Kritische Erziehungswissenschaft am Neubeginn?* (pp. 270–299). Frankfurt/M: Suhrkamp.

Weber, S. M. (1998). *Organisationsentwicklung und Frauenförderung. Eine empirische Analyse in drei Organisationstypen der privaten Wirtschaft*. Königstein and Taunus: Helmer.

Weber, S. M. (2000). 'Fördern' und 'Entwickeln'. Institutionelle Veränderungsstrategien und normalisierendes Wissen. *Zeitschrift für Erziehungswissenschaft*, (3), 411–428.

Weber, S. M. (2005a). *Rituale der Transformation. Großgruppenverfahren als pädagogisches Wissen am Markt*. Marburg (habilitation manuscript)

Weber, S. M. (2005b). Selbstoptimierende Subjekte, Labor-Gesellschaft, Markt-Universität. Ein Essay aus gouvernementalitätstheoretischer Perspektive. In A. Dzierzbicka, R. Kubac, & E. Sattler (Eds.), *Bildung Riskiert. Erziehungswissenschaftliche Markierungen* (pp. 237–244). Wien: Löcker.

Weber, S. M., & Maurer, S. (Eds.). (2006). *Gouvernementalität und Erziehungswissenschaft. Wissen – Macht – Transformation*. Wiesbaden: VS Verlag für Sozialwissenschaften.

Susanne Maria Weber
University of Applied Sciences
Fulda
Germany

Susanne Maurer
Department of Educational Science
University of Marburg
Germany

FABIAN KESSL

23. WHAT'S THE USE OF STUDIES ON GOVERNMENTALITY IN SOCIAL WORK?

A Critique on the Critique[1]

INTRODUCTION

Studies on governmentality have been established in the recent years in the field of social work, so this chapter will discuss the relevance such of an analysis of power for social work (and social policy) studies. This approach is not only helpful, but also systematically required for social work studies, because we are in need of more adequate analytical instruments to reconstruct and interpret the fundamental shift in the current transformation of 'the Social'. The former nation and welfare states – which are the context of social work as we know it since the 19th century – are in flux leading to an emergence of post-welfare and post-nation states. Studies on governmentality can offer an appropriate analytical basis for a new type of policy studies concerning these transformation processes. The chapter outlines the state of the art of German governmentality studies in social work. Two aspects are currently highlighted in that debate: an economisation of the social and a (re) integration of (former) emancipatory concepts in hegemonic political programs. The main objections raised against a governmentality approach will be discussed in the third part of this paper: the allegation of assuming a concept of totalistic power, the allegation of reducing its observations on political programs and an ambiguous analytical point of view. Finally, the chapter looks at the question of what resources a governmentality approach can provide for social work (and social policy) research will be discussed.

POLITICAL STUDIES BEYOND THE NATION STATE

Nikolas Rose begins his introduction on governmentality studies as follows. "As we enter the twenty-first century, many of the conventional ways of analysing politics and power seem obsolescent" (Rose, 1999, p. 1). Formerly policy studies have focused on three main dimensions, which have become more and more fragile: (1) the nation state as a quasi natural border of the political space, (2) 'subjects' as the individual and autonomous actors in that space and (3) the protection of the actor's freedom as a negative freedom guaranteed by the (nation) state agencies. These agencies, like human services and social work, were responsible in the

M.A. Peters et al. (eds.), Govermentality Studies in Education, 415–431.

welfare arrangement to care for the societal members and to secure the normalisation of their life conducts at the same time.

The nation state – especially in Europe – was always a welfare state. It was called to "intervene deliberately to protect the legitimate interests of the citizens", as the members of the *Verein für Socialpolitik*, one of the most influential think tanks in the process of establishing the German welfare state, have mapped out in their first invitation 1872 (Evers & Nowotny, 1987, p. 127)[2]. Beginning in the 1970s and reinforced in the 1990s this protection agreement, which was institutionalised in the welfare state agencies, is currently losing its base of legitimation. Social work as a printout of the publicly organized normalization process, established institutionally and professionally since the end of the 19th century, can therefore – beside social security systems – be seen as the main part of the new forms of "governing the social" (Krasmann, 2003, p. 99). The state is no longer seen as an opponent to society, but rather as an actor, who cares for 'the Social' (Donzelot 1979). During this time the state was transformed to a "state of the society" (Lemke, 1997, p. 195). This form of 'the Social' in a broad sense (society) was renewed in the new territories of the national frame through the implementation of the social sector –'the Social' on a specific note (i.e. social and human service organisations).

Since the last third of the 20th century institutional forms of welfare governing have fundamentally changed. Therefore, we can understand the present situation as an emerging post-welfare arrangement. On the background of this fundamental shift of the former welfare state, governmentality researchers like Rose worked on an alternative policy study approach. Earlier policy studies focussed on the distribution, enforcement and enhancement of the nation state's power, but such an analytical perspective no longer fits the transformed and diminished welfare states. The current shift shows clearly that the state itself is "only" a specific historical printout of the relations of power and domination and therefore we cannot take it as the given starting point of policy studies. Instead it may be appropriate to start with the question, "what authorities of various sorts wanted to happen, in relation to problems defined how, in pursuit of what objectives, through what strategies and techniques" (Rose, 1999, p. 20). Policy studies – in social work and social policy in general – should focus on questions regarding the processes of the political formation of 'the Social' such as:
- Who is in power to regulate and in what way is that regulation being done and legitimated?
- What kind of social relations are considered necessary to regulate?
- Finally, what is considered a social problem and what is not?

The processes of the transformation of former nation and welfare states is promoted by three trends: (1) a tendency to extended trans-national relations (globalization); (2) a tendency to privatization and devolution of the hitherto existing state based agencies; and (3) an accentuation of regional and local communities for social inclusion instead of the nation state as an integrative corpus. Regarding social work research, one immanent dynamic becomes apparent: at the beginning of the 21st century social participation rights are no longer automatically bound up with citizenship. Participation is now primarily relocated to private constellations, such as families, quasi-families, and associations in civil society. Institutions for education, like social work, are re-conceptualized in a specific way. They are called to activate these private spaces of inclusion as a substitute for the social integration support of the welfare states – as nation states have previously promised. Relevant parts of the national economy are transferred to the transnational level. Regional as well as local relations are re-defined as 'spaces of (re)production' (communities as locations of business) and the former national social integration policies are increasingly transformed to social inclusion policies. Regional and local spaces therefore become important in two ways: as bases for economic resources and as spaces for social inclusion. But these new spaces of inclusion are highly stratified. Wealthy people close off their communities (e.g. gated communities). At the same time it is assumed that the life style of the poor or new underclass is seemingly anti-civic and needs to be changed according to the main political programs. In light of this, a policy of territorialization was established in the 1980s and 1990s following the pacification and re-inclusion of the seemingly excluded parts of the population, living in specific city areas (Kessl & Otto, 2007).

In sum, the former arrangement of the social welfare state has been fundamentally re-shaped since the second third of the 20th century. The emerging post-welfare arrangements are therefore leading to a "fundamental new redefinition of the topography of the social" (Ronneberger, Lanz & Jahn, 1999, p. 215). Analytically we have to ask, how can we systematically describe and categorize ongoing transformation processes? Rose (1999) and others recommend that we should focus on the ways of thinking (including the ways of acting). For example, such a systematic perspective is offered by the studies on governmentality.[3] Michel Foucault called that perspective of analyzing the ways of governing 'governmentality' (see Foucault, 2004a & b).[4] Following Foucault and his successors, we are forced to re-think the focus of policy studies. Foucault recommends an alternative idea of the (nation) state as a "way of governing" (Foucault, 2004b, p. 359). We should understand the state in "its survival and (...) in its boundaries", Foucault argued (Foucault, 2000, p. 66). The Foucauldian concept of governing is therefore a broad one. Government as the key concept of the studies on governmentality is not reduced to the acting of institutionalized political administration. The forms of government, all "what is governed", refer in fact to "human beings" (Foucault, 2004b, p. 183). Lemke, Krasmann and Bröckling (2000, p. 10), leading German governmentality researchers, summarized that the broad understanding of government refers to "several and different forms of acting and fields of practices, which lead, control and conduct individuals and collectives in different ways and subsume forms of conducting the self as well as techniques of conducting the others" (also see Doherty, 2007).

In contrast to existing policy studies, governmentality researchers are interested in ways of thinking about political rationalities as they were developed in Europe since the 16th century and later realized in the 18th and 19th century in terms of human conduct as a conduct through the nation state (Kessl, 2005). It is this "conduct of the conduct" that characterizes the governmentality of welfare states, the interrelation of "freedom of the subjects" and the "power of the state" (Lemke, 1999, p. 425). Governmentality in welfare states and therefore in social work agencies is not primarily a state based disciplinarian strategy, but a way of normalizing the ways that life is conducted, the forms of conduct of both individual and collective subjects: "Government in this sense only becomes possible at the point at which policing and administration stops; at the point where government and self-government coincide and coalesce" (Peters, 2001, p. 1, quoted by Doherty, 2007, p. 197).

Governmental policy studies in that sense can show (Castel, 2000; Ewald, 1986) how a "civil society or rather a governmentalized society (...) have something implemented, what we can call the state – this fragile and pestering something" (Lemke, 1999, p. 420). The transformations of the welfare states have resulted in what we can call a post welfarist arrangement.

Policy studies on governmentality make it clear that the social order of nation states were a printout of specific political rationalities, because the "tactics of governing allow to define, wherefore the state is responsible or not responsible, what is public and what is private, what is part of the state and what is not part of the state" (Foucault, 2000, p. 66). And also such a governmentality approach can show that power relations of the nation state are not an opposite to society, but "the conditions of the possibility of the society" (Lemke, 1999, p. 427). In his understanding of society, Foucault follows Max Weber's definition of power (Weber, 1972) "that we can have influence on the action of the others. A society 'without power relations' can only be an abstraction" (Foucault, 1987a, p. 257). Foucault's critical analysis of the political is twofold. First, through his statement of an "overestimation of the problem of the state" (Foucault, 2000, p. 65): "For sure the state has never owned in history that unity, that individuality, that strict functionality and, as I would argue, that prominence; lastly the state is probably only a composed outcome, a mythical abstraction, which importance is much more reduced as we believe" (ibid.).[5] Second Foucault turned away from the repressive conception of power that he favoured in his earlier works (Sarasin, 2005). In contrast, he subsequently accentuates the productive site of power (Foucault, 1999). Power relations are seen as being (re)produced primarily through the freedom of subjects and not through their direct oppression: "Power is executed only against the 'free subjects' and only as far as they are 'free'" (Foucault, 1987b, p. 255). The everyday practice of subjects as "free" members of the society is therefore the structural basis of the governmental power. Power relations in a governmental state can only exist, Foucault suggests, as far as "subjects are free in it" (Foucault, 2005b, p. 890). If one would rule the other(s) in an absolute way and would become the object of the other(s) power relations would not exist. "The existence of power relations is based on a specific grade of freedom on both sides. Even if power relations are totally out of balance, if one is controlling the other, the power can only be executed as far as the other has the possibility to kill himself. Power relations therefore necessarily embrace the possibility of resistance. If there would be no such possibility, power relations wouldn't exist" (ibid).

To summarize at this point we can note five key elements of a governmentality approach. First the reconstruction of political rationalities (Dean, 1999). In what ways do people conduct the others and themselves (see Foucault, 2004 a & b)? Governmentality studies focus on specific historical forms of political rationalities, the "allowed" forms of reflexivity (Foucault, 2005a, p. 537). Second, the main issue of governmentality studies is a systematic observation of the contingent but powerful forms of what can be said and what can be seen. While the hegemonic form of subjectivation in nation and welfare states developed since the end of the 18th and the beginning of the 19th century was the *homo legalis,* the advanced liberal form of subjectivation is the model of the self entrepreneur (*homo oeco-nomicus*). Following Étienne Balibar (1991) we can characterize the systematic interest of governmentality studies as an analysis of the historical articulation of different practices of power and corresponding forms of subjectivity. This articulation occurs as a discourse about the "art of governing" (Foucault, 2004b, p. 353). Third, governmentality studies favour an anti-dualistic perspective. They argue against an imagination of state compared to society or of a realm of freedom to a realm of the economy. Governmentality research focuses instead on the specific historical formations of these dimensions. For example, we can ask, in what ways will balances of power be actualized? Such a relational research perspective is helpful in observing institutional forms of government and forms of subjectivation in general, such as forms of life conduct and how people put them into practice, how they arrange their everyday life. The subject is no longer seen as the basic unit of an even potentially autonomous action in opposite to the objects (e.g. structures or things). From a governmentality point of view the subject can be understood as a form, which can be "neither mainly nor continuous identical with itself" (Foucault, 2005b, p. 888). Fourth, governmentality studies can be categorized as analyses of power, because in contrast to former theories of power they are not based on an imagination of a prescriptive and repressive concept of power, but a radical historicized concept. Its interest is not "to tell the truth to the power. In fact it has to be examined how the different interdependences of truth, power, and ethics as a context of the thinker are formed and have been changed" (Rabinow, 2004, p. 81). As Foucault himself said, "power as an independent question is not from interest" (Foucault cited in Rabinow, 2004, p. 72). What is of interest is the different practice of power, which is ensured by the possibilities for the "subjects" (Rose, 1999, p. 93). Fifth, governmentality studies provide a radical relational approach, because they are based on the assumption of a "historicity of the occasion" that means they refuse an idea of trans-historical categories or theories (Balibar, 1991, p. 62).

In the rest of the chapter consideration of three main exceptions against a governmentality approach are introduced and evaluated on their persuasiveness, finally leading us to a critique on the critique.

STUDIES ON GOVERNMENTALITY IN SOCIAL WORK – STATE OF THE ART

The Foucault Effect, an edited collection by Graham Burchell, Colin Gordon & Peter Miller in 1991 can be seen as the starting point in implementing the governmentality approach in the English speaking world. A series of papers especially published in *Economy & Society,* a growing number of readers, and the works by Nikolas Rose (1999) and Mitchell Dean (1999) firmly established governmentality studies in the 1990s. In the German speaking countries a similar development occurred ten years later with the anthology by Ulrich Bröckling, Susanne Krasmann and Thomas Lemke, *Gouvernementalität der Gegenwart* (2000), which has a very similar structure to the *The Foucault Effect.* Subsequently there have been a number of introductions (e.g. Krasmann, 2003; Krasmann & Volkmer, 2007; Lemke, 1997; Opitz, 2004; Pieper & Rodriguez, 2005) and a growing number of single studies are available in different disciplines (e.g. Dzierzbicka, 2006; Gertenbach, 2007; Lemke, 2004; Michel, 2005). Even if there are only a very few systematic overviews in the field of a social work research till now (Kessl, 2005; Stövesand, 2007; Wilhelm, 2005), we can find a growing number of authors referring to a governmental perspective (Böhnisch, 2006; Heite, 2006; Herrmann, 2006; Maeder, 2004; Maurer, 2005; May, 2006; Otto & Seelmeyer, 2004; Richter, 2004; Ziegler, 2004).

In these papers, we can find at least two main aspects that are generally mentioned as being relevant for the debates on social work: First they diagnose a growing economisation of the social and of social work and second an absorption of former critical positions.

Economisation of the Social

Cora Herrmann defines the "economisation of the social" (Lemke, Krasmann & Bröckling, 2000, p. 25) as a process in which "cost-benefit calculations and the criteria of the market were extended on the decision making in fields they were thought as being not economically governable" (Herrmann, 2006, p. 20). To speak about an economisation of the social – and of social work – means to suggest that formerly separate systems, the systems of economy and the social, are merging. Economisation is called to be the *new leading paradigm*: "The economy is not any more only a part of the whole system, but the most important mainspring, how people and the society are currently organized" (Albert, 2006, p. 18). Such an analysis of what is called *economisation* is already done for a number of specific aspects of social work. Christoph Maeder for example shows clearly the establishment of a "managerial governmentality" (Maeder, 2004, p. 68). A new *regime of the management* can be seen, he argues (ibid., p. 67), which is realized as a *moral crusade*: "The administration is redefined as a public problem, to introduce new norms, habits and measuring standards and the adequate control system" (ibid., p. 76). Catrin Heite makes a similar argument regarding to the current hegemony of case-management programs, which aim at an implementation of a "managerial strategy of professionalization", including the demand "that among other aspects the professionals are successfully disciplined" (Heite, 2006, p. 206).

Holger Ziegler defines economisation as one out of two main new dimensions of the transformation processes of the former welfare states, especially the tendency of a growing re-programming of child and youth welfare in terms of prevention (see Ziegler, 2004, p. 177 & p. 581). In a similar way Martina Richter alludes to the phenomenon of a *re-familiarization* as a key of the increasing economisation of social work. As a part of the "dismantling of the welfare arrangements" families are more and more called to take over their self-responsibility: social problems are redefined as private (familiar) problems (Richter, 2004, p. 5). Finally Andreas Schaarschuch (2003) and Michael Lindenberg (2000) indicate a fundamental change in the forms of regulation of the state. State agencies like social work organizations tend to prefer and institutionalize a "steering at arm's length" (Schaarschuch, 2003, p. 58), that means an attempt to "let the others row and concentrate on the navigation" (Lindenberg, 2000, p. 105).

Often neo-liberalism is defined as a strategy of the violation of the social sectors through market and management principles and strategies. In contrast the named studies, using the analytical instruments of the governmentality approach, can clearly show that a more fundamental shift is going on. Economisation in that sense has to be seen as a new formation of the former historical connection of the economy and the social and not as a process of levelling a seemingly natural connection of two distinct spheres. The governmental diagnosis of an economisation of the social can make it clear that a systematic distinction of the political and the economy, which was constitutive for the welfare state since the 19th century, is a specific historical arrangement (see Castel, 2000).

Governmentality studies clearly provide a perspective of the political economy, an analysis of the specific historical formations of the constitutive connection of economy and politics (Althusser & Balibar, 1972). A governmentality perspective suggests such continuity, even if this was not often apparent in the available literature until now (Stenson, 2007). So we have to be aware of that blind spot in studies of governmentality. We will come back later to this point. Studies on governmentality should make it clear that the establishment of political economy has developed a different political program: "For sure Rose and Foucault are right in saying that the foundation of the 'political economy' is connected to an emerging new science, which focuses methods how to optimize the diverse nets of relations between population, territory and wealth" (May, 2006, p. 33).

The assumption of simple colonialization of the political and the Social through the economy – the "cost reduction of the welfare state on duty of the location Germany" (Krölls, 2000, p. 131) – ignores that economisation is part of changed political programs. The economisation of the Social, seen as a post-welfarist program includes much more than a simple model of marketization or a use of social work as part of a strategy of marketization. Marketization is undoubtedly predominant in advanced capitalistic states, but the process of economization contains a much more complex development of a political re-adjustment of the relation of spheres we have seen as given for a long time: the economy, the political and the social (in a narrow sense). These changed rationalizations of how social relations are governed have to be analyzed in detail.

(Re)Integration of Emancipatory Conceptions in Social Work

In her current work on social work as a social movement Susanne Maurer argues that there are remarkable similarities between the conceptions and semantics of what has been seen in the 1970s and 80s as naturally emancipatory and current hegemonic programs: "It is amazing to see how almost every single aspect in emancipatory concepts (not only in social work, I guess) is now answered in some sense in the neo-liberal promise" (Maurer, 2006, p. 241). In indicating this similarity Susanne Maurer, points out the second main aspect of the governmental studies in German social work. This aspect can clearly show how current concepts are able to adapt former critical concepts and semantics. Maurer highlights in that context the promise of "freedom" and of self-determination and the demand for flexibility (ibid.). Other authors extend the list in adding autonomy (Heite, 2006), self-organisation (Weber, 2006), participation (Sturzenhecker, 2003) and prevention (Ziegler, 2004). These concepts cannot be taken for granted any more as being critical per se. In contrast they are now often part of cultural hegemonies, as their normal use at main points in administrational papers can symbolize.

But even in regard to that second main aspect, governmentality studies in social work and social policy can show that we have to be careful not to reproduce a reduced analytical point of view. To diagnose the adaption of former, as critically understood positions can lead to the idea of a simple colonization of social work. Some authors mark ambiguities and insecurities in the current contexts, but call at the same time for specific forms of participation and empowerment as a remedy to the incorporation of these concepts. In the case of the economisation diagnosis some authors, indicate a clearly directed colonization and claim defence of the Social: "This shift is part of a strategy, the French thinker Michel Foucault called 'governmentality', an inducement and conduct of the ways of thinking and living a political, economical, scientific, and journalistic elite takes the responsibility for" (Brandhorst, 2005, p. 4).

In contrast to such assumptions of colonization and simplification we will argue that from the governmentality point of view just the immanence of power will be the focus. Social work cannot escape the texture of power, because it is part of the former welfare states and their current post-welfarist transformation. But it would be too easy to continue arguing that social work has just to be embedded in this texture. The loss of clearness, possibly deriving from a de-centered perspective, should not be seen as a relativistic position. To take over an ambiguous position does not mean we are at the end of critique, just because we cannot claim clearness any more. We have to argue against all attempts to simplify (Biesta, 2003). And therefore we have to accept the permanence of political struggles – in the institutionalized fields of analyses, the academic sphere, and in everyday life (*le quotidien*). Thus social work's task is to give support to the users, which can help them to become as fully fledged as it is possible, but within the texture of power.

BOUNDARIES OF AN ANALYSIS OF POWER: THREE EXCEPTIONS AGAINST THE PROJECT OF GOVERNMENTALITY STUDIES IN SOCIAL WORK

Exception No 1: 'The Totality of Power'

In the mid 1980s, twenty years before the German debate on governmentality began, in *Kritik der Macht,* Axel Honneth objected to the reductionist view on power of a Foucauldian perspective (Honneth, 1985). In the same year Jürgen Habermas (1985/1990) published his lectures on the philosophical discourse of modernity, where he accentuated Honneth's exception in arguing against Foucault as follows: "societal individuals can only be seen as standardized products of a discursive formation", if we would follow such a view.

This exception has been often repeated over the last years in current German critiques against studies on governmentality (see Lindner, 2006). The Foucauldian concept of power as productive is called to subdue all differences in human actions and therefore loose all analytical distinctions. For social policy and social work research such a perspective seems to be especially reduced, these authors argue, because such a totalistic concept of power would be the end of the project of Enlightenment: the autonomy of the subjects is announced to be a myth. If power is ubiquitous and every single action and all decisions are also only a printout of it, there can be no individual freedom and therefore every social political and social work intervention will lose its aim.

Exception No 2: 'The Reduction on the Observation of Political Programs'

Pat O'Malley, Lorna Weir & Clifford Shearing (1997) and John Clarke (2004) suggest a second systematic exception in the last years. The material basis of studies on governmentality is too restricted, they argue: only political programs seem to build research material for the reconstruction of political rationalities. Such materials could probably be helpful to illustrate intended practices "as a source (…), but not as an illustration of the reality of government", as a leading German educational scientist has argued (Tenorth, 2006, p. 40). Observations of political programs are not focussing the real execution of concrete educational or social work practice, these authors argue (see also Langemeyer, 2007). Ljubomir Bratic (Bratic & Pantucek, 2004) and Sabine Stövesand (2006) make the same argument in their current work. Both highlight that the existing studies on governmentality – not only in social work – are not tied to real social and political struggles, but they should be. The level of "practice that means the level of the empirical subjects, who are not the same subjects like the one, studies on governmentality focus" is systematically out of observed, they object (Bratic & Pantucek, 2004). Such a reduced observation perspective would ignore the "germ of restriction", but also of "resistance" – the space, in which the "empirical subjects are produced and constitute themselves" (ibid.).

To avoid such an analytical reduction Pantucek and Langemeyer recommend the use of analytical instruments, which a critical psychology can provide. If we would follow that attempt, we would have to overcome basic methodological ideas of the governmentality approach. Therefore authors like Stövesand (2006) and Stenson (2007), who are still interested in a critical governmentality perspective, recommend instead to follow on in the governmentality work, by comparing it to political economy and by taking into consideration regulation theory (see also Bischoff, Hüning & Lieber 2005): "The explosion of specific governmental technologies and semantics cannot only be seen in the context of the current dominant political rationalities. They are connected to a change of the regime of accumulation and the corresponding regime of regulation", (Stövesand, 2006, p. 329 et seq.).

Exception No 3: "Ambiguous Analytical Point of View"

In its 100th issue the board of the critical German journal *Widersprüche* has discussed methodological and theoretical contradictions the board members have been struggling with during the last years (see Redaktion der Widersprüche, 2006). The main cleavage was around the question of how adequate an analysis of power like the governmentality one can be for critical policy studies. Those board members who argue from a standpoint of ideology theory and therefore are critical against the governmentality approach, have made a third main exception.

Studies on governmentality couldn't make it clear, why, how far and in which way their interpretations can be historically adequate. To answer those questions adequately it would be necessary to accept the need of an expression of a criterion to prove what are the current basic motions of our history. But governmentality researchers would refuse the possibility of a theoretical construction of such a criterion, which brings them into an *aporia*. Governmentality researchers have no possibility of showing, whose interests are behind the analysed power strategies and how they probably can re-used. But that should be the task of critical social policy studies and therefore the precondition of social policy and social work, as far as the actors are obliged to a critical position.

CRITIQUE ON THE CRITIQUE – CONCLUDING REMARKS ON THE ANALYTICAL POTENTIAL OF THE GOVERNMENTALITY APPROACH

A few years after he held his lectures on governmentality at the *Collège de France* in an interview, Michel Foucault answered Rux Martin's question about conscious change, because his work seemed to be quite skeptical of such a possibility "I really don't know, how you could think, I couldn't imagine any change. Because what I observed was always connected to political action. *Discipline and Punish* is solely an attempt to answer that question and to determine, how new ways of thinking can emerge. We all are existing and thinking subjects", (Foucault, 2005c, pp. 963–964). This answer, which seems to be almost idealistic about the subject can be very surprising because this assumption comes to a head, when he lastly said, "I believe in the freedom of the people" (ibid., p. 965). How can it be possible for the same thinker to mention an "ubiquity of power" (Foucault, 1999, p. 114) *and* call for a "history of subjectivity" (Foucault, 2004c, p. 27)? Some authors like Axel Honneth state this being not possible and that we therefore should read Foucault as a thinker with a paradoxical concept of power. Foucault tried to include a model of action as a "permanent process of social struggles", Honneth suggests, and at the same time a social theory of "a boundless effectiveness of modern disciplinarian force" (Honneth, 1985, p. 195).

The majority of exceptions against a Foucauldian and the current governmentality approach are constructed around such an implicit or explicit diagnosis of a basic paradoxical structure. The main objections are (1) the governmental idea of a totality of power would ignore social struggles; (2) the restricted research material would reduce social practices only to a result of power (of the state); and (3) the Foucauldian (totalistic) concept of power would come out of the refusal to take over a speakers position which is normative.

The allegation of such a reduced concept of power draws on the governmental assumption of a decentered model of power and the idea that both types of governing, the governing of the others and the governing of the selves, are part of that power. But studies on governmentality do not assume a negative concept of power, but power as the analytical point of view to understand social relations as balances of power. Power in that sense is encompassing everything by saying that strategic actions are realized in all social relations. To talk about balances of power shall mark that power is encompassing everything indeed, but not in an absolute and deterministic sense. In contrast analyses of power focus on how relations at specific historical moments are affected, influenced and regulated and are influencing and regulating. In contrast to theories of power the governmentality approach is based on the assumption that strategic actions do not have a clear centre. They are not the result of intentional actions of single persons – such as a political leader, single interest groups or the management of one social deliverer. They are an effect of balances of power, which they again (re)produce.

The analytical fuzziness of this approach using a strict relational concept of power can be seen as a danger, when researchers do not distinguish clearly enough power and domination. Domination as coagulated power relations, especially institutionalized forms of power which influence social practices, are well known in fields of social work and social policy; for instance, the institutional structures of big welfare agencies (*Wohlfahrtsverbände*) as quasi-state agencies. These structures (of domination) have of course to be differentiated from power relations in general, a distinction Foucault himself has not made clear enough in his early work.

But we would completely misunderstand the theoretical assumption of govern-mentality studies if we understood it as a concept of total domination. To put ubiquitous power relations as the main point of analytical interest provides a basis to look systematically on *how* relations are currently formed and *where* their boundaries are. The often wrongly interpreted notion of Foucault (1999, p. 114) that "undoubtedly", we should have to be nominalists is "only" a reminder that we should place our reconstructions into their contexts. The Foucauldian concept of power means to focus on the "complex strategical situation in a society" (ibid.). That is what he has called nominalistic – a nominalism, which is interested in questioning identities, *the* man, *the* people or even *the* state. The analytical ambition is therefore of "pure relational nature", as Balibar says (1991, p. 63). At the same time Foucault calls for a nominalistic view to have a quasi anti-metaphysical self-protection to avoid that we deduce from "the materiality of bodies" to an "ideality of the life" (ibid.). Etienne Balibar shows that exactly such a transition designates often enough Marxist thinking, although Marxs considerations themselves do not necessarily lead to that kind of view.

The Foucauldian nominalism has to be differentiated from a stylized program called nominalism and is based on the idea of a methodological individualism – a program some of the leading neo-liberal thinkers prefer. Those radical nominalists assume that all subsuming terms are not more than convenient mnemonics (Ritsert, 2000), which cannot name specific things: "Only concrete single persons, we can see and listen to, exist – even if we are not able to stand them" (ibid., p. 14).

The second exception of a reduced material basis is touching a sore spot, because it can illustrate a main analytical weakness of some of the existing governmental work. Studies on governmentality are actually often concentrated on the observation of political programs, which is of course not at all illegitimate or unusable (Kessl & Krasmann, 2005). Nevertheless sometimes the authors forget to point out that they *only* observe that level and therefore they only can talk about that level. Until now we did not have German governmentality studies, where political rationalities were systematically analysed regarding political programs (administration papers or mission statements) and social practices as rationalities. To focus on forms of political rationalities which are constructed in committees, management meetings or user organizations would offer us an important extension of the observation of (political) programs. Such an extended version of governmentality studies would have to focus on the (re)construction of political rationalities in such communications.

Even if it is often argued – especially in educational science and social work contexts – that we should extend the governmental approach, we should understand that advice as compliance, because the exception of a reduced observation perspective may underestimate the level of political programs. If we analyse for example the (re)integration of former emancipatory concepts over the last years we focus on important logics on a very influential level – a level, where decision making is going on regarding to educational and social work agencies. It would not be persuasive, if we would deduce from such analyses that in all fields these logics are reproduced and put into practice in exactly that way. Governmentality studies should therefore mark their analytical boundaries, but at the same time should not fall into the trap of assuming the level of educational and social work practices are independent from political programs. That is probably a nice, but empirically an indefensible idea.

The third exception saying that the governmentality approach lacks a clear analytical point of view would also be adequate, if we assume that it can be theoretically resolved and how we should exceed the existing concerns. All critical positions have to take up such a position, if they insist on a rule of truth to evaluate alternative positions. But studies on governmentality question this possibility itself; instead they only focus on the identification of the boundaries of the existing. Are the existing rules the best? Or should we exceed them? And if so, in which way? All these questions cannot be answered analytically as a question of the truth because that claims the impossibility of a theoretical construction of a way out. Researchers can and should work on questions of normativity and ethics and should work from a distance (Habermas, 1972). But researchers should also be able to distinguish when they work primarily in an analytical way and when they work primarily on the basis of a specific ethical stance. They should not only be able to distinguish, but – because both perspectives are connected which each other – they should mark it explicitly (speech position). Even within the academe both perspectives are necessary because those academic fields are of course not beyond power. To be able to choose the issue of a research project and to publish about that issue has to be seen as a position of power which has to be reflected permanently. We therefore should make explicit our own position as a speaker. Nevertheless it would be a misunderstanding to base our analytical work on an uncommented ethical stance – a fundamental problem of critical theory, which does not focus the problem on critiques (Peters, 2003). The governmentality approach is committed to a reflection of moral foundations. Furthermore, governmentality studies should reflect on their own analytical reach.

Governmental policy studies attend to the eventfulness of practices, pointing out the regularities of what can be said and what can be seen (Waldenfels, 2004). They point out their regional availability, and their immanent forms of excluding, where something strange is sent back to legitimate the identity of the domestic. Therefore we can characterize governmentality studies as demarcation work. Their analytical and political work on the boundaries of the existing is what makes such kind of policy studies very attractive for social work and social policy research because social work as a profession is itself a worker on the boundaries (Kessl & Maurer, 2005). To work in that sense means to know about the boundaries that exist and to exceed them if possible. Governmental policy studies could offer a considerable aspect of adequate knowledge for this kind of social work, because they could show where the lines of demarcation are, what currently can be seen and what currently can be said – and therefore, where social work is called to work. Due to the changing lines of demarcation in the post-national and post-welfarist arrangements, it would be a fundamental and highly important task for social work and social policy to work in that sense as a worker on the demarcation lines.

NOTES

[1] My special thanks to David Rutkowski (Hamburg) for his great help in language editing. All the remaining errors are my own.

[2] All following quotes from German literature are translated by the author.

[3] At that point we clearly can see that the use of the term "governmentality" by Michel Foucault is inconsistent. As the editor of the two lectures on governmentaliy Michel Sennelart argues in his concluding considerations not only against the wrong German and English translation of the term as a semantic addition of "gouvernement" and "mentalité" (Sennelart, 2004. p. 564), but also on the confusing use of a broad and a narrow conception of governmentality. While Foucault in his famous "governmentality" lecture speaks about the "occasional and regional characteristic of the term" – governmentality therefore is a description of the governmental state as a successor of the forme

427

sovereign- and disciplinarion state, the broad concept of governmentality is used as an analytical frame regarding to relations of power in general (see ibid., p. 565). To avoid misunderstandings we use only the broad conception of governmentality in the following text – as a specific historical way of governing in form of welfare states.

[4] Ines Langemeyer has mentioned the earlier source of the neologism "governmentality" in Roland Barthes *Myth Today* (see Langemeyer, 2005, p. 38, footnote 15; see also Lemke, 2007). But it is not clear, if Foucault refers to Barthes implicit definition. The term governmentaliy" is used by Barthes to focus "the government, how it is seen by the mass media as the 'character of evidence'" (Barthes 1957, p. 216; quoted by Langemeyer, 2005, p. 38).

[5] When Foucault argues that the analysis of the ways of governing has to lead to a perception, which does see the state not any more as such a "cold-hearted monster", which still grows and evolves as a threatening organism above the civil society (Foucault, 2004b, p. 360), he argues in that way on the background of the quite influential materialistic critiques against the state in the 1970.

REFERENCES

Albert, M. (2006). *Soziale Arbeit im Wandel: Professionelle Identität zwischen Ökonomisierung und ethischer Verantwortung*. Hamburg: VSA.

Althusser, L., & Balibar, E. (1972). *Das Kapital lesen I*. Hamburg: Rowohlt.

Balibar, É. (1991). Foucault und Marx. Der Einsatz des Nominalismus. In F. Ewald & B. Waldenfeld (Eds.), *Spiele der Wahrheit. Michel Foucaults Denken* (pp. 39–65). Frankfurt/M: Suhrkamp.

Biesta, G. J. J. (2003). Jacques Derrida: Deconstruction = Justice. In M. A. Peters, M. Olssen, & C. Lanksheer (Eds.), *Futures of critical theory: Dreams of difference* (pp. 141–154). Lanham, MD: Rowman & Littlefield Publishers.

Bischoff, J., Hüning, H., & Lieber, Chr. (2005). Von der neoliberalen zur sozialistischen Gouvernementalität. Anforderungen an eine Rifondazione der Linken. *Prokla, 35*(4), 521–540.

Böhnisch, L. (2006). *Politische Soziologie: eine problemorientierte Einführung*. Opladen: Barbara Budrich.

Brandhorst, H. (2005). Geld und Geist. Anmerkungen zum schwierigen Spagat der Diakonie zwischen Ökonomie und Spiritualität. In *VEDD-Reihe*, Impuls II, 1–27.

Bratic, L., & Pantucek, P. (2004). *Sie haben ein Problem. Soziale Arbeit als Form des Regierens*. Retrieved December 19, 2006, from www.pantucek.com/texte/bratic_pant.html

Bröckling, U., Krasmann, S., & Lemke, T. (Eds.). (2000). *Gouvernementalität der Gegenwart: Studien zur Ökonomisierung des Sozialen*. Frankfurt/M: Suhrkamp.

Burchell, G., Gordon, C., & Miller, P. (Eds.). (1991). *The Foucault effect*. London: Harvester Wheatsheaf.

Castel, R. (2000). *Die Metamorphosen der sozialen Frage: eine Chronik der Lohnarbeit*. Konstanz: UVK.

Clarke, J. (2004). *Changing welfare, changing states: New directions in social policy*. London: Sage.

Dean, M. (1999). *Governmentality: Power and rule in modern society*. London: Sage.

Doherty, R. (2007). Critically framing education policy: Foucault, discourse and governmentality. In M. Peters & T. Besley (Eds.), *Why Foucault? New directions in educational research* (pp. 193–204). New York: Peter Lang.

Donzelot, J. (1979). *The policing of families*. New York: Random House.

Dzierzbicka, A. (2006). *Vereinbaren statt anordnen. Gouvernementalität macht Schule*. Wien: Löcker.

Evers, A., & Nowotny, H. (1987). *Über den Umgang mit Unsicherheit: die Entdeckung der Gestaltbarkeit*. Frankfurt/M: Surkamp.

Ewald, F. (1986). *L'Etat Providence*. Paris: Bernard Grasset.

Foucault, M. (1987a). Das Subjekt und die Macht. In H. L. Dreyfus & P. Rabinow (Eds.), *Michel Foucault* (pp. 243–261). Weinheim: Beltz.

Foucault, M. (1987b). Wie wird Macht ausgeübt? In H. L. Dreyfus & P. Rabinow (Eds.), *Michel Foucault* (pp. 251–264). Weinheim: Beltz.

Foucault, M. (1999). *Sexualität und Wahrheit I. Der Wille zum Wissen.* Frankfurt/M: Suhrkamp.

Foucault, M. (2000). Die Gouvernementalität. In U. Bröckling, S. Krasmann, & T. Lemke (Eds.), *Gouvernementalität der Gegenwart: Studien zur Ökonomisierung des Sozialen* (pp. 41–67). Frankfurt/M: Suhrkamp.

Foucault, M. (2004a). *Geschichte der Gouvernementalität. Band I: Sicherheit, Territorium, Bevölkerung. Vorlesung am Collège de France 1978–1979.* Frankfurt/M: Suhrkamp.

Foucault, M. (2004b). *Geschichte der Gouvernementalität. Bd. II: Die Geburt der Biopolitik. Vorlesung am Collège de France 1978–1979.* Frankfurt/M: Suhrkamp.

Foucault, M. (2004c). *Hermeneutik des Subjekts. Vorlesung am Collège de France 1981/1982.* Frankfurt/M: Suhrkamp.

Foucault, M. (2005a). Strukturalismus und Poststrukturalismus. In M. Foucault (Ed.), *Schriften in vier Bänden. Dits et Ecrits, Band IV: 1980–1988* (pp. 521–555). Frankfurt/M: Suhrkamp.

Foucault, M. (2005b). Die Ethik der Sorge um sich als Praxis der Freiheit. In M. Foucault (Ed.), *Schriften in vier Bänden. Dits et Ecrits, Band IV: 1980–1988* (pp. 875–909). Frankfurt/M: Suhrkamp.

Foucault, M. (2005c). Wahrheit, Macht, Selbst. In M. Foucault (Ed.), *Schriften in vier Bänden. Dits et Ecrits, Band IV: 1980–1988* (pp. 959–966). Frankfurt/M.

Gertenbach, L. (2007). *Die Kultivierung des Marktes. Foucault und die Gouvernementalität des Neoliberalismus.* Berlin: Parodos.

Habermas, J. (1972). Gegen einen positivistisch halbierten Rationalismus. In T. W. Adorno et al. (Eds.), *Der Positivismusstreit in der deutschen Soziologie* (pp. 235–266). Darmstadt and Neuwied: Luchterhand.

Habermas, J. (1985/1990). *The philosophical discourse of modernity: Twelve lectures.* Cambridge, MA: MIT Press.

Hayek, F. A. (1978). *The constitution of liberty.* Chicago: University of Chicago Press.

Heite, C. (2006). Professionalisierungsstrategien der Sozialen Arbeit. Der Fall des Case Managements. *Neue Praxis, 36*(2), 201–207.

Herrmann, C. (2006). Neoliberale Sicherheiten, neoliberale Qualitäten. Die Neuausrichtung Sozialer Arbeit. *Fantômas, 2*(9), 20–22.

Honneth, A. (1985). *Kritik der Macht. Reflexionsstufen einer kritischen Gesellschaftstheorie.* Frankfurt/M: Suhrkamp.

Kessl, F. (2005). *Der Gebrauch der eigenen Kräfte: eine Gouvernementalität Sozialer Arbeit.* Weinheim and München: Juventa.

Kessl, F., & Krasmann, S. (2005). Sozialpolitische Programmierungen. In F. Kessl, C. Reutlinger, S. Maurer, & O. Frey (Eds.), *Handbuch Sozialraum* (pp. 227–245). Wiesbaden: VS.

Kessl, F., & Maurer, S. (2005). Soziale Arbeit. In F. Kessl, C. Reutlinger, S. Maurer, & O. Frey (Eds.), *Handbuch Sozialraum* (pp. 111–128). Wiesbaden: VS.

Kessl, F., & Otto, H. U. (2007). *Territorialisierung des Sozialen: Regieren über soziale Nahräume.* Opladen & Farmington Hills: Barbara Budrich.

Krasmann, S. (1999). Regieren über Freiheit. Zur Analyse der Kontrollgesellschaft in Foucaultscher Perspektive. *Kriminologisches Journal, 31*(2), 107–121.

Krasmann, S. (2000). Gouvernementalität der Oberfläche. Aggressivität (ab-)trainieren beispielsweise. In U. Bröckling, S. Krasmann, & T. Lemke (Eds.), *Gouvernementalität der Gegenwart: Studien zur Ökonomisierung des Sozialen* (pp. 194–226). Frankfurt/M: Suhrkamp.

Krasmann, S. (2003). *Die Kriminalität der Gesellschaft: zur Gouvernementalität der Gegenwart.* Konstanz: UVK.

Krasmann, S., & Volkmer, M. (2007). *Michel Foucaults "Geschichte der Gouvernementalität" in den Sozialwissenschaften. Internationale Beiträge.* Bielefeld: Transkript.

Krölls, A. (2000). Vom Emanzipations-Zynismus über die Bestreitung des Sparzwecks zur Optimierung staatlicher Steuerungsfähigkeit. In M. Lindenberg (Ed.), *Von der Sorge zur Härte: kritische Beiträge zur Ökonomisierung Sozialer Arbeit* (pp. 111–133). Bielefeld: Kleine.

Langemeyer, I. (2005). *Kompetenzentwicklung zwischen Selbst- und Fremdbestimmung: Arbeitsprozessintegriertes Lernen in der Fachinformatik. Eine Fallstudie.* Münster: LIT.

Langemeyer, I. (2007). Wo Handlungsfähigkeit ist, ist nicht immer schon Unterwerfung. Fünf Probleme des Gouvernementalitätsansatzes. In F. Bettinger, J. Stehr, & R. Anhorn (Eds.), *Michel Foucaults Machtanalytik und Soziale Arbeit* (pp. 227–243). Wiesbaden: VS-Verlag.

Lemke, T. (1997). *Eine Kritik der politischen Vernunft. Foucaults Analyse der modernen Gouvernementalität.* Berlin and Hamburg: Argument.

Lemke, T. (1999). Der Kopf des Königs—Recht. Disziplin und Regierung bei Foucault. *Berliner Journal für Soziologie, 9*(3), 415–434.

Lemke, T. (2004). *Veranlagung und Verantwortung. Genetische Diagnostik zwischen Selbstbestimmung und Schicksal.* Bielefeld: Transkript.

Lemke, T. (2007). *Gouvernementalität und Biopolitik.* Wiesbaden: VS.

Lemke, T., Krasmann, S., & Bröckling, U. (2000). Gouvernementalität, Neoliberalismus und Selbsttechnologie. Eine Einleitung. In U. Bröckling, S. Krasmann, & T. Lemke (Eds.), *Gouvernementalität der Gegenwart. Studien zur Ökonomisierung des Sozialen* (pp. 7–40). Frankfurt/M: Suhrkamp.

Lindenberg, M. (2000). "Ökonomisierung Sozialer Arbeit?" Gegen die These der ausschließlichen Bestimmung dieser Diskussion aus staatlicher Zwecksetzung. In M. Lindenberg (Ed.), *Von der Sorge zur Härte: kritische Beiträge zur Ökonomisierung Sozialer Arbeit* (pp. 89–109). Bielefeld: Kleine.

Lindner, U. (2006). Alles Macht, oder was? Foucault, Althusser und kritische Gesellschaftstheorie. *Prokla, 36*(4), 583–609.

Maeder, C. (2004). Die Gouvernementalität des New Public Managements. In U. Mäder & C.-H. Daub (Eds.), *Soziale Folgen der Globalisierung* (pp. 7–80). Basel: Edition Gesowip.

Maurer, S. (2005). Soziale Bewegungen. In F. Kessl, C. Reutlinger, S. Maurer, & O. Frey (Eds.), *Handbuch Sozialraum* (pp. 629–646). Wiesbaden: VS.

Maurer, S. (2006). Gouvernementalität "von unten her" denken. Soziale Arbeit und soziale Bewegungen als (kollektive) Akteure "beweglicher Ordnungen". In S. Weber & S. Maurer (Eds.), *Gouvernementalität und Erziehungswissenschaft* (pp. 233–252). Wissen—Macht—Transformation. Wiesbaden: VS.

May, M. (2006). Woher kommt die Produktivität des Sozialen? Ansätze zu einer Analyse ihrer Produktivkräfte. In K. Böllert, P. Hansbauer, B. Hasenjürgen, & S. Langenohl (Eds.), *Die Produktivität des Sozialen – den sozialen Staat aktivieren* (pp. 31–48). Wiesbaden: VS.

Michel, B. (2005). *Stadt und Gouvernementalität.* Münster: Westfälisches Dampfboot.

O'Malley, P., Weir, L., & Shearing, C. (1997). Governmentality, criticism, politics. *Economy & Society, 26*(4), 501–517.

Opitz, S. (2004). *Gouvernementalität im Postfordismus. Macht, Wissen und Techniken des Selbst im Feld unternehmerischer Rationalität.* Münster: Westfälisches Dampfboot.

Otto, H.-U., & Seelemeyer, U. (2004). Soziale Arbeit und Gesellschaft. Anstöße zu einer Neuorientierung der Debatte um Normativität und Normalität. In S. Hering & U. Urban (Eds.), *"Liebe allein genügt nicht." Historische und systematische Dimensionen der Sozialpädagogik* (pp. 45–63). Opladen: Leske & Budrich.

Peters, M. A., Olssen, M., & Lanksheer, C. (Eds.). (2003). *Futures of critical theory: Dreams of difference.* Lanham, MD: Rowman & Littlefield Publishers.

Pieper, M., & Rodriguez Gutierrez, E. (Eds.). (2005). *Gouvernementalität. Ein sozialwissenschaftliches Konzept in Anschluss an Foucault.* Frankfurt/M and New York: Campus.

Rabinow, P. (2004). *Anthropologie der Vernunft: Studien zu Wissenschaft und Lebensführung.* Frankfurt/M: Suhrkamp. [English: (1997) *Essays on the anthropology of reason.* Princeton, NJ: Princeton University Press.]

Redaktion der Widersprüche. (2006). Anlass des Heftes 100: ein Blick auf einige methodologische und theoretische Widersprüche in der Redaktion. *Widersprüche, 26*(100), 209–222.

Richter, M. (2004). Zur (Neu)Ordnung des Familialen. *Widersprüche, 24*(92), 7–16.

Ritsert, J. (2000). *Gesellschaft: ein unergründlicher Grundbegriff der Soziologie.* Frankfurt/M and New York: Campus.

Ronneberger, K., Lanz, S., & Jahn, W. (1999). *Die Stadt als Beute.* Bonn: Dietz.

Rose, N. (1999). *Powers of freedom: Reframing political thought.* Cambridge, UK: Cambridge University Press.

Sarasin, P. (2005). *Michel Foucault zur Einführung.* Hamburg: Junius.

Schaarschuch, A. (2003). Am langen Arm: Formwandel des Staates, Staatstheorie und Soziale Arbeit im entwickelten Kapitalismus. In H. G. Homfeldt & J. Schulze-Krüdener (Eds.), *Basiswissen Pädagogik. Pädagogische Arbeitsfelder 3: Handlungsfelder der Sozialen Arbeit* (pp. 36–65). Baltmannsweiler: Hohengehren.

Sennelart, M. (2004). Situierung der Vorlesungen. In M. Foucault (Ed.), *Geschichte der Gouvernementalität. Band II: Die Geburt der Biopolitik.* Frankfurt/M: Suhrkamp.

Stenson, K. (2007). Das Lokale regieren. Der Kampf um Souveränität im ländlichen England. In F. Kessl & H. U. Otto (Eds.), *Territorialisierung des Sozialen. Regieren über soziale Nahräume* (pp. 117–142). Opladen and Farmington Hills: Barbara Budrich.

Stövesand, S. (2006). *Mit Sicherheit Sozialarbeit!* HAW Hamburg (PhD).

Sturzenhecker, B. (2003). Aktivierende Jugendarbeit?. In H. J. Dahme, H. U. Otto, A. Trube, & N. Wohlfahrt (Eds.), *Soziale Arbeit für den aktivierenden Staat* (pp. 381–390). Opladen: Leske & Budrich.

Tenorth, H. E. (2006). Macht und Regierung – oder die asymmetrische Ordnung der Bildung. *Zeitschrift für Pädagogik, 52*(1), 36–42.

Waldenfels, B. (2004). Foucault. Auskehr des Denkens. In M. Fleischer (Ed.), *Philosophen des 20.Jahrhunderts. Eine Einführung* (pp. 191–203). Darmstadt: Wissenschaftliche Buchgesellschaft.

Weber, M. (1978). *Economy and society: An outline of interpretive sociology.* Berkeley: University of California Press.

Weber, S. (2006). Gouvernementalität der "Schulgemeinde". Zwischen experimenteller Demokratie und Innovationstechnologie. In S. Weber & S. Maurer (Eds.), *Gouvernementalität und Erziehungswissenschaft. Wissen - Macht – Transformation* (pp. 77–100). Wiesbaden: VS.

Wilhelm, E. (2005). *Rationalisierung der Jugendfürsorge: die Herausbildung neuer Steuerungsformen des Sozialen zu Beginn des 20. Jahrhunderts.* Bern, Stuttgart and Wien: Haupt.

Ziegler, H. (2004). *Jugendhilfe als Prävention. Die Refiguration sozialer Hilfe und Herrschaft in fortgeschritten liberalen Gesellschaftsformationen.* Universitaet Bielefeld (PhD). Retrieved December 12, 2006, from http://www.bieson.ub.uni-bielefeld.de/volltexte/2004/533/

Fabian kessl
University of duisburg-essen
Germany

UTE KARL

24. LEARNING TO BECOME AN ENTREPRENEURIAL SELF FOR VOLUNTARY WORK?

Social Policy and Older People in the Volunteer Sector[1]

This chapter will concentrate on changes concerning the discourses and role models that deal with the demographic group of elderly and old aged people. The classification of a part of the population as 'older people', 'senior citizens', 'young elderly', 'oldest old' etc. is a power related construction that objectifies reality and makes "'it' available for cognitive grasp and practical action" (Katz & Green, 2002, p. 160). A perspective derived from the theory of governmentality brings into focus the specific measures of leading and steering those parts of the population which do not function by coercion or by general laws (see Foucault, 1991; Doherty, 2006). These measures are directed at the subjectivity of individuals and the influence the technologies of self-regulation, of self-government, and of the conduct of life.

> The term governmentality sought to draw attention to a certain way of thinking and acting embodied in all those attempts to know and govern the wealth, health and happiness of populations (Miller & Rose, 1992, p. 174).

Governmentality is closely related to the concept of power as developed by Foucault in his later years. According to Foucault, power is executed by influencing the conduct of subjects who are fundamentally free. The general meaning of 'governing' according to Foucault is "to structure the possible field of action of others" (Foucault, 1982, p. 221).

My considerations are mainly concentrated on discussions and programs related to Germany. It is apparent, however, that these have to be reflected in the context of international and in particular of Anglo-American debates.2 What I want to show is that the neoliberal rationale can be found more and more in the role models of age and ageing. The individual is made responsible for his/her well-being; taking care is a matter of private responsibility; and self-concept and self-management are prominent issues in the educational work with old people. It is intended to encourage people in community building and, without coercion, to lead the individual to socially useful behaviour. The political rationality connected with professional educational and social work with elderly people requires the development of a critical perspective. The role models of an 'active', 'successful' and 'productive age/ageing' have special significance for social policy programmes and for (model-) projects in the field of educational work with old people. Role models

M.A. Peters et al. (eds.), Govermentality Studies in Education, 433–451.
© *2009 Sense Publishers. All rights reserved.*

like these can show us how formations of knowledge gain power, how they shape social reality, and how they become reality itself. In this chapter I will discuss an exemplar which analyses a current practice-related project – an interface-project related to two discourses– the discourse on age/ageing, and the discourse on civic engagement and voluntary work.[3]

FROM ACTIVATION TO A SOCIALLY DEMANDED AND USEFUL PRODUCTIVITY

'Age(ing)' is a social construction. "Age is a phase of life produced by social arrangements" (Göckenjan, 2000, p. 376).[4] Images of old age and age(ing) discourses should be seen as moral and social policy discourses, in most cases with a polarising effect. They function as discourses on social order (see Göckenjan, 2000). The dichotomizing structure formed signifies a division between 'health' and 'disease' e.g. 'active' vs. 'in need of care'; 'young age' vs. 'old age'; or 'third age' vs. 'fourth age.' This structure, however, does not only refer to the process of inclusion and exclusion, but also to the social construction of the dividing line itself (Kondratowitz, 2002).

Societal expectations regarding conformity are expressed in images of old age. They execute pressure by way of discerning right or wrong behaviour. This social pressure is in fact not really visible in today's dominant images of old age. There are no sharply profiled and accepted negative images (Göckenjan, 2000, p. 427).

Recently, the discourses on age(ing) are dominated by an economic rationality.

In the existing programmes the role models of an 'active', 'successful', and 'productive' age(ing) are not conceived as clearly separated or strictly consecutive.

What they have in common is their reference to a 'close to healthy age(ing)' and their interest in varying strategies to maintain or to extend this situation. But it should be noted that in contemporary discourses the question of an individual's well-being is increasingly being accompanied by the question of what is socially desirable or useful.

'ACTIVE AGE(ING)'

The social-gerontological theory of activity can be seen as a central frame of reference for the 'active age(ing)' role model. This theory originated from empirical studies conducted in the USA and published in the 1950s (Kolland, 1996).[5] But it was not before the 1970s and early 1980s that this theory was developed and implemented in professional practice concepts. The activity theory is opposed to the theory of disengagement. This theory assumes a 'naturally' developing social retreat in old age and a new, pacifying balance between individual and society. In contrast, the activity theory fundamentally opposes the assumption of altered needs and norms and of reduced cognitive competencies (Backes & Clemens 1998; Lenz, Rudolph & Sickendieck, 1999). A retreat from social relations and the loss of competencies is seen as a result of a loss of roles and functions in old age. The central assumption of the activity theory is, that in old age the achievement capacities can be preserved or even extended in some areas by continuous demands and challenges and by a new construction of the meaning of life – to the extent that the limits are defined by factual physical developments (Lenz, Rudolph & Sickendieck, 1999).

In social work with older people, the role model of an 'active age' is instrumental in promoting participation in social life through activities, and for establishing a positive image of old age (Zeman & Schmidt, 2001). Educational activities regarding the individual are perceived as necessary for the development of activities desirable for society and they should not be evaluated on the basis of their utility for society (e.g. theatre productions, public readings, narration cafes, senior universities, tourism, new media). The point here is not whether these activities are useful to others, but that there are projects (see knowledge markets) that are seen to be harnessing the potential of old age as well as stimulating productivity (Glaser & Röbke, 1992; Braun, Burmeister & Engels, 2004).

The 'active ageing' policy of the WHO comprises more than "the ability to be physically active or to participate in the labour force." It explicitly includes those, "who are frail, disabled and in need of care" (WHO, 2002, p. 12). Nevertheless, there are programmes where the role model of 'active age(ing)' neglects the reality of life situations, biographies and careers. So indirectly individuals are made responsible for their success or failure in old age.[6] According to Gertrud Backes and Wolfgang Clemens (1998, p. 117) the end of ones' professional situation is perceived as "*the* central event," whereas the "middle part of life ... as point of reference is seen too positive[ly]."[7] In addition, the equation of activity and satisfaction, the implicit achievement-orientation, and the connection of activity and quality of life are problematic (Kolland, 1996). Regarding one's life as meaningful depends on a life full of activities (Kinsler, 2003). The connection of 'quality of life' and 'activity' is best illustrated in the book *Giving meaning to old age. How seniors can be culturally active* (Glaser & Röbke, 1992). The activities presented in this collection of articles clearly show that the central target group of the activity programmes is a healthy, achievement-oriented population. Thus the role model of 'active age(ing)' all too often contributes to a continuing neglect or a repeated exclusion of frailty, illness, and loneliness and conditions often connected with older age[8] The ethical problems of connecting 'activity' and 'quality of life' become evident, when the question is reversed: Is a non-active, passive life or a life in illness of elderly people meaningless?

Despite the numerous criticisms regarding the 'active age(ing)' role model and the social-gerontological theory of activity, a variety of programmes rely on this role model. The 'active senior' appears to be an unquestioned natural figure, *the illusio* (Bourdieu) in the field of social and educational work with older people.[9] At least two reasons may account for this situation. First, the image of older age accounts for new practice perspectives and is opposed to negative stereotypes despite the fact that it has normative implications (Göckenjan, 2000). Second, this role model is integral to the logic and rhetoric of an 'activating state'. So at the same time as the individual searches for possibilities in order to shape one's life, practices of government are aimed at activating individuals.

'SUCCESSFUL AGE(ING)'

The discourse on 'successful age(ing)' is omnipresent in the role models of 'active' and 'productive age(ing)' and cannot easily be separated from the two. Nevertheless, it is important to have a closer look at this concept. Klaus R. Schroeter (2002, p. 88) has shown that the term "successful aging" was introduced as early as 1961 by Robert J. Havighurst. In this early phase the focus was on satisfaction with life, the individual's well-being, and on difficult social situations. In the 1980s "successful aging" was conceived as a psychological model by Margret M. Baltes and Paul B. Baltes (1989; 1990). The key position of this model of a "selective optimization with compensation" is understanding aging and age as not being a defined and given situation. The essence and the very nature of age has to be seen in its adaptability and openness for change. According to Baltes & Baltes (1989), a negative stereotype of old age can not lead to the best way of aging for the individual or society.

Similar to the concept of active age, this model also opposes a negative stereotype of old age. Baltes & Baltes suggest "an encompassing definition of successful aging," which "requires a value-based, systemic, and ecological perspective. Both subjective and objective indicators need to be considered within a given cultural context with its particular contents and ecological demands," (Baltes & Baltes, 1990, p. 7). They offer general perspectives and strategies for successful aging with reference to a characterisation of psychological aging and age-related limitations. They recommend a "healthy life-style in order to reduce the probability of pathological aging conditions," and they suggest "educational, motivational, and health-related activities" in families and in situations of leisure and work to slow down negative aging processes and to "strengthen one's reserve capacities, be they physical, mental, or social reserves," (Baltes & Baltes, 1990, p. 19 et seq.; Baltes & Baltes, 1989, p. 7 et seq.). It is evident that in this concept individual strategies of optimization are essential. Activity and health are closely related, "development-enhancing societal opportunities and supports need to be offered" (Baltes & Baltes, 1990, p. 20) and "compensatory support" is essential (Baltes & Baltes, 1989, p. 8). This perspective is focused on the problem of how an individual can find best ways to cope with the process of aging and what role "the three interacting elements and processes" of selection, optimization, and compensation play (Baltes & Baltes, 1990, p. 21).[10]

In this context learning processes are the most important part of strategies to cope with limitations and losses and to compensate for these by developing new capacities. Thus their role is to contribute to retarding the negative implications of aging in order to lead an independent life as long as possible.

But the rhetoric of 'successful age(ing)' is misleading in so far, as it is only the strategies can be successful, but not aging itself. Reserve capacities are shrinking, regardless of whether or not the strategies are successful (Schroeter, 2002). And it should be kept in mind, that to talk about those who age successfully always implies there are others who do not (ibid., p. 93). Schroeter's question is: "Who then belongs to those who failed? ... At which age does one have to die, which mental and physical frailties does one have to endure, what amount of incompetencies must one display, to be stigmatised as a 'failure'?" (ibid.).

'PRODUCTIVE AGE(ING)'

'Productive age(ing)' is a role model of the 1990. The documentation of the conference "Old age and productive living", which was held at Hamburg in 1994 (Baltes & Montada, 1996), presents a great variety of definitions. It is interesting to see, how the concept, developed by Margret M. Baltes from a psychological perspective, is in accord with her concept of 'successful age(ing)'. She asks for "definitions of productivity, i.e. a taxonomy of multiple objectives of aging, by which the meaning of old age can be defined" (ibid., p. 402), and she emphasizes the issues of the meaning, of the aims and perspectives of old age, of individual resources and of societal contexts and arguments against understanding productivity closely related to paid work.

Baltes' concept of "successful aging" which leads to "productive, self-responsible aging" means a "successful adaptation to age-related losses and to define and to realize aims" (Baltes, 1996, p. 404 et seq.). Responsibility has a twofold meaning: self-responsibility, which is intended to reduce the burden on others; and responsibility towards others. Baltes is convinced that the emphasis on productivity brings into focus the marginalization of old aged people and shows that society, including the elderly, has no idea what the "aims of old age" might be (ibid., p. 407). But why should everyone focus on aims? And why is the question of aims related to the question of the meaning of life in old age? Are the phases of youth and of adult life always full of meaning and determination?

The conference contributions include an article by Hans Peter Tews who presents a sociological concept of "productivity in old age", and social usefulness (Tews, 2000). This concept bridges the gap between the discourses on old age and on civic engagement, and it confronts the problem of "the burden the aged represent for society" with the question of a reduction of this burden by "an independent lifestyle", by "individual productivity" in old age (Tews, 2000, p. 74). Regarding the "structural change in old age"[11] Tews asks for an understanding of "productivity in old age" which goes beyond the field of vocational and semi-vocational productivity and which should not include all fields of after- or extra-vocational activities:

> "We should define 'productive' as behaviour which creates 'value' and is socially useful. Values are dependent on exchange conditions. They can be expressed in money or ... by payment in kind. 'Time' is a service that can also be exchanged and something which the aged normally have a lot of. In principle they are marketable services which could or would have to be paid for were they not provided free of charge", (Tews, 2000, p. 74; see also Tews, 1996, p. 189).

He discerns the following "five forms of productivity in old age":

"Retention of an independent lifestyle" in old age, which aims at individual independence and is therefore supposed to „reduce the burden the aged represent for society";

"Inter-generational productivity";

"Intra-generational productivity";

"Community productivity", referring to social voluntary work, which should be retained;

"A further form of social productivity", which primarily relates to "self-organization in old-age and political influence" (Tews, 2000, pp. 74–76; Tews, 1996, p. 188 et seq.).

Tews describes productivity-oriented projects in old age. Among these are the senior co-operatives in Baden-Württemberg, senior citizens offices, knowledge markets, and initiatives for a productive use of the experience and expertise of older people (Tews, 1996). Thus the discourse on old age increasingly becomes a discourse of voluntary service and civic engagement.

Looking at the debates in the USA, Tews notices that the problem of usefulness and productivity is obviously accepted there since it is much easier "to integrate older people in productivity-oriented programmes and initiatives," "including the integration of older people as "productive elements", as "'underused active elderly', and as societal resource into educational programmes for seniors, activities older people are normally paid for" (Tews, 1996, p. 198)[12]. The following examples listed among others by the author, can give us an idea of the dimensions of the field of "productivity in old age" in the USA:

"older people work as tutors in ghetto schools to assist pupils with learning difficulties ....

they do installation and repair work in the households of older and handicapped people ...

they give classes for illiterate people ...

they work in Third World development programmes...

retired lawyers offer free professional legal services for poor people" (ibid., p. 197 et seq.).

This list of old age productivity-projects illustrates two important aspects: the target groups are often poor or very poor people and the services rendered rely on professional qualifications. In an underdeveloped welfare-state these professional activities for needy people can only be offered for free by a benevolent, voluntary engagement of individuals.

Tews asserts that education and educational activities are important not only for the development of old age, but also for the development of society through the redefinition of "productivity in old age" (Tews, 1996, p. 194). Education is seen as a prerequisite for productivity and being useful for society.

For Tews, the role model of a "productive old age" is helpful for a renewed sociological debate on the potential of old age (ibid., p. 208). In this debate the question of potential can be closely connected with the debate on the usefulness of productivity. Under economic perspectives, human beings are perceived as cost-returns factors as potentially negative dimensions of the usefulness and productivity concept. Ethical problems inherent to this dichotomy are evident.

Peter Zeman and Roland Schmidt's contribution to the Third Report on Old Age (2001) deals with the structures and lines of development of social work for the aged. For these authors, Tews' position belongs more or less to product-oriented approaches, whereas process-oriented approaches are characterised by a development-psychological and educational understanding of old age productivity. In my view, however, the position of Tews is process-oriented with respect to educational and learning processes of the individual. But in his approach process-orientation is functional for socially useful, market-oriented services.

In the final report of the Enquête-Commission, Demographic Change (Deutscher Bundestag, 2002a) "productivity in old-age" is the central theme, blending, the positions of Baltes & Montada (1996) and Tews (1996), and connecting productivity with resources and competencies which should be used more effectively. It should be noted that the Report strongly argues against a "re-engagement of old age" and a "social work period for elderly people" (Deutscher Bundestag, 2002a, p. 49).

But how can this understanding of the resources and competencies of old age people lead to an enhanced civic engagement in society? The project "Experience for Initiatives" (EFI) of the German "Federal Ministry for Family Affairs, Senior Citizens, Women, and Youth" discussed below, relies on learning processes to initiate a socially useful, civic engagement.

EDUCATIONAL GOALS OF ROLE –MAKING AND SELF-ORGANISATION OF AGED PEOPLE: SENIOR-TRAINERS IN THE EXPERIENCE FOR INITIATIVES (EFI) PROJECT

The model programme "Experience for Initiatives" (EFI) was scheduled for a five year period (2002–2006).[13] The main project participants were volunteer agencies in thirty-five municipalities, local Senior Citizen's offices, self-help contact points, agencies for civil involvement, and 12 educational institutions on a national scale. The twelve educational institutions were responsible for implementing the training programmes in accordance with the core curriculum. By the end of 2006, 942 persons were qualified as 'Senior-Trainers' and more than 3000 projects were initiated by this group (Engels, Braun & Burmeister, 2007, p. 53). In addition, Senior-Trainers are qualified in regional or communal programmes. Meanwhile some Senior-Trainer responsible for Senior Expertise teams are part of the nationwide model programme "Generationsübergreifende Freiwilligendienste." In the project "Den demographischen Wandel in Kommunen mitgestalten – Erfahrungswissen der Älteren nutzen" (2007-2009) implemented in former East German locations, the Robert-Bosch-Stiftung is sponsoring the qualification of additional 300 Senior-Trainers (ibid., p. 22 et seq., p. 187). The EFI Project is a member of the European co-operative project "Lifelong Learning and Active Citizenship in Europe's Ageing Society" (LACE, 2005-2007).[14] The development of similar projects in other European countries is encouraged by the experiences accumulated in this project.[15] The origins of this project are located in many international discussions "about the part volunteering can play in the transition from paid work to retirement" (Smith & Gay, 2005, p. 1).

The basic point of reference for the concept of the EFI project is the demographic change with its challenges for the social, health care, and educational systems. To cope with future-oriented tasks may depend "on the active integration and participation of the citizens and in particular of the people of old age to make good use of their potentials for the public good" (Braun, Burmeister & Engels, 2004, p. 15). So one central goal of the programme was to "assure people of old age of the value of their expertise and experience and to better use this knowledge for society" (ibid.).[16] The invention and the development of the role of Senior-Trainer serves the "re-discovery of the social position of people of old age and the public acceptance of their contribution to society", (ibid.).[17]

Above that, special aims and objectives are defined for a number of policy fields, i.e. senior citizens policy and educational policies, including the policy problems of enhancing the civic engagement. The objectives referring to senior citizens include the dimensions of meaningfulness, the alteration of a negative stereotype of old age, and the participation in society. The inter-relation of these three dimensions is vital for an engagement with others as well as for personal gains.

The EFI-project is closely connected to the 5. Report on Old Age by the Federal Government of Germany, focussing on "Potentials of old age in economy and society – The contribution of people of old age for the relationship of and solidarity between different generations". One aim of this report is to find answers to the following questions: What are the genuine capacities of people of age and how can these capacities be made useful for new social roles in a changing society? What are the necessary societal prerequisites for an increased readiness to nurture and to use the potentials of old age[18]? What educational programmes should be offered? It should be recognized, however, that the report of the expert commission explicitly mentions the danger of a biased, purpose-related, one-dimensional misuse of the debate on a reconstruction of the social state and on fairness among generations:

"The language reveals socio-economic, utilitarian positions – e.g. to perceive people of age as 'human resources', whose potentials must be used by society, thus neglecting their self-will and self-determination" (BMFSFJ, 2005, p. 373).

"Expertise and Experience" in the model programme is perceived as "personal resource" and "social capital"[19]. In the process of self-reflection, it is shaped by the role of the Senior-Trainer. The public promotion of this role will help to perceive the resources and potentials of old age in society in an appropriate way, and it is expected, that the EFI-project will oppose the "exclusion of people of age" (Braun,

Burmeister & Engels, 2004, p. 17). The role of the Senior-Trainer is defined within the spectrum of civic engagement which needs to be stabilised by sustainable development, enhanced by the EFI-project.

The EFI training programme is characterised by a "three-pillar-approach". In 3x3 days that include practical and theoretical learning periods, volunteers acquire role related competencies and qualify as Senior-Trainers. What is the essence of this new role and what is the training concept? The EFI-programme intended to use people of old age for the role of Senior-Trainers and to assist them in their role-finding process (Braun, Burmeister & Engels, 2004). The special responsibility inherent to this role concerns the engagement potential of the elderly and the fact that these all too often have a "roleless role" (similar to one of the assumptions of the activity theory). The concept and the core curriculum emphasize the necessity to individually develop responsibility in the process of *role making*. But the training process also includes elements of *role taking*. In addition the learning should hold the dimension of responsibility as the key element of the Senior-Trainer-role:

> "The 'Senior-Trainer'-role implies the emphasis on responsibility, essential for multiplying and initiating activities concerning the enhancement of civic engagement and for the transfer of experience and expertise into initiatives, societies, or organisations" (ibid., p. 32).

The first core curriculum had already outlined "possible role profiles and activities of Senior-Trainers" (Knopf, 2003, p. 5) and suggested "the development of the role by examples". The core curriculum of 2004 then presents five different role profiles[20], combined with a catalogue of the key competencies to be acquired in units two and three.[21] These defined guidelines for the development of an individual role profile and educational concept may well lack the openness needed for adult learning.

A closer look at the competencies shows that these are crucial for civic voluntary engagement. In addition, the first unit of the curriculum of 2004 suggested perceiving civic engagement and age(ing) "in a greater context", and understanding the "exemplary quality of the senior voluntary engagement" (Burmeister, 2004, p. 26):

> Whatever the practical activities of Senior-Trainers are, they should do it with a professional 'civic perspective' and look beyond their own interests and expectations, taking into account the public good by stimulating others (Burmeister, Heller & Stehr, 2004, p. 16).

The training also intends to promote the capacities of self-organisation for the participants and to qualify them for "self-organised individual or collective learning processes including local Senior expertise teams, experiments with future forms of engagement, organisation, as well as the reflection of perspectives" (Braun, Burmeister & Engels, 2004, p. 162). Though the important program and evaluative role of the voluntary agencies and their reduced resources are outlined, self-organisation appears to be an instrument to master the challenges of Senior-Trainers. In particular, self-organisation is to be promoted by local "Senior Expertise Teams" (ibid.). It is expected that these teams share the responsibility with the Agencies for civil involvement in monitoring the work of the Senior-Trainers (see Engels, Braun & Burmeister, 2007, p. 84).

Who are the project participants and what are their expectations? The report on the first phase of the programme illustrates the high expectations Senior-Trainers are confronted with:

> The EFI-Programme supports motivated and capable seniors to ask questions, to communicate problems, and to find fitting solutions together with others (Braun, Burmeister & Engels, 2004, p. 33).

The competencies needed for these tasks (e.g. management and organisation) cannot be fully achieved in the training period. Therefore these competencies should have been required beforehand and play a role the future life of the Senior-Trainers (Braun, Burmeister & Engels, 2004).[22] It is also expected that Senior-Trainers "communicate their expertise and experience in accord with the goals and objectives of the programme (e.g. the role profiles of the Senior-Trainers) and with reference to local needs and goals" (ISAB, 2003b, p. 6), which in some cases has led to declarations of self-commitment (Braun, Burmeister & Engels, 2004, p. 152). It is obvious that the EFI-project is characterised by an "Assist and demand"-structure. The nurturing of the potentials of the participants is connected with the expectation of volunteering and providing useful services for the community as Senior-Trainers.[23] With reduced economic support, the moral self-commitment is vital for the functioning of this interplay between "Assist and demand".

The numbers reveal that the high expectations connected with this programme can only be reached by a select number of old aged people, in particular by the "young aged" who are between 55 and 65 years with school and vocational certificates above average at the start of the programme. The interim report shows that in fact 69% of the participants had been volunteers for more than one year before they started the training programme (Braun, Burmeister & Engels, 2004). The local agencies testify that at this point 52% of the participants had been active in their organisation (ibid). This, however, proves that this group of people of age cannot be classified as a "roleless role" group. Such intended and demanded active engagement obviously contributes to a further segmentation of the group of aged people (Böhnisch & Schröer, 2002). For this group the EFI-project underlines the the connection of socio-economic factors and engagement (see Deutscher Bundestag). Questions arise: can negative stereotypes be altered by those who are among the objects of the process of social depreciation? Can such an exclusive project, not centrally focused on excluded elderly or old aged people, contribute to a more general perception of the problems of age(ing)? The creation of a positive image of older generations is exclusively related to the potential usefulness of old age people for society. This, again, implies a depreciation of those who cannot or who do not want to comply with this norm. The dichotomy of growth and reduction of the burdens of old age is inherent to this approach, too.

The major difference between those who are engaged in the volunteer sector and those who are qualified for the Senior-Trainer role is not so much that they are no longer working or that they are on their way from paid work to retirement.[24] Those who volunteer act self-organized, initiating, and supportive on the basis of a role profile which incorporates their expertise and experience offered to an existing or still to be created market.

The idea of *role making* is the key adult learning concept of this programme and is a qualitative leap in the understanding of educating the old aged. For actively engaged seniors the aspects of self-management, self-organization, and self-formation are essential for what they offer to potential markets and for the activation of others. The structures of honorary, volunteering, and self-help activities change such that the focus is no longer self-help projects or tasks to be tackled by engaged people, but by a group of people activated and trained for market services (see ISAB, 2004). "Active age" is still a central role model (see the public campaign on "Active Age" suggested for the second project phase), but the concept is no longer based on the activity theory of old age(ing). This may explain why critical assessments are without influence. The promises of "active age(ing)" seem to have reached a dynamic of their own.

REFLECTIONS ON GOVERNMENTALITY – A SUMMARY

The neo-liberal, managerial rationale (Bröckling, 2000) has not only found access to the field of paid work but also to the field of voluntary work and civil engagement, a field characterized by the transition from paid work to retirement. Voluntarily engaged people are constituted as Senior-Trainers. On this basis their experience and expertise can be offered free of charge, yet purposefully, and controlled. Accepting the role of a Senior-Trainer means seeing one's potential as resources, transforming them into a marketable product and offering this product in self-organized way. The reduction of responsibilities of the welfare-state imply that the policy options are concentrated in the fields of voluntary work, self-help activities, and civic engagement. These communal forms are an ideal field for a paradigmatic change "to transfer the steering capacity of state organs and institutions to 'responsible', 'circumspective', and 'rational' subjects" (Lemke, Krasmann & Bröckling, 2000, p. 30). The process of role making, effected by self-technologies, seems to be a very effective, conflict-free way of governing the individual by self-formation, self-organization, self-commitment and by stimulating desirable conduct rather than coercion or political discussions. Self-organization has always been prominent in the field of voluntary work. What is new is that state initiated programmes are promoting self-organization. In this case protest movements and public interest conflicts, which commonly happen in debates on civic engagement and voluntary work, have not occurred (Mayer, 2004; Böhnisch & Schröer, 2002). Moreover, the role of biographical patterns of activity for engagement is neglected (Aner, 2005), and there is no answer to the question, who is able or who should participate in the decision-making processes of a society and how this could be done.[25] So it is not surprising that the following aspects are neglected or are of marginal importance in this project. The relations between the structural changes of age(ing) and general structural changes of/in society and the responsibility of the state and the economy in these processes of change are not discussed in the model.

What is the responsibility of the actors promoting neo-liberal economic and labour-market strategies for the process of making old age "younger" and for the shrinking numbers of younger generations? Which are the contributions of the economic and political systems to a depreciation of old age and to the notion of old age as a burden for society? In particular, the EFI-project does not deal with the relationship and the characteristic differences of paid and voluntary work. It is insufficient to proclaim, that volunteer work is not a continuation of vocational activities or even an equivalent to qualified professional work because the differences between voluntary work and employment are continually fading away. The model-project "Self-organization of people of age" (2006) illustrates clearly, that in an ever increasing number publicly financed tasks and employment are going to be substituted by voluntary engagement.[26] In addition among the EFI-participants, more women than men located their activities in the social sector. But within this sector many women are employed under precarious conditions, are underpaid, or lose their employment in the reduction of welfare-state activities (Wessels, 1994). The EFI-project avoids discussing a re-distribution of paid and unpaid work and how work should be paid.

This project also throws light on a more general yet urgent question: what happens to the norms and values of a society when societal care work and social and educational work is increasingly situated in the field of civic engagement and so depends ever more on individual engagement?

The analysis of the EFI model programme shows that the availability of harnessing the abilities of people of age for the society is prominently discussed, and that the self-management of the individuals is essential for the activation and regulation of their availability.

It is one thing to discuss only varieties of a healthy age while ignoring the manifold and complex life situations of old age. It is something else to silently accept the implicit topic of old age(ing) as passive, failed, unproductive, or even superfluous. It becomes highly problematic to give old age a new value and appreciation by using criteria like 'activity', 'success', or 'productivity' and by an elaborated debate on the 'potentials' of old age.

ROOMS OF POSSIBILITIES: MANIFOLD VOICES

Despite a number of similarities concerning the process of role-making between the EFI-project and government technologies that regulate the labour market, the main difference is that for old age self-management and self-formation is not connected with income and that the participants who volunteer for training are not subject to legal regulations. A closer look at the interim report reveals that 232 out of a total number of 676 seniors interested in the project did not hand in their application. This may result from varying positions concerning the activities and the content matters of the training (Braun, Burmeister & Engels, 2004). The interim report also shows that participation in the project is not primarily motivated by training for the Senior-Trainer role, as 52% returned to the organizations they came from. It can be assumed, that their prime interest was in a high-quality training of valuable competencies. The second and third training periods with a focus on the acquisition of competencies, were highly praised (ISAB, 2003a; Engels & Machalowski, 2004). During the model project phase the percentage of people who discovered a relevant difference to other forms of voluntary work rose. However, the final report shows that this group comprises only 62% (Engels, Braun & Burmeister, 2007, p. 70 et seq.). The age and educational achievement of the participants suggests that quite a number have long standing experiences in project and self-help work dating back to the 1970s. This group may be looking for training and supporting activities and may even be ready to help others, but at the same time it might have developed an opposition to specific forms of community building activities and the methods of narrowly guided self-formation. This is the group which certainly would prefer a more prominent place of political participation in the model project.

These observations show that the possibilities offered by model projects like EFI can be used in quite different ways and that the programmatic orientations of such projects meet real people that they have to face very differently socialized and individualized subjects. These cannot be integrated easily and without alternative options in such programmes. The actual forms of practice may be much more varied than suggested by the model project and by quantitative evaluations and critical perspectives offered here. There is no doubt that voluntary engaged people ask for further education and *continuously* question their routines and use their experience to approach new dimensions of learning. There is no doubt either, that new and more learning opportunities for voluntary engaged people are needed.[27]

Translated by Dieter Keiner

NOTES

[1] This text is an extended version of Karl, 2006.

[2] See e.g. for a Foucauldian perspective on Enterprise Culture and the Entrepreneurial Self Peters, 2001, Doherty, 2006. See for a Foucauldian perspective on gerontology and volunteering Powell & Edwards, 2002, Powell & Biggs, 2003. See for Governmentality and Social Policy on Aging Katz & Green, 2002.

[3] In the German discussion, very often the terms 'bürgerschaftliches Engagement' and 'zivilgesellschaftliches Engagement' (civic engagement), 'neues Ehrenamt' (new honorary engagement), 'freiwilliges Engagement' (voluntary engagement), and 'Freiwilligenarbeit' (voluntary work) are used as equivalents, although these terms have different traditions. I will use the term 'voluntary work' in the sense that people work voluntarily, public welfare orientated, for themselves and others and without being paid. Voluntary work is part of civic engagement. The rationale of voluntary work is different from that of paid and subsistence guaranteeing work, although the examples will show that political practices at the intersection of notions of 'volunteering', 'citizenship', 'learning', and 'ageing' could lead to a reduction of civic engagement and of voluntary work to unpaid work.

[4] Gerd Göckenjan (2000: 362) emphasizes the importance of the German reform of pensions in 1957 for the increasing public debate on old age. Only in connection with economic developments and with social policy "a generalized social passage was constituted and provided with a budget" (ibid., p. 379). So the images of old age reflected here are closely related to welfare-state securities.

[5] Franz Kolland (1996, p. 21) observes a relation between 'activism' as a cultural value in the US-American society and the development of this concept.

[6] In the controversial debate on the concept of 'active age' in the 1st Interim Report of the Enquête Commission on "Demographic Change – challenges of our ageing society for the individual and for politics" (1994) this problem and the necessity become evident, that in the context of social policy 'activity' must be related to the life situations of old age (for a summary see Aner, 2005, pp. 42–46). For a critical assessment, see Lenz, Rudolph & Sickendieck, 1999; Backes & Clemens, 1998.

[7] The biographical interviews with players in theatre groups of aged people reveal that some of these are glad to have overcome the high vocational and family demands and challenges especially in the phase of adult age (see for my interviews Karl, 2005).

[8] See Tokarski, 1998 for criticism of programmes in social and cultural work

[9] The World Health Organization has adopted the term 'Active Ageing' as "Policy Framework". In this context 'active ageing' is understood in a very broad sense: "Active ageing is the process of optimizing opportunities of health, participation and security in order to enhance quality of life as people age" (WHO, 2002, p. 12).

[10] Selection "refers to an increasing restriction of one's life world to fewer domains of functioning (...). It is the adaptive task of the person and society to concentrate on those domains that are of high priority" (Baltes & Baltes, 1990, p. 21). Optimization "reflects the view that people engage in behaviours to enrich and augment their general reserves and to maximize their chosen life courses (and associated forms of behaviour) with regard to quantity and quality", (Baltes & Baltes, 1990, p. 22). Compensation „becomes operative when specific behavioural capacities are lost or are reduced below a standard required for adequate functioning. (...) The element of compensation involves aspects of the mind and technology", (Baltes & Baltes, 1990, p. 22).

[11] Five aspects of the structural change in old age are mentioned: 1. The old are getting younger; 2. Lack of employment; 3. Feminization in old age; 4. Singularization; 5. Very old age is increasing (see Tews, 2000, p. 81 et seq.; see also Tews, 1993).

[12] 'Underused active elderly':" Original quote from Tews, 1996, p. 198."

[13] This project is realized in 10 federal states in Germany. The Institute for Sociological Analysis and Consultancy (ISAB), Cologne, is responsible for co-ordination, consulting, and supervising, the University of Applied Sciences Neubrandenburg for the curriculum development, and the Institute for Social Research (ISG), Cologne, for the evaluation. There is also an advisory board.

[14] See: www.lace-project.net [Date of research: 08.01.2008]; www.efi-programm.de/dokumente/ Pr% E4sentation_ISAB_23.11.05.pdf [Date of research: 08.01.2008]; institut.de/ upload/Aktuelles/PDF/ Praesentation_Zwart_Brauers.pdf [Date of research: 22.10.2006]. See for recent projects: http:// www.isab-institut.de/front_content.php?idcat=65 [Date of research: 30.01.2008]. See for European perspectives on voluntary engagement by and for very old persons: Internationaler Rat für soziale Wohlfahrt; Deutscher Verein; Kuratorium Deutsche Altershilfe (Eds.) 2000.

[15] For international contacts of the project see Institut für sozialwissenschaftliche Analysen und Beratung, 2006.

[16] In a way, the well-known topic of the "wisdom of old age" (see Göckenjan, 2000, p. 413) is resumed and upgraded.

[17] The working areas of the "seniorTrainers" are quite different from those of traditional trainers, e.g. in further education.

[18] For the 5th Report on Old Age see Bundesministerium für Familie, Senioren, Frauen und Jugend, 2005, and for the Newsletter "Potenziale des Alters": http://www.bmfsfj.de/Politikbereiche/aeltere-menschen,did=65316.html [Date of research: 22.10.2006].

[19] For a detailed debate on "social capital", (Robert Putnam) in the context of social work see Kessl & Otto, 2004; for the interplay of social capital, humane capital and entrepreneurial assets see Deutscher Bundestag, 2002b; for the strategies of the World Bank: http://www1.worldbank.org/ prem/poverty/scapital/home.htm [Date of research: 22.10.2006].

[20] At the end of the project the following *role profiles* were suggested: 1. Supporters and counsellors of existing initiatives, NPOs; 2. Initiators of new projects; 3. Networkers in the voluntary sector; 4. Coordinators and facilitators of senior Expertise-Teams.

[21] 1. Communications; role of consultant, consultancy models; conflict management; group models, group dynamics. 2. Initiating projects and activities. 3. Rhetoric and presentation; 4. Networking in the volunteer sector. 5. Organizational learning; public relations work in the context of local senior Trainer-Teams; self-commitment and self-related communication.

[22] For the ad personam selection, perspectives of self-organization and of team and group work were decisive.

[23] For voluntary engagement and the activating state see Bußmann & Stöbe-Blossey, 2003.

[24] In the first course, 5.3% of the participants were employed, 9.9% unemployed, and 8.6% partly employed (Informationen der wissenschaftlichen Begleitung, Info Nr. 12, p. 5). The report for the first phase of the programme of 2004 (first and second course) notes an increased number of unemployed: "A significant number is unemployed; among the male participants almost every seventh". In the eastern part of Germany the unemployment rate is 18%, in the western part 8% (Braun, Burmeister & Engels 2004, p. 47 et seq.). According to Martin Brussig, Matthias Knuth and Walter Weiß (2006, p. 39) and with reference to the micro census of 1996-2001, 40% of the unemployed people at the age of 50 would like to be employed again, and 80% of the unemployed and ready to work group at the age of 50 to 60 would prefer to be full-time employed.

[25] For a detailed presentation of this complex relationship see Backes, 1998.

[26] See: www.bmfsfj.de/Kategorien/Presse/pressemitteilungen,did=67546,render=renderPrint.html [Date of research: 22.10.2006]

[27] In 2003, for example, only 237 of the 353 applicants could be accepted for the EFI-project (see Braun, Burmeister & Engels, 2004, p. 174 et seq.).

REFERENCES

Aner, K. (2005). *"Ich will, dass etwas geschieht". Wie zivilgesellschaftliches Engagement entsteht – oder auch nicht.* Berlin: Sigma.

Backes, G. M. (1998). Zur Vergesellschaftung des Alter(n)s im Kontext der Modernisierung. In G. M. Backes & W. Clemens (Eds.), *Altern und Gesellschaft. Gesellschaftliche Modernisierung durch Altersstrukturwandel* (pp. 23–60). Opladen: Leske+Budrich.

Backes, G. M., & Clemens, W. (1998). *Lebensphase Alter. Eine Einführung in die sozialwissenschaftliche Alternsforschung.* Weinheim and München: Juventa.

Backes, G. M., & Clemens, W. (Eds.). (1998). *Altern und Gesellschaft. Gesellschaftliche Modernisierung durch Altersstrukturwandel.* Opladen: Leske & Budrich.

Backes, G. M., & Clemens, W. (Eds.). (2002). *Zukunft der Soziologie des Alter(n)s.* Opladen: Leske & Budrich.

Baltes, M. M. (1996). Produktives Leben im Alter: Die vielen Gesichter des Alters – Resumee und Perspektiven für die Zukunft. In M. M. Baltes & L. Montada (Eds.), *Produktives Leben im Alter* (pp. 393–408). (Schriftenreihe/ADIA-Stiftung zur Erforschung Neuer Wege für Arbeit und Soziales Leben Bd. 3). Frankfurt/M and New York: Campus.

Baltes, M. M., Kohli, M., & Sames, K. (Eds.). (1989). *Erfolgreiches Altern. Bedingungen und Variationen.* Bern: Hans Huber.

Baltes, M., & Montada, L. (Eds.). (1996). *Produktives Leben im Alter* (Schriftenreihe/ADIA-Stiftung zur Erforschung Neuer Wege für Arbeit und Soziales Leben; Bd. 3). Frankfurt/M and New York: Campus.

Baltes, P. B., & Baltes, M. M. (1989). Erfolgreiches Altern: Mehr Jahre und mehr Leben. In M. M. Baltes, M. Kohli, & K. Sames (Eds.), *Erfolgreiches Altern. Bedingungen und Variationen* (pp. 5–10). Bern: Hans Huber.

Baltes, P. B., & Baltes, M. M. (1990). Psychological perspectives on successful aging: The model of selective optimization with compensation. In P. B. Baltes & M. M. Baltes (Eds.), *Successful aging: Perspectives from the behavioural sciences* (pp. 1–34). New York: Cambridge University Press.

Baltes, P. B., & Baltes, M. M. (Eds.). (1990). *Successful aging: Perspectives from the behavioural sciences*. New York: Cambridge University Press.

Böhnisch, L., & Schröer, W. (2002). *Die soziale Bürgergesellschaft. Zur Einbindung des Sozialpolitischen in den zivilgesellschaftlichen Diskurs*. Weinheim and München: Juventa.

Braun, J., Burmeister, J., & Engels, D. (Eds.). (2004). *seniorTrainerin: Neue Verantwortungsrolle und Engagement in Kommunen. Bundesmodellprogramm "Erfahrungswissen für Initiativen"*. Bericht zur ersten Programmphase. (ISAB-Schriftenreihe: Berichte aus Forschung und Praxis, Vol. 84). Köln

Bröckling, U. (2000). Totale Mobilmachung. Menschenführung im Qualitäts- und Selbstmanagement. In T. Lemke, S. Krasmann, & U. Bröckling (Eds.), *Gouvernementalität der Gegenwart. Studien zur Ökonomisierung des Sozialen* (pp. 131–167). Frankfurt/M: Suhrkamp.

Brussig, M., Knuth, M., & Weiß, W. (2006). Arbeiten ab 50 in Deutschland. Eine Landkarte der Erwerbstätigkeit auf der Grundlage des Mikrozensus 1996 bis 2001. In Deutsches Zentrum für Altersfragen (Ed.), *Beschäftigungssituation älterer Arbeitnehmer* (Expertisen zum 5. Altenbericht, Vol. 1, pp. 7–51). Berlin: LIT.

Bundesministerium für Familie, Senioren, Frauen und Jugend (BMFSFJ) (Ed.). (2005). *Fünfter Bericht zur Lage der älteren Generation in der Bundesrepublik Deutschland. Potenziale des Alters in Wirtschaft und Gesellschaft. Der Beitrag älterer Menschen zum Zusammenhalt der Generationen*. Bericht der Sachverständigenkommission. Berlin. Retrieved October 22, 2006, from http://www.bmfsfj.de/RedaktionBMFSFJ/Abteilung3/Pdf-Anlagen/fuenfter-altenbericht,property=pdf,bereich=,rwb=true.pdf

Burchell, G., Gordon, C., & Miller, P. (Eds.). (1991). *The Foucault effect. Studies in governmentality*. London: Harvester Wheatsheaf.

Burmeister, J. (2004). Ergebnisse der seniorTrainerinnen-Weiterbildungskonzeption. In ISAB-Berichte aus Forschung und Praxis, Nr. 87 *Halbzeitbilanz und Perspektiven des Modellprogramms "Erfahrungswissen für Initiativen"*. 3. Zentrale EFI-Fachtagung für alle EFI-Akteure vom 21–23 Juni 2004 in Lingen-Holthausen 2004.

Burmeister, J., Heller, A., & Stehr, I. (2004). Weiterbildung älterer Menschen zu seniorTrainerinnen: Rahmencurriculum 2004 im Modellprogramm "Erfahrungswissen für Initiativen" des Bundesministeriums für Familie, Senioren, Frauen und Jugend.

Bußmann, U., & Stöbe-Blossey, S. (2003). Aktivierung von Freiwilligenarbeit als Element eines aktivierenden Staates. In H.-J. Dahme et al. (Eds.), *Soziale Arbeit für den aktivierenden Staat* (pp. 127–147). Opladen: Leske & Budrich.

Dahme, H.-J., Otto, H.-U., Trube, A., & Wohlfahrt, N. (Eds.). (2003). *Soziale Arbeit für den aktivierenden Staat*. Opladen: Leske & Budrich.

Dallinger, U., & Schroeter, K. R. (Eds.). (2002). *Theoretische Beiträge zur Alternssoziologie*. Opladen: Leske & Budrich.

Deutscher Bundestag (Ed.). (2002a). *Herausforderungen unserer älter werdenden Gesellschaft an den Einzelnen und die Politik*. Schlussbericht der Enquête-Kommission "Demographischer Wandel" (BTDS 14/8800).

Deutscher Bundestag (Ed.). (2002b). *Bürgerschaftliches Engagement: auf dem Weg in eine zukunftsfähige Bürgergesellschaft*. Bericht der Enquête-Kommission "Zukunft des Bürgerschaftlichen Engagements". (BTDS 14/8900).

Deutsches Zentrum für Altersfragen (Ed.). (2001). *Lebenslagen, Soziale Ressourcen und gesellschaftliche Integration* (Expertisen zum Dritten Altenbericht der Bundesregierung, Vol. 3). Opladen: Leske & Budrich.

Deutsches Zentrum für Altersfragen (Ed.). (2006). *Beschäftigungssituation älterer Arbeitnehmer* (Expertisen zum 5. Altenbericht, Vol. 1). Berlin: LIT.

Doherty, R. A. (2006). Towards a Governmentality Analysis of Education Policy. In S. Weber & S. Maurer (Eds.), *Gouvernementalität und Erziehungswissenschaft* (pp. 51–61). Wiesbaden: VS.

Dreyfus, H. L., & Rabinow, P. (1982). *Michel Foucault: Beyond structuralism and hermeneutics.* Chicago: University of Chicago Press.

Engels, D., Braun, J., & Burmeister, J. 2000. *Senior*Trainer*innen* und *senior*Kompetenzteams; Erfahrungswissen und Engagement älterer Menschen in einer neuen Verantwortungsrolle. Evaluationsbericht zum Bundesmodellprogramm "Erfahrungswissen für Initiativen". (ISAB-Schriftenreihe: Berichte aus Forschung und Praxis, Vol. 102). Köln.

Engels, D., & Machalowski, G. (2004). *Ergebnisse schriftlicher Befragungen des Instituts für Sozialforschung und Gesellschaftspolitik zwischen September 2003 und März 2004.* Köln.

Foucault, M. (1982). The subject and power. In H. L. Dreyfus & P. Rabinow (Eds.), *Michel Foucault: Beyond structuralism and hermeneutics* (pp. 208–226). Chicago: University of Chicago Press.

Foucault, M. (1996). *Der Mensch ist ein Erfahrungstier. Gespräch mit Ducio Trombadori.* Mit einem Vorwort von Wilhelm Schmid. Frankfurt/M: Suhrkamp.

Foucault, M. (1991). Governmentality. In G. Burchell, C. Gordon, & P. Miller (Eds.), *The Foucault effect. Studies in governmentality* (pp. 87–104). London: Harvester Wheatsheaf.

Glaser, H., & Röbke, T. (Eds.). (1992). *Dem Alter einen Sinn geben. Wie Senioren kulturell aktiv sein können. Beiträge, Beispiele, Adressen.* Heidelberg: Hüthig.

Göckenjan, G. (2000). *Das Alter würdigen. Altersbilder und Bedeutungswandel des Alters.* Frankfurt/M: Suhrkamp.

Institut für sozialwissenschaftliche Analysen und Beratung (Ed.). (2003a). *Informationen der wissenschaftlichen Begleitung 12.*

Institut für sozialwissenschaftliche Analysen und Beratung (Ed.). (2003b). *Informationen der wissenschaftlichen Begleitung. 13.*

Institut für sozialwissenschaftliche Analysen und Beratung (Ed.). (2004). *EFI-Newsletter. 4.*

Institut für sozialwissenschaftliche Analysen und Beratung (Ed.). (2006). *Informationen der wissenschaftlichen Begleitung. 34.*

Internationaler Rat für Soziale Wohlfahrt, Deutscher Verein für öffentliche und private Fürsorge, & Kuratorium Deutsche Altershilfe (Eds.). (2000). *Voluntary engagement by and for very old persons – a european comparision.* Documentation of the conference of experts of the International Council on Social Welfare.

Karl, U. (2005). *Zwischen/Räume: Eine empirisch-bildungstheoretische Studie zur ästhetischen und psychosozialen Praxis des Altentheater.* Münster: LIT.

Karl, U. (2006). Soziale Altenarbeit und Altenbildungsarbeit – vom aktiven zum profilierten, unternehmerischen Selbst. In S. Weber & S. Maurer (Eds.), *Gouvernementalität und Erziehungswissenschaft. Wissen – Macht – Transformation* (pp. 301–319). Wiesbaden: VS.

Katz, S., & Green, B. (2002). The government of detail: The case of social policy on aging. *Journal of Aging and Identity, 7*(3), 149–163.

Kessl, F., & Otto, H.-U. (Eds.). (2004). *Soziale Arbeit und Soziales Kapital. Zur Kritik lokaler Gemeinschaftlichkeit.* Wiesbaden: VS.

Kinsler, M. (2003). Alter – Macht – Kultur. Kulturelle Alterskompetenzen in einer modernen Gesellschaft (Schriften zur Kulturwissenschaft; Bd. 49). Hamburg: Dr. Kovač.

Knopf, D. (2003). Erfahrungswissen nutzen – ein innovativer Bildungsansatz. In ISAB (Ed.), *EFI-Newsletter, 1:* 3–6.

Kolland, F. (1996). *Kulturstile älterer Menschen. Jenseits von Pflicht und Alltag.* Wien, Köln and Weimar: Böhlau.

von Kondratowitz, H. J. (2002). Konjunkturen – Ambivalenzen – Kontingenzen: Diskursanalytische Erbschaften einer historisch-soziologischen Betrachtung des Alter(n)s. In U. Dallinger & K. R. Schroeter (Eds.), *Theoretische Beiträge zur Alternssoziologie* (pp. 113–137). Opladen: Leske & Budrich.

Lemke, T., Krasmann, S., & Bröckling, U. (2000). Gouvernementalität, Neoliberalismus und Selbsttechnologien. In T. Lemke, S. Krasmann, & U. Bröckling (Eds.), *Gouvernementalität der Gegenwart. Studien zur Ökonomisierung des Sozialen* (pp. 7–40). Frankfurt/M: Suhrkamp.

Lemke, T., Krasmann, S., & Bröckling, U. (Eds.). (2000). *Gouvernementalität der Gegenwart. Studien zur Ökonomisierung des Sozialen*. Frankfurt/M: Suhrkamp.

Lenz, K., Rudolph, M., & Sickendieck, U. (1999). Alter und Altern aus sozialgerontologischer Sicht. In K. Lenz, M. Rudolph, & U. Sickendieck (Eds.), *Die alternde Gesellschaft. Problemfelder gesellschaftlichen Umgangs mit Altern und Alter* (pp. 7–96). Weinheim and München: Juventa.

Lenz, K., Rudolph, M., & Sickendieck, U. (Eds.). (1999). *Die alternde Gesellschaft. Problemfelder gesellschaftlichen Umgangs mit Altern und Alter*. Weinheim and München: Juventa.

Mayer, M. (2004). Vom Versprechen lokaler Kohäsion. Blindstellen in der internationalen Debatte. In F. Kessl & H.-U. Otto (Eds.), *Soziale Arbeit und Soziales Kapital. Zur Kritik lokaler Gemeinschaftlichkeit* (pp. 63–78). Wiesbaden: VS.

Miller, P., & Rose, N. (1992). Political power beyond the state: Problematics of government. *British Journal of Sociology, 43*(2), 172–205.

Naegele, G., & Tews, H. P. (Eds.). (1993). *Lebenslagen im Strukturwandel des Alters. Alternde Gesellschaft – Folgen für die Politik*. Opladen: Westdeutscher Verlag.

Powell, J. L., & Edwards, M. M. (2002). Policy narratives of aging: The right way, the third way or the wrong way? *Electronic Journal of Sociology* (ISSN: 1198 3655).

Powell, J. L., & Biggs, S. (2003). Foucauldian gerontology: A methology for understanding aging. *Electronic Journal of Sociology* (ISSN: 1198 3655).

Peters, M. (2001). Education, enterprise culture and the entrepreneurial self: A foucauldian perspective. *Journal of Educational Enquiry, 2*(2), 58–71.

Rauschenbach, T. (1995). Sozialengagement zwischen gestern und morgen. Das soziale Ehrenamt auf dem Prüfstand. *aej-Studientexte, 2*, 25–41.

Schroeter, K. R. (2002). Zur Allodoxie des "erfolgreichen" und "produktiven Alterns". In G. M. Backes & W. Clemens (Eds.), *Zukunft der Soziologie des Alter(n)s* (pp. 85–107). Opladen: Leske & Budrich.

Smith, J. D., & Gay, P. (2005). *Active ageing in active communities*. Bristol, Avon: The Policy Press.

Tews, H. P. (1993). Neue und alte Aspekte des Strukturwandels des Alters. In G. Naegele & H. P. Tews (Eds.), *Lebenslagen im Strukturwandel des Alters. Alternde Gesellschaft – Folgen für die Politik* (pp. 15–42). Opladen: Westdeutscher Verlag.

Tews, H. P. (1996). Produktivität des Alters. In M. Baltes & L. Montada (Eds.), *Produktives Leben im Alter* (Schriftenreihe/ADIA-Stiftung zur Erforschung Neuer Wege für Arbeit und Soziales Leben; Bd. 3, pp. 184–210). Frankfurt/M and New York: Campus.

Tews, H. P. (2000). Introductory speech on the subject of old age. In Internationaler Rat für Soziale Wohlfahrt, Deutscher Verein für öffentliche und private Fürsorge, & Kuratorium Deutsche Altershilfe (Eds.), *Voluntary engagement by and for very old persons – a european comparision* (pp. 74–83). Documentation of the conference of experts of the International Council on Social Welfare.

Tokarski, W. (1998). Alterswandel und veränderte Lebensstile. In G. M. Backes & W. Clemens (Eds.), *Altern und Gesellschaft. Gesellschaftliche Modernisierung durch Altersstrukturwandel* (pp. 109–119). Opladen: Leske and Budrich.

Weber, S., & Maurer, S. (Eds.). (2006). *Gouvernementalität und Erziehungswissenschaft. Wissen – Macht – Transformation*. Wiesbaden: VS.

Wessels, C. (1994). *Das soziale Ehrenamt im Modernisierungsprozeß. Chancen und Risiken des Einsatzes beruflich qualifizierter Frauen.* Pfaffenweiler: Centaurus.

World Health Orgaization. (2002). *Active ageing. A policy framework.* Madrid.

Zeman, P., & Schmidt, R. (2001). Soziale Altenarbeit – Strukturen und Entwicklungslinien. In Deutsches Zentrum für Altersfragen (Ed.), *Lebenslagen, Soziale Ressourcen und gesellschaftliche Integration* (Expertisen zum Dritten Altenbericht der Bundesregierung, Vol. 3, pp. 235–277). Opladen: Leske & Budrich.

*All translations of quoted German texts by Dieter Keiner.

Ute Karl
Institute for Social and Organizational Pedagogy
University of Hildesheim
Germany

SUSANNE MARIA WEBER

25. FREE PLAY OF FORCES AND PROCEDURAL CREATION OF ORDER: THE DISPOSITIVE OF DEMOCRACY IN ORGANIZATIONAL CHANGE

Today, participatory pedagogical learning arrangements can be found in all social fields of action. Throughout all sub-disciplines of educational science, there emerges a program and practice of particular forms of learning which is proactive, democratic, participatory and knowledge-generating, and it emerges within an innovative type of event that is skillfully designed to address methodic-didactic issues and to activate resources (Weber, 2005a). In educational science debates, these forms of learning are addressed as part of a new "culture of learning" (Arnold & Schüssler, 1998), of "network learning" (Siebert, 2003), of professional and vocational education (Dobischat & Husemann 1997), of citizens' participation in civil society (Elsen, 2000) within community work (Lüttringhaus, 2003) or organizational development (Senge, 1996) as well as of "learning regions" (Matthiesen & Reutter, 2003) and the transformational society (Schäffter 2001a; 2001b).

Those practices of participatory and transformational procedures give insight in an educational rationality, we not only can observe today taking place in contexts of organizational transformation. In a historical perspective, we can start from the organizational practice of a reform-pedagogical and basic-democracy experiment, the children's home Kinderheim Baumgarten, which was established by Siegfried Bernfeld, a Jewish socialist, activist and educator in the 1920's. It will become clear that this democracy based concept of community development over time will combine with other rationalities and shift into an improvisational technology within organizational development.

Let us start out with the pedagogical learning arrangements today and the state of the debate within educational sciences. It will be shown that the discussion of new pedagogical learning arrangements is based on the certainty of uncertainty: the uncertainty of the situation, the development, of possible directions; the uncertainty about what could be objects of learning, what they could represent for learners and what could be the right knowledge under today's conditions. One thing is evident: moments of certainty are increasingly hard to find.

M.A. Peters et al. (eds.), Governmentality Studies in Education, 453–472.

NEW PEDAGOGICAL LEARNING ARRANGEMENTS IN TIMES OF UNCERTAINTY AND TRANSFORMATION

The pedagogical element today has to be analysed in areas that are structured contradictorily, that become the "challenge and defining mark of pedagogically oriented design and of reflection in educational science" (Helsper, Hörster & Kade 2003, p. 8). Instead of "unequivocal orientation and stable behavioural patterns" we find "dynamic mixes of certainty and uncertainty, of knowing and not knowing, of security and insecurity". In new pedagogical arrangements pedagogical fields become unclear. Borders come out of focus, new interspersions and new boundaries appear (ibid., p. 18).

Transformation represents a diagnosis of the present that embraces uncertainty as a category of pedagogy and educational science and opens a connection to questions of methodical-didactical learning arrangements (Schäffter 2001a; 2001b). The transformational society is characterized by fields of uncertainty and degrees of uncertainty that, in relation to the original situation and the objective of processes of learning and transformation, produce variations of non-transparency and make different forms of planning and control necessary. Accordingly, transformational patterns change but transformation per se remains structurally uncertain.[1]

As opposed to linear models of transformation, a reflexive model assumes that learning has to be accompanied by continuous self-ascertainment since from a point of departure that is unknown and demands definition, a reflective process of permanent change runs a course whose goal is open and that will never reach an end but will, in principle, remain in demand of a definition. Points of departure as well as points of arrival of interventions lie within the area of not-knowing, and thus need a process of self-ascertainment. Particularly in view of possible futures, transformation remains a process that cannot be completed. For this reason the organization of learning is drawn into an unending iteration of permanent change and self-guided learning as well as nurturing support "accompanying the development" of the learner.[2] Nurturing and developing become pedagogical rationality and government practice (Weber, 1998; 2000a), aiming at subjects as well as at organizations as collective subjects that are given over to learning. This becomes evident in the programmatic approach to the learning organization (Senge, 1996; Weber, 2005a). Interactive didactic arrangements now address subjects and organizations in all social fields of action. The central principles of such procedures dealing with learning organizations (Königswieser, 2000, p. 43) and network learning in transformational contexts will be presented first, in order to explain the mode and rationality of those methods.

In the mid-1990's, approaches to collective learning known as Large Group Interventions became popular in German-speaking countries. They can be regarded as rituals of transformation because the practice they utilize is generative, community-building, and symbolic; as transitional spaces on the way to the new (Weber, 2005a), because as didactic arrangements they assume uncertainty and open transformation for the initial situation as well as for the objective. They start with the analysis of the present that is yet to be defined and design futures which are also yet to be defined, within a planned process of dialogic self-ascertainment.

Aided by principles of system and field orientation, of solution and future orientation, of participation and collective resource development, they attempt to strengthen individual and collective responsibility and to promote joint development of new solutions. From a reflexive, transformation-theoretical perspective they are, in this sense, forms of network learning and network events.

As a practical convention, it has been agreed on defining Large Group Interventions by group size, i.e. using this term on collective, interactive approaches that work with groups from 30 people up (Königswieser & Keil, 2000). The best-known approaches in Germany are 'Open Space Technology' (OST), "Appreciative Inquiry Summit" (AI), the 'Future Search Conference' and 'Real Time Strategic Change' (RTSC) (Weber, 2000b). The working of Large Group Interventions can be described by the principles of self-organization, community-building and system learning. The approaches refer back to a variety of theories but they all are dialogic practices by design. The following sections will offer an outline of their central principles – self-organization, the community of experts and the learning laboratory, followed by a trip back in time in order to rediscover in another place the rationality here employed.

Self-organized Processes of Education by Means of Learning from Experience in a "Free Play" of Powers

Large Group Interventions are generally interactively and not frontally designed events; they are always about making room for knowledge in all its variations and diversity. Knowledge is not addressed as something to be transmitted but as something pre-existent and pervasive that is to be generated collectively. Their hallmark is that they do not start out from what is known for certain but from what is not known. For this reason they all begin by establishing that which is. Their starting point is irritation, for example, at the entrance to an event like this you might find a poster telling you: "Be prepared to be surprised!"

Knowledge and understanding are conceived as something to be generated by one's own initiative. 'Open Space' (Owen 1997; 2001) may serve as an example for a minimalist learning arrangement with a well-developed sense of self-organization.[3] All in all, volition is seen as the precondition for participation. The rules of the game generalize the principle of freedom. Every participant is thrown back on her own responsibility for the design of the self and the situation. The intervention aims at (self-)formation and the level of learning that can be called a self-relatedness in dealing with power, authority, self and the design of 'open' situations and themes. It is expected that just participating in such an event can bring about a personal transformation on the level of one's own learning attitude and reflexivity. Owen points out that control is not desirable because it stymies learning. Life without limitations, on the other hand, produces new problems. Chaos as a starting point leads to learning (Owen 2000). Within the mode of learning by experience, taking responsibility for oneself is mediated by the design of minimalist learning arrangements. As a context for learning on one's own, this model consciously follows a non-interventionist design. In 'Open Space' there should be no moderation of the process, just somebody who accompanies the process, who keeps the space open and protects the group from individual strategies of dominance. This mostly symbolic function of keeping the space open reduces the role of the supervisor to an energetic function of strong presence and greatest invisibility. According to its fundamental principles then, the design of this intervention is egalitarian and dialogic. Everything is permitted with the exception of dominating the open space. Institutional power, hierarchies and positions are neither reflected by the event's social space, nor are they represented on its stage – forms of heteronomy by formal structures, hierarchies, and institutional power do not have a formally designated status here. Large Group Interventions open up the space to new experimental and alternative practices of the generation of knowledge and the constitution of norms.

Forces should unfold freely and learning should organize itself – although this takes place within a formally defined event framework – according to the mode of informal learning and game playing. Self-organization in this context means to choose themes and groups entirely freely, even to decide whether one wishes to work thematically at all. Learning should follow subjective intrinsic interests and self-motivation, under the motto: whoever feels 'passion and responsibility' for themes and contents will champion them (Owen 2001; 1997). "Commitment, performance, and excellence only emerge when the heart is engaged meaningfully, and that is called passion" (Owen, 1997, p. 27). The principle of the energetic game and of passionate commitment is tied to the principle of responsibility as an individual and collective project. "Having fun and doing something useful" are construed not as contradictory but as forming a connection full of tension and productivity (ibid., p. 28). Following from the basic assumption that interpretations of a problematic "status quo" reflect subjective experiences and thus necessarily differ, a collective dialogic process is needed. Especially 'Open Space' (Owen, 1997; 2001) explicitly promotes the principle of constituting a community of responsibility which shapes itself from chaos to order during the process as a 'chaordic organization.'

Dialogic Constitution of the Collective Community of Responsibility

Large Group Interventions are based on the premise of complex problems that build at the borders and along management gaps of organizations. Unlike classic approaches that remain within predefined borders, these procedures with their principles of systemic intervention aim at getting the system into one space, addressing the variety of participant perspectives, expertise, concerns and needs in order to work out sustainable solutions.

Thus Large Group Interventions generally work with the circle that surrounds the theme as the spatial structure of the learning arrangement. The borders of the system are no longer determined by the borders of the organization. It is rather the interfaces and transitions at the institutional borders which are criteria for the spatial structure, in order to facilitate complex strategies of problem-solving. They are sometimes systematically and methodically included and prescribed in seating arrangements.[4] The small circles of chairs or the large plenary circle make it clear that not a single speaker is addressing the masses but that the individual members are talking to each other and with each other. The criteria for participation is concern with and a stake in the theme, it is the thematic involvement, the appropriateness to the subject, personal concern and individual commitment.

These events are experience-oriented and knowledge-generating and they do not address individual participants but the group, the collective community of responsibility that is made up of (partial) experts for the problem at hand.[5]

The methodical principle that is expressed in these procedures can be called a dialogic search within the community of responsibility. Disciplinary and subjective fragmentation of knowledge is to be de-fragmented by a dialogic communication style (Bohm, 1998) which is contrary to the communicative style of discussion (literally, shattering, dividing, taking apart). By dealing with the preceding assumptions behind statements, the ability to create something new is promoted. Isaacs, head of the dialogue project at MIT, Boston, sees the use of the dialogic approach for the development of the learning organization in the fact that it employs collective intelligence (Hartkemeyer, Hartkemeyer & Dhority, 1998).

Constitution and Declaration of Norms in the Process of the "Learning Laboratory"

The mode of learning by experience as a collective project utilizes experimental and game elements. Imagination and ideas are to create 'concrete utopias' that can be realized. Visions and possible futures are sketched out to create a 'pull' into the future. The way the problems are dealt with is on the one hand creative, playful, and constructive. The practical elements of the generative game, on the other hand, achieve a connection to a systematizing analysis. The designs of the interventions themselves follow the principle of systematic testing, starting out from problems at hand, analyzing them collectively, and systematically looking for alternative actions.

In a planned and systematic way, a topic is worked on which constitutes itself as a problem without borders, as a concern that transcends cross sections and systems borders and in which a large number of actors have to be involved in order to find reasonable solutions. Starting from a not-knowing stance, the sounding out and the analysis of what 'is' takes up a lot of space, before the development of solutions and futures is made an issue. Learning is conceptualized systematically in so far as the problem, alternative solutions and agreements for the future are designed in a process. The planning mode is iterative – not a master plan for the future is created, but the future has to be designed along the lines of problems at hand that have to be managed and solved. Agreements on how to proceed further and how to deal with the problems that arise throughout the process are addressed in the mode of the democratic community of responsibility as a project of learning and of collective problem solving.[6] The interventions are explicitly termed 'learning laboratory' (Weisbord & Janoff, 2001; 2000; 1995).

This process of collective norm constitution is not about changing individual actors but about improving the options for action of entire fields. Nothing is prescribed from above, instead a normalizing practice is put in place. The dialogic community of responsibility communicates the norm-building process and the agreements that are reached as the application of norms and in this way has an effect on the field, in a practice that does not pursue the individual with orders or advice but works, by the principle of collective insight, towards sensible solutions that are supported by everybody. The validity of norms is related to a norm-reflective practice. The rationality apparent in Large Group Interventions is a norm-constituting as well as norm-declarative practice. These interventions provide a stage and a staging practice for new norm validity, they create a new symbolic order of action in community. As rituals of transformation (Weber, 2005a) their operation is expressive, dramatizing and quite emotionalizing. Interventions take place on the level of metaphors that systematically generate actions (Barrett & Cooperrider, 1990; Hammond & Royal, 1998). In such rituals of transformation – which are by no means just reproductive but mainly generative – organizations are staged and generated as informal communities. Interventions take place on the level of metaphors that systematically generate actions (Barrett & Cooperrider, 1990; Hammond & Royal, 1998).

In these approaches, a democratic rationality is employed which is based on processes of self-organization, of collective formation of experience and its systematic evaluation and re-evaluation, and on procedural norm-constitution. This type of government will now be analyzed in a completely different setting. Taking a trip through time – to the 1920's and the *Kinderheim Baumgarten* experiment that took place in a reform-pedagogical setting – we will undertake a reconstruction of the democratic rationality within the dispositive of the school community.

THE NEW, THE COMMUNITY, DEMOCRACY: COMMUNITY- AND SELF-EDUCATION IN THE *KINDERHEIM BAUMGARTEN* EXPERIMENT

The following, genealogical view is concerned with the practice of community- and self-education within the socio-pedagogical experiment *Kinderheim Baumgarten* in the 1920's. In this way we can take a look at the alternative rationality and the mode of government that were practiced here, from the other end of the time line.

"... A new kind of Disciplinary Guidance": Self-organization and Co-determination as an Alternative Practice of Government

As a socio-pedagogical experiment, the *Kinderheim Baumgarten* attempts something new. The "most prominent feature of our school is a serious and extensive design for a novel interaction between the adults (teachers) and the children" (Bernfeld, 1921, p. 40). Bernfeld's school community experiments with an alternative pedagogical practice, an alternative rationality of action, an alternative social space (Hörster, 1997). "Characteristic for the socio-pedagogical experiment is that we did not start out from order" (Bernfeld, 1921, p. 109). Bernfeld's "fact-mindedness" is determined by a procedural production of order:

> Order not as an unmotivated demand enforced by the principal who happens to possess the power to demand and enforce, but as an expression of a progressively more civilized, more enlightened community of adolescents and young adults (Bernfeld, 1927, p. 109 et seq., quoted by Hörster, 1992, p. 150).

The school community should run on self-organization and co-determination. Bernfeld himself sees the term school community as a

> name for a new kind of disciplinary guidance, ... which wants to substitute the authoritarian system of punishment, reward, prescription and proscription by students' co-administration, co-determination as far as the school order and the discipline and life of the students are concerned. This system is called student self-management (Bernfeld, 1928, p. 940, quoted by Hörster, 1992, p. 151).

In Bernfeld's attempt to create openness, "the masses" are educated "... only by themselves, by the life that surrounds them and the way it is structured" (ibid.), here the "new educator's course of action is the relinquishment of action" (Bernfeld, 1921, p. 108).

Constitution of Norms and Formation of Will

A different rationality is put up against an authoritarian or agitating and manipulative[7] approach. Bernfeld tells us about the indescribable chaos ruling the first days and weeks: "Chaos has always come prior to creation, and it is certainly a test of talent for the organizing pedagogue whether or not he has the courage to allow this chaos" (ibid., p. 50 et seq.). In the beginning there are no rules for communal life, they are to be set collectively. A different way of dealing with time and social constellations has to accompany this approach:

> We would all assemble weekly, on the same day, and that would be called the school community. Whenever anyone had a problem with anything, this assembly would be the place to speak up (ibid., p. 56).

To allow a procedural creation of order, spontaneous, every-day situations are treated as sources of productivity.[8] "Slowly, very slowly but just as noticeably, order and quiet was established in the dining-hall, spreading in concentric circles from certain points, those places where the teachers were sitting" (ibid., 36). Step by step catalogues of rules are developed from the "chaos" and the experience of pressing problems. They lead to the establishment of institutions and procedures, like schedules for the dining-hall, rotational schedules for tasks and responsibilities and the like. Within the forum of the school community sessions, a remarkable number of laws and rules are established that order the children's lives (ibid., p. 62) and that, at the same time, make it manageable democratically (Hörster, 1992).

Field interventions and the Creation of a new Social Place

There are weekly 'court' sessions on the inhabitants' behavior. Court is formed by a pupils' association, the secretary of the school community and Bernfeld as chairman (Bernfeld, 1921, p. 59). Plaintiffs appear before the full assembly, defendants have an opportunity to represent their side, and witnesses are heard. After the hearing, the court meets behind closed doors to discuss the case. Bernfeld casts his vote last, the majority rules. Then the verdict is presented by the chairman in the court room where the benches are filled with residents of the *Kinderheim Baumgarten*. Quasi-theatrical stagings also have their place here. Zander (1992) compares the school community to a theater, a moral institution of cleansing and catharsis and last but not least of thrill for the spectators: by norm-constituting as well as theatrical practice, not only the individual's behavior is corrected, but a field is designed. The effect of the presentation is aimed not so much at those directly concerned but rather at the emotions of those who participate in the presentation. Zander sees the stuff of myths and fables at work here, not that of the logos.

Bernfeld sees the educational institution, on the one hand, as the "living and acting space of a libidinously connected group of leader and followers" (Bernfeld, 1928, p. 456, quoted by Hörster, 1992, p. 158). This, on the other hand, stands in "correlation and association to the democratic principle of will-formation in the school community" (ibid.). The developing order is a constitutive "expression of affect and mind-set" (ibid., p. 150).

The school community becomes the organization of the "pedagogical mind-set of compromise" (Bernfeld, 1921, p. 52), mediating in the "antinomy between the justified will of the child and the justified will of the teacher" (ibid., p. 52 et seq.) and seeking an "equilibrium of currents between parts of the masses, between masses and leader".

Active communicative processes are opened up instead of ordained from without, what is normal is not predefined but created as an alternative social place (Hörster & Müller, 1996). A pedagogy that emancipates and explains status instead of producing power-knowledge is to be brought to life here, designing a new social place of education in the process (Müller, 1992).

Approaches in a socio-pedagogical discourse "first and foremost aim at creating living conditions that give individuals not only existential security but avenues of learning and development that lead to a self-determined life" (ibid., p. 68 et seq.). The experiment creates a new social place that can provide counter-experiences to an outer or inner reality and that finds a position of compromise between the justified will of the child and the justified will of the teacher within the framework of the school community. "The socio-pedagogical task would be to create the possibility of a formative life" in this design (ibid., p. 69). Socio-pedagogical interventions are not aimed directly at the individual but at the socio-pedagogical field. In openly structured beginnings of social education, new 'social places' (Bernfeld, 1921) and a 'nurturing environment' (Winnicott, 1995) become a possibility.

THE SCHOOL COMMUNITY AS A DIAGRAM OF DEMOCRATIC WILL-FORMATION

This social education experiment differs from other social reform measures with utopian ambitions by its diagrammatic regulation (Hörster, 1992). A diagram is a map, a formula, a design which is temporalized within a normative context or a dispositive, thus making it possible to work on it socially or educationally. A diagram is a power mechanism reduced to its ideal form, an "internalized model of a function, which defines the relationship between power and people's daily lives" and which can block or facilitate people's positioning within the real relationships, the social structures mentioned above (ibid., p. 154). Strategic analyses of a discourse-analytical program are descriptions of the diagram "intricately tied up between process maintenance and process transformation" (Foucault, 1992, p. 39).

The alternative practice of the school community is a "special form of administration and organization of pupils' lives" (Hörster, 1992, p. 152 et seq.) that is different from a juridical or socio-disciplinary practice of intervention or rationality. How the beginnings are designed within a pedagogical context, shows that this reform-pedagogical concept follows a normalizing rationality (Hörster & Müller, 1996).

Normalizing Rationality: Norm Constitution and Declaration as Naming Practice

From a discourse-analytical point of view the school community works as a naming practice. Rules are generated as part of a process and they are directed at problems. They declare themselves vis-à-vis the members, according to their relation to the matter at hand and to the sense they make, as "sensible rules" in a manner that "makes it possible to manage the social problems created by disorder democratically and at the same pace as they arise" (Hörster 1992: 154). By "declaratively creating normality by constituting a norm", the school community generates and reproduces itself as a place of democratic will-formation (ibid., p. 152).

Using the violation of the norm-to-be, the regulating function of the norm can be clarified and declared. Not so much the violator of the norm is the focal point but rather the witnesses, the addressees of the declaration. By declaratively displaying the transgression in the stage setting of the collective tribunal's court rulings, these stagings have a normalizing effect on the spectators. They point out the deviation and thus create normality. The obligation is placed on the school community, the organization of pedagogical compromise-mindedness in which the respective norms are created, declared and accepted. As a place of norm constitution the school community becomes educationally effective (Hörster, 1992). The order established throughout the process is an "expression of affect and mind-set" (Bernfeld, 1921, p. 110, quoted by Hörster, 1992, p. 150).

The active process of communication is the beginning of social education because it is not prescribed from without; normality is not imposed but created. The school community proves to be a monument in a Foucauldian sense because as a diagram of a specific handling of the pedagogic antinomy between leader-followers and democratic will-formation it can be passed down and generalized socially (Hörster, 1992, p. 154).

Normalizing Rationality as a 'Program of Action' for Social Generalization

Bernfeld writes his essay on the school community as a "program of action" (Bernfeld, 1921, p. 12), i.e. his objective is the social generalization of the school community as an "educational principle", he wants to make it the "general form of organization in all of the educational fields" (Bernfeld, 1928, quoted by Hörster, 1992, p. 156). It is supposed to assume a central role in economic and methodic regulation, and so he elevates it to the position of a procedural norm. He sees this approach of democratic discipline as one whose rationality can be fused with other forms of discipline:

> The democratic discipline allows for the incorporation of the advantages of other forms of discipline, limited to their fields. It is diverse and avoids being just rational or just irrational; at the same time it remains a pure form complete in itself – while the introduction of irrational facts in the military or of rational facts in the familial discipline, almost unavoidably leads to an increase in hidden despotism. (Bernfeld, 1927, p. 233, quoted by Hörster, 1992, p. 159)

The democratic community of education as a type of government works in the mode of procedural norm constitution and links the "(self-)production of the subject to government goals" (Lemke, Krasmann & Bröckling, 2000, p. 29). The school community as a dispositive of the democratic community is an experiment, a living, concrete utopia. From a discourse-analytical perspective though, it is impossible to grasp it unfragmented in its utopian quality. Since the discourse has no 'outside,' utopias can only be analyzed as 'heterotopias' expressing utopias (Foucault, 2005; Hörster, 1997). For this reason, the following section looks at the 'school community dispositive' as a heterotopia that fuses with other rationalities along the "timeline of transformation".

ALONG THE TIMELINE OF TRANSFORMATION: THE SCHOOL COMMUNITY DISPOSITIVE AS A HETEROTOPIA

The experiment of the alternative social space is an object of discourse and entwined with a discursive practice, in spaces that are created throughout the active process of the constitution of knowledge, as spaces for storing and positioning as an outer space, a space "including the real, the effective places inscribed in the institutions of society" (Hörster, 1997, p. 102). "Space for Foucault equals the possibility to structure contexts of action" (ibid., p. 106). Utopian designs such as the democratic community are, as a "speech on utopias", objects of the discourse. They appear as reflections, as "different places", as "mirror images of utopias", as "heterotopias" (ibid., p. 110). Just as a mirror shows me in a virtual point where I am not, heterotopias reflect utopias in the discursive structure. In the "utopia of the mirror" the mirror actually, really exists, and it is a heterotopia (ibid., p. 107).

As Bernfeld works towards the social generalization of the school community as an "educational principle", the school community dispositive experiences its own social generalization. This can serve the establishment of order (Hörster, 1992, p. 157 et seq.). But the dispositive of this procedural norm does not follow a rigid trajectory; it works with "variable creativity". What constitutes the school community as an experimental practice is, anyway, the orientation towards the new. The design of the school community will provide a starting point for the realization of educational elements of a transitory society – while crossing over to a new level of existence.[9] Since the heterotopological instrument has its function rather in the analysis of real relationships, as they can be found in the complementary space of society (Hörster, 1997), the following section will address the topic of the school community diagram, its transformation and displacement. In other words, it deals with the transformation of the dispositive during the "cycle of positivity", the transition from the "fact of acceptance to a system of acceptability" (Foucault, 1992, p. 34).

On the level of primary social relations, a program that is oriented towards uncertainty, complexity and process, an institutional practice can be identified, in which the dispositive of democratic will-formation can be fused or interfaced with other rationalities. It leads into a program for dealing with a given complexity and uncertainty in an adequate fashion, thus entering into an existence as functional knowledge.

FROM EXPERIMENT TO IMPROVISATIONAL TECHNOLOGY[10]

Starting from a singular experiment that can be observed in the *Kinderheim Baumgarten*, the dispositive presents itself as a planned, method-infused, temporally and organizationally limited mode which incorporates itself in other structures and compensates for the weaknesses and shortcomings of the hierarchical, authoritarian governmental rationality. Here we encounter the system of acceptability, in the establishment of the problem of uncertainty as an epochal economic challenge.

A new era is dawning, bringing with it challenges that most companies are as yet unable to face. Whoever attempts to solve the increasingly complex problems of economy and society with outdated methods of management, will fail! What kind of difficulties does a non-transparent environment pose – for the individual, for companies, organizations and for society as a whole? What possibilities are there to face these difficulties with success? Management by complexity is the answer to these questions (Ahlmeyer & Königswieser, 1997).

"Management **by** complexity" is regarded by representatives of systemic transformations of organizations as much more adequate to the problem than "management **of** complexity" that tries to rule complexity, non-transparence and impossibility of guidance by "domination". Instead one tries to establish a field of "structural tension" and "variable response".

"Management of complexity cannot mean solving the problem of complexity once and for all. It has to mean building the problem of complexity in such a way, structuring it in such a way that it continuously solves itself and simultaneously rebuilds itself. It is about building structural tension into the organization which allows the organization, in face of its own complexity and that of its environment, to choose different reductions all the time, thus reacting in a complex fashion." (Baecker, 1999, p. 171).

Complexity should not be regarded as a problem or a solution but "as the shape of the world itself" and as "the way the world handles itself" (Baecker, 1997, p. 21 et seq.). In this way, organization is turned into the field "where impediments to action can be used to generate action" (Baecker, 1999).

Uncertainty is viewed as a new opportunity, a new horizon on which strategies for the creation of certainty can be employed. Uncertainty and its potential put the event, the possibility, the surprise into focus. Thinking in uncertainty is a radical thinking of "perhaps", of the possible-impossible which is not yet integrated in the horizon of knowledge (Helsper, Hörster & Kade, 2003, p. 10). The "creative, emergent potential of uncertainty" is seen as a "place for the creation of the new" (ibid., p. 16).

The "Productivation" of the Experimental Democracy

The rationality that is expressed in Large Group Interventions is based on the productive force not of order but of chaos. Openness or the opening of the space as a starting point for self-organization and dialogue facilitates re-combinations and new patterns of order for knowledge. Encounters and relations that are energetically self-guiding and self-regulating provide a framework and a context for the *free play* of forces in Large Group Interventions (Burow, 2000, p. 71).

Creative fields are characterized by a mutual interest (product-orientation), by a multitude of different skill profiles (diversity and personnel-centeredness), by a concentration on unfolding the common creativity (synergetic process), by equal participation without paternalism by 'experts' and by a social and ecological environment that promotes creativity (sustainability). (Burow, 1999, p. 123).

Here as well, a problem in the process of action is usually used as a starting point for learning by dealing with and working on the problem. The type of rationality implied in e.g. 'Open Space' systematically works with openness and an open beginning.

Apart from the practice of game playing, the experience of those involved is systematically used for experimenting. The mode of intellectual problem solving is supposed to be based on the complexity of concrete problems, problems and situations stemming from real-life cases. Part of a casuistic productivity are, for Hörster (2003, p. 319).

Those activities of deliberation which make it possible to experience a special situation (a case) of crisis or conflict that is morally significant and burdened by uncertainty, in such a way that its contents remains relevant for a practical solution or for practical decision making.

Situations of conflict are then discussed in a situation of practical learning instead of being argued and concluded theoretically. The "network of thinking" starts out "from the specifics of a case that has been experienced to arrive at a practical argumentation" (ibid.). In this way, a practical, substantial cognitive and problem-solving mode is not only permitted but privileged.

This mode has uncertainty at its basis and establishes a relationship to the world and the self that is characterized by research and by discovery. In the governmental type of democratized expertise, the search for solutions is cooperative and experimental. The problem itself is the starting point for the process of problem solving, which is infinite and procedurally open since new problems pose themselves for further deliberation during the process. According to Dewey (1949) this practice develops the process of civilization by systematic employment of a rationality of the commonwealth. He regards local communities as the birthplace of democracy; refunding political action in a democratic, epistemic fashion and thus causing the transformation of the Great Society into the great community (Jörke, 2003). Politics as cooperative, problem-solving actions are methodically realized through social inquiry. The method of learning by experience in the sense of systematic evaluation is expected to facilitate intelligent growth in democratic communities. This method is particularly marked by its experimental, research character, which can be determined by three elements:

Experimenting as an open activity that achieves certain changes in the environment or in our relation to it.

The experiment as an activity guided by ideas that have to be adequate to the conditions demanded by the problem that has initiated the research process.

This guided activity creates a new empirical situation in which objects are related to each other in a specific way: the consequences of the guided actions become the objects which have the characteristic of being recognized (Dewey, 1998, p. 89).

While the *Kinderheim Baumgarten* is a social experiment that generates the new and aims at creating a different social place for the pupils, Large Group Interventions develop the experimental practice methodically and its procedures can be separated from the situation to be integrated in different institutional contexts. The rationality of experimental democracy can now be employed *technologically* in order to balance the shortcomings of the hierarchical, segmented and static organization (Weber, 1998) and as a transitory space for the transformation into the new. For this objective it integrates the rationality of the game, the experiment and the dialogue as systematic procedures for the generation of knowledge and for problem solving.

Norm Constitution in Transitory Spaces that Stage Democracy

In the social process of education the Normal is constituted as a norm formation that is represented in the fact of living together and is maintained by the group in symbolic reference to equality. The pupils of social education are involved in its creation. Their participation has an educational effect and contributes to the creation of the Normal since the constitution of norms becomes intelligible to the participants, and in a self-regulating fashion structures the chaos that they had been suffering from" (Hörster & Müller, 1996, p. 631).

The democratic diagram of the constitutive creation of order as a normalizing practice is maintained in its normalizing function but it changes its place, from being an experiment to being a transitional space that stages democracy and to being a generatively designed ritual of transformation (Weber, 2005a). Embedded in an existence that has been made methodical, temporal, transitive and organizationally nested, the dispositive of democracy remains exposed to the anterior social places, and as a technology it risks being functionalized – e.g. by tilting towards the libidinously charged group of leader-followers that Bernfeld had already discussed as problematic. The employment of the technology and the question whether a legitimizing or an innovative function is to be its main feature, is now uncertain.

Field Interventions: Normalization as Naming Practice

The mode of normalization as naming practice that intervenes in the field of the spectators, the observers, the participants, is kept in the practice of Large Group Interventions. But where in the school community activity may only be directed from within the group of pupils, some method-infused variations of the democratic rationality are open to the risk of manipulative influence from without.[11] This possibility appears as a staged ritualistic practice in the context of Large Group Interventions: the staging lets the emotional amplitude grow exponentially and creates contagious emotions, suggestibility, enthusiasm, fascination, readiness to love or to hate. The dynamic that is at work here turns the system into a wave, into motion, it produces transformational energy. On the other hand, the "risk of regression" that recreates the "primal horde" is never far (Boos & Königswieser, 2000, p. 24 et seq.). The reason given for having interventions like this is that people "hunger for sensuality" (Königswieser, 2000, p. 35). "Complex contents" become "intelligible" and "the hearts" are opened. In a public, participatory event, the message that one is needed can be conveyed much better and more strongly. Messages (or myths) – e.g. "We're all in the same boat" – are made credible, since management and staff come together at one table. The credibility of management increases, while at the same time the place in the community fosters self-assurance and creates motivation (ibid.). To give living examples of values leaves traces in the entire system (Königswieser, 2000). Normalization also works via mimetic practice as the educators in the *Kinderheim Baumgarten* have shown – their character is not manipulative but norm-constitutive.

Bernfeld points to the entanglement of bourgeois pedagogy and social power relations. Social pedagogy must always deal with stronger forces, pedagogues are systematically relegated to particular social places within whose boundaries they have to stay and act. This defines what pedagogic action is and can be (Müller, 1992). Opportunity for the addressees of pedagogic action opens up when their social place is changed.

The transformation-theoretical perspective holds that in a transformational society, uncertainty is permanent (Schäffter, 2001a; 2001b). In a reflexive transformational model, learning has to take place in constant self-ascertainment. Starting point and objective both are unknown and have to be defined. The temporalized school community is a transitional ritual and a transitive space. It takes a methodical approach to the way in which uncertainty is productively dealt with and connects the democratic dispositive with an educational mode that increases performance.

	Experimental democracy	Improvisational technology
Finality	Democracy as experimental experience	Staging of democracy to increase performance
Space of opportunity	Experiment	Productive and functional transformational ritual as "transitory space"
Transformational potential	Transformative in the sense of a "new social place"	Transitory and compensating in the sense of an increase in performance
Practice	Generative practice from within	Generative practice and risk of manipulation from without
Normalizing activity	Procedural constitution of norms	Procedural constitution of norms – risk of staging of constitution, communication and declaration of norms
Libidinous group of leader-followers	Mimetic practice	Potentially symbolic politics

Figure 1. The school community dispositive on the timeline of transformation

With the two points on the timeline we could show how the utopia of the school community can be described as a heterotopia and how the type of government represented by a democratic community of education can be methodically generalized in terms of improvisational technology (Dell, 2002; 2003). The power-knowledge practice uses the game as well as the systematic research and experimental practice of the social inquiry in the sense of casuistic productivity (Dewey, 1998; Hörster, 2003). It utilizes the collective community of responsibility that constitutes itself through dialogic problem-solving. In the learning laboratory, norm constitution can take place throughout a process.

Tactics are embedded in strategies and simultaneously co-create them within the power-knowledge complex. These are the strategies of freedom and self-organization, of loose coupling and systems development that can be achieved in the mode of context guidance (Weber, 2005b).

Tactics of knowledge	Games of discovery Experimental research	Dialogic constitution within the collective community of responsibility	Norm constitution in the "learning laboratory"
Strategies of knowledge	Freedom and self-organization	Loose coupling	Systemic development by context guidance

Figure 2. The governmental type of the democratic community of education

With this type of government, the democratic community of education, a practice of subjectification in the sense of improvised subjects and of creative self-transformation is laid out (Dell, 2002; 2003). Here, the connection between the democratic dispositive and the dispositive of creativity shows itself.

> Within the framework of neo-liberal governmentality self-determination, responsibility and freedom of choice do not signal the limits of governmental action, but they are themselves vehicles and instruments to transform the relationship of the subjects to themselves and to others. (Lemke, Krasmann & Bröckling, 2000, p. 30).

Improvisation and a life "in preparation of doing the unforeseen" highlight a design of creative self-transformation, an "aesthetic rationality" that includes the "irrational" and a "rationality in a broader sense" (Heubel, 2000, p. 185). Criticism and resistance can be productively integrated into an energetic rationality. The speech of creative rationality allows to overcome the limitations of an ascetic model of the self and to resolve the contradiction between vitality and rationality. A new type of energetic structure emerges in whose center we find the ideal of optimal and satisfying realization of one's skills, befitting the "trivialization of creativity" (ibid., p. 188 et seq.). The integration of work ethic and pleasure principle is part of the "positive, knowledge-generating, discourse-increasing, pleasure-stimulating and power-creating mechanisms" of the "dispositive of creativity", "which includes that of sexuality" (ibid., p. 189) and is fit to be the principle of a new capitalist work ethic of "non-alienated work" and the performance principle of "creative productivity". Human energy as a resource can thus be exploited more thoroughly and contributes to the further economization of the self. "Creativity" combines "aesthetic individuality and energetic efficiency" (ibid., p. 204).

So the practices of self-emanation stand between energetic art of living and bio-technology. Whether the type of government the democratic school community creates, as an improvisational technology, new social places for the subjects, remains uncertain. But it does carry with it subjectifying practices of creative productivity.

We have the certainty that there will be continued uncertainty in further transformations and displacements of the dispositive of the school community: the genealogy does "not work with closure because the network of relations that is supposed to make a singularity intelligible as an effect, does not form one single level. They are rather relations that keep unhooking from each other" (Foucault, 1992, p. 38). Each one of them can enter into a game that goes beyond it. Inside the entanglements of process maintenance and process transformation, the discourse is eternally flexible and fragile – just as democracy is.

NOTES

[1] The "linear transformation" model is based on a known object of learning and demand for learning and identifies a known and future-oriented learning objective (Schäffter, 2001a, p. 19 et seq.). Schäffter points to goal-oriented transformation as a second structure of change within this model: Starting from unknown possible points of departure a process of education takes its course that is modeled on known examples. The third transformational process, on the other hand, shows a pattern of change that represents a transformation whose goal is open. Learning is a search. Starting from a given, definable point, the process of goal attainment leads into a space of possibilities in an uncertain future, a diffuse departure. Despite the openness of the future objective, this third model is based on the assumption of a development that can lead to new securities and new structures of order if the "shore" is recognizable at all. But just this is what becomes more and more difficult in a transformational society.

[2] On the governmentality of "nurturing and developing" see Weber 1998 and 2000a.

[3] Only the theme of the event is fixed in advance. Contents, selection of topics, group formation are all left to "voting with one's feet". The event likes to be regarded as an "organized coffee break" – as would be the case during a coffee break, forces of attraction and repulsion should unfold order from chaos. If one has "nothing to learn and nothing to contribute", one should leave the group one has joined, thus "honoring the group by one's absence" (Owen, 2001).

[4] Mornings and evenings the plenary circle in Open Space serves as a framing for the "chaotic" process of self-organization. During the Future Search Conference participants are seated in small circles (Weisbord & Janoff, 1995; 2000; 2001).

[5] Not just those (formally) in charge, not just "functionaries" are to support the transformation, but all those committed to it. People are to meet each other not primarily as representatives of functions but also as persons. In order to lend a more informal mode to these encounters, the "dress code" is also less formal and status differences are rather denied than expressed.

[6] Open Space is described as "a new way to hold better meetings", and as a "natural laboratory" which is suitable "to perceive and explore the emerging potential of our common humanity in a transforming world". Better meetings then are the starting point of a process that ends in "a richer way of being together in that wonderful thing we call organization" (Owen, 1997, p. 1).

[7] This would be, for instance, the display of "ideal behavior" of a norm-constituting avant-garde as practiced by Lazarsfeld and Wagner in a holiday camp in 1924: the supervisors get a group of children and adolescents to exert a positive influence on the whole holiday camp by functioning as "normalizing agents". Lazarsfeld and Wagner solve the problem of a "howling horde milling about" by according privileges to a group of 12- to 14-year-olds in exchange for their help in creating peace and quite and by calling a meeting of the older children to discuss the camp (Hörster & Müller, 1996, p. 624).

[8] The strategy of "mimetic ability" (as Hörster & Müller call it) is invented by the educator Gusti Bretter-Mändl in the "Kinderheim Baumgarten" founded by Bernfeld in 1919 (Hörster & Müller, 1996, p. 626). Bretter-Mändl participates in the noise, chats with the neighbors and gets to know the children. In the dining-hall, there is rowing and grabbing for spoons, bread, etc.: "I never took a spoon; when I got one, as "the teacher", I gave it to the children, the same with the bread and so on –

only when everybody had what they needed, I started to eat. Initially the children looked at me with astonishment and suspicion, then they took the spoon with a certain shyness of gesture – that was a great progress, they began to detect something. And eventually nobody wanted to take anything from me, they even outdid each other to hand me a spoon. At that point I had won the game. We loved each other." (Bernfeld, 1921, p. 35).

[9] Hörster shows such timelines with reference to children's games: they are not the same as the institution of a "constructed playground" – the city, loaded with "staged play situations", is a place quite different from the game utopias that they refer to. In staging the game, the focus shifts from the developmental and illusionary space of playing freely towards a space that compensates for lacking familial education and care (Hörster, 1997, p. 111).

[10] I am indebted to Reinhard Hörster for pointing out the "improvisational technologies" to me.

[11] Rituals and symbols, celebrations and Jewish rhythms have a specific value, status and place for Bernfeld when they are "expressions of living emotions and behavior" (Bernfeld, 1921, p. 110).

REFERENCES

Ahlemeyer, H. W., & Königswieser, R. (1997). *Komplexität managen. Strategien, Konzepte und Fallbeispiele*. Wiesbaden: Gabler.

Arnold, R., & Schüßler, I. (1998). *Wandel der Lernkulturen*. Darmstadt: Wissenschaftliche Buchgesellschaft.

Baecker, D. (1997). Einfache Komplexität. In H. Ahlemeyer & R. Königswieser, Roswitha (Eds.), *Komplexität managen. Strategien, Konzepte und Fallbeispiele* (pp. 17–50). Wiesbaden: Gabler.

Baecker, D. (1999). *Organisation als System*. Frankfurt/Main: Suhrkamp.

Barrett, F. J., & Cooperrider, D. L. (1990). Generative metaphor intervention: A new approach to intergroup conflict. *Journal of Applied Behavioral Science, 26*(2), 223–244.

Bernfeld, S. (1921). *Kinderheim Baumgarten. Bericht über einen ernsthaften Versuch mit neuer Erziehung*. Berlin: Jüdischer Verlag.

Bohm, D. (1998). *Der Dialog. Das offene Gespräch am Ende der Diskussion*. Stuttgart: Klett-Cotta.

Boos, F., & Königswieser, R. (2000). Unterwegs auf einem schmalen Grat: Großgruppen in Veränderungsprozessen. In R. Königswieser & M. Keil (Eds.), *Das Feuer der großen Gruppen. Konzepte, Designs, Praxisbeispiele für Großveranstaltungen* (pp. 17–29). Beratergruppe Neuwaldegg/synetz. Stuttgart: Klett-Cotta.

Bröckling, U., Krasmann, S., & Lemke, T. (Eds.). (2000). *Gouvernementalität der Gegenwart. Studien zur Ökonomisierung des Sozialen*. Frankfurt/Main: Suhrkamp.

Burow, O.-A. (1999). *Die Individualisierungsfalle. Kreativität gibt es nur im Plural*. Stuttgart: Klett-Cotta.

Burow, O.-A. (2000). *Ich bin gut – wir sind besser – Erfolgsmodelle kreativer Gruppen*. Stuttgart: Klett-Cotta.

Dell, C. (2002). *Prinzip Improvisation*. Köln: Verlag der Buchhandlung Walther König.

Dell, C. (2003). Für eine Technologie der Improvisation. In N. Killius, J. Kluge, & L. Reisch (Eds.), *Die Zukunft der Bildung* (pp. 251–256). Frankfurt/Main: Suhrkamp.

Dewey, J. (1949). *Demokratie und Erziehung. Eine Einleitung in die Philosophische Pädagogik*. Braunschweig, Berlin and Hamburg: Westermann.

Dewey, J. (1998). *Die Suche nach Gewissheit*. Frankfurt/Main: Suhrkamp.

Dobischat, R., & Husemann, R. (Eds.). (1997). *Berufliche Bildung in der Region. Zur Neubewertung einer bildungspolitischen Gestaltungsdimension*. Berlin: Ed. Sigma.

Elsen, S. (2000). Zivile Gesellschaft gestalten. Gemeinwesen als Lern- und Handlungsort nachhaltiger Entwicklung. In S. Elsen, H. Ries, N. Löns, & H.-G. Homfeldt (Eds.), *Sozialen Wandel gestalten – Lernen für die Zivilgesellschaft* (pp. 94–125). Neuwied and Kriftel: Luchterhand.

Foucault, M. (2005). *Die Heterotopien. Der utopische Körper*. Frankfurt/Main: Suhrkamp.

Foucault, M. (1992). *Archäologie des Wissens* (5th ed.). Frankfurt/Main: Suhrkamp.

Hammond, S., & Royal, C. (Eds.). (1998). *Lessons from the field: Applying appreciative inquiry.* Plano, TX: Practical Press, Inc. (Distribution by Thin Book Publishing Company).

Hartkemeyer, M., Hartkemeyer, J., & Dhority, L. F. (1998). *Miteinander denken. Das Geheimnis des Dialogs* (2nd ed.). Stuttgart: Klett-Cotta.

Helsper, W., Hörster, R., & Kade, J. (2003a). *Pädagogische Felder im Modernisierungsprozess.* Weilerswist: Velbrück.

Helsper, W., Hörster, R., & Kade, J. (2003b). Einleitung: Ungewissheit im Modernisierungsprozess pädagogischer Felder. In W. Helsper, R. Hörster, & J. Kade (Eds.), *Ungewissheit. Pädagogische Felder im Modernisierungsprozess* (pp. 7–20). Weilerswist: Velbrück.

Heubel, F. (2002). *Das Dispositiv der Kreativität.* Darmstadt: Wissenschaftliche Buchgesellschaft.

Hörster, R., & Müller, B. (Eds.). (1992). *Jugend, Erziehung und Psychoanalyse. Zur Sozialpädagogik Siegfried Bernfelds.* Neuwied: Luchterhand.

Hörster, R. (1997). Bildungsplatzierungen. Räume, Möglichkeiten und Grenzen der Heterotopologien. In J. Ecarius & M. Löw (Eds.), *Raumbildung. Bildungsräume. Über die Verräumlichung sozialer Prozesse* (pp. 93–122). Opladen: Leske & Budrich.

Hörster, R. (2003). Fallverstehen. Zur Entwicklung kasuistischer Produktivität in der Sozialpädagogik. In Helsper et al. (Eds.), *Ungewissheit. Pädagogische Felder im Modernisierungsprozess* (pp. 318–344). Weilerswist: Velbrück.

Hörster, R., & Müller, B. (1996). Zur Struktur sozialpädagogischer Kompetenz. Oder: Wo bleibt das Pädagogische der Sozialpädagogik? In A. Combe & W. Helsper (Eds.), *Pädagogische Professionalität. Untersuchungen zum Typus pädagogischen Handelns* (pp. 614–648). Frankfurt/Main: Suhrkamp.

Jörke, D. (2003). *Demokratie als Erfahrung. John Dewey und die Politische Philosophie der Gegenwart.* Wiesbaden: Westdeutscher Verlag.

Königswieser, R. (2000). Das Feuer von Großgruppen. In R. Königswieser & M. Keil (Eds.), *Das Feuer der großen Gruppen. Konzepte, Designs, Praxisbeispiele für Großveranstaltungen* (pp. 30–44). Beratergruppe Neuwaldegg/synetz. Stuttgart: Klett-Cotta.

Königswieser, R., & Keil, M. (2000). *Das Feuer großer Gruppen. Konzepte, Designs, Praxisbeispiele für Großveranstaltungen.* Beratergruppe Neuwaldegg/synetz. Stuttgart: Klett-Cotta.

Lemke, T., Krasmann, S., & Bröckling, U. (2000). Gouvernementalität, Neoliberalismus und Selbsttechnologien. Eine Einleitung. In U. Bröckling, et al. (Eds.), *Gouvernementalität der Gegenwart. Studien zur Ökonomisierung des Sozialen* (pp. 7–40). Frankfurt/Main: Suhrkamp.

Lüttringhaus, M. (2003). Sozialdarwinismus durch Partizipation? Anmerkungen zu fördernden und behindernden Faktoren von Beteiligung und zur Methode der Bewohnerversammlung. In W. Hosemann & B. Trippmacher (Eds.), *Soziale Arbeit und soziale Gerechtigkeit* (Series: Grundlagen der Sozialen Arbeit. Vol. 8). Baltmannsweiler: Schneider Hohengehren.

Matthiesen, U., & Reutter, G. (Eds.). *Lernende region – mythos oder lebendige Praxis?* Bielefeld: Bertelsmann.

Müller, B. (1992). Sisyphos und Tantalus – Bernfelds Konzept des "Sozialen Ortes" und seine Bedeutung für die Sozialpädagogik. In R. Hörster & B. Müller (Eds.), *Jugend, Erziehung und Psychoanalyse. Zur Sozialpädagogik Siegfried Bernfelds* (pp. 59–74). Neuwied: Luchterhand.

Owen, H. (1997). *Expanding our now: The story of open space technology.* San Francisco: Barrett-Koehler Publishers.

Owen, H. (2000). *The power of spirit. How organizations transform.* San Francisco: Berrett Koehler Publishers.

Owen, H. (2001). *Open Space Technology. Ein Leitfaden für die Praxis.* Stuttgart: Klett-Cotta.

Schäffter, O. (2001a). *Weiterbildung in der Transformationsgesellschaft. Zur Grundlegung einer Theorie der Institutionalisierung.* Baltmannsweiler: Schneider Hohengehren.

Schäffter, O. (2001b). Transformationsgesellschaft. In J. Wittpoth (Ed.), *Erwachsenenbildung und Zeitdiagnose* (pp. 39–68). Theoriebeobachtungen. Bielefeld: Bertelsmann.

Senge, P. M. (1996). *Die fünfte Disziplin. Kunst und Praxis der lernenden Organisation.* Stuttgart: Klett-Cotta.

Siebert, H. (2003). *Vernetztes Lernen. Systemisch-konstruktivistische Methoden der Bildungsarbeit.* München: Luchterhand.

Weber, S. M. (1998). *Organisationsentwicklung und Frauenförderung. Eine empirische Analyse in drei Organisationstypen der privaten Wirtschaft.* Königstein: Ulrike Helmer.

Weber, S. M. (2000a). Fördern und Entwickeln. Institutionelle Veränderungsstrategien und normalisierendes Wissen. *Zeitschrift für Erziehungswissenschaft, 3,* 411–428.

Weber, S. M. (2000b). Power to the people!? Selbstorganisation, Systemlernen und Strategiebildung mit großen Gruppen. *Sozialwissenschaftliche Literatur Rundschau, 41,* 63–89.

Weber, S. M. (2005a). *Rituale der Transformation. Großgruppenverfahren als pädagogisches Wissen am Markt.* Postdoctoral lecture qualification thesis. 408 pages.

Weber, S. M. (2005b). Selbstoptimierende Subjekte, Labor-Gesellschaft, Markt-Universität. Ein Essay aus gouvernementalitätstheoretischer Perspektive. In A. Dzierzbicka, R. Kubac, & E. Sattler (Eds.), *Bildung Riskiert. Erziehungswissenschaftliche Markierungen* (pp. 237–244). Wien: Löcker.

Weisbord, M., & Janoff, S. (1995). *Future search. An action guide to finding common ground in organizations and communities.* San Francisco: Berrett-Koehler Publishers.

Weisbord, M., & Janoff, S. (2000). Zukunftskonferenz: Die gemeinsame Basis finden und handeln. In R. Königswieser & M. Keil (Eds.), *Das Feuer großer Gruppen. Konzepte, Designs, Praxisbeispiele für Großveranstaltungen* (pp. 129–145). Beratergruppe Neuwaldegg/synetz. Stuttgart: Klett-Cotta.

Weisbord, M., & Janoff, S. (2001). *FutureSearch. Die Zukunftskonferenz. Wie Organisationen zu Zielsetzungen und gemeinsamem Handeln finden.* Stuttgart: Klett-Cotta.

Winnicott, S. W. (1995). *Vom Spiel zur Kreativität* (8th ed.). Stuttgart: Klett-Cotta.

Zander, H. (1992). Katharsis und Entsühnung. Siegfried Bernfelds Beobachtungen über das innere Wirken von Erziehungskollektiven. Ein Beitrag zur Grundlegung der Sozialpädagogik. In R. Hörster & B. Müller (Eds.), *Jugend, Erziehung und Psychoanalyse, Zur Sozialpädagogik Siegfried Bernfelds* (pp. 163–180). Neuwied: Luchterhend.

Susanne Maria Weber
University of Applied Sciences
Fulda
Germany

DANIEL WRANA

26. ECONOMIZING AND PEDAGOGIZING CONTINUING EDUCATION[1]

Reviewing the German discussion surrounding the key term 'economizing,' one finds two positions, and thereby, two ways of using the term. On the one hand are the critics of economizing, those who see it as a sort of hostile takeover of adult education by market logics. They see the economic aspect, for example, as a superficial '*Verzweckung*' (appropriation of finality) of the learning process, which as a process of '*Bildung*'[2] should actually simply be an end in itself. Or they see dwindling public support for continuing education as leading to the danger of market-orientation and thereby criticize the privatization of adult education as a simultaneous de-professionalization (e.g. Pongratz, 2003; Ahlheim, 2001; Hoffmann, 2001; Weiland, 2001). The other position, which comprises the proponents of economizing, points out that 'we' inevitably live in a world of scarce resources and that educators who do not take this into account obviously fancy themselves to be in some sort of paradise (e.g., Mühlenkamp, 2005; Wagner, 2006). Pragmatists try to join the two positions. They place value on the fact that personality development is always an integral part of vocational education and that one best achieves goals, such as equal opportunity and emancipation, by implementing dwindling resources as effectively as possible (e.g. Arnold, 2002; Dohmen, 2005).

I would like to approach the issue from a fundamental perspective founded in a theory of power. I do not understand economizing as either creating greater operational efficiency or mandating a market-orientation of educational processes, but rather as a historical process in which adults in civil society have become the site for implementation of an economic form. My particular thesis here proposes that economizing and pedagogizing are not opposing processes, but a doublet – two sides of the same coin, so to speak. I understand the economic and simultaneously pedagogic form that is suggested to adults for subjectivation as the result of a historical social process and of the power relations in a society, and not as a universal constant, for example, 'the pedagogic' or 'the economic.' For Foucault, power is not an ominous, otherworldly entity that forces its law on humanity – although this is a common assumption made by critics. The quite abstract concept of power is distinguished and concretized in two concepts: on the one hand are the power practices, i.e., social acts of practicing power, which also include the pedagogic practices, and, on the other hand, the power relations, which as relations, connect utterly diverse elements – institutions, discourses, programs, buildings, and artifacts. Although as Foucault says, power relations run throughout the entire social body, they should not be comprehended as a unified power inevitably shaping the whole. Instead, they are always plural; they can be understood – as

M.A. Peters et al. (eds.), Govermentality Studies in Education, 473–486.

formulated by Engels – as "innumerable intersecting forces, an infinite series of parallelograms of forces" (Engels, 1975, p. 692). A *"dispositif"* (Foucault 1977, p. 299) or apparatus in a Foucauldian sense does not identify a society's deep structure; it is an arrangement of power relations, relations of subjects, and a current "state-of-the-battles" (Foucault ibid.). Such an analysis therefore constructs a multi-part, fleeting, and contradictory object, in order to make the object of analysis – power relations – intelligible and comprehensible.

I would like to begin by pointing out a misconception and introduce a shift in meaning by grasping the pedagogic and the economic as two sides of an implementation process, two moments in the establishing of practices of governing subjectivity, rather than as an opposing pair or two fundamentally different approaches.

POWER BASED ON THE ECONOMY AS ROLE MODEL

Foucault's analysis of the modes of governmental practices works out the history and the functioning of a specific knowledge and specific practices with which 'things' – to put it quite generally – are to be 'governed,' 'negotiated,' and 'managed.' Government encompasses the ensemble of institutions and practices for conducting and directing humans in all areas of society – from administration to education (Foucault, 1996, p. 118). The formation of an art of governing dates back to the eighteenth century. It is no mere coincidence that pedagogy and economy became established in this same period.

First of all, I would like to describe an essential moment of governing practices from the late eighteenth century. A belief that had been around since antiquity (see Foucault, 1993) proposed that those who want to govern the state well, must first govern themselves well, the people in their surroundings, their own goods and chattels. The sovereign must be a good educator. And if the sovereign rules the state well, then the individuals within this state will also rule themselves well. But what does that mean, to rule well? Rousseau, writing the article on 'political economy' for Diderot's encyclopedia, established that economy actually means: "Wise ... government of the house for the common good of the entire family."

Rousseau then poses the question of how this principle of wise government could be introduced for the welfare of all within the state and its administration (see Foucault, 2004a). For Quesnay and many others, a good government is an economic government. The art of governing is the art of exercising power in the form of economy and according to its model – *"d'èxercer le pouvoir dans la forme et selon le modèle de l'économie"* (Foucault 2004a, p. 98). Economy is understood here as a way of dealing with things, as a form of government. What characterizes the economic form of government? La Perrière – a much earlier author – stated that government was the "right disposition of things" – to conduct them to their appropriate ends. *"Gouvernement est la droite disposition des choses, desquelles on prend charge pour les conduire jusqu'à fin convenable"* (p. 99, quoted from Foucault, 2004a, p. 99). But what are these "things" – what is to be conducted? They are the relations people have to customs, habits, wealth and their health. The relations they have to opportunities and developments, misfortunes and hazards, which are to be led to appropriate ends (ibid.). With the emergence of the art of governing as economic governance, these appropriate ends multiply. Good government must arrange itself so that people are sufficiently taken care of, wealth is multiplied, and the population's health continues to improve. This plurality of ends, however, finds common ground in the following argument: the goal of the government is not brought in from outside and applied to matters, it lies within the things that are controlled, it can be found in the perfecting, maximizing and intensifying of the governed processes: "...*la fin du gouvernement est dans les choses qu'il dirige, elle est à rechercher dans la prefection ou la maximalisation ou l'intensification des processus qu'il dirige*" (Foucault, 2004a, p. 103).

AUTOFINALIZATION AND THE PLURALITY OF ENDS

The pedagogic classics, too, drafted their approaches against a horizon of emerging governing practices. In pedagogy, one begins – as in economy, too – to discover that the things – the individuals, their educational processes, the markets, the circulation of goods – have an inherent logic that must be accentuated and perfected. Thus, for Kant and Rousseau, the seed of educability is found within individuals. The idea is to cultivate their nature and thereby, their inherent finality. In Rousseau's economy article for the encyclopedia, he demanded the expansion of government as public economy to all social realms. *Emile* (Rousseau, 1993) can be seen as a thought experiment with which Rousseau attempted to show how an educator can successfully cultivate and perfect an inner nature's singular end and, at the same time, associate this end with an ensemble of ends, or a common public spirit, as described in the social contract (Buck, 1984). The same discursive figure led both the newly emerging pedagogic discourse of this era and the governmentality discourse as a whole: developing the inner finality of things.

This principle is not restricted to children's education: it also applies to the bourgeois adult's self-education, as the implementation of governmentality practices is closely connected with the middle class struggle to advance. Adult education in Germany has its origins and heritage in the practices of the early bourgeoisie, such as, working on one's own self-rule in reading groups and discussion circles (Olbrich, 2001; Pongratz, 2003; Otto, 2005). The adult citizen, too, was meant to recognize the inner finality of things and then govern things in such a way that this end would be achieved – the citizen should rule himself or herself. But the factions of the bourgeoisie were split. The educated bourgeoisie (*Bildungsbürgertum*) emphasized that the citizen should develop, work on, and perfect his or her self, that citizens should permanently care for themselves. This, in effect, sets up a pedagogic definition of self-rule. Other bourgeoise factions emphasized that citizens are ruling themselves per definition, and thereby drafted a legal definition of self-rule (Sennett, 1978; Bollenbeck, 1994). With the different understandings and realizations of self-rule in the factions of the bourgeoisie, the further education practices of different groups within civil society do diverge. But the pedagogic form of taking care of oneself is likewise an economic form, for the idea is to lead one's self to an end befitting this self. The educated bourgeoisie radicalized the economic-pedagogic doublet on the side of self-care with the neo-humanist educational concept of *Bildung*, where self-care is the only end and an end in itself. However, this radicalization conceals the economic side of this doublet. Foucault describes this movement in which the end becomes a finality per se as *autofinalization*. He writes: "*Dans le souci de soi on est son propre objet, on est sa propre fin. ... une auto-finalisation de soi par soi dans la pratique qu'on apelle le souci de soi*" (Foucault, 2001, p. 170).

But the bourgeois society lives with its contradictions. Even the '*autofinalized Bildung*' – the bourgeoisie's nobility – has always been impure, for it is a moment in the assertion of the bourgeoisie's power. The educated adult has never existed beyond bourgeois society, which would thereby also mean capitalist mode of production and the economy. But through the contradictions of bourgeois society that accompany its increased complexity and differentiation, the ends multiply and overlap. In the discourses of the newly independent social fields, ends are given an artificial purity. Governing practices differentiate between economy and pedagogy as fields of intervention (Forneck & Wrana, 2005.). Now the conflict of ends can re-stage its antagonism as a conflict of social fields, whereas the battle for education's own value, independent from the ends of external fields such as that of the economy, is a battle for the autonomy of the pedagogic field, the behavioral logic of a profession, and the interpretational power of a group of actors. The field's common governmental form of rule over subjects is harbored and, at the same time, concealed in the field.

A field's struggle for autonomy is thus always likewise a battle for the hegemony of a certain finality. The illusion emerges in the discursive battle, that an individual action can have a single, isolatable end, can be reduced to one single end. But this illusion is an effect of the reductionist perspective of a field-specific discourse, which has a similar mono-finalizing function, such as, the intentionality of the subject. But if one analyzes concrete actions within social ensembles, then one must admit that their intended ends are over-determined. The exertion of bourgeois society is the assurance of the plurality, qua contradictoriness of the intended ends in the fields rather than their purity. Critical theory has always emphasized this double character of aims in bourgeois society. Where critical theory does not fall back behind itself, it attempts to grasp the over-determination of aims as the driving force of a critical movement rather than simply lament over economization (e.g. Pongratz, 2003).

BIOPOWER AND GOVERNING THE POPULATION

At the beginning of the nineteenth century, new governing practices arose. Foucault worked out a series of characteristics for them. They thus have a new subject, or more precisely, two new subjects. The new governing practices begin, on the one hand, with the individual, and on the other, with the 'population.' As Foucault explains, one begins to recognize the population as a complex social body, as an unstable, dynamic form that one cannot manipulate directly. Instead, one must control it indirectly. The aim is to lead the things, which are now the populations, to "their ends": enhance the lives of the many, increase opportunities, multiply wealth. Since the governing of the population has to do with the potential of life, Foucault calls this form of power "biopower" (Foucault 1997, p. 220).

This discovery of the population as the government's subject was accompanied by new ideas on the best ways of governing: liberalism. The liberal governing practices introduce a new relationship of freedom and power as compared with the old "reason of state." Their credo is that one governs the population best, most economically, by leaving the individual "free" – in that one governs as little as possible, rather than as much as possible (Foucault, 2004b). More precisely, one does not govern the population by placing all individuals under a uniform law, but instead, by viewing laws as tactics as framework conditions within which the individuals are able to consume their freedom. But liberal government does not simply produce pure freedom. Liberal government also possesses a constant awareness of the "danger" that individuals are not using their freedom properly. As a consequence, in a liberal government, governing practices are installed as "counter weights," which Foucault identifies as security technologies. They make it possible to govern the freedom that is meant to be initiated in the populations; they make it possible to capture the monsters that freedom is capable of spawning (Foucault, 2004b).

But governing practices are practices of control and their establishment goes along with the development of relations of forces. For a fairly long time, in the German bourgeoisie, the 'government of one's self' as the augmentation of individual subjectivity was considered dangerous and was restricted. The government's reigning practices were disciplinary practices that directly formed the body and soul - the school being the most prominent site of these disciplinary practices. On the one hand, that can be attributed, to the early capitalist industrial modes of production, which demanded a simple subjugation of the labor force, and on the other hand, to the liaison of the bourgeoisie with the conservative, monarchic state. Within this constellation, national public and adult education became an instrument of the relevant social groups in their struggle for hegemony – the work force and also the bourgeoisie (Axmacher, 1974). The *"Gesellschaft für Volksbildung"* (Society for Education of the *'Volk'*[3]) placed itself at the service of the German nation and became part of a self-appointed *'ordnungspolitische Kraft'* (power-political force). It contributed to generating acquiescence within society, gave the work force the key qualifications, as it were, for subjugation to the given order – without ever losing sight of education as an end in itself. That has great significance, since the program of national public education has its origins in liberalism. Yet for the entire nineteenth century and for most of the twentieth, the education of adults was not a topic of concern for actors in the economic and political fields. Contrary to school-based education, adult education was not recognized and assimilated as a means of governing populations – or at least, not yet.

ADULT/CONTINUING EDUCATION IN LIBERALISM

This relative lack of interest in general and adult education by those in power first changed with the educational reforms, that is, with West Germany's recognition in the 1950s that a *German Educational Catastrophe* (Picht, 1964) was ahead since the economic system required a more qualified work force than the population could supply. A gap developed because a governmental matter – wealth – had a requirement that was not fulfilled: the qualifications and competences in individuals as a precondition for the production of this wealth in the population.

The plan of the *Deutscher Bildungsrat* (German Educational Committee) which was installed to direct the reforms, fulfilled all criteria of a liberal governing of individuals with regard to their competences. Within this, society was designed as a flat space in which every individual can, in principle, achieve every position. In other words, he or she was free to achieve every position if he or she was willing to offer the corresponding capacities. Understood as a general competence, here is 'mobility,' which consists of the ability to abstract, communicate, and learn, the willingness to cooperate, sensitivity, and imagination (*Deutscher Bildungsrat* [German Educational Committee], 1972, see p. 52). This mobility frees one from those constraints that individuals without mobility are more strongly at the mercy of. Individuals should continue their education throughout their entire lives.– Lifelong learning is necessary then, as the promise goes, so there will be no contradiction between the 'economic-technical demands' and individual interests. At this historic point, it appears that pedagogizing and economizing are not only constructed following the same principles of governing, but are one and the same thing. Pedagogizing is now the ability to permanently re-envision and to revise all personal variables for the purpose of mobility, and economizing the orientation of these revisions toward the common social goal of increasing wealth. The contradiction of bourgeois society has been redefined as consonance.

The mobility that is at issue, the freedom, is one that must be secured in compliance with liberal governing practices. The individual is viewed as being fundamentally free and the institutions that are now being set up should secure this freedom. Belonging to this system of safeguards are the continuing education institutions of the fourth sector, a building block system of offered courses, a rational educational plan, a strong profession, and a separate program for continuing or adult education science at universities. The autonomy that the continuing education of adults is meant to secure implies a freedom that is ceaselessly threatened and thereby a base for ever new, never ending, and thus, lifelong interventions.

The draft of the educational committee is the epitome of liberal governing, which judges things according to the economy by increasing individuals' freedom. It implies that continuing education should be part of national and economic considerations. Not in the sense of forcing individuals to educate and govern themselves, but in giving them the right and the resources to do so. This was based in the belief that individuals want to be educated and self-governed, not least, for economic considerations. The fact that many of these plans and strategies were never realized does not mean that these strategies are without relevance. Instead, they shape the horizon of awareness of the problem against which continuing education was designed. The fact that realization lags behind this awareness of the problem has to do with the actual development of the relations of forces and interests.

CONTINUING EDUCATION UNDER PRESSURE

Here I will now cross the 1980's with their moment of renewed conservatism, with the so-called 'postmodern,' with 'experience society,' the 'immaterialist transformation of values,' etc. Whereas reforms based on neoliberal concepts were made mainly in the U.S. and England, the former West Germany continued, for the most part, along its path of a socialist market economy and was perceived as doing so in public awareness. The economic realm remained largely unproblematic and was in the background of public awareness. In his analysis of experience society, Gerhard Schulze summarizes this state of affairs of social discourse: the material securing of life seems to have become unproblematic, everybody's "existential problem" (Schulze, 1992, p. 34) had to do with the style of living, the ways in which one designed their experience.

That changed fundamentally in the course of the 1990s. The educational system and also the continuing education system came under increasing pressure from social and educational policy. On the one hand, this is connected with internal restructuring and simplification within public governance and dismantling of the social state. On the other hand it is connected with a public discourse about the economy, the social realm, education, and the future that reaches through a series of national and international studies, reports, analyses, and expert opinions through to the entertainment programs of private broadcasters.

Similar to the other sectors of the educational system, continuing education ended up in an increasingly problematic contradiction resembling a double bind. The emphasis was on the enormous economic significance of life-long continuing education in the context of the knowledge society – competence must be produced, reserves of talent must be set free – and it should happen at all levels. Subject to classical, liberal governmentality, the state had to once again invest enormously in its educational system. But that is exactly what did not happen. Action was thwarted when a rearrangement of taxation saw the state argue that it had an empty purse. It could not and did not want to continue to finance liberal safeguards such as continuing education. The program then followed new, neo-liberal taxation imperatives: its central thesis was, to put it bluntly, that wealth for all increases when one grants the individual complete freedom to act in accordance with their entirely personal success.

Expenses for continuing education were thus frozen, reversed, and rearranged. If public continuing education wanted to exist at all, then it would have to pull in other financial resources and produce more output with fewer investments. In this regard, economizing – understood as streamlining operating procedures in continuing education facilities – gained in importance. A further economizing was the financing of continuing education efforts by the students themselves rather than by the public hand.[4] Added to these two forms was one more: the form of subjectivation launched in governmental practices. Neo-liberal economic subjectivation took up a special position because a simple streamlining of the hitherto means for continuing education cannot balance out the crisis into which liberal government had fallen. The new subjectivation refers to a practically Copernican turn in the use of pedagogic means, as represented by the concept of informal, self-guided learning. The discipline of continuing education reacted to this situation in recent years. In keeping with the educational policy of the socialist-green coalition German government from 2000–2005, it has relied on concepts such as "self-guided learning," "informal learning," "continuing education as infrastructure," etc. The associated economizing of "continuing education" goes deeper than the organization as it affects the learning adults themselves. This is an economizing of continuing education in that the individuals are oriented on the end of increasing wealth, but at the same time, it is a pedagogizing in that all individuals within a society are subjected to an imperative of permanent flexibility, an advancing of the self, of one's strengths and activities. What is new about this pedagogic form, however, is that a profession is no longer responsible. Instead, every individual must take over responsibility for their own formation.

THE SELF-EMPLOYED EMPLOYEES: THE NEW COMPETITIVE RELATIONS OF INDIVIDUALS

In self-guided learning the individual decides what, when, and towards what he or she learns. Individuals are responsible for themselves. But this freedom has another aspect to it – as does the associated responsibility. And this entails setting up a new form of fallback system. How is it possible to assure that the ends toward which the individual directs their desires are headed in the right direction? That is, that in the end this leads to increased affluence and wealth for all? What is the counterweight that restricts the individual's freedom in a neoliberal sense? It is no longer a norm along which the individual is to be objectified, or which limits his or her free actions – which liberalism tends toward. The new counterweight to freedom is not a norm, but a form, and indeed, one that assumes the subject's reference to itself. I would like to demonstrate this based on two theories that play a central role in the new arrangement of relations – metacognition theory and human capital theory.

Metacognition theory positions an ideal of learning and hence of the 'learner.' The end point of both metacognitive strategies and consciousness is optimal deployment of the financial resources for learning and a streamlining of the individual learning process. This form must assume reflexivity. Almost all research designs are laid out in such a way to prove an optimizing of the learning process. This is their only relevant application, whereby the ideal of the learner – that of 'good-strategy-users' – implies a learner who always decides rationally, with reference to himself or herself. The concept of metacognition is oriented on the self-optimizing subject. It takes up an economic position in a new sense: first, because the aim is a maximum of benefits with a minimum of resources, and second, because one's self should become the means of optimization. The actual content of the learner's success does not play a role as long as it is achieved in the most effective way possible (Wrana, 2006).

The subject is summarized in quite a similar way in human capital theory, which can be considered the theoretical core of neoliberalism and has been economics' hegemonic approach for quite some time. Its basic assumption is that the degree of verifiable competence, that is the stock of individual human capital, precipitates in a person's earnings and that individuals behave rationally by investing (or not) in their own human capital (Becker, 1996). The entire stock of human capital in a population, or at least its competence profile, grows optimally when the individuals make their own decisions about their educational investments; the competitive relations are made as visible as possible, for example, through rankings; and individuals actually bear the possible negative consequences of their investment decisions. Although it has never been possible to empirically prove the central allegation of the human capital theory – the connection of income and level of education – most educational policy reform suggestions and the activities of the international organizations are based on the logic of this theory.[5]

The subject of metacognition and the rational choice subject are free and, at the same time, coerced in making their decisions. But the illusion is rarely maintained. Even the theory carries the function of production within it: subjects do not simply behave as rational decision makers; they must be brought to this form. Metacognition theory and metacognition research, for example, can be understood as a set of practices that produce a specific knowledge about the possibilities and borders of economic regulation of subjects. They can supply information about how the economic subject functions, the constraints of the subject's existence, the degree to which the subject can be maximized, how the subject can be motivated to engage in self-production, and how to motivate the subject to invest in the means of his or her own self-production.

Precisely at this point, public continuing education is able to enter the action, and it does so with self-guided learning – for since the end of the 1990s it has accurately determined that subjects must first be placed in a position to learn of their own accord. And this contradiction now runs throughout the entire debate – on the one hand, subjects are self-determined, and on the other, they first have to be led to this position. At first glance, this looks like a pedagogic idea – to produce the economic attitude toward one's self. But a glance at other areas of activity in society shows that everywhere, practices are being installed that first and foremost bring the self to assume an economic approach.

The new freedom thus goes hand in hand with an arsenal of practices with which subjects should be able to control themselves and with which this control can be controlled. Among these are adequate mediation, measurement, evaluation, and certification of competences, the use of learning journals, the introduction of educational coupons, etc. For example, when Erpenbeck demands that all biographically acquired competences should be included "100 percent" (Erpenbeck 2001, p. 211) – and then reminds us that the issue is not a comprehensive summation and control of all competences, but instead, that such a system's mode of functioning is one of distributed self-stimulation. The demand is for a pass in which competences are acknowledged whereby individuals can recognize themselves as having certain competences and can compare their competence profiles with other individuals. Competence becomes an integral feature of individual identity and a marker of an individual's position in society.

Continuing education understood in this way should enable individuals to permanently observe and optimize themselves by multiplying their metacognitive strategies, documenting themselves in portfolios and journals and working out their core competences through educational counseling. Such practices are moments of self-disciplining. Through learning journals, self-surveys, quality guidelines, and the like, subjects are required to subject themselves to a grid and perceive themselves as both particular and at the same time, capable of being characterized in a ranking system. Subjects are expected to carry out their own profiling. Subjective intentionality and self-reflectivity are not simply continuing education's vanishing line in the direction of freedom; they become the area of achievement, the self-relationship to relations of capital. The learning power becomes labor power that can and should be used, and which requires lifelong maintenance and care. This process can be understood as self-capitalization since not only the knowledge and skills, but also the self and the self's subjectivity become human capital. To the extent that the learners are required to make themselves a permanent investment site, and thus comprehend not only their skills as capital, but also their relationship to themselves, that is, their self-relationship, they can be considered self-entrepreneurs (Wrana, 2006).

Neoliberalism becomes involved with new forms of security technologies. Whereas liberalism drafted regulating and limiting security technologies for the market from outside, such as the further education laws and financing programs, neoliberalism introduces security technology that is inherent to the market. This works only when those who do not take adequate care of themselves are threatened by tough sanctions. For that reason, the discussion of neoliberal taxation modalities becomes inflamed precisely over the so-called Hartz-Laws – which integrated unemployment compensation and welfare payments within a new system of inclusion and exclusion at society's lower rungs. The fear of social exclusion, or the permanent danger of decline, is the most effective means to induce subjects to care for themselves in the right way.

In the face of this threat, individuals will indeed care for their educational portfolio, themselves and the employability resulting from this. The market will then decide, ultimately, on the employment possibilities and value of this education.

THE BUSINESS LOCATION: THE POPULATION'S COMPETITIVE RELATIONSHIP

Not only individuals, but also populations are set into a new, competitive relationship which occurs through practices of ranking, the Program for International Student Assessment (PISA) being the most well-known. Rolf Arnold and Henning Pätzold have shown that the associated debates seldom lead to well-grounded reforms, as everyone interprets the results from their own inherited perspective. The debates remain at the level of symbolic politics (Arnold & Pätzold, 2004, see

p. 11). The most important demand voiced is merely that Germany must "place among the top five" (ibid.) in the next comparison, yet that demand is void of content.

The effect of neoliberal security technologies such as PISA is an empty competitive relationship. International populations are set in a competitive relationship through comparative studies and rankings. What is suggested by this is that those who do not win will necessarily perish. Nation states are constituted as units that have things such as a state of knowledge, of literacy, a competence profile, and the assumption is that their future ability depends on these factors. There can only be one 'first five' and that Germany must belong among these first five is never in question – it is an expectation. "You are Germany," (http://www.du-bist-deutschland.de) a major public campaign was launched in 2005 by leading public personalities in private enterprises in Germany to increase the engagement of the masses, then becomes an appeal for a collective sense. An appeal was made to every individual in society to invest his or her power in the power of the population. Ranking practices such as PISA are part of symbolic politics that syndicate populations as an entity and are meant to mobilize these populations. Nonetheless, what we are dealing with are symbolic politics with an inherently symbolic force.

CONCLUSION

The first conclusion is that in bourgeois society, adult education and further education has always had an intensive and somewhat unavoidable relationship to the economy. Therefore, an analysis and critique of power leads to the realization that one cannot simply reject economizing across-the-board and understand the economic as the opposite of the pedagogic.

Another conclusion that can be drawn is that there are various forms of economizing, of liberalism, and of subjectivation. The neoliberal forms of subjectivation are not naturally given or unavoidable. There is an entire set of reasons why a neoliberal form of government is problematic. Here, I will offer three of them:

– Neoliberalism produces inequality coupled with income differences. This is, indeed, a permanent factor in bourgeois society, in principle, but neoliberal government practices – such as rankings – maximize this effect rather than counterbalance it. The increasing gap in living standards both within industrial societies as well as in a global context cannot be justified by an economic standpoint of good government for the welfare of all.

– An essential instrument of a neoliberal government is not the will to progress, but the fear of decline. Fear rules. Yet fear is a form of symbolic violence – to remain in the value horizon of bourgeois society – that devalues the promised freedom.

– In a neoliberal form of government, partial ends – those of streamlining and optimizing – are set as global ends. The optimizing loop, the empty form that the perfectible subject of metacognition falls into, simultaneously conceals that which it excludes. But democracy lives from an antagonism of aims and their differences. It is not education's lack of finality that comprises the self-will of the pedagogic realm – but instead, keeping open the conflict among the ends (see Lyotard, 1988, p. 178 et seq.).

In addition, the circumstances are not at all clear. My previous reconstruction of the forms of government of continuing education is unsparingly terse. In some areas it is substantiated by more extensive analyses, in other areas this is not the case. A division into epochs, which would distinguish an era of liberalism from one of neoliberalism, makes little sense. For one, comparisons with other investigations of governmentality show that the social fields in question and the geographic regions would demand entirely different treatment as epochs. The history of governing practices of continuing education in Germany has its own rhythms and even these are in no way distinct. Once again, it is necessary to point out that every field of practice is a result of power relations and, as such, it always encompasses hegemonic positions, discursive struggles, and lines of resistance. It is much too easy to say that we live in an era of neoliberalism; precisely the discourse about self-guided learning is full of maneuvers and has numerous redefinitions and transformations within it (on reflexive practices, see Wrana, 2006).

I do not argue against an economizing of continuing education – it is just as unavoidable as a pedagogizing of society. Nonetheless, one must question the economy of the economy, and that does not amount to an expansion of the special economy, but to a general economy that follows the aim of governing things for the welfare of all. The final question would then be whether an economy of the educational realm is possible – and what this might comprise. The economization of the subject seems inevitable. Thus the question is – which forms and modes of economization are possible and imaginable? The relative autonomy of the pedagogic realm does not signify independence from the economy, but instead, the ability to define modes of economization – or at least to a certain point.

NOTES

[1] This is a reworked version of a paper delivered at the panel "Continuing Education and Governmentality" at the congress of the DGFE (German Association of Educational Science), 2006 in Frankfurt/Main.

[2] Bildung is a German notion with no direct correlation in English. It originated in neo-humanist and idealist philosophy and is used to identify personal development related to (high) culture and implicates an attitude of reflexivity.

[3] The German word 'Volk' has its origins in an early nineteenth-century romantic nationalism. The connotations of the term are: 'nation,' 'people' and 'folk.' The early German term 'Volksbildung' was used to denote the liberal and conservative fractions of adult education. Its goal was not only to educate all, like in general education, but to create a unified, educated 'Volk.' This education of the 'Volk' as a unity was mostly anti-intellectual, rationality was considered a hindrance to forming a sense of belonging to the 'Volk.' It would be wrong to call these conservative groups of adult education an early form of the national socialist movement, but it was a reason for the more or less ambivalent reactions of some actors of German 'Volksbildung' in the spring of 1933 (see Langer & Wrana, 2005)

[4] In an expert report for the DIE, the German Institute for Adult Education, Dieter Dohmen comes to the conclusion that this aspect is overestimated (Dohmen, 2005).

⁵ Timmermann shows the attempts to empirically guarantee human capital theory and the tendency for this endeavor to fail (Timmermann, 2002). International Organizations such as the World Bank and OECD have followed neoliberal imperatives since the 1960s. The interplay of these policies with national policies, or those of the European Union still require more precise reconstruction (see Schemmann, 2006).

REFERENCES

Ahlheim, K. (2001). Mehr als Qualifizierung. Profil und Chancen öffentlich verantworteter Weiterbildung. *Erwachsenenbildung, 47*(4), 184–188.

Arnold, R. (2002). Mehr als Ökonomisierung: eine Replik auf Klaus Ahlheim. *Erwachsenenbildung, 48*(2), 79–81.

Arnold, R., & Pätzold, H. (2004). PISA und Erwachsenenbildung – Verlockungen und offene Fragen. *Report Weiterbildung, 27*(4), 9–17.

Axmacher, D. (1974). *Erwachsenenbildung im Kapitalismus.* Frankfurt/M.: Fischer.

Becker, G. S. (1996). *The economic way of looking at behavior. The nobel lecture.* Stanford: Hoover.

Bollenbeck, G. (1994). *Bildung und Kultur. Glanz und Elend eines deutschen Deutungsmusters.* Frankfurt/M.: Suhrkamp.

Buck, G. (1984). *Rückwege aus der Entfremdung. Studien zur Entwicklung der deutschen humanistischen Bildungsphilosophie.* Paderborn: Schöningh.

Deutscher Bildungsrat. (1972). *Strukturplan für das Bildungswesen.* Stuttgart: Klett.

Dohmen, D. (2005). *Ökonomisierung und Angebotsentwicklung in der (öffentlichen) Weiterbildung.* Bonn: DIE. Retrieved March 5, 2006, from http://www.die-bonn.de/esprid/dokumente/doc-2005/dohmen05_01.pdf

Engels, F. (1975). Letter to J. Bloch, London, Sept. 21, 1890. In K. Marx & F. Engels (Eds.), *Selected correspondence.* Moscow: Progress.

Erpenbeck, J. (2001). Selbstorganisiertes Lernen – Ausdruck des Zeitgeistes oder geistiger Ausdruck der Zeit? In D. Hoffmann et al. (Eds.), *Ökonomisierung der Bildung* (pp. 199–214). Weinheim: Beltz.

Forneck, H., & Wrana, D. (2005). *Ein parzelliertes Feld. Eine Einführung in die Weiterbildung.* Bielefeld: Bertelsmann.

Foucault, M. (1993). Technologien des Selbst. In M. Foucault et al. (Eds.), *Technologien des Selbst* (pp. 24–63). Frankfurt/M: Fischer.

Foucault, M. (1996). *Der Mensch ist ein Erfahrungstier.* Frankfurt/M: Suhrkamp.

Foucault, M. (1997). *Il faut défendre la société. Cours au Collège de France (1976).* Paris: Gallimard/Seuil.

Foucault, M. (2001). *L'herméneutique du sujet. Cours au Collège de France (1981–1982).* Paris: Gallimard/Seuil.

Foucault, M. (2004a). *Sécurité, Terretoire, Population. Cours au Collège de France (1977–1978).* Paris: Gallimard/Seuil.

Foucault, M. (2004b). *Naissance de la biopolitique. Cours au Collège de France (1978–1979).* Paris: Gallimard/Seuil.

Gonon, P. (2002). Pädagogisierung, eine Erfolgsgeschichte. Einfluss der Pädagogik auf Berufswelt und Weiterbildung. *Neue Zürcher Zeitung* (Internationale Ausgabe. Beilage Bildung und Erziehung), *18*(49).

Hoffmann, D. (2001). Die Auswirkungen der 'unsozialen Marktwirtschaft' auf den pädagogischen Zeitgeist. In D. Hoffmann et al. (Eds.), *Ökonomisierung der Bildung* (pp. 23–48). Weinheim: Beltz.

Langer, A., & Wrana, D. (2006). *Diskursverstrickung und diskursive Kämpfe—Nationalsozialismus und Erwachsenenbildung. Methodologische Fragen zur Analyse diskursiver Praktiken.* Retrieved August 20, 2006, from http://www.wb-giessen.de/dokumente/langerwrana_verstrickungenkaempfe.pdf

Lyotard, J.-F. (1988). *The differend: phrases in dispute.* Manchester, Lancashire: University Press.

Mühlenkamp, H. (2005). *Zur "Ökonomisierung" des öffentlichen Sektors: Verständnisse, Mißverständnisse und Irrtümer*. Speyer: DHV.

Olbrich, J. (2001). *Geschichte der Erwachsenenbildung in Deutschland*. Bonn: BPB.

Otto, V. (2005). Autonomie als Prinzip. Zur Geschichte des Autonomiebegriffs in der Erwachsenenbildung. *Hessische Blätter für Volksbildung*, *1*, 5–15.

Picht, G. (1964). *Die deutsche Bildungskatastrophe. Analyse u. Dokumentation*. Freiburg/Br: Walter.

Rousseau, J.-J. (1993). *Emile*. London: J.M. Dent.

Pongratz, L. A. (2003). *Zeitgeistsurfer. Beiträge zur Kritik der Erwachsenenbildung*. Weinheim: Beltz.

Schemmann, M. (2006). Bildung als Wirtschaftsfaktor oder Bildung für Alle. Die Perspektive der Weltbank auf Entwicklung und Aufgabe der Weiterbildung. In H. Forneck, G. Wiesner, & C. Zeuner (Eds.), *Teilhabe an der Erwachsenenbildung und gesellschaftliche Modernisierung* (pp. 98–106). Baltmannsweiler: Schneider Hohengehren.

Schulze, G. (1992). *Die Erlebnisgesellschaft. Kultursoziologie der Gegenwart*. Frankfurt/M: Campus.

Sennett, R. (1978). *The fall of public man*. New York: Vintage.

Timmermann, D. (2002). Bildungsökonomie. In R. Tippelt (Ed.), *Handbuch Bildungsforschung* (pp. 81–122). Opladen: Leske & Budrich.

Wagner, G. (2006). Ökonomie(sierung) und Bildung – Plädoyer für ein entspannteres Verhältnis. *Zeitschrift für Pädagogik*, *52*(1), 43–51.

Weiland, D. (2001). Der 'Arbeitskraftunternehmer' – ein neuer Leittypus für Wirtschaft und Schule? *Die Deutsche Schule*, *93*(4), 390–394.

Wrana, D. (2006). *Das Subjekt schreiben*. Baltmannsweiler: Schneider Hohengehren.

Daniel Wrana
Departement of Primary Education
University of Education
Northwest Switzerland

HERMANN J. FORNECK

27. FROM PASTORAL TO STRATEGIC RELATIONS IN ADULT EDUCATION?

Governmentality Theory-Based Thoughts on a Changing Relationship

"Whereas pastoral power, I believe, is defined entirely through its beneficence, its right to exist lies merely in doing good, and in actually doing it. For pastoral power, the salvation of the herd is, indeed, the most essential goal" (Foucault, 2004, p. 189).

INTRODUCTION

The following analysis from a governmentality perspective sheds light on the changing relationship between adult education providers and adult education recipients emanating from an adjustment in the structure of full-time personnel in further education. After a functional analysis of the field, I will thematize a specific type of relationship between further education providers and participants, which will be identified and analyzed as a secular pastorate. Subsequently, and in contrast to this pastoral relationship, I will examine the new form of provider-participant relationship and show that entirely new strategic relations are emerging there.

STRUCTURAL TRANSFORMATION OF THE FIELD

Nittel's analysis from a profession-theory perspective poses the thesis that there are two bases of knowledge in adult education. This limits the profession's power in so far as multilinguality leads to a divided knowledge base (Nittel, 2000). Nittel's theory targets the different discourses that full- and part-time employees in adult education refer to and simultaneously generate and maintain. Bastian's empirical study of trainer profiles shows, among other things, that most part-time trainers draw their knowledge from a professional base (Bastian, 1997), whereas studies by Giesecke (2002; 2005) suggest that actors in the field employed on a full-time basis generally do refer to adult-education knowledge.

These different knowledge bases used by the field's actors are not coincidental or voluntary, but instead correspond with the position and function of these actors within the field. Part-time instructors are remunerated compensated mainly for their material knowledge of, for example, a foreign language or rose growing, etc., whereas full-time instructors are recognized for their professional expertise based upon their pedagogic qualifications as adult educators in the broadest sense.

M.A. Peters et al. (eds.), Govermentality Studies in Education, 487–498.

Table 1. Knowledge bases

	Adult education knowledge base		Professional knowledge base	
	public adult education	private further education	public adult education	private further education
Full-time employees	high	high	low	low
Part-time employees	low	low	high	high

If we now also add in a further difference, that of public as opposed to private adult education, at first the change that results does not seem to be qualitative but rather quantitative. The percentage of full-time personnel employed in private adult education is quite high. In recent decades, an actual quantitative growth has occurred in this sector. It appears as though full-time actors in both sectors fulfill a function that is largely similar and draws on an identical knowledge base.

According to Schäffter's systems-theory inspired approach to analyzing transformation, modern society is involved in a process of constant transformation:

> In society's contemporary developmental phase, vastly different structural developments mutually influence one another, each with their partial effects and thus overlap to a highly complex tension-laden structure. (Schäffter, 2001, p. 16)

As Schäffter explains, great potential opens up in a society in which the borders of possibilities for arrangements are clearly perceptible. The greater opportunities for participation cannot be taken advantage of because there are too many choices. The dynamics that emerge must be taken up once again and processed in the educational system, and especially in further education.

A crucial characteristic of modern society, which Schäffter identifies as transformation society, is the change in social conversion processes. The system of adult education, in particular, is meant to react to this second order change primarily with reflexive, non-targeted transformations. In this way,

> Adult education becomes responsible for guaranteeing a historical, social, and personal identity that can be constantly newly acquired through learning processes (Schäffter, 2001, p. 146).

Here Schäffter's analysis changes and becomes a normative determination of the function of adult education and the (full-time) profession. Schäffter's analysis shows that further education is involved in a process described by sociologists as individual or subjective modernity, which is linked with macro-theory-oriented economic and social science research on growth and development in a third world context. It is concerned with the role of the individual in the modernization process, more concretely, the process of psychosocial transformation and adaptation of individuals who will come into increasing contact with modern institutions (see Inkeles, 1984). The theory states that there is a "syndrome of individual modernity" evident throughout the world in which modern people "[are] informed citizens participating in political life. They exhibit a distinctive sense of efficiency and are highly independent and autonomous in their relationship to tradition, especially when they make fundamental decisions about personal affairs; and they are open for new experiences and ideas, which means that they are relatively open-minded and cognitively flexible" (Inkeles, 1984, p. 363; Schöfthaler & Goldschmidt, 1984, p. 465).

Adult education, and also the profession, function to determine what has yet to be determined, to generate a subject's subjectivation (construction as a subject), and thereby to guarantee a subject's modernity. Additionally, a specific autonomy is granted to the field. In the context of this autonomy, the profession constitutes a modern subject by specific practices, "that is continually subjected to networks of obedience — a subject that is subjectivated by acquiring the truth that is imposed on him" (Foucault, 2004, p. 269). The outlined structures of the field lead beyond the full-time and part-time workers' distinct knowledge bases, as diagnosed by Nittel, to a further differentiation and dynamics of the adult education knowledge base: The full-time actors in public adult education, according to the theory pursued here, understand their function primarily as a materially determined mission: full-time actors in private further education define their function as a procedural mission. Since there is a growing influence of full-time actors in private adult education, a transformation occurs in the adult-education discourse, in the professional knowledge base, and in the relation between the profession and its clientele.

THE SECULAR ADULT-EDUCATION PASTORATE IN PUBLIC ADULT EDUCATION

Foucault develops the concept of pastoral power in the fifth to the eighth lecture of his 1978 lecture series "*Sécurité, Territoire et Population*"[1]. Historically, this form of leadership is not new. What is new is its Christian version that is not directed toward territory or security, but instead, toward the guidance of souls.Foucault's aim is to show that the Christian pastorate is composed of a "subtle economy of merit and lapses, an economy that presupposes the detailed analysis of transfer mechanisms, inversion procedures, and supportive functions between opposing elements" (Foucault 2004: 252). There are three general traits that characterize every pastorate: first, the pastorate has a relationship to salvation; its fundamental goal is for people to advance on their path to salvation. Second, the pastorate has a relationship to the law, and third, to truth. "The pastor leads to salvation, he disposes the law, he teaches truth" (Foucault, 2004, p. 244). Reading Kant's "Lectures on Pedagogics" and his essay on Enlightenment from the perspective laid out here, it is entirely possible to understand the secular expectations of salvation associated with the bourgeois project of education, which is meant to lead all the way to "eternal peace," in the same vein. Pedagogy, including adult education, with its didactics and repertoire of methods, is thereby understood as a set of instructions (laws) for the teaching of this education. The inner-disciplinary terms such as "subject," "individualization," "emancipation," "maturity," and "autonomy" represent the secular pendants to religious salvation. In this inter-pretation, the material concretization of the content of adult education, which German adult education science continues to enact even today, represents the secular pendant to religious truth. From a governmentality perspective, such pretensions of social function become transformed in the profession's secular mission[2] "to direct and to determine" (Foucault, 1985, p. 25) people's behavior by governing their mental state, and thus to practice a governmentality. In order to follow the analytical possibilities of this kind of perspective, in the following I understand "mission" and the form of influence that adult education has on subjects — specifically corresponding with this mission — as a secular adult-education pastorate.[3]

Yet this perspective yields analytical results only if one follows the further characterization of the Christian pastorate as presented by Foucault. Foucault is interested in the reciprocity relations that distinguish the pastorate and establishes five such relations: distributiveness, analytical responsibility, transfer, inversion, and correspondence. In analyzing adult education with the help of these five relations, integral and simultaneously paradoxical distributiveness, identifies the fact that a paradox occurs when the adult education instructor takes on a particular responsibility for all of the participants in the course to learn something and also for each individual to learn. The instructor guides the learning experience of the entire group, structures the content and method for what happens in the course as a whole and also for each participant. Yet pursuing both of these aims equally leads to a paradoxical situation. For example, when course instructors have to decide whether to proceed with their program, one person might not be able to follow what is happening in the lessons, or instead, might not orient what happens in the course to the learning needs and learning development of the others. The adult-education professional habitus cares for the whole as well as the individual; the course, as well as each participant; the environment as well as the biotope; humanity as well as the individual biographies; thereby embodying one of the basic traits of every pastorate, namely, integral and paradoxical distributiveness.

'Analytical responsibility' of adult educators comprises having to take on a 'representative interpretation of the world', for all issues that students have not yet made their own. The educators are made responsible for this in the name of their clientele.

'Exhaustive and immediate transfer' refers to the fact that the student's success or failure always equates with the teacher's success or failure. In the pastorate, it is not possible to differentiate between cause and effect. For this reason, the quantitative empirical research on teaching/learning, with regards to public educational processes, after a certain point always returns to the fact of a multifunctional relational dependence of factors and the implosion of the difference between dependent and independent factors.

The humanities postulate of a pedagogic province can be understood as an 'inversion of a sacrificial act.' Regardless of whether we are dealing with children, youths, or adults, in the project of formalized education aiming at the creation of mature/responsible individuals, implies that it is somehow a special project, protected from real life, if only to enable a different time regime than the industrial one and accentuate the self-will of learning. It is also applicable in those cases where concepts of job-related education attempt to implement a 'pedagogic province' into the sequencing of the labor process. Adult education instructors represent the protectors of these adult education spaces; they safeguard them, protect them against the rigors of the world; they are the ones that stand in resistance to society's functional demands. The 'alternating correspondence' denotes the fundamentally deficient construction of the subject. Participants are always construed as deficient in terms of a certain matter (knowledge, skill, competence, behavior, etc.). This is necessary for them to become legitimate objects of adult education activities. On the other hand, the topos of the instructor's lack of knowledge runs throughout (adult) education literature, from the new trend to the latest adult-education constructivism. This has become a programmatic point of departure for the program of self-guided learning with its core statement: in the end it is the learning subjects who know best how they learn most effectively.

Adult education pastoral relations, although always limited in terms of time and content, are nonetheless relations of subjugation. They constitute a subject under explicit political, legal, and economic power, "a subject that is subjectivated by acquiring the truth that is imposed upon him" (Foucault, 2004, p. 269).[4] This reality is present in adult education's claims of responsibility/maturity and emancipation and implies a subtle economy of foreign-will and self-will. On the one hand, it has to be responsive to the diverse, contradictory needs of its clientele and at the same time disregard these, as the profession's aim is to "apply symbolic and instrumental regulatory knowledge and societal norms to individual cases" (Dewe, 1988, p. 144). Along with tasks oriented on mediation and comprehension, negotiations are characterized by a respect for the clientele's autonomous lives: Kade states that "Adult education institutions are interstitial worlds between obligations and options" (Kade, 1997, p. 118). With this formulation, he thus thematizes participants' ambiguous, ambivalent, and pluralistic utilization of available adult education opportunities. Yet that is only the one side, that of appropriation. The paradoxical task of the professional impact can be found in everyday life, in making it likely that for the clientele, "ideas about behavior will be formed and/or changed" (Habermas, 1971, p. 75) while simultaneously respecting the self-will of learning (Sesink, 1990).

The pastorate, however, does not want to govern. It understands and stylizes itself as an institute of advancement, qua self-improvement, in which "we arrive at the growth of all powers, abilities, and skills, at the growth of knowledge, insights, and perspectives, that surpass mere functionality" (Meueler, 1993, p. 157). The pastorate has "only" the secular salvation of the subject in mind. Thus a requirement for the success of subjectivation processes is the lack of a governing technology, which Luhmann identified as a technology deficit of pedagogics (see Luhmann, 1982, p. 31).

As Herrmann (1996) states, inside the field, these processes are understood as self-formation processes and professional activity is understood as merely enabling or yielding. However, the adult-educational secular pastorate organizes self-improvement in the context of higher-level cultural ideals and social demands and does so to their advantage. But these social demands are coded as having to do with the quality of learning, which, for example, has to take place within and not on the individuals. At the same time, however, the paradox is that every autonomous activity (*Selbsttätigkeit*) is always also the result of adult education practices, which are foreign practices, thus implying a temporary mutuality and constantly raising the question for the discipline of the boundary between adult-educational practices and other practices.

The Relationship of Further Education Providers and Clientele

The relations analyzed above continue at the level of provider—addressee. This remains linked with a paradoxical relation which, on the one hand, assumes a functioning public discussion whose aim, on the other hand, is "always the enabling of ... adults to participate in these kinds of public debates" (Groothoff, 1978, p. 517). Also in the area that was known as public relations, which, as we will see, could no longer survive, the adult is positioned as both capable and incapable, he or she is simultaneously object and subject in this relationship.

The heterogeneity and diversity of the providers does not serve to create competition within the field: "The legally recognized pluralism of the providers makes sense in that it guarantees a variance and diversity in the structure of what is offered that is suitable to the dynamics of socio-cultural, economical, and political processes..." (Wirth, 1978, p. 520). Publicly presenting the field's heterogeneity serves to once again safeguard the socially present and desired plurality, and with that, the actual mission, of the production of modernity. The provider's public relations – e.g. course brochures – are again functionally oriented on the mission of a secular modernity. They are meant to visibly present in the public space the actual heterogeneity of pedagogic events taking place. This public visibility is then the template against which participants decide for or against specific educational offers and, at the same time, "learn" that they have to decide from within a plural value-order (*Werteordnung*). In this respect, the course brochures from the 1960s and 1970s are characterized by a materiality that one no longer finds today.

"Adult education institutions are, namely, not only reliant on public relations, but also have a duty to carry out public relations" (Wirth, 1978, p. 520).

The adult education system's provider-orientation is a specific relationship in the context of the secularized pastorate. In this, the provider understands itself to be the carrier of the system and it must offer public content and objectives of responding actors regarding their needs. Need always means a balancing of public and private demands and thereby contains at a system level what Foucault refers to as the foundational characteristic of every pastorality – integral and paradoxical distributiveness or concern for the whole and the individuals.

Yet at the present time, the pastorate appears increasingly dysfunctional. The field actors in the area of private further education eclipse the secular pastoral discourse in adult education and decisively transform it.

FUNCTIONALITY ORIENTED ON DEMAND

The "syndrome of individual modernity" is experiencing a decisive transformation in recent decades through a neo-liberal governmentality which configures the self-subjectivating subject in a new dispositif as a self-employed entrepreneur (Masschelein & Simons 2002, p. 590). What this implies is a fundamental change in the relationship of the learning individual to the materiality of knowledge and to the individual's own subjectivity. Both are integrated in a complex of self-economizing (Voß, 2000).

The concept of subject hereby experiences an essential shift. Subjects are no longer understood as resistant, but as structurally determined (see e.g. Ludwig, 1999, p. 671). Their anthropological determination as subjects with reference to maturity/responsibility becomes translated in an empirical definition and thus attains a specific functionality. The normatively charged but materially empty arsenal of concepts in adult education that refer to the 'self' (self-direction, self-determination, self-organization, etc.) define the learner as autonomous. However, this is an abstract autonomy, void of society, and empirically bypassed. Autonomous subjects choose from available content, times, etc., for learning, are self-directed and judge and observe themselves, develop meta-cognition of their own learning, create portfolios on their own learning processes to achieve a transparency for themselves and for others on the outside that extends into the regions of informal learning through a process of 'certification of informal learning.' The subjectivity subjectivated in this way is, for all of its deficits, autonomous. The pastoral relation of alternating correspondence is therefore no longer present. What was formerly only available to the individual, what was not public, has now been turned outward, made visible, and been transferred from the informal realm to the public space. This is the first essential transformation. This turning outward of the inside is tied to a change in the position of the content of learning. It is no longer a specific materiality defined in the cultural field, which is linked with a specific form of appropriation that should be effective in a process of subjectivating the subject. The position of materiality becomes exchangeable. The field has lost its power to internally define materiality; the profession is no longer analytically responsible for the content of the educational process. The new position of materiality lies outside of the field of adult education. That is the second transformation.

Shifting to the center of the new subjectivation process are specific competences that have been demanded from the outside. The subjectivated subjectivity is thus no longer oriented toward differentiating itself from the environment – in as small a difference as it may be – but instead, toward a specific fit with the environment, toward its exploitation, toward a demand that comes from outside. That is the third transformation. Learning is oriented toward subjectivities that are desired by the market and useful within it.

It is through this that the *need* for further education is replaced by the *demand* for further education. Just like the concept of need, demand is not flatly empirical. Demand is not something sought by those who potentially participate in further education. Demand is the need for competence indicated by other fields that subjects subjectivated as entrepeneurs want to exploit. The concept of demand thus creates new ways of relationing subjects, materiality of content, and demands for competence from outside the field.

Therefore, three essential transformations are important in the context of our problem:

Table 2. Field and Discourse Structure

Field and discourse structure	
Public adult education	Private adult education
Privacy	Transparency
Self-realization	Self-valorization
Need	Demand

And they lead to entirely new constellations of learners, course content to be acquired, and its consumption outside of the field.

The suggested transformations also change the provider-participant relationship. For example, a current fundamental adjustment as a consequence of the marketing concept is represented by the further education providers' usage of a term for participant that corresponds with the learner being made a subject and being made responsible. This occurs in the discourse by construing a client-subject from the participant. The new talk of a client is more than just a shift in nomenclature. The changed term represents changed rationalities that are then linked with technologies (concepts, models) and techniques (methods, procedures). The pastoral concern for each and every individual no longer relates providers and recipients in a disciplinary discourse identified as participant-oriented, but instead, a specific interest of the provider meets with one of the recipient/client. It is at that moment, namely, when the participants are constituted as client-subjects that they are inquiring customers with specific interests in an educational market.

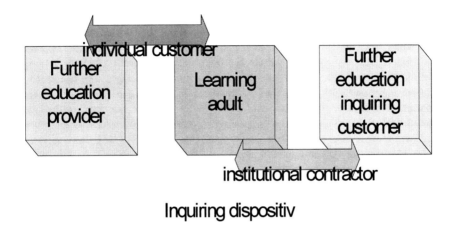

Figure 1. Inquiring dispositif

The conceptual adjustment from participants to customers (clients) represents the fourth essential transformation, simultaneously viewing the relationship of participants and providers (or lecturers) homologous to a relationship of consumers and producers. The main concern here is the customer's satisfaction, no longer their disturbance. There is no longer the pastoral concern for their higher-level secular 'salvation' (maturity, emancipation), their development as educational subjects, since the orientation toward the client re-constitutes further education institutes as businesses (Opitz, 2004). In this way, a new demand-dispositif emerges that is fundamentally different than that of the secularized pastorate and leads to internal resistance within the field. The new dispositif emerges when concern is with an 'innovative' form of further education, the so-called in-house offers. Institutional contractors (firms, authorities) purchase so-called in-house programs. They provide the participants and determine the content and goals. The adult education facility merely contributes their methodological know-how and instantiates the further education measures. Disappearing in this relationship is the original customer (the subjectivated subject). The profession has lost its jurisdiction over that which in a didactic triangle was still considered a unit, the professional organization of an event comprising material and formal content, its integral distributiveness.

In the implementation of the new relationship at the provider-recipient level, the new technologies of quality management, quality development, and quality assurance play a decisive role.

New Relationship of Those Seeking and Supplying Further Education

Quality management stands for an ensemble of social practices intended primarily to effect an orientation of the supplier on the customer. Found within the changeover from a secular pastorate to an interest-driven client relationship via the implementation of quality assurance processes is a new formation of the supplier. This changeover comprises no longer thinking about the further education client in the same way as the further education participant, capable of appropriating a cultural identity as one who should be concerned with forming him or herself and developing this found reality. Instead, the customer is thought of empirically as a person equipped with free choice in the form of educational coupons and credits making investment decisions. The addressee concept at the base of pedagogic-theoretical thought is entirely supplanted by the idea of a customer, whereby, learners choose between various offers (contents, course types, lecturers, institutes with a particular reputation, and paths and forms of learning). In this way, the governmental strategy of subjectivation of those seeking further education corresponds with the strategy of subjectivation of suppliers, who are oriented toward the clients' changing requests. Quality assurance procedures now steer the behavior of actors in the field toward a continuous responsiveness to fulfilling the customer's requests.

The changeover from participant orientation to customer orientation implies a new quality regime for the provider. Whereas participant orientation indicates the unreasonable demand of a materially-defined ideal subject, customer orientation forces behavior oriented on needs along with an accompanying, calculated security. In this way, customers as potential purchasers are freed from inconveniences or secondary activities that might distract them from buying. Also the concept of satisfaction is hereby newly constructed. Until now, participant satisfaction referred to the emotional state that set in after a phase of successful subjective effort, now customer satisfaction refers to the learning entrepreneur's assessment of the supplier since, for the learning entrepreneur, studying is a personal investment that must promise a return. This transfer also causes a change in the character of further education's addressee; the participating student becomes a (co)paying client. The client concept thus simultaneously shapes addressee and addresser of further education and sets them into a new relationship.

The image of the (future) customer in further education includes that of the entrepreneur. Customers actively work on their education, which increasingly becomes their own responsibility to compile. Quality concepts demand a certain ideal type of participant-customer: "Quality concepts assume an educated and sovereign customer who largely (co)determines what is offered, and how and where" (Gnahs, 1997, p. 18). But the relationship itself is a different one. Adult entrepreneurs are integrated between a diversified offer and their preconditioned demands. Their freedom is not found in the free choice of a further education program; their choice comprises the cleverest individual relationship of demand and supply in order to market their subjectivity as profitably as possible.

Quality assurance procedures serve essentially to lead education providers to respond with market strategies that refer to customers' selection mechanisms. Included in this is their understanding of themselves as further education service providers. The customer/service provider concept implies a strategic relationship to selecting customers. The new market rationality forces the provider to establish practices of corporate identity in order to win over customers and bind them to the institute. A new, strategic relationship is established between supplier and client that no longer has anything to do with the pastoral relationship of traditional educational institutes and participants, which also contained an integral, mutually strategic relationship. Additionally, the institute has to maintain a brand reputation that operates with an identification strategy. Following these types of concepts that originated in the area of marketing, such as corporate identity and branding, activities shift from pedagogic problems to management issues. Suppliers now search for strategies to maintain their "market share," to expand it, to form brands, evaluate the images of the suppliers on the market, establish controlling for education, and evaluate investment decisions with the help of economic prognoses.

The full-time profession in further education draws from this newly emerging knowledge base, actually fundamentally co-produces it. In the process, pastoral discourse seems to be eroding steadily and it isn't necessary to invoke clairvoyant power to predict that the discursive battles have only just begun.

NOTES

[1] This lecture was published simultaneously in German and French, the English translation should follow in 2007/08, see: http://www.palgrave.com/philosophy/foucault.asp

[2] To this extent, it can deal "only" with the relationing of mission and profession, not with a replacement.

[3] Foucault emphasized that the pastorate does not coincide with the pedagogic (Foucault, 2004, p. 241), yet nonetheless develops in his analysis characteristics of a Christian pastorate that encompasses also traits of adult education.

[4] While examining the history of the pastorates, the development of a secularized pedagogic pastorate coming from the Christian, will not be the topic here.

REFERENCES

Bastian, H. (1997). *Kursleiterprofile und Angebotsqualität*. Bad Heilbrunn: Klinkhard.

Dewe, B., & Ferchhoff, W. (1988). Dienstleistungen und Bildung – Bildungstheoretische Betrachtungen über personenbezogene Dienstleistungsberufe. In O. Hansmann & W. Marotzki (Eds.), *Diskurs Bildungstheorie I: Systematische Markierungen* (pp. 135–157). Weinheim: Deutscher Studienverlag.

Foucault, M. (1985). *Freiheit und Selbstsorge. Interview 1984 und Vorlesung 1982* (H. Becker, Ed.). Frankfurt/M: Materialis.

Foucault, M. (1987). *Table round du 20 mai 1978* (conversation with A. Farge, A. Fontana, J. Léonard, M. Perrot et al.). quoted by Lemke 1997, 146.

Foucault, M. (2004). *Geschichte der Gouvernementalität I. Sicherheit, Territorium, Bevölkerung. Vorlesung am Collège de France 1977–1978* (M. Sennelart, Ed.). Frankfurt/M: Suhrkamp.

Gieseke, W. (2005). Professionalität und Fortbildungsbedarf. In K. Baldauf-Bergmann, F. von Küchler, & C. Weber (Eds.), *Erwachsenenbildung im Wandel: Ansätze einer reflexiven Weiterbildungspraxis* (pp. 28–51). Baltmannsweiler: Schneider Hohengehren.

Gieseke, W. (2002). Was ist erwachsenenpädagogische Professionalität? In H.-U. Otto, T. Rauschenbach, & P. Vogel (Eds.), *Erziehungswissenschaft: Professionalität und Kompetenz* (pp. 197–208). Opladen: Leske & Budrich.

Groothoff, H.-H. (1978). Öffentlichkeit und Erwachsenenbildung. In I. Wirth (Ed.), *Handwörterbuch der Erwachsenenbildung* (pp. 517–519). Paderborn: Schöningh.

Habermas, J. (1971). Der Universalitätsanspruch der Hermeneutik. In K.-O. Apel et al. (Eds.), *Hermeneutik und Ideologiekritik* (pp. 120–159). Frankfurt/M.

Herrmann, U. (1996). Die Schule – eine Herausforderung für das New Public Management (NPM). *Beiträge zur Lehrerbildung, 14*(3), 314–329.

Inkeles, A. (1984). Was heißt 'individuelle Modernität'? In T. Schöfthaler & D. Goldschmidt (Eds.), *Soziale Struktur und Vernunft* (pp. 351–378). Frankfurt/M.

Kade, J. (1997). Riskante Biographien und die Risiken lebenslangen Lernens. *Literatur- und Forschungsreport Weiterbildung, 39,* 112–124.

Klafki, W. (1972). *Studien zur Bildungstheorie und Didaktik.* Weinheim: Beltz.

Lemke, T. (1997). *Eine Kritik der politischen Vernunft. Foucaults Analyse der modernen Gouvernementalität* (4th ed.). Berlin: Argument.

Ludwig, J. (1999). Subjektperspektiven in neueren Lernbegriffen. *Zeitschrift für Pädagogik, 45*(5), 667–682.

Luhmann, N., & Schorr, E. (Eds.). (1982). *Zwischen Technologie und Selbstreferenz: Fragen an die Pädagogik.* Frankfurt/M: Suhrkamp.

Maschelein, J., & Simons, M. (2002). An adequate education in a globalised world? A note on immunisation against Being-Together. *Journal of philosophy of education, 36*(4), 589–608.

Meueler, E. (1993). *Die Türen des Käfigs: Wege zum Subjekt.* Stuttgart: Klett-Cotta.

Opitz, S. (2004). *Gouvernementalität im Postfordismus. Macht, Wissen und Techniken des Selbst im Feld unternehmerischer Rationalität.* Hamburg: Argument.

Schäffter, O. (2001). *Weiterbildung in der Transformationsgesellschaft. Zur Grundlegung einer Theorie der Institutionalisierung.* Baltmannsweiler: Schneider Hohengehren.

Schöfthaler, T., & Goldschmidt, D. (Eds.). (1984). *Soziale Struktur und Vernunft.* Frankfurt/M: Suhrkamp.

Sesink, W. (1990). *Der Eigensinn des Lernens.* Weinheim: Deutscher Studienverlag.

Voß, G. G. (2000). Unternehmer der eigenen Arbeitskraft. Einige Folgerungen für die Bildungssoziologie. *Zeitschrift für Soziologie der Erziehung, 20*(2), 149–166.

Wirth, I. (1978). Öffentlichkeitsarbeit. In I. Wirth (Ed.), *Handwörterbuch der Erwachsenenbildung* (pp. 519–524). Paderborn: Schöningh.

Hermann J. Forneck
Department for Primary Teacher Education
University of Applied Sciences
Basel
Switzerland

THOMAS HÖHNE AND BRUNO SCHRECK

28. MODULARIZED KNOWLEDGE

INTRODUCTION

The modularization of curricular knowledge and the transformation of Diplom/ Magister degrees into internationally accredited Bachelor's/Master's degree programs at German universities are structural elements of current international educational reforms of the academy. As a result of these reforms, curricular knowledge is subject to structural transformation which up to the present has hardly been researched.

The aim of this chapter is to trace the transformations of knowledge from its more classical curricular appearances to its modularized forms, and to give a theoretical account of these transformations from the perspective of theories of governmentality. We will attempt to understand the findings of this enquiry in light of the issue of structural transformations of the university in the neoliberal context.

We hypothesize that modularization is an indicator for tendencies to restructure knowledge in a Tayloristic manner. Modularization also represents the commodification of knowledge, since by this very process, knowledge becomes a part of the structure of economic exchange, and its value is only acknowledged in terms of its status as an object of that exchange.

In order to understand these processes and the resulting transformations in the structure of knowledge, we will particularly focus on the changes subsequent to the educational reforms of the 1960s and 1970s.

In what follows, we are mainly concerned with the effects of the educational reform on the discourse of education following the Bologna declaration in Germany.

Our thesis is that the modularized way of the production of knowledge can no longer be accounted for in terms of the classical form of critique of rationalism as it is presented in the *Dialectic of Enlightenment* (Adorno, 1987). The reason for this impasse is that we are dealing with new forms of knowledge production, new practises of knowledge transmission and new ways of building networks of relations between protagonists and forms of knowledge.

MODULARIZATION AND THE TRANSNATIONAL REFORM OF THE EDUCATION SYSTEM

Modularization of education is one structural feature, among a whole set of measures, programmatically bound to the Bologna process and its accompanying reforms. Part of this package of measures is the introduction of Bachelor-/Master programs, which provide a structure of successive degrees, and a unified system of accreditation of credit points the European Credit Transfer System (ECTS). The

M.A. Peters et al. (eds.), Govermentality Studies in Education, 499–508.

stated objectives of Bologna are to advance student mobility, to enhance the capacity of universities to compete internationally, and to expedite the employability of graduates.

It is quite evident that the aforementioned transformations aim at the globalization of labor and educational processes in creating a global knowledge society which should now be implemented within a 'Europe of knowledge'.

A necessary precondition for this implementation is the standardization of curriculum contents and subjects of knowledge in order to render them comparable and calculable. This is accomplished by means of a unified system that helps to assess and compare coursework achievements by using credit points. The transcript of courses and the respective credit points and hours earned by each student thus operate like money: as standardized units of barter, completely transferable to other universities. Credit points and hours reflect the amount of time invested, and help officials to appropriately determine the level of each student's matriculation. Insofar as study time is always personally incorporated, credit points come to represent individual time acquisition and gain of time for the student: One can 'save' time and thus, capital.

Practises of knowledge do not stay untouched by such reforms. This includes the manner in which knowledge is dealt with and controlled by educational policies, internal institutional decisions, teaching, and to a great extent by students' study behaviour ranging from subjective connotations of studying and learning to the decision for studying in accordance to the criteria of employability. The whole system is subject to a rigid time regimen determined by outside actors.

The Conference of the Ministers of Education and Arts (*Kultusministerkonferenz*) has determined three to four years as standard duration for a BA program, and an additional one to two years for an MA program. If completed consecutively, the time spent at a university adds up to a maximum of five years (see KMK, 2003). The rationalizing influences of the reforms have been found to have positive effects on students, especially in regards to their use of time.

The accreditation process and evaluation process are among the factors that are supposed to optimize the educational conditions at the university. They suggest by implication that the university is a 'preparatial field,' a place where students can develop their profiles and where their degrees can help enhance access to a transnational employment market.

The supposed time-frame for completion and the standardization of essentially required knowledge certainly implies predictability insofar as the accomplishment of the objective – the development of competences – means one does not need to invest more time than predetermined.

The question arises: how does this form of standardization affect knowledge? And more specifically: how is academic knowledge taught at the university affected by such standardizations. Does knowledge take on decisively new forms? What new knowledge practises and practises of subjectivation are tied to it? This leads us to the notion of the 'module.'

The term module is derived from classical Greek architecture where it signified "a measuring unit that served to define the proportion within column-arrangements by criteria of height, distance, frames and capitals" (Kokemohr 2005, p. 102). In technical terminology the expression "module" stands for an "integrated group of components" or rather just a particular component of a unit assembly system which has to be compatible to other elements to form a working system of construction elements" (ibid.).

For the academic field, the German Federal and State Committee (Bund-Länder-Kommission) defines a "module" as "(…) a cluster of courses which are dedicated to one topic or thematic focus." Thus "module" is defined as a "content-specific, self-contained temporal unit, possibly composed of a combination of different courses. It is qualitatively (contents) and quantitatively (credit points) specifiable and needs to be assessable (by exams)" (Kokemohr, 2005, p. 103). To Michael Ehrke modularization is an "iridescent expression", used to describe various sets of problems which, although entirely different from each other, become mixed up in the academic discourse (Ehrke, 2005, p. 2).

Unlike the didactical notion of modules, where modules are content units, formed to serve didactical or learning-theoretical purposes (e.g. by means of the development of the curriculum, or content specific internal differentiation), the definition of modules which is portrayed above is solely formal in character. Modularized contents thus receive a temporally self-contained, calculable and assessable form. In this way, quantitative parameters of time, exchange and performance represent essential structural elements of modularization. This process was also described as commodification of knowledge (Lyotard, 1984). In contrast to the traditional qualitative and didactic designation of modules, in recent educational discourse we find a paradigmatic shift in which modules become more and more functionally oriented towards the attainment of competences.

The declared goal of the educational reform is for modules or individual university courses to provide students with certain competences. The ubiquitous, increasing lists of desirable skills (social skills, communicative, management, reflective or problem-solving skills, self-skills, etc.) represent psychologically abstract terms whose operationalization and evaluation would take as much effort, would demand as much organizational complexity as the university courses apparently designed for their transmission and acquisition. So the discourse on assigned competences remains at an abstract distance from the subject of capabilities and obligations since a definition of the subject matter that would serve as the foundation of the subjects' skills is lacking. Still, the focus on the subject in the context of the academic modularization discourse is remarkable because it determines a specific range of socially acknowledged self-government and acceptable autonomy as the range of skills that a competent subject is characteristically expected to possess (*homo competens* vs. the rational decider, *homo economicus*).

Contents become fluid, fleeting under the pressures of competence-orientation and the unyielding time-restrictions of a six-semester BA course, of permanent content-ratings and evaluability and the clear assignation of credit points. These rigid structural requisites have a fragmentizing effect on knowledge, uncoupling it from its structural components, time and contents. Unlike the dogmatic-canonical structure of the classical curricular knowledge, this formally modularized knowledge shows hardly any coherence beyond its functional connections. At the same time, the emphasis on the subjects' formal skills shifts the focus away from the distinctive internal logic of knowledge and its content- and domain-specific structure. A critical, qualitative concept of learning that embraces multitude of variations in understanding and interpretation is replaced by a technocratic concept that puts its decisive emphasis on the outcome of learning. Output-orientation in learning corresponds to the idea of functional, performance-oriented, flexible subjects (in the sense of Sennett, 1998) who can rationally choose "their knowledge" and "their competences," who are able to track necessary knowledge within a given range systematically and who are capable of acquiring the respective competences and of transforming them into performance. But if we go by the assumption that subjectivity is mainly or at least also defined by resistance, that it is characterized by how the subject deals with and how it transforms the objects of knowledge, then the functional, technocratic lopsidedness of this kind of modularization becomes obvious.

As far as the individual management of study courses is concerned, the range of possibilities for rational choice is rather pre-regulated by organizational restrictions like universities' entrance standards and admission restrictions. Selective pressure grows. Changing to a different major and the connected time loss will be penalized by more tuition fees. Repeatedly failing an obligatory exam will lead to ex-matriculation. All these practices point to the paradox of 'regulated autonomy' the name we give for the space for individual action that we have described above. which is a matter of a temporal-spatial transformation of the structure of knowledge and practices as part of the modularization program.

TAYLORIZATION OF KNOWLEDGE AND SUBJECTIVATION EFFECTS

Studying in Germany has always been determined by curricula, schedules, by economic (e.g. the tuition fees that existed in Germany until 1970) as well as by political guidelines (the associated student body, too, has a political mandate). There have always been courses which imparted canonical and dogmatic knowledge, such as medicine and law – the classic professions. However, their systematic structure was based on the ideal of an academic education as well-founded as possible. Research into the development of the notion of competence shows which conceptual transformations have taken place in educational discourses since the 1970s.

Individual skills clearly associated with specific activities used to be the decisive qualifications when looking for a job. The additional concept of key qualifications has expanded the field of professional knowledge and skills to include comprehensive skills (extra-functional 'meta-skills'), but until the dawn of the competence discourse of the 1990s profession and theory specific knowledge and skills were conceptually marginalized in favor of individualized powers of self-organization. The former forms of knowledge have not just disappeared, they have rather been substituted as "necessary but by far no longer sufficient prerequisites for adequate expertise on the subject's part" (Höhne, 2006a, p. 301).

Since the 1980s, and more so following the Bologna processes of the 1990s, the fundamental, central metaphor for the knowledge base of the professions, in general ,academic and political discourses, focuses on notions of 'core and key' as reflected in words like 'core competence', 'key qualifications', 'core subjects', and 'core topics' etc. Such metaphors stand for universal skills that are not tied to specific contents, in effect reflecting a process of the pragmatization of knowledge, such that the functionality of knowledge is reduced to employability.

However, a reflexive awareness of basic knowledge that has to be transmitted is fundamental; knowledge of its system and the didactic structuring within a specific domain of knowledge, and the abstract functional abilities that can be deduced only by dealing with this basic knowledge.

In the process of a functional orientation of competence and through the principle of modularization, the acquisition of knowledge and of skills becomes detached from knowledge itself, from its forms and structures. The deduction process is reversed, or at least its point of reference shifts away from contents and towards objectives of competence. Questions of coherence, systematization, compatibility of knowledge move into the background. At this point the idea that the acquisition of knowledge is (on the side of the subject) necessarily accompanied by an assimilation of a certain order of meaning, of a certain pattern of interpretation, a context, thus a social structure (all of this does, after all, characterize learning processes), this idea then becomes secondary to the normative goal that structure, context and meaning are established and even have to be established by the competent subjects themselves.

In this sense twenty years ago J. F. Lyotard delivered the hypothesis of the disrupture of knowledge and 'Bildung' as a consequence of the commodification of knowledge (Lyotard, 1984).

A look at vocational training in Germany illustrates the effects of modularization. Michael Ehrke correctly points out that modularization in the area of vocational training means the fragmentation of formalized, degree-oriented courses of education. Regarding consecutive courses of study, i.e. the BA/MA-structure, he sees the practice of consecutive education in vocational training as leading to a *dequalification*. Therefore since the 1980s such courses have been widely cut back. Discussion about the limits of Taylorism affected this policy. True to the motto: "Back to Taylorism" the call for modularization is a roll-back strategy as well (Ehrke, 2005, p. 4).

If modularization is generally a kind of *Taylorization of knowledge* then it is a *neo-liberally modernized Taylorism*. This *Neo-Taylorism* is characterized by its ability to join apparently contradictory principles, thus presenting itself as a *hybrid* form. On the one hand there is a visible increase of measures of external control by accreditation procedures, evaluation and the hierarchization of organizational decision-making processes (requirements of educational policies, the presidency model). On the other hand we find an almost emphatic embrace of a concept of subjectivity which incorporates powers of self-organization, individual competence, permanent mobilization and individual responsibility.

In our view this hybrid form, which we have called regulated autonomy, represents the basis of a *new type of student* who is to be created by modularization and who is also, as an ideal, at the heart of the current academic reforms. Although there will certainly still be a continuity between the individual modules and meaningful connections will always be made by the subject, the *practice of modularization* creates an attitude or a *habitus* of pragmatic utilitarian knowledge, a market value consciousness on the part of students. One effect of this is the devaluation of *theoretical knowledge* since its existence is not legitimized by any kind of practical applicability. Research into professionalization and the usage of scientific knowledge has made it abundantly clear that theoretical knowledge and practical know-how have to be seen as *two completely different forms of knowledge* (Beck & Bonß, 1989; Dewe, Ferchhoff & Radtke, 1992; Neuweg, 2000). In our judgement this important difference is about to disappear, to be sacrificed to a concept of BA-employability. Employability is part of an education market where individuals use their *competences as capital* to compete against each other. As *homo competens*, as self-manager the *entrepreneur* represents new forms of subjectivation in the market place of options that have gained predominance as social models.

The market metaphor and the liberal notions of the subject reveal a trend to make the social element anathema. Together with a roll-back of the political this is an eminent goal and effect of neo-liberal change. What is demanded is self-knowledge gathered through permanent self-observation and self-scrutiny which thus facilitates 'self-rationalization.' The necessary knowledge is not regarded as connected to specific contents or domains, but as universally functional; tied up with this is the question of the knowledge base for (partial) competences needed for professionalization.

COMPETENCE INSTEAD OF KNOWLEDGE?

The *capital of competence* consists of nothing less than a conglomerate of different forms of knowledge, accumulated over a lifetime and permanently integrated and organized by the learners. Against this, Dirk Rustemeyer rightfully accentuates the necessity to differentiate forms of knowledge in order to make them available for the reflection of both action and thinking (Rustemeyer, 2002).

Reflective knowledge is characterized by its 'non-functional' functionality, by its resistance to technologization – it cannot be directly exploited. In the face of knowledge that invites technologization, Rustemeyer continues, "ideas of a good life, of sound judgment that do not easily conform to a cost-benefit calculation" (ibid.) are equally "devalued as processes of aesthetic education that are as time-consuming as they are hard to judge in terms of efficiency and that interface perceptive and reflective competences" (ibid.). In this we recognize a break with the tradition of knowledge transmission and acquisition. In the course of this process an amalgamation of forms of knowledge and a one-sided emphasis of practical knowledge, in terms of *applicability*, takes place. Notions of universal competence engender a dichotomy of general knowledge that is regarded as functional for developing competences, and specialized knowledge (de Haan & Poltermann, 2002; Höhne, 2003; 2006b).

The devaluation of theoretical knowledge leads to a normative valorization of functional competence as a 'form of knowledge' that to a large extent departs from content-based knowledge as a basis for integration and organization.

Ewald Terhart remarks about academic teacher-training in Germany, that "questions of structure and questions of contents cannot be discussed separately" (Terhart, 2002, p. 21). According to Terhart, employability cannot be the central goal of university education in the context of job-oriented study courses without "didactical and pedagogical knowledge preceding specialized knowledge" (ibid.) in a well-organized relational system. A reduction of professional expert knowledge to formal and functional transmission of knowledge or transmission techniques is de-professionalizing in more ways than one:

a) Contents become arbitrary and thus avoid all need for legitimization; and

b) As professional transmission of knowledge of this kind becomes more and more unbounded, a kind of blank space is created that could affect all those *professionals who identify themselves as educators*. Analogous to multi-disciplinarity there would emerge a kind of 'multi-professionalism' or 'multi-expertise' that lacks content and thereby misses the central point of *professional knowledge transmission*.

Werner Helsper (2002) comments on Gabriele Behler's suggestion to introduce a BA whose central criteria for the facilitation of employability would be the provision of transmission knowledge, thus creating possible links to teaching but also to personnel management. Helsper describes the habitualizing effect of a professional 'culture of transmission' as a technical short-cut to knowledge transmission that dissolves the "structure of pedagogical professionalism" (Helsper, 2002, p. 83) where this transmission was formerly indifferent to different logics of action and forms of knowledge.

PROBLEMS IN THE IMPLEMENTATION PROCESS OF MODULARIZATION IN ORGANIZATIONS

So far, our comments have primarily dealt with possible and conceivable effects of the modularization program. Modularization – as we have mentioned in the beginning – is part of those academic reforms which have been initialized since the Bologna declaration, if not before, and which are at present being implemented at German universities. "Implementation is the realization of predetermined structures and (work) processes within a system and in consideration of a certain framework of conditions, rules and goals, in other words of a specification" (Wikipedia. Die freie Enzyklopädie – The free encyclopedia, 8/21/2006).

This definition shows that 'realization' may also include the modifications of structures and work processes on the level of organization. This is the case with the modularization program, which is part of the Bologna process and has its primary impact on organizations of education in EU-countries. The concept behind modularizing courses of study is to create a process of transmission and formation of specific competences that are mainly geared to enhance the university graduate's employability. But these competences, in addition to being the main goals to be reached by the student, also represent the leverage point for the organizational units in the implementation process of the modularization of study courses.

In this hybrid form, the definition of competences becomes a problem of subject matter as well as of the planning and management of modularization. The concept's normative objectives are counteracted by the given initial conditions at the universities as well as by the lack of a binding code of practice for the individual universities' efforts to reorganize and restructure the curriculum into units. The problem of organizational structure lies in the fact that the subject matter of the courses which are to be restructured into modular units has to be conceived with regard to criteria that are deduced from the requisite competence objectives. Modules have to deliver predefined (partial) competences that need to accumulate, over time, to grow into a portfolio. Following this "deductive logic" (Kokemohr, 2005, p. 105), the subject matter and methodology of academic teaching have to be goal-oriented in their definition, structure, scheduling, and they have to be permanently evaluated in terms of their adequacy for the goals that are to be obtained. As far as the practical realization of this abstract concept is concerned, a uniform framework of guidelines for the necessary organizational stages is lacking. Hence, an important point to consider is the uncertainty about the fundamental knowledge for the (pre-)definition of specific competences and their structural embedding in the module contents. As universities find themselves in a transitional period that causes excessive demands on their organizational structure, the implementation process of the modularization concept requires a cautious, empirical 'step-by-step approach.'

Ewald Terhart describes the specific problems of modularization practice as a lack of fit between the organizational point of departure and the concept's normative objectives. There is likely to be a rush for academic instruction since the credit-point system will force students into regular attendance of the lectures; and this is another reason why modularization will require, in terms of contents and quantity, a "demand-oriented allocation of courses" (Terhart, 2005, p. 91). The number of examinations (so-called 'efficiency controls') accompanying the learning process, both as part of particular modules and of the academic course as a whole will probably increase. To safe-guard module content coherency, universities, individual departments and institutes will have to agree on instruments of standardization. They will need to coordinate curricula and module and competence descriptions while maintaining lectures and examinations given current staff and capacities.

In striking contrast, there are no unified procedural guidelines for management offset out by the modularization program's initiators. The likely result is divergent practices of module implementation, depending on the respective states, universities, departments or institutes. Universities are structurally forced to react to this lack of guidelines or to this excessive freedom of decision which goes beyond their organizational capacities, by adopting standardization. Time constrictions force universities to follow a *top-down logic*, according to Rainer Kokemohr:

> By this definition, the job market dictates the desired qualifications and hence the educational profile; politics transfer these job market demands into a framework of guidelines which, in turn, are elaborated by commissions of specialists in such a way as to modify professional, institutional and local conditions; until commissions for structural and academic reform, in accord with the teaching body, finally provide the academic courses of the individual universities with a concrete shape that is ideally marketable throughout Europe (Kokemohr, 2005, p. 105).

The effects of the market principle are thus indirectly extended to the university management's own domain of responsibility, where they create policies, procedures and directives for the autonomous university institutions to adopt (see Radtke, 2003, p. 114 et seq.). Here, the formal execution of these diffuse guidelines, as far as they exist, is undertaken, and local practices of organization and problem-solving are established before they are turned over to the responsibility of those further down in the organizational hierarchy who are directly affected by the uncertainty inherent in the universities' practices of handling the organizational problems: i.e. to teachers and students.

Within this "culture of agreement" we find an oscillation between the framework of rather unspecific, restricting as well as empowering requirements on the one hand and local or regional practices for the realization of the core concept of modularization on the other hand. In order to manage the practical requirements of modularization, universities in this situation will have to fall back on further standardizations that may vary locally.

If these predictions prove to be accurate, the goals and promises of inter-disciplinarity, flexibility, mobility and transnational comparability have to be regarded as structurally imperiled from the very outset (and globalization's motto to "think globally and act locally" is turned into its own caricature).

As authors of this article, we have been confronted with the problems of implementing the modularization concept in our own department. We have gained experience from more or less successful stages of the implementation process, and we have discovered that one important issue is the massive problems caused by having to calculate and reconcile available staff and capacities and the need to offer a curriculum of courses with coherent subject-matter.

So far, the concept of modularization has consisted mainly of program definitions of objectives, of assumptions about the causal effects of formal definitions of competences and of standardized module content descriptions aiming at highly specific employability. But all in all we feel that the possible effects of a modularization of knowledge on the structure of knowledge itself and on the practices of knowledge transmission have not yet been sufficiently reflected upon. We urge that this should be one of the essential tasks for theoretical, practical, and empirical research that accompanies the Bologna process.

REFERENCES

Adorno, T. W., & Horkheimer, M. (1987). *Dialektik der Aufklärung. Philosophische Fragmente*. In Gunzelin Schmid Noerr (Hrsg.): *Gesammelte Schriften*. Band 5 *Dialektik der Aufklärung und Schriften 1940–1950*, Frankfurt am Main: Fischer.

Beck, U., & Bonß, W. (Eds.). (1989). *Weder Sozialtechnologie noch Aufklärung? Analysen zur Verwendung sozialwissenschaftlichen Wissens*. Frankfurt/M: Suhrkamp.

Bund-Länder-Kommission für Bildungsplanung und Forschungsförderung (BLK). (2002). *Handreichung zur Modularisierung und Einführung von Bachelor- und Master-Studiengängen – Erste Erfahrungen und Empfehlungen aus dem BLK-Versuchsprogramm „Modularisierung"*. Bonn.

Dewe, B., Ferchhoff, W., & Radtke, F.-O. (Eds.). (1992). *Erziehung als Profession: Zur Logik professionellen Handelns in pädagogischen Feldern*. Opladen: Leske & Budrich.

Ehrke, M. (2005). *"Modularisierung" – Paradigmenwechsel in der Bildungspolitik?* Retrieved August 22, 2006, from http://www.uebergebuehr.de/de/themen/schulpolitik/modularisierung-paradigmenwechsel-in-der-bildungspolitik/

Haan, G. De, & Poltermann, A. (2002). Bildung in der Wissensgesellschaft. In Heinrich Böll Stiftung (Ed.), *Gut zu wissen. Links zur Wissensgesellschaft* (pp. 310–341). Münster: Dampfboot.

Helsper, W. (2002). Wissen. Können, Nicht-Wissen-Können: Wissensformen des Lehrers und Konsequenzen für die Lehrerbildung. In Zentrum für Schulforschung und Fragen der Lehrerbildung (Eds.), *Die Lehrerbildung der Zukunft. Eine Streitschrift* (pp. 67–86). Opladen: Leske & Budrich.

Höhne, T. (2003). *Pädagogik der Wissensgesellschaft.* Bielefeld: Transcript.

Höhne, T. (2006a). Wissensgesellschaft. In A. Dzierzbicka & A. Schrirlbauer (Eds.), *Pädagogisches Glossar der Gegenwart. Von Autonomie bis Wissensmanagement* (pp. 297–305). Wien: Löcker.

Höhne, T. (2006b). Der Leitbegriff 'Kompetenz' als Mantra neoliberaler Bildungsreformer: Zur Kritik seiner semantischen Weitläufigkeit und inhaltlichen Kurzatmigkeit. In L. A. Pongratz (Ed.), *Bildung – Wissen – Kompetenz. Bildungsphilosophie in der Wissensgesellschaft* (pp. 136–149).

Kokemohr, R. (2005). Internationalisierung der Universität, Standardisierung des Wissens und die Idee der Bildung. In A. Liesner & O. Sanders (Ed.), *Bildung der Universität. Beiträge zum Reformdiskurs* (pp. 101–122). Bielefeld: Transcript.

Kultusministerkonferenz (KMK). (2003). 10 Thesen zur Bachelor- und Masterstruktur in Deutschland. Beschluss der Kultusministerkonferenz vom. Retrieved August 20, 2006, from http://www.kmk.org/doc/beschl/BMThesen.pdf#search=%22kmk%2010%20thesen%22

Lyotard, J.-F. (1984). *The postmodern condition: A report on knowledge.* Manchester: Manchester University Press.

Neuweg, G. H. (Ed.). (2000). *Wissen – Können – Reflexion. Ausgewählte Verhältnisbestimmungen.* Innsbruck: Studien-Verlag.

Radtke, F.-O. (2003). Die Erziehungswissenschaft der OECD – Aussichten auf die neue Performanz-Kultur. In DGFE (Ed.), *Erziehungswissenschaft* (Vol. 14, Issue 27, pp. 109–136). Opladen: Leske & Budrich.

Rustemeyer, D. (2002). Neues Lehrerwissen in der "Wissensgesellschaft"? In Zentrum für Schulforschung und Fragen der Lehrerbildung (Ed.), *Die Lehrerbildung der Zukunft. Eine Streitschrift* (pp. 87–96). Opladen: Leske & Budrich.

Sennett, R. (1998). *The corrosion of character. The personal consequences of work in the new capitalism.* New York: Norton.

Terhart, E. (2002). Was müssen Lehrer wissen und können? In Zentrum für Schulforschung und Fragen der Lehrerbildung (Ed.), *Die Lehrerbildung der Zukunft. Eine Streitschrift* (pp. 17–23). Opladen: Leske & Budrich.

Terhart, E. (2005). Die Lehre in den Zeiten der Modularisierung. *Zeitschrift für Pädagogik. Hochschullandschaft im Wandel* (Vol. 50, pp. 87–102). (Beiheft). Weinheim/Basel: Beltz.

Wikipedia. Die freie Enzyklopädie: Implementation. Retrieved August 21, 2006, from http://de.wikipedia.org/wiki/Implementierung

Thomas Höhne
University of Education
Freiburg
Germany

Bruno Schreck
Center for Self-Directed Learning
Offenbach am Main
Germany

ANDREA LIESNER

29. HOW TO GOVERN THE PROFESSOR?

Reflections on the Alma Mater Bolognese

The state of Europe's higher education is changing. The aim is to develop the continent to be the leading worldwide knowledge-based economy by 2010. Then a network of universities all over Europe will provide a high-quality education of the academic youth and, at the same time, centres of excellence will guarantee innovation, growth, and employment. Since the Bologna Declaration of 1999, the construction of this new landscape of higher education has been actively promoted – from Lisbon to Moscow, from Glasgow to Athens–universities are involved in a process of establishing comparable curricula and diplomas. The introduction of Europe-wide compatible modules of credit points for BA and MA certificates aims at a concept of studies which is effective, transparent, and, most importantly, mobile, because international experiences are seen as the cornerstone of the future employability of academics. At the same time, official proclamations insist on the principle of unity and variety of the European Higher Education System although it is not intended to abolish the existing cultural differences between the various national systems of higher education.

However, in the process of the ongoing construction of this new system of Higher Education more and more critical voices can be heard. Their prime issue is the dominance of an economic rationale determining this process. One faction, mostly concerned with university transformations, refers implicitly or explicitly to Foucault and to his concept of 'governmentality' (Dzierzbicka 2006; Liesner 2006/2007; Masschelein & Simons 2002/5; Masschelein 2001; Weiskopf 2005). This chapter illustrates the critical and stimulating potentials inherent to Foucault's approach. The first part will show an actual reform position, followed by a critical annotation and, in a third part, reflections on the strengths and weaknesses of a perspective based on the theory of governmentality are presented.

HOW TO GOVERN THE PROFESSOR? THE TEACHING POINTS MODEL
ACCORDING TO THE "CENTRUM FÜR HOCHSCHULENTWICKLUNG" (CENTRE
FOR UNIVERSITY DEVELOPMENT", "CHE")

Since the 1990s German higher education policy has been more and more influenced by recommendations of the CHE, an agency actively involved in the promotion of university rankings. This 'think tank' (a self-attribution) operates on two levels: within the legal construction of a public interest company (gGmbH) as part of the Bertelsmann Stiftung (Bertelsmann Foundation), assisted by the "Foundation for

M.A. Peters et al. (eds.), Govermentality Studies in Education, 509–514.
© *2009 Sense Publishers. All rights reserved.*

the Promotion of the Hochschulrektorenkonferenz," and as a privately operating consultancy, initiating and realizing joint venture projects with universities and ministries.

This combination of a privately operating business and a foundation is symptomatic of changes in the relationship between the private and the public sector which can be observed all over Europe. At this point, I will not deal with the rather complex question of what the implications of these changes might be for the future of education as a public good. Instead, I would like to illustrate the strategies of such a twofold business structure to establish structural analogies between public educational institutions and private businesses.

Some time ago the CHE presented a working paper to promote the introduction of "Teaching Points" for the academic staff similarly in analogy to "Credit Points" for students (Handel et al. 2005). The traditional German way to offer classes (i.e. the "teaching load") by defining teaching hours per week was criticized as an "inherent obstacle to reforms", because modularized curricula lead to new "teaching demands" (ibid., p. 1). In their evaluation of the traditional system, the authors of the working paper concentrated on the following five problems:

> The "supply oriented reflection of a teaching unit ... neglects all demand oriented factors", i.e. time for examinations, for consultations, and for the preparation and evaluation of classes (ibid., p. 3);

> "a professor's weekly teaching for which he is personally responsible" is no longer the non plus ultra, because "new ways to teach and to learn ... have been achieved", asking for "new incentives to be realized" (ibid., p. 3);

> the teaching hours per week model does not allow to describe "the scope and structure of modules", because modules "primarily are defined by Credit Points for students which are resulting from the workload". Regarding the workload of the staff, however, i.e. "consultation, individual mentoring, control of self-reliable studies, and advisory activities", are classified within the traditional system as "supplementary duties", which cannot, due to their secretive quality, be integrated into the planning of the curricula;

> the immobile teaching hours per week model "does not offer room for the definition of strategic priorities and incentives within the planning of curricula according to the university profile" (ibid.). In this model, neither further education and e-learning projects nor a discrimination of the "specific relevance of classes for the study course (compulsory/free)" are properly attributed to the teaching load (ibid., p. 4);

> the per week model does not encourage the integration or cooperation of different "types of universities (Applied Sciences, Universities, Art Academies)", because "the teaching load is individually attributed to a person acknowledging neither the actual teaching situation nor a reform perspective" (ibid.).

The CHE Teaching Points model is an instrument to calculate "the individual teaching load", regardless of the personal status or the type of university. Teaching Points are a "new measuring unit" to adjust the teaching load to "the demands of classes resp. modules" by developing and applying "standards" as "part of the development of study courses" (ibid., p. 4). Nevertheless, "different teaching loads" can be attributed to certain status groups. However, a further "individualization" is intended to define the teaching load "not with reference to status groups but with reference to the individual profile" (ibid., p. 6).

For the implementation of this program the authors suggest developing the Teaching Points model in conjunction with a given "time budget". The "arithmetic mean" is "1.800 hours per year". For a university professor the teaching load would be 50% of this budget, whereas 900 hours would remain for "research, administration, and services" (ibid., p. 6). The calculation of the "whole workload" of a professor under given prerequisites leads to the following results:

"Advisory time per module 0,25 hours, per paper 0,5 hours, and per final assignment 24 hours (Bachelor)" (ibid., p. 8);

"Preparatory and evaluation time for lectures ... 1 hour per lecture hour";

"Exercises" 0,25 hours;

"Classes or similar events" 0,5 hours;

"Examinations": exam paper 1 hour, oral exam 0,5 hours, paper 1,5 hours, final assignment (Bachelor) 7,5 hours.

Under these prerequisites, a module existing of a lecture (1 hour), attended by 50 students, and an integrated exercise, attended by 15 students, leads to a calculated teaching load of precisely 236,5 hours which is equivalent to 7,88 Teaching Points. Thus, according to the CHE working paper, the "strategic aims were accomplished" (ibid., p. 9) and "universities resp. faculties, departments, or schools have the opportunity for a strategic planning of study courses" (ibid., p. 10).

THEORY OF GOVERNMENTALITY: APPROACHING AN ANALYSIS

The proposed introduction of the Teaching Points model is characterized by elements, which qualify it as part of a governmental regime. With reference to the analysis of recent transformations in the educational sector presented by Jan Masschelein and Maarten Simons (Masschelein & Simons, 2005) this chapter deals with two characteristic traits of this transformation.

To begin with the universities and their members: They are perceived as autonomous actors who are willing to strengthen their profile in a global competition to work effectively and to offer high-quality products. The educational policy discourse promotes the acceptance of entrepreneurship as the guiding image by highlighting steering techniques directed at the individual's environment. The university is presented as an organization, which can be free, if it will be so, and by doing the right things: "Directives are no longer needed, when the university accepts the quantitative aims defined by the regional government" (Handel et al., 2005, p. 5). Autonomy is thus defined as the freedom to creatively react to state prerequisites. Government takes place via an encouragement that is helpful for reaching the goals. The market defines success or failure: success leads to high rankings; failure implies a loss of attractiveness. This kind of competition asks for individual and for continuous investment. Entrepreneurship, also perceived as the guiding image for the individual subject, seems necessary for the promotion of a state of the art self-perception. The CHE working paper offers the perspective that a professor can influence his or her teaching load by individual profile building. A reduction of the teaching load is subject to negotiations; the administration in those cases where new forms of teaching and learning are integrated and classes are qualified as innovative. The same applies to a category of research, which is supply-oriented and promises added value. As an individualized and evaluated achievement, it offers the opportunity to regulate individually the time budget for teaching and for research.

In the second place the introduction of modularized study courses is central for this kind of approach for professors. Modularization not only allows for the control of students and their acquisition of credit points, but also for the control of professors by standardizing the subjects which are compulsory for students. According to Masschelein and Simons "a module is a unit of subject matters, of teaching-/learning and of evaluation methods, having to contribute to a certain set of knowledge, capacities, and attitudes" (Masschelein & Simons, 2005, p. 75). The CHE working paper addresses the professor as an individual. To bring into account his/her real time investment for teaching implies that at the same time there is a forced transparency. In an autonomous market-oriented university, teaching is by definition a service. Teaching Points are a means to calculate the module related efforts of any individual, promising to measure and to control the quality of the service. So the message is obvious. Teaching Points are good for students and professors alike; enabling the university to offer permanent incentives for quality improvement through strategic management.

THEORY OF GOVERNMENTALITY – SOME QUESTIONS

From a point of view derived from the theory of governmentality, the CHE recommendations are part and parcel of the steering strategies connected with a successful implementation of the Bologna Process. It illustrates that the invention and realization of the European Higher Education Area cannot be attributed to individual actors not to neo-liberal governments during the times of Schröder or Blair, not to an international association of Education Ministries as part of a "New Mainstream". In fact, there are "numerous agencies, from national authorities to Universities, Universities of Applied Sciences, and students movements", all requested to "adopt an active part in the creation of this area" (ibid., p. 49). The CHE is among these agencies.

Traditionally, the anonymity of the actual regime and the reluctance to discern primary actors and protagonists is underpinned by studies in governmentality. The state and actors like the CHE are perceived as effects of this regime; as agencies and individuals they are evaluated according to their entrepreneurial potentialities in the face of the 'permanent economic tribunal'.

On the one hand that marks the strengths of these studies. They offer an important general orientation by introducing the analytical figure of the entrepreneurial self, which is helpful for a systematic approach towards numerous and often contradictory reform attempts in present day educational discourses in Europe. The discovery of a strategic interplay between external and internal steering mechanisms is a valid contribution, which draws attention to problematic implications of the Bologna Process and sets up warnings, not to neglect the repressive elements of the kind of freedom promised in this process.

On the other hand this perspective risks ignoring some important dimensions of the economic steering regime. Numerous governmentality studies concentrate their critique upon the programs and strategies to reform the European universities, and doing so they keep distance from other forms of critique, especially from a critique of ideology or a critique of capitalism. But it should be noted that conflicts preceding the analyzed programs are not longer visible within them: Dissenting arguments and real struggles against the transformation of the educational sector can not be seen in the reform-strategies. Focusing on these strategies as an effect of an omnipresent entrepreneurial regime without actors (ibid.), conjures an intangible empire and thus could strengthen exactly those hegemonic powers, which are criticized. A possible implication, though unintended, is the transformation of Foucault's "Critique of Liberations" into a "Liberation from Critique" (Messerschmidt, 2007). Such Liberation would indicate a squeamish weakness of governmentality studies. Therefore: Why not being critical towards 'the' regime in the same way as towards 'the' system? Why not apply a critique of ideology and of new capitalistic formations in cases where real actors can be discerned, actors who promote the process of a capitalization of social life? Protagonist actors like the CHE with 75% of its annual budget of €3,2 millions provided by the Bertelsmann Foundation?

Translated by Dieter Keiner

REFERENCES

CHE. (2007). *Mission statement.* Retrieved February 17, 2009, from http://www.che.de

Dzierzbicka, A. (2006). Neoliberalismus light. Die Kunst des Regierens in wissensbasierten Wirtschaftsräumen. In S. Weber & S. Maurer (Eds.), *Gouvernementalität und Erziehungswissenschaft. Wissen – Macht – Transformation* (pp. 101–120). Wiesbaden: VS Verlag für Sozialwissenschaften.

Handel, K., Hener, Y., & Voegelin, L. (2005). *Teaching Points als Maßstab für die Lehrverpflichtung und Lehrplanung. Arbeitspapier Nr. 69 des Centrums für Hochschulentwicklung.* Retrieved from http://www.che.de/downloads/CHE_TeachingPoints_AP69.pdf

Keller, A. (2004). alma mater bolognaise. Perspektiven eines Europäischen Hochschulraums im Rahmen des Bologna-Prozesses. GEW-Landesverbände Berlin, Brandenburg, Hessen, & Niedersachsen (Eds.). Frankfurt/M.

Liesner, A. (2006). Education or Service? Remarks on teaching and learning in the entrepreneurial university. In J. Masschelein, M. Simons, U. Bröckling, & L. Pongratz (Eds.), *The learning society from the perspective of governmentality* (pp. 69–82). Malden, UK: Blackwell Publishing.

Liesner, A. (2007). Governmentality, European politics, and the neo-liberal reconstruction of German universities. *Policy Futures in Education*, *5*(4), Oxford, UK.

Masschelein, J. (2001). The discourse of the learning society and the loss of childhood. *Journal of Philosophy of Education*, *35*(1), 1–20.

Masschelein, J., & Simons, M. (2002). An adequate education for a globalized world? A note on the immunization of being-together. *Journal of Philosophy of Education*, *36*(4), 565–584.

Masschelein, J., & Simons, M. (2005). *Globale Immunität oder Eine kleine Kartographie des Europäischen Bildungsraums*. Berlin and Zürich: Diaphanes.

Messerschmidt, A. (2007). Von der Kritik der Befreiungen zur Befreiung von Kritik? *Erkundungen zu Bildungsprozessen nach Foucault. Pädagogische Korrespondenz*, *36*(2), 44–59.

Weiskopf, R. (2005). Unter der Hand: Aspekte der Gouvernementalisierung der Universitäten im Zuge der Hochschulreform. In H. Welte, M. Auer, & C. Meister-Scheytt (Eds.), *Management von Universitäten. Zwischen Tradition und (Post-)Moderne* (pp. 171–186). München and Mering: Hampp.

Andrea Liesner
Department of Educational Science
University of Hamburg
Germany

ANDREAS FEJES

30. FABRICATING THE EUROPEAN CITIZEN[1]

One of the major changes in higher education today is the Bologna process, a declaration signed by 46 nations, both members of the European Union and several other countries (London Communiqué, 2007). It aims at harmonising the higher educational systems in Europe. In texts on this issue, there are ideas of comparability, mobility, transparency, flexibility, shared European values and diversity put forward as means of creating a European educational space. However, deciding about this policy area is outside the competence of the EU. Consequently, each nation has to choose whether or not to sign it. According to some researchers (Nóvoa, 2002; Ahola & Mesikämmen, 2003), the narratives about harmonisation are in some respects taken for granted and many universities in Europe have accepted this process and see it as inevitable. As the narratives about this issue seem to construct the Bologna process as a process in which sameness is to be created out of difference where inclusion is seen as the output, it would be interesting to study the ordering of such a process and what the effects of such ordering are. Thus, questions of a European citizen and subjectivity become central and the overall aim of this chapter will be to analyse the construction of the European citizen and the rationality of governing related to such a construction. The specific focus will be on the rules and standards of reason in higher education reforms, which inscribe continuums of values that exclude as they include (Popkewitz, 2006).

I perform a discourse analysis where I analyse official documents concerned with the Bologna process and higher education in Europe and Sweden. These documents construct views of various aspects of the future, the European citizen, the ones not 'European', etc. In what way do ideas circulating in the discourse of higher education (the Bologna process) construct the European citizen as a way of solving the problem posed? Who should the European citizen become and how should this be realised through the practice of higher education? More specifically, I ask the following questions in the analysis, based on Foucault (1983) and Dean (1999):
- What is the problematic of governing and why govern (the teleos of government)?
- What should be governed?
- How should governing be practised?

The case of Sweden is used as a way of analyzing how the Europeanization of citizens is constructed discursively in a 'local' cultural practice. Based on such a governmentality analysis (Foucault 2003a) I will argue that the texts about the

M.A. Peters et al. (eds.), Govermentality Studies in Education, 515–526.

Bologna process construct a practice of exclusion and otherness. 'The European' is defined and thus excludes those nations and citizens, within and outside Europe, who do not have the 'European essence'. Inclusion and exclusion are discursively constructed as binary concepts, although exclusion as the effect of inclusion is not acknowledged in policy documents. Thus, I believe analysis of such discursive constructs is needed as to make visible how power operates and what the effects of such operations are. Further, I argue that the Bologna process is part of a neoliberal rationality of governing where each subject (which can be an individual, a higher education institution or a nation) is fostered to self-govern.

I have analysed material from the European Union and Sweden in order to compare the relation between texts from two different subject positions, the European and the Swedish. Further, by analysing the Swedish documents it is possible to see how the Europeanization of the citizens is discursively constructed in a 'local' cultural practice. I have chosen to analyze official documents as they are assigned a specific position in the discourse. All positions in a discourse are part of the construction of the discourse itself, but some positions are created as more important than others. Such a construct is specific to time and space. In Sweden, official documents are assigned an important role in the decision-making process (Olsson, 1997) and, as will be illustrated, ideas from the European documents are inscribed in the Swedish ones in specific ways. Five European documents are analysed; the *Bologna Declaration* (1999), *Making a European Area of Lifelong Learning a Reality* (2001), the *Berlin Communiqué* (2003), *Standards and guidelines for quality assurance in the European higher education area* (2005) and the *Bergen Communiqué* (2005). The second and fourth of these documents are not about the Bologna process per se. However, I have chosen to analyse them as they are two central documents in the policymaking of education on a European level and they are closely related to the Bologna process and discourses of lifelong learning (for detailed governemntality analyses of discourses of lifelong learning see Fejes & Nicoll, 2008). Two official documents from the Swedish Ministry of Education are analysed. One is a document produced as a foundation for gathering opinions on the Bologna process in Sweden (Ministry of Education, 2004) and the other is a proposal made by the government to the Swedish parliament on this issue (Ministry of Education, 2005).

The analysis is divided into three parts. In the first part, the focus is on the problematic of government. What is it the Bologna process is supposed to solve? In the second part, I analyse what kind of subject is constructed in the European and Swedish texts. And lastly, the focus is on how the technique of diversity constructs a specific kind of subject.

THE BOLOGNA PROCESS – STANDARDISATION AS A WAY OF HANDLING RISK AND CONSTRUCTING A EUROPEAN CITIZEN

Texts concerning higher education in Europe stress the need to create a Europe of knowledge. So far, Europe has made extraordinary progress, but an even greater effort needs to be made. According to the texts, such a growing awareness can be seen especially in the political and academic world. What has to be done in particular is building "upon and strengthening its intellectual, cultural, social and scientific and technological dimensions" (Bologna Declaration, 1999, p. 1). It is emphasised that:

A Europe of Knowledge is now widely recognised as an irreplaceable factor for social and human growth and as an indispensable component to consolidate and enrich the European citizenship, capable of giving its citizens the necessary competences to face the challenges of the new millennium, together with an awareness of shared values and belonging to a common social and cultural space (Bologna Declaration, 1999, p. 1).

The idea of a Europe of knowledge is something taken for granted and it is seen as an essential part of the construction of a European citizen. Such a subject should be able to handle the challenges of the new millennium and should feel a sense of belonging to a common cultural space. Further, this space should be created as a means for Europe to be able to compete with the surrounding world. Europe needs to become the most competitive and well-developed knowledge society (European Commission, 2001). Here, we can discern an idea of threats from the surrounding world. There are other parts of the world, and in this case the entire world, that have to be competed with. Therefore, Europe has to become a "Europe of Knowledge" (Berlin Communiqué, 2003, p. 2). Similar ideas are repeated in the Swedish texts. Competencies are seen as essential and are closely related to the universities. If Sweden does not have good universities, there will be a risk of marginalisation in relation to the rest of the world, which is illustrated in the following quotation.

In a society constantly measured in relation to other societies, the individual competence becomes the most significant factor for the future development of the society. Therefore, well-run and highly qualitative universities are essential for us if our society is to keep up with the competition in the future (Ministry of Education, 2005, p. 26).

We could say that both the European and Swedish texts present the Bologna process as a solution to threats in the future. Through it, Europe and individual countries, in this case Sweden, will attain/maintain top positions in the world. The narratives of threat contain an idea of risk. If certain measures are not taken, there is a risk that something bad will happen. These narratives are projections of the present on the future – someone writes about a future that does not exist as natural and real. It is written as a fact and some measures will have to be taken to avoid this risk. The future is constructed as a technique for governing and the result is that what is in the unknown future is seen as a fact and a truth. This imaginary truth is then part of the basis of certain conclusions of how to act. Such ideas can also be seen in texts about municipal adult education in Sweden, where the need to properly educate the citizens is stressed as a means of competing with the surrounding world (Fejes; 2005, 2006a, b).

At first glance, one might regard such an idea of risk as an external risk, something that comes from the outside. But, as Giddens (2000) argues, today, risk is manufactured based on the knowledge we create concerning ourselves and our world. Thus, the production of 'bad' visions of the future is not something that comes from the outside. Instead, it is a manufactured risk made into a fact which fosters individuals into becoming active subjects who have to address these risks based on knowledge produced about them. As Giddens (2000) argues, risk has not become more dangerous than before; instead, it has taken on new shapes and today we create our own risks. Such a way of reasoning about risk is part of the construction of a specific neoliberal rationality of governing. It acts as an argument for why certain measures should be taken and it constructs specific subjects.

Further, the European texts argue that comparability and compatibility between different educational systems are part of the solution to the problem concerning the future:

> Ministers welcome the various initiatives undertaken since the Prague Higher Education Summit to move towards more comparability and compatibility, to make higher education systems more transparent and to enhance the quality of European higher education at institutional and national levels (Berlin Communiqué, 1999, p. 3).

Transparency is central and the projected consequence is good quality. We can see this as a central part of the current rationalities of governing where the things to be governed need to be made visible. Through a transparent higher educational system, knowledge can be produced about the individual universities. Higher education is made into a calculable and governable space. Further, the focus should be on structural aspects such as degree cycles and grading systems as well as on content aspects such as criteria of what a student should know after obtaining a certain degree (Bologna Declaration, 1999, ENQA, 2005). There is, in other words, an idea to standardise higher education in Europe. Such a system would create good quality and a prosperous Europe. Standardisation can be seen as a way of governing and regulating behaviour in specific ways (Brunsson & Jacobsson, 2000). For example, it can be seen as risk management that addresses the manufactured risks (Giddens, 2000) concerning the future. In other words, there is an ambition to create sameness out of difference. At the same time as sameness is created, there is a practice of exclusion. The one who is not, does not want to or cannot become, the same will be created as 'the other' (Popkewitz, 2003), the excluded one who needs correction. He/she should be placed in programs of ethical re-programming (Rose, 1996), as a way of being transformed into the desirable citizen. The ambition to include as it is expressed in policy, has a double effect which is inseparable but not acknowledged in social policy and educational practices; efforts to bring about an inclusionary society also have exclusion as an effect.

Thus, the problem, according to the texts, is how to handle threats and risks in the future. The way to meet these risks and threats is to create a European area of higher education, a prosperous Europe and a specific kind of subject. In the following parts, I will analyse what kind of subject is constructed in the texts about the Bologna process and what kinds of techniques are constructed to fabricate this subject.

THE FLEXIBLE, EMPLOYABLE EUROPEAN CITIZEN

As mentioned earlier, the European citizen is constructed as one who has to be able to face a new and uncertain future and who feels a sense of belonging to a common cultural space. Such a subject is constructed through the creation of a Europe of knowledge. Further, the texts construct the desirable subject as one who is employable and mobile. This mobile and employable subject is created at the same time as a European area of higher education is created. There should be a "creation of the European area of higher education as a key way to promote citizens mobility and employability and the Continent's overall development" (Bologna Declaration, 1999, p. 1–2). It is essential to satisfy the employment market and this is done by constructing subjects that develop transferable skills, e.g. in doctoral programs. "We urge universities to ensure that their doctoral programmes promote inter-disciplinary training and the development of transferable skills, thus meeting the needs of the wider employment market (Bergen Communiqué, 2005, p. 4)." The employable citizen is also constructed in the Swedish texts. In a constantly changing society, people need to be prepared to change jobs and to become mobile. Education is seen as a way of constructing such a subject, which the following quotation illustrates:

> The speed of change in society is increased by globalisation. New work opportunities and companies evolve and other disappears. No one can depend on keeping a job with the same content for a long time. Therefore, educational policy becomes important. Education becomes one of the most important assets for people to be strong and secure in a time of rapid change (Ministry of Education, 2005, p. 27).

In this text, the future is seen as something that is unknown and not possible to plan. The only thing certain is change, compared to the discourses dominating educational policy during the early 20th century in Sweden. Then, the future was seen as known and possible to plan (Fejes, 2006a). At the same time, society is seen as constantly changing and uncertain. "Given the current uncertain economic climate, investing in people becomes all the more important" (European Commission, 2001, p. 6). Therefore, the subjects constructed need to be able to handle these changes by becoming flexible citizens. The emphasis is placed on the subjects themselves. All of them have to adapt to these changes and the established patterns of behaviour need to be changed. This implies that the subjects are their own actors in their own local welfare (Hultqvist et al., 2003).

It is stated that knowledge and competencies are essential in order to become employable. At the same time, the subjects are encouraged to take advantages of the opportunities created as a way of becoming competent. It is argued that citizens:

> Have vast new opportunities in terms of communication, travel and employment. Taking advantage of these opportunities, and actively participating in society,

is reliant on the ongoing acquisition of knowledge and competences (European Commission, 2001, p. 6).

If the citizen does not take advantage of these opportunities, there is a risk that he/she will not become employable and thus become 'the other', the one who is in need of a remedy. These 'others' are especially the ones without a basic level of education: "but almost 150 million people in the EU without this basic level of education face a higher risk of marginalisation" (European Commission, 2001, p. 6). To avoid marginalisation, investments have to be made in people (e.g. through education) as a means of making them active participants in society. But the citizen her/himself must actively choose participation. Further, we could say that this discourse is almost a totalising one where there is only one thing about the future the citizen can be certain of and that is a future of change. A citizen cannot remain outside the changing future, but he/she can meet it by making choices and thus becoming flexible.

This way of reasoning constructs active subjects who are encouraged to participate in the Bologna process. However, not only citizens as subjects but also higher education institutions are constructed as active subjects. This is seen as essential for making the endeavour a success. Universities are seen as partners in a joint venture that will create a good future. "Ministers welcome the commitment of Higher Education Institutions and students to the Bologna Process and recognise that it is ultimately the active participation of all partners in the Process that will ensure its long-term success" (Berlin Communiqué, 2003, p. 5). Universities as subjects are central to the success in reforming higher education in Europe in order to create EHEA, the European Higher Education Area.

> We underline the central role of higher education institutions, their staff and students as partners in the Bologna Process. Their role in the implementation of the Process becomes all the more important now that the necessary legislative reforms are largely in place, and we encourage them to continue and intensify their efforts to establish the EHEA (Bergen Communiqué, 2005, p. 1).

As a partner, different subjectivities are constructed as being active and responsible for the implementation of the Bologna process. We could say, drawing on Rose (1999), that there is a process of responsibilisation in which the subjects themselves are made the vehicles of action. If they do not act in a responsible way and contribute to the process, there will be a risk of failure. There is no 'direct' governing where the subjects are told exactly how to act. Instead, a prosperous future is presented as desirable and combined with different options for how it is possible to act. It is then up to the subjects to make their own choices.

Such ways of speaking construct 'the EU' as 'the enabling state' that should make it possible for the subjects to make their own choices, and it is in the choices and actions of the subjects themselves that the state (EU) inscribes itself (Rose, 1999). 'The state' is not referred to as an entity or an actor that does things. Instead, I view the state as a changing epistemological pattern of assumptions about how to govern and what to govern. Over time and space, it changes, taking on new shapes and meanings (Hultqvist, 2004). It could be said that 'the state' is a mode of governing. 'The enabling state' is an epistemological pattern constructed today, which is made up of ideas about how to govern and what to govern. By enabling the subjects to become autonomous, self-regulated actors responsible for their own future, the future can be controlled, but not planned. Here, we see the construction of an autonomous, self-choosing subject, which can be related to a neoliberal governmentality. Governing is not conducted through lawmaking; instead, the freedom of each citizen is a necessary starting point for regulating and governing behaviour. By fostering the will to make choices, governing becomes something which everyone carries out by him/herself – the conduct of conduct – we govern ourselves and others. However, this does not mean that the state governs less than before. Instead, governing has assumed new shapes, and today the 'state' governs at a distance.

However, we should not view such expressions of power as repressive. Power is not something that a person inherits and which can be used against others. Nor is it a thing, commodity or position. Instead, power is productive and it works through our desires in all relations and it produces the limits of what is possible and not possible to say and do, e.g. what subjectivity is desirable, although these limits are constantly changing and put into question (Foucault, 1980). Everyone should desire to be a flexible and mobile subject, but other positions (subjectivities) in the discourse are possible. As Foucault, (1980; 2003b) argues, there is always a space for resistance in discourses. Without resistance there can be no power relations. Other positions than the flexible subject are possible, but such positions might be categorised as being part of 'the others' who are in need of a remedy. However, in the analysis performed in this chapter, the focus is on the desirable subject constructed through the policy documents.

In this section, I have illustrated how there is a construction of an autonomous, flexible and mobile European citizen in the European and Swedish documents. Such a desirable citizen, together with a standardised higher education system in Europe, is seen as a solution to threats in the future. In the next section, I will discuss how the technique of diversity operates so as to construct such a standardised system and such a citizen.

DIVERSITY AS A WAY OF CREATING A COMMON EUROPEAN EDUCATIONAL SPACE

In this part, I will illustrate how the idea of diversity operates in different ways in the European and the Swedish texts so as to construct a European citizen. However, the effects are the same in both.

In the European texts there is a construction of a subject that has "an awareness of shared values and belonging to a common social and cultural space" (Bologna Declaration, 1999, p. 1). Such an idea constructs a 'cultural subject' with specific European values. It is intertwined with an idea that there are cultural differences within Europe that should be respected. In the Bologna declaration it is stated that:

> We hereby undertake to attain these objectives - within the framework of our institutional competences and taking full respect of the diversity of cultures, languages, national education systems and of University autonomy – to consolidate the European area of higher education (Bologna Declaration, 1999, p. 4).

Together, these ideas represent a view that there is an essence of the European citizen that needs to be acknowledged; a Euro-centrism. There is something 'specifically European', which is related to shared values and a common cultural space at the same time as cultural differences are acknowledged – the same but different. There is an ambition to make the difference more alike and at the same time to respect this difference. In such narratives, diversity operates as a way of realising a standardised higher education system and a desirable European citizen. Respect for diversity is a condition of the possibility to start speaking about standardisation.

Such ways of speaking also create 'the other', the one who does not have this European essence (i.e. people from other parts of the world), or the one who is not aware of it. The specific power relations in the discourse define what is normal and abnormal, what is to be included and what is excluded (Foucault, 2003b). In this case, this division is based upon ideas about cultural affiliation. Based on my analysis, I argue that texts on the Bologna process express ideas about inclusion, at the same time as they also create exclusion. Countries outside Europe and their citizens are excluded, as they do not have the 'European values'. If they are to be included, these values need to become part of those nations and those citizens. What we see is how the efforts to achieve inclusion have exclusion as one of their effects, which is not recognized in social policy and educational practices. Such effects have implications for the practices of reflection and action. The rules of conduct that produce principles of exclusion in efforts to achieve an inclusionary society are embodied in the very strategies of reform. This implies that researchers, policymakers and academics take part in the production of subjectivities (Popkewitz, 2006).

In the Swedish documents, we can see how the technique of diversity operates in a slightly different way where there is a 'Swedish European' created. Instead of creating a 'European space' (common social and cultural space), a 'national space' is created through ideas of systems. These can be seen as national stories (Balibar, 2004) acting as imaginary techniques in the creation of a national identity. For example, it is argued, with reference to Swedish tradition, that the specificity of the system in Sweden needs to be protected. An example of this can be found in the discussion about the European credit transfer system and the idea of having a common grading scale in all the countries participating in the Bologna process. In the Swedish texts, it is argued that the Swedish grading system (which is goal-oriented) is better than the one suggested in the Bologna process (which is a norm-referenced grading system) (Ministry of Education, 2004, 2005). This is discussed by the Swedish Minister of Education in a news article. He argues that: "another pedagogy is needed for such a fine grading scale, and it diverges from the Swedish tradition to work in such a way (SvD, 10/4 2005)". Further, the article states that the minister "wants to increase the competitiveness and the mobility of the Swedish students by 'other means'. Nevertheless, he does not think the 7-grade scale will solve the problems as only two countries, Italy and Norway, have introduced it" (SvD, 10/4 2005). What we see is the construction of a Swedish citizen made up of 'traditional' Swedish ideas. The texts construct something 'specifically Swedish' related to ideas about systems. Nevertheless, the Swedish texts present an ambition to be part of Europe and the Bologna process. Accordingly, what we see is a Swedish European under construction. The Swedish subject is supposed to become a European based on Swedish traditions.

We can also see how an idea of differences (cultural diversity) is present in the Swedish texts, as it is in the European texts. "When more and more people obviously do not share a common cultural and ethnic background it is necessary to develop a higher education that is relevant irrespective of the students background" (Ministry of Education, 2005, p. 27-28). Higher education needs to be developed in a way that can handle such a population of students. Further, the students need to gain knowledge of, and show respect for, these cultural differences where exchange studies are seen as leading to "personal development, increased general knowledge, improved language knowledge, knowledge and understanding of people in other countries and the circumstances they live in, attitudes and values" (Ministry of Education, 2005, p. 61). Such a student is part of the solution of how to solve the problems of the future and of how to make higher education more alike. Diversity operates so as to harmonise the Swedish system of higher education in relation to Europe, and to construct a desirable European citizen.

What my analysis illustrates is that diversity is constructed as a technique, which fosters nations to desire to participate in standardising their higher education system at the same time as it fosters students to desire to become a specific European citizen – one who is mobile, flexible and shows respect for diversity. Diversity is a condition of possibility to start speaking about harmonisation and standardisation of higher education in Europe. Further, the analysis illustrates how the narratives of the European citizen produced in European and Swedish documents are similar, even if they appear to be different. For example, the construction of a European space and a Swedish space seems to differ. Nevertheless, the same techniques operate in the discourse as a way of creating a standardised higher education system and flexible and mobile citizens.

CONCLUDING REMARKS

In this chapter, my aim has been to show how the European citizen is constructed through texts on the Bologna process and what rationality of governing is related to such a construction. I have illustrated how texts on the Bologna process construct a neoliberal rationality of governing. Such rationality seeks to de-emhazise the state and its different practices of governing. Governing should not be conducted by a legislative institution or by a 'state/EU' dictating what to do. Instead, governing should be conducted through the choices and actions of each subject. It is in these choices that the 'state/EU' is inscribed.

Such a statement has been supported in my analysis where I show how different texts present the Bologna process as a solution to several threats in the future. By making higher educational systems in Europe more standardised it is argued in the texts that Europe will maintain a leading position in the world. Further, an uncertain and constantly changing future is created, which can be handled by constructing the Bologna process. These different threats in the future can be handled by fostering subjectivities (citizens) who are flexible, mobile and adaptable. Universities and nations, as subjects, should desire to become active partners in such an enterprise. They need to take responsibility for making a good future for Europe a reality. Thus, government is conducted through the freedom of each citizen and subjectivity. By making choices, citizens, universities and nations participate in governing themselves and others.

I have also illustrated how the technique of diversity operates as a way of fostering desirable subjectivities. Such a technique operates in the discourses constructed by both the European and Swedish documents, but in slightly different ways. By analysing European and Swedish documents, I have been able to show these differences and how they are part of the same rationality of governing. I argue that diversity is a condition of possibility to speak about harmonisation and standardisation of higher education. In the discourse of higher education today, it would not be possible to speak about harmonisation without any reference to respect for diversity. Such a narrative is excluded from the discourse.

Further, I have shown how power operates and produces specific subjectivities. At the same time as subjectivities are produced, there are exclusionary effects. Inclusion and exclusion are discursively constructed as binary concepts, but the exclusionary side is something not acknowledged in policy documents. The analysis shows how the rules and standards of reason in higher education reforms inscribe continuums of values that exclude at the same time as they include. At the same time as there is a construction of the European citizen, there is also a construction of 'the other', the one without the European values who is in need of ethical reprogramming to become what is desirable.

In this chapter, I have made an attempt to contribute to an ongoing debate on how higher education in Europe is governed, based on a governmentality perspective. The discussions and analysis I have presented might point to a new trajectory in research on the Bologna process. Using the concept of governmentality allows us to analyse the specific relations of power that operate in the discourse of higher education, what pictures of reality they create and what the expressions of power set in motion are. Such an approach is limited in this field of research. I have shown how complex the current discussion is concerning how higher education in Europe should be governed. There are changes taking place that have different effects in terms of power. We need to analyse these effects more thoroughly as a way of opening up a critical space for reflections about our present. What discourses are the dominating ones today, how do they operate, what is made possible to say and do, and what is being excluded. Thus, it is possible to show how the very trivia of everyday ways of constructing a better world leave untouched and intact the rules and standards for ordering conduct. As illustrated in this chapter, the ambition to include also excludes, something not acknowledged in social policy. Consequently, a critical task such as the one carried out in this chapter is necessary as it gives us another starting point (it makes visible the rules and standards of reasong and ordering of conduct) for discussion than do other kinds of perspectives, e.g. several of those adopted by researchers mentioned in my research overview. Instead of prescription and foundational critique, I give 'exemplary' criticism, which is normative in the sense that I do not prescribe what the results of my questioning are (Dean 1999). What such a project is about is best illustrated by Foucault.

My point is not that everything is bad, but that everything is dangerous, which is not exactly the same as bad. If everything is dangerous, then we always have something to do. So my position leads not to apathy but to a hyper- and pessimistic activism (Foucault, 1983, p. 231–232).

NOTES

[1] This chapter is a slightly revised version of the article European citizens under construction: the Bologna process analyzed from a governmentality perspective published in Educational Philosophy and Theory 2008.

REFERENCES

Ahola, S., & Mesikämmen, J. (2003). Finnish higher education policy and the ongoing Bologna process. *Higher education in Europe, 28*, 217–227.

Balibar, É. (2004). *We, the people of Europe? Reflections on transnational citizenship*. Princeton, NJ: Princeton University press.

Bergen Communiqué. (2005). *The European higher education area: Achieving the goals. Communiqué of the conference of European ministers responsible for higher education.*

Berlin Communiqué. (2003). *Realising the European Higher Education Area. Communiqué of ministers responsible for higher education.*

Bologna declaration of 19 June 1999.

Brunsson, N., & Jacobsson, B. (Eds.). (2000). *A world of standards*. Oxford, UK: Oxford university press.

Dean, M. (1999). *Governmentality: Power and rule in modern society*. London: Sage publications.

ENQA. (2005). *Standards and guidelines for quality assurance in the European higher education area*. Helsinki: European association for quality assurance in higher education.

European Commission. (2001). *Communication from the commission: Making a European Area of Lifelong Learning a Reality*. Brussels: European commission, Directorate – general for Education and Culture and Directorate – general for Employment and Social Affairs.

Fejes, A., & Nicoll, K. (Eds.). (2008). *Foucault and lifelong learning: Governing the subject*. London: Routledge.

Fejes, A. (2006a). The planetspeak discourse of lifelong learning in Sweden: What is an educable adult? *Journal of Education Policy, 21*(6), 697–716.

Fejes, A. (2006b). *Constructing the adult learner: A governmentality analysis*. Linköping: LiU-Tryck.

Fejes, A. (2005). New wine in old skins: Changing patterns in the governing of the adult learner in Sweden. *International Journal of Lifelong Education, 24*, 71–86.

Foucault, M. (1983). On the genealogy of ethics: An overview of work in progress. In H. L. Dreyfus & P. Rabinow (Eds.), *Michel Foucault: Beyond structuralism and hermeneutics* (pp. 229–252). Chicago: University of Chicago Press.

Foucault, M. (2003a). Governmentality. In P. Rabinow & N. Rose (Eds.), *The essential Foucault: Selections from the essential works of Foucault 1954–1984* (pp. 229–245). New York: The New Press.

Foucault, M. (2003b). The subject and power. In P. Rabinow & N. Rose (Eds.), *The essential Foucault: Selections from the essential works of Foucault 1954–1984* (pp. 126–144). New York: The New Press.

Foucault, M. (1983). On the genealogy of ethics: An overview of work in progress. In H. L. Dreyfus & P. Rabinow (Eds.), *Michel Foucault: Beyond structuralism and hermeneutics.* Chicago: University of Chicago Press.

Foucault, M. (1980). *Power/knowledge: Selected interviews and other writings 1972–1977.* New York: Pantheon.

Giddens, A. (2000). *Runaway world: How globalization is reshapening our lives.* Routledge: New York.

Hultqvist, K. (2004). The traveling state: The nation, and the subject of education.' In B. M. Baker & K. E. Heyning (Eds.), *Dangerous coagulations? The uses of Foucault in the study of education* (pp. 153–188). New York: Peter Lang.

Hultqvist, K., Olsson, U., Petersson, K., Popkewitz, T., & Andersson, D. (2003). Deciphering Educational thought in Sweden in the early 2000: Fabricating subjects in the name of history and the future. Presented at *Philosophy and History of the Discipline of Education: Evaluation and Evolution of the Criteria for Educational Research,* Leuven.

Hultqvist, K., & Petersson, K. (1995). *Foucault, namnet på en modern vetenskaplig och filosofisk problematik: Texter om maktens mentaliteter, pedagogik, psykologi, medicinsk sociologi, feminism och bio-politik.* Stockholm: HLS Förlag.

London Communiqué. (2007). *Towards the Eruopean higher education area: Responding to challenges in a globalised world.*

Ministry of Education. (2005). *Ny värld – ny högskola. Prop. 2004/05:162.* Stockholm: Ministry of education.

Ministry of Education. (2004). *Högre utbildning i utveckling – Bolognaprocessen i svensk belysning. DS 2004:2.* Stockholm: Ministry of education.

Nóvoa, A. (2002). Ways of thinking about education in Europe. In A. Nóvoa & M. Lawn (Eds.), *Fabricating Europe: The formation of an education space* (pp. 131–155). Boston: Kluwer Academic Publishers.

Olsson, U. (1997). *Folkhälsa som pedagogiskt projekt: Bilden av hälsoupplysning i statens offentliga utredningar.* Uppsala: Uppsala universitet.

Popkewitz, T. S. (2006). Hope of progress and fears of the dangerous: Research, cultural theses and Planning different human kinds. In G. Ladson-Billings & W. F. Tate (Eds.), *Education research in the public interest. Social Justice, action, and policy* (pp. 119–141). New York: Teachers College Press.

Popkewitz, T. S. (2003). Governing the child and pedagogicalization of the parent: A historical excursus into the present. In M. Bloch, K. Holmlund, I. Moqvist, & T. S. Popkewitz (Eds.), *Governing children, families and education: Restructuring the welfare state* (pp. 35–61). New York: Palgrave Macmillan.

Rose, N. (1996). Governing "advanced" liberal democracies. In A. Barry, T. Osborne, & N. Rose (Eds.), *Foucault and political reason: Liberalism, neo-liberalism and rationalities of government* (pp. 37–64). Chicago: The University of Chicago Press.

Rose, N. (1999). *Powers of freedom: Reframing political thought.* Cambridge, UK: Cambridge University Press.

SvD. (2005). *Pagrotsky backar om nya betyg.* Retrieved December, 5, 2005, from http://www.svd.se/dynamiskt/inrikes/did_9505441.asp

Andreas fejes
Linköping university
Sweden

MAARTEN SIMONS AND JAN MASSCHELEIN

31. "THE ART OF NOT BEING GOVERNED LIKE THAT AND AT THAT COST"

Comments on Self-Study in the Studies of Governmentality

"Work in philosophy – like work
in architecture in many respects –
is really more work on oneself"
Ludwig Wittgenstein

INTRODUCTION

The aim of this chapter can be formulated simply as follows: to re-introduce, or at least to draw attention to, an 'ethos of enlightenment' or 'critical attitude' within the line of research that is commonly referred to as 'studies of governmentality'. The point of departure for our study indeed is that what is often missing or lost out of sight in 'studies of governmentality' is a critical concern with the present, related to what according to Foucault is "the art of not being governed like that and at that cost" (Foucault, 2007/1978: 45). Thus, we will try to clarify that studying processes of governmentalisation could be motivated by an attitude of 'de-governmentalisation' (Gros, 2001, 520-523).[1] The attitude of de-governmentalisation can be described in a very classical way as an 'attitude of enlightenment', that is, bringing to light mechanisms of power or speaking truth to power.

Speaking broadly (and, thus somewhat inaccurately), governmentality studies seem to fall apart into two registers. On the one hand, there are studies that are merely descriptive and incorporated within the broader domain of sociological and political analysis. In this register, an ongoing debate seems to be whether and/or how studies of governmentality can rely more on 'empirical methods' in order to be able to grasp the 'reality' of governmentalities (and not merely what they refer to as 'the programmes'). On the other hand, studies of governmentality seem to be integrated within broader critical programmes that want to resist political, cultural and social hegemony (and ultimately the consequences of different sorts of capital accumulation). In this register, ongoing debates include (1) the issue of how agency (and the possibility of resistance towards forms of hegemony) can be thought of in the context of an analysis of governmentality, and (2) the explanation (instead of description) of processes of governmentalisation by drawing upon materialist or idealist social and political theories (see also Reichert, 2001; Osborne, 2001).

M.A. Peters et al. (eds.), Governmentality Studies in Education, 527–548.

In our view, giving shelter to studies of governmentality in these disciplinary registers becomes tempting precisely when the particular critical heart is removed from these studies, or when that critical heart remains unnoticed. The two registers, then, are welcomed as providing an intellectual and methodological context, an explicit normative foundation or just the common and safe ground of classical scholarly work. Additionally, because the critical attitude underlying these studies is a 'practical' and even 'existential' attitude and not a more common theoretical or normative one, as we will elaborate further on, the tendency to integrate studies of governmentality within one of the two registers (or even to assimilate these studies) is somehow understandable. It is understandable indeed that, from the perspective of classic normative and critical (social, political, educational) theory, studies relying upon a 'practical' and 'existential' critical attitude are often disqualified for being relativist or crypto-normative (e.g. Fraser, 1981; Habermas, 1985). Although we recognize and understand this temptation, this kind of integrationist and assimilating attitude towards studies of governmentality is not necessary, at least as long as one acknowledges that the critical attitude, being a kind of virtue (Butler, 2004; Simons et. al., 2005), lies at the very heart of studies of governmentality. Without this critical attitude these studies run the risk of becoming empty or blind, and probably hence the attempts to bring them under in one of common disciplinary registers.

Apart from our focus on the 'attitude of de-governmentalisation' that could underlie studies of governmentality, the chapter has also another objective. We want to argue that exactly the attitude of de-governmentalisation (and, therefore, conducting research in view of de-governmentalisation) is itself to be seen as a form of education or 'self-study'. In other words, we want to develop the thesis that 'studies of governmentality' include a particular 'self-study' (for the one doing the study, and probably also for the people invited to read the study). In view of this thesis, the chapter will focus on governmentality and education, yet not on governmentality in education nor on education from the viewpoint of govern-mentality, but on the educational dimension (that is, the critical practice of self-study) that could be part of studies of governmentality.

FOUCAULT, STUDIES OF GOVERNMENTALITY, CONDUCT

During the courses at the *Collège de France* in the late seventies (*Sécurité, Territoire et Population (1977-1978)* and *Naissance de la biopolitique (1978-1979))*, Michel Foucault elaborated his analysis of power-relations (Foucault 2004a, 2004b; cf. 1978, 1981). While previously he analysed disciplinarian forms of power (giving shape to modern institutions such as schools, hospitals and the prison), later his interest shifted to broader governmental issues, such as to addressing the exercise and development of power relations throughout the modern state. His point of departure however was not to analyse the power of the state or the growing 'etatisation of society', and his aim was not to discuss the legitimacy of the state's power. Instead, and broadly speaking, Foucault's main interest was the analysis of the exercise of power by focusing on the development of governmental rationalities, on related governmental technologies and on how the objects and subjects of government are being shaped. For this domain of analysis he introduced the term 'governmentality', and opened up the perspective to analyse processes of govern-mentalisation.[2]

In order to analyse processes of governmentalisation it is important to stress that there is no single and universal mode of governing. As Foucault (2004a; 2004b) has elaborated in detail, the governmental state and its rationalities and mentalities have continually transformed throughout history: a governmentalisation in the name of 'reason of state' in the early modern period, in the name of 'individual freedom and security' (finding its intellectual rationalization in the reflections on political economy) in the modern era and in the name of 'the social' in the twentieth century. Foucault (2004b) noticed a new phase in the governmentalisation of the state in the second part of the twentieth century and meanwhile many scholars (Gordon, 1991; Rose, 1999; Dean, 1999; Lemke, 1997; Bröckling et al., 2000) have elaborated Foucault's indications.

In current processes of governmentalisation the role of the state is for instance no longer rationalised as a central agency of government that should 'intervene' in society in the name of 'the social' and in order to align individual freedom and social welfare (Rose, 1996). Instead, the state today is increasingly regarded as a 'managerial' agency that should 'enable' an 'entrepreneurial' type of freedom (at the individual level, and at the level of organisations, communities...) through for example 'marketisation', 'investment in human capital' and in collaboration with other agencies (both local and global, public and private) of 'governance' (Olssen et al., 2004). Thus in the current context, the state does not disappear, but its task is rationalised in a new way (towards global and local agencies), new technologies are being used and those being governed are required to 'conduct' themselves in new ways. This 'advanced liberal' (Rose, 1996) forms of governmentalisation can help to understand the current phase in the governmentalisation of the state. Additionally, it is important to focus on processes of governmentalisation in other domains and at other scales as well: global processes of governmentalisation, processes related to 'Europeanisation' and forms of governmentalisation at more local levels (Perry & Maurer, 2003; Masschelein & Simons, 2003, 2005; Larner & Walters, 2004; Simons, 2007). In view of the scope of the chapter, it is important to focus in more detail on the conception of government underlying the studies of governmentality.

Foucault describes government as *"conduire des conduite"* or "the conduct of conduct" (Foucault, 1982, p. 237). This formula expresses clearly that the object of government is not a passive pole (outside), but that government acts upon people who are governing themselves (or 'conducting', behaving) in a specific way. Government thus is acting upon the self-government or 'conduct' of people. This self-government however is not something that is given (as a kind of natural resource that government has at its disposal), but it is being shaped historically. Hunter has clearly and convincingly indicated how the school (and its spiritual discipline) played a major role in 'producing' people with the 'ability' to govern themselves, and (relatively new in history) people who came to see themselves in terms of rational and moral autonomy (Hunter, 1994). In this Hunter was profoundly inspired by Foucault's studies of the 1980s explicitly focusing on (the history of ethical) technologies of the self which allow human beings to relate in a particular way to themselves and to constitute themselves as self-governing subjects (cf. Foucault, 1984a, b; 2001).

In line with these ideas on government and governmentality different topics have been studied; by Foucault himself, by his close collaborators (such as Burchell, Donzelot, Procacci, Ewald) and from the 1990s by scholars like Rose, Miller, Dean up into the 21st century (where studies of governmentality– at least as part of the self-understanding of a group of researchers – took shape) (Simons & Masschelein, 2006a). Additionally, several scholars started to focus on processes of governmentalisation in education particularly in relation to educational policy and to restructurings in the wake of so-called neoliberal and neo-conservative governance (e.g. Marshall, 1995; Popkewitz, 1998; Popkewitz & Brennen, 1998; Peters, 2000; Edwards, 2002; Olssen et al., 2004). Also our own research can be situated here, and we want to discuss this research briefly in order to able to start focusing on the critical attitude.

In our studies, the focus on processes of governmentalisation (related to quality assurance and performance management in education, managerialism, feedback mechanism, lifelong learning and learning society policies) helps to describe what was and is happening *to us*. It helped us to focus on how our educational present (that is, the present that we refer to in terms of –'the learning society', or 'quality education' or 'lifelong learning') is related to particular governmental rationalities, governmental technologies and forms of self-government (Simons, 2002, 2006; Masschelein & Simons, 2002; 2003; Masschelein et al., 2006). The perspective of governmentality thus allowed to look at educational ideas and programmes as being part of the history of the ways in which we, as human beings, conduct and govern oneself and others. It is possible to describe the intrinsic relation between the intellectual and practical educational technologies on the one hand and the way in which political power is wielded in our societies as well as the way in which we govern ourselves on the other side. In this way, studies of governmentality can indicate how educational practice, educational theory (and science) and current policies actually ask us to behave or conduct ourselves in a particular way; how for instance we are asked to understand ourselves as (lifelong) learners (and for instance no longer as social citizens), to look at schools as productive sites to be judged in terms of added value (instead of institutions for instance), to look at learning as an ongoing capitalization of life, to regard students as customers in need of quality education, etc.

Rather than elaborating on these studies at the level of their results and conclusions, it is our aim to elucidate the particular critical attitude of de-governmentalisation that motivates these studies – at least Foucault's work, the works of some others working in line of this, and also what we, in all modesty, tried to do in our own work (and motivated by questions such as: how not to be governed as a lifelong learner? and, what is the cost of being governed in the name of permanent quality control?). In order to clarify this attitude, Foucault's description of his own work will be used as a point of departure.

EXPERIENCE, DE-SUBJECTIVATION, THE PRESENT

Being asked what writing and doing research meant for him, Foucault states his studies and books work as experiences, and that throughout his studies and writings he is transforming himself: "What I think is never quite the same. (...) for me my books are experiences (...). And experience is something that one comes out of transformed." (Foucault, 2000, 239). The term experience is important here, and is related more specifically to 'putting something to the test', that is, putting oneself and one's thinking to the test. Because 'experience' is his main focus, he is very clear about the way he understands himself: "(...) I am an experimenter and not a theorist. I call a theorist someone who constructs a general system, either deductive or analytical, and applies it to different fields in a uniform way. That isn't my case. I'm an experimenter in the sense that I write in order to change myself and in order not to think the same thing as before."(Ibid., p. 240) Hence, for Foucault a theorist is not someone who writes in order to change him/herself, and hence, the theorist is someone who does not put his/her own thinking and his/her own mode of being at the test. One could say that the theorist puts instead reality to the test in the carefully constructed theoretical system. Further in the interview, Foucault tells that theorists deliver us 'books of truth' or 'books of demonstration', while he regards his books as 'books of experience'. This distinction is important to explore in view of the critical attitude motivating his studies (of governmentality) (cf. Masschelein 2006, Simons 2004).

For Foucault, the term experience should be understood in a strong sense, that is, it refers to rather particular, challenging events in one's life. Experience for him, does not refer to what someone has ('I have an experience' and 'this experience enriches me'), but precisely to what actually destroys the 'I' and 'me'. Experience does not lead to a kind of enrichment or development of the 'I' or 'the subject'. This way of understanding experience is captured very well in the following: "For Nietzsche, Bataille, Blanchot (...) experience is trying to reach a certain point in life that is as close as possible to the 'unlivable,' to that which can't be lived through. (...) experience has the function of wrenching the subject from itself, of seeing to it that the subject is no longer itself. (...) This is a project of desubjectivation. (...) The idea of a limit-experience that wrenches the subject from itself." (Ibid., p. 241–242) The experience Foucault has in mind is a process of de-subjectivation, and throughout his studies and through writing his books he becomes someone else. This means that he takes his own understanding of the world, and for instance the common understanding of 'madness' and the current practices to deal with 'madness', as a point of departure (in *Madness and Civilization*). His study meant that he was no longer able to relate in the same way to 'madness'; the 'I' that took the current way of dealing with 'madness' as evident or necessary, disappeared during his studies and throughout his writing. What is at stake is "to construct myself and to invite others to share an experience of what we are, not only our past but also our present, an experience of our modernity in such a way that we might come out of it transformed", and this means, he goes on, "that at the end of the book we would establish new relationships with the subject at issue; the I who wrote the book and those who have read it would have a different relationship with madness, with its contemporary status, and its history in the modern world." (Ibid., p. 244) Thus, although Foucault wrote very much historical work, the point of departure is clearly the present, and in particular, the way he and his contemporaries understand the present (and how he and his contemporaries look at the past of their present). In that sense, he stresses that his work is "inspired by direct personal experience", and experience here (and in a weaker sense) referring to a taken for granted perception and understanding of the world. However, his work is not about these kind of personal experiences (such as stories about one's personal experience with madness), but inspired by them and directed to finding a point at which one no longer is able to relate in the same way to one's opinions and perceptions.

Being an experimenter and not a theorist, Foucault regards his book as books of experience and not as truth books or books of demonstration. The latter want to pass true knowledge to the readers by way of demonstration; these theoretical books are focused on argumentation and proof. Hence, the theorist regards the readers as being in a state of ignorance about a particular subject, or as an audience that has to be convinced (based on a careful demonstration of the truth). The theorist, by using his/her truth books, thus is in a particular way a teacher; someone who claims a position of authority based on access to the truth and transferring knowledge to others in order that they have access to the truth too, and know how to think about a particular subject. In describing his own position and books, Foucault makes the following remark: "I don't accept the word 'teaching' (...), my books don't exactly have that value [method, demonstration, lessons]. They are more like invitations or public gestures." (Ibid.,) The experimenter invites people to read a book of experience in order to transform oneself, that is, one's relation to oneself and to the topic under investigation. It is not a 'lesson' based on 'authority', but an 'experience' based on 'invitation'; not a kind of 'intellectual service' but a 'public gesture'. In view of such an invitation and gesture, readers are not addressed (as subjects of knowledge and in needs of true knowledge about a particular thing), but invited to have an experience. This experience, of course, does not tell the readers how they should think about a particular thing, but is a process of de-subjectivation due to which one is no longer able to relate in the same way to oneself and the world.

It is really important to stress that books of experience should not be regarded as popular collections of narratives about one's experiences on a particular topic, neither as (auto)biographical stories to reveal the truth about the world taking one's on experience as a point of departure. Such kind of 'personal experience' books are actually 'truth books' because based on 'personal experiences' they want to 'demonstrate' or 'proof' something to the reader. Instead, the term experience in 'books of experience' refers to the books' transformative or 'de-subjectifying' force in at least two directions. Firstly, they are an experience for the writer and researcher herself as explained earlier. However, secondly they can function as experiences for the readers: "to read it as an experience that prevented them from always being the same or from having the same relation with things, with others, that they had before reading it." (Ibid., 243) In short, Foucault doesn't want to prove something, does not want to teach his readers a lesson, but wants to invite people to have an experience in relation to specific topics under investigation, an experience that puts not just the common knowledge of himself and his readers, but actually their subjectivity to the test.

This short preliminary depiction of Foucault's understanding of his own work brings several important aspects to the foreground. We will mention them briefly in order to set the scene to discuss the critical attitude that might inspire studies of governmentality.

Firstly, Foucault's work and hence also his elaboration of governmentality is guided by a concern for the present. In relation to governmentality, it means clearly that the concern is the way in which he and his contemporaries have been and are being governed: should we take the freedom in which we are governed for granted?, should we see it as an evident task for governments to 'take care of our lives' from the cradle to the grave?, what are the effects of governments acting in the name of security and social and mental hygiene that we actually support today? Hence, questions like these, and starting from what is taken for granted (or at least not being questioned explicitly) today by himself and his contemporaries, are the point of departure for these studies. Again the aim is not to reveal the truth about what is going on (and to demonstrate what is right or wrong), but to question instead the truths we live by and take for granted.

Secondly, this concern for the present is what Foucault described elsewhere as a (historical, critical) 'ontology of the present' or an 'ontology of ourselves' (Foucault, 2007/1983/1984, 95/113). This kind of ontology, as we will explain in more detail below, starts from the things that 'we' (at a particular moment in time and in a particular context) take for granted (or regard as "'fundamental' or as 'ontological'), and how 'we' came to see those things as fundamental; which 'we' or which 'subject' came to see these things (e.g. the prison, the hospital, sexuality) as evident or fundamental. The 'ontology of the present' thus is related to the notion of experience, since showing that what we regard today as given or being self-evident (part of our 'ontology') leads to a kind of de-subjectivation. It destroys the subject, or the 'we', that takes for instance a particular way of dealing with sexuality or madness for granted. In view of this, the thesis we want to develop is that the originality and strength of 'studies of governmentality' is their reliance on such an 'ontology of ourselves' and the possibility to result in 'books of experience'.

Thirdly, the 'ontology of the present' and de-subjectifying work of experience clearly refer to a particular conception of critique on the one hand and education on the other hand. Critique here is first of all an attitude (and even "akin to virtue") and more specifically a task one is taking up (Foucault, 2007/1978, p. 43; Butler, 2004; Masschelein, 2004). The critical task, according to Foucault, "requires work on our limits, that is, a patient labour giving form to our impatience for liberty." (Foucault, 2007/1984, p. 119). Works on our limits means studying what we regard as evident or as part of our ontology today and hence what functions as a limit. We mentioned earlier indeed that de-subjectivation is a 'limit-experience'; not a (personal) experience of limits, but an experience that exposes someone to one's foundations (and to who one is, and to how one relates to things) and consequently opens up a space to relate in a different way to oneself (and to things). This clarifies there is indeed a clear educational dimension at stake here. Education however is not about the transfer of knowledge (and it is not an education based on truth books or 'school books'). Instead of education being the accumulation of knowledge (and strengthening the subject), education here is about the transformation of the subject (and destroying one's knowledge basis). Importantly, this education is at stake for both the researcher (conducting an ontology of the present) and the readers (reading an experience book). Therefore, we want to pay attention to the 'self-study' that is part of 'studies of governmentality'.

Finally, the above distinction between books of experience and truth book may give the impression that Foucault, and studies of governmentality in line with his work, are not concerned about truth. This is certainly not the case. It is precisely by taking the angle of truth that we want to elaborate the 'critical attitude' underlying books of experience and studies of governmentality (Simons & Masschelein, 2007). We will elaborate that studies of governmentality consist in 'speaking truth to power', although it is important to be very clear about the term truth and truth-telling (and not to mix it up with 'truth books').

ACCESS TO THE TRUTH, SELF-TRANSFORMATION, KNOWLEGDE

In studies of governmentality (at least in their form as books (or articles) of experience) it is the researcher herself who is at stake, that is, the relation to herself and to things in her present. Studies of governmentality thus include a kind of self-study, and a transformation of the researcher herself. Exactly this transformation of the researcher involving a particular kind of experience and truth telling is however hard to think within an academic context that values 'objectivity', 'method' and 'knowledge' (and as mentioned earlier, this explains probably why studies of governmentality are often being integrated in other disciplinary registers). We will elaborate this alternative way of truth telling by drawing on the research of the later Foucault and particularly on his 1981–1982 courses at the *College de France* under the title *The hermeneutics of the subject* (Foucault, 2001). As is well known, Foucault worked in his later work and contrary to his earlier work on topics he sympathised with such as *parrhesia* and care of the self (although not aiming at transposing these ideas to the present). One leading question in the series of courses where he studied carefully Greek and Roman antiquity is: how can people have access to the truth? how can people become truth-tellers?, or what is the price of having access to the truth? Foucault distinguishes two traditions that each answers this question in its own particular way. Let us focus in more detail on these traditions in view of clarifying the truth telling at stake in the ontology of the present (and studies of governmentality).

The first tradition, that emerged in Greek antiquity and is dominant today, claims that it is 'knowledge' that offers access to the truth and that in order to have 'true knowledge' specific (internal and external) conditions related to the act of knowing and the position of the knower have to be taken into account. It probably needs no more clarification that this tradition culminated in modern scientific research and academic inquiry that relies for the 'production' of true knowledge on (scientific) method and on a disinterested and objective research ethos. This tradition has been institutionalised at the modern 'research university', and is playing a major role in the production 'truth book' or 'books of demonstration'. Perhaps due to the familiarity with this tradition, we lose out of sight that it is but one, very particular way of having access to the truth.

A less common tradition claims that access to the truth requires a transformation of the self. While the first knowledge-based and knowledge-oriented tradition assumes in principle everyone has access to truth on the basis of being a human being (at least if conditions at the level of knowledge are taken into account), the second tradition, which could be called the 'existential-ethical', 'spiritual' or 'ascetic' tradition, assumes that the transformation of the 'mode of being of the subject' is required.[3] From this viewpoint (and unlike the first one) there is no access to the truth without transforming oneself. Truth telling based on self-transformation however does not lead to the production of 'truth books' (in view of the distribution of knowledge) but to books of experience (having their own truth value, as we will elaborate below). Thus in both traditions people have to meet certain conditions or have 'to pay a price' in order to have access to the truth, but the conditions and price differ: either a transformation of the self, either conditions related to know-ledge. It will come as no surprise that we want to look at the ontology of the present and studies of governmentality in line with the existential-ethical tradition, and consequently, to regard indeed the particular transformation of the self as the ('educational') price that the researcher has to pay in order to have access to the truth or to become a truth-teller.

We want to stress again that today *the* existential-ethical tradition does not exist, or at least not in an institutionalised form. Thus in referring to the existential-ethical tradition, to which the ontology of the present belongs, we do not have a tradition at hand that has developed in a similar way as, at the same level of and alongside the dominant knowledge-oriented/based tradition (institutionalised at the academia). It is a tradition that lives instead in its shadows and margins – not necessary outside the university but certainly not having a central position. As far as the knowledge–based/oriented studies of power, governance and education have a dominant position, as long as the dominant academic tradition reconfirms its exclusive position by telling stories about its own great origins, the existential-ethical tradition not just remains marginal but keeps on being disqualified for being 'not scientific', 'not academic' and for producing knowledge and understanding that is not according to the 'internal and external conditions of true knowledge production'. In short, the existential-ethical tradition we want to focus on seems permanently to run the risk of being disqualified for having missed (or ignored) "Enlightenment" and "humanity's passage to its adult status" led by true reason and scientific method and rigidity. At this point and in line with Foucault, it is important to refuse the "blackmail of Enlightenment" – "you either accept the Enlightenment and remain within the tradition of its rationalism (…); or else you criticize the Enlightenment and then try to escape from its principles of rationality" – and thus to resist any marginalizing of other forms of truth telling in the name of "rationality" (Foucault, 2007/1984, 110) Instead, what we want to indicate is that also the existential-ethical tradition is related to 'enlightenment' on the one hand and to a 'critical attitude' on the other hand, and also this tradition has a clear political relevance in terms of speaking truth to power; however not precisely what the knowledge-oriented/based tradition has in mind.

SPEAKING TRUTH TO POWER, ENLIGHTENMENT, CRITIQUE

Let us, first, elaborate a bit more on the term 'enlightenment'. At stake is not the relation between knowledge and truth (or enlightenment based on true knowledge) but the relation between ethics and truth. In other words: in the knowledge-based/oriented tradition the subject is regarded as someone who is *a priori* capable of having access to the truth and only *additionally* an ethical subject who can and should know what to do (Gros, 2001, 504). The basic assumption is that everyone (in principle) can obtain knowledge, and based on this knowledge that everyone is in a position to know what to do (be it technically, politically or ethically). It is indeed in accordance with the dominant modern way of understanding enlightenment (and probably 'The Enlightenment'); the transition from a state of dependency or heteronomy ('dark ages' or 'oppressive dogmatism' and 'enslaving tradition') to a state of independency or autonomy guided by the principles of (universal) reason that is incarnated in true knowledge (on ourselves, others and the world). This is the enlightenment of the theoretician, of the truth books and its ultimate version 'The handbook of reason'; it is the enlightenment related with the political project of emancipation where everyone submits oneself to the 'law within', that is, the law of reason.

In the second tradition, ethical work of the self on the self and a transformation of oneself is the main condition to have access to the truth. In order to grasp the kind of enlightenment at stake here, it is important to say more about the particular meaning of ethics (as well as truth) in this tradition. The term ethics has to be distinguished from the terms morals (and morality) (Foucault, 1984a). The latter are about the set of rules, norms and values of just behaviour (and in view of their morality). The term ethics instead refers to the relation of the self to the self and how this relation is modified or transformed by the self in order to become an ethical subject, that is, a subject of action (and not merely a knowing subject). In line with Foucault (and his genealogy of ethics in Ancient Greece) the domain of ethics understood in this way can be referred to as field of practices related to 'care of the self' and 'self-mastery' (Foucault, 1984a/b, 2001).[4] The relation of the self to the self, as we will indicate further on, is a relation of care and not a relation of knowing; one has to look at the self not as an object of knowledge but as a matter of concern and care; and the point of departure is not oneself as a knowing subject but as an ethical subject of action.

The aim of care or work upon the self is to bring into alignment what one thinks and what one does, one's actions and one's thoughts. What is at stake is: "The test of one self as a thinking subject, who acts and thinks accordingly, who has as his goal a certain transformation of the subject such there is a self-constitution as an ethical subject of truth." (Foucault, 2001, 442; cf. Rabinow, 2003, 9) In Ancient Greece, this 'test of one self' is assumed to be an ongoing concern, and is focused on 'self-mastery' or living a 'true life'; the notion true means that one's thinking (and relation to oneself and to the world, including one's understanding of that world) is in accordance with what one is doing, and that one lives an 'enlightened' life. The figure of Socrates is described in Foucault's studies as someone living a life of self-care and self-mastery in view of living a 'true' and 'enlightened' life'. Enlightened refers not to 'based on true knowledge or according to the principles of reason', but to the process of self-transformation in view of the incorporation of knowledge in self-mastery. Self-mastery therefore is a state in which one has access to the truth and in which this truth has a function of 'enlightenment'; it transforms the subject in its way of being or it saves the subject. As a consequence, someone who masters the self is someone whose life is a true life or a life inspired by truth; it is someone who actualises truth in her life and during her whole life; someone whose life is animated by truth. Truth is thus a 'reason for living', the *logos* that is actualised in existence and that animates, intensifies and proves life; it is what 'verifies life' (Gros, 2001, p. 510). As we will explain later, this care for the self is required to have access to the truth and to become a truth-teller, but the authority of this truth-telling is based on self-mastery (and not on the strength of the demonstration or proof).[5]

Secondly, in the ethical-existential tradition being 'critical' and 'speaking the truth to power' is first of all a task or even a matter of virtue, and not merely the consequence of generating true knowledge. It is helpful to recall here another practice in Greek antiquity: the practice of *parrhesia* or free speech. This practice involves the duty to speak openly and frankly, on issues that are of public relevance and even if one's own life is at risk, the latter being precisely an indication that one is 'truly' critical (Foucault, 2001, p. 388; cf. Foucault, 2004c; cf. Peters, 2003). Without discussing the historical and contextual details, self-mastery and care of the self could be regarded as the condition for *parrhesia*; the *parrhesiast* is someone who lives and acts as truth wants her to act and therefore her truth-telling implies a correspondence between the 'subject of speech' and the 'subject of action'. This engaged speech, or this speech in which the subject who speaks commits herself to the truth, articulates courage and a kind of freedom or independency. The attitude of independency and critique is what the master articulates when she says: "this truth that I say to you, well, you see it in myself" (Foucault, 2001, 391). The master is someone who in a specific way has everything to lose (and puts herself at stake) and nevertheless feels a duty to speak truth (to power). She is not saying: 'this truth that I say to you, well, the method and my disinterested research attitude proof it to be based on true/valid knowledge.' Hence, truth telling for the *parrhesiast* relies on existential-ethical conditions, and is a mode of speaking truth to power.

Although Foucault retraces the roots of the critical attitude back to the practice of parrhesia, he is particularly interested in the practice of critique emerging during modernity and in correlation with the processes of governmentalisation (including the birth of the modern 'governmental' state) (Foucault, 2007/1978, 44-47). According to Foucault, the question 'how to govern people?' became a real concern in early modern times and was related to the development of particular 'arts of government', that is, rationalities and technologies of government that seek to modify the conduct of people (children, workers, populations, households, etc). Modern critique, at least as a task and practice, correlates exactly with these processes of governmentalisation. Instead of being led by the question 'how to govern people?' the leading question of the critical attitude however was "how not to be governed like that, by that, in the name of those principles, with such and such an objective in mind and by means of such procedures, not like that, not for that, not by them." (Ibid., 44) This question articulates for Foucault the birth of the critical attitude as "art of not being governed like that and at that cost." (Ibid., 45) A main element of this art is clearly the art to speak truth to power by questioning at the same time 'the truths' (and technologies) in the name of which people are governed.

This historical elucidation of the terms enlightenment and critique, as well as the practice of speaking truth to power, is helpful for us today because it opens up a space and offers tools to re-think the specific attitude of critique and enlightenment in relation to the 'ontology of the present' and 'studies of governmentality'. It is the attitude that is perhaps best captured in the terms 'ethics of de-governmentalisation' (Gros, 2001, 520). Ethics here referring to the existential-ethical work on the self or the 'test of oneself' in view of resisting the type of subject one is asked to be and at the same time speaking truth to these processes of governmentalisation. Foucault formulates it this way: "(...) If governmentalization is indeed this movement through which individuals are subjugated in the reality of a social practice through mechanisms of power that adhere to a truth, well, then! I will say that critique is the movement by which the subject gives himself the right to question truth on its effects of power and question power on its discourses of truth." (Ibid., 47) And he goes on by defining critique as "the art of voluntary insubordination", the art of "reflected intractability" or as that what would "insure the desubjugation of the subject in the context of what we could call, in a word, the politics of truth." (Ibid., 47) The art of voluntary insubordination or the ethics of de-governmentalisation is in fact the resistance towards 'power' by resisting the kind of subjectivity or conduct that is imposed on us. Understanding resistance in this way – that is resisting who one is and what one takes for granted as well as the governmental relation relying on that self-understanding – means it is a kind of limit-experience that works as a process of de-subjectivation. In other words, the ethics of de-governmentalisation is at the same time an 'ethics of de-subjectivation'.

Based on the elements brought together thus far, the next sections outline briefly a few 'essential features' of the critical attitude motivating studies of governmentality whereas the final section explores the political and public dimension of the ethics of de-governmentalization.

CURIOSITY, LIMIT ATTITUDE, EXPERIMENTAL ATTITUDE

Studies of governmentality require an existential-ethical transformation of the researcher. This is to say that the form of reflexivity of the researcher is not to be determined by (intellectual) method and that the researcher is not guided primarily by conditions and criteria of knowledge production and knowledge about fixed norms. Additionally, the critical dimension of studies of governmentality is not about a *judgmental attitude* (based on criteria of validity), and hence, should not be judged (by other disciplines) in view of lacking such an attitude. The researcher's reflexivity instead takes the form of 'an exercise of thought' in view of exposing one's thoughts (and what one's is taking for granted), and this supposes an *attentive attitude* to the present of which the researcher herself is part. Studies of governmentality thus are concerned with the present. It is important however to stress what is meant with 'concern' and 'the present'. The present is neither what appears as such and before us (the present here is not an object of knowledge), nor that what appears from a longitudinal or temporal approach (the present is not the moment between a past/tradition and a future). The present instead is what appears in a kind of 'sagittal relationship', and what is experienced when we are attentive or when we are 'present in the present' (Foucault, 2007/1983, 86). The present hence refers to what is 'actual' for us today.

In view of this relation to the present, the type of question leading studies of governmentality could have the following form: who are we today, including me as a researcher, and what is distinctive and singular in our current understanding of who we are? It is a question about 'our ontology', or about what we 'are' in the sense of what we take for granted about our being today. Such a question however is always very specific. It is a question that should articulate the distinctiveness of our present. An example from the field of education of what articulates the singularity of who we are in the present, is the issue of 'quality education' or the evident concern with 'quality' in education. Teachers, researchers as well as policy makers use the notion 'quality' constantly to position themselves and to talk about what they are doing in and with regard to education. Even if the definition of the term quality is most of the time unclear, fact is that this term has become indispensable today to speak about education, and thus it seems to be part of our 'ontological make-up' (cf. Simons, 2002; Simons & Masschelein, 2006b). A question therefore could be: who are we, we for whom quality is important, for who educational quality is what is permanently at stake, we who discuss continuously about the adequate indicators of educational quality? Another exemplary question could be related to the issue of 'learning': who are we, we for whom (as researchers, policy-makers, parents, teachers, citizens…) learning is an indispensable notion to position and reposition ourselves today and to talk meaningful about what we are, what we do and what we want to become? In short, the terms 'quality' and 'learning' seem to become referring to something that is fundamental 'for us' (including oneself as a researcher) and it is the 'for us' that will be studied.

To be able to ask such a question (and to put something that is evident, including one's own subjectivity, at stake) implies a particular 'care of the self' or 'work upon the self' from the part of the researcher, and focusing on how 'the self' is part of the present (and the current way of acting and thinking). Although these questions aim at finding knowledge (who are we?), the underlying attitude is an attitude of attention or care and not an attitude of knowing or judging. It is the notion 'curiosity' that captures very well this attitude of care towards the present (cf. Rajchman, 1991, 141). Curiosity, as Foucault explains, is not to be situated at the level of knowledge and the ongoing assimilation of what is proper to know: "To me it suggests something altogether different: it evokes "concern"; it evokes the care one takes for what exists and could exist; a readiness to find strange and singular what surrounds us; a certain relentlessness to break up our familiarities and to regard otherwise the same things; a fervor to grasp what is happening and what passes; a casualness in regard to the traditional hierarchies of the important and the essential." (Foucault, 1997, 325) The term curiosity thus refers to care; care is derived from the Latin word *cura* that is still part of 'curiosity' and the French word *curiosité* (Foucault, 1980, 108). An attitude of care or curiosity encloses a concentrated, accentuated gaze on what is happening today in education, what is happening with us in the world and a willingness to become a stranger in the familiar present, to regard who we are and what we do, and what we regard as our foundations, as no longer evident. As such curiosity combines both distance (towards oneself in the present) and vigilance or attention (cf. Gros, 2001, 512).

Driven by this curiosity for the present, studies of governmentality could be regarded as embodying "an attitude, an ethos, and a philosophical life in which the critique of what we are is at one and the same time the historical analysis of the limits that are imposed on us and an experiment with the possibility of going beyond them."(Foucault, 2007/1984, 118) Hence, and referring clearly to the ideas on experience and de-subjectivation discussed earlier, the attitude at stake combines a 'limit-attitude' and an 'experimental attitude'. The limit-attitude refers to becoming sensitive for what presents itself as a necessity nowadays in order to explore a possible transgression of these limits. Critical work, then, refers to the work that is done at the limits of ourselves and our present: "(...) It will separate out, from the contingency that has made us what we are, the possibility of no longer being, doing, or thinking what we are, do, or think. (...) it is seeking to give new impetus, as far and wide as possible, to the undefined work of freedom." (Foucault, 2007/1984, 114) But this limit-attitude should at once be combined with an 'experimental attitude' or an attitude that seeks to transform or modify one's mode of being and how one lives the present. As such the studies of governmentality involve as well an experimental work of the self on the self, and this work done at the limits of ourselves must (...) put itself to the test of reality, of contemporary reality, both to grasp the points where change is possible and desirable, and to determine the precise form this change should take." (Foucault, 2007/1984, 114).

In order to illustrate the particular kind of critical attitude at stake we can reconsider a question such as 'who are we, we for whom quality is important?' The question itself is both an expression of limits and an experiment of the self with the self, and as such at the heart of an ethics of de-governmentalisation. However, the common critical attitude towards for instance the impact of quality control on education, reformulates this radical question immediately in terms of knowledge-oriented/based questions of validity: how to make legitimate use of the notion educational quality?, what are the valid indicators of educational quality?, are the ruling conceptions and existing opinions on education quality in accordance with what education or schooling essentially is about? This reformulation in fact transforms the critical limit-attitude and experimental attitude into a 'limiting attitude towards one's current experience'; critique here becomes determining (in an almost Kantian sense) what legitimately can be known (and be done) with regard to educational quality. Reformulated this way, the assumption is that 'our experience of educational quality' is blind without orientating, fundamental knowledge, without a 'real handbook on quality assurance'. It is a recuperation of (and immunisation towards) an attitude and question that are rooted in what we earlier called the existential-ethical tradition into the common ground of the knowledge-based/oriented tradition. Thus, emerging from an experimental and limit-attitude, a question such as 'who are we, who am I, for whom educational quality is indispensable to talk meaningful about education?' has a different and more radical meaning; it may lead to trying to escape from the term quality and related practices itself. It is a question that includes the subjectivity of the researcher in the critical inquiry, and works as an experience that makes it no longer possible to relate in the same way to issues of quality in education. It is an attempt to displace oneself in the present and to disengage oneself from oneself, or more precisely, the question itself displaces (and transform) one's mode of being.

ESSAY, ETHICAL DISTANCE, SELF-STUDY

This explains why Foucault refers to the critical ontology of the present (and by extension we want to add studies of governmentality) as a kind of 'essay'. An essay – as the French word *essayer* or 'to try' indicates – is a careful attempt to modify our mode of being in the present. It is a "transforming test of oneself in the play of truth" or and "askesis, an exercise of the self, in thought" (Foucault, 1984a, 15). Again, it is important to stress that the researcher's relation of the self to her present self is a relation of care and not a relation of knowledge. In order to answer the question ('who are we, we who…?'), of course, knowledge is required. But it is a particular kind of knowledge having a particular function. The value (and 'validity') of this kind of knowledge does not reside in its conformance with scientific method, but in its usefulness for the care of the self and for the self-mastery that one aspires. As such it should be labeled as 'experimental knowledge' for the self. It functions as a touchstone to test whether it is still possible to take care of the self in the present and to establish a relation of rectitude between what one does and thinks. Here, the term ethics of de-governmentalization receives its positive meaning; it is on the one hand a work of de-subjectivation but on the other hand an attempt to take care of the self in view of self-mastery. Hence, the ethics aims not at all at a withdrawal from the world, but its aim is to "live the present otherwise" (Foucault, 1979a, 790).

Finally, we have to focus briefly on the truth-telling that is based upon the ethics of de-governmentalisation and on its educational dimension, and foremost the dimension of self-study (for the researcher involved). In order to indicate the particular scope of truth-telling, it is important to recall the major importance of curiosity. It is a curiosity that is related to an experience of 'deconversion' or a loss of assurance or certainty as to who we are or have to be today (Rajchman, 1991, 141). In other words, it is a curiosity that assumes that it is not knowledge (and its conditions) that guarantees access to truth but care of the self and a modification of the self. Being engaged in a study of governmentality is in view of this not about wanting to accumulate and transfer knowledge (and processes of govern-mentalisation), but to live a true life and to be a touchstone for others to take care of the self and to live a true life oneself. Hence, in her truth-telling the researcher addresses others (readers, students) not as subjects of knowledge (in need of a handbook on educational quality for instance) and does not judge their involvement in education matters (based on true knowledge). Studies of governmentality along the existential-ethical tradition do not assume the kind of truth-telling that addresses people as (potentially) intellectual beings that should become enlightened by valid knowledge for better understanding, neither are these studies addressing human beings as in need of (practical) knowledge that is useful for better action.

Based upon on experiment of oneself in the present the truth-telling and true knowledge functions as a book of experience or touchstone, i.e. it can be used as an experiment or test by others in their care for the self. In this context, Foucault's claim that "knowledge is not made for understanding; it is made for cutting" is illuminating (Foucault, 1984c, 88). Understanding is about accumulating knowledge or including new experiences and ideas, while cutting refers to the (indeed almost physical activity) questioning of who we are and what we regard as fundamental in our understanding of ourselves and the world. It is about cutting in our present and how we live the present; knowledge that cuts "introduces a discontinuity", or works as process of de-subjectivation (Ibid., 88). In other words, it opens up spaces to take care for the self, to live the present otherwise. At this point, the ethics of de-governmentalisation is mirrored in a "governmentality of ethical distance" (Gros, 2001, 520-523). This is about a way of behaving oneself where the ethical distance limits the ambition and absorption of the self in tasks and modes of conduct that are imposed, thus an attitude of ethical distance that disconnects self-government from government. The distance resides in a conversion to the self and one's ability to take care of the self. What is at stake is not just to free oneself from the power that is being exercised, but from the subjectivity and individuality it imposes (cf. Foucault, 1982).

This brings us finally to the educational dimension of the studies of governmentality motivated by the critical ontology ourselves. Because (and as far as) it is engaged in the study of the present in which one is partaking oneself, this research is always a kind of education or pedagogy or self-study for the researcher herself (cf. Rabinow, 2003, 9). It is important to frame education or self-study not within the knowledge-oriented/based tradition. Instead of looking at education as an activity of knowledge transfer or accumulation, it could be regarded as 'work on the self' and hence opening up space to take care for the self through limit-experiences or processes of de-subjectivation. The act of displacement and of disengagement with the self in order to be exposed to the limits of (oneself in) the present, could be regarded as a mode of self-study. Hence, education in this existential-ethical tradition refers to, as the etymology of the Latin verb *e-ducere* shows, being led out of ourselves, leading us outside, out of position, exposed (Masschelein & Simons, 2002). E-ducation as the experimental self-study included in studies of governmentality.

The ethical-existential transformation is the condition to become – as a touchstone or through one's book of experience – a teacher or truth-teller for others as well. Again, studies of governmentality do not lead to knowledge that additionally serves as the basis for a 'lesson' or a 'demonstration of the truth'. As Foucault mentions regarding his own work, he is not giving a 'lesson' (in view of understanding), but inviting others (in view of cutting in their self-understanding and their taken for granted relation to the present). E-ducational truth-telling takes care for others, however not by telling them what to do (based on true knowledge) but by opening up spaces to take care for oneself and to verify one's life. While the authority of the knowledge-based/oriented teacher is based on her access to true knowledge, the authority of critical studies of governmentality is different; critical studies of governmentality can function as true touchstone or books of experience to the degree that this work is based on experimental research in which the self (of the researcher) and her present is at stake. Then, and we use the term that Foucault uses in relation to his own work, the studies of governmentality can become 'public gestures'. It is the public dimension of these gestures that will be the subject of the concluding thoughts of this paper.

TOWARD A POLITICS OF 'MAKING THINGS PUBLIC'

Hopefully we made a convincing case on the particular critical attitude of de-governmentalisation that could inspire studies of governmentality, and preventing these studies (for their lack of explicit normative responsibility, political orientation or methodological and empirical scope) to be integrated within or assimilated to traditional registers of sociological, political and philosophical research. Taking studies of governmentality that are motivated by a particular existential-ethical self-study into protection against that disciplinary integration or assimilation does not mean we want to prevent any elaboration or further development of these studies and the critical attitude at stake. It is our contention that this elaboration at least should try to grasp the specificity of these studies. In conclusion, we want to formulate two outlines for further elaboration that seem to be interesting to us and both are related to the public or political scope of studies of governmentality.

What studies of governmentality attempt to do is to cut in our present being, to introduce a discontinuity, and hence to open up spaces for care of oneself or spaces to live the present otherwise. Maybe there is another way to open up such spaces, in addition to 'cutting' in our present. Instead of the cutting activity of the *critical* ontology (of ourselves), we could think of a *creative* ontology (Hacking, 2001). This type of ontology aims at the articulation of (inspiring) 'ideas' for people to take care of oneself (and to develop a governmentality of ethical distance). As Hacking states: "With new names, new objects come into being. Not quickly. Only with usage, only with layer after layer of usage." (Hacking, 2001, 8) In view of this, the aim would be to invent new words and concepts, a new language (of education) that articulates what is at stake in the care of oneself today. Instead of a destructive act, these studies would be motivated by the 'creative act' of forming, inventing and fabricating new concepts as well as by the aim to introduce new techniques and practices to govern oneself (disconnected from processes of governmentalisation) (cf. Deleuze & Guattari, 1991). This creative (positive) attitude could be underlying 'studies of governmentality of ethical distance'. But similar to the critical ontology of the present, it would be worthwhile to explore how these studies could look like if they want to function as gestures inviting people to take care for oneself (instead of being an attempts to transfer knowledge in view of (better) understanding).

Except for trying to develop positive next to negative 'public gestures', it would also be interesting to elaborate the term 'public'. Common reactions towards studies of governmentality include the questioning of their so-called a-political character, their crypto-normativity (hence their being politically dangerous) and, related particularly to the work of the latter Foucault, the insistence on ethics and aesthetics (and the so-called private dimension of the care of the self) at the dispense of politics and issues of public concern. The complaint in fact is that studies of governmentality want to criticize processes of governmentalisation without clearly mentioning on what basis and hence not giving any direction of more humane or just processes of governmentalisation. This complaint is related to the tendency to integrate these studies within a broader, more 'solid' and 'complete' programme of critical (educational, social, political) research. It will come as no surprise that we do not agree with these complaints – although we do think some more elaboration is welcome at this point.

In fact, and as the term 'public gestures' clearly indicates, there is a public concern. The care of the self, and the concern for the present, is not a private or a-social activity, but includes precisely a relation to a 'we' and to 'our present' (see also Gros, 2001, 519). By questioning the present ('who are we, we...?') what is opened up is a space for a possible future 'we' and for a future relation of oneself to that 'we'.[6] Due to this point of departure ('our present') the gestures resulting from studies of governmentality will always be public gestures; not just because these are gestures to a public of contemporaries, not only because they articulate something of public concern, but foremost because throughout these gestures 'public space' is created. Studies of governmentality indeed do not have a particular 'we' (or normative framework, or procedure) in mind that they use to judge the present and to shape a knowledge-based/oriented guidance of future politics or of processes of governmentalisation. Instead, studies of governmentality precisely by relying on the existential-ethical work of the researcher could be regarded as attempts, and we rely for this on a formulation of Latour, to 'make things public' (Latour, 2005).

Making things public, in line with Latour, is not about formulating (like in the knowledge-based/oriented tradition) 'matters of facts' that should lead to a public agreement or understanding in view of knowledge-based/oriented political reform or resistance. Making things public instead is about 'matters of concern' and their becoming public correlates with the constitution of a public, that is, people invited to share this concern. Making things public (as matters of public concern) is thus the result of existential-ethical work on the self that breaks open the horizon of our self-understanding and taken for granted practices (that is, what 'we' regard as matters of fact) and hence transforms it into a matter of concern i.e. "an issue to talk about" (Latour & Sanchez-Criado, 2007, 368). In this regard, Foucault's work on madness, prisons and sexuality contributed in one way or another to the transformation of these issues into matters of public concern. And maybe, although this needs further elaboration too, it is possible to regard these 'public gestures' (resulting from studies of governmentality) as what Rancière would call "demonstrations of equality" or "democratic acts" of taking part in the whole although one has no part in the current whole according to the present distribution of parts (Rancière, 2005).

Indeed, the art of de-governmentalisation (and not wanting to be governed in this or that way) results in introducing new concerns (and not (knowledge-related) facts) into the field of governmentality and in its organisation of ways of thinking, directing and acting. As such, these gestures function as a demonstration of equality and verify the idea that there is ultimately no (rational, ethical, divine) reason to stick to the existing form of governmentality or way of governing people. An elaboration of this line of thinking, could indicate that studies of governmentality do not just have a public concern but as well a democratic one.

It is however important to consider that the elaboration of these lines of thinking only make sense if one is prepared to pay a price to have access to the truth. The prices for studies of governmentality is not the submission to (methodological, deontological) rules of scientific knowledge production, but the transformation of oneself and putting oneself at risk in one's research.

NOTES

[1] The authors translated themselves the quotations from French texts, including some of Foucault's own text.

[2] There are several discussion around this term; for instance on the question whether the neologism is a combination of 'government' and 'mentality' or whether it refers to a kind of potential (similar to for instance the term 'musicality'), or on the question whether governmentality is a perspective on (and framework to analyse) power relations or whether it refers first of all to a particular (historical) configuration of power relations (Osborne, 2001; Senellart, 2004).

[3] In line with Foucault, and contrary to our current (Christian or New Age) understanding of the concepts, 'spiritual' and 'ascetic' do not refer to practices of self-denial and self-renunciation, but (in line with the classic Greek understanding of the term) to intellectual (and other) exercises or practices in order to become attentive to the self and to transform the self (cf. Rabinow, 2003).

[4] For the ancient Greek the context of this idea of care of the self is the problem of finding and describing an 'art of living' or 'technique of existence' (tekhnê tou biou). Care of the self is a general principle to develop a kind of tekhnê or art to master the self, others or life as such. While initially, this principle and the art of existence were located within the domain of education (the preparation of governing others and often to compensate for the lack of adequate education), in the Hellenistic period it gradually became a prescript for the whole duration of on's life (Foucault, 2001, 428-430). These ideas and their subtle transformations have been discussed in detail (cf. Adorno, 1996, 119-138; in the field of education: Peters, 2003; Peters & Besley, 2008). Within the scope of this paper we limit the focus to a general discussion.

[5] The focus on the ethical, spiritual level and the relation to the self also means that this concept of ethics has to be distinguished from concepts and ideas introduced by other French philosophers (Levinas, Lyotard and Derrida) that stress the relation with the Other (cf. Biesta, 2003; Standish, 2002). These philosophers focus, each in their own way, on the limits of knowledge (representation and language), on ethics (as a unconditional, infinite relation of responsibility to the Other) that precedes ontology (the totality of being) or on justice as an unconditional condition of truth (Lyotard, 1983; Levinas, 1991, Derrida, 2001). It is not our aim however to discuss at a theoretical level the differences between Foucault on the one hand and other theories on ethics on the other hand. For present purposes, it should be sufficient to indicate that we discuss ethics at the level of the immanent relation of the self to the self, the work of the self upon the self and its influence on the mode of being of the subject and not at the level of the fundamental relation of transcendence that 'works' on the self and transforms it into a subject of responsibility.

SIMONS AND MASSCHELEIN

6   Foucault stresses that his writings receive their truth once they have been written and not before (as if the book would just articulate what was known before or what can be said within a regime of truth): "I hope that the truth of my books is in the future." (Foucault, 1979b, p. 805)

REFERENCES

Adorno, F. P. (1996). *Le style du philosophe: Foucault et le dire vrai*. Paris: Kimé.

Biesta, G. J. J. (2003). Learning from Levinas. *Studies in Philosophy and Education, 21*(1), 61–68.

Bröckling, U., Krasmann, S., & Lemke, T. (Eds.). (2000). *Gouvernementalité der Gegenwart. Studien zur Ökonomisierung des Sozialen*. Frankfurt am Main: Suhrkamp.

Butler, J. (2004). What is critique? An essay on Foucault's virtue. In S. Salih (Ed.), *The Judith Butler reader* (pp. 302–322). Malden, Oxford and Victoria: Blackwell Publishing.

Dean, M. (1999). *Governmentality. Power and rule in modern society*. New Delhi: Sage.

Deleuze, G., & Guattari, F. (1991). *Qu'est-ce que la philosophie ?* Paris: Les Éditions de Minuit.

Derrida, J. (2001). *L'université sans conditions*. Paris: Galilée.

Edwards, R. (2002). Mobilizing lifelong learning: Governmentality in educational practices. *Journal of Education Policy, 17*(3), 353–365.

Foucault, M. (1978). La "gouvernementalité". In D. Defert, F. Ewald, & J. Lagrange (Eds.), *Dits et écrits III 1976–1979* (pp. 635–657). Paris: Gallimard.

Foucault, M. (1979a). Vivre autrement le temps. In D. Defert, F. Ewald, & J. Lagrange (Eds.), *Dits et écrits III 1976–1979* (pp. 788–790). Paris: Gallimard.

Foucault, M. (1979b). Foucault étudie la raison d'état. In D. Defert, F. Ewald, & J. Lagrange (Eds.), *Dits et écrits. II: 1977–1988* (pp. 801–805). Paris: Gallimard Quarto.

Foucault, M. (1980). Entretien avec Michel Foucault. In D. Defert, F. Ewald, & J. Lagrange (Eds.), *Dits et écrits IV 1980–1988* (pp. 104–110). Paris: Gallimard.

Foucault, M. (1981). "Omnes et singulatim": vers une critique de la raison politique. In D. Defert, F. Ewald, & J. Lagrange (Eds.), *Dits et écrits IV 1980–1988* (pp. 134–161). Paris: Gallimard.

Foucault, M. (1982). Le sujet et le pouvoir. In D. Defert, F. Ewald, & J. Lagrange (Eds.), *Dits et écrits IV 1980–1988* (pp. 222–243). Paris: Gallimard.

Foucault, M. (1984a). *Histoire de la sexualité 2. L'usage des plaisirs*. Paris: Gallimard.

Foucault, M. (1984b). *Histoire de la sexualité 3. Le souci de soi*. Paris: Gallimard.

Foucault, M. (1984c). Nietzsche, genealogy, history. In P. Rabinow (Ed.), *The Foucault reader* (pp. 76–100). New York: Pantheon.

Foucault, M. (1997). The masked philosopher. In M. Foucault, *Ethics* (P. Rabinow, Ed. R. Hurley et al., Trans.), *Essential Works of Foucault* (Vol. I., pp. 321–328). New York and London: Penguin.

Foucault, M. (2000). Interview with Michel Foucault. In *M. Foucault, Power* (J. D. Faubion, Ed. R. Hurley et al. Trans.), *Essential works of foucault* (Vol. III, pp. 239–297). New York/London: Penguin.

Foucault, M. (2001). *L'herméneutique du sujet. Cours au Collège de France (1981–1982)*. Paris: Gallimard.

Foucault, M. (2004a). *Sécurité, territoire, population, Cours au Collège de France (1977–1978)*. Paris: Gallimard/Le seuil.

Foucault, M. (2004b). *Naissance de la biopolitique, Cours au Collège de France (1978–1979)*. Paris: Gallimard/Le seuil.

Foucault, M. (2004c). *Parrèsia. Vrijmoedig spreken en waarheid*. Amsterdam: Parrèsia.

Foucault, M. (2007). *The politics of truth*. Los Angeles, CA: Semiotext(e).

Fraser, N. (1981). Foucault on modern power: Empirical insights and normative confusions. *Praxis International, 1*(3), 272–287.

Gordon, C. (1991). Governmental rationality: An introduction. In G. Burchell, C. Gordon, & P. Miller (Eds.), *The Foucault effect: Studies in governmentality* (pp. 1–51). London: Harvester Wheatsheaf.

Gros, F. (2001). Situation du cours. In M. Foucault (Ed.), *L'herméneutique du sujet. Cours au Collège de France (1981–1982)* (pp. 488–526). Paris: Gallimard.

Habermas, J. (1985). *Der philosophische Diskurs der Moderne. Zwölf Vorlesungen.* Frankfurt am Main: Suhrkamp.

Hacking, I. (2001, January 16). Inaugural Lecture: Chair of Philosophy and History of Scientific Concepts at the Collège de France. *Economy and Society, 31*(1), 1–14.

Hunter, I. (1994). *Rethinking the school. Subjectivity, bureaucracy, criticism.* St. Leonards: Allen and Unwin.

Larner, W., & Walters, W. (Eds.), *Global governmentality: Governing international spaces.* London: Routledge.

Latour, B. (2005). From realpolitik to dingpolitik or how to make things public. In B. Latour & P. Wiebel (Eds.), *Making things public. Atmospheres of democracy* (pp. 14–41). Karlsruhe and Cambridge, MA: ZKM & MIT Press.

Latour, B., & Sanchez-Criado, T. (2007). Making the 'Res Public'. *Ephemera. Theory & Politics in organization, 7*(2), 364–371.

Lemke, T. (1997). *Eine Kritik der politischen Vernunft. Foucault's Analyse der modernen Gouvernementalität.* Berlin and Hamburg: Argument.

Levinas, E. (1991). *Anders dan zijn.* Ambo: Baarn.

Lyotard, J.-F. (1983). *Le différend.* Paris: Les Éditions de minuit.

Marshall, J. (1995). Governementality and liberal education. *Studies in the Philosophy of Education, 14*(1), 23–24.

Masschelein, J. (2004). How to conceive of critical educational theory today? *Journal of Philosophy of Education, 38*(3), 351–367.

Masschelein, J., & Simons, M. (2002). An adequate education for a globalized world? A note on the immunization of being-together. *Journal of Philosophy of Education, 36*(4), 565–584.

Masschelein, J., & Simons, M. (2003). *Globale immuniteit. Een kleine cartografie van de Europese ruimte voor onderwijs.* Leuven: Acco.

Masschelein, J., & Simons, M. (2005). *Globale Immunität oder Eine Kleine Kartographie des europäischen Bildungsraums.* Zürich and Berlin: Diaphanes.

Masschelein, J. (2006). Experience and the limits of governmentality. *Educational Philosophy and Theory, 38*(4), 561–575.

Masschelein, J., Simons, M., Bröckling, U., & Pongratz, L. (Eds.). (2007). *The learning society from the perspective of governmentality.* Oxford, UK: Blackwell.

Olssen, M., Codd, J., & O'Neill, A.-M. (2004). *Education policy: Globalization, citizenship, democracy.* London: Sage.

Osborne, Th. (2001). Techniken und Subjekte: von der 'Governementality Studies' zu den 'Studies of Governmentality. *Mitteiungen des Instituts für Wissenschaft und Kunst, 56*(2–3), 12–16.

Perry, R., & Maurer, B. (Eds.). (2004). *Globalization under construction: Governmentality, law, and identity.* Minneapolis, MN: University of Minnesota Press.

Peters, M. A. (2000). Neoliberalism and the constitution of the entrepreneurial self: Education and enterprise culture in New Zealand. In C. Lankshear, M. Peters, A. Alba, & E. Gonzales (Eds.), *Curriculum in the postmodern condition.* New York: Peter Lang.

Peters, M. A. (2003). Truth-telling as an educational practice of the self: Foucault, parrhesia and the ethics of subjectivity. *Oxford Review of Education, 29*(2), 207–224.

Peters, M. A., & Besley, A. C. (2008). *Subjectivity and truth: Foucault, education and the culture of the self.* New York: Peter Lang.

Popkewitz, T. S. (1998). *Struggling for the soul. The politics of schooling and the construction of the teacher.* New York: Teachers College Press.

Popkewitz, T. S., & Brennan, M. (Eds.). (1998). *Foucault's challenge: Discourse, knowledge, and political projects of schooling.* New York: Teachers College Press.

Rabinow, P. (2003). *Antropos today. Reflections on modern equipment.* Princeton, NJ: Princeton University Press.

Rajchman, J. (1991). *Truth and eros: Foucault, Lacan and the question of ethics.* London: Routledge.

Rancière, J. (2005). *La haine de la démocratie.* Paris: La fabrique.

Reichert, R. (2001). Die 'Governmentality studies': Grundlagen-und Methodenprobleme. *Mitteiungen des Instituts für Wissenschaft und Kunst, 56*(2–3), 2–11.

Rose, N. (1996). Governing 'advanced' liberal democracies. In A. Barry, T. Osborne, & N. Rose (Eds.), *Foucault and the political reason: Liberalism, neo-liberalism and rationalities of government* (pp. 37–64). London: UCL Press.

Rose, N. (1999). *The powers of freedom. Reframing political thought.* Cambridge, UK: Cambridge University Press.

Senellart, M. (2004). *Situation de cours, M Foucault (2004) Sécurité, Territoire, Population: Cours au Collège de France (1977 – 1978)* (pp. 381 – 411). Gallimard, Paris.

Simons, M. (2002). Governmentality, education and quality management: Toward a critique of the permanent quality tribunal. *Zeitschrift für Erziehungswissenschaft, 5*(4), 617–633.

Simons, M. (2004). *De school in de ban van het leven. Een cartografie van het moderne en actuele onderwijsdispositief* (unpublished doctoral thesis, Leuven).

Simons, M., Masschelein, J., & Quaghebeur, K. (2005). The ethos of critical research and the idea of a coming research community. *Educational Philosophy and Theory, 37*(6), 817–832.

Simons, M. (2006). Learning as investment. Notes on governmentality and biopolitics. *Educational Philosophy and Theory, 38*, 523–540.

Simons, M., & Masschelein, J. (2006a). The learning society and governmentality: An introduction. *Educational Philosophy and Theory, 38*, 417–430.

Simons, M., & Masschelein, J. (2006b). The permanent quality tribunal in education and the limits of education policy. *Policy Futures, 4*, 294–307.

Simons, M. (2007). 'To be informed': understanding the role of feedback information for Flemish/European policy. *Journal of Education Policy, 22*, 531–548.

Simons, M., & Masschelein, J. (2007). Only love for the truth can save us: Truth-telling at the (world)university. In M. Peters & T. Besley (Eds.), *Why Foucault? New directions in educational research.* New York: Peter Lang.

Simons, M., & Masschelein, J. (2008). Our ,will to learn' and the assemblage of a learning apparatus. In A. Fejes & K. Nicoll (Eds.), *Foucault and adult education.* London: Routledge.

Standish, P. (2002). Disciplining the Profession: Subjects subject to procedures. *Educational Philosophyand Theory, 34*(1), 6–23.

Maarten Simons
Center for Educational Policy and Innovation
Center for Philosophy of Education
Catholic University of Leuven

Jan Masschelein
Center for Philosophy of Education
Catholic University of Leuven

CONTRIBUTORS

EDITORS

A.C. (TINA) BESLEY is a Research Professor in Educational Policy Studies at the University of Illinois, Urbana Champaign, currently working in Global Studies in Education. She was Professor of Counseling in Educational Psychology and Counseling at California State University, San Bernardino and Research Fellow and Lecturer in the Department of Educational Studies at the University of Glasgow, Scotland, UK. Tina's research interests include: youth issues, in particular notions of self and identity in a globalised world; educational policy and philosophy, especially poststructuralism and the work of Michel Foucault. Her books include *Counseling Youth: Foucault, power and the ethics of subjectivity* (Praeger, 2002) is now in a paperback edition (Sense Publishers) and, *Assessing the Quality of Educational Research in Higher Education: International Perspectives* (Sense Publishers, 2009).

MARK OLSSEN is Professor of Political Theory and Education Policy in the Department of Political, International and Policy Studies, University of Surrey. He is author of *Toward A Global Thin Community: Nietzsche, Foucault and the Cosmopolitan Commitment*, (2008); *Michel Foucault: Materialism and Education*, (2006); *Education Policy: Globalisation, Citizenship, Democracy*, (2004), with John Codd and Anne-Marie O'Neill; *Critical Theory and the Human Condition: Founders and Praxis* (2006), and *Futures of Critical Theory: Dreams of Difference*, (2006) with Michael Peters and Colin Lankshear. He has published extensively in leading academic journals in Britain, America and in Australasia.

MICHAEL A. PETERS is Professor of Education at the University of Illinois at Urbana-Champaign. He is the executive editor of *Educational Philosophy and Theory* (Blackwell) and editor of two international ejournals, *Policy Futures in Education* and *E-Learning* (both with Symposium) and sits on the editorial board of over fifteen international journals. He has written over thirty-five books and three hundred articles and chapters, including most recently: *Global Citizenship Education* (2008) with H. Blee and A. Britton; *Global Knowledge Cultures* (2007) with Cushla Kapitzke; *Subjectivity and Truth: Foucault, Education and the Culture of Self* (2007) with Tina Besley; *Why Foucault? New Directions in Educational Research* (2007) with Tina Besley, *Building Knowledge Cultures: Educational and Development in the Age of Knowledge Capitalism* (2006) with Tina Besley. He has research interests in distributed knowledge systems, digital scholarship and elearning systems and has acted as an advisor to government on these and related matters in Scotland, NZ, South Africa and the EU.

SUSANNE MAURER is Professor for Social Pedagogy in the Department of Educational Science at the University of Marburg. Her main research interests are studies on power, knowledge and social movements. She is working on a critical historiography of social work in a feminist perspective, focusing the nexus between gender and welfare regimes in a social policy as well as in an epistemological view. Main publications are *Genderzukunft. Zur Transformation feministischer Visionen in der Science Fiction (Genderfuture : Transformations of feminist visions in Science Fiction)* (2008), co-edited with K. Maltry, B. Holland-Cunz, N. Köllhofer and R. Löchel; *Gouvernementalität und Erziehungswissenschaft (Governmentality and educational science. Power - Knowledge – Transformation)* (2006), co-edited with S. Weber; *Handbuch Sozialraum (Compendium Social Space)* (2005) co-edited with F. Kessl, C. Reutlinger and O. Frey.

SUSANNE MARIA WEBER is Professor for Social Management, Networks and Transformational Change in the Social Studies Department at the University of Applied Sciences in Fulda, Gerrnany. The focus of her work addresses the nexus of power, knowledge and transformation from the angles of discursive knowledge, institutional dynamics and subjectivity. She has contributed articles and chapters to many collections and journals.

BERNADETTE BAKER is a Professor at the University of Wisconsin in the Center for Global Studies, The Holtz Center for the Social Studies of Science and Technology, and the Dept of Curriculum and Instruction. Her research interests lie in philosophy, history, and sociology of education, science, and cosmology, trans-national curriculum studies, and 'post' literatures.

STEPHEN J. BALL is Karl Mannheim Professor of Sociology of Education in Faculty of Policy and Society, Dept. of Educational Foundations and Policy Studies, Institute of Education, University of London. His main work is in the field of 'policy sociology'; the use of sociological theories and methods to analyze policy processes and outcomes. His specific research interests focus upon the effects and consequences of the education market in a variety of respects including; the impact of competition on provider behaviour; the class strategies of educational choosers; the participation of private capital in education service delivery and education policy; and the impact of 'performativity' on academic and social life. Stephen Ball is also the convenor of the BERA Education and Social Theory SIG.

MARIE BRENNAN is Professor of Education at the University of South Australia, where she recently completed a five year term as Dean of Education. She currently teaches in curriculum studies and educational policy at graduate and undergraduate levels. A key researcher in the Centre for Studies in Literacy, Policy and Learning Cultures within the Hawke Research Institute, her research interests include: political sociology of school reform, especially curriculum; democratic and participatory forms of research, including action research; teacher education; and 'global south' issues. With Tom Popkewitz she co-edited the book *Foucault's Challenge: Discourse, Knowledge, and Power in Education.*

DAVID LEE CARLSON is an assistant professor in secondary education at Arizona State University. He has published several articles on methods that prepare teachers to teach literature and multiple forms of writing in secondary urban schools. He continues to do research on how Foucault's ideas can be useful to English studies.

ROBERT DOHERTY teaches in the Department of Educational Studies at the University of Glasgow, Scotland. His research interests include education policy, social exclusion and the politics of education.

JACQUES DONZELOT is professor of political science at the University of Paris-X, Nanterres, and an urban planning advisor in Paris. He is a founder, along with Michel Foucault, the Prison Information Group (G.I.P). He is the author of a comparison of urban policies in the United States and France, *Faire société. La politique de la ville aux États-Unis et en France* (2003), as well as a book proposing an analysis of the riots in the French suburbs in November 2005 and an alternative policy *Quand la ville se défait. Quelle politique face à la crise des banlieues?* He has directed several special issues of the periodical *Esprit* on urban, social and security issues, of which the best known is entitled 'La ville à trois vitesses' (March-April 2004). His books also include *L'invention du social* and, with Philippe Esthbe, *L'Itat animateur.*

RISTO ERÄSAARI is Professor in the Department of Social Policy at the University of Helsinki. His recent publications include: 'Objectivity, experts and institutions', 'Concept of Context', 'Representations of Society', 'Logics of Cultural Policy', 'Risk as expectation and as proposal'. He has a major research project called 'Society and Contingency' (2006–2009).

ANDREAS FEJES is Associate Professor at Linköping University, Sweden. His research explores lifelong learning and adult education, in particular drawing on poststructuralist theory. He recently published (with co-editor Katherine Nicoll) the book Foucault and lifelong learning: Governing the subject (London: Routledge) and his articles recently appeared in Journal of Education Policy, Educational Philosophy and Theory, International Journal of Lifelong Education, Teaching in Higher Education, Studies in the Education of Adults and the International Journal of Higher Education in the Social Sciences. He is also the secretary of the European Society for Research on the Education of Adults (ESREA).

HERMANN J. FORNECK is Director of the Department for Primary Teacher Education at the University of Applied Sciences at Basel. His fields of research are the governmentality of adult education, the theory of professionalization and the organizational development of universities. A few of his main publications are *Ein parzelliertes Feld* (*A divided field*) (2005), with D. Wrana; *Lernwiderstand – Lernumgebung – Lernberatung* (Resistance to/of learning) (2005), co-edited with

Faulstich & Knoll; *Selbstlernarchitekturen. Lernen und Selbstsorge* (*Architectures of self learning*) (2005).

COLIN GORDON is a programme manager in medical informatics at Royal Brompton Hospital, London. He edited *Michel Foucault: Power/Knowledge*, was co-editor, co-author, and translator of *The Foucault Effect*, and selected and wrote the Introduction to *Michel Foucault: Power*.

LINDA GRAHAM is a Macquarie University Research Fellow with the Children and Families Research Centre in the Faculty of Human Sciences, Macquarie University, Sydney, Australia. Linda specializes in the medicalization of childhood and the nature and quality of educational responses to students who are difficult to teach. Her doctoral research investigated the relationship between educational policies, pedagogical practice and the increase in diagnosis of behaviour disorder. A key contribution of her work has been to outline the relationship between categorical resource allocation methods and the increase in medical categorization of difference through relatively new categories of disability which include behaviour disorder, emotional disturbance, and autistic spectrum disorders. Her current research is an international comparative project examining the political economy of special educational needs across four international contexts: New South Wales, England, Finland and Alberta.

ADAM DAVIDSON-HARDEN is a Social Sciences and Humanities Research Council of Canada postdoctoral fellow in the Faculty of Education at Queen's University, Kingston, Ontario. His principal research interests are in the political economy and shifting culture of education, and particularly postsecondary education, under neoliberalism and 'knowledge capitalism'. His postdoctoral program of work encompasses qualitative investigations at three public universities in Ontario, Canada, engaging in dialogue with active and retired faculty and administrators toward exploring their perceptions of the shifting realities of their workplace and the directions of their universities under the push to situate universities in a global 'knowledge economy'. The analytical framework for this research takes inspiration from Marxism and neoliberal governmentality.

THOMAS HÖHNE is Professor of Educational Science at the University of Education in Freiburg (Pädagogische Hochschule). He is author of *Pädagogik der Wissensgesellschaft* (*Pedagogy of the Knowledge Society*) (2003) and many articles.

UTE KARL is Assistant Professor of Social Pedagogy in the Institute for Social and Organizational Pedagogy at the University of Hildesheim. She is author of *Zwischen/Räume. Eine empirisch-bildungstheoretische Studie zur ästhetischen und psychosozialen Praxis des Alttentheaters* (*Between/Spaces. An empirical-bildungstheoretical study of the aesthetical and psychosocial practice of seniors' theater*) (2005) and editor of *Lebensalter und Soziale Arbeit. Ältere und alte Menschen* (*LifeAge and Social Work, Elderly and old people*) (2008).

552

FABIAN KESSL is Professor for Theory and Practice of Social Work at the School of Social Work and Social Policy, University of Duisburg-Essen. His basic interest is in the current transformation of welfare and quasi-welfare arrangements since the 1970s and the Governmentality of Social Work, the Spatial Formation-Shifts of Social Policy, and Neo-Social Patterns of Life Conduct. Recent published works include: *De- and Reterritorialization of the Social* (2008), Special Issue for Social Work & Society, edited with J. Clarke; *Territorialisierung des Sozialen: Regieren über soziale Nahräume/Territorialization of the Social: Governing local spaces* (2007), edited with H.-U. Otto, and *Der Gebrauch der eigenen Kräfte: eine Gouvernementalität Sozialer Arbeit (The use of one's own strengths: a governmentality of social work)* (2005).

THOMAS LEMKE is Heisenberg-Professor of Biotechnologies, Nature and Society at the Social Sciences Department of the Goethe-University Frankfurt/Main in Germany. He did his PhD 1996 in political science at the Johann Wolfgang Goethe-University in Frankfurt/Main. From 1997 to 2006 he worked as an assistant professor for sociology at Wuppertal University and was a visting professor at New York University, Goldsmiths College in London and the Copenhagen Business School. From 2002 to 2008 he was also a Senior Researcher at the Institute for Social Research in Frankfurt/Main. His research interests include social and political theory, sociology of organization, biopolitics, social studies of genetic and reproductive technologies. His book publications include: *Eine Kritik der politischen Vernunft*: Foucault's *Analyse der modernen Gouvernementalität*, (4th edition 2003); *Die Polizei der Gene. Formen und Felder genetischer Diskriminierung*, (2006); *Gouvernementalität und Biopolitik, Wiesbaden: Verlag für Sozialwissenschaften* (2nd edition 2008); *Biopolitik zur Einführung*, (2007); *Der medizinische Blick in die Zukunft. Gesellschaftliche Implikationen prädiktiver Gentests* (together with Regine Kollek), (2008).

ANDREA LIESNER is Professor in the Department of Educational Science at the University of Hamburg. The focus of her work lies on the relationship between education and economy. She is author of a historical and systematic study about the needs for security from the Antique until the Present: *Zwischen Weltflucht und Herstellungswahn*, (2002) and many articles.

JAN MASSCHELEIN is Professor for Philosophy of Education at the Catholic University of Leuven. His primary areas of scholarship are educational theory, political philosophy, critical theory, studies of governmentality and social philosophy. His current research concentrates on the 'public' character of education in the age of networks. He is the author of many articles, special journal issues and books in these fields including: *Pädagogisches Handeln und Kommunikatives Handeln* (1991), *Alterität, Pluralität, Gerechtigheit. Randgänge der Pädagogik* (1996), with M. Wimmer, *Globale Immunität. Eine kleine Kartographie des Europaischen Bildungsraums* (2004), with M. Simons.

MAJIA HOLMER NADESAN, of Arizona State University, studies biopolitics and has authored *Governmentality, Biopower and Everyday Life* (2008) and *Constructing Autism: Unravelling the "Truth" and Understanding the Social* (005). A current project addresses children, risk, and biopolitics.

THOMAS OSBORNE is Professor of Social and Cultural Theory at the University of Bristol, UK. He is the author of *Aspects of Enlightenment: Social Theory and the Ethics of Truth* (1998) and *The Structure of Modern Cultural Theory* (2008) as well as numerous articles in the fields of the history of ideas and the sociology of knowledge.

THOMAS S. POPKEWITZ, Professor at The University of Wisconsin-Madison, studies the systems of reason that govern educational reforms and research. His most recent book, *Cosmopolitanism and The Age of Reform* explores historically present reforms and sciences of pedagogy and teacher education as simultaneous processes of abjection and inclusion. He is also working on a collaboratively with colleagues in Europe, Latin America, and North America on a historical volume concerned with the political cultures in schooling during the long 19th century.

BRUNO SCHRECK works as Learning Consultant at a Center for Self-Directed Learning in the Learning Region Offenbach am Main. He is author of several articles and has research interests that focuses on private actors in the educational sector.

MAARTEN SIMONS is Professor at the Centre for Educational Policy and Innovation and the Centre for Philosophy of Education, Catholic University of Leuven, Belgium. His research interests are educational policy and political philosophy with special attention on governmentality and schooling, autonomy and higher education and performativity in education. Together with Jan Masschelein he is the author of *Globale Immunität. Ein kleine Kartographie des Europaischen Bildungsraum* (2005). He is the co-editor of the books *Europa anno* (2006), *E-ducatieve berichten uit niemandsland* (2006), *The learning society from the perspective of governmentality* (2007), *De schaduwzijde van onze welwillendheid* (2008), and the special issue 'The university revisited: questioning the public role of the university in the European knowledge society' (2007, *Studies in Philosophy and Education*), and the author of several articles in journals and edited books.

JAMES WONG is associate professor in the Department of Philosophy, Wilfrid Laurier University. His current research focuses on the question of 'autonomy' in late Foucault, with particular emphasis on the notion of 'care' in Foucault's conception of 'Care of the Self'. Representative publications include "Paradox of Capacity and Power: Critical Ontology and the Developmental Model of Childhood" which appeared in *Why Foucault? New Directions in Educational Research* (2007), edited by Michael Peters and Tina Besley.

DANIEL WRANA is Professor of Self Regulated Learning in the Department of Primary Education, University of Education (PH FHNW) in Northwest Switzerland. He recently published *Ein parzelliertes Feld (A Divided Field – a governmentality of the field of adult education)* (2005), with Hermann Forneck; *Das Subjekt schreiben* (Writing the Subject – a discourse analysis of learning journals) (2006); *Autonomie und Struktur (Autonomy and Structure – Empirical studies to processes of self regulated learning in teacher education)* (2008), edited with C. Maier Reinhard.

QIZHI YU is Professor of Philosophy, Institute of Philosophy at South China Normal University, Guangzhou. He has strong research interests in the work of Michel Foucault and Jacques Derrida and has published widely on their work.

LEW ZIPIN lectures in sociology and policy of education at the University of South Australia where he is a key researcher in the Centre for Studies in Literacy, Policy and Learning Cultures within the Hawke Research Institute. His research interests include critical theories of power in education; issues of governance, ethics and work in schools and higher education; and education for social justice. His previous publications on issues of Foucauldian analytics include a chapter in the book *Foucault's Challenge: Discourse, Knowledge, and Power in Education.*

9 789087 909833